NETFLIX
STRANGER THINGS

THE COMPLETE SCRIPTS
SEASON 4

NETFLIX
STRANGER THINGS

THE COMPLETE SCRIPTS
SEASON 4

CREATED BY THE DUFFER BROTHERS

RANDOM HOUSE
WORLDS

NEW YORK

Random House Worlds
An imprint of Random House
A division of Penguin Random House LLC
1745 Broadway, New York, NY 10019
randomhousebooks.com
penguinrandomhouse.com

2025 Random House Worlds Trade Paperback Original

STRANGER THINGS™ / © 2025 Netflix. Used with permission.
Introduction © 2025 by the Duffer Brothers

Penguin Random House values and supports copyright. Copyright fuels creativity, encourages diverse voices, promotes free speech, and creates a vibrant culture. Thank you for buying an authorized edition of this book and for complying with copyright laws by not reproducing, scanning, or distributing any part of it in any form without permission. You are supporting writers and allowing Penguin Random House to continue to publish books for every reader. Please note that no part of this book may be used or reproduced in any manner for the purpose of training artificial intelligence technologies or systems.

Published in the United States by Random House Worlds,
an imprint of Random House, a division of
Penguin Random House LLC, New York.

RANDOM HOUSE is a registered trademark, and
RANDOM HOUSE WORLDS and colophon are trademarks
of Penguin Random House LLC.

ISBN 978-0-593-98409-3
Ebook ISBN 978-0-593-98410-9

Printed in Canada

BOOK TEAM: Editor: Jacinta O'Halloran • Production editor: Abby Duval • Managing editor: Susan Seeman • Production manager: Angela McNally • Proofreaders: Alissa Fitzgerald, Jacob Reynold Jones, Taylor McGowan, Darcie Robertson

Book design by Elizabeth A. D. Eno

2 4 6 8 9 7 5 3 1

The authorized representative in the EU for product safety and compliance is Penguin Random House Ireland, Morrison Chambers, 32 Nassau Street, Dublin D02 YH68, Ireland. https://eu-contact.penguin.ie

CONTENTS

Introduction by the Duffer Brothers	vii
Chapter One: The Hellfire Club	3
Chapter Two: Vecna's Curse	81
Chapter Three: The Monster and the Superhero	167
Chapter Four: Dear Billy	243
Chapter Five: The Nina Project	333
Chapter Six: The Dive	411
Chapter Seven: The Massacre at Hawkins Lab	501
Chapter Eight: Papa	587
Chapter Nine: The Piggyback	667

INTRODUCTION

Season four was our toughest season to write, with the possible exception of season two. We had wanted to shake things up at the end of season three to challenge ourselves, but as we began to brainstorm this season, panic set in. For the first time, our characters were split up geographically—in California, Russia, and Hawkins. How were these storylines going to weave together in a coherent way? Even more challenging, our "kids" were no longer kids, but young adults. We could no longer rely on the middle school joy that defined the heart of the first three seasons. This was new, scary territory.

We also knew that this was the penultimate season. We needed to lay track for the ending, and that meant finally pulling back the curtain on the show's ultimate villain. From the beginning, we knew there was a dark, sentient being behind all the evil in Hawkins: One, the first child in Brenner's program, a twisted reflection of Eleven. We had always compared him to Pennywise, Pinhead, and Freddy Krueger. When we were kids, even hearing about these monsters freaked us out and gave us so many sleepless nights. We wanted One to be just as scary. But what would make our monster unique? We didn't know his appearance, the extent of his powers, or his backstory. For weeks, we were stuck.

The answer, it turned out, lay inward—back in our own high school years. Unlike our middle school experience, which was so fun and hopeful, high school was a far darker period. We weren't bullied, not exactly, but most of our closest friends drifted away. Some went to different schools, while others joined sports teams and made cooler friends. Gone were the days of playing Magic: The Gathering and making horror movies over the weekend. We felt left behind, lost, scared, and worst of all, invisible. Our experience was hardly unique—many kids had it much, much worse. This is the time in life when social pressures peak at the precise moment your body and mind are undergoing intense change. Inevitably, you're plagued by self-doubt and insecurity.

While it was scary to reopen old wounds, we knew this would be rich, new territory to explore with our heroes. But how could our villain embody it? We spitballed with the writers: What if he fed on all of that—your darkest thoughts, your deepest fears? What if he could slip inside your mind and turn it against you? What if he sought out the kids who were already struggling, the ones most vulnerable? And what if he didn't just haunt you, but killed you—a supernatural serial killer? That was our answer. Now he just needed a name. We opened our D&D book one more time and found it: one of its most infamous villains, a dark, spell-casting wizard known as Vecna.

We now had a narrative drive: a supernatural serial killer terrorizing Hawkins. But then came another question: If dead bodies are popping up all around Hawkins, how would the town respond? There needed to be a scapegoat, a character in the tragic vein of Damien Echols and the satanic panic of the eighties, something we'd long wanted to bring into the show. At first, we weren't sure what would make this character worth adding to an already sprawling cast. We could hear the internet screaming at us, *Stop adding new characters!* Then our writer Curtis Gwinn told us about his older brother—a long-haired, D&D-obsessed metalhead. Curtis reminded us that we had leaned into stereotypes by having bad boy Billy blast Metallica in season two. It was time to do metalheads justice. It was time for the freaks. It was time for Eddie Munson.

The season was at last coming together, and we were energized by the new directions the show was still capable of taking. We were pivoting away from the blockbuster neon fun of season three and into darker, scarier, psychological territory. This was going to be old-school eighties horror. No more giant CGI monsters and evil Russians; it was time for prosthetics, practical effects, and stories that felt leaner and more grounded. At least, that was the plan. The deeper we got into breaking the story, the more massive it became. Eleven's journey—tying her back to Henry Creel—kept expanding. Hopper's Russia arc added even more weight and scale. The scripts grew longer and longer—and longer—until, for the first time since season two, we realized we had to add a ninth episode to fit it all in. The only problem? We had no time to write this extra script because production had already begun in Atlanta. The train was already speeding down the track.

And then . . . the pandemic hit, and production shut down. Suddenly, we went from having not enough time to having more time than we'd ever had. As difficult and isolating as that period was, it allowed us to return to earlier scripts and refine them even further. By then, we had cast the brilliant Joseph Quinn, and Eddie became sharper, more distinct, more original—tailored for Joe. And for the first time in *Stranger Things* history, we entered production with every script finished.

Which brings us here, to this book. These scripts hold some of our favorite moments in the series: Chrissy's brutal death, Max "running up that hill," the triple reveal of Henry/One/Vecna, Eddie shredding "Master of Puppets" on his trailer roof. It was exhilarating to write. But it was also bittersweet—we knew we were steering the ship toward the end. Toward saying goodbye.

But that's a story for another time, for season five.

Until then, we hope you enjoy the longest, darkest trip we've taken yet.

Over and out,
Matt and Ross Duffer

NETFLIX
STRANGER THINGS

THE COMPLETE SCRIPTS
SEASON 4

EPISODE ONE

CHAPTER ONE:
THE HELLFIRE CLUB

WRITTEN BY **THE DUFFER BROTHERS**

EXT. SUBURBAN NEIGHBORHOOD - MORNING

We FADE UP on a Hawkins suburb. Quaint. Happy. *Normal.*

WHOOSH! A NEWSPAPER BOY zips past on a bicycle, cutting a path through a carpet of burnt yellow fall leaves.

He tosses newspapers at passing houses with pinpoint accuracy. They bounce off door after door. THUMP, THUMP --

EXT. QUAINT SUBURBAN HOUSE - MORNING

THUMP. A newspaper drops onto the doorstep of an ordinary one-story house.

The door opens and a MAN'S hand reaches down from out of frame and retrieves the paper. The door closes.

INT. UNKNOWN MAN'S HOUSE - MORNING

A series of CU SHOTS as the Man goes about his morning routine. (NOTE: THE MAN'S FACE REMAINS HIDDEN THROUGHOUT.)

-- A tea kettle WHISTLES.

-- The Man pours tea into a cup.

-- The Man opens the newspaper to the crossword section.

-- The Man sets a timer and begins to fill out the crossword.

-- The timer ends. The puzzle is finished.

INT. ENTRY - MORNING

-- The Man prunes an indoor plant. Careful, exacting.

INT. MAN'S BATHROOM - MORNING

-- The man shaves. A sharp razor blade skims across his cheekbone.

INT. MAN'S HOUSE - BEDROOM - MORNING

-- The Man opens a closet. It's lined with a ROW OF SUITS.

-- The Man wraps a necktie around his neck. Pulls it tight.

-- The Man slips on a blue blazer. He adjusts the blazer, his head lifts. And now, at last, we see him. It's...

DR. BRENNER. He is several years younger than he was in season one. Handsome. Still some color in his hair. And something else seems different about him. His spirit is lighter somehow. Less *haunted*. Off a CU of Brenner, CUT TO --

EXT. HAWKINS LABS - DAY

We're soaring through the sky now. Flying toward Hawkins Labs. It's bustling with cars, people, *life*.

CHYRON: HAWKINS NATIONAL LABORATORIES. SEPTEMBER 8, 1979.

CUT TO a direct overhead shot of the lab. It looks like a giant X. As our camera drifts toward this X, DISSOLVE TO --

INT. HAWKINS LABS - RAINBOW ROOM - DAY

A LARGE PAINTING OF A RAINBOW. We PULL BACK from the rainbow to reveal that we are in some kind of COLORFUL PLAYROOM.

Our camera slowly PANS, methodically surveying the room. There are about a DOZEN CHILDREN and TEENS in here, happily watercoloring, playing puzzle games, interacting. It almost seems like a normal elementary school. *Almost*. There are cameras on walls... a STERN ORDERLY... the children are dressed in lab gowns... their heads are shaved... these are NUMBERS.

Brenner enters. He walks over and takes a seat beside a YOUNG BOY, age 11. This boy seems lonelier than the others, playing by himself with a MAGIC 8 BALL. Brenner smiles softly.

      DR. BRENNER
  That's your favorite, isn't it?

The Young Boy nods shyly.

      DR. BRENNER (CONT'D)
  How are we feeling today?

      BOY
  Okay.

      DR. BRENNER
  Up for some more lessons?

The Boy shakes the 8 Ball again. Holds it up for Brenner. It reads: "SIGNS POINT TO YES."

INT. HAWKINS LABS - HALLWAY - DAY

CLOSE ON: Brenner's hand and the boy's hand, now clasped as they walk together down a hallway. The boy's wrist is tattooed with the number 010. We will now refer to this boy as TEN.

Dr. Brenner and Ten pass by a FEMALE DOCTOR and another YOUNG NUMBER (also female), who are walking in the opposite direction.

></br>
>   DOCTOR ELLIS
>   Morning, Doctor Brenner --
>
>   DR. BRENNER
>   (nodding)
>   Doctor Ellis.

A HIGH WIDE TRACKING SHOT reveals rooms on either side of the hallway. Each room is marked with a number.

We focus on a familiar number: 011. The door is shut, locked.

As we push toward the closed door, *toward that 011*, we PRE-LAP an UNNERVING SCRATCHING SOUND...

INT. HAWKINS LABS - LAB ROOM - LATER

CHH! CHH! CHH! An EEG machine scribbles electrical activity.

Ten is now sitting at a table with electrodes affixed to his head. His eyes are closed. Brenner sits opposite him with a CLIPBOARD, a SHEET OF PAPER, and some CRAYONS.

Brenner draws a simplistic picture of the sun.

>   DR. BRENNER
>   What do you see?

The boy hesitates. The EEG jumps a bit.

>   DR. BRENNER (CONT'D)
>   Don't force it. Let it *come to you*.
>   Just as we practiced.

Ten slows his breathing.

>   TEN
>   It's... a yellow... circle. The...
>   sun.

>   DR. BRENNER
>   Good. Very good.

Brenner draws a simple dog.

>   DR. BRENNER (CONT'D)
>   Now what do you see?

>   TEN
>   A... cow?

Brenner smiles.

>   DR. BRENNER
>   It's supposed to be a dog.

>   TEN
>   Looks like a cow.

>   DR. BRENNER
>   It does, doesn't it?
>   (small laugh)
>   Never was much of an artist.

Brenner pushes away his drawings.

>   DR. BRENNER (CONT'D)
>   Alright -- let's try something a
>   little more challenging now. Is
>   that alright with you?

Ten nods. *Yes.*

>   DR. BRENNER (CONT'D)
>   I want you to find *Doctor Ellis*.

Ten nods. He steadies his breathing and focuses his mind. ECU on his eyelids. His eyes dart back and forth beneath them.

The EEG spikes a bit.

>   DR. BRENNER (CONT'D)
>   Have you found her?

>   TEN
>   ... Yes.

>   DR. BRENNER
>   What is she doing?

>   TEN
>   Lessons with... Six. In her room.

                    DR. BRENNER
          What kind of lessons?

                    TEN
          Six is trying... to move a block. A
          red block.

Brenner scribbles notes onto his pad: *Block, red, 11:27 AM.*

                    DR. BRENNER
          Can you hear what they're saying?

Ten starts to respond when -- his breath catches.

The EEG spikes a bit. CHH CHH CHH!

                    TEN
          Something is... wrong --

                    DR. BRENNER
          If you lost the visual, just let it
          go, try to reorient --

Ten starts to get visibly upset, flinches --

                    TEN
          They're screaming.

Brenner shifts in his seat. Concerned.

                    DR. BRENNER
          "Screaming"? Why are they
          screaming? *Ten?*

AN ALARM BEGINS TO BLARE. *What the hell?* A now *very concerned* Brenner pushes to his feet and strides over to an INTERCOM and presses the CALL button --

                    DR. BRENNER (CONT'D)
          What is going on out there? Peter??
          Alec??

No answer. Only static. Ten opens his eyes. Looks to Brenner. His face is pale. His voice trembles.

                    TEN
          Dead. They're both dead.

BAM! SOMETHING SUDDENLY SLAMS INTO THE LAB DOOR.

Brenner turns. Someone -- *something* -- is trying to force their way in here. Before Brenner even has time to react --

ANOTHER IMPOSSIBLY POWERFUL FORCE STRIKES THE DOOR AND --

BOOM! THE DOOR EXPLODES OPEN -- SLAMS HARD INTO BRENNER -- HIS BODY FLIES BACKWARDS -- AND THE WHOLE WORLD GOES --

BLACK

WE HEAR SCREAMS, RUNNING, THE ALARM, THEN --

INT. LAB ROOM - DAY

A SHARP GASP as Brenner blinks awake. He's now lying on the ground. Blood spills from a GAPING WOUND in his forehead.

Brenner crawls over to a fallen body. It's Ten. Brenner lifts him into his arms, cradles him. He is as limp as a rag doll.

HE IS DEAD. As Brenner takes this in, CRASH TO --

INT. HAWKINS LABS - HALLWAY - DAY

Dr. Brenner, dazed, bleeding, staggering down the hallway.

It looks like a war zone out here. There are DEAD LAB TECHS and DEAD GUARDS everywhere. The doors to all of the rooms have been BLOWN WIDE OPEN. Inside each room, more DEAD NUMBERS. Brenner can hardly stand to look. Then --

A SHARP, PIERCING SCREAM OF A CHILD. He turns. The scream came from --

DOUBLE DOORS (painted the colors of a rainbow) at the far end of the hallway. *The rainbow room. The electricity is going wild,* and a STRANGE ORANGE LIGHT begins to glow from within.

Off Brenner, his horror growing, we SMASH TO --

INT. RAINBOW ROOM - DAY

The big painted rainbow -- now spattered in blood. Our CAMERA PULLS BACK AND PANS, surveying the room as before. There is no more screaming. Because THE NUMBERS ARE ALL DEAD.

Our CAMERA lands on Brenner as he steps into the room.

He can hardly breathe. Can hardly speak. Tears well.

      DR. BRENNER
    (low, scared)
 ... What have you done?

We now REVERSE TO REVEAL that there is ONE CHILD still alive in this room, standing tall amongst the pile of dead bodies.

The child's back is turned to us.

> DR. BRENNER (CONT'D)
> *What have you done*?

Our camera drops down the child's back and lands on a close-up of her wrist, which is engraved with a familiar tattoo: 011. *It's...*

YOUNG ELEVEN. She turns to Brenner. To *us*. She is seven years old. HER FACE IS PAINTED IN BLOOD. SHE LOOKS FEROCIOUS. *ANGRY*. A *KILLER*. And now, it hits us. *Eleven did this.*

As she locks eyes with Brenner, *ferocious*, we CRASH TO --

MAIN TITLES

INT. BYERS HOUSE - HALLWAY - MORNING

We move out of titles to find ourselves gently drifting down a hallway toward a BEDROOM DOOR. It's cracked three inches.

> ELEVEN (V.O.)
> Dear Mike. Today is day one hundred eighty-five. *One hundred eighty-five!* I had to check five times to make sure that was right, because it feels more like ten years.

We slink through this crack into...

INT. BYERS HOUSE - ELEVEN'S BEDROOM - MORNING

We pass a desk, where we find a GIANT STACK OF LETTERS. All addressed TO ELEVEN, FROM MIKE.

> ELEVEN
> Joyce says time is funny like that. Emotions can make it -- speed up or slow down. We are all -- time travelers, if you think about it.

We drift past the letters to at last find --

A PRESENT-DAY ELEVEN, seated at a small desk below a window. She's finishing up a DIORAMA OF HOPPER'S CABIN! It's made from a shoebox and looks like something a second grader might make. As El bites her lower lip, focusing in...

                    ELEVEN (V.O.)
            For example, this week is going
            very fast, I think because I am so
            busy. But do not worry -- it is a
            good busy!

Eleven adds a TINY CLAY SQUIRREL outside the cabin.

                    ELEVEN (V.O.)
            I have to make something called a
            "visual aid" for class. Joyce said
            I should make a "diorama." I hope
            Missus Gracey will give me an A.

Eleven places the finishing touch: A TINY CLAY HOPPER FIGURE.
Finished! As El smiles, proud, CUT TO --

INT. BYERS HOUSE - JOYCE'S "OFFICE" - LENORA HILLS - MORNING

JOYCE seated at the little office table, a cordless phone
pressed to her ear and an Encyclopedia Britannica
telemarketing book by her side.

                    ELEVEN (V.O.)
            Some exciting news. Joyce got an
            amazing new job -- she gets to work
            at home.

                    JOYCE
            ... If you're concerned about
            budget, Mister Taylor, let me assure
            you, we have some payment plans
            that will --

She sits back in her chair, growing agitated now --

                    JOYCE (CONT'D)
            I'm not a robot, you do realize
            that right?

                    ELEVEN (V.O.)
            She says she loves the "freedom."

                    JOYCE
            PRICK!!

BAM! Joyce slams down her phone and --

INT. BYERS HOUSE - WILL'S ROOM - CONTINUOUS

Quiet as WILL paints on a canvas in his room.

> ELEVEN (V.O.)
> Will is painting a lot -- but he
> won't show me what he's working on.
> I think whatever it is, it must be
> *very special*.

CLOSE SHOTS ON: the paintbrush sweeping across the canvas and Will's intensely focused eyes.

> ELEVEN (V.O.)
> Maybe it is for a girl. I think
> there is someone he likes because
> he has been acting... weird.

INT. BYERS HOUSE - JONATHAN'S ROOM - MORNING

A framed photo of Jonathan and Nancy smiling together, in love. A CLOUD OF SMOKE crosses frame as our camera begins to DOLLY AWAY FROM THE PHOTOGRAPH.

> ELEVEN (V.O.)
> Jonathan is acting weird also. I
> think he is just nervous about
> college. He is still waiting for
> his big letter. I hope he and Nancy
> get to go together.

... We find JONATHAN. He is indeed acting *weird*. His eyes are bloodshot, and he is coughing while frantically trying to clear smoke out his window.

EXT. BYERS HOUSE - MORNING

Jonathan's car sits in the driveway, gathering dust.

> ELEVEN (V.O.)
> But I don't know how he will ever
> get to college, because his car is
> still broken. Me and Will think it
> is ready for the car graveyard. Do
> cars have funerals?

SCREECH! A PIZZA VAN swerves up to the Byers house. A ridiculous logo reads: SURFER BOY PIZZA! Behind the wheel --

> ELEVEN (V.O.)
> His funny friend Argyle has been
> taking us to school.

ARGYLE, 17, a SoCal stoner with hair down to his waist. Surfer music blasts out the window.

> ELEVEN (V.O.)
> His hair is longer than mine and he and Jonathan like to smoke smelly plants together.

Argyle pounds his horn, honking --

BACK IN JONATHAN'S ROOM

The HONKING carries inside. Jonathan finishes clearing his room of smoke --

> ELEVEN (V.O.)
> Jonathan says the plants are super safe because they come from the earth -- but to not tell Joyce.

He shuts the window and grabs up his backpack.

EXT. BYERS HOUSE

Jonathan, El, and Will hurry to the idling "Pizzamobile," their overstuffed backpacks slung over their shoulders. We begin to glimpse some desert scenery around them --

> ELEVEN (V.O.)
> And me? I am twice as *happy now*.

INT. PIZZAMOBILE

Eleven climbs into the Pizzamobile, cradling her diorama. She seems nervous, but also excited for the day.

> ELEVEN (V.O.)
> You were right -- it just takes time.

> ARGYLE
> Buckle up my three amigos!

Argyle kicks his van into reverse and --

EXT. BYERS HOUSE

Squeals away. An irritated Joyce watches from the porch.

> JOYCE
> SLOOOW DOWN!!!

As the Pizzamobile zooms off down the street, not slowing down but rather *speeding up*, we CRANE UP to reveal they are now living in a dusty California suburb, a la *E.T.*!!

CHYRON: LENORA HILLS, CALIFORNIA. MARCH 21, 1986.

>   ELEVEN (V.O.)
>   I think... I have finally
>   "adapted." Do you know that word?

INT./EXT. PIZZAMOBILE - MORNING

Eleven rides in the back of the van. She holds the diorama protectively in her lap.

>   ELEVEN (V.O.)
>   You are so smart I am sure you do.
>   I just learned it and -- I think
>   that is what I am doing. *Adapting*.

She looks out the window at the passing scenery. Large mountains loom over an expansive desert landscape.

>   ELEVEN (V.O.)
>   At first -- I missed all the spring
>   flowers. But now -- I find it
>   *pretty here too*.

EXT. LENORA HILLS HIGH - MORNING

Eleven, Will, Jonathan, and Argyle head into a BUSTLING HIGH SCHOOL, nestled between some low, rolling brown hills.

>   ELEVEN (V.O.)
>   I even like school now. I am still
>   best at math but my grammar is
>   getting good now also.

INT. LENORA HILLS HIGH - MORNING

Eleven wades through a packed hallway.

>   ELEVEN (V.O.)
>   It helps that everyone is so nice
>   here. I have made *lots* of friends.

A FRIENDLY GIRL waves at Eleven. El waves back, but then --

The girl *strides past El*. She was waving at ANOTHER GIRL!

Eleven looks away, disappointed, then presses on. *Alone*.

                        ELEVEN (V.O.)
                Even so -- I am ready for spring
                break --

She passes by a colorful sign that reads:

                "COUNTDOWN TO SPRING BREAK! 1 DAY."

As we PUSH IN on the "1"...

                        ELEVEN (V.O.)
                Mostly because I get to see *you*.

INT. LENORA HILLS HIGH - CLASSROOM - MORNING

Eleven pushes her way through bodies as she fights her way to her desk.

                        ELEVEN (V.O.)
                I am so excited to see you it is
                hard to breathe. Are you excited
                too?

She finally sits. *Catches her breath.*

                        ELEVEN (V.O.)
                I think you will love it here like
                me. I think... we will have the
                best spring break ever.

SPLAT! A spitball smacks El right in the face!

Eleven turns to find a POPULAR GIRL and BOY (who we will come to know as ANGELA and JAKE) giggling at Eleven. *Jerks.*

Off Eleven, trying to stay positive, CUT TO --

INT. MIKE'S BEDROOM - DAY

MIKE, reading his "Dear Mike" letter in bed...

                        ELEVEN (V.O.)
                I hope my spelling was better this
                time. Miss you. Love, El.

Mike beams dreamily, still clearly very much in love, when --

WHOOM! His bedroom door explodes open -- violently jarring him out of his spell. It's NANCY. She's wearing an EMERSON COLLEGE T-SHIRT. And she *doesn't look happy.*

                    NANCY
          The hell are you doing? It's ten
          after!!

                    MIKE
          Shit -- *SHIT*!!

Mike scrambles out of bed --

                    NANCY
          You have *thirty seconds* or I'm
          leaving without you! *THIRTY
          SECONDS*!

Mike yanks pants over his Joe Boxers and --

INT. WHEELER HOUSE - KITCHEN - MORNING

Mike races downstairs, pulling on a hand-made T-shirt that reads HELLFIRE CLUB. It's aggressively edgy, emblazoned with FIRE and DEVIL HORNS, like the cover of a heavy metal album.

As Mike grabs a Pop-Tart from the kitchen pantry --

                    KAREN
              (cleaning up dishes)
          Michael, I know you have your D&D
          Club tonight --

                    MIKE
              (correcting)
          Hellfire --

                    TED
              (to himself)
          Why don't you just call it High
          School Dropout Club --

                    KAREN
          But I want you home no later than
          nine tonight.

                    MIKE
          Yeah I'll try --

                    KAREN
          No -- *no trying* -- you need to get
          to bed early tonight --

                    MIKE
          Why -- ?

                    TED
          It's a six-thirty flight Michael --

                    MIKE
          Yeah I know but --

                    KAREN
          No buts. Nine or no California --

                    TED
          And no sweetie pie.

Mike stares. *Sweetie pie?* Nancy screams from the door --

                    NANCY
          MIKE LET'S GOOO!!!

Mike is gonna explode --

                    MIKE
          How am I going to survive a whole
          week without you guys?

Mike storms out the house, SLAMS the door.

Ted looks at Karen --

                    TED
          Remind me, when do they become
          reasonable human beings again?

Karen shrugs, resumes scrubbing, and --

EXT. HENDERSON HOUSE - MORNING

We PUSH IN on the Henderson home. We can't help but notice --

A GIANT RADIO TOWER AFFIXED TO THE ROOF. This is CEREBRO 2.0!!!!

                    VOICE (V.O.)
          That's a negative Dustybun.

                    DUSTIN (V.O.)
          Sonofabitch.

INT. DUSTIN'S ROOM - MORNING

Inside, DUSTIN (wearing the same Hellfire Club T-shirt) scratches out a word from a LIST OF PASSWORD IDEAS.

                        DUSTIN
                     (into CB)
              Okay -- try "TIGERS86."

                        VOICE (OVER CEREBRO)
              TIGERS86, copy that.

We now CUT TO --

INT. SUZIE'S ROOM - MORNING

SUZIE!!! She is on _her_ Cerebro -- which sits beside a BRAND-NEW COMPUTER!!! On the computer monitor, blue text reads:

              ROANE COUNTY DISTRICT DATANET.
              PLEASE LOG IN WITH USER PASSWORD.

Holy shit, Suzie is a _hacker now????_ Her fingers fly as she types TIGERS86. She punches ENTER and --

A FLURRY OF BLUE TEXT flies across the screen!

                        SUZIE
              I'm in.

INT. DUSTIN'S ROOM - DAY

                        DUSTIN
              Holy shit --

BAM BAM BAM! A LOUD KNOCKING on his door. It's --

INT. HALLWAY - OUTSIDE DUSTIN'S ROOM

Dustin's mom, CLAUDIA!

                        CLAUDIA
              Dusty, what's going on in there??
              You're gonna be late!!!

Claudia starts to open the door but --

                        DUSTIN
                     (shrieking)
              DON'T COME IN I'M _NAKED_!!

Claudia yanks the door shut in horror as --

INT. DUSTIN'S ROOM/SUZIE'S ROOM - INTERCUT

                        DUSTIN
              I'm running out of time here --

                    SUZIE
          Just hold your horsies, Dustybun --

Suzie types "Henderson, Dustin" into the database and --

BEEPBOOP! Dustin's ENTIRE CLASS CURRICULUM pops up on
screen... followed by his CORRESPONDING GRADES!!!!

                    DUSTIN
          Do you see it?

Suzie scrolls down to his LATIN GRADE. It's a big fat D.

                    SUZIE
          Yeah -- I see it. *Yikes Dusty*.

She goes to change the grade, when her eyes shift to a LARGE
PHOTO OF JESUS on the wall. Jesus stares at her. *Judging*.

Suzie sighs.

                    SUZIE (CONT'D)
          I will repent later.

She turns back to the computer. *And* --

Punches an A on the keyboard. As Dustin's grade transforms
into an A, we PRE-LAP ROCK MUSIC AS --

EXT. COUNTRY ROAD - DAY

WHOOSH! Steve's BMW rockets down the road, passing a COLORFUL
FIELD OF SPRINGTIME FLOWERS.

INT. BMW - MORNING

STEVE'S beautiful hair flows in the wind. He's wearing a
FAMILY VIDEO VEST, but that hasn't deterred him -- he's cool
and confident again!

                    STEVE
          -- And then there's Heidi tomorrow
          night, but, you know, the problem
          with Heidi is she's going out of
          state for college --

We PULL BACK to reveal Steve is talking to ROBIN, seated
passenger, wearing a HAWKINS HIGH MARCHING BAND OUTFIT!

She's acting very un-Robin like, fussing with her make-up in
the mirror. She's not listening, just letting Steve ramble.

                    STEVE (CONT'D)
          -- And I just don't know if I can
          get into another relationship that
          has no point besides sex, you know?
          I mean, does that make sense?

Steve looks at the distracted Robin.

                    STEVE (CONT'D)
          Hey! Can you pay attention to me??

                    ROBIN
          I'm paying attention --

                    STEVE
          What'd I just say -- ?

                    ROBIN
          Something about sex with... Linda?

                    STEVE
          Heidi -- I was talking about Heidi!

                    ROBIN
          Okay can you cut me some slack
          please? Your dating life is one
          of labyrinthine complexity and it's
          seven in the morning and we have
          this stupid pep rally and I woke up
          looking like a -- <u>a corpse</u>.

Robin goes back to doing her make-up. Steve eyes her.

                    STEVE
               (skeptical)
          You're worried about how you look
          for a *basketball pep rally* -- ?

                    ROBIN
          Yeah, so -- ?

                    STEVE
          So don't sell me that bullshit.
          This is about Vickie --

                    ROBIN
          No <u>it's not</u> --

                    STEVE
          You know what else I think -- ?

                    ROBIN
          I don't care --

                    STEVE
          I think you gotta stop pretending
          to be someone else. You gotta just
          be yourself around her, you know?

Robin shoots Steve a look.

                    ROBIN
          You're quoting *me* to *me*, you do
          realize that, right -- ?

                    STEVE
          Well maybe you need to listen to
          yourself, you ever think about that,
          smarty-pants? I listened to you and
          now look at me: *back in business* --

                    ROBIN
          It's not the same thing, okay? When
          you ask a girl out, if she says no,
          it's not a big deal. I ask the
          wrong girl -- *bam* --

Robin slaps the mirror away.

                    ROBIN (CONT'D)
          I'm suddenly the *town pariah*.

                    STEVE
          I'd buy that *except* Vickie is
          definitely not the wrong girl --

                    ROBIN
          We *don't* know that --

                    STEVE
          She returned *Fast Times* and it was
          paused at fifty-three minutes and
          five seconds. You know who pauses
          Fast Times at fifty-three minutes
          and five seconds?
                    (beat)
          People who like boobies.

                    ROBIN
          Please don't say boobies.

> STEVE
> Why not? I like 'em. You like 'em.
> Vickie likes 'em.
>   (beat)
> Boobies.

Robin sighs as Steve swings a left and pulls into --

EXT. HAWKINS HIGH - DAY

-- The school drop-off. It's jam-packed with cars and buses and a HERD OF STUDENTS -- all flocking toward the school gym.

A kind-eyed counselor, MS. KELLEY, redirects traffic --

> MS. KELLEY
> TO THE GYM, EVERYONE TO THE GYM!

We find MAX as she steps out of a school bus. She's got WALKMAN HEADPHONES on and is listening to Kate Bush's "Running Up That Hill."

Max starts to follow the herd, when --

> MS. KELLEY (CONT'D)
> Max. MAX -- !

Max winces. She turns back and pulls off her headphones as --

Ms. Kelley approaches.

> MS. KELLEY (CONT'D)
> Where were you yesterday?

> MAX
> Oh yeah, sorry, I just --
>   (uhhh)
> Forgot it was Thursday.

> MS. KELLEY
> Well, I'd like to see you today.
> Come straight from lunch, okay?

Max nods unenthusiastically, then slips her headphones back on and heads to the gym. As a concerned Ms. Kelley watches Max go, PRE-LAP the sound of DRUMS AND TRUMPETS and CUT TO --

INT. HAWKINS HIGH - GYMNASIUM - MORNING

The pep rally in FULL SWING:

-- A RAUCOUS CROWD (dressed in school colors) cheers and claps from the bleachers!!!

-- An ATHLETIC CHEERLEADER performs impressive flips!

-- CHRISSY, 17, head cheerleader, strikingly pretty, excitedly shakes her pom-pom!

-- "GO TIGERS!!!" flags and banners wave back and forth!

-- A TIGER MASCOT dances!

-- Robin plays her trumpet with the band. She eyes a cute drummer girl with short hair -- this is VICKIE! Vickie looks over in her direction, but Robin quickly looks away, flustered.

-- Dustin and Mike clap unenthusiastically.

>   DUSTIN
>   Listen -- I'm not saying my
>   girlfriend is better than yours,
>   but Suzie is a certified *GENIUS* --
>
>   MIKE
>   You realize El saved the world
>   *twice*, right -- ?
>
>   DUSTIN
>   And yet, you still have a C in
>   Spanish.

THE CROWD NOW ERUPTS IN CHEERS AS --

ON THE COURT - CONTINUOUS

The HAWKINS HIGH BASKETBALL TEAM races out in uniform!

They're jumping up and down and shouting. In the lead: JASON, 17, a preppy, handsome rich kid. Close behind him, the rest of the starters, including ANDY, 16, and PATRICK, 17. Then, trailing the pack, the younger bench warmers, including --

LUCAS?! Holy shit, Lucas plays basketball now?? Before we even have much time to take in this new development --

Jason grabs a center-stage microphone.

>   JASON
>   GOOOD MORNING HAWKINS HIGH!!!

THE CROWD GOES NUTS!! Jason is clearly *very* popular.

Jason takes the mic off the stand and begins to walk back and forth like he's some sort of inspirational speaker.

                    JASON (CONT'D)
              First off, I'd like to thank each
              and every one of you. Without your
              support, we wouldn't be here... so
              give yourselves a big hand.

Jason leads the crowd in applauding themselves. As Lucas claps along, his eyes roam the bleachers and lock onto Max.

He smiles and waves at her, but she looks away. *Oh no what happened with LUMAX???*

                    JASON (CONT'D)
              And of course I gotta give a
              special shout-out to the best and
              prettiest fans of all: The Tiger
              Cheer Squad!!!

More APPLAUSE! The Cheer Squad shake their pom-poms.

Jason locks eyes with Chrissy.

                    JASON (CONT'D)
              Chrissy -- love ya babe.

Jason blows a kiss to Chrissy. She blows one right back.

The crowd OOOHS and AWWWWS. Robin tries not to vomit.

Jason walks back to the center of the stage and places his mic back in the stand. He gives a dramatic pause, then:

                    JASON (CONT'D)
              You know... I think I can speak for
              all of us when I say -- it's been a
              tough year for Hawkins. So much
              loss. Sometimes I wonder -- how
              much loss can one community take?

The bleachers are silent. The kids are holding on to his every word.

                    JASON (CONT'D)
              ... In dark days like this, we need
              something to believe in.
                         (MORE)

                    JASON (CONT'D)
          So last night, when we were down by
          ten points at half to Christian
          Academy, I told my team: Think of
          Jack... think of Melissa...think of
          Heather... think of Billy --

Max shifts uncomfortably at the mention of her brother.

                    JASON (CONT'D)
          Think about our heroic police chief
          Jim Hopper...think about each and
          every one of our friends who
          perished in that fire. What did
          they die for? For us to lose to
          some crap school? For us to return
          home with our heads hung low in
          defeat? No. *NO*. Let's win this game
          -- let's win it *for them*. And
          that's exactly what we DID.

The crowd cheers. Jason rips the mic back off the stand --
back to pacing.

                    JASON (CONT'D)
          We embarrassed those candy asses in
          THEIR OWN HOUSE!!! And tonight --
          TONIGHT -- we're gonna bring home
          that CHAMPIONSHIP TROPHY!!!

THE CROWD LEAPS TO THEIR FEET. WOOO!!!!!

ON THE BLEACHERS,

Dustin and Mike share shocked looks --

                    MIKE
          Did he just say "tonight" -- ?!

                    DUSTIN
          How is that possible?!

                    MAX
          They call it a "tournament" -- if
          you win one game, you play another,
          until only one team is left.

Mike and Dustin can't believe it. Their eyes shift to --

Lucas, high-fiving his teammates on the court.

As we PUSH IN ON Mike, irritation growing, CUT TO --

EXT. GYM - DAY

A herd of students leaving the gym, headed back to class.

A frustrated Mike and Dustin are walking with Lucas --

                LUCAS
I don't get the big deal -- just talk to Eddie, get him to move Hellfire to another night --

                DUSTIN
             (scoffing)
"Just talk to Eddie."

                MIKE
Why don't you "just talk" to your coach, get HIM to move the game --

                DUSTIN
That's a great idea, Mike --

                MIKE
Thank you, Dustin --

                LUCAS
This is the *Championship Game* --

                DUSTIN
And this is the end of Eddie's campaign!! A *semester* of adventuring has led to *this moment*! We *need* you --

                MIKE
And the Tigers *don't* -- you haven't come off the bench all year --

                LUCAS
That's not the point --

They head inside now --

INT. HAWKINS HIGH SCHOOL - HALLWAY - DAY

                DUSTIN
Please -- *arrive at the point* --

              LUCAS (CONT'D)
-- If I get in good with these guys, I'll be in the *popular crowd*. And then you guys will be too --

                    MIKE
          Did it ever cross your mind that
          maybe we don't _want_ to be popular??

                    LUCAS
          So you want to be stuck with the
          nerds and the freaks for three more
          years?

                    DUSTIN
          We ARE nerds and freaks --

                    LUCAS
          Yeah but maybe _we don't have to be_.

Lucas pauses by a classroom. He turns back to his friends,
his tone softening a bit -- _vulnerable_.

                    LUCAS (CONT'D)
          I'm just -- tired of being bullied,
          tired of girls laughing at us,
          tired of feeling like a -- a _loser_.
          I mean, we came into high school
          wanting things to be different,
          right?

Mike and Dustin hesitate --

                    LUCAS (CONT'D)
          Now we have that chance. I skip
          tonight, that's _all_ out the window.
          So I'm asking you guys, _as a friend_
          -- just get Eddie to move Hellfire
          and _come to my game_.
               (beat)
          Please.

Off Mike and Dustin, sharing looks, CUT TO --

EXT. LENORA HILLS - STREET - DAY

VROOM! A MAIL TRUCK speeds down a bumpy, dusty road.

We're back in Lenora Hills.

EXT. LENORA HILLS - STREET - DAY

The mail truck parks out front of the Byers'.

INT. MAIL TRUCK - DAY

WHOOM! The back door to the mail truck opens as --

The MAILMAN starts to gather his mail. As he works...

We PUSH IN ON a STRANGE BROWN PARCEL labeled: JOYCE BYERS.

> JOYCE (PRE-LAP)
> ... Missus Ergenbright, now -- let me ask you a question --

INT. BYERS HOUSE - JOYCE'S OFFICE - DAY

We find Joyce seated at her little office table, cordless phone pressed to her ear. She has her TELEMARKETER SCRIPT open.

> JOYCE
> Have you ever wished you had the answer to any question <u>right at your fingertips</u>?

Joyce listens a beat, then smiles --

> JOYCE (CONT'D)
> That's right -- those big fancy books you see on the TV --

DING DONG! The doorbell rings. Joyce rises to her feet --

INT. LIVING ROOM - MOMENTS LATER

Joyce continues her conversation as she heads for the door --

> JOYCE
> -- Just imagine, no more trips to the library -- I mean, the money you'll save on gas alone --

Joyce opens the door to reveal the Mailman on the other side. He's carrying a LARGE STACK OF MAIL for her -- letters and various magazines piled on top of that odd brown parcel.

Joyce cups the phone receiver as she takes the mail --

> JOYCE (CONT'D)
> *Anything* -- ?

                    FRIENDLY MAILMAN
          Nothin' -- but these acceptance
          letters tend to come end of week,
          just to make ya sweat. It's coming
          Missus Byers -- don't you worry.

                    JOYCE
          Oh, you know me -- *still gonna
          worry.*

She smiles, then shuts the door with her elbow, and --

INT. KITCHEN - MOMENTS LATER

THUNK! The stack of mail hits the kitchen counter.

                    JOYCE
          -- And how old is your grandchild?
          Five grandkids, *my GOODNESS* --

Joyce begins to casually sort through the mail,

                    JOYCE (CONT'D)
          -- Now Carol -- can I call you
          Carol? Do you think you'd like to
          start with A through C? Or should
          we just go for the whole alphab --

Joyce's voice catches in her throat. She's reached the brown parcel -- it looks battered to hell and it's SMOTHERED IN STAMPS. Whatever this is, it's been on *quite a journey.*

Joyce's heart nearly stops in her chest.

                    JOYCE (CONT'D)
          Yes, I -- I'm here -- I'm so sorry
          but -- can I call you right back?

WHAM! Joyce hangs up the phone. And...

INT. KITCHEN - MOMENTS LATER

Joyce lays the parcel down on her office table. Grabs scissors... opens the package... pries open the box... and...

Her eyes narrow. Inside: A CREEPY PORCELAIN RUSSIAN DOLL, COMPLETE WITH USHANKA HAT, TRADITIONAL DRESS, BEADY EYES.

As Joyce lifts up the doll, turning it around, baffled...

Our CAMERA PUSHES IN on one of the parcel's STAMPS.

It's a *HAMMER AND SICKLE*. Whatever this thing is...

IT'S FROM RUSSIA.

EXT. LENORA HILLS HIGH - DAY

WHOOSH! An American flag dances outside Lenora Hills High.

> ANGELA (PRE-LAP)
> ... After learning to speak, she traveled the world to spread her message...

INT. LENORA HILLS HIGH - CLASSROOM - DAY

Eleven is in class with her diorama. Her knees bop as...

Star student Angela gives a SLICK PRESENTATION to the class. She clicks through a SERIES OF PROFESSIONAL SLIDES.

> ANGELA
> ... And along the way *changed* how the world perceived those like her with disabilities. And that is why I have chosen Helen Keller as MY HERO.

CLICK! Angela switches to a final slide: THE END.

The class APPLAUDS. The history teacher, MRS. GRACEY, kicks on the lights.

> MRS. GRACEY
> That was wonderful Angela, truly wonderful! What an inspiring story.

As a beaming Angela returns to her chair, the Teacher walks over to her desk and dips her hand into a BOWL.

> MRS. GRACEY (CONT'D)
> Okay, now let's see who has to follow *that*...

The Teacher pulls out a SLIP OF PAPER --

> MRS. GRACEY (CONT'D)
> JANE!!

El's heart rises into her throat as the teacher leads the class in unenthusiastic applause. El shoots a nervous look to Will, but he gives her an encouraging nod: *You've got this!*

El stands and shuffles her way to the front of the class, clutching her diorama tight as she looks out at all those staring eyes. *Gulp.*

                    ELEVEN
          For my hero -- I -- I chose my dad.

People in the class share looks, *uhhhh...* Even the Teacher seems a bit thrown by this. *Hmmm.*

                    ELEVEN (CONT'D)
          And for my visual aid -- I made a
          direyama of his cabin --

                    ANGELA
               (low, to Jake)
          "Direyama" -- ?!

                    JAKE
               (low)
          More like "diarrhea" --

Angela and others LAUGH at this.

                    MRS. GRACEY
          Quiet everyone -- be respectful!

Eleven's anxiety spikes. *Rough start*. But she presses on. As she speaks, she motions to the relevant parts of her diorama.

                    ELEVEN
          This is my dad. His name is Hopper.
          And this is Mister Fibbly -- he is a
          squirrel -- he visited us every
          day.

More giggles. *Mr. Fibbly?* Will winces, feeling bad for El. As El continues, he looks down to find another foot grazing his own. He looks over to find --

A CUTE GIRL, 15. She inches her foot closer to his, playing footsie! Will smiles awkwardly at her, then --

<u>Pulls his foot away</u>. The Girl looks offended, but Will either doesn't notice or doesn't care as he returns his attention to --

El, who is still stammering through her report:

                    ELEVEN (CONT'D)
          ... And this is -- the alarm that
          my dad made -- to tell us if any
          bad men came -- but I was never
          scared -- because -- because --

Her voice catches, distracted by Angela -- who has an arm
raised high in the air.

                    MRS. GRACEY
          Angela, why don't we save questions
          until the end of Jane's
          presentation?

                    ANGELA
          Yeah sorry, I'm just, like,
          confused -- I thought this was a
          presentation about a historical
          hero?

                    MRS. GRACEY
          Well --

                    ELEVEN
          My dad -- was in the paper.

                    ANGELA
          Your *local* paper?

GIGGLES from the class.

                    ANGELA (CONT'D)
          I just don't think that's what Missus
          Gracey meant by historical -- this
          is supposed to be about *famous
          people* --

                    ELEVEN
              (defensive)
          My dad is famous -- he saved --
          lots of lives -- in a mall fire --
          he died for them -- he was a hero --
          for people -- and he was -- my hero
          too --

                    ANGELA
          That's not what I'm saying at all --
          but forget it. I'm *so* sorry Missus
          Gracey, I didn't mean to interrupt.
          I just wanted clarity on the rules
          of the assignment.

                    MRS. GRACEY
          Okay. Well -- technically you're
          right, Angela, but... Jane has
          decided to do her father so...
          please continue with your
          presentation Jane.

Off Eleven, completely humiliated, SMASH TO --

EXT. LENORA HILLS HIGH - DAY

Eleven bursts out of class. Upset. Will tries to keep up
with her --

                    WILL
          It wasn't that bad --

                    ELEVEN
          Friends *don't lie* --

                    WILL
          I'm not lying. El, come on -- *El* --

El picks up her pace and breaks away from Will. We hold with
El as she weaves through a crowd of students, trying not to
cry. PRE-LAP Kate Bush's "RUNNING UP THAT HILL" and CUT TO:

INT. HAWKINS HIGH - OUTSIDE COUNSELOR'S OFFICE - DAY

Max, listening to her favorite song on her Walkman as she
weaves her way through her own crowded hallway. She looks
around as she walks, sees various happy imagery that
juxtaposes with her dark mood:

-- TEEN GIRLS SMILING AND LAUGHING

-- A TEEN BOY AND GIRL KISSING

-- LUCAS LAUGHING WITH ANDY AND PATRICK. HE CLOCKS HER, BUT
SHE QUICKLY LOOKS AWAY AND TOWARD --

-- Her first "unhappy" sight: Chrissy the Cheerleader exiting
an office, fighting tears. Chrissy slips on her hoodie and
hurries away down the hall.

Max watches her go, then heads into the same office.

A sign reads: COUNSELING.

                    MS. KELLEY (PRE-LAP)
               Can you remove the headphones
               please?

INT. HAWKINS HIGH - COUNSELOR'S OFFICE - DAY

Max slips off her headphones. The music abruptly stops.

                         MAX
               ... Sorry.

WIDEN: Max is sitting across from Ms. Kelley.

Max's feet bounce as Ms. Kelley shuffles through Max's file.

                    MS. KELLEY
               ... A C in English -- a C *minus* in
               Spanish --

                         MAX
               Yeah --

                    MS. KELLEY
               That's not normal for you.

                         MAX
               If you say so.

Ms. Kelley pushes aside the papers, shifts tactics.

                    MS. KELLEY
               How is your mom holding up?

                         MAX
               She's fine. I mean -- she hates our
               new place. Which -- yeah. It's
               terrible. But she's fine.

                    MS. KELLEY
               Is she still drinking?

Max tightens, gets defensive --

                         MAX
               Like -- yeah -- a little. I mean...
               she's working two jobs so... it's
               not easy --

                    MS. KELLEY
               It must not be easy for you either,
               not having your stepdad around
               anymore --

                    MAX
          It's... kinda better, honestly --

                    MS. KELLEY
          Better how?

                    MAX
          He was an asshole? So I guess now
          there's less -- assholery.

                    MS. KELLEY
          Are you sleeping better --

                    MAX
          Yeah -- fine --

                    MS. KELLEY
          So no more headaches?

Max shakes her head. Nope.

                    MS. KELLEY (CONT'D)
          Nightmares -- ?

*WE FLASH TO BILLY DYING -- MAX WATCHING HELPLESSLY --
SCREAMING -- TENTACLES SHOOTING INTO HIS CHEST AND --*

                    MAX
          ... Nope.

Ms. Kelley looks at Max. Concerned.

                    MS. KELLEY
          Max. What you've been through --
          what you're still going through --
          it's a lot for *anyone*. And it's
          okay to not be okay. But I can only
          help you if you're truthful. If
          you... open up to me.

                    MAX
          Yeah... I, I know. I'm being open.

Ms. Kelley gives Max a look, *challenging her*. But --

                    MAX (CONT'D)
          I'm being open.

Off Ms. Kelley, frustrated, CUT TO --

INT. HAWKINS HIGH - HALLWAY - DAY

Max escapes the counselor's office, only to find --

Lucas waiting for her. *Jesus can she catch a break??*

> LUCAS
> Hey, Max --

Max keeps walking, moving fast. Lucas pursues, keeping pace.

> MAX
> What are you stalking me or something -- ??

> LUCAS
> No, I just, uh, wanted to give you...

He excitedly hands her a TICKET --

> MAX
> What is this -- ??

> LUCAS
> (duh)
> A ticket to the game --

Max shoots him a look. *Really?*

> LUCAS (CONT'D)
> I know you never want to go to my games, but this one is kinda a big deal --

> MAX
> A *big deal*. Lucas, you *seriously* care about this -- ?

> LUCAS
> Yeah. *I do*. You know -- maybe you should find something you care about too --

> MAX
> What is *that* supposed to mean -- ?

> LUCAS
> You're just -- not even here anymore. It's like -- you're a *ghost* or something --

                    MAX
          A ghost. *Really?*

                    LUCAS
          Max. I *know* something is wrong.

                    MAX
          Right. Something must be wrong
          because I broke up with you --

                    LUCAS
          That's not what I meant --

                    MAX
          People just -- *change, Lucas*. Okay?
          I've changed. It's *that simple*.

Max hands him the ticket back.

                    MAX (CONT'D)
          Good luck.

She ducks into the girls' bathroom and --

INT. HAWKINS HIGH - BATHROOM - DAY

WHOOM! Max drops in front of the sink. Can *finally breathe*.

She opens her backpack, removes a BOTTLE OF TYLENOL. She pops two pills, quickly swallows them with water, takes a beat to gather her composure, and --

She hears something: GAGGING. *VOMITING*. She turns. The awful sounds are coming from a bathroom stall. She can see the back of shoes; someone is kneeling by the toilet in there.

                    MAX
          Hey? Are you... alright?

INT. BATHROOM STALL

It's Chrissy. She wipes her mouth, looks back, breathing hard.

                    CHRISSY
          Yes -- I -- I'm fine --

INT. BATHROOM

Max is unsure what to do here --

>   MAX
>   Are you sure -- ?
>
>   CHRISSY
>   Yes -- please just -- *go away*.

Max hesitates for a beat, then exits. But we stay behind as --

INT. BATHROOM STALL

Chrissy wipes spittle from her mouth, flushes the vomit down the toilet, and --

KNOCKING on her stall.

>   CHRISSY
>   Are you deaf??? I said go away!
>
>   WOMAN'S VOICE (O.S.)
>   *Chrissy?*

Chrissy stops, turns -- confused as all hell --

>   CHRISSY
>   ... M-mom??
>
>   CHRISSY'S MOM (O.S.)
>   You ready to try on the dress
>   again? I loosened the back a little
>   for you...

Chrissy now looks down under the stall to find --

THE FEET STANDING OUTSIDE THE STALL ARE NOT HER MOM'S -- THEY ARE PALE, GNARLED, SLIMY, LONG TOES. FLESH PEELING AWAY --

IT'S A MONSTER. SUDDENLY --

BZZZT! The fluorescent light begins to flicker above.

Chrissy, scared, pulls herself up onto the toilet seat as --

Her Mother's voice turns guttural, distorted:

>   "CHRISSY'S MOM" (O.S.)
>   *CHRISSY? DID YOU HEAR ME???*

The stall door begins to SHAKE and RATTLE --

Chrissy fights tears, fear --

                    CHRISSY
          PLEASE -- LEAVE ME ALONE --

BAM BAM!!! The door rattles more --

                    "CHRISSY'S MOM" (O.S.)
                    (voice distorting, becoming
                    monstrous)
          OPEN THE GODDAMN DOOR CHRISSY OR
          I'LL GUT YOU LIKE THE FAT PIG YOU
          ARE YOU HEAR ME!! YOU HEAR ME??!!

                    CHRISSY
          GO AWAY GO AWAY GO AWAY -- !!!!

The banging on the door gets louder and LOUDER --

Chrissy covers her ears and squeezes her eyes shut, then --

THE BANGING ABRUPTLY STOPS.

Chrissy peels open her eyes and...

INT. BATHROOM - OUTSIDE THE STALL - MOMENTS LATER

The stall door opens and Chrissy steps out. Looks around.

WIDEN: The bathroom is empty. No one is in here.

                    DRAMATIC VOICE (PRE-LAP)
          THE DEVIL HAS COME TO AMERICA.

INT. HAWKINS HIGH SCHOOL - CAFETERIA - DAY

CLOSE ON: EDDIE, 20, charismatic but "scary looking" with long hair, heavy metal T-shirt, and a guitar pick necklace.

He is reading a magazine article to a table of FREAKS and OUTSIDERS. They all wear HELLFIRE CLUB SHIRTS.

                    EDDIE
                    (over-the-top news anchor
                    voice)
          Dungeons and Dragons, at first
          regarded as a harmless game of make-
          believe, now has both parents and
          psychologists concerned. Studies
          have linked violent behavior to the
          game, saying it promotes satanic
          worship, ritual sacrifice, sodomy,
          suicide, and even... MUUUUUURDER!

Everyone at the table CHUCKLES as --

ACROSS THE CAFETERIA,

We find Mike and Dustin, holding their food trays, watching Eddie from afar. They look nervous.

> DUSTIN
> He looks revved up today.
>
> MIKE
> He's *always* revved up. Just -- act casual.
>
> DUSTIN
> Casual, right. Totally.

Our boys walk forward, not casual at all, and --

AT THE TABLE - MOMENTS LATER

CLOSE ON: Trays hitting a table --

Dustin and Mike join the "freak" table.

> FREAK
> Society has to blame something, we're an easy target --
>
> EDDIE
> Exactly -- we're the "freaks" because we like fantasy games --

Eddie hops up on his chair so he can survey the whole cafeteria. He proceeds to point out the various cliques scattered about the cafeteria --

> EDDIE (CONT'D)
> But as long as you're into band, or science, or parties, or GAMES WHERE YOU TOSS BALLS INTO LAUNDRY BASKETS --

Eddie points to a GROUP OF JOCKS at a nearby table -- including Jason and Lucas.

> JASON
> You want something freak?!

Eddie sticks out his tongue and makes devil horns above his head with his fingers, freaking out those jocks, then --

He drops back down into his chair, smiles --

>   EDDIE
>   Then you're all good. It's forced
>   conformity -- THAT'S what's killing
>   kids. *That's* the real monster --

Dustin suddenly breaks in --

>   DUSTIN
>   I think you hit the nail right on
>   the head there Eddie -- and uh --
>   (glances to Mike)
>   Speaking of monsters --
>   (way too fast, NOT casual)
>   Lucas has to play in his ball-in-
>   laundry-baskets game so he can't
>   come to Hellfire tonight and no way
>   we can beat your sadistic campaign
>   without him so Mike and I have been
>   talking and we think we have no
>   choice but to -- to --

>   MIKE
>   *Postpone*.

MOANS and JEERS from the "Freaks" --

>   EDDIE
>   Whoa whoa whoa -- hold up hold up.
>   Let me get this straight --
>   Sinclair's been taken in by the
>   dark side -- ??

>   MIKE
>   Something like that --

>   EDDIE
>   And rather than find a sub for him
>   you want to... *postpone* "THE CULT
>   OF VECNA"??

Mike and Dustin share nervous looks.

>   MIKE
>   Yeah, I mean, we'd find a sub, but,
>   like *everyone's* going to this
>   championship game --

>   EDDIE
>   The cool kids aren't.

Laughter from the table.

                    EDDIE (CONT'D)
          Listen guys -- I'll level with you.
          Jeff graduates this year, Gareth's
          got what? A year left?

                    GARETH
          If I'm lucky --

                    EDDIE
          Meanwhile, me, I'm army crawling my
          way toward a D in Miss O'Donnell's.
          I don't blow her final, I'm gonna
          walk the stage next month -- and
          then I'm gonna look Principal
          Higgins dead in the eyes, flip him
          the bird, snatch that diploma, and
          run like hell --

                    GARETH
          You said that last year --

                    JEFF
          And the year before --

                    EDDIE
          Yeah and I was full of shit -- but
          this year is different. I can *just
          feel it*. This is my year. *Eighty-
          six*. And you know what that means?
               (points at Dustin and Mike)
          It means you boys are the future of
          Hellfire.

Dustin and Mike light up. This means the world to them.

                    EDDIE (CONT'D)
          I knew it from the moment I saw you
          two sitting alone at that table
          over there, lookin' like two lost
          little sheep --
               (to Dustin)
          Dustin you were wearing your Weird
          Al shirt, which I thought was
          brave --
               (to Mike)
          And Mike, you were wearing whatever
          shit your mom bought you at the
          goddamn Gap --
               (Dustin laughs, Mike
                blushes)
                    (MORE)

                    EDDIE (CONT'D)
          And we showed you that this school
          didn't have to be the worst years
          of your lives, right?

               DUSTIN   MIKE
Right --   Totally --

                    EDDIE
          Well -- I'm here to tell you --
          there are other lost sheepies out
          there that need help. That need
          you. All you guys got to do is get
          your Bo-peeps on and find *one*. And
          you've got approximately --
               (checks watch)
          Six hours.

Mike and Dustin share looks. Worried. But --

                    EDDIE (CONT'D)
          Oh -- and hey -- if you need help
          convincing anyone --

Eddie tosses them the magazine article. The headline reads: "D AND D: THE DEVIL'S GAME." An illustration depicts a table of kids playing D&D in Hell. Off this, MATCH CUT TO:

INT. BYERS HOUSE - LENORA HILLS - DAY

FWOOM! EXTREME CLOSE ON: A FLAME LIGHTING UP AS --

Joyce lights a cigarette. She drags on it as she paces in her living room. Back and forth. Back and --

BRRRRRRING! The phone rings. Joyce rips it up --

                    JOYCE
          -- The hell have you been???

INT. MURRAY'S HOUSE - DAY - CROSSCUT

It's MURRAY!! He's wearing a KARATE UNIFORM -- and he's *very sweaty*.

                    MURRAY
          I have karate from three to five on
          Fridays.

Murray grabs a GIANT BAG OF ICE from the freezer, then proceeds to limp across his house --

MURRAY (CONT'D)
So let me see if I have this right:
You received a doll in the mail?

JOYCE
Yes --

MURRAY
And it's creepy -- ?

JOYCE
Yes --

MURRAY
And you believe it's from Russia?

JOYCE
I know it is.

She crosses over to the parcel --

JOYCE (CONT'D)
There's a -- a stamp with that
hammer and -- curved sword thing-a-
ma-jig --

MURRAY
Sickle --

JOYCE
Whatever --

MURRAY
Sounds like it came from Russia --

JOYCE
Wow I'm so glad I called --

Murray enters his --

BATHROOM - CONTINUOUS

He dumps the ice into a running bath --

JOYCE
Should I be worried?

MURRAY
I would be. It could be a threat.
After all, we did sabotage their
U.S. operation and killed about two
dozen "comrades" --

44

Joyce drags hard on her cigarette, getting nervous.

      JOYCE
  How -- how could they know my name?

      MURRAY
  If it's the KGB, Joyce -- if they
  want to find out who you are, they
  will.

Murray strips off his karate robe. Which gives him an idea --

      MURRAY (CONT'D)
  Can you undress her?

      JOYCE
  What -- ?

      MURRAY
  The creepy doll -- can you remove
  her dress??

      JOYCE
  I -- I think so --

Joyce unbuttons the doll's dress and pulls it off and --

      JOYCE (CONT'D)
  Jesus --

      MURRAY
  What -- ?

      JOYCE
  She has... *nipples.*

Murray settles into the bath. Exhales. *Feels good.*

Joyce is unsettled by his noises.

      MURRAY
  Okay now -- do you see anything
  taped to her -- wires or a bug or
  something?

Joyce rotates the doll. Sees no bugs but --

      JOYCE
  She's -- cracked --

      MURRAY
  Cracked -- ?

                    JOYCE
          The porcelain. It's -- it's been
          broken -- glued back together.

Sure enough, we see a crack cutting across the doll's
abdomen, like she's had an appendectomy or something.

                    MURRAY
          Do you have rope? And something
          heavy?

                    JOYCE
          ... For what?

                    MURRAY
          Smashing.

INT. LENORA HILLS HIGH - WOODSHOP CLASS - DAY

WHAM-WHAM-WHAM! A HAMMER SMASHES a nail.

WIDEN: We're in woodshop class with Jonathan now. He's making
a bird feeder. Working beside him --

Argyle. He holds up his bird feeder. It looks, uhhh... hemp-
shaped.

                    ARGYLE
          What do you think, Byers? I call it
          a weeder -- get it, man?? Not a
          feeder. Weeder -- !!

Argyle is clearly very pleased with himself but Jonathan
offers only a small smile.

                    JONATHAN
          Clever --

                    ARGYLE
          Just tryin' to turn that frown
          upside down, man.

Jonathan carries a piece of wood to another table, not
smiling. Argyle traipses after him in his flip-flops.

                    ARGYLE (CONT'D)
          Come on dude -- you gonna mope
          around all break man or what -- ?

Jonathan lines up some wood to cut.

                    JONATHAN
          I'm not -- moping --

                    ARGYLE
          This about your girl ditchin' you
          or what -- ?

                    JONATHAN
          Nancy is *not ditching me* --

                    ARGYLE
          Oh so she's coming now -- ?

                    JONATHAN
          No --

                    ARGYLE
          Sooo she's DITCHING you --

                    JONATHAN
          Dude -- no. She wants to come,
          okay? She just has to work --

                    ARGYLE
          She a lady of the night or
          something -- ?

                    JONATHAN
          What? No -- !

                    ARGYLE
          Who else works over spring break,
          man???

                    JONATHAN
          Nancy. Nancy does.

As Jonathan begins to saw --

INT. JOURNALISM CLASS - DAY

SWOOSH! An EXACTO KNIFE slices through paper.

WIDEN: We're in a busy journalism classroom as a GAGGLE OF STUDENTS work to put together the school paper's SPRING BREAK EDITION. The leader of it all:

Nancy. As she moves around the room, inspecting various students' work, she is trailed by --

FRED BENSON, 16. He's scrawny, wears glasses, and he's got a SCAR on his face. We've caught them mid-conversation --

FRED
Maybe I'm just missing something
here... but why can't Jonathan just
come *out here* for break?

Nancy hesitates, as if wondering this herself, then --

NANCY
A lot of reasons.

Nancy moves up to a FEMALE STUDENT and inspects her page
layout. The headline reads: "TIGERS WIN!!!" She frowns; the
organization is clunky.

NANCY (CONT'D)
You mind if I take a crack at this,
Candace -- ?

CANDACE
All yours.

As Nancy begins to rearrange the layout to her liking --

FRED
Such as -- ?

NANCY
What -- ?

FRED
You said there were "lots of
reasons" he's not coming. *Such
as -- ?*

Nancy turns to him, annoyed --

NANCY
Why are you being so nosy -- ??

FRED
Let's just call it -- *journalistic
instincts* --

NANCY
Well -- there's no *story here*, if
that's what you're after, at least
not a very interesting one.
         (returns to rearranging as
          she talks, playing off)
              (MORE)

                    NANCY (CONT'D)
          His mom has to work, and he needs
          to watch over his brother -- on top
          of that, he wasn't early decision
          like me, so he's still waiting for
          his acceptance letter -- he's
          nervous and wants to be there when
          it comes, which I *totally get* --

                        FRED
          Well -- um   *I don't*. It just --

INT. WOODSHOP CLASS - DAY

                      ARGYLE
          -- *Doesn't make sense*, dude. Let me
          just -- sift through this madness,
          yeah? Nancy is the supposed love of
          your life -- in fact you're so
          smitten you've got this grand plan
          to go to some fancy schmancy
          college AKA money pit together --

INT. JOURNALISM CLASS - DAY

                        FRED
          -- And yet he's so nervous about
          this acceptance letter he can't
          visit the *number one most desired
          girl in Hawkins*?? I mean, you don't
          have be in Mensa like yours truly
          to realize --

INT. WOODSHOP CLASS - DAY

                      ARGYLE
          -- That doesn't pass the smell
          test. In fact, it stinks to high
          heaven my dude. I mean, I haven't
          even seen you look at girls all
          year, you've been a good boy, and
          it is past time you give your right
          hand a vacation and get some well-
          deserved *hanky-panky* --

INT. JOURNALISM CLASS - DAY

Nancy grimaces --

NANCY
Okay -- first of all, Fred, I'm going to pretend you didn't just say any of that... about me... being... *desired*. It's --

INT. WOODSHOP CLASS - DAY

JONATHAN
Gross dude -- super gross. And --- you just don't understand Nancy --

INT. JOURNALISM CLASS - DAY

NANCY
He's not like you or other guys -- he's *caring* and *compassionate* and --

INT. WOODSHOP CLASS - DAY

JONATHAN
-- *Incredibly ambitious*. She's never done a single thing halfway in her life --

INT. JOURNALISM CLASS - DAY

NANCY
-- He's so protective of everyone he loves, especially his mom and brother --

INT. WOODSHOP CLASS - DAY

JONATHAN
So if she takes on something like the editor of the school paper -- she's going to make that the best damn school paper that's ever existed --

INT. JOURNALISM CLASS - DAY

NANCY
And he will never back down from what's right -- what's moral -- no matter the pressure, no matter the personal cost --

INT. WOODSHOP CLASS - DAY

> JONATHAN
> And that's why I love her --

INT. JOURNALISM CLASS - DAY

> NANCY
> That's why I love him.

INT. WOODSHOP CLASS - DAY

> JONATHAN
> Everything between us is totally and completely --

INT. JOURNALISM CLASS - DAY

> NANCY
> -- Perfect.

Nancy finishes her layout for the first page of the paper. She studies it, clearly pleased, but --

> FRED
> Eh. I'm still rooting for my alt.

Fred holds up another article. The headline reads: "TIGERS DEVOURED. BLOOD AND TEARS SHED." Before Nancy can respond --

BOOM! The door suddenly bursts open. Nancy whirls to find --

Mike barging into her class. Everyone turns --

> MIKE
> Sorry but -- Nancy -- you want to join Hellfire tonight??

Nancy stares. Mike holds up some crumpled one-dollar bills.

> MIKE (CONT'D)
> I can pay.

Nancy continues to stare at her brother and --

FAST-PACED, BUILDING SYNTH MUSIC NOW BEGINS AS:

EXT. HAWKINS HIGH

Dustin is on the payphone talking to someone...

                    DUSTIN
          Just move your date this *one time*!

INT. FAMILY VIDEO - DAY - INTERCUT

Steve is on the other end at Family Video!

                    STEVE
          To hang out with you and *Eddie
          "the Freak" Munson*?? Yeah, I think
          I'll pass --

                    DUSTIN
          You're just jealous that I have
          another older male friend --

                    STEVE
               (wincing)
          Dude. That sounds wrong. Also
          I *really* dig this chick, I think
          she could be, like, *the one* --

Steve looks up as a GAGGLE OF COLLEGE GIRLS enter the store.

                    STEVE (CONT'D)
          Got some customers, call ya back --

                    DUSTIN
          You can't call me back I'm --

DIAL TONE.

                    DUSTIN (CONT'D)
          ... At *school*.

Dustin slams the phone back onto the hook in irritation as --

INT. GYM - WRESTLING CLUB - DAY

WHAM! Two WRESTLERS slam into one another. On the sidelines, Mike tries to convince a skeptical WRESTLER TEEN to play.

                    WRESTLER TEEN
          So you fight -- with dice -- ?

                    MIKE
          Yeah but these are not normal dice
          -- they have *up to TWENTY SIDES*.

The Wrestler Kid stares at Mike and --

EXT. HAWKINS HIGH - DAY

Dustin talks to Max, who is skateboarding outside.

>   MAX
>   If I play, do I get one of those
>   cool T-shirts?

>   DUSTIN
>   Yeah, everyone gets --
>   (realizing)
>   You're being sarcastic.

Max gives Dustin a "no shit" look, then glides away and --

INT. SCIENCE CLUB - DAY

Mike is talking to a nerdy KID IN GOGGLES.

>   KID IN GOGGLES
>   My mom says that game promotes
>   satanism and animal cruelty --

>   MIKE
>   That's just bullshit media
>   propaganda --

>   KID IN GOGGLES
>   *60 Minutes* begs to differ --

BOOM! A FOUNTAIN OF FIRE ERUPTS from the test tube and --

INT. HAWKINS HIGH - MATH CLASSROOM - DAY

A MATH STUDENT shoots down Dustin --

>   MATH STUDENT
>   Nah --

INT. HAWKINS HIGH - ART CLASS - DAY

An ART KID shoots down Mike:

>   ART KID
>   No --

INT. HAWKINS HIGH - CHESS CLUB - DAY

>   CHESS KID
>   (to Dustin)
>   NO --

INT. HAWKINS HIGH - THEATER - DAY

                    DRAMA KID
            (to Mike)
  NO!!!

EXT. HAWKINS HIGH - DAY

The synth music crashes to an end as --

Mike and Dustin drop down on a bench outside school.

Out-of-breath. *Failures both.*

                    MIKE
    I hate high school.

Dustin eyes the MIDDLE SCHOOL up the street. *Lightbulb.*

                    DUSTIN
    So *screw* it.

                    MIKE
    What -- ?

                    DUSTIN
    Screw *high school*.

With that, Dustin is off and racing for the middle school!

                    MIKE
    Dustin -- where are you going --
    DUSTIN???

Mike chases after him, sprinting right past --

CHRISSY. She is walking in the other direction. Hoodie up.

Our CAMERA TRACKS HER. *What is she doing out of class?*

EXT. FOOTBALL FIELD

Chrissy heads across the field -- *for the woods*.

EXT. WOODS BEHIND SCHOOL - DAY

Chrissy makes her way through the woods behind the school.

She comes to a stop at an OLD PICNIC TABLE, half claimed by the forest, CIGARETTE BUTTS, and EMPTY BEER CANS.

She looks around, calls out --

                    CHRISSY
            ... Hello? HELLO...?

Her call goes unanswered. *Wait*. She hears something. A CHIME.
It echoes through the forest. *Eerie*. She turns now, sees --

THE FACE OF A GRANDFATHER CLOCK EMBEDDED IN A TREE. *What the
hell?* The clock continues to chime as she walks over to it.
Then, on the fourth chime, it happens: The glass begins to
crack in an unusual pattern, spreading *inward* from four
corners of the clock. A BLACK WIDOW SPIDER crawls out of the
EPICENTER OF THE CRACK. She backs up in terror and --

WHAM! SLAMS INTO SOMEONE!!! SHE WHIRLS WITH A GASP BUT IT'S
JUST --

Eddie!!

                    EDDIE
            Hey -- sorry -- didn't mean to
            startle you.

Chrissy whirls back. The clock is gone. Just a regular tree.

                    EDDIE (CONT'D)
            You okay...?

Off Chrissy, obviously *not okay*...

A LITTLE LATER

WHAM! A metal lunchbox hits the picnic table. WIDEN: Eddie
and Chrissy are now seated across from one another. As Eddie
unsnaps the lunchbox hinges, he eyes Chrissy with concern.
She is looking around, still on edge, her legs bouncing --

                    EDDIE
            Listen -- there's nothing to be
            worried about, no one ever comes
            out here -- *promise, alright?*

Chrissy gives a shaky nod. Eddie now opens the lunchbox,
revealing BAGS OF WEED. LOTS OF WEED. Holy crap -- Eddie is a
drug dealer!! Chrissy shifts a bit, uncomfortable --

                    CHRISSY
            So... how -- how does this work
            exactly?

                    EDDIE
          Just like any other ol' sale, but
          cash only, and for obvious reasons,
          no receipts. I'll give you half an
          ounce for an even twenty. Good bang
          for your buck, last you awhile,
          whaddaya say?

Chrissy is about to respond when she hears a RUSTLING SOUND.
Her eyes snap to the sound, but it's only a SQUIRREL,
scrambling up a tree. Eddie softens --

                    EDDIE (CONT'D)
          Hey. We don't have to do this you
          know -- give me the word and I'll
          walk away, this <u>never happened</u> --

                    CHRISSY
          No, it's not that, I don't want you
          to go... it's just --
               (beat, fighting tears)
          You ever feel like... you're losing
          your mind?

                    EDDIE
          Ohhh ya know -- just pretty much on
          a *daily basis*. Shit, I think I'm
          losing my mind right now, doing a
          drug deal with Chrissy Cunningham,
          the *Queen of Hawkins High* --

Chrissy smiles a bit at this, feeling a little better...

                    EDDIE (CONT'D)
          Though I don't know if you
          remember, but this actually isn't
          the first time we've hung out --

                    CHRISSY
          Oh? Sorry -- I don't --

                    EDDIE
          It's cool, I wouldn't remember me
          either. Middle school talent show,
          you were doing this cheer routine,
          it was pretty cool actually, and I
          was with my band --

                    CHRISSY
               (suddenly remembering)
          The Dirty Scabs --

                    EDDIE
          The Dirty Scabs yeah --

                    CHRISSY
          Oh my God -- yes!! Wow. With a name
          like that how could I forget? You
          just -- you looked so --

                    EDDIE
          Different? Well, my hair was buzzed
          and I didn't have these sweet tats
          yet --

                    CHRISSY
          You played -- *guitar, right* -- ?

Eddie holds up a GUITAR PICK NECKLACE.

                    EDDIE
          Still do. You should come see us
          sometime -- we play the Hideout on
          Tuesdays, we usually draw a crowd
          of about five drunks. It's not
          quite the Garden, but hey -- I
          figure you gotta start somewhere,
          right?

                    CHRISSY
          You know ---- you're... not what I
          thought you'd be like --

                    EDDIE
          Mean and scary?

Chrissy nods -- *sorry*.

                    EDDIE (CONT'D)
          Well, I thought you'd be mean and
          scary too, so... guess we were both
          wrong.

A shared smile.

                    EDDIE (CONT'D)
          And, in other good news --
          flattery gets you a twenty-five
          percent discount! So -- fifteen for
          the half ounce? What do ya say?

Chrissy hesitates, then -- feeling more comfortable with
Eddie now -- asks:

                    CHRISSY
          Do you have anything... maybe...
          stronger?

Off Eddie, surprised once more by Chrissy, CUT TO --

EXT. LENORA HILLS HIGH - DAY

BRRRRRING! The bell rings outside Lenora Hills and --

INT. LENORA HILLS HIGH - MATH CLASSROOM - DAY

Excited students pour out of class as --

A MATH TEACHER hands out tests as everyone leaves --

                    MATH TEACHER
          Nice job, Kate -- *excellent work*.
          Paul, nice improvement --

Eleven steps up and the teacher's mood turns dark --

                    MATH TEACHER (CONT'D)
          -- Let's talk after break.

She hands El her test. It's an F. Off Eleven --

EXT. LENORA HILLS HIGH - COURTYARD - DAY

Eleven heads out of school, *all alone*, clutching tight to her diorama, when --

WHOOM! An OUTSTRETCHED LEG trips her! She crashes face-first onto the sidewalk, falling RIGHT ON TOP OF HER CABIN DIORAMA!

The culprit: Angela. *Of course*. She's with her mean posse.

                    ANGELA
          Oh my God, I'm soooo sorry -- I
          hope Mister Fibbly is okay!

LAUGHTER from the mean posse as they continue on their way --

ACROSS THE WAY

Will, just now walking outside, sees this happen. *Shit.*

BACK WITH ELEVEN,

Eleven pushes to her knees, sees --

THE CABIN HAS BEEN DESTROYED. Her sadness gives way to *anger*.

She stands and turns to the mean girls and:

                    ELEVEN
    <u>ANGELA</u>.

Angela and the mean girls spin back around as --

Eleven lets out a furious scream --

                  ELEVEN (CONT'D)
    AHHHHHHHH!!!

She thrusts out an open hand and --

<u>NOTHING HAPPENS.</u> <u>HER POWERS STILL DON'T WORK.</u>

But Eleven's scream has drawn the attention of *everyone nearby*. It feels like the *WHOLE SCHOOL* is staring at her.

An ERUPTION OF LAUGHER.

                  ANGELA
    Holy shit -- !!

                  MEAN GIRL
    What the hell was that????

The LAUGHTER GROWS when suddenly --

                  MRS. GRACEY (O.S.)
    What's going on here???

Silence falls as everyone turns to find Mrs. Gracey pushing her way through the crowd. She sees the broken diorama -- turns to El --

                  MRS. GRACEY (CONT'D)
    Did someone do this, Jane?

El quickly looks at Angela, then away --

                  ELEVEN
        (fighting tears)
    I tripped. It was... just... an
    accident --

But Mrs. Gracey knows better. She looks at Angela.

                  MRS. GRACEY
    Alright, Angela, come with me --

                         ANGELA
              What? Why -- I didn't do anything --
              tell her, Jane -- !

But Eleven doesn't say anything --

                         MRS. GRACEY
              LET'S *GO* --

As Mrs. Gracey takes Angela by the arm and drags her away, soundtracked by the "OOOOOOOOH" of students--

Eleven kneels down to pick up her diorama. Will comes over, kneels to help.

                         WILL
              Are you... okay?

El manages a small nod. Picks up --

The Hopper figurine. He's been <u>shattered in half</u>. The first tear falls as she places him back in the diorama and --

EXT. LENORA HILLS HOUSE - DAY

EEEE! A rope carrying a PAINT CAN drags across a tree limb.

WIDEN TO REVEAL: Joyce is pulling on the other end of the rope -- she has devised a MAKESHIFT PULLEY SYSTEM to crush this doll! To top it all off, she has her cordless phone cupped between her shoulder and her ear and she's wearing safety goggles and gardening gloves.

She's looking very... well... *Joyce*.

ACROSS THE STREET,

A NEIGHBOR, helping her small kids out of the car, catches this bizarre sight. Joyce shoots her a friendly smile, but --

The Mom pulls her kids toward the house.

                         MOM
              Come on, Timmy -- don't stare --

BACK OVER AT THE BYERS HOUSE,

                         JOYCE
                      (into phone)
              Was this really necessary??

INT. MURRAY'S HOUSE - DAY - INTERCUT

Murray is pacing in his towel.

>   MURRAY
>   If that porcelain belly is pregnant
>   with an explosive device, you will
>   soon be THANKING ME.

EXT. BYERS HOUSE - DAY

Joyce finishes pulling the paint can to the top of the tree --

>   MURRAY
>   And remember, you're not lowering
>   this bucket. You're --

>   JOYCE
>   Releasing -- I got it --

>   MURRAY
>   We want to make sure we destroy
>   that doll with as much force as
>   possible --

>   JOYCE
>   Yep GOT IT --

>   MURRAY
>   Oh one more thing --

Too late. Joyce release the rope and --

SHOOM! The paint can *ROCKETS DOWNWARD* toward the doll. As metal collides with porcelain, a freaked Joyce drops the phone and covers her face and --

INT. MURRAY'S HOUSE

CHHHHH! Murray hears crazed static on the other end!

>   MURRAY
>   Joyce -- talk to me -- are you
>   there?? Joyce?!

EXT. BYERS HOUSE

CLOSE ON: A GLOVED HAND grabs the phone up out of the grass.

It's Joyce. She's out of breath -- but very much alive.

                         JOYCE
              Hi.

                         MURRAY
              What happened??

                         JOYCE
              It broke.

Joyce walks over, kicks the paint can away, and stares down
at the remains of the doll. Amidst the shattered porcelain...

A GREASY FOLDED-UP PIECE OF PAPER.

                         MURRAY
              Do you see a bug? Anything with
              wires?

Joyce is too transfixed to answer.

She picks up the paper, unfolds it. It's a NOTE.

                         MURRAY (CONT'D)
              Joyce, what's going on? Do you see
              anything? *Joyce?*

As she starts to read, we PUSH IN on the note. It's been
written with cut-out magazine letters, like a ransom note. On
the top of the letter, a "headline" of sorts reads:

              "HOP IS ALIVE."

Joyce can hardly believe what she's reading. The phone slips
off her shoulder... her eyes fill with shock and emotion.

                         MURRAY (CONT'D)
              Joyce? *Joyce???*

As the *FIRST TEAR* slips down her cheek, we pre-lap the SOUND
OF APPLAUSE AND CHEERING as --

INT. HAWKINS HIGH - GYMNASIUM - NIGHT

Tiger fans are on their feet -- CHEERING!

We're back in the Hawkins High gym and it's almost game time!
The gym is JAM-*PACKED* with excited parents and kids. Our
CAMERA ROAMS, checking in with all of our characters here:

Lucas -- Jason -- Chrissy -- Robin -- Vickie -- Nancy --

And Steve, who is here with a DITZY DATE!

                    DITZY DATE
          Does it bother you that, like, we
          might win a championship like _right_
          after you graduated??

                    STEVE
          You know -- that's an interesting
          point, thank you _so much_ for
          bringing that up, Brenda.

Steve smiles big and fake as --

The band wraps up with a flourish.

An ANNOUNCER (at the scoring table) speaks into a mic:

                    ANNOUNCER
          Everyone now -- please rise for our
          national anthem.

Everyone stands. Hats are removed from heads.

                    ANNOUNCER (CONT'D)
          Singing for us tonight, we have a
          very special guest -- she has come
          allllll the way from Nashville --
          our very own _TAMMY THOMPSON_!

A stunned Robin shoots a look to a stunned Steve as --

TAMMY THOMPSON struts out to mid-court to BIG CHEERS! She is cute and _annoyingly cheery_. She wraps a hand around the mic. Closes her eyes. And begins:

                    TAMMY
          O, SAYYYYY CAN YOU SEEEEE/ BY THE
          DAWN'S EARLY LIGHT!!!/ WHAT SO
          PROUUUUUUDLY WE HAILED /AT THE
          TWILIGHT'S LAST GLEAMING...

Her voice is everything we've hoped for -- nasally, out-of-tune, and just generally..._unpleasant_.

                    DITZY DATE
          Wow -- she sounds _amazing_, doesn't
          she??

Steve stares at his date in horror. Meanwhile --

ACROSS THE COURT,

A grinning Robin leans over to Vickie.

> ROBIN
> She sounds like a muppet --

Vickie smirks.

> VICKIE
> Oh my God totally, like Kermit --

> ROBIN
> I was thinking more Miss Piggy --

Vickie laughs. Robin can't believe it -- Steve's advice to use *her own advice* is working!

> ROBIN (CONT'D)
> It's so funny, I used to think she sounded good because I had this massive cru --

Robin catches herself --

> VICKIE
> Sorry -- ?

> ROBIN
> Class -- I had a class with her. Tammy. It was massively... hard.
> (wince)
> Sorry, wait -- what was your question?

> VICKIE
> Oh -- nothing.

Vickie forces a smile, then looks away. Robin winces. *Disaster.*

BACK ON THE COURT,

Lucas scans the bleachers. Looking for his friends...

<u>But they're nowhere</u>.

As Tammy belts out a high note, we lay some ELECTRIC GUITAR CHORDS into the National Anthem and make a HARD CUT TO --

INT. HAWKINS HIGH - HALLWAY - NIGHT

Mike and Dustin walking down a hallway in SLOW MOTION.

Positioned between them and walking with real swagger:

ERICA SINCLAIR. WEARING AN AMERICAN FLAG AS A CAPE!!

Off an epic final three-shot of our nerdy "heroes," the National Anthem crashes to a dramatic end and --

INT. AV ROOM - NIGHT

CLOSE ON: Eddie, staring in disbelief.

> EDDIE
> Absolutely not.

REVERSE TO REVEAL cape-wearing Erica with Mike and Dustin, now in the AV room, which is packed with NERDS and has been decked out in Hellfire Club paraphernalia -- candles, banners, skulls, you name it.

> DUSTIN
> You asked for a sub, we delivered.

> EDDIE
> This is Hellfire Club, not Babysitting Club --

> ERICA
> I'm eleven you long-haired freak --

Everyone laughs. Holy shit the gall of this girl!

> EDDIE
> My my, the child speaks.

Eddie steps toward her.

> EDDIE (CONT'D)
> What's your name, child?

> ERICA
> Erica Sinclair --

> EDDIE
> Ah so this is Sinclair's infamous sister --

                    ERICA
              (to Dustin)
          He's sharp --

Some laughter from the nerds. *Is she winning them over?*

                    EDDIE
          What's your class and level? Level
          one *Dwarf*?

The room laughs; it seems Eddie has the edge now. But Erica isn't intimidated by this metalhead. No sir. She steps toward him.

                    ERICA
          My name is Lady Applejack and I'm
          a chaotic good half-elf rogue level
          fourteen and I will sneak behind
          any monster you throw my way and
          stab them in the back with my
          poison-soaked kukri and then I'll
          smile as I watch them die a slow,
          agonizing death -- and oh yeah, I
          particularly enjoy killing
          cultists.
              (beat)
          So? We gonna do this? Or we gonna
          keep chit-chatting like this is
          your mommy's book club?

A tense beat. Then --

Eddie cracks a smile. Holds out a hand.

                    EDDIE
          Welcome to Hellfire.

Erica takes his hand. A WHISTLE BLOWS and --

INT. HAWKINS HIGH - GYMNASIUM - NIGHT

A basketball is tossed into the air! THE GAME IS ON!!!

The Tigers grab the ball. The POINT GUARD passes to Jason, who fires off a jump shot. SWOOSH! *Nothin' but net!*

The CROWD GOES WILD! A cocky Jason winks at Chrissy, who does her best to cheer for him.

Back on the court, a COCKY OPPOSING PLAYER nails a three.

Jason shouts at his teammate --

                    JASON
          WHAT WAS THAT? YOU GOTTA STAY ON
          HIM MAN!!! STAY ON HIM!!

Fred leans over to Nancy.

                    FRED
          Looks like my headline has a shot.

INT. AV ROOM - NIGHT

In the AV room, a very different game is underway.

                    EDDIE
               (dramatic)
          The hooded cultists chant... "HAIL
          LORD VECNA... HAIL LORD VECNA..."

Shared looks. Everyone is on edge, *transported* --

                    EDDIE (CONT'D)
          They turn to you and remove their
          hoods. You recognize most of them
          from Makbar, but one... one you do
          not recognize. His skin is
          shriveled, desiccated. And
          something else. He is missing both
          his left arm -- and *his left eye*.

The table goes crazy -- shouting and chaos --

          DUSTIN   GARETH
WHAT?? -- !!!   BULLSHIT!

                    JEFF
          Vecna's dead -- !!!

                    MIKE
          He was killed by Kas -- !!!

                    EDDIE
          So it was thought, my friends! So
          it was thought. But Vecna... *LIVES*.

Eddie SLAMS down a Vecna figurine as --

INT. HAWKINS HIGH - GYMNASIUM - NIGHT

Jason passes the ball to the POINT GUARD. He goes for a
layup, but the Cocky Player FOULS HIM HARD, knocking him to
the ground. A WHISTLE BLOWS. EEEEE. Time for a free throw
but --

The Point Guard isn't getting off the ground. As concerned teammates race to his side, Jason gets in the face of the Cocky Player --

>   JASON
>   The hell was that huh??? THE HELL
>   WAS THAT??

As the injured player limps off court with the help of his teammates --

>   EDDIE (PRE-LAP)
>   You are injured, you are tired...
>   you are *hurting*...

INT. AV ROOM - NIGHT

Eddie leans forward.

>   EDDIE
>   Do you flee Vecna and his cultists
>   -- or do you <u>stand your ground --
>   and fight</u>?

Our nerds share looks, uncertain as --

INT. HAWKINS HIGH - GYMNASIUM - NIGHT

>   COACH
>   Sinclair!

Lucas looks up at his COACH in surprise --

>   COACH (CONT'D)
>   You're in!!

>   LUCAS
>   Wha -- ?

>   COACH
>   YOU'RE IN! LET'S GO!!!

A stunned Lucas leaps up off the bench. He yanks off his overshirt and pants, nearly tripping as he races onto court.

INT. AV ROOM - NIGHT

>   DUSTIN
>   I say we fight -- <u>to the death</u>.

>   MIKE
>   To the death.

                    ERICA
          To the death.

                    EVERYONE
               TO THE DEATH!

WAR CRIES ERUPT as our nerds get pumped up for this final
confrontation. We now move into a FAST-PACED MONTAGE as --

WE INTERCUT THE BASKETBALL GAME AND THE D&D GAME:

-- Lucas passes to Jason, who makes another jump shot.
SWOOSH!

-- Gareth high-fives Dustin after a good roll --

-- SWOOSH! The opposing team scores -- the Cocky Player
taunts Jason again -- the tension rising --

-- Another basket -- 45-45 -- another basket -- 58-56 --

-- Eddie knocks over a nerd's figurine -- another -- heroes
and villains trading victories as --

-- The basketball teams trade baskets --

-- A dice is tossed -- a basket is scored --

-- Dice -- basket -- dice -- basket --

-- Faster and faster *and* --

-- The scoreboard is now 68-69. Tigers down 1.

-- Only TEN SECONDS left --

-- Jason grabs a rebound, makes a T and shouts --

                    JASON
          TIME OUT, TIME OUT!!!

EEEEE!!! The REF blows a whistle as --

INT. AV ROOM - NIGHT

Gareth makes a T with his hands --

                    GARETH
          Time out, time out -- !!!!

MOMENTS LATER

The group huddles --

                    GARETH
          Guys, I hate to say this, but we
          have <u>got to flee</u> --

                    ERICA
          Was I dreaming or did we just agree
          "to the death" -- ??

                    GARETH
          That wasn't <u>literal</u> --

                    JEFF
          Vecna just decimated us -- we can't
          kill him with two players --

                    DUSTIN
          You too? He only has fifteen hit
          points left, don't be pussies--

                    GARETH
          Pussies *really*?? Because we're not
          delusional -- ??

                    ERICA
          Delusional?? How about <u>not
          cowards</u> --

                    EDDIE
          Hey HEY -- if I MAY interject,
          gentlemen and -- *Lady Applejack* --
          while I respect the passion, you'd
          be wise to take Gareth the Great's
          concern to heart. I'm telling this
          to you as a friend, not your DM,
          okay: There's no shame in running.
          Don't try and be heroes. *Not today.*

This weighs heavy on our group...

                    DUSTIN
          ... What do you think, Mike?

                    MIKE
               (considering)
          How many hit points between you and
          Applejack?

70

ERICA/DUSTIN
Twelve --

INT. HAWKINS HIGH - GYMNASIUM - NIGHT

The Coach scribbles on a small whiteboard --

          COACH
They're gonna try to shut down Jason, double-team him -- that'll free up Patrick on the left --

          JASON
No no no -- you gotta let me take the shot Coach. You *gotta let me*.

          COACH
They're gonna be all over you *son* -- !

INT. AV ROOM - NIGHT

          MIKE
It's risky as hell. But you're on the battlefield, so -- your call.

Dustin, pondering, swivels to Erica.

          DUSTIN
Lady Applejack, what do you say?

          ERICA
You *really gotta ask?*

Dustin hardens.

          DUSTIN
Screw it. Let's kill the sonofabitch.

INT. HAWKINS HIGH - GYMNASIUM - NIGHT

          JASON
Winners find a way to win, coach. Let me *find a way*.

INT. AV ROOM - NIGHT

          JEFF
Chances of success are *twenty to one* --

                    DUSTIN
          Never tell me the odds.

INT. HAWKINS HIGH - GYMNASIUM - NIGHT

                    JASON
          Just get me the ball.

INT. AV ROOM - NIGHT

                    DUSTIN
          Get me the D-20.

As Eddie passes the D-20 to Dustin --

INT. HAWKINS HIGH - GYMNASIUM - NIGHT

Jason is passed the ball. The defense is all over him, but he breaks free with some fancy dribbling, fires a shot, and --

INT. AV ROOM - NIGHT

Dustin throws the die. It scatters and spins as --

INT. HAWKINS HIGH - GYMNASIUM - NIGHT

The basketball rolls out of the rim, *MISSES* --

INT. AV ROOM - NIGHT

The die lands and --

                    EDDIE
          It's a MISS!

Dustin pounds the table in frustration as --

INT. HAWKINS HIGH - GYMNASIUM - NIGHT

Everyone scrambles for the rebound and --

LUCAS COMES UP WITH IT! Only two seconds left on the clock --

Everyone in the crowd rises to their feet as --

INT. AV ROOM - NIGHT

All nerds rise to their feet as Erica shakes the D-20, blows on it for luck, as...

INT. HAWKINS HIGH - GYMNASIUM - NIGHT

Lucas dribbles free from a defender, jumps and --

INT. AV ROOM - NIGHT

Erica rolls and --

INT. HAWKINS HIGH - GYMNASIUM - NIGHT

Lucas releases! All eyes follow the ball as it soars through the air in SLOW-MO as --

INT. AV ROOM - NIGHT

The die scatters across the table in SLOW-MO, lands on --

TWENTY!!!

>   ERICA
>   CRIT HIT!!!!

INT. HAWKINS HIGH - GYMNASIUM - NIGHT

THE BALL GOES THROUGH THE NET!!! SAWOOOSHH! THE CROWD GOES ABSOLUTELY WILD as --

INT. AV ROOM - NIGHT

EVERYONE GOES *EQUALLY WILD* IN HELLFIRE. Eddie bows to Queen Erica. She *beams* as --

INT. HAWKINS HIGH - GYMNASIUM - NIGHT

Lucas *beams* as more and more people race over to him.

As we PUSH IN on Lucas, stunned and proud, we hear...

>   LOCAL BROADCASTER #1 (V.O.)
>   Lucas Sinclair... I haven't even
>   heard of this kid, Don, have you?
>
>   LOCAL BROADCASTER #2 (V.O.)
>   Never, no -- I don't think he's
>   even come off the bench before
>   tonight --

EXT. HAWKINS HIGH - PARKING LOT - NIGHT

SLOW MO: Jason, Lucas, and the other players walking from the gym, Jason's got his arm around Lucas's shoulders --

                    LOCAL BROADCASTER #1 (V.O.)
               And then -- he comes out of nowhere
               and makes the game-winning play --

                    LOCAL BROADCASTER #2 (V.O.)
               He's gotta be feeling on top of the
               world right now --

Lucas's smile abruptly fades as he sees his friends excitedly
leaving the school in their Hellfire shirts... and they're
with Erica! HOLY SHIT. Lucas is both surprised by this --

And *hurt*. He tears his gaze away and climbs into Jason's car
as --

INT. TRAILER - NIGHT

CLOSE ON: A RADIO. The voice continues to talk excitedly --

                    LOCAL BROADCASTER #1 (ON RADIO)
               After a tragic year for our town,
               Hawkins High has brought home the
               conference title for the first time
               in twen --

SWITCH! The radio is switched off. WIDEN to find --

Max, lying in bed. She seems unsure how to feel about Lucas's
success, when she hears --

THE SOUND OF A WHIMPERING DOG. Max sighs.

                    MAX
               Alright alright, I hear you...

She pushes out of bed. We now TRACK with Max as she makes her
way through her new house. Or what little house there is...

She's living in a CRAMPED, SHITTY TRAILER.

INT. MAX'S TRAILER - MAIN ROOM - CONTINUOUS

MAX'S MOM is asleep in front of the TV, with just beer
bottles and cigarettes for company. It's a mess. *She's* a
mess. Max opens the fridge, grabs some LEFTOVERS, and --

EXT. TRAILER PARK - NIGHT

Max heads outside. WIDEN TO REVEAL: a ratty trailer park.
It's spooky at night. Old laundry flutters on clotheslines.

Max crosses to a tied-up mutt named REX.

                    MAX
          Here ya go --

As she scrapes the leftovers onto the ground, HEAVY METAL
MUSIC drags her eyes to --

A DODGE VAN (rusty, spotted with primer), pulling up beside a
neighboring trailer. The van door opens and Eddie steps out
with --

Chrissy??? Seeing these two together is... *weird*.

Rex whines again. Max looks back down. He's finished his
leftovers and he's now looking up at Max with hopeful eyes.
She makes a frowny face.

                    MAX (CONT'D)
          That's all I got. Sowwy.

She ruffles his head, heads back to her trailer as --

                    EDDIE (PRE-LAP)
          Sorry about the mess -- maid took
          the week off --

INT. EDDIE'S TRAILER - NIGHT

Eddie leads Chrissy into his messy, cramped trailer.

Chrissy looks around.

                    CHRISSY
          You... live here alone -- ?

                    EDDIE
          With my uncle -- but he works
          nights at the plant. Bringin' home
          the big bucks --

WHOOM! Eddie riffles through some drawers, looking for drugs.

                    CHRISSY
          How -- long does it take?

                    EDDIE
          Sorry -- ?

                    CHRISSY
          The Special K -- how long to...
          kick in?

                    EDDIE
          Depends on if you snort it or not.
          You snort it -- you'll feel it
          pretty qu --
               (annoyed)
          Shit.

Eddie tosses aside the medicine basket.

                    CHRISSY
          You sure you have it?

                    EDDIE
          Yeah yeah, it's here *somewhere* --

Eddie heads down a small hallway and enters --

INT. EDDIE'S BEDROOM - CONTINUOUS

It's a total shit-mess in here, everything dirty, disorganized -- that is, with the exception of a KILLER B.C. RICH WARLOCK ELECTRIC GUITAR, which hangs from the wall like a prized piece of art.

                    EDDIE
          Hey sweetheart, *sorry I'm late* --

He kisses his hand, touches the guitar, then starts to rummage through the drawers while --

INT. EDDIE'S TRAILER - NIGHT

Chrissy waits by herself in the living room. And that's when she hears it: that CHIME again. It sounds like it's coming from outside.

Chrissy tenses. *Shit.* She walks up to the window.

OUTSIDE - CHRISSY POV

It's spooky out there. Laundry billows. The chimes continue, seemingly coming from nowhere. *Three more times.*

INT. EDDIE'S TRAILER - NIGHT

Chrissy closes the window curtains, calls out.

                    CHRISSY
          Eddie?? You find it?

No answer. But she can hear him RUSTLING AROUND back there.

                        CHRISSY (CONT'D)
                ... Eddie??

Still no answer. What the hell?? Chrissy follows THE RUSTLING
SOUND into --

A BEDROOM - CONTINUOUS (MINDSCAPE)

She freezes. Her face goes pale. It's not Eddie. It's --

A MIDDLE-AGED WOMAN. This is Chrissy's Mom. Her back is
turned to us as she sews a cheerleader dress.

                        CHRISSY'S MOM
                Just loosening this up for you,
                sweetheart --

Her Mother looks up at Chrissy. Something is VERY WRONG with
her eyes. They are sunken in. Pure white. _MONSTROUS_.

Chrissy STIFLES A SCREAM and stumbles back and slams the door
and locks it and --

INT. CHRISSY'S HOUSE - NIGHT (MINDSCAPE)

She looks around. She's no longer in Eddie's trailer -- she's
in an _upstairs hallway_. A row of happy family portraits of
her family lines the walls. This is _her house_.

BAM BAM BAM! Her "mother" bangs on the door, voice
distorted --

                        CHRISSY'S MOM
                Chrissy!! CHRISSY!! OPEN THE
                DOOR -- !

Chrissy doesn't dare, instead she runs and --

MOMENTS LATER (MINDSCAPE)

CLOSE ON FEET as Chrissy races down a flight of stairs.

She flies down the steps and into --

INT. LIVING ROOM - DOWNSTAIRS - NIGHT (MINDSCAPE)

Her DAD is down here -- watching TV on a LA-Z-BOY.

                        CHRISSY
                Dad?? DAD -- ??

She runs up to him and grabs his shoulder, turning him toward her, and --

HER FATHER'S MOUTH AND EYES HAVE BEEN SEWN SHUT AND HIS HANDS HAVE BEEN SEWN INTO THE ARMS OF THE CHAIR.

Chrissy stifles a scream as --

INT. EDDIE'S TRAILER - BEDROOM - NIGHT

WHOOM! A drawer shoots open. We're back with Eddie in the real world.

> EDDIE
> *Gotcha* --

He shakes the pillbox as he makes his way back to Chrissy --

> EDDIE (CONT'D)
> *Found it*! Peaceful bliss is just
> moments away --

INT. EDDIE'S TRAILER - MAIN ROOM - CONTINUOUS

Eddie freezes.

> EDDIE
> Chrissy...?

REVERSE TO REVEAL: CHRISSY. She's still here. But something is very wrong. She's frozen in place, not moving or reacting, and her eyelids are half closed and fluttering wildly. The sliver of eye we do see is solid white. It's like... she's <u>in a trance</u>.

Eddie walks up to her, freaked --

> EDDIE (CONT'D)
> -- Chrissy? Chrissy?!

As he waves a hand in front of her, the lights in the trailer flicker and --

INT. CHRISSY'S HOUSE - DINING ROOM - NIGHT (MINDSCAPE)

FWOOM! The lights flicker in the nightmare house too.

> VOICE (O.S.)
> *CHRISSY...*

Chrissy whirls away, toward the voice, sees --

A SHADOWY FIGURE -- just visible through the wooden railings -- making its way down the staircase. Any trace of her mother is gone. We glimpse a large gnarled hand ... dark, wet flesh... <u>A MONSTER</u>.

Chrissy flees, leaving her dad, racing into --

INT. CHRISSY'S HOUSE - DINING ROOM - NIGHT (MINDSCAPE)

-- Where a fancy BANQUET OF FOOD has been laid on a long dining table -- only the food is ROTTEN. SPIDERS of all shapes and sizes crawl out of moldy cakes and spoiled meats --

Chrissy trying not to gag, sprints away into --

INT. CHRISSY'S HOUSE - KITCHEN - NIGHT (MINDSCAPE)

She races up to the back door, only --

It's been boarded up by OLD, GNARLED BOARDS. *What the hell?*

                    CHRISSY
        No no NO -- !!!

She begins to frantically tear at the boards as --

INT. EDDIE'S TRAILER - NIGHT

Eddie begins to frantically shake Chrissy --

                    EDDIE
      Chrissy -- CHRISSY!! WAKE UP!!
      COME ON!! CHRISSY -- !! CHRISSY!!

INT. CHRISSY'S HOUSE - KITCHEN - NIGHT (MINDSCAPE)

Chrissy continues to struggle with the door when --

                    VOICE
      CHRISSY...

She turns. <u>THE MONSTER IS HERE</u>. As he walks toward Chrissy, we reveal more and more of him. He's THE MOST HUMANOID MONSTER YET. SIX FEET TALL. WRINKLED WHITE SKIN. SUNKEN WHITE EYES. BLOODY FLESH WHERE HIS JAW SHOULD BE. STRANGE FLESH DROPPING FROM HIS NECK. A LARGE MUTATED LEFT HAND WITH <u>*SHARP*</u> FINGERS. AND HE WALKS WITH A METHODICAL GAIT -- with *PURPOSE*.

As our monster steps up to poor, whimpering Chrissy...

He speaks.

>   MONSTER
>   (guttural, very deep)
>   Don't cry, Chrissy. It's time...
>   for your suffering... *to end*...

Chrissy lets out a BLOOD-CURDLING SCREAM as --

The Monster places its mutated left hand over her face and --

INT. EDDIE'S TRAILER - NIGHT

Back in the real world, CHRISSY SUDDENLY LIFTS UP AND SLAMS INTO THE CEILING. EDDIE BACKS AWAY IN HORROR, WATCHING HELPLESSLY AS --

INT. CHRISSY'S HOUSE - KITCHEN - NIGHT (MINDSCAPE)

CLOSE ON: The Monster's long fingers dig into Chrissy's skin and --

INT. EDDIE'S TRAILER - NIGHT

WHOOM! CHRISSY FLINGS UPWARD -- SLAMS INTO THE CEILING --

AS HER BODY PRESSES AGAINST THE CEILING -- PINNED --

HER BONES VIOLENTLY *SNAP* --

HER EYES POUR BLOOD --

THEN SUCK INWARD --

AND --

<u>END EPISODE</u>

EPISODE TWO

CHAPTER TWO:
VECNA'S CURSE

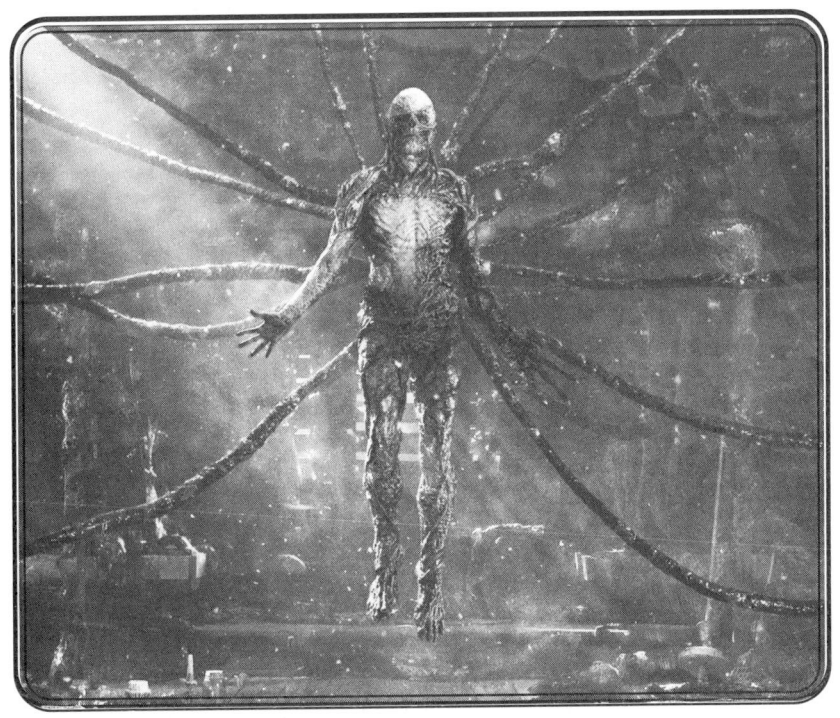

WRITTEN BY **THE DUFFER BROTHERS**

PRE-LAP the SOUND OF CRACKLING ELECTRICITY, then SMASH TO --

INT. RIFT CHAMBER - LOWER BALCONY - NIGHT (FLASHBACK)

HOPPER.

He is wearing the Russian uniform and he's trapped out on the catwalk -- yep, we're BACK IN TIME, at the end of season three!!

He locks eyes with JOYCE.

A final, emotional look between them.

Then Joyce closes her eyes....

And TURNS THE KEYS.

But we don't cut to black this time. This time --

We stay with Hopper. The machine BEGINS TO ERUPT. But Hopper isn't giving up. Not yet. He SPRINTS for the edge of the catwalk with everything he's got -- machine parts EXPLODE all around him -- barely missing him -- he THROWS his body off the ledge just as --

KABOOM! A MASSIVE TIDAL WAVE OF ELECTRICITY ERUPTS FROM THE MACHINE -- and right here we CRASH TO --

BLACK

After a long beat, a spark illuminates the darkness -- then another. It's the RUSSIAN MACHINE, spitting electricity. Busted, broken. We begin to DRIFT FORWARD -- traveling along the barrel of the machine, moving toward the closed Rift.

It seems like we're headed straight for the Rift, but then -- abruptly -- we DIVE DOWN. And that's when we see him...

HOPPER. He's lying on a platform below, about fifty feet below us. Quite the fall -- and he's not moving. Is he dead?

We keep moving toward him, right up to his eyes. We hold for a beat.

Then his eyes move ever so slightly.

And, then --

THEY OPEN.

MAIN TITLES

INT. MAX'S TRAILER - MAX'S BEDROOM - DAY

WHOOM! MAX bolts awake in bed, drenched in sweat, breathing hard. *Another nightmare.*

INT. MAX'S TRAILER - MAIN ROOM - DAY

Max opens a kitchen cabinet. Grabs Tylenol. Dumps two into her hand. Swallows them with some water, then --

She hears the *SOUND OF SIRENS*. Growing louder. *Coming.*

EXT. TRAILER PARK - DAY

Max exits her trailer just in time to see --

Cop cars swarming into the trailer park. SIRENS SCREAMING. They speed past Max and up to Eddie's trailer.

MAX'S MOM, looking hungover in a robe, walks up to her.

> SUSAN
> Looks like that Munson boy's up to
> no good again...

Off Max --

EXT. MAX'S TRAILER - DAY

FWOOM! Car doors fly open as CHIEF POWELL and OFFICER CALLAHAN exit their vehicles. They approach a lower-class bearded man, who is pacing and smoking by Eddie's trailer, on edge.

This is WAYNE MUNSON, 50s.

> POWELL
> Mister Munson -- where is she?

Wayne shakily motions to the trailer --

> WAYNE
> ... I just found her there, I, I
> swear to you. I don't even know her
> name, never even seen her 'fore --

> POWELL
> Just calm down and -- stay back --

As Powell and Callahan leave Wayne and approach the trailer --

EXT. MAX'S TRAILER

Max walks closer to Eddie's trailer as...

INT. EDDIE'S TRAILER - DAY

Powell draws his gun, pushes open the door, and...

... Enters. Whatever he sees _shocks him_.

Callahan steps up beside him --

>   CALLAHAN
>   Holy mother of God...

As we PUSH IN on our stunned cops --

EXT. MAX'S TRAILER

-- We also PUSH IN on Max. Whatever our cops see, _she_ sees too. As her eyes grow wide with fear --

WHAM! A HAND GRABS HER FROM BEHIND, STARTLING HER, BUT --

It's just a STERN COP. This is OFFICER DANIELS.

>   OFFICER DANIELS
>   Hey -- you can't be here -- get
>   back inside -- _back inside_ --

As a disturbed Max hurries back to her trailer --

INT. EDDIE'S TRAILER - A LITTLE LATER - DAY

Powell is now on the phone as MORE COPS inspect the trailer.

>   POWELL
>   (disturbed)
>   Hey Frank -- listen -- we caught a
>   body over here at the Munsons'
>   trailer --

INT. SURVEILLANCE ROOM - UNKNOWN - DAY

CLOSE ON: A TAPE REEL spins -- _recording_ this conversation.

                    POWELL (ON TAPE)
                  (filtered)
            -- I -- don't even know how to
            describe it... I've just -- I've
            never seen anything like it...

WIDEN TO REVEAL we're in a government surveillance room, much like in season one, only this place is larger, more sophisticated.

A GOVERNMENT MAN scribbles notes.

                    POWELL'S VOICE
            I just -- I need you down here ASAP
            to tell me what the hell I'm
            lookin' at -- or how someone could
            even do something like this --

We PUSH IN on the recorder which is taping the conversation.

The reels spin *FASTER* and *FASTER* and --

EXT. LENORA HILLS AIRPORT - DAY

EEEE!! Wheels hitting pavement, fast, skidding, as --

A PASSENGER JET touches down on a tarmac in Lenora.

INT. LENORA HILLS AIRPORT - ARRIVAL GATE - DAY

JONATHAN, WILL, ELEVEN, and ARGYLE wait by the gate as passengers deplane. We DOLLY LATERALLY, surveying each one --

-- Jonathan is looking miserable.

-- Argyle is looking stoned.

-- Will is nervous, clutching his painting.

-- And El is *so excited* she can barely breathe!

Finally, through the crowd, *he* emerges:

                    EL
            MIKE!!!

That's right, it's MIKE! And boy is this Hawkins kid ready for California: He's wearing a Hawaiian shirt, flip-flops, zinc under the eyes, the *works*! He carries a BOUQUET OF FLOWERS.

El races toward him. They hug, then KISS!

                    MIKE
          Careful, careful -- you're
          squishing my present --

He pulls out of her tight embrace and holds out his present:
It's a BOUQUET OF FLOWERS. Eleven's eyes light up, excited --

                    MIKE (CONT'D)
          Fresh from Hawkins! Picked them
          myself -- I went, kinda heavy on
          the yellow, I'm seeing that now --
          I think you like yellow, right --
          it was that or purple -- I sorta
          went for a seventy/thirty split to
          be safe and --

As Mike rambles, Eleven notices there's a tag that reads: TO
EL. FROM MIKE. We can tell something about that upsets her --

                    MIKE (CONT'D)
          Shit it's too much yellow isn't it?
          I knew it was too much yellow --

El shakes it off, smiles --

                    ELEVEN
          No. *It is perfect*. Thank you.

Mike smiles, then at long last he notices the rest of the
party waiting for him. Will in particular seems awkward,
clutching that painting.

                    MIKE
          Well well well -- what a
          coincidence you guys are here too!

          JONATHAN   WILL
Hey dude --   Hey --

Our old friends share a quick, awkward half-hug. It's not
exactly the warm welcome that Will was hoping for. As Mike
pulls away from Will, he clocks the painting --

                    MIKE
          What's that?

                    WILL
          Oh just -- some painting I'm
          working on. It's -- nothing.

Before Mike can press further --

                    ARGYLE
          Rad shirt, my man. Ocean Pacific?

Argyle goes to check his tag, weirding Mike out --

                    JONATHAN
          Oh -- sorry -- Mike -- this is my
          friend, Argyle --

                    MIKE
          Oh -- hey --

                    ARGYLE
          Nah it's just some shitty knock-
          off. Bummer. We'll get you the real
          threads.
               (then abruptly)
          I've heard a lot about your sister.

Mike stares -- *uhhh?* Then Argyle, not sure what to do here, moves in and hugs Mike. It's as awkward as you'd imagine. Then -- he pulls away.

                    ARGYLE (CONT'D)
          Alright. Shall we escape this
          awkwardness or what?

He grabs Mike's bag and --

EXT. LENORA HILLS AIRPORT - DAY

WHOOSH! Luggage wheels skip across concrete as our gang heads out of the airport and toward a parking garage.

El is holding Mike's hands, pulling him she's so excited.

                    ELEVEN
          I have our whole day planned.
          First, El Rodeo for burritos --

                    MIKE
          Burritos for breakfast??

                    ELEVEN
          Yes. *Trust me* --

                    MIKE
          It's just weird, but I trust you, I
          trust you --

                    ELEVEN
          Then after burritos, I want to go
          to Rink-o-Mania --

                    MIKE
          Rink-o-Mania -- ?

                    ELEVEN
          The most fun place in Lenora --
          they have -- skating and games --

                    MIKE
          Sounds awesome. Your friends coming
          too?

Will reacts to this --

                    WILL
          Friends? What friends?

Eleven shoots Will daggers --

                    ELEVEN
          You know -- Angela and... Stacy.

                    WILL
          Angela -- ?

Eleven has had enough -- turns back to Mike.

                    ELEVEN
          You'll meet them. *Promise*. But not
          today. I want today to be *about us*.

This is a dagger to Will. He shrinks. He clutches that painting closer, crumpling the paper, as our oblivious gang passes --

A FAMILIAR-LOOKING MAN -- loading luggage into a taxi. As he slams the trunk, we reveal --

It's MURRAY! Holy shit! BALD EAGLE HAS LANDED!

INT. TAXI - MOMENTS LATER

Murray drops into the taxi.

                    TAXI DRIVER
          Where to?

                    MURRAY
          Forty-eight-nineteen Lonzo Street.
          Let's go, this is life or death --
          snap, snap!

                    TAXI DRIVER
          Yes _sir_.

The annoyed TAXI DRIVER adds two bucks to the counter then --

EXT. LENORA HILLS AIRPORT - DAY

EEEE! The taxi speeds off, rubber burning, and --

EXT. FAMILY VIDEO - DAY

WHOOSH! A car speeds down a road, racing past --

Family Video. _We're back in Hawkins_.

                    ROBIN (PRE-LAP)
          And then Vickie laughed -- and it
          wasn't a fake laugh either --

INT. FAMILY VIDEO - DAY

We find a uniformed STEVE and ROBIN moving through the store, chatting as they put VHS tapes back onto shelves.

                    ROBIN
          Like a real, _genuine_ laugh --

                    STEVE
          Of course she laughed -- that's MY
          muppet joke --

                    ROBIN
               (ignores him)
          Point is -- Vickie laughed and it
          was all just, like, _perfect_.

                    STEVE
          But...

                    ROBIN
               (wincing)
          I have this problem where, like, I
          should stop talking, like I said
          everything I needed to say, but
          then -- I guess I get nervous?
                    (MORE)

ROBIN (CONT'D)
-- And the words keep spilling out and it's like my brain is moving faster than my mouth or rather my mouth is moving faster than my brain and it's like I'm digging this hole for myself but I can't stop digging so I just keep going and --

Robin catches herself, looks to Steve -- *shit*.

ROBIN (CONT'D)
I'm doing it now aren't I?

STEVE
Yep.

Robin sighs, drops back against a wall.

ROBIN
I'm hopeless.

Steve joins her against the wall.

STEVE
We both are.

Robin turns to Steve, mind racing --

ROBIN
We just need to somehow -- *combine*.

STEVE
Combine -- ?

ROBIN
I mean, think about it -- I know what I want and I've found the *girl of my dreams*, but just can't get the courage to ask her out -- meanwhile, you go on, like, a million dates, but *you have no idea what you want*. So like, if we just combined -- all our problems would be solved. Because alone, I mean, let's face it --

STEVE
We suck.

ROBIN
Totally and *utterly*.

Robin's eyes suddenly light up.

> ROBIN (CONT'D)
> OOOO -- I just found our morning movie!

Robin excitedly rushes forward and grabs a movie off the shelf. She holds it up for Steve. It's *DOCTOR ZHIVAGO*. Steve grimaces --

> STEVE
> You *know* I don't do double VHS --

> ROBIN
> Yeah, but it's about *doomed love*.

> STEVE
> (intrigued)
> Relatable --

> ROBIN
> *Precisely* --

Robin heads over to the TV as she keeps talking --

> ROBIN (CONT'D)
> Also Julie Christie is like *bonkers hot* in this -- like *seriously* the most beautiful creature you've ever seen in your life --

Robin hits on the TV and --

Immediately stops talking. Her excitement drops. REVERSE TO REVEAL:

ON TV, A NEWS REPORTER is standing outside the trailer park at the scene of the crime. A bold red banner reads:

POLICE INVESTIGATING POSSIBLE HAWKINS MURDER.

> NEWS REPORTER (ON TV)
> *... We are in the Forest Hills Trailer Park in East Roane County... We don't have a lot of details right now -- but we do know a body of a Hawkins High student was found early this morning...*

Steve walks up and joins Robin.

                              STEVE
                    Holy shit...

As their eyes grow wide --

EXT. BENNY'S BURGERS - DAY

We PUSH IN on Benny's Burgers, which has been long boarded up. But it's not abandoned -- there are a ton of cars parked out front, and the house has been spray-painted with things like -- TIGERS FOREVER! '86 CHAMPS!!!

INT. BENNY'S BURGERS - BATHROOM - DAY

BLAAARGH! A HUNGOVER LUCAS vomits in a toilet. Wipes his mouth, then -- KNOCKING on the bathroom door. It's --

INT. BENNY'S BURGERS - VARIOUS

JASON, eating from a box of cereal, clearly amused --

                              JASON
                    You alright in there, Sinclair?

                              LUCAS
                    Yep, uhh... I'm good.

                              JASON
                    First hangover feels like you're
                    gonna split in two. But you'll
                    live.

Jason leaves Lucas, carrying his cereal through the restaurant, munching away. We now reveal that Benny's has been transformed into a full-blown party house, with colorful lights hanging from the ceiling, kegs everywhere, empty beer bottles, red cups, discarded food, and other evidence from what was clearly a long night of partying. A shirtless player lies passed out on the floor; someone has scribbled a mustache above his lip with permanent marker.

-- Jason steps over another player as he makes his way into the main dining area, where we find PATRICK, ANDY, and other HUNGOVER BASKETBALL PLAYERS watching the same NEWS REPORT on a SMALL TV SET.

                              JASON (CONT'D)
                    What's this, I thought we were
                    watching *ThunderCats* --

                              PATRICK
                    A Hawkins student got murdered --

                        JASON
            <u>What</u> -- ?

                        ANDY
            Yeah it's all over every channel --

Jason darkens a bit as he takes in the news --

                        NEWS REPORTER (ON TV)
            ... *As you can see behind me, the
            Hawkins Police Department is
            actively investigating. They have
            completely blocked off access to
            this trailer behind me...*

                        JASON
            They say who it is -- ?

                        PATRICK
            Not yet --

                        ANDY
            Hey -- maybe Chrissy didn't stand
            you up after all -- !!!

Andy cackles at his own poor taste joke.

                        PATRICK
            Don't even say that man --

                        ANDY
            It was a joke, dude, *relax* --

As the jocks continue to bicker over the news report, Jason notices something out the window. He walks over. It's...

TWO COP CARS. PULLING UP TO THE PARTY.

Off Jason, heart-in-throat, CUT TO --

INT. HAWKINS HIGH - JOURNALISM CLASS - DAY

A PHOTO OF JASON -- triumphant and happy -- holding a trophy.

It's Nancy's SPRING BREAK EDITION. *Almost finished.* Only --

<u>NANCY isn't working on it</u>. Instead, she and FRED have their eyes glued to the same TV report, same as everyone else --

> PARANOID NEIGHBOR (ON TV)
> Ever since that girl Barb died a
> few years back, it's been one thing
> after the other, I tell you -- it
> almost makes you believe all that
> stuff they say -- that this town is
> cursed. That the devil is here...
> in Hawkins --

This statement triggers a flood of memories for Nancy -- BARB GETTING YANKED INTO THE POOL -- NANCY IN THE TREE -- THE DEMOGORGON IN THE UPSIDE DOWN -- THE MONSTER IN THE MALL --

> FRED
> -- I don't think anyone is gonna
> care about a basketball game
> anymore --

Nancy doesn't respond, too lost in her own dark memories ---

> FRED (CONT'D)
> Nancy -- *earth to Nancy*.

She finally turns to Fred.

> NANCY
> What -- ?

> FRED
> (holding up paper)
> I said I don't think anyone's gonna
> care about this anymore --

> NANCY
> Yeah. No. I know.

She looks back to the TV for a beat. Then --

> NANCY (CONT'D)
> (back to Fred)
> You up for a field trip?

Off Fred --

EXT. HAWKINS HIGH - DAY

Fred and Nancy are now headed to Nancy's car, moving fast --

> NEWS REPORTER (V.O.)
> Many of the residents we spoke to
> voiced similar concerns to us.
> (MORE)

> NEWS REPORTER (V.O.) (CONT'D)
> Grief -- shock -- disbelief --
> anger --

EXT. TRAILER PARK - CRIME SCENE - DAY

Disturbed onlookers watch as Chrissy's body (now zipped up) is carried via stretcher toward a medical examiner's van --

> NEWS REPORTER (V.O.)
> Everyone wants to know the same
> thing -- how can so many tragedies
> befall a once peaceful town? All
> eyes are now on the police for
> answers --

Our camera finds Powell in the crowd. He looks *overwhelmed*.

> NEWS REPORTER (V.O.) (CONT'D)
> Is the new Chief of Police Powell
> in over his head? Or is he the very
> savior this town needs?

As the medical van door closes on Chrissy's body --

INT. HENDERSON HOUSE - LIVING ROOM - DAY

A distraught CLAUDIA (clutching TEWS THE CAT) watches the report with DUSTIN --

> NEWS REPORTER (ON TV)
> We'll keep you posted on all the
> latest developments -- in the
> meantime -- we recommend you keep
> your doors and windows locked
> tight. This is Beverly Moss,
> signing off for WDHB --

> CLAUDIA
> My heart can't take it anymore --
> it just can't take it...

DING DONG! The doorbell rings, startling them.

MOMENTS LATER

Dustin swings open the door to find --

Max. She is out-of-breath. *And scared.*

Off Dustin...

                    DUSTIN (PRE-LAP)
          Chrissy Cunningham??

INT. DUSTIN'S ROOM - DAY

Dustin paces in his room, panicked --

                    DUSTIN
          Are you sure it was *Chrissy*?

                    MAX
          Yes, she was in her cheerleader
          outfit, the *same thing* she was
          wearing when I saw her with Eddie --

Dustin is having trouble processing this.

                    DUSTIN
          Did you tell all this to the
          cops -- ?

                    MAX
          No but I can't be the only one who
          saw them together. They... stood
          out --

                    DUSTIN
          *Eddie the freak with Chrissy the
          cheerleader --*

                    MAX
          Exactly -- his name's not in the
          news yet -- but I *guarantee you*
          Eddie is suspect number one right
          now --

                    DUSTIN
          That's crazy!! Eddie didn't do this
          -- no way -- NO WAY-- !!

                    MAX
          We can't rule it out --

                    DUSTIN
          YES WE CAN -- !!!

                    MAX
          Dustin -- !

                    DUSTIN
          You don't know him like I do, Max,
          okay???
                         (MORE)

                    DUSTIN (CONT'D)
          When we got to high school, Lucas
          made all his sports friends, but
          Mike and me... I mean, no one was
          nice to us -- *no one but Eddie*.

                    MAX
          Didn't they say similar shit about
          Ted Bundy?? He's a "super nice
          guy" -- but then, like, he was
          murdering women on the weekend -- ?

                    DUSTIN
          You're saying Eddie is like Ted
          Bundy -- ???

                    MAX
          I'm saying -- we can't presume
          anything. But it doesn't look good
          for Eddie.

Dustin drops head in hands, having trouble processing all of this. When suddenly --

Dustin realizes something. Looks back at Max.

                    DUSTIN
          Why haven't you told the cops this?

                    MAX
          I -- don't know --

                    DUSTIN
          You "don't know"?

Max hesitates. He's caught her. She drops down beside him. She's clearly scared, and doesn't want to say this, but...

                    MAX
          After I saw Eddie and Chrissy go in
          the trailer -- something... else...
          happened.

EXT. MAX'S TRAILER - NIGHT (FLASHBACK)

We're now BACK IN TIME as Max watches Eddie take Chrissy into the trailer --

                    MAX
                (to Rex)
          That's all I got. Sowwy.

She heads back into the trailer...

INT. MAX'S TRAILER - NIGHT (FLASHBACK)

Max sits down to watch TV. The image stutters.

                    MAX
        Ah come on --

As Max gets up and starts to bang it -- the lights in the trailer flicker. She looks around, a bit spooked, then --

THE SOUND OF A SLAMMING DOOR. SCUFFLING FEET.

She heads over to the window, looks through the blinds.

MAX POV: Eddie sprints into his car, terrified, and squeals off. As Max watches him go --

                MAX (PRE-LAP) (CONT'D)
    I mean -- nothing was *that* weird or
    anything...

BACK AT DUSTIN'S

                    MAX
        Eddie always drives like a maniac.
        And the power goes off in my place
        all the time -- it's a piece of
        shit. But then -- this morning -- I
        started to think back and... I
        don't know. The look on his face.
        He was *scared, Dustin*. I mean --
        really scared. Maybe he was just
        scared because he just... killed
        someone. Or maybe he was scared, I
        don't know... because --

                  DUSTIN
    Something else killed her.

Max nods. Relieved Dustin is the one who said it.

                  MAX
    ... But... that's impossible,
    right?

Dustin thinks it over.

                  DUSTIN
    I don't know. It *should* be.
        (beat)
    Only one person knows for sure what
    happened.

                        MAX
            Eddie.

Dustin nods, and --

INT. HALLWAY - DAY

Dustin and Max now hurry through the house, *fast* --

                        DUSTIN
            Have you talked to anyone else -- ?

                        MAX
            No, I can't find Lucas or Nancy, and
            Mike's --

                        DUSTIN
            In California. *Shit shit shit* --

INT. LIVING ROOM - DAY

They race past Claudia, still watching the news --

                        CLAUDIA
            Dusty where are you going -- ??

                        DUSTIN
            To see a friend --

                        CLAUDIA
            You heard the TV -- it's not
            safe -- !

                        DUSTIN
            Right good point we'll be extra
            careful thanks Mom love you bye!

As Dustin *SLAMS* the door on a flustered Claudia --

EXT. BYERS HOUSE - DAY

WHOOM! The taxi cab trunk flies open as --

Murray fetches a LARGE SUITCASE from the taxi's trunk, which now idles outside the Byers house. As he hauls it toward the house, those wheels skipping across pavement, we PRE-LAP:

                        MURRAY (V.O.)
              "Hop is alive. He looks ford too
              date. Pleez to make resarvazion
              call four one five two blah blah."

INT. BYERS HOUSE - LIVING ROOM - LATER

Joyce paces and drags on a cigarette as --

Murray reads the "sketchy" note.

                        MURRAY
              "Open twelve day PETT. No govnt
              pls. Kind regard, ENZO..."

Murray puts down the letter. Shakes his head.

                        MURRAY.
              I like it even *less* in person --

                        JOYCE
              You don't *"like it"* -- ??

                        MURRAY
              I don't *TRUST IT*. For starters --
              who the hell sent this??

                        JOYCE
              I think it must be a friend --

                        MURRAY
              A "friend" -- ???

                        JOYCE
              A *friend of Hop's* --

                        MURRAY
                  (reading note, Russian
                   accent)
              "Hop is alive." "No government."
                  (back to regular voice)
              This looks and reads like a ransom
              note, and a *bad one* at that --
              there's no *proof of life* here --

                        JOYCE
              Yes -- yes *there is* --

Joyce walks up, taps the note vigorously --

                        JOYCE (CONT'D)
              It's signed *Enzo*.

MURRAY
So -- ?

JOYCE
SO only two people know about our Enzo's date -- *me and Hop*. Whoever sent this -- Hop trusted them enough to tell them about our date. He's *sending me a message* --

Murray looks firmly at Joyce.

MURRAY
You saw him die, Joyce --

JOYCE
There wasn't a body --

MURRAY
Because he *EVAPORATED* --

JOYCE
OR he survived.

MURRAY
Okay, let's indulge this fantasy for a moment -- he's Houdini, he's a cat-man with nine lives, whatever it is, he survives -- what's he doing in Russia? He was *CAPTURED*, that's what! Then he probably made some new "friends," and by friends, I mean *the KGB,* and believe me when I tell you, these guys are *the worst of the worst*. I'm talking *torture*, Joyce.

Joyce flinches at this word. Doesn't like this thought.

MURRAY (CONT'D)
And no matter how strong you think Jim is, believe me, they *will* break him. They'll get his whole life story -- and yes that might very well include a planned date at Enzo's with you, his co-conspirator -- making this all an elaborate ruse to capture you as well!

Joyce stares at him.

> JOYCE
> You just made all that up.

> MURRAY
> It's a *theory* --

> JOYCE
> <u>I prefer mine</u>.

> MURRAY
> So do I. Doesn't make it right.

> JOYCE
> Either way --

Joyce grabs the letter from Murray --

> JOYCE (CONT'D)
> This might be real. Hop might be <u>alive</u>.

Murray sighs.

> MURRAY
> I suppose there's only one way to find out.

He crosses to his luggage, works to unsnap its *many* locks.

> JOYCE
> What are you doing?

> MURRAY
> We're going to call that number and find out <u>who the hell</u> sent you that letter --
> (more unsnapping)
> But we're <u>doing it *MY WAY*</u>.

WHOOM! Murray flings open his suitcase and --

INT. RIFT CHAMBER - LOWER BALCONY - NIGHT (FLASHBACK)

WHAM! A BLOODY HAND GRABS THE RUNG OF A METAL LADDER.

We're back in time as a barely conscious Hopper claws his way back up onto the catwalk. He heaves from the effort, and...

WHOOM! He finally hauls himself up onto the platform, only to find himself face to face with BLACK BOOTS. He looks up to find --

A CADRE OF RUSSIAN GUARDS AIMING RIFLES AT HIM.

A RUSSIAN GUARD SMIRKS.

> SMIRKING RUSSIAN GUARD
> <Where do you think you're going?>

The Guard SLAMS Hop in the face with his rifle butt and

INT. INTERROGATION ROOM - UNKNOWN LOCATION - NIGHT

WHAM! A fist SLAMS Hopper in the gut. As he SCREAMS IN PAIN, widen to reveal that his hands are tied up to the ceiling in a shadowy and blood-spattered torture room. His shirtless body is bruised and bleeding, broken from days of torture.

There are several Russians in this room -- including a LEAD INTERROGATOR. He hisses at Hopper in accented English --

> LEAD INTERROGATOR
> Tell us who you work with?

> HOPPER
> I told you -- NO ONE --

WHAM! A SOLDIER punches him again. Hopper grits his teeth.

Lead Interrogator holds up a BLURRY SURVEILLANCE PHOTO of him and Joyce in the Russian base.

> LEAD INTERROGATOR
> This woman -- who is she?

> HOPPER
> You... you tell me. She's wearing a
> Russian uniform.

Lead Interrogator stares, then turns to INTERROGATOR #1.

> LEAD INTERROGATOR
> <Get the Elephant.>

INT. INTERROGATION ROOM - UNKNOWN LOCATION - NIGHT

Soldiers drop Hopper onto a chair -- handcuff him under the seat -- strap a CREEPY WHITE RUSSIAN GAS MASK over his face.

It's a long breathing tube that looks like the trunk of an elephant.

                    LEAD INTERROGATOR
          *You want to die for this woman,
          American? Is she worth it?*

Hopper doesn't say another word. Just braces himself.

Lead Interrogator nods at INTERROGATOR #2, who closes off the
mask's breathing tube. Hopper begins to choke, unable to
breathe --

He yanks frantically at the handcuffs -- desperate to yank
off that fucking mask -- but he's stuck, there's nothing to
do --

His bloodshot eyes go wide with pain and fear and --

His vision begins to stutter -- and blur --

A HIGH-PITCHED NOISE fills the soundscape --

EEEEEEEEEEEE --

EXT. RINK-O-MANIA - PARKING LOT - DAY

A wide-open sky, framed by mountains. We're back in
sunny California. We TILT DOWN to find --

Argyle's Pizzamobile pulling up to a large building. The
parking lot is packed and a bright neon sign reads:

              RINK-O-MANIA EAT! SKATE! PLAY!!

The van door slides open and our kids leap out. As an excited
El drags Mike toward the roller rink entrance, Jonathan calls
out to Will, who is noticeably lagging behind his friends. He
looks, well, *mopey*.

                    JONATHAN
          We'll be back at five -- have fun,
          okay?

                    WILL
          Yeah okay --

Will forces a smile, then follows El and Mike.

Jonathan watches his brother go, a touch worried. Argyle then
hits the gas and --

INT. RINK-O-MANIA - DAY

FAST POP MUSIC blares as we show QUICK SHOTS of TEENS playing arcade games, ordering ice cream, eating CHEAP PIZZA, flirting, and, of course, skating around a colorful neon-lit roller rink! It's jam-packed and everyone's getting spring break off to a helluva start. A skater leads our camera over to --

THE COUNTER,

Where we find our kids receiving their skates from a FRIENDLY EMPLOYEE.

     ELEVEN
  Thanks!

     FRIENDLY EMPLOYEE
  Have fun!

As they head off toward the rink with skates in hand, Mike observes all the hopping activity around him.

     ELEVEN
  Bitchin', right?

     MIKE
  Yeah yeah -- bitchin'. You come here
  a lot -- ?

    ELEVEN   WILL
Yes --   No --

Eleven shoots Will a look, then, "clarifying"

     ELEVEN
  Will does not. But I -- I go to --
  parties here. It's a big -- party
  place.

Will can't help but roll his eyes, then --

MOMENTS LATER

Our friends drop down by a bench near the rink. They begin removing their shoes, but Mike just has on his flip-flops and --

     ELEVEN
  Oh -- you need socks --

MIKE
Socks, socks -- shit --

ELEVEN
Sorry I forgot --

WILL
They sell them at the counter I think --

MIKE
Right, right --

Mike hustles off, and we're left with Eleven and Will. It's a bit awkward and tense here as they pull on their skates. Finally Will can't hold it in anymore.

WILL
How'd you forget about the socks? I mean, since you come here all the time --

ELEVEN
(playing off)
I don't know. I just -- forgot --

WILL
Right.
(beat, then)
Why do you keep lying?

ELEVEN
What -- ?

WILL
Why do you keep lying? To Mike.

ELEVEN
I'm *not lying* --

WILL
You're "friends with Angela and Stacy"? You come to parties here?

ELEVEN
I have been to a party here --

WILL
For *Mom's work*. That's not what you implied.

Eleven looks away, upset.

                    WILL (CONT'D)
          I just -- I don't think Mike is
          gonna like that you're lying to
          him. And -- and he doesn't deserve
          that. And when he finds out -- he's
          gonna be mad.

Before a worried Eleven can respond, Mike comes sprinting
back. He's now wearing some very thin gross-looking NEON
GREEN socks.

                    MIKE
          So I asked if they had any in vomit-
          puke color and *they did!* Nice,
          right?!

Mike drops down onto the bench and begins to slip on his
skates over those awful socks. Eleven forces a smile here,
trying to forget what Will said. As her excitement for the
day slowly returns, we PRE-LAP the SOUND OF SKATES and --

ROLLER RINK - MOMENTS LATER

WHOOSH! Mike and Eleven are now holding hands as they skate
across the rink, laughing, just thrilled to be back together.
An annoyed Will skates further behind, the forgotten third
wheel. As our friends skate, we CUT WIDE and PAN to find...

ANGELA, JAKE, and the rest of the SCHOOL BULLIES entering
Rink-o-Mania. Angela's eyes light up as she spots El.

                    ANGELA
          Well well well... would you look at
          that?

Jake follows her gaze to the skate floor.

                    JAKE
          Who's that twig with her?

                    ANGELA
          I don't know. But seems like the
          snitch has a boyfriend...

                    JAKE
          Told ya spring break was gonna be
          fun...

Off Angela, her eyes glinting like a little psychopath, CRASH
TO --

EXT. BENNY'S BURGERS - DAY

COP CARS, still parked outside Benny's. Lucas, Patrick, Andy, and other players have been booted from the restaurant and are waiting outside, on edge, watched by a few cops.

Lucas paces, clearly on edge -- Patrick comes up to him. Comforts --

                PATRICK
I'm sure it's nothing man -- some neighbor probably just complained about the noise or some shit --

Lucas nods. But he knows better. His eyes go back to the restaurant as...

                POWELL (PRE-LAP)
And you were here all night?

INT. BENNY'S BURGERS - DINING ROOM - DAY

An emotional, scared Jason is seated across from Powell in the empty dining area. Callahan leans against a wall, his arms crossed.

                JASON
Yes -- *ask anyone* --

                CALLAHAN
We will -- but thank you for the suggestion.

POWELL
I see a whole lot of alcohol around. You have fun last night?

JASON
You gonna arrest me for drinking?

POWELL
It is against the law, so we could.
(to Callahan, casual)
Should we -- ??

CALLAHAN
I'd vote for trespassing myself -- don't think Benny's family'd be too thrilled to see what you've done to his place --

JASON
People have been using this shithole for years, man -- act like you guys didn't know --

POWELL
(ignoring this)
What about your girlfriend -- she party here last night?

Jason shifts, uncomfortable with this new line --

JASON
Chrissy? No --

CALLAHAN
That's odd, what with her being your girlfriend and all --

JASON
(getting more freaked now)
Why are you asking about Chris -- ?

POWELL
When's the last time you talked to her -- ?

JASON
After the game. This -- this doesn't have to do with that dead student does it -- ?

> POWELL
> (ignoring)
> What did Chrissy say? When you
> talked to her?

> JASON
> She said she was going home to --
> to get changed, something like
> that --

> CALLAHAN
> Did she mention anything about
> buying drugs for the party,
> something like that?

> JASON
> Drugs?? No -- no way -- Chrissy
> doesn't mess with that crap --

> POWELL
> Maybe someone talked her into
> it -- ?

> JASON
> NO -- she's straight as an arrow --

> POWELL
> What about Eddie Munson -- you ever
> seen her talking to him?

This is out of left field for Jason.

> JASON
> That freak??? No, no way --

And suddenly it hits Jason --

> JASON (CONT'D)
> What does Eddie have to do with all
> this?

The cops share looks. Jason begins to understand. Panic sets in.

> JASON (CONT'D)
> Did that freak hurt her? He hurt my
> Chrissy? *Did he hurt my Chrissy*??

Off Powell, about to break some really bad news --

EXT. BENNY'S BURGERS - DAY

The back door swings opens and Jason stumbles out of the restaurant in a daze.

Lucas and the others players look up, startled --

> PATRICK
> Jason -- dude, you alright?

> LUCAS
> What's going on -- ?

> ANDY
> Are they gonna call our parents?

Jason ignores all of them. Striding right past them. Lucas and the others share concerned looks as --

Jason heads into the woods where Eleven first appeared all those years ago. Shaken. Breathing hard. As the tears start to fall --

He drops to the ground... grabs his hair...

And STARTS TO *SCREAM* --

EXT. FAMILY VIDEO - DAY

WHOOSH! Bike wheels cut past as Dustin and Max race up to the video store --

INT. FAMILY VIDEO - DAY

Dustin and Max burst inside, moving fast.

Steve and Robin, still watching the news, look up.

> STEVE
> (re: TV)
> Dude, you see this -- ?

> DUSTIN
> (ignoring him)
> How many phones do you have -- ?

> STEVE
> Someone was *murdered* --

DUSTIN
HOW MANY PHONES DO YOU HAVE?!

STEVE
Two -- why -- ????

ROBIN
(correcting)
Well technically three if you count Keith's in the back --

Max and Dustin share looks.

MAX
Three will work.

Dustin nods in agreement, then shoves his way behind the counter --

STEVE
Whoa whoa -- the hell do you think you're doing, Henderson -- ?

DUSTIN
We're setting up our base of operations here --

ROBIN
"Base of operations" -- ???

Dustin drops behind the computer.

STEVE
Hey -- get off that -- !

Dustin swats Steve away.

DUSTIN
NO I need it --

STEVE
Need it for WHAT --??

DUSTIN
To get phone numbers for all of Eddie's friends --

STEVE
Eddie? Your best new friend Eddie who you think is cooler than me because he plays your nerdy games -- ?

                    DUSTIN
          Eddie, yes -- and I NEVER SAID
          THAT.

Dustin types in a name, punches enter --

                    ROBIN
          Seriously, guys -- maybe like on
          Monday you can play around in here
          like toddlers but it's *Saturday*,
          this is our busiest day --

                    DUSTIN
              (still typing away)
          Yeah sorry I empathize and all
          Robin but this simply *cannot* wait
          until Monday --

                    ROBIN
          Because calling all of Eddie's
          friends is... an emergency?

                    DUSTIN
          Correct --

Steve turns to Robin.

                    STEVE
          You want me to strangle him or do
          you want to?

                    ROBIN
          We could take turns?

As Dustin continues to type like a madman --

                    DUSTIN
          Max while I get these you want to
          maybe fill them in?

Robin and Steve turn to Max.

                    ROBIN
          Fill us in on... what?

As Max takes a deep breath, about to explain, CUT TO --

EXT. COUNTRY ROAD - DAY

WHOOSH! The Wheeler Wagon races past camera --

                    FRED (PRE-LAP)
          So what's our game plan -- ?

INT. WHEELER STATION WAGON - DAY

Nancy is driving, Fred sits passenger --

                    NANCY
          Game plan -- ?

                    FRED
          Yeah like what did you and Jonathan
          do when you investigated stuff for
          Hawkins Post -- did you split up
          or -- ?

                    NANCY
          Okay, first of all, you're *not*
          Jonathan --

                    FRED
          Well clearly not, I'm here --
          present and accounted for.

Nancy shoots him a look.

                    NANCY
          I've gone through a lot of managing
          editors, you know --

                    FRED
          Someone's testy. *Curious*.

Nancy stews in silence for a beat, then whips back to Fred --

                    NANCY
          I'm annoyed he's not here, okay? Is
          that what you wanted to hear?
          Something's been going on with him
          but guess what -- that's not the
          mystery we're investigating today.
          A classmate died. And the game plan
          is you let me do the talking and
          you take notes in your little pad
          there and you follow my lead *at all
          times*, is that understood?

                    FRED
          Yep, totally and completely --
          shit --

Fred has spotted something out the front windshield: Officer Daniels from earlier (and his car) is blocking the road that leads to the trailer park.

>   FRED (CONT'D)
>   Slow down, slow down --

Nancy pumps the brakes, her hands clenching around the steering wheel --

>   NANCY
>   Just act casual and --

>   FRED
>   Follow your lead. Got it.

EXT. TRAILER PARK ENTRANCE - DAY

Nancy slows as she approaches the cop.

She rolls down the window, flashes a smile --

>   NANCY
>   Hi Officer --

Officer Daniels leans down --

>   OFFICER DANIELS
>   You can't get through here, we got
>   a crime scene --

>   NANCY
>   Yeah. I'm actually here to...
>   (shit, wait, got it!)
>   See Max Mayfield? A friend. She
>   lives in there --

>   OFFICER DANIELS
>   We're restricting access to
>   residents only --

>   NANCY
>   I understand, it's just -- her mom
>   has work today -- and we wanted to
>   check in on her.

>   FRED
>   We're basically her nanny. *Nannies.*

The cop now shifts his attention to Fred.

                    OFFICER DANIELS
            Hey, don't I know you -- ?

                    FRED
            I -- I don't think so --

                    OFFICER DANIELS
            Yeah. Yeah. I do know you. You're
            Fred Benson -- you killed that kid
            last year --

Fred's breath catches.

                    FRED
            Wh- what -- ?

The cop leans in closer to the window. His voice has dropped
into a deeper range.

                    OFFICER DANIELS
            That ugly scar on your face -- it's
            from that crash --

Fred can barely breathe.

                    FRED
            It -- it was an accident --

A VINE now begins to slither its way out of the officer's
collar -- coiling up his neck. *What the hell?*

                    OFFICER DANIELS
            An "accident." That why you ran all
            the way home 'stead of calling us,
            huh?

Fred is too scared to respond --

                    OFFICER DANIELS (CONT'D)
            You're a murderer is what you are --
            everyone thinks so. I SHOULD ARREST
            YOU RIGHT NOW --

And that's when Fred feels it -- blood dripping down his
forehead. He looks in the rearview mirror to find that --

HIS SCAR HAS GRUESOMELY OPENED UP AGAIN. JAGGED GLASS JUTS
FROM THE SLICED SKIN AND --

                    OFFICER DANIELS (CONT'D)
            You alright there -- ?

                         FRED
             What -- ?

Fred spins back to the officer -- the vine is gone, and the
cop's voice has returned to its natural register. Fred checks
the rearview mirror -- his scar is totally healed. *Like
nothing ever happened.*

                         OFFICER DANIELS
             I said you alright, kid? You're
             looking a little peaked.

                         FRED
             I'm f-fine --

Nancy smiles --

                         NANCY
             He's just -- on edge. We all are.

The officer turns back to Nancy, sighs --

                         OFFICER DANIELS
             I'll let you check in on your
             friend -- but *be fast*.

                         NANCY
             Of course, Officer. Thank you.

As Nancy drives forward, she shoots Fred an annoyed look.

                         NANCY (CONT'D)
             What was that? I said act *casual* --

                         FRED
             Yeah, I just -- s-sorry.

Off Fred, totally shaken, CUT TO --

EXT. LENORA HILLS - CAR GRAVEYARD - DAY

WHACK-CRASH! A GOLF CLUB SLAMS A GOLF BALL into a rusty car.

WIDEN: Jonathan and Argyle are whacking golf balls in the
desert, aiming at a graveyard of abandoned cars. Their eyes
are very red -- they're obviously *super high*. Argyle's
Pizzamobile is parked nearby.

JONATHAN
I don't know, a part of me expected her to be on that plane or something -- like surprise, here I am, you know -- ?

ARGYLE
Uh huh --

Argyle whacks a ball. It goes way sideways.

ARGYLE (CONT'D)
SHIT SHIT SHIIIIT. Golf is IMPOSSIBLE man. Like, in all sports -- it's the smallest ball and yet also the biggest playing area. Like -- *what?*

JONATHAN
But I also -- I don't know. I felt this intense -- *relief* -- when she wasn't there.

ARGYLE
Oh that's just the Purple Palm Tree Delight working its magic, my man. It makes your troubles *float away* -- like the seed pods of a dandelion in the wind --

JONATHAN
No -- this was *pre*-Purple Palm Tree Delight. ... If I show you something, you won't tell anyone right -- ?

ARGYLE
Who would I tell, we have no friends -- ?

Jonathan nods. *Fair.* He reaches into his pocket, pulls out a letter, hands it over. Argyle scans it, blinks.

ARGYLE (CONT'D)
What is this?

JONATHAN
An acceptance letter -- to Lenora Community.

ARGYLE
That's where I'm going dude.

                    JONATHAN
          I know.

                    ARGYLE
          But this is addressed to you, dude.

                    JONATHAN
          I know.

                    ARGYLE
          But you're going to Emerson with
          Nancy --

                    JONATHAN
          No -- I'm not. She just -- doesn't
          know it yet.

                    ARGYLE
          Dude -- wait -- reverse, *beep beep*
          -- <u>what</u> -- ?

                    JONATHAN
          I can't go to Boston -- leave my
          mom -- my brother -- to... to chase
          a dream that's not mine, you know?

                    ARGYLE
          You applied though, right?

                    JONATHAN
          ... No --

                    ARGYLE
          Oh dude -- dude you are <u>*so dead*</u> --

                    JONATHAN
          What was I supposed to do??

                    ARGYLE
          <u>Not lie</u> -- !

Jonathan is pacing now, the pot paranoia is kicking in.

                    JONATHAN
          Not lie -- and then what?? If I
          told her the truth -- she'd throw
          her dreams out the window and come
          out here and be with me...
                    (MORE)

                    JONATHAN (CONT'D)
And -- this -- this knot of
resentment would build -- growing
like some -- some cancer -- she'd
eventually hate me -- I'd hate
myself -- I'd hate her -- before
you know it, we'd become my mom and
dad -- we get divorced -- our kids
would hate me -- I'm building
sports cars in my overgrown
backyard. Don't you see -- _the
cycle never ends_ --

                    ARGYLE
So to stop this nightmare cycle you
were... gonna... slow-motion break
up with her -- ?

                    JONATHAN
I guess -- I don't know --

                    ARGYLE
But you still love her -- ??

                    JONATHAN
I mean yeah --

                    ARGYLE
Oh dude --

                    JONATHAN
I know --

                    ARGYLE
SHIT I'm stressed now dude --

                    JONATHAN
What do I do -- ??

                    ARGYLE
More Palm Tree Delight! Pronto!!
Pronto!!!

Argyle claps urgently. And --

INT. PIZZAMOBILE - DAY

Jonathan clambers into the back of the Pizzamobile, which is
a total mess. He scrounges for ARGYLE'S COLORFUL KILIM
BACKPACK and, in doing so, accidentally drives his knee right
into --

WILL'S ROLLED-UP PAINTING.

                    JONATHAN
          Shit -- shit --

Jonathan does his best to undo the damage, then places the
painting safely onto the bench. As Jonathan resumes rummaging
for his weed, our CAMERA RACKS FOCUS onto the half-smushed
painting, still unopened. Off this sad image, CUT TO --

INT. RINK-O-MANIA - DAY

WHOOSH! Skaters ripping past camera, taking us to --

Mike, El, and, Will, who are now taking a break from skating
and sitting on a bench. El and Mike are having milkshakes,
while a miserable Will eats an ice cream cone.

                    VOICE (O.S.)
          Milkshakes, yummmmm!!!

El's head snaps up as she sees Angela and Jake skating over
to her. *Uh oh*. El's whole body tenses -- but she fights to
keep it together for Mike.

                    ANGELA
             (re: Mike)
          Where oh where have you been hiding
          this handsome *thing*?

                    ELEVEN
          Oh -- this is Mike. My --
          boyfriend.

Will braces himself. This... can't be going anywhere good.

                    ANGELA
             (taking his hand)
          Angela -- pleasure.

                    MIKE
          Heard a lot about you. It's cool to
          finally meet El's friends.

                    ANGELA
          "Friends." Yeah. Super cool.
             (pivoting to El)
          Come on, *friend* -- let's skate,
          shall we -- ?

Angela grabs El's hand and yanks her up onto her feet --

                    ELEVEN
                (re: milkshake)
        I need to finish --

                    JAKE
        I'll hold onto that --

Jake grabs her milkshake and speeds out onto the rink. And before El knows what is even happening, Angela has pulled her out onto the rink, *fast* --

BACK ON THE SIDELINES,

Will stands and watches, anxiety rising. His eyes swivel, scanning the building. He sees more BULLIES. They're everywhere. A TEEN BOY ominously films the rink with an RCA VIDEO CAMERA.

                    WILL
        Oh no.

                    MIKE
        What -- ?

Screw it. Will turns to Mike --

                    WILL
        El -- she hasn't been telling you
        everything --

                    MIKE
        What are you talking about?

                    WILL
        I mean -- she's been *lying to you*
        Mike.

BACK ON THE RINK,

Angela pulls El toward the center of the rink. She smiles big. As El tenses --

BACK ON THE SIDELINES,

                    MIKE
        Bullshit --

                    WILL
        No, Mike, listen to me. She's having
        problems here.

                    MIKE
        Problems?? What kinda problems -- ?

Before Will can respond, the current pop song ends and --

                    DJ
          Alright everyone, this next song is
          dedicated to -- JANE!! THE LOCAL
          SNITCH!!!

CHOOM! A spotlight hits El in the center of the rink and "WIPEOUT" begins to play.

WHOOSH-WHOOSH-WHOOSH! SKATERS suddenly swarm onto the rink, coming from every nook and cranny of this place, absolutely flooding the rink. They encircle Eleven, forming what can only be described as a SKATER CYCLONE. Then --

They narrow their eyes and throw their hands out at her -- mocking her power move from the day before.

                  BULLIES
         AHHHHH!!!! AHHHHHH!!!!!

ON THE SIDELINES,

A horrified Mike watches. *Shit.* He doesn't know what to do. But then his eyes snap to --

The DJ. Bobbing his head, watching all of this unfold with sadistic pleasure. Mike starts to skate toward him as --

ON THE RINK,

The teens continue to relentlessly mock Eleven, throwing out those hands, adding in some insults for good measure --

TEEN 1 Snitch -- !	TEEN 2 Freak -- !
TEEN 3 Weirdo -- !	TEEN 4 Moron --

El fights back tears as she whirls around, looking for escape but finding none as --

BACK ON THE SIDELINES,

Mike finally reaches the DJ --

                  MIKE
          Turn it off -- !

                  DJ
          (motioning to his ears)
          Sorry, can't hear ya, dude --

                    MIKE
          I SAID *TURN IT OFF*!!!

                     DJ
                  (shrugs)
          If you say so --

The DJ kills the song and then leans into the mic and --

                  DJ (CONT'D)
          WIPPEEEEEOUT!!!

BACK ON THE RINK,

On cue, Jake throws the chocolate milkshake at El with enough force that it explodes open --

WHOOM! She TOPPLES to the floor, covered in chocolate. *Wipeout indeed.*

Angela skates up to El, leans over her.

                   ANGELA
          Didn't you see the sign, dummy? No
          drinks or food on the rink.

With that, Angela skates away with her evil, giggling posse.

                    MIKE
          El! EL!

Our miserable El looks up to find Mike skating over to her. *Coming to the rescue.* But El doesn't want to face Mike now. She just.... *can't*. She clambers to her feet and skates away at full speed. She stumbles out of the rink, pushes through the giggling crowd, fighting back an onrush of tears, and --

EXT. BYERS HOUSE - DAY

Quiet outside the Byers house.

> JOYCE (PRE-LAP)
> Murray, it's time -- we have to make the call.

INT. BYERS HOUSE - DAY

Joyce is smoking, pacing, on edge. She crosses over to --

Murray, who is typing away furiously on a bulky computer -- *so that's what was in that luggage of his!* Tangled wires connect the computer to an ACOUSTIC COUPLER, which cradles Joyce's phone receiver!

> MURRAY
> *One moment please --*

Another flurry of typing, then he hits enter, and --

> MURRAY (CONT'D)
> Walah! Okay -- you are now calling from... Durham, North Carolina.

He looks back at Joyce.

> MURRAY (CONT'D)
> But if this is KGB they'll still be able to trace us eventually -- so keep it brief --

> JOYCE
> How brief?

> MURRAY
> A minute max. And don't forget --

> JOYCE
> <u>Proof of life</u>. I got it.

Joyce starts to dial the number on her phone's keypad. Murray hits record on a tape recorder. The tape spins as --

EXT. KAMCHATKA, RUSSIA - DAY

WHOOSH! Cars zip through the snowy streets of Kamchatka.

BRRRING! A phone rings in an empty phone booth. We PUSH TOWARD the phone as it rings and rings and --

INT. BYERS HOUSE - LIVING ROOM - DAY

Joyce and Murray share looks, nervous, then --

EXT. KAMCHATKA, RUSSIA - DAY

WHOOM! A gloved hand grabs the phone.

A handsome RUSSIAN MAN pulls the phone to his ear.

We will come to know him as DMITRI. But for now --

> DMITRI
> (heavy accent)
> This is Enzo.

INT. BYERS HOUSE - DAY - INTERCUT

Joyce and Murray share looks. *Holy shit this is really happening!* Joyce tries to steady her nerves --

> JOYCE
> Hi... Enzo. This is -- Joyce. I received your message and... I'd like to make a reservation.

> DMITRI
> Yes, good, good. But for reservation you need to make deposit --

Joyce and Murray share another look.

> JOYCE
> What -- kind of deposit -- ?

> DMITRI
> Forty thousand dollar. You have money in girl Jane's trust. From Hopper? Yes?

Murray shoots Joyce a questioning look, but --

JOYCE
Yes -- yes -- forty thousand --

DMITRI
Good. Bring to Yuri's Fish N Fly in
Nome, Alaska --

JOYCE
Alaska -- you -- you want me to
come to Alaska -- ??

DMITRI
Yes -- you give Yuri money, Yuri
brings me money, I give him your
friend. Simple trade. Understand?

Murray frantically mouths "proof of life" at Joyce.

JOYCE
We're going to need to speak to
Hopper first. We need to know he's
alive --

An ANNOYED WOMAN knocks on Dmitri's phone booth, talks at him
in Russian, but Dmitri waves her off --

DMITRI
I am afraid not possible --

JOYCE
Why not -- ?

DMITRI
Your friend is... stuck. But you
get me money -- I make him unstuck.
You must trust me --

JOYCE
How can I trust you?? I don't even
know who are you -- !

Dmitri looks up -- the annoyed woman is still banging on the
booth, demanding to be let in --

DMITRI
Forty thousand. Yuri's Fish N Fly.
Two days. Do not call again.

He hangs up and shoves his way out of the phone booth and --

INT. BYERS HOUSE

A shaken Joyce hangs up the phone. Turns to Murray --

> JOYCE
> That wasn't KGB --

> MURRAY
> But it wasn't a friend either.

> JOYCE
> So we're both wrong.

Murray nods.

> JOYCE (CONT'D)
> Then who the hell was that?

Off this burning question, we CRASH TO --

INT. INTERROGATION ROOM - NIGHT (FLASHBACK)

WHUMP! Hopper collapses to the floor. Unmoving. Dead?

Lead Interrogator stands by as a RUSSIAN DOCTOR examines Hopper with a stethoscope. Checking for life. After a tense beat --

He looks up at Lead Interrogator --

> DOCTOR
> <Still alive. But only just. More of this -- he will die.>

Lead Interrogator takes this in. Kneels by Hopper. Into his ear:

> LEAD INTERROGATOR
> You are strong, American.
> Perhaps... the Motherland could use that strength.

He turns to his friends.

> LEAD INTERROGATOR (CONT'D)
> <Send him to Kamchatka.>

INT. HALLWAY OUTSIDE INTERROGATION ROOM - NIGHT (FLASHBACK)

Guards drag Hopper's lifeless body down the corridor.

Lead Interrogator and the doctor watch him go.

                    DOCTOR
          <I never knew you to be generous.>

Lead Interrogator smirks a bit.

                    LEAD INTERROGATOR
          <You clearly do not know Kamchatka,
          Doctor. This man does not deserve
          the peace of death.>
                    (beat)
          <So I have sent him to Hell.>

INT. BENNY'S BURGERS - DAY

WHAM! A yearbook slams down, opened up to a PHOTO OF LAST YEAR'S HELLFIRE, with hand-drawn flames all around them.

A finger points at the "freak" in the center --

                    JASON
          Eddie Munson -- he's a part of that
          freak devil cult -- _Hellfire_.

WIDEN: Jason and the other basketball starters surround a table, looking at the photo. Lucas, meanwhile, hovers a few feet away -- this is all making him very anxious.

Jason looks up at his team. His eyes are bloodshot from crying and his voice is so tense it shakes.

                    JASON (CONT'D)
          The cops -- they say Chrissy went
          to him to buy drugs --

                    PATRICK
          Drugs? _Come on_ --

                    JASON
          That's what I said. Chrissy would
          never touch that shit. And they
          wouldn't even show her parents her
          face -- I don't know what this
          freak did to Chrissy, but... he did
          something... _sick_ --

                    ANDY
          He probably sacrificed her --
          drained her blood for the devil --
          I hear satanists do that shit --

                    JASON
          That's what I'm saying -- it's this
          cult he's in --

                    LUCAS
               (blurts out)
          Hellfire isn't a cult.

Everyone turns to Lucas. He swallows. *Shit*. You could hear a fucking pin drop in here.

                    LUCAS (CONT'D)
          And it has nothing to do with
          Satan. It's just... a D&D club.

More stares.

                    LUCAS (CONT'D)
          D&D? Dungeons and Dragons? It's
          just a game and it's... fantasy.
          Like... Lord of the Rings --

Patrick looks at Lucas, suspicious --

                    ANDY
          And how exactly is it you know all
          that, Sinclair?

Lucas hesitates, flustered --

                    LUCAS
          I just -- my sister, she's like --
          a total nerd. She plays.
          Sometimes --

                    JASON
          And I'm sure your sister isn't
          killing people. But shit, I've
          read, the wrong person plays this
          game -- it can *warp their mind*.
          They confuse fantasy and reality.
          And innocent people die. It's been
          happening all over the country,
          like an -- an epidemic --

                    PATRICK
          I've read about this, it's true --

Jason holds up the picture of Eddie.

                    JASON
          And I think Eddie -- he's the wrong
          kind of person. He got lost,
          thought Chrissy was just... part of
          his *sick game*. And chances are --
          he's still in the game. Meaning --

                    PATRICK
          He's gonna kill again.

                    JASON
          But not if we can help it.

Jason paces, back in leader mode.

                    JASON (CONT'D)
          Would Chrissy want us to just --
          stand by while the cops go around
          and follow up their bullshit leads?
          Spreading rumors saying she was
          some -- some druggie -- ??

                    TEAMMATES
          NO --

Jason rips out the Hellfire page from the yearbook, then looks around at his team, eyes burning.

                    JASON
          She'd want us to go out there and
          do something about it, wouldn't
          she -- ?!

                    TEAMMATES
          YEAH -- !!!

                    JASON
          THEN LET'S HUNT SOME FREAK!!! FOR
          CHRISSY!!!

The team ROARS with approval as Jason takes out a lighter and SETS THE PAGE ON FIRE, burning the picture of Hellfire Club.

Lucas watches, feeling trapped and scared and alone as --

We PUSH IN on the burning picture of Eddie as the flames *RIP THROUGH* Eddie's smiling face and --

EXT. FAMILY VIDEO - DAY

We PUSH IN on Family Video.

DUSTIN (PRE-LAP)
          Have you seen or heard from Eddie?

INT. FAMILY VIDEO - DAY

Dustin is talking on the phone in Family Video, in full
detective mode --

                    DUSTIN
          I'm, uh, trying to locate him -- uh
          huh -- and when did you last talk
          to him?

As a disappointed Dustin continues his conversation, our
CAMERA SWIVELS past a white board -- which reads *HELLFIRE
(with a list of names below)* -- and over to Robin, who is
on phone #2 --

                    ROBIN
          ... Yeah, I don't think he's at the
          arcade -- yeah, *pretty sure* --

As Robin continues to talk, our camera moves to Max,
who is on phone #3, scribbling notes --

                    MAX
          Reefer Rick? Okay -- um -- does
          this *Reefer Rick* have a... last
          name?

As Max continues, our CAMERA CONTINUES over to --

Steve, who is... flirting with a CUTE COLLEGE GIRL?! He
holds up a copy of *DOCTOR ZHIVAGO* --

                    STEVE
          I know it's long but that's because
          it's got a little bit of everything
          -- romance, suspense, action...

                    CUTE GIRL
          So my boyfriend won't, like,
          totally puke when I bring it home?

Steve deflates.

                    STEVE
          "Boyfriend" -- yeah, no -- he'll...
          love it.

Steve flashes a forced smile and --

EXT. FAMILY VIDEO - DAY

DING! The bell rings as Cute College Girl heads outside, *Doctor Zhivago* in hand. Steve waves bye, then shuts the door as --

INT. FAMILY VIDEO - DAY

WHOOM. Max hangs up the phone, spins to Robin and Dustin --

> MAX
> Hey guys -- I might have a lead --

Dustin practically leaps out of his chair --

> DUSTIN
> Seriously -- ???

> MAX
> Yeah -- so evidently Eddie gets his drugs from a guy named Reefer Rick -- and sometimes Eddie crashes there --

> DUSTIN
> At Reefer Rick's?

> MAX
> Yeah --

> ROBIN
> Well, that's promising. Where's this Reefer Rick guy live -- ?

> MAX
> That's the thing -- no one knows -- he's more... legend than, like... someone people *actually know* --

> DUSTIN
> What about a last name -- ?

> MAX
> No one knows that either --

> STEVE (O.S.)
> I bet the cops know his last name.

Everyone turns to find Steve approaching the counter.

> MAX
> What -- ?

                    STEVE
          The cops. If this guy Reefer Rick's
          actually a drug dealer, I *guarantee
          you* he's been busted at some point
          and is in the system --

Dustin stares.

                    DUSTIN
          The *cops?* Really, Steve? *That's*
          your suggestion?

                    STEVE
          I just think at this point they
          should be filled in on what we know
          and what's going on --

                    DUSTIN
          Just admit it -- you think Eddie's
          guilty, don't you -- ?

                    STEVE
          I mean -- I believe innocent until
          proven guilty and all that
          constitutional shit... I just don't
          think we can rule it out --

                    MAX
          That's *precisely* what we're trying
          to do here, Steve --

                    DUSTIN
          Maybe we'd have more luck if you
          were spending less time looking for
          a girlfriend and more time *looking
          for Eddie* --

                    STEVE
          Someone has to attend to our
          customers --

                    ROBIN
          Especially if they're babes, right?

                    STEVE
          HEY! Not fair! I attend to ALL our
          customers, babes and non-babes
          alike -- we have a big selection,
          it can be, like, super
          overwhelming!

Suddenly -- a lightbulb goes off for Robin.

                    ROBIN
          Yeah. *It can be.*

She drops down by the computer and starts typing.

The others gather behind her --

                    MAX
          What are you doing?

                    ROBIN
          Maybe we don't need a last name.

She types in "RICK" under search. A list of RICKS appear, listed in alphabetical order.

                    ROBIN (CONT'D)
          Twelve Ricks have opened accounts
          here --

                    MAX
          That's *a lot of Ricks* --

                    ROBIN
          So let's narrow it down --

Robin clicks on the first Rick on the list.

                    ROBIN (CONT'D)
          Rick Alderman. Last rentals were...
          Short Circuit and... *Dumbo*.
               (spins to others)
          What are the chances our drug
          dealer has a family?

                    MAX
          Not likely --

Robin swivels back to the computer, clicks on the next Rick.

                    ROBIN
          Rick Conroy. Recent rentals --
          Teen Wolf, *Sixteen Candles*,
          Romancing the Stone --

                    MAX/DUSTIN/STEVE
          Nope --

                    ROBIN
          Rick Joiner. *Mask*, *Footloose*,
          Grease --

                    MAX/DUSTIN/STEVE
          Nope --

                    ROBIN
          Rick Kimbrough. *Howard the Duck* and
          -- *Splash* -- ?

                    MAX/DUSTIN/STEVE
          <u>Definitely not</u> --

                    ROBIN
          Rick Lipton. *Fast Times at
          Ridgemont High... Cheech and
          Chong's Up in Smoke... Cheech and
          Chong's Next Movie... Cheech and
          Chong's Nice Dreams...*

Shared looks. *Bingo.*

                    MAX
          Lipton?

                    ROBIN
          (nods)
          Spelled like the tea -- he lives on
          twenty-one twenty-one Holland
          Road --

                    DUSTIN
          That's out by Lover's Lake --

                    MAX
          In the middle of nowhere --

Robin spins back to them.

                    ROBIN
          <u>The perfect place to hide</u>.

More shared looks, *and* --

EXT. FAMILY VIDEO - DAY

DING! The group race out of the store. As they pile into Steve's BMW, we PUSH PAST them to Family Video, where --

A CLOSED SIGN swings back and forth.

136

EXT. HAWKINS - DAY

CH-CH-CH-CH-CH! Rotors *cutting air* as --

A MILITARY CHOPPER soars over Hawkins.

MOMENTS LATER

The chopper sets down on a field.

MOMENTS LATER

The door opens and LIEUTENANT COLONEL SULLIVAN, 40s -- intimidating, draped in medals -- steps out. A few other MILITARY MEN exit with him.

A PAIR OF SOLDIERS and VEHICLES are waiting for them.

A SOLDIER approaches -- holds out a hand --

>   SOLDIER
>   Lieutenant Colonel. Welcome to
>   Indiana.

As their hands CLASP FIRMLY --

INT. MORGUE

CLOSE ON: A ZIPPER SLOWLY PEELING OPEN AS --

AN ARMY MEDICAL EXAMINER opens CHRISSY'S body bag.

WIDEN: Her corpse has been laid out on a slab in a windowless room. Sullivan and his men hover around the table. *It sure seems like a lot of people for an autopsy.*

As the medical examiner sets about this work, an ASSISTANT ARMY MEDICAL EXAMINER snaps photographs of the corpse --

A SERIES OF TIGHT SHOTS show us abstract yet sufficiently GROTESQUE GLIMPSES OF CHRISSY'S BODY --

-- HER SKIN IS COVERED IN DARK SPIDER-WEB-LIKE VEINS --

-- HER LIMBS BROKEN AT ODD, HORRIBLE ANGLES --

-- ONE OF HER FEET IS *TWISTED TOTALLY BACKWARDS* --

-- HER RIBS ARE CAVED IN --

-- HER CHEEKS ARE UNNATURALLY GAUNT --

-- HER MOUTH IS WIDE OPEN -- UNNATURALLY WIDE -- AS IF FROZEN IN A SCREAM --

-- AND, PERHAPS WORST OF ALL, HER EYES ARE COMPLETELY REMOVED -- JUST DARK BLOODY EYE SOCKETS IN THEIR PLACE --

-- As Sullivan takes it all in, a final BRIGHT FLASH of the camera's bulb takes us to --

EXT. TRAILER PARK - ESTABLISHING - DAY

The sun, now setting outside the trailer park. It's getting spooky out here. We PRE-LAP the SOUND OF KNOCKING as --

EXT. TRAILER PARK - WINNEBAGO - DAY

Nancy raps on the door to a Winnebago. An ANNOYED NEIGHBOR opens it a crack, peers out.

     NANCY
  Hi, I'm Nancy Wheeler, I work for
  the Hawkins Tiger --

     ANNOYED NEIGHBOR
    (cutting off)
  I've talked to enough reporters --

The door shuts on Nancy. *Shit.*

MOMENTS LATER

Nancy and Fred walk away from the trailer, discouraged --

     FRED
  I think that's... everyone --

     NANCY
  Nope. Not *everyone.*

Nancy walks over to Rex the dog. She kneels down, pets him.

     NANCY (CONT'D)
  You see something last night? Huh?

     FRED
  Nancy, come on, let's get out of
  here --

Nancy starts to respond when her eyes narrow. She sees Wayne smoking by a ratty picnic table, looking like a mess.

She looks back at Fred --

                    NANCY
            Stay here --

Off Fred --

A FEW MOMENTS LATER

Wayne takes a drag, sees Nancy approaching. She waves.

                    NANCY
            Hi.

Wayne gives a half-hearted nod --

                    NANCY (CONT'D)
            I'm friends with Max -- over there.

Nancy motions to Max's trailer. Wayne nods again. *Okay.*

                    NANCY (CONT'D)
            You're -- Wayne Munson aren't you,
            Eddie's uncle -- ?

                    WAYNE
            That's right.

                    NANCY
            I heard you -- found the body. The
            neighbors --

                    WAYNE
            Like to gossip. And I'm not
            interested in gossiping no more.
            Certainly not to a reporter.

                    NANCY
            What gave me away?

Wayne motions to her notebook --

                    NANCY (CONT'D)
            Oh. Right.

A beat. *Shit.* But Nancy doesn't give up, sits beside him.

                    NANCY (CONT'D)
            Listen. I'll level with you, Mister
            Munson. The paper I work for is...
            small. We don't have the staff to
            compete with the big guys. And
            I'm...
                        (MORE)

                    NANCY (CONT'D)
          I'm just looking for something --
          anything really -- about what
          happened last night.

                    WAYNE
          Why? As far as I can tell -- you
          all have it figured out already --
          my nephew is a freak, and he killed
          that girl, in't that about right?

                    NANCY
          Let me guess -- you've been talking
          to the Hawkins Post.

Wayne doesn't respond.

                    NANCY (CONT'D)
          Chuck Bailey?

He looks away. Bingo.

                    NANCY (CONT'D)
          I used to work with him. He doesn't
          know his ass from his elbow.

Wayne looks up at her, surprised.

                    NANCY (CONT'D)
          Let me tell *your side of the story.*

Off Wayne, CUT TO --

BACK BY MAX'S TRAILER,

Fred is waiting by Rex, anxious, when --

He hears: DONG. DONG. DONG. DONG. *The same four chimes Chrissy heard.*

Fred turns toward the sound. It's coming from the adjacent woods. *What the hell?* As Fred begins to follow the sound, walking across the trailer park...

                    WAYNE (PRE-LAP)
          My nephew, he may look...
          dangerous. But he didn't do this --
          it just -- *ain't in his nature.*

BACK BY WAYNE'S TRAILER

Wayne is now opening up to Nancy...

                    WAYNE
          No matter what anyone says... and
          they *will* say things, believe you
          me. But this wasn't Eddie. The man
          who did this -- who killed that
          poor girl -- he's pure evil --

                    NANCY
          "Man"? You... think you know who
          might have done this?

Wayne hesitates... cigarette trembling in his hands as --

                    WAYNE
          You ever hear the name Victor
          Creel?

Off Nancy --

EXT. WOODS BY TRAILER PARK - DAY

Fred enters a small clearing in the woods. His breathing catches. His eyes go wide. REVERSE TO REVEAL:

A LARGE WOODEN CASKET. It has a familiar CLOCK embedded on top of it -- the same one that Chrissy saw in the woods. It ticks. *Tick, tock, tick, tock.*

Off Fred, taking this in...

EXT. TRAILER PARK - DAY

                    WAYNE
          Guess you're too young. But back
          when I was your age -- everyone
          here knew the name Victor Creel. He
          lost his mind, killed his whole
          family -- kids and wife. Took their
          eyes. Cut 'em right out.

                    NANCY
          God --

                    WAYNE
          And that poor girl I found this
          mornin' -- *same exact thing.*

Nancy stares. Shocked.

                    WAYNE (CONT'D)
          So I'm thinking -- maybe he broke
          out --

                    NANCY
              (surprised)
          Victor Creel -- is still alive -- ?

                    WAYNE
              (nods)
          They locked him away in Pennhurst
          Asylum, and yeah, as far as I know,
          he's still there. That is -- 'less
          he broke out. Like what's his name
          -- white mask, kills babysitters --

                    NANCY
          Michael Myers.

                    WAYNE
          Yeah. *Michael Myers*. You ask me --
          Victor's like that. A real
          boogeyman. And <u>he's</u> who the cops
          should be lookin' at. *Not my
          nephew.*

Nancy takes this in when suddenly --

BARK BARK BARK BARK! She turns to find Rex barking like crazy. Tugging on his chain. <u>But Fred is no longer there.</u>

                    NANCY
              (to Wayne)
          Sorry -- I'll be right back --

MOMENTS LATER

Nancy walks back over to Rex. Looks around, but --

Fred has vanished.

                    NANCY
          Fred? Fred?!

As Nancy begins to search the trailer park for Fred...

EXT. WOODS BY TRAILER PARK - DAY

A DARK CLOUD seems to swallow the forest as --

Fred hears something -- SOBBING. He looks to find --

He is no longer alone out here. He is surrounded by --

GRIEVERS. They are all dressed in black, their heads bowed.

A YOUNG GIRL looks up at him. Something is wrong with her eyes. They are milky white. *Angry.*

>						YOUNG GIRL
>				*Murderer.*

She points at Fred. Only there is something wrong with her finger -- it's gnarled and grotesque, horribly distended.

>					YOUNG GIRL (CONT'D)
>			*MURDERER! MURDERER!! MURDERER!!*

All the grievers now look up at Fred. Their faces are twisted, horrific -- their noses gone, skin shriveled and covered in veins. <u>Demons.</u>

>					MONSTROUS MOURNERS
>			*MURDERER!! MURDERER!! MURDERER!!!*

Fred turns and scrambles away, those voices crying out behind him as he flees deeper into the woods --

He shoves through *TANGLED BRUSH* and --

EXT. RINK-O-MANIA - DAY

We CRANE DOWN from the RINK-O-MANIA sign to find --

The Surfer Boy Pizzamobile idling by the entrance. WE PRE-LAP THE SOUND OF COUGHING.

INT. PIZZAMOBILE - RINK-O-MANIA - DAY

The Pizzamobile van is absolutely CHOKED WITH SMOKE. Argyle gets his coughing under control, checks his watch --

>						ARGYLE
>				It was a five o'clock pickup right?
>				Byers? *Byers??*

Through the parting smoke, he now sees that Jonathan is passed out, totally relaxed. Argyle smirks to himself --

>					ARGYLE (CONT'D)
>				What'd I say... like *dandelions in the wind... dandeeelions in the wind...*

He cranks his seat back, lowers his hat over his eyes, and starts to nap himself as...

INT. RINK-O-MANIA - DAY

WHOOSH! A wooden ball flies up a Skee-Ball.

WIDEN: We're back in the Rink-o-Mania arcade, where we find Mike, urgently knocking on the door to the girls' bathroom --

>   MIKE
>   El?? You in here? _EL_??

He opens the door and --

GIRLS' BATHROOM - CONTINUOUS

There are GIRLS are in here alright, but not El --

>   ANNOYED GIRL
>   What the hell???

Mike ducks to check under the stalls --

>   MIKE
>   EL -- ??

>   ANNOYED GIRL
>   Get OUUTTT!!!!

The girls start to chase Mike.

RINK-O-MANIA ARCADE - CONTINUOUS

Mike shuts the door, quickly walks away.

>   WILL
>   Not there -- ??

>   MIKE
>   No.

Mike walks fast. He's getting frustrated. Angry.

>   MIKE (CONT'D)
>   You should've told me she was
>   having trouble.

Will can't believe this is coming back on him. Now he's upset --

>   WILL
>   I, I didn't know they were going to
>   be here, Mike --

> MIKE
> Yeah but you knew she was having trouble for like, a year, and you didn't tell me --

> WILL
> I didn't know she was lying to you, Mike --

> MIKE
> So that's why you decided to be a douche to her all day --

> WILL
> I wasn't being a douche --

Mike spins on Will here.

> MIKE
> You *were*. Barely talking -- moping, rolling your eyes and stuff. Basically sabotaging the whole day --

> WILL
> She was lying to you, Mike, straight to your face, ever since you got here -- and I've been a total third wheel all day -- it's been *miserable*. So sorry if I wasn't -- you know -- smiling.

> MIKE
> Right. Whatever, man.

Mike starts to walk away when Will calls out --

> WILL
> What about us?

Mike stops, turns back --

> MIKE
> What?

Will works up the courage, steps up to Mike.

> WILL
> You're mad that I didn't talk to you? Well -- you've made it super clear you're not interested in anything I have to say.

                    MIKE
          That's just -- not true --

                    WILL
          You've called maybe -- a couple
          times. It's been over a year Mike.
          Meanwhile, El has like -- a book of
          letters from you --

                    MIKE
          That's different. She's my
          girlfriend, Will.

                    WILL
          And us -- ?

                    MIKE
          We're friends, Will. *Friends* --

                    WILL
          We used to be best friends.

An awkward beat here as this sinks in, Mike, unsure what to
say, pivots --

                    MIKE
          Then -- you should have reached out
          to me. Why is it all on me? Stop
          making me the bad guy. Let's just --
          find her okay?

Mike turns and presses on, continuing his search for El.

Will starts to follow. We hold on a CU of Will as he walks.
We can tell he hates himself right now -- in his mind, he
just made a bad day worse. Off Will's heartbreak, CUT TO --

INT. RINK-O-MANIA - STORAGE ROOM - DAY

An even more *miserable-looking* El.

WIDEN: She's sitting in a messy storage room, her dress drenched in that chocolate milkshake, surrounded by broken arcade machines and old neon signs. All alone. Eyes bloodshot from crying. When --

She hears FAMILIAR VOICES, *LAUGHTER*.

MOMENTS LATER

Eleven inches open the door and peers out. It's Angela and her cronies, standing by a lunch table, watching the video recording back, giggling --

> MEAN BOY
> Look at her face oh my God --
>
> ANGELA
> She looks like she shit
> herself -- !

As the bullies laugh, El's sadness morphs to anger, and --

INT. RINK-O-MANIA - LUNCH AREA - DAY

WHOOM! Eleven bursts out of the storage room and stomps over to the bullies --

> ELEVEN
> *Angela* --

Angela and her cronies whirl, see El.

> ANGELA
> Uh oh look who it is --
>
> JAKE
> She looks upset --

El stops a few feet from Angela. Then --

> ELEVEN
> You -- you ruined my day.

                    ANGELA
          Oh NO -- did we embarrass you in
          front of your boyfriend??

El tries not to cry, maintains her composure.

                    ELEVEN
          I -- I want you -- to say sorry to
          me. And -- I want you to tell my
          boyfriend -- it was just a joke --
          that we are -- really friends --

                    ANGELA
          Or... *what?* You gonna hurt us with
          your mean stare again?

Angela then holds out her hand and narrows her eyes, mocking
El's power move. Her friends cackle. Needless to say --

El is not amused.

                    ANGELA (CONT'D)
          Sorry you can't cry to teacher
          today. You'll have to just cry to
          daddy instead -- oh wait -- can't
          do that either!

MORE LAUGHTER as the bullies walk away. Eleven watches them
go, her anger reaching a new level. Her eyes swivel to the
front counter, where a HAPPY FAMILY is getting their skates.

El walks over, snatches one of the skates --

                    FRIENDLY EMPLOYEE
          Hey, those aren't yours! HEY!

Eleven doesn't even respond. She walks fast toward the
bullies, carrying the skate, driven by pure rage.

                    ELEVEN
          ANGELA --

Angela turns and --

Eleven swings the skate and --

WHACK! THE HARD WHEELS OF THE SKATE SLAM ANGELA HARD ACROSS
THE FACE. THE FORCE OF THE IMPACT SNAPS HER HEAD BACKWARDS.

A moment of shock, stillness, then --

Angela's face twists and she SCREAMS IN PAIN --

ACROSS THE ROOM

Mike and Will hear the SCREAM as --

BACK WITH ELEVEN,

BLOOD BEGINS TO POUR FROM ANGELA'S NOSE.

>   JAKE
> Holy shit -- holy shit!!

This is not a hero moment. This is violent -- scary.

>   JAKE (CONT'D)
> Angela, are you okay?! ANGELA?!

Angela cries out -- definitely NOT okay.

Eleven drops the skate as --

A stunned Mike and Will race up, take in what happened --

>   WILL
> Oh my God --

Mike stares at El --

>   MIKE
> What did you do???

Off Eleven, breathing hard, we abruptly CRASH --

BACK IN TIME

A SERIES OF QUICK POPS FROM OUR OPENING SCENE THIS YEAR -- THAT BLOOD SPLATTERED RAINBOW -- THOSE DEAD NUMBERS -- ELEVEN STANDING TALL AMONGST THEM -- FEROCIOUS. <u>*ANGRY. A KILLER.*</u>

>   DR. BRENNER
> <u>What have you done</u>?

BACK TO PRESENT

                      MIKE
             What did you do??

We're back in the present. Eleven doesn't say anything -- she just stands there, shaken and overwhelmed and scared as --

The SCREAMS OF ANGELA grow LOUDER and LOUDER and --

INT. BYERS HOUSE - DAY

WHOOSH! A CASSETTE TAPE WHEEL SPINS. PLAYING --

                  DMITRI (ON TAPE)
         Your friend is... stuck. But you
         get me money -- I make him unstuck.
         You must trust me --

CLOSE ON: A finger hits *stop* on the tape recorder. Then *rewind*.

WIDEN: Joyce is obsessively playing and replaying the recording. And Murray is getting *very* impatient --

                  MURRAY
         Joyce, whoever Enzo is, the
         answer's *not* on that tape --

Joyce ignores him -- *stays focused.*

                  JOYCE
         Do you not hear that -- in the
         background -- ?

                  MURRAY
         The car horn -- ?

                  JOYCE
         Yes yes -- but -- also -- there's
         another voice -- someone else is
         there with him. LISTEN --

                  MURRAY
         Okay -- so he's outside, someone's
         talking -- not surprising --

                  JOYCE
         I think she's talking to Enzo --

Murray's interest is piqued now.

                    MURRAY
          Play it again --

Murray listens as she plays again ---

Joyce looks at Murray, hopeful.

                    JOYCE
          Can you translate -- ?

                    MURRAY
               (shakes head)
          I, I can't understand it -- it's
          too low.

Joyce suddenly has an idea. She pops the tape out and --

INT. JONATHAN'S ROOM

-- Carries it into Jonathan's room.

-- Kneels by his FISHER SOUND SYSTEM.

-- Pops open the tape door.

-- Slots in the cassette, slams it shut, hits play and --

INT. UNKNOWN ROOM - DAY

CHOOM! Sharp scissors chop hair.

WIDEN TO REVEAL: Hopper, strapped in a chair, is having his hair roughly cut by a grim-looking BARBER. Hop's hair drops to the floor, piling up around his dirty, bare feet.

                    WARDEN MELNIKOV (O.S)
          <...You are no longer men. You
          are... cogs in a machine...>

A LITTLE LATER

ZZZZZMMM! An ELECTRIC RAZOR shaves off his remaining hair.

                    WARDEN MELNIKOV (O.S.)
          <...a machine in service of our
          great Motherland...>

INT. SHOWERS - UNKNOWN - DAY (FLASHBACK)

CHOOM! A RUSSIAN GUARD yanks the LEVER on a HIGH-PRESSURE WATER HOSE and --

WHOOM! A BARRAGE OF WATER pummels a newly shaved Hopper. We're back in time again, in some unknown location.

> WARDEN MELNIKOV (O.S.)
> <If you are sick, you work. If you are tired, you work. If you refuse, you will die.>

Hopper shuts his eyes and grits his teeth as water pounds his wounded body --

INT. RUSSIAN PRISON - PRISON FLOOR - DAY (FLASHBACK)

Hopper now stands in a row of other men, now all wearing the same decrepit, colorless prisoner uniforms.

WARDEN MELNIKOV, 50s, intimidating, strides before them.

                    WARDEN MELNIKOV
          <And if you are foolish enough to
          attempt escape... well... you will
          be hunted down... you will be
          captured... and then you will
          suffer greatly as you perform your
          final act for the Motherland. There
          will be no second chances.>

He stops in front of Hopper, looks him square in the eye.

                    WARDEN MELNIKOV (CONT'D)
                      (broken English)
          Run. Die. You hear, American?

Hopper gives a faint, defeated nod --

INT. PRISON - LATER (FLASHBACK)

A pair of guards now lead Hopper through a prison corridor FILLED WITH SCARY-ASS RUSSIAN PRISONERS. THEY BANG ON THE BARS, CURSE AT HIM, SPIT AT HIM. Lead Interrogator was right -- this place is Hell.

As Hopper looks away from them, fighting back his fear, finding what little strength remains...

                    DMITRI (PRE-LAP)
          Your friend is... stuck. But you
          get me money -- I make him unstuck.

INT. BYERS HOUSE - DAY

Murray is now listening back to the conversation on headphones.

                    MURRAY
          Turn it up --

Joyce does. Murray listens harder.

FLASHBACK TO THE ANNOYED WOMAN TALKING TO DMITRI.

Murray's eyes narrow.

                    MURRAY (CONT'D)
          She -- she wants to use the
          phone... she's mad at Enzo....

                    MURRAY (CONT'D)
            Calls him "moosor" --

                    JOYCE
            "Moosor" -- ??

Murray looks up -- eyes wide.

                    MURRAY
            It's slang.

                    JOYCE
            For what -- ?

EEEEE! PRE-LAP the sound of a BUZZER as --

INT. RUSSIAN PRISON - DAY (FLASHBACK)

Hopper is led through a new corridor, toward a cell.

                    MURRAY (PRE-LAP)
            Literally, moosor translates to
            "trash" or "garbage" --

INT. BYERS HOUSE - DAY

                    MURRAY
            It's like pig here. Often directed
            at cops --

                    JOYCE
            Cops -- ?

                    MURRAY
            Or *guards*.

The puzzle pieces are beginning to click.

                    JOYCE
            Hopper's "*stuck*" --

INT. RUSSIAN PRISON - DAY (FLASHBACK)

Hopper is marched up to his cell --

INT. BYERS HOUSE - DAY

                    MURRAY
            And Enzo can get him "*unstuck*" --

INT. RUSSIAN PRISON - DAY (FLASHBACK)

Hopper enters his cell. He turns back to the guard who escorted him, and for the first time, we see ---

IT IS <u>DMITRI</u>.

>   DMITRI
>   Welcome to your new home --
>   American.

Dmitri smiles, then shuts the door on Hopper. CLANG!

INT. BYERS HOUSE - DAY

Joyce and Murray share looks as they realize at the same time --

>   MURRAY
>   Enzo's a <u>prison guard</u>.
>
>   JOYCE
>   Maybe Hopper bribed him --
>
>   MURRAY
>   Sounds like Jim doesn't it?
>
>   JOYCE
>   Yeah -- *it does*.

INT. BYERS HOUSE - LIVING ROOM - DAY

WHOOM! Joyce grabs her purse as she heads for the door --

>   MURRAY
>   Where are we going -- ?
>
>   JOYCE
>   The bank. We're going to get Enzo
>   his damn money -- and then we're
>   <u>getting Hopper back</u>.

Joyce slams the door behind them and --

BLACK

WHOOM! A pair of headlights punch through the night as --

EXT. COUNTRY ROAD - LOVER'S LAKE - NIGHT

Steve's BMW tears down a dark country road.

MOMENTS LATER

The BMW pulls onto a dirt driveway, driving past a mailbox that reads "Lipton," and toward a low-slung house.

EXT. LIPTON HOUSE - NIGHT

DING DONG! Dustin rings the doorbell, but there's no answer.

He rings again. DING DONG! Still nothing.

          STEVE
  Well, guess that settles it, he's
  not here...

But the others aren't giving up yet. Dustin bangs on the door, calling out --

          DUSTIN
  EDDIE?? You in there??? It's
  Dustin! We're just here to help!!
  No cops, I swear, just us!!!

As Robin peers in a smudged window, Max walks to the far end of the porch. Her eyes narrow.

          MAX
  Hey guys...

The others join her. They follow her gaze. In the distance, a RICKETY BOATHOUSE sits on the edge of a mist-covered LOVER'S LAKE. A _dim light_ glows from inside the boathouse...

Everyone shares looks, Steve sighs, and --

INT. BOATHOUSE - NIGHT

EEEEEE. The door to the boathouse swings open as...

Our gang slips inside. The light is coming from a single naked bulb that hangs from the ceiling, casting more shadows than light.

There is no one in here. Just a small boat, draped in blue tarp. It bobs in the water, knocking against the dock.

          ROBIN
  Hello? Anybody home??

No answer. Steve pulls a cobwebbed oar off the wall and
begins to poke at the blue tarp. One jab, two jabs --

                    DUSTIN
          Steve, *what* are you doing?

                    STEVE
          He might be in there --

                    DUSTIN
          Just take off the tarp --

                    STEVE
          You're so brave, you take off the
          tarp -- *you take it off* --

                    MAX
          Guys! Over here --

The others follow Max over to a shelf. There are some FOOD
WRAPPERS, a couple of DRAINED BEER BOTTLES, and a SMALL
RADIO.

                    MAX (CONT'D)
          Someone was here --

                    ROBIN
          Maybe he heard us, got spooked, ran
          off?

                    DUSTIN
          Don't worry, Steve will find him
          with his oar --

Steve continues to jab the tarp, talking as he works --

                    STEVE
          I know you think you're funny
          Henderson, but considering the fact
          everyone in this room has nearly
          died like a hundred times,
          personally, I don't find it funny
          in the slight --

WHOOOM! THE BLUE TARP SUDDENLY EXPLODES UPWARDS and --

                    EDDIE
          AHHHH!!!!!

EDDIE BURSTS OUT FROM BENEATH THE TARP, SCREAMING -- WIELDING
A BROKEN BEER BOTTLE! HE CHARGES STEVE WITH A CRAZED LOOK
AND --

WHAM! HE SLAMS STEVE AGAINST THE BACK WALL OF THE BOATHOUSE
AND THRUSTS THE SHARP GLASS AGAINST HIS THROAT AND --

                   DUSTIN
    EDDIE! STOP!!

Eddie freezes at the sound of Dustin's voice, that jagged
glass pressed right up against Steve's neck --

                   DUSTIN (CONT'D)
    It's me -- it's, it's Dustin!!!
    And that's Steve -- Steve
    Harrington, he's with me -- he
    won't hurt you, right Steve -- ??

                   STEVE
    R-right -- !

Steve tries to suck in his neck as the jagged glass begins to
cut into his skin, drawing its first drop of blood --

                   DUSTIN
    Why don't you drop the oar, Steve?

Steve drops the oar.

                   DUSTIN (CONT'D)
    See, he's cool --

                   STEVE
    I'm c-cool -- I'm real c-cool --

Eddie looks a bit crazed himself, anything *but* cool. Finally,
he speaks. His voice is pitched, frenzied:

                   EDDIE
    What are you doing here?

                   DUSTIN
    We're -- looking for you --

                   ROBIN
    To <u>help</u> --

                   DUSTIN
    Yeah -- these are my friends. You
    know Robin, right? From band? And --
    and Max? Our friend Max who never
    wants to play D&D?

Robin and Max hold up their hands awkwardly. "Hi."

                    DUSTIN (CONT'D)
            We're on your side. Swear on my
            mother, right, everyone???

                        MAX
            Yes -- we, we swear --

                      ROBIN
            On Dustin's mother --

Eddie looks from Dustin back to the terrified Steve... then
finally lowers the broken bottle. Steve staggers away,
catching his breath and feeling his throat as --

Eddie slumps back against the wall, breathing hard.

Dustin approaches him, very gentle:

                     DUSTIN
            We -- we just... want to talk,
            that's all... okay, Eddie?

                      ROBIN
            Yeah -- we just want to know what
            happened...

Eddie catches his breath. Fighting tears.

                      EDDIE
            ... You -- you won't believe me.

A beat, then --

                       MAX
            Try us.

EXT. TRAILER PARK - NIGHT

Night has now fallen on the trailer park.

An increasingly frantic Nancy hurries around, searching the
area for Fred. She approaches a nearby NEIGHBOR --

                      NANCY
            Sorry -- have you seen my friend
            wandering around-- nerdy, glasses,
            scar across his face?

A head shake. Nope.

Off Nancy, spinning around, totally lost as to what to do --

EXT. TRAILER PARK ENTRANCE - NIGHT

Nancy hurries back to the stern cop --

>   NANCY
>   Hey -- Officer -- Officer --

Officer Daniels turns, surprised to see her again --

>   OFFICER DANIELS
>   What're you still doing here -- ??

>   NANCY
>   My -- my friend. The one with me in
>   the car. I, I can't find him --

>   OFFICER DANIELS
>   What do you mean... "can't find
>   him"?

>   NANCY
>   He was there, then he was just --
>   gone. Did you see him maybe --
>   leave with someone or -- ?

>   OFFICER DANIELS
>   I told you kids to go home. *Jesus
>   Christ* --

The cop pulls his radio off his belt --

>   OFFICER DANIELS (CONT'D)
>   Hey, it's Glenn. We might have a
>   situation here --

Off Nancy, growing increasingly freaked, CUT TO --

EXT. WOODS - NIGHT

Fred, who is *truly freaked,* stumbling through the dark woods, exhausted and soaked with sweat. He shoots a panicked look behind him, looking for those monstrous people, but --

There's no one there. Then, up ahead -- lights! Thank God! He hurries forward, explodes out of the woods, and bursts out --

EXT. HAWKINS ROAD - NIGHT

Onto a COUNTRY ROAD. His face falls. *Something is wrong.*

Our CAMERA rises over his back to reveal he's looking at...

A HORRIBLY WRECKED CAR. MANGLED, ON FIRE, COUGHING SMOKE.

We PUSH IN on Fred as he looks on in horror, those flames reflected in his glasses...

                  EDDIE (V.O.)
          Her body... it just... lifted up
          into the air...

INT. BOATHOUSE - NIGHT

CLOSE ON: A pale Eddie. He's so scared his voice shakes.

The others sit around him. Intensely listening.

                  EDDIE
          -- And then she just -- she hung
          there in the air, and her bones --
          her bones just started to... snap --

QUICK FLASHES OF CHRISSY'S BONES BREAKING --

                  EDDIE (CONT'D)
          And her eyes...

Eddie takes a deep, shaky breath.

                  EDDIE (CONT'D)
          It was almost like -- there was
          something... inside her head --
          just... *pulling*.

QUICK FLASHES OF CHRISSY'S EYES SUCKING INWARD --

Eddie tries to shake off the awful memory.

                  EDDIE (CONT'D)
          I -- I didn't know what to do -- so
          I just ran -- I just ran --

Eddie fights an onrush of tears.

                  EDDIE (CONT'D)
          You -- you all think I'm crazy
          don't you?

                  DUSTIN
          No. We don't think you're crazy at
          all --

                    EDDIE
          Don't bullshit me, I, I know how it
          sounds --

                    MAX
          We're not bullshitting you--

                    ROBIN
          We believe you.

Dustin nudges Steve --

                    STEVE
          Yeah, we, uh, *believe you.*

Eddie looks at these eyes looking back at him with empathy.

                    DUSTIN
          What I'm going to tell you... might
          be difficult for you to take at
          first... okay?

Eddie stares at Dustin, uncertain. But he gives a small nod.

                    DUSTIN (CONT'D)
          But... you know how people say
          Hawkins is... cursed?
                    (Eddie nods)
          They're not... *way off* --

EXT. HAWKINS ROAD - NIGHT (MINDSCAPE)

Fred slowly approaches the burning car... fear in his eyes...

He can hear CRIES OF PAIN coming from within...

                    DUSTIN (PRE-LAP)
          There's... another world... a
          world... hidden beneath Hawkins --

INT. BOATHOUSE - NIGHT

                    DUSTIN
          And sometimes... it bleeds into our
          world --

Eddie shifts. His voice low.

                    EDDIE
          ... Like... ghosts and shit -- ?

                    MAX
          There are some things... *worse than
          ghosts.*

EXT. HAWKINS ROAD - NIGHT (MINDSCAPE)

WHAM! A bloody hand hits the pavement as a DYING
TEENAGER begins to crawl out of the burning car. His face is
slashed and bloody, his limbs broken, screaming at Fred --

                    DYING TEEN
          HELLLP HELLPPPP!!!

The Dying Teen reaches out a desperate hand --

Fred staggers away in horror and --

WHAM! He trips over his bike and falls backwards. But --
impossibly -- he doesn't land on the pavement below.

He keeps tumbling through darkness, down, down, *down* --

INT. GRAVE - NIGHT (MINDSCAPE)

WHAM! Fred lands in mud -- directly beside the ROTTING CORPSE
OF HIS FRIEND. MAGGOTS AND WORMS CRAWL OUT OF HIS EYES.

Fred screams and scrambles to his feet, backing away in
horror, only to slam right into --

A DIRT WALL. He spins around. There are walls around him on
all sides. He looks up to find a square of moonlight above,
the headstone from earlier.

HE'S INSIDE AN OPEN GRAVE.

                    DUSTIN (V.O.)
          These... monsters... from this
          other world...

INT. BOATHOUSE - NIGHT

                    DUSTIN
          We thought they were gone... but
          they've come back before. That's
          why we needed to find you --

                    MAX
          If they're back again -- we need to
          know --

INT. GRAVE - NIGHT (MINDSCAPE)

                    GUTTURAL VOICE
    FREDDDDD...

Fred whirls around, terrified. THE GRAVE BEHIND HIM NOW EXTENDS, TUNNELING INTO DARKNESS. We see the faint outline of something moving in that tunnel darkness. It's THE MONSTER...

                    ROBIN (V.O.)
    That night -- did you see anything?

INT. BOATHOUSE - NIGHT

                    MAX
    Dark particles maybe?

                    DUSTIN
    It would almost look like dust --
    swirling dust.

Eddie shakes his head. "No."

                    EDDIE
    There was nothing, nothing you
    could see... or, or touch --

INT. GRAVE - NIGHT (MINDSCAPE)

The MONSTER emerges out of darkness and steps into the grave, its gnarled face dimly lit in the moonlight.

Fred is so scared he is shaking and crying now.

                    FRED
    Wh-- what do you want???

And then something shocking. Our Monster *speaks*:

                    MONSTER
    I want you to join me.

The Monster thrusts out his large, mangled hand. His sharp fingers plunge like knives *into* Fred's face and head and --

EXT. HAWKINS ROAD - NIGHT

Back in the real world, Fred -- whose eyes are half shut and fluttering like Chrissy's -- begins to lift up, levitating in the middle of the dark street --

                    EDDIE (V.O.)
          I, I tried to wake her. But she
          couldn't move --

INT. BOATHOUSE - NIGHT

                    EDDIE
          It's like... she was in a trance or
          something...

                    DUSTIN
          Or under a spell.

Eddie looks up. Tracking Dustin's logic.

                    EDDIE
          A curse.

Dustin's mind races.

                    DUSTIN
          Vecna's curse.

EXT. ROAD - NIGHT

One by one, Fred's limbs begin to SNAP, his eyes pour blood, then --

His eyes SUCK INWARD and --

He drops to the road. Limp as a rag doll. DEAD.

INT. BOATHOUSE - NIGHT

                    STEVE
          ... Who's Vecna?

                    DUSTIN
          An undead creature of... great
          power --

                    EDDIE
          ... A spellcaster --

                    DUSTIN
          A dark wizard.

As everyone takes this in, terrified --

INT. VECNA'S LAIR - NIGHT (UPSIDE DOWN)

ECU ON: Milky, cold eyes slowly peel open.

We PULL AWAY to reveal our monster -- who we will now refer to as VECNA. Only he is not in the grave.

His body is hovering in mid-air, held up by slimy vines which are hooked to various parts of his body, like supernatural umbilical cords. The cords lower him down and detach and --

WHOOM! Vecna drops to his hands and knees. As his body heaves from the effort of his kill, we continue to PULL AWAY from him, drifting backwards through an opening in rotted wall, slipping --

OUTSIDE (UPSIDE DOWN) - CONTINUOUS

We now reveal that Vecna lives in a room at the very top of the decrepit attic of a Victorian House. The house is choked in fog and spores, and vines slither along its walls.

If it wasn't clear before, it is now.

Vecna lives in THE UPSIDE DOWN.

A storm rages overhead. A bolt of red lightning scars the sky, illuminating a flock of winged bat-like creatures. We will call these --

DEMOBATS. They circle Vecna's lair like vultures.

As one of them swoops right by camera with a SHRIEK we --

<u>END EPISODE</u>

EPISODE THREE

CHAPTER THREE:
THE MONSTER AND THE SUPERHERO

WRITTEN BY **CAITLIN SCHNEIDERHAN**

EXT. OWENS HOUSE - NIGHT

We open on a small adobe house. Alone in the desert.

CHYRON: RUTH, NEVADA

INT. OWENS HOUSE - NIGHT

We find a woman, CATHY, 60s, quietly cleaning dishes while listening to the radio.

She puts a plate on the drying rack when she notices something odd: The dishes on the rack are *trembling*. A LOW-END RUMBLING fills the house.

She looks out the window. Her eyes grow and --

MOMENTS LATER

Cathy hurries into living room, where we find --

DOCTOR SAM OWENS! He's fallen asleep on the couch in front of the TV. She shakes him --

      CATHY
 Sam -- Sam!

He jolts awake -- and promptly clocks the worried look on his wife's face. Then he hears it too. THAT LOW-END RUMBLING. LOUDER NOW. His eyes swivel to an end table -- it is vibrating. The entire house is now. *Oh shit.*

EXT. OWENS HOUSE - NIGHT

Owens and Cathy step outside. We PUSH TOWARD THEM as they look up toward --

THREE MILITARY HELICOPTERS. HEADLIGHTS ON. SOARING TOWARD THEIR LITTLE HOUSE.

Off Sam, a look of worry building on his face --

MOMENTS LATER

Dust and sand swirl as the choppers settle down near the house. The doors open and --

LT. COLONEL SULLIVAN, 40s, steps out, followed by three intimidating MILITARY MEN.

Sullivan walks up to Owens, who is now approaching --

He shouts over the rotor noise --

>   SULLIVAN
>   Doctor --

>   DR. OWENS
>   Lieutenant Colonel --

They <u>shake hands</u> and --

INT. OWENS HOUSE - LIVING ROOM - NIGHT

CLOSE ON: MORGUE PHOTOS OF CHRISSY'S TWISTED, EYELESS BODY, EACH MORE GRUESOME THAN THE LAST AS --

Owens sifts through the photos in his living room, his face pale, as Sullivan explains --

>   SULLIVAN
>   -- There were no signs of an
>   attacker -- no bruises -- no sign
>   of any struggle -- it's as if her
>   attacker was a ghost.
>   (beat)
>   Does this remind you of anything,
>   Doctor?

We PUSH IN on Owens, shaken by what he's seeing. Lost in thought.

>   SULLIVAN (CONT'D)
>   Doctor Owens? *Doctor?*

Owens finally snaps out of it. Gathers his composure. Puts down the pictures.

>   DR. OWENS
>   (lying)
>   It doesn't. No.

He tosses the photos back onto the table. Sullivan stares at Owens. He seems to see *right through him.*

>   SULLIVAN
>   Are you sure about that?

Things are getting oddly tense.

>   DR. OWENS
>   Why are you here? *Really* --

> SULLIVAN
> I'd like your opinion. You're the
> expert on Hawkins after all --
>
> DR. OWENS
> *Was*. I was fired, in case you
> forgot --
>
> SULLIVAN
> Thirty civilians died last year --
> a foreign government invaded our
> country -- all under your watch.
> There had to be consequences,
> certainly you understand that --
>
> DR. OWENS
> I understand something is happening
> in that town that nobody -- *nobody*
> fully comprehends -- and I also
> understand that military strength
> is not the answer --
>
> SULLIVAN
> So what's the answer then -- more
> scientists? It was *men of science*
> who created this problem in the
> first place.

Sullivan tosses out a photo of Eleven from 1983 -- lab gown, shaved hair.

> SULLIVAN (CONT'D)
> Everything that has happened in
> Hawkins can be traced back to
> Brenner's little pet, wouldn't you
> agree?

Before Owens has a chance to respond --

Sullivan tosses down crime scene photographs of DR. BRENNER'S MEN -- CONNIE AND THE OTHER AGENTS -- lying dead on the floor of Hawkins Middle School. Like Chrissy, they are bleeding from their eyes.

FLASHCUT TO ELEVEN KILLING THE AGENTS IN SEASON ONE.

> SULLIVAN (CONT'D)
> The similarities are striking,
> aren't they? Doctor Brenner trained
> her for this very thing -- *remote
> assassinations*.

                    DR. OWENS
          What you're suggesting is
          impossible.

                    SULLIVAN
          Is it -- ?

                    DR. OWENS
          Eleven is dead.

                    SULLIVAN
          I'm not convinced --

                    DR. OWENS
          Not convinced. Okay. And where has
          she been this whole time?

                    SULLIVAN
          There are rumors she's received
          help. From someone on the inside.

Owens tenses. And then -- suddenly -- it hits him --

                    DR. OWENS
          You think I helped her.

                    SULLIVAN
          If I just wanted to chat I would've
          picked up the phone.
                    (beat)
          Now... you can make this easy and
          tell us where she is. Or we can do
          this the hard way.

Off Owens, shocked, getting angrier by the moment --

LATER - VARIOUS

WHOOM! A SERIES OF FRANTIC HANDHELD shots as Sullivan's men search the house --

Opening attic space -- pantry -- closet -- grabbing a computer -- searching a basement -- collecting files --

MOMENTS LATER

An upset Cathy chases after a soldier who is carrying boxes up from their basement --

                    CATHY
          Those are Peter's old school
          projects -- you don't need those --
          hey!!

The soldier doesn't listen -- just keeps walking out the
house with the boxes. Cathy shoots Owens a panicked look, but
he's helpless here. We PRE-LAP the SOUND OF SPINNING ROTORS
as --

MOMENTS LATER

The choppers take off again. As dust kicks into the air --

We PUSH IN on a distraught Sam, watching from his doorstep,
holding hands with Cathy as --

                    SULLIVAN (PRE-LAP)
          He's lying. He knows where she is.

INT. MILITARY HELICOPTER - NIGHT

Sullivan talks to one of his men.

                    SULLIVAN
          I want to know everything he's done
          and everyone he's spoken to in the
          past year. If we're lucky -- he'll
          lead us right to the girl.

As his man nods, we PUSH IN on that PHOTO OF ELEVEN. *Their
target.* The ROAR OF THE BLADES grows LOUDER and LOUDER and --

MAIN TITLES

EXT. RINK-O-MANIA - NIGHT

We open on the bright and happy Rink-O-Mania sign.

An AMBULANCE is now parked outside.

INT. RINK-O-MANIA - NIGHT

A small team of PARAMEDICS tends to the injured, sobbing
ANGELA.

                    PARAMEDIC
          Where does it hurt, sweetie -- can
          you tell us where it hurts?

Our CAMERA DRIFTS AWAY from Angela as the paramedics continue to tend to her, moving through a crowd of worried onlookers, surveying...

A frightened JAKE... a very stoned and confused JONATHAN and ARGYLE... an angry WILL... a shocked MIKE... and last but certainly not least...

ELEVEN. She doesn't seem to know what to do... she just looks around, only to find that --

Everyone keeps looking at her. With fear. With *disgust*. Like... she's a monster.

She turns to Mike, but he looks *away*. As if, he too, is ashamed. In this moment, it's like a GUT-PUNCH.

We PUSH IN on Eleven -- feeling very alone and very lost.

                    ARGYLE (PRE-LAP)
      Listen... I know it's upsetting and
      shit... like, in the moment, right
      now -- but I'm sure that future
      prom queen is gonna be TOTALLY
      fine --

INT./EXT. PIZZAMOBILE - NIGHT

They're now driving through Lenora. Everyone is sitting in silence except for Jonathan and Argyle, who are still *high as kites*:

                    ARGYLE
      I mean it was just, like, rubber
      wheels.

                    JONATHAN
      Or plastic. But like a soft
      plastic. Not hard plastic.

                    ARGYLE
      Totally. I mean why do you think
      those wheels aren't wood dude? Or
      metal? SO people don't get hurt
      when they get smacked. Because it
      happens more than you think --
      roller skate attacks.

                    JONATHAN
      Yeah absolutely. And like -- what
      if it was an ice skate -- ?

                    ARGYLE
          DUUUDE. Her nose woulda been sliced
          right off --

                    JONATHAN
          Blood everywhere --

                    ARGYLE
          Gushing -- spraying --

                    JONATHAN
          R.I.P. *R.I.P.*

                    ARGYLE
          See, coulda been so much worse --
          like, waaaay worse.

This obviously doesn't make *anyone* feel any better. Mike
shoots Eleven a look, but she just --

Looks away. Fighting tears. Then --

INT. BYERS HOUSE - NIGHT

Our screwed-up California gang shuffles into the Byers house,
where they're greeted by blasting ITALIAN MUSIC. *Ummmm...*

                    WILL
          Mom...?

Our confused teens trail the music into --

                    THE KITCHEN

Their eyes go wide. REVERSE TO REVEAL: It's not Mom, it's--

MURRAY! HE'S IN THE KITCHEN, WEARING A WOMAN'S APRON,
STIRRING A POT OF RICE AS A RECORD PLAYER SPINS NEARBY.

His eyes light up as he sees them --

                    MURRAY
          Well well -- aren't you lot a sight
          for sore eyes!

He raises up his pot of steaming rice.

                    MURRAY (CONT'D)
          You kids like risotto??!!

Off our kids, stunned and baffled --

                    MURRAY (PRE-LAP)
          So *there I was*, headed down the I-5
          to see a client out in Ventura --

INT. DINING ROOM - NIGHT - LATER

CLOSE ON: A spoon digs into risotto as --

The "family" -- which now includes Murray and Argyle -- eats the meal together at the dining table. Jonathan and Argyle are absolutely DEVOURING their risotto, barely looking up.

> MURRAY
> I was looking for a motel for the night and suddenly -- bam -- it hit me. Didn't the Byers move here???

> JOYCE
> Small world, isn't it -- ??

> MURRAY
> So I thought, you know what, hey -- why not drop in and say hello to my old friends -- ?!!

> JOYCE
> Isn't that sweet of him?

> MURRAY
> Sweeter of you to let me stay.

The kids share looks. This is weird. And... gross.

> JOYCE
> And as it turns out -- he cooks --

> MURRAY
> Cleans too! A regular ol' housewife!

> JOYCE
> Maybe you should just stay --

More horrified looks.

> MURRAY
> Well, I'd be tempted, Joyce, except you know, you have that -- uh --

He shoots her a look. Her cue.

> JOYCE
> Business trip -- I know --

The kids stare in confusion.

> WILL
> "Business trip"? What business trip?

JOYCE
Oh, gosh, I almost forgot to tell you guys! A last minute thing came up at work. They're having a conference tomorrow -- in Alaska --

WILL/MIKE
Alaska -- ??

JOYCE
Yeah! It turns out -- they're based there. The -- Britannicas. Brian and Joan. Britannica.

ARGYLE
Do Eskimos still live in igloos or are they, like, full-blown living in suburbs now -- ?

JOYCE
(ignoring Argyle)
So this means Jonathan -- *Jonathan.*

Jonathan looks up from his risotto.

JOYCE (CONT'D)
I'm going to need you to take charge here while I'm gone --

JONATHAN
Totally. Wait. What -- what's going on?

Joyce stares at her son --

WILL
Business trip --

ARGYLE
Your mom's going to Alaska dude --

JONATHAN
Alaska -- why Alaska?

JOYCE
Okay -- what is wrong with you -- ?

JONATHAN
Nothing -- I just. Sorry. We had a crazy day.

                    ARGYLE
          This girl got smacked in the head
          at the roller rink. Another of
          those -- skate attacks.

                    JONATHAN
          But not *ice skates*. Just -- plastic
          skates.

                    ARGYLE
          Or maybe rubber. Not sure. But yeah
          so she's gonna be totally fine.

                    MIKE
          She didn't look fine.

El has heard enough. She pushes up off of her seat --

                    JOYCE
          El -- you need to finish your --

But she's already gone. The kids all share looks. Murray and
Joyce are totally confused.

                    MURRAY
          I sense tension -- is it my
          risotto? Everyone hates my risotto?

                    JONATHAN
          Are you kidding -- this is
          incredible.

                    ARGYLE
          Increddddible.

Joyce stares at them in horror and --

INT. ELEVEN'S ROOM - NIGHT

WHOOM! Eleven bursts into her room and --

She drops down onto the bed, fighting tears, mind racing.

FLASHCUT OF MEMORIES: HITTING ANGELA -- MIKE YELLING --

                    MIKE (FLASHBACK)
          What did you do?

Eleven grabs a pillow -- squeezes it as --

MORE MEMORIES FLASH PAST US -- WE SEE THE RAINBOW ROOM -- DR.
BRENNER SHOUTING -- BLOOD -- FLASHES OF VIOLENCE -- THE
IMAGES PASS US FASTER AND FASTER -- LOOPING BACK -- AND --

EXT. HAWKINS - NIGHT (UPSIDE DOWN)

BOOM! RED LIGHTNING *SCARS THE SKY*.

We're back in the Upside Down.

EEEEEE! A DEMOBAT *SWOOPS* by camera with a SHRIEK. We travel with it for a bit as it flies over the wasteland that is downtown Hawkins, but soon it overtakes us, headed toward --

VECNA'S LAIR.

INT. VECNA'S LAIR - ATTIC - NIGHT (UPSIDE DOWN)

THUMP! Slimy, gnarled feet slap wood as --

VECNA steps into the attic. He lowers his head. Then --

HISS. Vines peel off the walls of the attic, hissing, *alive*, as if called to him. They slink through the fog like snakes through water, then sharp, hook-like bones protrude from their ends and --

SHOOM! They *CLAMP* onto various parts of his body and then contract, lifting Vecna into the air. As he rises, another FLASH OF LIGHTNING fills the attic with RED LIGHT and --

EXT. HAWKINS - DAY

A *BLOODRED* SUN rises outside Hawkins. It's a *new day*.

INT. BENNY'S BURGERS - DAY

CLOSE ON: The *burnt* photograph of the Hellfire Club. We DRIFT PAST it, over a few empty beer bottles, until we find --

LUCAS, blinking awake on the couch. He hears NOISES. VOICES.

EXT. BENNY'S BURGERS - DAY

Lucas tracks the noises outside, where he finds --

JASON, PATRICK, and ANDY, tossing various items -- TIRE IRONS, DUCT TAPE, CROWBARS -- into the trunk of Jason's car.

      ANDY
    (clocking Lucas)
  Well well, look who's decided to
  join --

                    LUCAS
          What are you doing?

                    PATRICK
          Gearing up --

                    ANDY
          Preparing for *the hunt*.

Jason clocks Lucas's unease.

Approaches, takes his shoulder --

                    JASON
          Hey man, *relax*... we're not killers
          like Eddie. We just want to talk to
          him. Get him to admit to his
          crime --

                    ANDY
          Yeah, a *friendly neighborhood chat*.

Some chuckles, but not from Lucas. *This is getting scary.*

Jason looks deep into his eyes, a private moment:

                    JASON
          Hey. You didn't know Chris -- if
          you're not up to this, you can go
          home. No judgment. You'll still be
          one of us, alright?

Lucas hesitates. A moment of truth. Then --

                    LUCAS
          No -- I'm good.
               (beat)
          I want to help.

Jason nods -- *more like it*. He turns back to the others.

                    JASON
          Alright. Let's *capture us a freak*.

Jason slams the trunk closed and --

INT. BOATHOUSE - DAY

WHOOM! EDDIE bolts upright inside the boat. Sweating. Scared.

He hears RUSTLING. VOICES. *Someone is approaching.*

MOMENTS LATER

He grabs his broken bottle and heads to the smudged window.
He looks into the trees -- sees nothing out there. And --

WHOOM! The door kicks open behind him --

He whirls, startled as hell, but --

It's just DUSTIN, STEVE, ROBIN, AND MAX!!! They're carrying GROCERIES. Dustin holds up an overstuffed bag as he flashes a classic Dustin smile.

                  DUSTIN
        Delivery service!

Off Eddie --

                DUSTIN (PRE-LAP) (CONT'D)
        So we have some good news, and, uh,
        some bad news --

A LITTLE LATER

Eddie gobbles cereal and other junk food, ravenous, washing it all down with Yoo-hoo as the gang fills him in --

                DUSTIN
        How do you prefer it -- ?

                EDDIE
            (mouth stuffed)
        Bad news first, *always* --

                DUSTIN
        Okay. Bad news. We tapped into the
        Hawkins PD dispatch with my Cerebro
        and they're *definitely* looking for
        you -- and they're pretty convinced
        you killed Chrissy.

                MAX
        Like... *a hundred percent* kinda
        convinced...

Eddie takes this in, scared, tries to stay calm --

                EDDIE
        Okay. And -- the good news?

                ROBIN
        Your name hasn't gone public yet --

ROBIN (CONT'D)
But if *we* found out about you, it's a matter of time before others do too. And once that gets out, everyone and their shallow-minded *mother* is gonna be gunning for you --

EDDIE
Freak hunt --

ROBIN
Exactly --

DUSTIN
Basically, it's a matter of time before you're found -- SO before that happens, we have to just find Vecna and kill him and prove your innocence.

EDDIE
Oh yeah? That's all, huh?

DUSTIN
(missing the sarcasm)
Yeah. I think so.
(to the group)
Did I leave anything out -- ?

MAX
No, I, uh, think you got it Dustin.

Robin leans forward.

ROBIN
Listen, Eddie, I know what Dustin says sounds totally delusional -- but we've actually dealt with this kinda thing before -- or rather, they have a few times -- I have once, well, sorta, it was a different thing -- related -- but either way, I feel like -- you know -- collectively... *we've got this*.

STEVE
We usually rely on a girl with superpowers, but those went bye-bye so --

                    ROBIN
          Yeah, I mean -- I guess technically
          we're still --

                    MAX
          In the *brainstorming* phase --

                    DUSTIN
          But there's nothing to worry about.

They force smiles. Eddie looks anything *but* reassured when --

SIRENS interrupt. Shared looks and --

                    ROBIN
     Tarp --

MOMENTS LATER

Eddie scrambles back into the boat -- Dustin and Robin toss the tarp back over him -- Steve grabs his trusty oar and --

MOMENTS LATER

Our gang crowds around the window, peering out. They listen as the sirens grow louder. And LOUDER. Then --

WHOOSH! An AMBULANCE zooms past. Then a COP CAR. Then another COP CAR. Then *another*. They're not coming for Eddie -- *they're headed somewhere else.* Shared, knowing looks, and --

EXT. CRIME SCENE - SIDE OF ROAD - DAY

CHOOM! A crime scene photographer snaps photos of --

FRED'S CORPSE. Eyes sucked in. Bones twisted. Dead.

WIDEN: We're at the road where was Fred was killed last night. It's now a CRIME SCENE -- swarming with cops, ambulances, firetrucks. A *real zoo.*

As more cop cars roll in our CAMERA TRACKS --

BEHIND A WALL OF CARS,

Where we find CHIEF POWELL taking NANCY'S statement alongside CALLAHAN and the stern cop, OFFICER DANIELS. Nancy looks scared, pale -- and *very tired*. She hasn't slept a wink.

                    POWELL
          And after you talked to Wayne --
          what happened?

                        NANCY
            I heard barking -- from the dog.
            And then he was -- just -- gone --

                        CALLAHAN
            You see... anyone lurking about?
            Anyone who looked like they
            shouldn't be there -- ?

                        NANCY
                 (getting frustrated)
            No -- no -- there was -- no one --
            I already told all of this to
            Officer Daniels --

She turns to Officer Daniels --

                        NANCY (CONT'D)
            Did you look into Victor Creel -- ?

                        POWELL
            Sorry -- what's that?

                        OFFICER DANIELS
            Victor Creel -- Wayne got it in her
            head that that old nut did this --

                        POWELL
            Victor's locked away tight, hun --
            you don't need to worry about him,
            alright? Now -- you said last you
            saw Fred -- he was by the picnic
            table -- do I have that right?

Nancy is about to snap back when, through the chaos, she sees a car pulling up. It's --

A FAMILIAR BMW. The doors open and --

STEVE, MAX, AND DUSTIN step out.

                        POWELL (CONT'D)
            Miss Wheeler? It was by the picnic
            tables, is that correct? *Miss
            Wheeler?*

But Nancy isn't listening to Powell anymore. She's just looking at her friends. About to cry with relief.

As they walk up to the crime tape, they see her.

She awkwardly holds up a hand. "Hi."

And right here, we CRASH TO --

EXT. BYERS NEIGHBORHOOD - DAY

WHACK! A stick slamming a puck as --

NEIGHBORHOOD KIDS play street hockey, LAUGHING, having fun.

We PUSH PAST them to the Byers house, where --

INT. BYERS HOUSE - DAY

Jonathan flips through the paper, checking out today's movie times. Mike and Will sit nearby, quietly eating breakfast.

A plate of Eggo waffles sits by Mike, untouched -- Eleven is *conspicuously absent*.

>   JONATHAN
>   ... There's a three PM showing of
>   *Cobra*, that could be fun.

Will glances at Mike -- who just looks away. Not talking.

>   WILL
>   Maybe we just -- stay home today.

Jonathan eyes the situation here.

>   JONATHAN
>   So -- what is this? You guys are
>   just gonna mope all break now?

>   WILL
>   No one's moping. *Cobra* is just
>   supposed to suck.

Mike shifts his gaze to the untouched Eggo waffles, and...

He grabs El's plate, heads off.

Will watches him go, a bit sad, then returns to his meal.

INT. BYERS HOUSE - OUTSIDE EL'S ROOM - DAY

Mike walks up to El's door. Still *open three inches*. Knocks.

>   MIKE
>   El...? I made you Eggos. But
>   they're kinda... getting cold.

There's no answer. Mike gently opens the door...

INT. ELEVEN'S ROOM - DAY

He finds El sitting at her desk, working to repair her diorama. She doesn't look at him -- just keeps working on it.

> MIKE
> Hey, that's cool... Hop's cabin, right?

A small nod from El. Mike places the Eggos down next to her, sits down on the bed. An awkward beat, and then --

> MIKE (CONT'D)
> So... are we just gonna just... not talk about it?

El keeps her eyes on the cabin.

> ELEVEN
> ... About... what?

> MIKE
> Yesterday? I don't know. *Everything*.

> ELEVEN
> There is... nothing to say.

> MIKE
> Yeah... I guess I just -- don't understand. I mean -- why didn't you just tell me about what's going on here?
> (no response)
> You know I'm not exactly, like, mister popularity back home. I've been bullied my whole life okay? I, I *know* what it's like --

Eleven snaps a bit at this --

> ELEVEN
> No. You don't.

She then returns to her cabin.

> MIKE
> Okay... what... don't I understand?

                        ELEVEN
                ... I am different.
                        (beat)
                I do... not belong --

                        MIKE
                You mean, like -- in Lenora -- ?

El shakes her head. Tears in her eyes.

                        ELEVEN
                Anywhere.

A beat.

                        MIKE
                You can't actually believe that --

                        ELEVEN
                They all look at me like... I am...
                a monster --

                        MIKE
                They just -- don't know you --

                        ELEVEN
                You think I am a monster too --

                        MIKE
                What -- ?

                        ELEVEN
                Yesterday -- the way you looked at
                me you -- you were scared *of me*.

                        MIKE
                That's -- not true... I -- I was
                surprised, I mean -- maybe I was
                upset -- in the moment. I just -- I
                didn't know what to do -- I'm
                sorry, okay? It was crazy -- it
                happened so fast -- but it doesn't
                matter, it doesn't change anything.
                I care for you. So much.

She looks at him --

                        ELEVEN
                "Care." But you do not -- love me
                anymore -- ?

Mike grows flustered --

                    MIKE
          What -- of course -- who said that
          -- I didn't?

                    ELEVEN
          You never -- say it --

                    MIKE
          Yes I have --

                    ELEVEN
          Not -- to me.

Before a stunned Mike can respond, she grabs up his pile of
letters from her desk and starts to flip through them --

                    ELEVEN (CONT'D)
          You can't even write it. "From
          Mike" -- "From Mike" -- "From Mike"
          -- "From from from -- "

Now she's tossing letters to the floor, getting more and more
upset. Mike has no idea what to do here as those letters pile
up at his feet --

                    MIKE
          El -- stop -- stop! Come on -- what
          is this??? You're -- being
          ridiculous. You're -- you're the
          most incredible person in the world
          and you know how I feel about you --
          you can't let these mouth breathers
          ruin you -- ruin us. They're --
          they're nobodies, nobodies, okay?
          And you -- you're a superhero.

She finally stops with the letters, turns back at Mike.

A tear slips down her cheek.

                    ELEVEN
          Not anymore.

As Mike realizes he's said the *exact wrong thing* --

DING DONG! The doorbell rings.

As Mike and El turn --

INT. BYERS HOUSE - DINING/LIVING ROOM - DAY

Jonathan stands, crosses to the door --

                    WILL
        Ten bucks says Mom forgot
        something --

                  JONATHAN
        Yeah I'm not taking that bet --

Jonathan reaches the door, swings it open, and --

His face falls. It's TWO LENORA COPS.

                LENORA COP #1
        Hi. Does a Jane Hopper live here?

Will stands now -- holy shit.

                  JONATHAN
        Yeah -- what -- is this about?

BACK DOWN THE HALLWAY,

An anxious Eleven and Mike edge their way toward the front of the house. They can hear Jonathan speaking to the cops --

              LENORA COP #1 (O.S.)
        Is Jane's father or mother around?

                    JONATHAN (O.S.)
            -- No no, her mom's out of town --
            I'm her -- brother. Stepbrother.

BACK AT THE DOOR,

Things are getting tense --

                    JONATHAN
            Can you please just -- tell me what
            this is about??

                    LENORA COP #1
            As you may or may not be aware,
            there was an incident last night
            involving Jane at Rink-O-Mania --

                    WILL
            That was an accident --

Cop #2 holds up a WARRANT.

                    LENORA COP #2
            We have a warrant here that says
            otherwise.

Cop #1 now spots Eleven. She's inched out into the hallway alongside Mike. She looks like a frightened animal.

                    LENORA COP #2 (CONT'D)
            Hey there. You Jane Hopper?

Off El, managing a scared nod, dramatic music rises and we CUT TO --

EXT. BYERS HOUSE - PORCH - MOMENTS LATER

Handcuffs snapping around Eleven as she's arrested --

Mike and the others look on with shock --

                    LENORA COP #1
                (heavy reverb)
            You have the right to remain
            silent. Anything you say can and
            will be used against you in a court
            of law. You have the right to an
            attorney. If you cannot afford an
            attorney, one will be provided for
            you --

MOMENTS LATER

The hockey kids now watch *slack-jawed* as --

A stunned, handcuffed Eleven is marched across the walkway toward a COP CAR. As they duck her head down and help her into the back seat, a panicked Mike attempts to console --

>   MIKE
>   It's gonna be okay, El -- okay?
>   We're gonna find you, I promise --
>   we're gonna find you and fix
>   this!!! We're gonna FIX THIS --

Eleven looks away. She can't face Mike. Not now. The first tear falls as --

The cop car drives away. As Mike watches in disbelief --

A panicked Will fires Jonathan a look --

>   WILL
>   *Mom*. Has her flight left -- ??

Jonathan doesn't waste time with a response -- he's already SPRINTING back to the house *as fast as he can* and --

INT. PASSENGER JET - FLIGHT 673 - DAY

THWICK! Joyce spins a lighter flint wheel.

WIDEN TO REVEAL: Joyce is smoking -- yes, in the plane! *God bless the '80s.* She is seemingly waiting for takeoff, anxious as hell, her mind racing a million miles an hour.

Finally she can't take the silence anymore -- she turns to Murray, who is reading next to her --

>   JOYCE
>   You think I should have just --
>   told them -- ?

>   MURRAY
>   Told who -- what -- ? Sorry?
>   (re: magazine)
>   I was engrossed.

>   JOYCE
>   The kids -- about Hopper. I mean it
>   just -- felt *wrong*. Last night --
>   lying to them like that --

                    MURRAY
          Well, I'm *not exactly* an expert in
          parenting.

Joyce blinks -- *that's very true.*

                    MURRAY (CONT'D)
          But for what little it may be worth
          -- I think you did the right thing.
          The *responsible thing* --

                    JOYCE
          "Responsible" -- ?

                    MURRAY
          Absolutely. Your children -- bless
          their mischievous souls -- like to
          get involved. This way, what --
          they play too much Nintendo? Eat
          too much junk food? Smoke some
          ganja? Pound some beers? Experiment
          -- sexually? I mean, really, what's
          the worst that can happen?

Before an *absolutely horrified* Joyce can respond --

                    STEWARDESS (O.S.)
          Excuse me, ma'am --

Joyce looks up to find a concerned STEWARDESS approaching.

                    STEWARDESS (CONT'D)
          Sorry to interrupt... but I'm gonna
          need you to fasten your seatbelt.
          Turbulence.

                    JOYCE
          Oh -- right --

As the Stewardess walks off, Joyce mutters --

                    JOYCE (CONT'D)
          Like if we crash *this* is gonna save
          me --

As she buckles her seatbelt, we PULL AWAY, moving through the window beside Murray to reveal --

EXT. SKY - CONTINUOUS - DAY

THE PLANE IS IN FACT ALREADY MID-AIR. *OH* NO!

AS SWIRLING SNOW OVERTAKES CAMERA, DISSOLVE TO --

EXT. KAMCHATKA, RUSSIA - DAY

We're PUSHING through blistering snow. We soar *over treetops* as we make our way toward...

A LONG LINE OF PRISONERS -- working to build a long railroad track. *It's a Russian chain gang!* CHYRON: KAMCHATKA, RUSSIA.

WORKSITE - MOMENTS LATER

Our camera surveys the worksite. There are armed guards, snowmobiles, makeshift tents, a watch tower, and seemingly endless snowy tundra in all directions. *No escape.* We TRACK DOWN the line of prisoners until we find --

HOPPER. He's barely recognizable now: He has a long, tangled beard, he's lost seventy pounds, he's malnourished, and the cold has begun to erode his skin. This is a raw shell of the man we once knew. As he methodically slams in a railroad tie --

DMITRI makes his way down the line, calmly inspecting everyone's work. He pauses by Hopper, narrows his eyes...

>   DMITRI
>   (Russian)
>   <What is this, American? What is
>   taking you this long? Are you tired
>   today?>

Hopper mutters --

>   HOPPER
>   <Scum -->

>   DMITRI
>   <*What* do you say??>

Hopper glares at him.

>   HOPPER
>   I said leave me be... <scum.>

Dmitri stares. Then he lunges forward, grabs Hopper, and drags him away from the tracks, flinging him back against --

A PILE OF RAILROAD TIES - CONTINUOUS

-- Out of sight of the other guards. And it is here, abruptly, that Dmitri drops the "angry guard" act --

>   DMITRI
>   Your Russian is getting better. So
>   is your acting --
>
>   HOPPER
>   What is it?

Dmitri looks around, making sure no one is watching, then --

>   DMITRI
>   I bring news -- from America. I
>   hear from your friends. They are
>   bringing your money to Alaska --

Hopper can scarcely believe it --

>   HOPPER
>   ... When -- ?
>
>   DMITRI
>   Today -- I hope.

A beat as Hopper absorbs this -- *holy shit*.

>   DMITRI (CONT'D)
>   If my pilot gets the money, he will
>   bring it to me in his plane
>   tomorrow. Then you hitch a ride
>   with him back to your country -- I
>   get rich -- you are free man --
>   sound too good to be true yes??
>
>   HOPPER
>   Yeah... it does. This pilot you
>   found -- you can trust him?
>
>   DMITRI
>   You getting cold feet, American? It
>   is *a bit late* for that --
>
>   HOPPER
>   I just want to know who it is I'm
>   trusting with my life --

DMITRI
His name is Yuri Ismaylov. He is a smuggler, supplies American goods for some of us guards here -- including me on lucky occasion -- cigarettes, peanut butter, *Playboys* -- the best America has to offer --

HOPPER
So he's a criminal -- ?

DMITRI
Of course!! Who else do you want to do this job??? Gandhi??

Dmitri laughs, but Hopper is unamused. Dmitri suddenly understands --

DMITRI (CONT'D)
You're worried about your woman -- is that it?

Hopper doesn't answer. Doesn't have to --

DMITRI (CONT'D)
I see why you like her, American. When I talk to her, I can tell by voice she is *very pretty*. *Feisty* too. I like that. It is a shame we won't meet -- shame for *her* that is --

Dmitri chuckles --

HOPPER
You promised she'd be safe --

DMITRI
And she will be.

Hopper looks anxious as hell, but --

DMITRI (CONT'D)
Let me handle Yuri -- you have more important things to worry about. Remember, you miss that plane tomorrow, I am still rich man -- and *you are still stuck in Kamchatka*. So whatever it is you are planning, American -- best get to it, yes?

Dmitri grins. Before Hopper can respond --

                    MEAN GUARD (O.S.)
    <Antonov!>

Heads swivel to find a MEAN GUARD approaching --

                    MEAN GUARD (CONT'D)
    <Finish with your American toy! We
    need him on the tracks!!>

                    DMITRI
    <Yes yes -- I am just -- putting
    him in his place.>

As the Mean Guard shuffles off, clearly irritated --

                    DMITRI (CONT'D)
        (under breath)
    <Nosy bastard.>

Dmitri turns back to Hopper --

                    DMITRI (CONT'D)
    Where do you want it?

Hopper sighs. *Fuck*. He motions to his left cheek. Dmitri SLAMS him with his fist. As knuckles meet bone, CRASH TO --

EXT. TRAILER PARK - DAY

Quiet. Laundry dances in the wind.

We PUSH THROUGH the laundry to find our Hawkins gang crowded around a picnic table in the trailer park.

Nancy is still clearly shaken from seeing Fred's body -- and even more so by what she's now been told...

                    NANCY
    ... And you think this... thing
    that killed Fred and Chrissy --
    it's from the Upside Down?

                    STEVE
    If the shoe fits --

                    DUSTIN
    Our working theory is that he
    attacks with a spell -- or curse.
            (MORE)

                    DUSTIN (CONT'D)
          Now whether or not he's doing the
          bidding of the Mind Flayer -- or
          just loves killing teens -- we
          don't know --

                    MAX
          All we know is -- this is something
          different -- *something new.*

A beat as Nancy absorbs this new information.

                    NANCY
          It just... it doesn't make sense --

                    DUSTIN
          It's only a theory --

                    NANCY
          No. I mean, Fred and Chrissy don't
          make sense. Why them?

                    DUSTIN
          Maybe they were both just in the
          wrong place -- they were both at
          the game --

                    MAX
              (picking up)
          And near the trailer park.

Steve looks around -- suddenly spooked.

                    STEVE
          Uh yeah, maybe we shouldn't... be
          here?

                    NANCY
          There *is* something about this
          place. Fred started acting weird
          the second we got here --

                    ROBIN
          "Acting weird" as in -- ?

                    NANCY
          Scared, on edge -- upset --

                    DUSTIN
          Max said Chrissy was upset too.

Nancy looks to Max --

                    MAX
            But not here. She was... crying in
            the bathroom. At school.

The pieces are starting to click.

                    ROBIN
            Before they strike, serial killers
            stalk their prey, right? So maybe
            Fred and Chrissy... saw this -- Vec-
            man --

                    DUSTIN
            Vecna --

                    STEVE
            Yeah, I don't know about you guys --
            but if I saw a wizard monster
            freak, I'd mention it to someone --

                    MAX
            Maybe they did.

Everyone now looks to Max.

                    MAX (CONT'D)
            I saw Chrissy leaving Miss Kelley's
            office. If you saw a monster... you
            wouldn't go to the police -- they'd
            never believe you. But you might go
            to --

                    ROBIN
            Your shrink.

Max nods. *Exactly.* And off this, CUT TO --

MOMENTS LATER

The group is fast walking across the trailer park. They start to climb in Steve's BMW, piling inside. That is, all but --

Nancy. Who continues on her way --

                    STEVE
            Hey -- where are you going??

                    NANCY
                (fast)
            There's something I want to check
            on first, I'll catch up --

She starts to continue on her way when Dustin calls out:

                    DUSTIN
          Something you maybe want to share
          with the rest of us??

Nancy turn back again, hesitates --

                    NANCY
          I don't want to waste your time,
          it's a real shot in the dark --

                    STEVE
          Yeah okay -- have you *lost your
          mind?* Flying solo with this Vecna
          creep on the loose? No no nopity
          NOPE --

Steve crosses to Robin, hands her his car keys --

                    STEVE (CONT'D)
          I'll stick with Nance. Take my car,
          check on the shrink --

                    ROBIN
          I'm not sure you want me driving
          your car --

                    STEVE
          Why not -- ?

                    ROBIN
          I don't have a license -- ?

                    STEVE
          Why is that again --??

                    ROBIN
          I'm -- poor?

                    MAX
          I can drive --

                    STEVE
          NO. Anyone *BUT* you --

                    DUSTIN
          I'll give it a whirl --

                    ROBIN
          This is just *stupid* --

Robin hands the keys back to Steve, grabs Dustin's walkie, and crosses to Nancy --

>   ROBIN (CONT'D)
> Us ladies will stick together --
>   (back to Steve)
> Or do you think we need *you* to
> protect us?

Steve watches them go in slack-jawed disbelief.

>   DUSTIN
> Are you just gonna stand there and
> gawk Harrington? Let's GO!!

INT. STEVE'S CAR - DAY

Steve grumbles as he drops back into his car.

>   STEVE
>   (to himself)
> Always the babysitter -- always the
> *goddamn* babysitter --

He turns the keys and the engine growls to life and --

EXT. TRAILER PARK - DAY

Steve drives away. Passing by --

Eddie's trailer. The crime scene tape flutters eerily in the breeze. We slowly push toward the trailer. Beneath the flapping of the tape, we hear a STRANGE LOW-END RUMBLE...

INT. EDDIE'S TRAILER

We're now drifting through Eddie's trailer. The rumble is much more intense now. The lights flicker and our camera moves up to the ceiling, honing in on some strange ROT AND MOLD. The rumble grows louder and louder and THE ROT BEGINS TO SPREAD AND --

EXT. UPSIDE DOWN - NIGHT

BOOM! RED LIGHTNING STRIKES.

Back in the Upside Down. Outside that Victorian house.

INT. ATTIC (UPSIDE DOWN)

We PUSH TOWARD Vecna, who is now hanging from his gross "spiderweb." We move toward his closed eyes. His eyelids move very rapidly back and forth, back and forth *and* --

INT. VECNA'S MIND LAIR

WHOOM! We're SUDDENLY HURTLING through what can only be described as a HIGHWAY OF RED FOG. Bloodred spores whip past us at dizzying speed, strange rib-like structures jut up out of the swampy earth, lightning crashes above us, and...

All around us, SEMI-TRANSLUCENT IMAGES OF PEOPLE flitter in and out of view. Every time we glimpse a person, we hear awful sounds *scraped* from their minds: SCREAMING, CRYING, SHOUTING. But only briefly -- almost as soon as we latch onto a person, they vanish once more beneath a curtain of red fog.

But then -- suddenly -- we find ourselves racing toward the back of a familiar car. *Jason's car. Like we're chasing it on the freeway.* As we draw closer, we hear:

> DISTORTED MALE VOICE (V.O.)
> You out drinking again?? HUH?
> You're an embarrassment -- a
> disgrace to this entire family --

We fly through the windshield *into the back of a head and* --

INT. JASON'S CAR - LOWER CLASS NEIGHBORHOOD - DAY

WHOOM! PATRICK SUDDENLY GASPS. Wincing. Blood spills from his nose.

Andy, seated next to him, speaks to him -- but his voice is buried a bit beneath a TINNITUS-LIKE RINGING.

> ANDY
> Patrick, your nose --

> PATRICK
> Huh -- ?

> ANDY
> Your nose is bleeding dude --

Patrick wipes it.

> ANDY (CONT'D)
> Gross --

As a disturbed Patrick tries to gather his composure --

BACK IN THE FRONT,

Jason's eyes narrow. Through the front windshield, he spots GARETH, JEFF, and TWO OTHER HELLFIRE "FREAKS" playing heavy metal music in a garage.

> JASON
> And -- hello there.

He swerves to the side of the road and --

INT./EXT. GARETH'S GARAGE - MOMENTS LATER - DAY

The freaks' music slows to a stop as they see the jocks approaching up the driveway -- Gareth stands up in front of his drum kit. He's wearing a DIRTY SCABS T-shirt; the name of the band has also been spray-painted on the head of the bass drum.

                    GARETH
          You're a bit early, fellas. Show's
          not until next week --

                    ANDY
          Oh that was *music* you were playing?

                    JASON
          We're looking for Eddie Munson.
          He's in this band, if that's what
          you can even call this, right -- ?

                    GARETH
          What do you care -- ?

                    JASON
          That's our business --

Gareth suddenly spots Lucas --

                    GARETH
          Lucas -- what are you doing with
          these douchebags -- ?

Jason and the others look at Lucas, surprised --

                    JASON
          You know these freaks, Sinclair??

Lucas hesitates, feeling caught, quickly evades --

                    LUCAS
          They know my sister, and they tried
          to recruit me to their -- club --
          cult --

Gareth can't believe *what* he's hearing -- a *betrayal*.

                    JEFF
          Lucas, man -- *the hell* -- ?

                    LUCAS
          We -- we just need to find Eddie --

                    GARETH
          Well, you got eyes don't you? He's
          not here --

WHAM! Jason suddenly SUCKER PUNCHES Gareth, then slams him
against the garage wall. The other freaks move to defend
their friend -- but Andy and Patrick easily grab them and
hold them back.

                    JEFF   FREAK #1
LET US GO -- STOP IT!!   GET OFF -- !

Lucas hovers back, shocked, not sure how to stop this as --

Jason gets in Gareth's now bleeding face, *inches away* --

                    JASON
               Where IS he -- ???

                    GARETH
          I DON'T KNOW -- I -- I SWEAR --

That's NOT the answer Jason was looking for. He throws Gareth backwards into his drum set, cymbals CRASHING. Gareth tries to scramble back up to his feet but --

WHAM! Jason slams one foot on his back, pinning him to the ground. Then -- WHAM! He slams his other foot on top of GARETH'S HAND --

                    JASON
               Gonna be hard to play those drums
               with a broken hand --

He presses harder. Gareth screams, then, finally, *breaks* --

                    GARETH
               Dustin -- *Dustin* --

Lucas's heart rate spikes. *Dustin??*

                    JASON
               What -- ??

                    GARETH
               Dustin -- Henderson -- he was
               calling around -- looking for Eddie
               -- maybe, maybe he found him.

Jocks share looks -- a lead. Lucas's breath catches. *Fuck.*

                    JASON
               See that wasn't so hard was it?
               Now...

Jason kneels down right by Gareth --

                    JASON (CONT'D)
               Where do we find this *Dustin*?

Off Lucas, terrified now for his friend, CRASH TO --

EXT. LENORA HILLS POLICE STATION - DAY

A flag waves outside a Lenora police station.

                    LENORA COP #1 (V.O.)
                -- And that's when you struck her?

INT. LENORA HILLS POLICE STATION - INTERROGATION ROOM - DAY

EXTREME CLOSE ON: A SHELL-SHOCKED ELEVEN. She nods. "Yes."

                    LENORA COP #1 (O.S.)
                I need you to give a verbal
                response.

REVERSE: The Lenora cops are questioning El in a windowless room.

                    ELEVEN
                Yes -- that is when -- I hit her.

As the cops scribble notes --

                    LENORA COP #2
                And why did you hit her -- ?

                    ELEVEN
                ... I don't know.

                    LENORA COP #1
                You don't know -- ?

                    LENORA COP #2
                You know that girl you hit -- she
                got a grade two concussion? Doctors
                say she might not be able to hear
                out of her right ear anymore -- did
                you know that?

                    ELEVEN
                No.

Cop #1 looks at Cop #2 --

                    LENORA COP #1
                She doesn't seem too upset about it
                does she?

                    LENORA COP #2
                No she doesn't --

Back to Eleven --

                    LENORA COP #1
          Did you want to kill her?

                    ELEVEN
          ... I don't know --

                    LENORA COP #1
          You don't know if you wanted to
          kill her or not?

FLASHCUT: DEAD CHILDREN -- BLOOD SPLATTERED ON THE RAINBOW --

                    ELEVEN
          No.

                    LENORA COP #1
          No, you didn't want to kill her --
          or no you don't know?

                    ELEVEN
          I... do not know.

As our cops share looks, MUSIC RISES and --

INT. LENORA HILLS POLICE STATION - MUGSHOT ROOM - DAY

CHOOM! A MUGSHOT PHOTO is taken of Eleven.

-- She turns her body. CHOOM!

-- Another turn. CHOOM!

                    POLICE RECEPTIONIST (PRE-LAP)
          Jane Hopper -- okay -- yes I see
          her now.

INT. LENORA HILLS POLICE STATION - RECEPTION - DAY

A stressed Jonathan, Mike, and Will crowd a reception desk, where an unsympathetic POLICE RECEPTIONIST reads data off a computer --

                    POLICE RECEPTIONIST
          Looks like she's still being
          processed --

                    JONATHAN
          Processed -- okay -- and -- what
          does that mean exactly -- ?

INT. LENORA HILLS POLICE STATION - BACK OF STATION - DAY

A SERIES OF SHOTS INTERCUT WITH THE RECEPTIONIST:

-- *EL ROLLS HER FINGER IN INK.*

          POLICE RECEPTIONIST (V.O.)
  It means they're putting her in the
  system --

-- *PRESSES HER INKED FINGER ON PAPER* --

          POLICE RECEPTIONIST (V.O.)
  ... After which point she'll be
  transferred to juvenile hall --

-- *THE OTHER FINGER NOW AND* --

INT. LENORA HILLS POLICE STATION - RECEPTION - DAY

          MIKE
  Jail -- *you're putting her in*
  jail -- ???

          POLICE RECEPTIONIST
        (correcting)
  A detention hall for juveniles --

EXT. LENORA HILLS POLICE STATION - BACK - DAY

Eleven is now led outside in handcuffs with a few other JUVENILES. She looks lost in a cloud of dark thoughts.

As she's placed into the back of a POLICE TRANSPORT VAN --

          JONATHAN (V.O.)
  Can we see her -- ?

INT. LENORA HILLS POLICE STATION - RECEPTION - DAY

          POLICE RECEPTIONIST
  Are you a parent or guardian -- ?

          JONATHAN
  No but --

          WILL
  We're her brothers -- *family* --

                    POLICE RECEPTIONIST
          That's not enough. You have to be a
          parent or legal guardian --

EXT. LENORA HILLS POLICE STATION - BACK - DAY

The door slams shut on the police transport van -- locking in
El and the other juveniles --

INT. LENORA HILLS POLICE STATION - RECEPTION - DAY

                        MIKE
          You have to be kidding. That --
          that is *ridiculous* --

                    POLICE RECEPTIONIST
          That is the <u>law</u>. And you're not
          gonna change it complaining to me.
          You want to see Jane --
                  (back to Jonathan)
          <u>Find your mother</u>.

EXT. LENORA HILLS POLICE STATION - DAY

Doors fly open as our angry, defeated teens exit the station.

A somber Mike slows to a stop. He sees --

The POLICE TRANSPORT VAN. It is now driving away from the
station, turning out. Its windows are dark and tinted -- we
can't see in -- but it's like... he knows she's in there. *He
can feel it.* As the van passes them, Mike hurries out onto
the middle of the road, as if he might just catch her --

INT. POLICE TRANSPORT VAN - DAY

El watches Mike out the back window. A single tear slips down
her cheek as Mike gets smaller and smaller and...

INT. PASSENGER JET - DAY

Sunlit clouds gently drift past camera.

WE SLOWLY PULL BACK to reveal we're back inside the plane,
looking out that small window. We continue to PULL BACK to
find...

Murray, fast asleep next to Joyce. He's snoring a bit, and
his head slips in her direction... closer... and closer...
and WHUMP. It lands on her shoulder. HELL NO.

She pushes him away. Murray doesn't even wake. Just keeps
snoring --

                    STEWARDESS
            Alright -- and *here you go* --

Our Stewardess hands Joyce a PREPACKAGED LUNCHBOX.

                    JOCYE
            Thanks. Um -- how much --
            longer -- ?

                    STEWARDESS
            Oh. Just a few more hours. Almost
            there! You and your husband have
            exciting plans?

Joyce winces at that -- husband?

                    JOYCE
            Yeah -- we're, uh -- seeing an old
            friend. *I hope.*

The stewardess smiles and heads off as --

Joyce peels open her lunchbox. Inside: green peas, a roll, and -- *is that chicken*? Whatever it is, it *hardly looks like food*. As a disturbed Joyce pokes at it, we CUT TO --

EXT. WORKSITE - KAMCHATKA - DAY

SPLAT! GROSS SLOP splashing into a dirty bowl.

WIDEN: Hopper is in line for lunch. Each prisoner receives a portion of the gross slop and --

                    MEAN GUARD
            <One bread each -- one bread!>

Hopper takes his slop and his stale bread, then --

A LITTLE LATER

The shivering prisoners now eat their meager meal amidst the falling snow. Hopper -- looking for a place to sit like a kid in a school cafeteria -- zeroes in on a STRONG PRISONER. *That'll work.*

MOMENTS LATER

Hopper sits beside him. A moment of silence. Then --

                    HOPPER
            <Here.>

Hopper passes the Strong Prisoner an additional bread. But the Strong Prisoner swats it away --

                    STRONG PRISONER
          <I am no fairy.>

Hopper persists.

                        HOPPER
          <No -- you -- hit -->

Hopper motions hitting. Then motions to his ankle iron.

                    HOPPER (CONT'D)
          <Hit. I give -- bread. Trade. Yes?>

The Strong Man seems to understand now. But --

                    STRONG PRISONER
          <I will break your leg.>

Hopper doesn't understand, reiterates --

                        HOPPER
          <Hit. I give -- bread. Yes?>

The Strong Man considers. Then --

                    STRONG PRISONER
          <And soup.>

He looks down at Hopper's slop. That's ALL of Hopper's food. But... screw it. Hopper hands him the soup --

The Strong Man shakes his head, mutters --

                  STRONG PRISONER (CONT'D)
          <Crazy American.>

The Strong Man devours Hop's soup, slurping it down, and --

EXT. KAMCHATKA TUNDRA - TRAIN TRACKS - DAY

WHAM! Spike mauls slam ties again. *Back to work.*

Hopper looks around, makes sure the guards aren't watching. Not even Dmitri. *It's now or never.*

Hopper places his leg up against the track, and --

                        HOPPER
          <<u>Now</u>.>

The Strong Prisoner pulls back on his big mallet.

As Hopper braces for the coming hit, he remembers back and --

FLASHBACK: JOYCE IN MELVALD'S. TALKING TO A CUSTOMER. THE SUNLIGHT CATCHING HER PERFECTLY.

The Strong Prisoner brings the spike crashing down and --

WHAM! THE MALLET SLAMS HARD INTO HOPPER'S LEG IRON.

It jolts Hopper out of his memory. That hurt like <u>fucking hell</u>. But he can't stop. Not now.

>   HOPPER (CONT'D)
>   (growls)
>   <Again.>

The Strong Prisoner brings the mallet back as Hop recalls --

FLASHBACK: HOP RUBBING EL'S HEAD IN THE KITCHEN. EL SMILES.

SLAM! The maul hits metal and flesh again.

Hopper fights back tears, then, switches legs --

>   HOPPER (CONT'D)
>   <AGAIN.>

FLASHBACK TO: HOPPER'S FINAL GOODBYE TO JOYCE.

The Strong Man swings again --

The mallet hits *AND* --

EXT. HAWKINS LIBRARY - DAY

WHOOSH! Birds scatter atop the Hawkins Library clocktower.

>   ROBIN (PRE-LAP)
>   -- So let me just make sure I have
>   all this straight, just because
>   *it's a lot...*

DOWN BELOW,

We find Nancy and Robin hustling up the library steps, on mission, mid-conversation. Nancy seems tense -- *annoyed*.

                    ROBIN
          Eddie's Uncle Wayne thinks this...
          Victor Creel escaped from Pennhurst
          Asylum and is now running around
          Hawkins committing these murders --

                    NANCY
          Pretty much --

                    ROBIN
          Okay, it's just... Victor committed
          these eyeball murders or whatever
          way back in the *fifties* --

                    NANCY
          Fifty-nine --

Nancy throws open the double doors as our girls head into --

THE LIBRARY - CONTINUOUS - DAY

Robin doesn't take a breath to stop talking.

                    ROBIN
          -- So that means these murders
          predate Eleven and the Upside Down
          by about thirty years --

                    NANCY
          Yep --

                    ROBIN
          And it would also make this scary
          Victor Creel... about *seventy years
          old* --

                    NANCY
          Yep --

The girls have reached the front desk -- but nobody is here.
Nancy looks around, desperate -- she needs another human to
speak to *pronto*.

                    ROBIN
          So Victor Creel is, like... a
          Grandpa Murderer... who can... turn
          invisible and lift people into the
          air -- ??

                    NANCY
          It <u>doesn't make sense</u>. I <u>know</u>. This
          is why I said it was a *shot in the
          dark* --

DING! Nancy rings a call bell.

                    ROBIN
          Yeah I guess I just thought by
          "shot in the dark" you were being
          modest, or hiding something awesome
          up your sleeve that you'd like wow
          us with later --

DINGDING! Nancy rings the bell more now, desperate --

                    ROBIN (CONT'D)
          But like -- this really is truly a
          shot in the dark, like, we're
          snipers with blindfolds on and
          we've been spun around fifty times
          or something --

DINGDINGDING! Nancy rings the bell more until AT LAST --

                    MARISSA
          COMMMMING!

MARISSA, our trusty librarian, hurries to the desk, balancing a stack of books in her arms.

                    NANCY
               (smiles, then)
          Sorry -- in a bit of a hurry --
          could I get keys for the basement
          archives?

                    MARISSA
          'Course, uh, one sec --

As Marissa rummages for the keys, Robin turns back to Nancy, lowers her voice --

                    ROBIN
          Sorry -- did I come off mean or
          condescending or something -- ?

                    NANCY
               (yes)
          No --

>   ROBIN
>   You just seem annoyed. Sorry -- you
>   don't know me very well -- but I
>   don't really have a filter or like
>   a strong grasp of social cues --
>
>   NANCY
>   Okay --
>
>   ROBIN (CONTINUOUS)
>   -- So like, if I say something
>   that upsets you, just know *I know*
>   it's a flaw -- I mean, believe me,
>   my mother *reminds me DAILY* --
>
>   NANCY
>   Right, <u>got it</u> --

Nancy fakes a smile, this is going to be a LONG DAY --

>   MARISSA
>   Alright, ladies, here ya go --

Marissa returns with a set of keys, passes them to Nancy --

>   MARISSA (CONT'D)
>   Have fun -- !
>
>   NANCY
>   Yep. We'll... *try.*

Nancy grabs the keys, then heads off. Robin sighs, then trudges after Nancy, knowing she's made a <u>terrible</u> first impression, and --

EXT. COUNSELOR KELLEY'S HOUSE - DAY

DING DONG! CLOSE ON: Max is ringing a doorbell outside an unknown house. A bit nervous. The door opens to reveal --

COUNSELOR KELLEY. She seems shaken -- and also surprised to see Max.

>   MS. KELLEY
>   Max... hi --
>
>   MAX
>   Hey -- I'm... so sorry to bother
>   you over break, but... do you have
>   a second -- to talk?

                    MS. KELLEY
          Um -- yeah. Of course, *of course.*

She opens the door for Max and --

                    STEVE (PRE-LAP)
          She's in.

INT. STEVE'S CAR - DAY

Steve and Dustin are watching from across the street --

                    DUSTIN
          I'm missing collarbones not eyes.

Steve taps the wheel. Awkward silence. Finally Dustin breaks it:

                    DUSTIN (CONT'D)
          So... are we gonna talk about it or
          what?

                    STEVE
          I'm sorry? Talk about -- ?

                    DUSTIN
          Your *temporary insanity* earlier
          today when you practically threw
          yourself at "Nance" --

                    STEVE
          Excuse me -- ?

                    DUSTIN
          You heard me.

Steve stares at Dustin. *Irritated* would be putting it lightly.

                    STEVE
          Okay first of all -- uh -- that's
          not what happened --

                    DUSTIN
          Pretty sure that's what happened.
          It was very public -- there were
          multiple witnesses --

                    STEVE
          I was making sure she was *SAFE* --

                    DUSTIN
          Safe? Have you seen Nancy fire a
          gun --

                    STEVE
          If you're implying I still have a
          thing for Nancy --

                    DUSTIN
          I'm not implying, I'm *stating* --
          and honestly, as it relates to your
          steadfast refusal to date Robin,
          it's the *only* logical explanation --

                    STEVE
          Not the *only one*. And as for Nancy,
          I was trying to protect a friend --
          a FRIEND -- 'cause I didn't want to
          find her in the morning with her
          eyes ripped out of her skull by
          this Vecna creep --

                    DUSTIN
          You're bright red in the face right
          now -- you do realize that, right?

                    STEVE
              (flustered)
          Yeah -- I -- I'm bright red with
          anger --

                    DUSTIN
          With anger, really -- ?

                    STEVE
          Yes -- ANGER. Look away from me
          right now or I will punch you so
          hard your teeth fall back out.
          Swear to God. Look AWAY, HENDERSON!
          AWAY!

Dustin looks away, *annoyed*, as --

INT. COUNSELOR KELLEY'S HOUSE - STUDY - DAY

CLOSE ON: A clock ticks forward. Stark, quiet in here.

WIDEN: We're in Ms. Kelley's private study. She sits across from Max, listening --

                    MAX
          ... It's just everything that's
          happening -- the murders. It's --
          it's making it all... *worse again* --

                    MS. KELLEY
          You've experienced trauma, Max. And
          when you keep your feelings -- your
          pain -- bottled up the way you do,
          it doesn't take much to trigger
          them again. So now -- when it rains
          it *storms* --

                    MAX
          Yeah, I -- I know --

                    MS. KELLEY
          Do you think -- you're ready to
          talk more? About that night?

VIOLENT FLASHCUT TO BILLY GETTING KILLED -- MAX SCREAMS --

Max shakes off the memory, then looks at Ms. Kelley -- back on mission mode --

                    MAX
          I live next door to where it
          happened.

                    MS. KELLEY
          I'm sorry -- ?

                    MAX
          To where Chrissy was murdered.

Counselor Kelley is taken off guard by this -- tenses.

                    MAX (CONT'D)
          The cops, they were asking me all
          these -- questions and stuff. Did
          they -- talk to you too? I mean --
          you were -- seeing Chrissy, right?

Counselor Kelley shifts in her chair.

                    MS. KELLEY
          Max, you know -- I can't talk to
          you about Chrissy or -- any other
          student --

                    MAX
          I know -- but -- what if, like...
          there's some serial killer loose in
          my neighborhood? I mean -- did
          Chrissy say anything to you? Like
          who she thinks might have done
          this -- ?

                    MS. KELLEY
          Max... I'm sorry, I -- I really
          can't discuss this. You wouldn't
          want me talking to any other
          students about *you*, right?

                    MAX
          If I were dead and it would help
          catch the killer -- I most
          definitely would.

Counselor Kelley smiles a bit -- this is getting awkward.

                    MS. KELLEY
          Well, let's leave that up to the
          police, shall we?

                    MAX
          Yeah. You're right. The police --
          totally have this under control.
               (beat, then hard pivot)
          Can I use your bathroom?

Off Ms. Kelley --

INT. COUNSELOR KELLEY'S HOUSE - HALLWAY - DAY

Ms. Kelley opens the door, letting Max out of her study --

                    MS. KELLEY
          Down the hall, to the right --

                    MAX
          Thanks --

Max heads down the hall, but then, instead of going right, she swerves *left* into --

THE KITCHEN - CONTINUOUS

She quickly looks around, spots --

A BOWL FILLED WITH MAIL. Atop the mail: a KEY RING. She picks it up, flips through it. The keys are labeled. One reads --

"OFFICE." *Bingo!* She grabs the keys and --

INT./EXT. STEVE'S CAR - OUTSIDE KELLEY'S HOUSE - DAY

WHOOM! Max leaps back into the car --

              DUSTIN
      What'd she say -- ?

              MAX
      Nothing -- just drive --

              STEVE
      Nothing -- ??

              MAX
      DRIVE -- !

Steve hits the gas, they SQUEAL off, and --

EXT. HENDERSON HOUSE - MOMENTS LATER

BAMBAMBAM! A fist pounds on a door.

WIDEN: Jason is knocking on the door to Dustin's house. No one answers. *Phew.* Andy cups his hand, peers into a window --

              ANDY
      No one's home --

              PATRICK
      So now what -- ?

              JASON
      We keep looking. Town's not that
      big. Only so many places these
      freaks can burrow.

MOMENTS LATER

The jocks head back to Jason's car, only to realize --

              JASON
      -- Where's Sinclair?

Sure enough, CUT WIDE to find: <u>Lucas is missing</u>.

INT. HENDERSON HOUSE - BEDROOM - MOMENTS LATER

WHOOM! Lucas topples through an open window and --

Into Dustin's room!! He scrambles over to Cerebro, grabs the CB, smashes Talk --

>   LUCAS
> Dustin, it's Lucas, do you copy?

A voice crackles in response --

>   DUSTIN (O.S.)
>   (filtered)
> Lucas -- ?? ?

INT. STEVE'S CAR - DAY - INTERCUT

Dustin is on the other end in Steve's car.

>   DUSTIN
> Where THE HELL have you been -- ??

>   LUCAS
> Listen -- are you guys looking for
> Eddie -- ??

>   DUSTIN
> Yeah and we found him -- no *thanks
> to you* --

>   LUCAS
> You found him?? Where??

>   DUSTIN
> A boathouse on Cole Mill Road --
> don't worry he's safe --

>   LUCAS
> *Safe?* You guys know he *killed*
> Chrissy right -- ?

Max and Steve share WTF looks --

>   DUSTIN
> That's bullshit -- Eddie tried to
> save Chrissy --

>   LUCAS
> Then why do the cops all say he did
> it -- ??

Max can't listen to this anymore -- she grabs the walkie from Dustin --

                    MAX
          Lucas you're so behind it's
          RIDICULOUS -- just meet us at
          school and we'll explain
          everything --

                    LUCAS
          I -- I can't right now. I -- I
          think some real bad shit's about to
          go down --

                    MAX
          What are you talking about -- what
          bad shit -- ??

INT. DUSTIN'S ROOM - DAY

Before Lucas can respond, a SUDDEN RAPPING on the window --

Lucas looks up to find Jason and the others giving him WTF looks. *Shit.* Lucas drops Cerebro and --

INT. STEVE'S BMW - DAY

                    MAX
          Lucas -- ?? LUCAS??

EXT. DUSTIN'S HOUSE - DAY

Lucas jumps back out of the window --

                    JASON
          The hell are you doing?

                    LUCAS
          Looking for -- *clues* --

                    PATRICK
          Clues? This freshman thinks he's
          Sherlock Holmes or some shit --

The jocks chuckle and head off. Lucas hesitates, mind racing. He *really* doesn't want to do this, but he's out of options --

                    LUCAS
          I found one.

Our jocks pause, swivel back.

                    JASON
          What -- ?

                        LUCAS
            A clue.
                (beat)
            I know where Eddie's hiding.

Off a surprised Jason, SMASH TO --

EXT. LENORA HILLS ROAD - DAY

WHOOSH! THE POLICE TRANSPORT VAN speeds down a long, straight, empty desert road.

INT. POLICE TRANSPORT VAN - DAY

Eleven sits in the back, staring off into space. Her body jostles with each bump in the road, but her expression remains fixed, distant. Lost in her own thoughts, memories.

As we PUSH IN on her face --

FLASHCUT TO: Hitting Angela --

                        MIKE (V.O.)
            What did you do??

FLASHCUT TO: The blood-splattered rainbow --

                        DR. BRENNER (V.O.)
            What have you done??

FLASHCUT: Angela's SCREAMS, which then suddenly become --

EEEEEE! The sound of SQUEALING TIRES. El looks up and out the rear window, sees --

A BLACK SEDAN *hurtling* toward them. It looks like it's going to crash right into them, but then, at the last second --

EXT. ROAD - DAY

It swerves *around them*, pulling in front of the van --

INT. POLICE TRANSPORT VAN - DAY

                        DRIVER
            The hell -- ??

The sedan slams on its brakes, forcing our DRIVER to a stop. Panicked, he looks out his side window as --

EXT. ROAD - DAY

SCREECH! Another black sedan pulls up alongside him, then --

SCREECH! Another closes in behind them, and we CUT TO --

AN OVERHEAD which shows the transport van surrounded on all sides by the black sedans.

MOMENTS LATER

CLOSE ON: A black door opens and government agents exit. Our camera zeroes in on the clear leader: AGENT STINSON. She's severe looking, sharp. She is flanked by two men who look like bodyguards. We will come to know these heavies as AGENT WALLACE and AGENT HARMON. They are very clearly <u>ARMED</u>.

IN THE BACK OF THE VAN

Eleven waits nervously in the back, trapped, getting scared now. She watches through the barred partition as AGENT STINSON approaches the Driver, who has now rolled down the window --

> AGENT STINSON
> Hey there. Are you transporting a
> Jane Hopper?

> DRIVER
> Yeah -- what is this?

Agent Stinson flashes a badge --

> AGENT STINSON
> I'm taking her off your hands.

Off Eleven in the back, terrified, CUT TO --

OUTSIDE - MOMENTS LATER

JANGLING KEYS as --

The Driver walks around to the back of the van, following his orders. Stinson and her heavies trail close behind --

The Driver slots the keys in the door, unlocks it, starts to open it, and --

WHOOM! ELEVEN EXPLODES OUT OF THE VAN WITH FORCE. THE DOORS SLAM INTO THE DRIVER, KNOCKING HIM BACK. EL LEAPS ONTO THE ROAD AND STARTS TO RUN BUT --

WHAM! The heavies grab her -- holding her back --

> ELEVEN
> LET GO -- LET ME GO!

El struggles in their arms, but without her powers, <u>she is helpless</u>.

                    VOICE (O.S.)
          Eleven.

Eleven looks up. Her eyes widen. Her struggle slows.

Standing outside one of the black sedans...

DR. SAM OWENS. He flashes a small smile.

                    DR. OWENS
          Hey, kiddo.

Off Eleven, breathing hard, stunned, CUT TO --

EXT. HAWKINS LIBRARY - NIGHT

BLACK. Quiet. A few stars twinkle. *It's night now.*

TILT TO FIND we're outside the Hawkins Library. *Spooky.*

INT. HAWKINS LIBRARY - BASEMENT - NIGHT

We drift through the dark basement, where we find --

Nancy and Robin, all alone down here, sitting across from one another at a long desk, scrolling through microfiche, scanning through *article after article* about the Creel Murders --

                    ROBIN
          Anything... juicy over there -- ?

                    NANCY
          ... Nothing new.

                    ROBIN
          Yeah same here -- dead family,
          missing eyes, Victor seemed like a
          normal guy, made a plea deal, sent
          to Pennhurst -- blah blah --

The girls scroll in silence for a few more beats, then --

Robin pops her head around her microfiche machine.

                    ROBIN (CONT'D)
          What are we looking for exactly?
          Just -- any mention of dark wizards
          from alternate dimensions or
          something in that vein?

                    NANCY
               (sighs, frustrated)
          I don't know, okay? It's looking
          like this was a waste of time and
          you're obviously bored -- so why
          don't you just call Steve? I'm sure
          he'll pick you up and I'm not
          exactly in danger here.

Nancy pops out her microfiche, shuffles away --

INT. BASEMENT - DEEPER IN LIBRARY - NIGHT

SHOOM! An annoyed Nancy opens up a cabinet drawer, scouring for more microfiche slides when --

Robin pops around the corner -- startling her --

                    ROBIN
          You do know me and Steve are like --
          totally not a thing, right?

Nancy is taken aback by this sudden pivot --

                    NANCY
          What -- ?

                    ROBIN
          I mean -- I figure you and Jonathan
          are still going strong since
          you're, you know, going to college
          together and stuff and you seem
          like one of those <u>unstoppable power
          couples</u> --
               (Nancy winces at this)
          I just -- yeah just -- I wanted to
          make sure you knew that me and
          Steve are just friends, like
          Platonic with a capital P -- in
          case it, you know, was adding to
          any tension between us --

                    NANCY
          Okay -- yeah -- it *wasn't* --

                    ROBIN
          Oh *shit* --

We think for a half-second Robin is responding to Nancy, but then she races to another cabinet aisle, this one labeled --

                    ROBIN (CONT'D)
          The Weekly Watcher -- I *can't*
          believe they have this --

Robin opens the drawer, thumbs through the collection. Nancy eyes her, very skeptical.

> NANCY
> Don't they... write about, like --
> Bigfoot and UFOs -- ?

> ROBIN
> Meanwhile the Hawkins Post is the bastion of truth??
> (Nancy blinks -- *fair*)
> Also UFOs are absolutely real -- though I'm on *the fence* about Bigfoot. But if someone's going to write about dark wizards --

Robin finds some microfiche from 1959 --

> ROBIN (CONT'D)
> -- It'd be these <u>weirdos</u>.

She rips out the microfiche and --

MOMENTS LATER

FWOOM! Robin quickly scrolls through the microfiche as a skeptical Nancy skims the outrageous headlines --

> NANCY
> Ah, Elvis cloned by aliens, nice--

> ROBIN
> You never know --

She scrolls further down and --

> ROBIN (CONT'D)
> Okay -- *here we go.*

A headline reads:

> ROBIN (CONT'D)
> "<u>VICTOR CREEL CLAIMS *VENGEFUL DEMON* KILLED FAMILY.</u>"

Robin skims the article, speed-reading:

> ROBIN (CONT'D)
> "The murder that shocked a small community" -- blah blah -- wow okay *get this.*
> (MORE)

ROBIN (CONT'D)
According to several insiders, Victor believed his house was haunted by an ancient "demon" --

Nancy leans in, eyes wide. Intrigued --

ROBIN (CONT'D)
"Victor allegedly hired a priest to exorcise the demon from the home --"

Robin looks back at Nancy, excited --

ROBIN (CONT'D)
Pretty novel back in the fifties -- I mean *The Exorcist* wasn't *even out yet* --

NANCY
Keep going --

Robin whips back, scrolls to the next page, summarizing --

ROBIN
Okay, so -- Victor claimed this exorcism failed -- but it angered this demon -- which then murdered his family, removing their eyes. Victor Creel believed he was "spared as punishment."

NANCY
That's pretty convenient for Victor --

ROBIN
Yeah. Or super *inconvenient*.

Robin spins back to Nancy, spitballs --

ROBIN (CONT'D)
I mean -- Victor was declared legally insane by the court, right? So what if this is *why* -- I mean this story sounds pretty *insane*. It just didn't go public because --

NANCY
The plea bargain -- *the records were sealed* --

Robin nods -- exactly.

                    ROBIN
          What if a demon *did* invade Victor's
          home? Only this demon wasn't just
          any old demon --

                    NANCY
          It was Vecna.

Our girls share looks and --

EXT. LIBRARY - NIGHT

The door to the library flies open as Nancy and Robin race
out, moving fast down the steps, printed articles in hand. As
they head for Nancy's car, Robin is on the walkie --

                    ROBIN
          Hey Dustin -- you copy???

INT. HAWKINS HIGH - NIGHT - INTERCUT

We find Dustin at the school walking alongside Steve -- Max
is a maybe five feet ahead of them, leading them through the
dark hallways, flashlights sweeping around --

                    DUSTIN
                (voice low)
          Yeah I copy --

                    ROBIN
          So listen -- Nancy's a genius and
          her shot-in-the-dark may have just
          been a *bullseye* -- turns out
          Vecna's first victims date back to
          nineteen fifty-nine --

                    DUSTIN
          Okay that's, uh, totally bonkers,
          but I can't really talk right now--

                    ROBIN
          What are you doing -- ?

                    DUSTIN
          Breaking and entering at school to
          retrieve some confidential and
          extremely personal files --

Max slots the key into the front office door, opens it --

                    ROBIN
          Can you -- repeat that??

                        DUSTIN
            Just get over here *stat* and we'll
            explain everything --

He switches off the walkie, follows Max into the office.

EXT. LIBRARY - NIGHT

Robin and Nancy share baffled looks --

                        NANCY
            I thought they were talking to Miss
            Kelley?

                        ROBIN
            We leave them alone for *two*
            hours...

The girls climb into Nancy's car, slam their doors, and --

INT. HAWKINS HIGH - FRONT OFFICE - NIGHT

CHUNK! A key slots into the counselor's office door as --

INT. COUNSELOR'S OFFICE - NIGHT

Our school "burglars" sweep inside Kelley's office.

As Dustin sweeps his flashlight around --

                        DUSTIN
            This feels like a mini Watergate or
            something... *Hawkins-gate* --

                        STEVE
            Didn't those burglars get caught??
                (suddenly worried)
            Should we be wearing gloves or
            something -- ?

                        DUSTIN
            Shit -- yeah -- *oh God* --

As a suddenly panicked Steve and Dustin start to wipe down everything they've touched, Max pulls out the top drawer of a filing cabinet and begins to flip through students' files, which have been sorted alphabetically. She passes several names on her way to CUNNINGHAM, CHRISSY, and --

Wait a minute. She flips back to another file.

                    MAX
          Holy shit --

Dustin looks up --

                    DUSTIN
          You found it?

                    MAX
          Yeah. And <u>not just Chrissy's</u>.

Max removes FRED'S FILE from the cabinet, holds it up.

                    MAX (CONT'D)
          Fred was seeing Miss Kelley too.

Max tosses the files onto Kelley's desk and --

EXT. AIRPORT - ALASKA - NIGHT

SCREECH! Airplane wheels touch down on a snowy tarmac.

INT. PASSENGER JET - NIGHT

DING! A FASTEN SEATBELT sign blinks off.

Joyce shakes Murray awake --

                    JOYCE
          Come on -- *we're here* --

MOMENTS LATER

WHOOM! Joyce opens the storage compartment above her seat. The bag's zipper has slid open a bit -- exposing some of the cash inside -- *shit*. She zips it shut and --

MOMENTS LATER

Joyce and a groggy Murray deboard the plane with the other passengers as the Stewardess welcomes them like a robot --

                    STEWARDESS
          Welcome to Alaska!! Welcome to
          Alaska!! Welcome to Alaska!!

EXT. PLANE - NIGHT

-- They take steps down onto a tarmac. Murray and Joyce clutch their arms, slapped in the face by the cold wind -- and like that, Murray is suddenly *very awake*.

                        MURRAY
            Oh God -- oh God -- this is
            spring??

As our LINE OF PASSENGERS *march* across the cold tarmac en route to the adjacent terminal, MATCH CUT TO:

EXT. RUSSIAN PRISON - NIGHT

Our prisoners *marching* through the snow -- returning from work. We find Hopper -- limping a bit, his chains noticeably bent -- but still tight enough that they're not falling off.

A LITTLE LATER

They arrive at the prison entrance, where --

The MEAN GUARD inspects their shackles.

He shakes the Strong Prisoner's shackles --

                        MEAN GUARD
            <Next!>
                  (checks another)
            <Next!>

Hopper tenses -- he's up. *This is do or die* --

The Mean Guard inspects his shackles, yanking them, and --

                        MEAN GUARD (CONT'D)
            <Next!>

Hopper -- doing his best to mask his intense relief -- proceeds into the prison and --

INT. HOPPER'S CELL - A LITTLE LATER - NIGHT

Hopper is now in his cell -- seated on his bed. He pulls up his pants to inspect his legs. They are horribly bruised from those hits earlier; in areas, flesh torn, *bleeding*. He attempts to pull the bent iron off his ankle but --

It doesn't slip off. But Hopper isn't giving up. He spits into his hand and slicks down his leg. Then pulls again. Harder -- and HARDER -- blood spilling -- flesh tearing --

He bites back a SCREAM -- the iron starts to pull off --

Almost there.

Just as we think it's about to PULL OFF, HARD CUT TO --

EXT. SIDE OF ROAD - NEAR WOODS - NIGHT

WHOOM! A trunk swinging open, revealing --

FLASHLIGHTS, ROPE, DUCT TAPE, BAT, TIRE IRON, HUNTING KNIVES.

WIDEN TO REVEAL: Jason's car is now parked on the side of the road by some woods. Our jocks grab their weapons and --

A LITTLE LATER

A stick drags through dirt, carving a square outline as --

Jason -- lit by the headlight of his car -- scratches out their plan of attack in the dirt. His boys huddle around him -- *it's like this is some high stakes basketball play.*

> JASON (O.S.)
> Okay -- if Sinclair is right -- the freak is hiding <u>here</u> -- we move through the woods here together, then Patrick, Andy -- you split up, head around this way --
> (drags line to show)
> Sinclair and me -- we keep going -- then we flank his ass from both sides --
> (the lines converge on the house)
> <u>The freak won't know what hit him.</u>

Shared looks. *Hell yeah.* And...

MOMENTS LATER

Our jocks head into the woods with their weapons. We hold on Lucas -- who appears nervous as hell. His hand tightens around a TIRE IRON as his body vanishes into darkness and --

EXT. LENORA DINER - NIGHT

Quiet. We're outside a lonely OLD SCHOOL DINER, in the middle of the valley. A neon sign glows above it, illuminating --

A pair of black sedans. The two heavies -- Wallace and Harmon -- keep an eye on the road, as still as statues.

> DR. OWENS (PRE-LAP)
> Sorry for the theatrics back there... didn't meant to scare ya...

INT. LENORA DINER - NIGHT

We find Owens and Eleven sitting at a booth in the back.

Owens has a cup of coffee; El has a lemonade.

                    DR. OWENS
          But you got yourself in quite the
          predicament, didn't you?

El gives a sheepish nod.

                    DR. OWENS (CONT'D)
          I relocated you guys to Lenora
          because I thought, you know -- safe
          town, small, dull, far from
          Hawkins, nothing could happen here
          -- but uh -- a roller skate was it?

El nods. A WAITRESS approaches, smiles --

                    WAITRESS
          Ready to order some food?

                    DR. OWENS
          Yeah, I think so... I'll have more
          coffee and uh -- how about the club
          special?

All eyes then go to Eleven, uncertain --

                    DR. OWENS (CONT'D)
          Whatever you want, kiddo -- it's on
          me.

                    ELEVEN
          The... blueberry waffles... with...
          whip cream. Please.

The waitress smiles, then heads off --

                    DR. OWENS
          Never too late for breakfast, I
          say. Cathy, my wife -- she
          disagrees. Probably a good thing.
          Otherwise all I'd eat is pancakes.

Owens smiles, but Eleven doesn't.

                    ELEVEN
          Am I -- in trouble?

                    DR. OWENS
          Oh -- over this roller skate
          incident? Nah. We'll make that go
          away. Don't you worry about that.

                    ELEVEN
               (surprised)
          That is not -- why you are here?

                    DR. OWENS
          To be honest with you, kid -- I
          wish that it was. Last night, I saw
          something -- something I've been
          dreading for some time now.

Owens shifts a bit in his seat, a little uncomfortable.

                    DR. OWENS (CONT'D)
          ... I don't know how to say this,
          other than to just say it.
               (beat)
          Hawkins is in danger.

Off Eleven, taking this in, terrified --

EXT. VECNA'S LAIR (UPSIDE DOWN)

THUNDER CRASHES in the Upside Down. The Demobats swoop overhead.

                    DR. OWENS (V.O.)
          You've fought this evil before --
          and you've won...

INT. VECNA'S LAIR - ATTIC (UPSIDE DOWN)

We PUSH IN on Vecna, still being held up by those vines. We can tell his eyes are moving beneath those grotesque eyelids. *He's searching. Hunting.* As we move closer...

                    DR. OWENS (V.O.)
          But this evil is like a virus. Each
          time it returns, it comes back
          stronger. Smarter. *Deadlier.*

INT. DINER - NIGHT

Eleven is listening -- riveted -- *scared*.

                    DR. OWENS
          And I fear... the worst is still
          ahead. A *war* is coming to Hawkins.

EXT. WOODS - NIGHT

WHOOSH! Jason and his goons move through dark woods.

Jason signals to Patrick and Andy -- who break off, following the plan. Jason and Lucas, meanwhile, continue on a straight path. Up ahead, lit in the moonlight, we can make out the faint outline of a building --

> DR. OWENS (V.O.)
> And to win this war, we're going to need all the help we can get...

INT. UNKNOWN LOCATION - NIGHT

WHOOM! JASON KICKS open a wooden door. He sweeps inside with his teammates, weapons out, ready to attack Eddie, but -- Eddie's not here.

WIDEN: We're not in the boathouse or Reefer Rick's house. We're in HOPPER'S CABIN! Holy shit, <u>Lucas tricked them</u>!! The group fans out throughout the house, kicking open doors -- finding nothing, and --

EXT. HOPPER'S CABIN - SHED - NIGHT

BOOM! The door to the outdoor shed is kicked open -- nothing in here either. Jason storms over to Lucas (we get our first wide shot of the cabin here).

> JASON
> You sure this is the right place??

> LUCAS
> Positive --

Jason turns to Patrick, the others, yells --

> JASON
> (furious)
> Let's check around the back -- around the back!

The jocks head around the back of the cabin. But Lucas doesn't follow them. Instead, he begins to walk in the opposite direction -- leaving his "friends." We hold tight on him as his walk morphs into a run --

>   DR. OWENS (V.O.)
>   There are good people -- brave
>   friends -- who have helped you
>   fight your battle in the past --

INT. HOPPER'S CELL - NIGHT

We PUSH PAST shackles... now *off*... to find...

Hopper, legs at last free, doing push-ups in his cell, strengthening himself for his coming escape --

>   DR. OWENS (V.O.)
>   But they alone can't win this war --
>   not <u>without you</u>.

INT. DINER - NIGHT

>   DR. OWENS
>   I know it is not fair to ask more
>   of you. But I wouldn't be here if I
>   didn't think this was the only
>   way --
>   (MORE)

                    DR. OWENS (CONT'D)
          -- If I didn't think you were the
          only one who might just have a shot
          to hit this thing so hard it can't
          get back up.

Eleven doesn't understand --

                         ELEVEN
          But -- my powers --

                    DR. OWENS
          What if... I told you there was a
          way. A way to bring them back.

Off Eleven, processing this --

EXT. OWENS HOUSE - NIGHT (FLASHBACK)

We're suddenly back in time as --

FWOOMFWOOMFWOOM! Lt. Colonel Sullivan's helicopter takes off. Owens watches from the porch and -- then --

INT. OWENS HOUSE - OFFICE - NIGHT (FLASHBACK)

FWUMP! A flathead screwdriver is thrust into the floor as --

A frantic Owens pries open the floorboard, revealing a hidden METAL BRIEFCASE.

                    DR. OWENS (V.O.)
          I feared this moment would come. So
          I've been preparing... developing a
          means to restore your abilities.

He lifts up the briefcase and --

MOMENTS LATER (FLASHBACK)

He set the briefcase down on his desk and flips it open and suddenly the briefcase is --

A COMPUTER. Not fancy by our standards, but certainly fancy for the 1980s. He turns it on and BEEEP! A crude, cryptic EMAIL SITE pops up. He prepares to send a message.

                    SUBJECT: NINA

                    DR. OWENS (V.O.)
               A program that has the potential to
               not just bring them back -- but
               bring them back stronger than
               before --

INT. HELICOPTER - NIGHT (FLASHBACK)

SHOT OF Sullivan riding in the chopper --

                    DR. OWENS (V.O.)
               But there are others who don't
               believe in you -- who think you are
               the cause. But I believe they're
               wrong. I believe -- you're <u>the
               cure</u>.

INT. DINER - NIGHT

                    DR. OWENS
               That's why... if we're really going
               to do this... I'm going to ask
               that you leave with me now --

INT. BYERS HOUSE - NIGHT

We survey Jonathan on the phone --

                    JONATHAN
               The reservation's under Byers --
               Joyce Byers. Yes I -- I can wait --

As Jonathan paces away, our camera finds Mike, waiting
nearby, a nervous wreck; Will is too afraid to comfort him --

                    DR. OWENS (V.O.)
               But you should know -- there is a
               very real possibility that this
               program *fails* --

INT. DINER - NIGHT

                    DR. OWENS
               And if it does -- <u>you will never
               see your friends again</u>.

A beat as El absorbs this -- then looks back at Owens --

                    ELEVEN
               My friends... in Hawkins... are
               they in danger?

As Owens darkens at the mention of this, return to --

INT. COUNSELOR'S OFFICE - NIGHT

Max flipping through Chrissy's file. Her eyes narrow, surprised and scared at what she reads.

CLOSE ON SCRIBBLED WORDS: "Past Trauma" -- "Terrible Nightmares" -- "Difficulty Sleeping," -- "Headaches" --

She looks up at Dustin, urgent --

>   MAX
>   *Can I see Fred's file* -- ??

As Dustin passes her Fred's file --

>   DR. OWENS (V.O.)
>   I'm afraid your friends in Hawkins
>   are very much... in the eye of the
>   storm.

INT. DINER - NIGHT

Eleven looks like she's about to bolt.

>   DR. OWENS
>   You may feel you need to go to them
>   now. But if you do -- you risk
>   everything. You risk... *everyone*.

INT. COUNSELOR'S OFFICE - NIGHT

An increasingly worried Max now flips through Fred's file.

CLOSE ON MORE SCRIBBLED WORDS: "Traumatic Past" -- "Nightmares" -- "Can't Sleep" -- "Bad headaches" -- *the exact same as Chrissy's file*. As the terrible truth sinks in for Max, FLASHBACK TO --

INT. HAWKINS HIGH - CLASSROOM - DAY (FLASHBACK)

Max taking a test, when she feels a subtle psychic sting. She winces and --

PLOP. Blood drops onto the test. She reaches up, finds --

Her nose is bleeding. Just like Patrick's. She wipes it away, then -- after a moment of concern -- returns to her test, thinking hardly anything of it, and --

INT. COUNSELOR'S OFFICE - NIGHT

Max's mind races as she goes back through the events of the past few days, *everything* now taking on a dark new meaning:

MAX POPPING TYLENOL -- WAKING UP TO NIGHTMARES -- RELIVING BILLY'S ATTACK -- MS. KELLEY COUNSELING HER --

THE IMAGES FLASH PAST US FASTER AND FASTER AND --

>			DUSTIN
>	Max, what is it? *Max -- ??*

Max is about to respond when she hears something off-screen. A very faint *CHIME*. As she rises to her feet...

>			DR. OWENS (V.O.)
>	They are not the only ones in
>	danger, Eleven --

INT. DINER - NIGHT

>			DR. OWENS
>	It is life as we know it. This is
>	why I am here -- because I believe
>	you are our best hope. Our <u>only
>	hope</u>.

A heavy beat as El absorbs all this.

>			ELEVEN
>	What if I am... not good. What if I
>	am -- the monster?

Owens takes this in.

>			DR. OWENS
>	I don't know you that well,
>	kiddo... but I'm betting the fate
>	of the planet that you're one of
>	the good ones. But you've spent too
>	much of your life being told what
>	to do by people like me. So say the
>	word and I'll take you right back
>	home. Or... come with me now. And
>	find out for yourself.
>			(beat)
>	Your call, kiddo.

As El takes this in --

A LITTLE LATER

The waitress comes back with the waffles and -- *stops*.

REVERSE TO REVEAL: Owens and Eleven are gone -- just a wad of cash on the table. Off the surprised waitress, CUT TO --

INT. BYERS HOUSE - NIGHT

As a frustrated Jonathan hangs up the phone --

HEADLIGHTS WASH across the room. Our three boys turn toward the window, eyes narrowing, and --

EXT. BYERS HOUSE - NIGHT

Mike, Jonathan, and Will step outside to find --

A PAIR OF SEDANS parked in the driveway. Doors open and Agent Wallace and Agent Harmon exit -- one of them has a metal briefcase (the same as Owens had in the opening). *But Eleven is not with them.* Off Mike, confused and scared, CUT TO --

EXT. DESERT ROAD - NIGHT

Owens's black sedan tearing down an empty desert road --

INT. SEDAN

Owens sits passenger; Eleven is alone in the back. She looks out the window, a new look of uncertainty on her face as --

INT. HAWKINS HIGH - HALLWAY - NIGHT

Max steps out of the front office with a new look of fear in her eyes. At the end of a long hallway, lit by the beam of her flashlight: THE GRANDFATHER CLOCK.

The second hand ticks -- methodical -- *unstoppable*.

Tick tock... tick tock...

And then, it CHIMES.

BLACK

Four chimes echo over credits.

<u>END EPISODE</u>

EPISODE FOUR

CHAPTER FOUR:
DEAR BILLY

WRITTEN BY **PAUL DICHTER**

EXT. BYERS HOUSE - NIGHT

We TILT DOWN from the stars to find a PAIR OF BLACK SEDANS still parked outside the Byers house.

> JONATHAN (PRE-LAP)
> I'm sorry -- I guess I'm having trouble understanding *any of this*.

INT. BYERS HOUSE - LIVING ROOM - NIGHT

AGENT STINSON is seated across from MIKE, WILL, and JONATHAN. Her heavies -- AGENT HARMON and WALLACE -- hover nearby, quietly intimidating. Our teens have been updated now, and they're freaking out. Especially Mike, whose anger is building --

> JONATHAN
> What exactly is going on in Hawkins?? What's doing this killing -- ?

> AGENT STINSON
> That's what we're trying to ascertain. That's why we need Eleven --

> MIKE
> And where is El -- like, *right now* -- ?

> AGENT STINSON
> With Doctor Owens, en route to his laboratory to begin her training --

> MIKE
> Yeah -- but where is that exactly -- this laboratory??

> AGENT STINSON
> For her safety it's best you don't know --

Mike pushes up off the couch, panicking --

MIKE
This is *insane* --

JONATHAN
And how long will it take -- for this training, for El to get her powers back?

AGENT STINSON
It depends on how she responds to the program. It could take weeks. It could take months.

WILL
Months -- ??

MIKE
Jesus -- *Jesus* --

AGENT STINSON
Until then --
    (motioning to agents)
Agents Harmon and Wallace here will stay with you. They are our very best and they will make sure you're safe.

Mike whirls around, furious --

MIKE
Make sure "we're" safe??? We're not the ones in danger!!

WILL
Our friends live there -- *in Hawkins* --

MIKE
My family --

AGENT STINSON
I will be going to Hawkins and will work to contain the situation until Eleven is ready. In the meantime, the best thing you can do is and remain calm. It is of vital importance that you don't speak to anyone about this -- and that includes your family in Hawkins --

MIKE
No way -- *no way* --

JONATHAN
They're in danger -- we have to
warn them --

AGENT STINSON
I know this is difficult to
understand --

MIKE
It's not difficult -- it's
impossible --

AGENT STINSON
There are factions within our
government -- within the DOD -- who
are working against what we are
trying to achieve -- who are
working directly against Eleven.
(MORE)

                        AGENT STINSON (CONT'D)
                    Who are -- in fact -- searching for
                    her as we speak. And they are
                    closely monitoring Hawkins. We
                    can't risk contact. If they learn
                    about any of this -- it will
                    jeopardize Eleven. And if Eleven is
                    jeopardized -- so are your friends.
                    So is your family.

This hits Jonathan and Will hard. They're between a rock and
a hard place here.

                            MIKE
                    And -- what -- we're supposed to
                    just -- trust that you're the good
                    guys? Whoever you are --

                        AGENT STINSON
                    We're friends of Owens.
                        (beat)
                    Eleven trusted us. Now we're asking
                    the same from you.

Agent Stinson reaches into her jacket pocket, removes an
envelope with Mike's name on it.

                        AGENT STINSON (CONT'D)
                        (to Mike)
                    For you.

Mike takes the envelope.

INT. ELEVEN'S ROOM - NIGHT

Mike sits down on El's bed and opens the envelope. He pulls
out a folded piece of paper, opens it. A message has been
scrawled in El's unmistakeable (bad) handwriting --

   "Dear Mike. I have gone to become a superhero again.

                    From, El."

We PUSH IN on Mike, taking this in, heartbroken, then CUT
TO --

EXT. HAWKINS HIGH SCHOOL - NIGHT

SCREEEEEECH! The Wheeler station wagon speeds up to the school, slams to a stop.

NANCY and ROBIN leap out. As they race toward the school --

> MAX (PRE-LAP)
> It was here -- *right here* --

INT. SCHOOL HALLWAY - NIGHT

Flashlights illuminate a blank concrete wall -- *right* where the grandfather clock was in Max's vision.

REVERSE TO REVEAL: MAX, DUSTIN, STEVE, Nancy, and Robin holding the flashlights, staring at that blank wall.

> NANCY
> A *grandfather clock?*

Max nods, and suddenly --

INT. HALLWAY - NIGHT (FLASHBACK)

We're now back in time as Max slowly walks toward the clock. TICK TOCK TICK TOCK.

> MAX (V.O.)
> It was -- *so real*... but when I got close -- I suddenly... *woke up.*

INT. GUIDANCE COUNSELOR'S OFFICE - NIGHT (FLASHBACK)

Max startles awake -- she's back in the guidance counselor's office. She never left.

Dustin is shaking her -- as Steve looks on with concern.

> DUSTIN
> (filtered with reverb)
> Max are you alright?? Max -- MAX???

As Max comes to, blinking, disoriented --

> DUSTIN (V.O.)
> It was like -- she was in a *trance* or something --

INT. SCHOOL HALLWAY - NIGHT

                  DUSTIN
        Exactly what Eddie said happened to
        Chrissy --

                  MAX
        And that's not even the bad part.

Off Nancy and Robin --

INT. GUIDANCE COUNSELOR'S OFFICE - NIGHT

WHOOM! Max drops Chrissy's and Fred's files onto the desk in front of Robin and Nancy --

                  MAX
        Fred and Chrissy -- they came to
        Miss Kelley for help.

CLOSE ON a few important scribbled words: "HEADACHES" -- "MIGRAINE" -- "DIFFICULTY SLEEPING" -- "NIGHTMARES" --

                  MAX (CONT'D)
        They were *both* having headaches.
        Bad headaches that just -- wouldn't
        go away. Then -- nightmares,
        trouble sleeping. They'd wake up in
        a cold sweat. Then -- they both
        started *seeing things*. Bad things --
        from their past. *Traumas.* These...
        visions just got worse and worse...
        until eventually...
            (beat)
        Everything ended.

A beat as this sinks in.

                  ROBIN
        ... *Vecna's curse*.

Max nods.

                  MAX
        Chrissy's headaches started a
        week ago. Fred's six days ago.
            (beat)
        I've been having them for <u>five
        days</u>.

A chill goes through the room. Max is fighting tears.

                    MAX (CONT'D)
          I don't know how long I have -- all
          I know is, Chrissy and Fred died
          less than twenty-four hours after
          they had their first vision. And I
          just saw that *goddamn clock,* so...
                    (beat, then, fuck it)
          Looks like I'm going to die
          tomorrow.

A hard beat as this sinks in. No one knows what to say. It's too *earth-shattering*. Nancy is about to finally speak when --

A CRASH ECHOES from somewhere off-screen, startling our group. Shared, frightened looks, then --

                    STEVE
          Stay here.

Steve grabs a lamp, strips it of its shade, and --

INT. HAWKINS HIGH SCHOOL - HALLWAY - MOMENTS LATER

Steve steps out into the hallway, wielding the lamp like a baseball bat! One by one, the others step up behind him --

                    STEVE
                (low)
          What part of *stay* didn't you
          understand -- ?

          DUSTIN   ROBIN
      (low)   (low)
  Shut up Steve --   Shut up Steve --

They shine their flashlights ahead. The hallway is dark, but they hear the DRUMBEAT OF FOOTSTEPS. *Something* is coming.

Steve pulls his lamp back, ready to attack, and --

WHOOM! A FIGURE suddenly rounds the corner at HIGH SPEED -- BARRELING STRAIGHT FOR THEM! Steve is about to swing, but --

                    FAMILIAR VOICE (O.S.)
          WHOA WHOA WHOA -- !!!

It's --

          DUSTIN   NANCY
  LUCAS??   LUCAS??

LUCAS skids to a stop in his sneakers -- drenched in sweat, out of breath. Steve lowers his "weapon."

>   STEVE
>   Jesus, dude!! What is wrong with
>   you?????
>
>   LUCAS
>   (catching breath)
>   I've been biking for like -- *eight
>   miles* -- we've got a <u>code red</u>!

Lucas pushes past Steve and grabs Dustin by the shoulders --

>   LUCAS (CONT'D)
>   (fast)
>   I've been with Jason and Patrick
>   and Andy and they've gone like
>   totally off-the-rails and they're
>   trying to capture Eddie and they
>   think you know where he is you're
>   in <u>terrible TERRIBLE danger</u> --
>
>   DUSTIN
>   Okay. That definitely... *sucks*. But
>   we've got bigger problems right now
>   than Jason.

Lucas now notices the energy in the group -- and Max. She's standing away from everyone, hovering back in the front office. Her face is ghost white. Her eyes wet with tears.

And suddenly Lucas is very, very scared.

>   LUCAS
>   ... What happened?

We PUSH IN on Max, more scared than we've ever seen her, and then --

MAIN TITLES

INT. SINCLAIR HOUSE - ERICA'S ROOM - DAY

A PAINTBRUSH sweeps across a D&D miniature. WIDEN TO REVEAL --

ERICA! She's a full nerd now -- and not ashamed of it!!

DING DONG! The doorbell rings. Erica ignores it, but --

>   SUE (O.S.)
>   Erica, can you get that, baby?

                    ERICA
          I'm BUSY!

                    SUE (O.S.)
          ERICA! NOW!!

Erica groans, drops the paintbrush, and --

INT. SINCLAIR HOUSE - FOYER - DAY

Erica swings open the door in annoyance to find --

<u>JASON</u>. Not who she -- or *we* -- were expecting.

                    JASON
          Hey there. Is Lucas here?

                    ERICA
          Negative --

Erica starts to shut the door but --

                    JASON
          You know where he is? We're
          supposed to go out --

                    ERICA
          "Go out"? You two dating? I see
          he's taken a step down from Max --

Erica once more goes to shut the door, but --

Jason catches it with his hand. Flashes a smile --

                    JASON
          You're the little sister who plays
          Dungeons and Dragons, huh?

                    ERICA
          ... What's it to you?

                    JASON
          You know Dustin Henderson?

                    ERICA
          Know him? I've <u>bled</u> with him. And
          before you ask -- no I don't know
          where he is *either* but chances are
          he's with your *cheater boyfriend*
          Lucas.

Before a shocked Jason can react to this --

                    ERICA (CONT'D)
               (fast)
          Oh -- if and when you do find Lucas
          -- please tell him I've been
          covering his ass for two days now --
          and per our binding contract, each
          day of covering costs ten bucks,
          with a DPR -- that's daily
          percentage rate -- of seven point
          nine percent. So another week of
          this and he's buying me a GODDAMN
          NINTENDO -- *with Duck Hunt.*

And with that, she slams the door and --

INT./EXT. JASON'S CAR

A shocked Jason drops back in the car with PATRICK (popping Tylenol, looking a little sickly) and ANDY.

                    ANDY
          Where the hell's Sinclair?

                    JASON
          ... That's what we're about to go
          find out.

He turns the car keys -- the engine growls to life.

                    JASON (CONT'D)
          We've been tricked, boys.

Jason shifts into drive and -- VROOM! His car SQUEALS out of the neighborhood at high speed, and we SMASH TO --

INT. WHEELER HOUSE - BASEMENT - DAY

WHOOM! A phone is slammed back into its cradle by --

Lucas, *the traitor.*

                    LUCAS
               Still busy --

He turns to Steve and Dustin, who are busy reading up on the printed Victor Creel microfiche. Steve looks like his head hurts --

                    LUCAS (CONT'D)
          You guys don't think that's weird?

DUSTIN
Not particularly. Joyce is a
telemarketer, she's on the phone
all the time --

STEVE
Even if we *could* get hold of them --
what would we tell them?

He waves around the printed material on Victor Creel.

STEVE (CONT'D)
None of this makes any sense --

DUSTIN
No? It seems rather straightforward
to me.

Steve shoots Dustin a look --

                    STEVE
Straightforward? *Really?*

                    DUSTIN
What's confusing to you? So far, everyone Vecna has cursed has died -- except for this old Victor Creel dude Nancy found. <u>He's the only known survivor</u>. If anyone knows how to beat this curse -- it's him.

                    STEVE
Yeah that's assuming he *was* cursed. I mean -- how can Vecna have existed back in the fifties??

                    DUSTIN
As far as we know, Eleven didn't *create the Upside Down* -- she just opened a Gate to it. The Upside Down has probably been around for thousands of years -- millions -- I wouldn't be surprised if it predated the dinosaurs --

                    STEVE
      (what)
Dinosaurs -- ??

                    LUCAS
Okay but if a Gate didn't exist in the fifties -- how did Vecna get through -- ??

                    STEVE
And how's he getting through now?

                    LUCAS
And <u>WHY</u> now -- ?

                    STEVE
And WHY *then*? He popped his head out in the fifties -- killed this one family -- then was like, "eh I'm good," and, poof, vanished -- only to return thirty years later to start killing some *random teens*? And where the hell has he been these past three years? Is he like, working for the Mind Flayer, or is he flying solo here?

Dustin hesitates. He doesn't have the answer to ANY of this.

                    STEVE (CONT'D)
          "Rather straightforward" *my ass*.
          You know -- a little humility every
          now and then would do you some
          good, Henderson.

Steve tosses the articles back onto the coffee table as --

Lucas's gaze now shifts to Max. She is sitting at the
workbench in the far corner of the basement, scrawling a
note.

Lucas looks concerned. *Deeply* concerned.

                    DUSTIN
               (low)
          Any idea what she's writing?

Lucas shakes his head.

                    DUSTIN (CONT'D)
          Did she sleep?

                    LUCAS
          Would *you*?

Before anyone can answer this --

WHOOM! The basement door flies open. Everyone turns, finds --

Nancy and Robin pounding down the stairs.

As they reach the landing --

                    NANCY
          Okay so -- we have a plan.

Synth music builds as we CUT TO --

A BIT LATER

Everyone (including Max) now passing the papers around. We
see that they are FAKE RESUMES for Nancy and Robin --
including *fake names* --

                    ROBIN
          Thanks to Nancy's little newspaper
          minions, we're now rockstar
          psychology students at the
          University of Notre Dame --

NANCY
I'm now Ruth --

ROBIN
And I'm Rose --

STEVE
Ruth??

DUSTIN
Nice GPAs --

ROBIN
Thanks. Lots of hard work and *long nights* --

NANCY
We called Pennhurst Asylum -- told them that we'd like to speak to Victor Creel for a thesis we're co-writing on paranoid schizophrenics.

ROBIN
They said, uh... *no* --

NANCY
<u>BUT</u> we landed a twelve o'clock with the director --

ROBIN
Now all we've got to do is charm his pants off and convince him to let us talk to Victor --

NANCY
-- And then maybe we can rid Max of this curse.

STEVE
Yeah about -- *that*. We've been going through our Victor Creel homework and, uh -- we have *questions* --

LUCAS
<u>Lots</u> of questions.

NANCY
Yeah -- <u>so do we</u>.
    (beat)
Hopefully Victor has the answers.

Steve flips through the resumes. Once again -- *he's confused*.

> STEVE
> ... Where's mine?

Off Nancy and Robin, CUT TO --

INT. NANCY'S ROOM - DAY

A door flies open as Nancy and Robin head into Nancy's room. A very annoyed Steve trails --

> STEVE
> You're out of your mind if you think I'm babysitting again --

> NANCY
> First of all -- they're not babies anymore. And Max is in *real danger* -- she needs people around her --

As Nancy throws open her closet and starts rummaging for something, Robin explores with her jaw hanging open --

> ROBIN
> *Oh my God* -- is that Tom Cruise??
> You have a Tom Cruise poster -- ???

> NANCY
> (embarrassed)
> That's -- *old*. Just -- can you please not touch anything -- ??

As Robin proceeds to touch everything, Steve whines to Nancy.

> STEVE
> I just think -- there's nothing I can do here, but maybe I can be helpful with this asylum director dude -- turn on my charm --

> NANCY
> Yeah that's not the kind of charm we need.

Nancy continues to flip through her clothes as she talks --

                    NANCY (CONT'D)
          I did a little digging last night --
          and this Doctor Hatch is a
          distinguished fellow of the
          American Psychiatric Association
          and a Harvard visiting scholar.
          This is a lifelong student of the
          world -- to win him over, we're
          gonna need to convince him that we
          are too. That, like him, we are
          true academic scholars.

Nancy pulls out an extremely preppy, conservative outfit --
think Nancy season one. Steve looks from the outfit to Robin
-- who is now fiddling with NANCY'S MUSIC BOX, repeatedly
opening and shutting it.

                    ROBIN
          Holy shit, there's a little
          ballerina in here!

Steve fires Nancy an incredulous look.

                    STEVE
          Academic scholar? She gives off
          "academic scholar" vibes?

                    NANCY
          No. But she will.

Nancy walks up to Robin, holds up the outfit.

For the first time, Robin realizes what's going on.

                    ROBIN
                (to Nancy)
          Please tell me you're joking.

Off Nancy, not joking, we PRE-LAP a growing growl as --

EXT. ALASKA MOTEL - DAY

WHOOSH! A truck ROARS past camera, revealing --

A SHITTY ALASKAN MOTEL.

                    JOYCE (PRE-LAP)
          It's busy, why is it still busy??

INT. ALASKA MOTEL - DAY

JOYCE is on the phone. An antsy MURRAY waits nearby, holding the money bag, clearly ready to go.

WHAM! She slams the receiver back down onto the cradle --

> JOYCE
> Am I doing something wrong -- I dialed one -- it says *dial one then your number* --

She tries again as Murray's impatience grows --

> MURRAY
> You can check in on your kids when we're back, okay?

> JOYCE
> It's just, it's *still busy* --

Joyce tries dialing again. Murray sighs.

> MURRAY
> Joyce... there are certain things one can be late for in life -- a dentist's appointment, a one-year-old's birthday party -- but for what is essentially a RANSOM EXCHANGE -- for *that* -- FOR THAT -- I think you very much need to be ON TIME!

Murray takes the phone receiver from Joyce -- then hangs it up. WHAM! A smile.

> MURRAY (CONT'D)
> Now. Let's go save Hopper, shall we?

With that, he turns away and marches out into the cold. Joyce sighs, takes one more look at the phone, then --

Hurries after him. As she slams the door, HARD CUT TO --

INT. RUSSIAN PRISON - DAY

EEEE! A prison door OPENING. HOPPER steps out.

EXT. PRISON - NEAR BACK GATES

CLOSE ON: Chains are tugged.

WIDEN: PRISON GUARDS are once more checking chains as our prisoners head back out of the prison gate for work.

> PRISON GUARD
> <Next.>

HOPPER's turn. The Guard inspects his chains.

<u>His leg irons are back on</u>. The Guard tugs them. And --

> PRISON GUARD (CONT'D)
> <Next.>

Hopper trudges forward and --

EXT. TUNDRA - DAY

EPIC WIDE SHOT as Hopper and the other prisoners march through the vast snowy tundra en route to the railroad worksite.

Hopper hears the CRUNCH OF SNOW. It's --

DMITRI. He matches Hopper's gait. He speaks quickly, not too loud, *not looking* at Hopper --

> DMITRI
> Beautiful morning for an escape, American, yes?

Hopper just nods. Keeps walking, keeps those eyes straight ahead.

> DMITRI (CONT'D)
> Head west through forest -- twenty miles -- there you will find a town. In this town you will see a church with a blue roof. It will look abandoned. It is not. This is where Yuri stores his goods. Out front, you will see a headless statue. Find its head, and you will find the key. Wait inside. As soon as money is delivered -- Yuri will meet you there.

> HOPPER
> Have you heard from him?

                    DMITRI
          Yes. Your friends arrived last
          night -- they are meeting Yuri
          soon. All goes well -- by tomorrow
          night, you're at home eating Enzo's
          with your sexy woman.

                    HOPPER
          She's not my woman --

                    DMITRI
               (sarcastic)
          Of course not. She saves your life
          because of friendship.
               (then)
          But -- do not put too much hope
          into this dream. I have thought
          long about this -- and I give your
          odds of success *fifty to one*.

Hopper doesn't respond to this. Much less react. Just keeps marching.

                    DMITRI (CONT'D)
          You don't even look *nervous,*
          American. I am impressed. You are a
          cool cat. Like Steve McQueen. *The
          Cooler King.* Yes?

                    HOPPER
               (low)
          ... Let's hope not.

                    DMITRI
          Ah, of course. Because Cooler King
          went back to cooler!! So -- you
          must be better than McQueen today.
          I change mind. Now give you odds a
          hundred to one.

Before Hopper can snap back --

                    DMITRI (CONT'D)
          <*Shit.*>

                    HOPPER
          What -- ?

Dmitri has clocked the MEAN GUARD looking back at them --

                    DMITRI
          Our nosy friend again. Where do you
          want it?

                    HOPPER
               (fuck)
          Just not the face --

                    DMITRI
          Ah, yes, must be pretty for your
          woman --

                    HOPPER
          She's *not* my wo --

WHAM! Dmitri SHOVES Hopper to the ground, then --

                    DMITRI
          <LAZY AMERICAN PIG!!!>

Dmitri KICKS HIM in the ass.

                    DMITRI (CONT'D)
          <MOVE YOU PIECE OF SHIT!! MOVE!!!>

The Mean Prison Guard watches as --

Hopper scrambles to his feet and rejoins the rest of the prisoners.

The Mean Guard tears his eyes away, walking on.

But we hold on him. He seems *suspicious*.

                    ANNOUNCER (V.O.)
          You can just... *feel the tension*
          here in the stands...

INT. BYERS HOUSE - LIVING ROOM

ON TV: Jack Nicklaus putts!

WIDEN: Agent Harmon and Agent Wallace are watching golf in the Byers living room. Wallace glances up as Jonathan walks in, headed for the kitchen.

                    AGENT WALLACE
          Where're you going -- ?

                    JONATHAN
          Just... getting something to drink.
          That allowed, or how does this
          house arrest work -- ?

                    AGENT WALLACE
                You're not under arrest.

                    JONATHAN
                Right, you're here to protect us --
                and watch TV. I remember now --

Jonathan opens the fridge, grabs a soda, then shuts the
fridge and --

He pauses. He's suddenly found himself staring straight at a
picture of him and Nancy, hanging from a magnet on the
fridge. They are holding each other, smiling. His breath
catches, his heart skips. His gaze then shifts from Nancy's
photo to a coupon hanging nearby. And not just any coupon:

A SURFER BOY PIZZA COUPON. SURF'S UP -- 30 MINUTES OR LESS!

As we PUSH IN ON Jonathan, an idea forming, the SOUND OF
APPLAUSE from the golf match echoes behind him and --

INT. JONATHAN'S ROOM - MOMENTS LATER

THUMP! A rubber band ball bounces against the ceiling and
back down into Will's hand, who is lying flat on his bed.

Nearby, we find Mike is on the floor, staring at El's letter.
"*I have gone to be a superhero again. From, El.*" He re-reads
those words over and over as Will worries behind him --

                    WILL
                ... I mean, I just don't think
                they've actually thought this
                through -- if this goes on for a
                month, or months, and people can't
                get hold of us, they're going to
                totally freak out. My mom's
                probably having a panic attack
                already. And what about Hawkins --
                that lady is just gonna keep it
                "contained," like you can contain
                any of this without El --

                    MIKE
                    (low)
                ... Yeah.

Will stops bouncing the ball, looks over at Mike. Sees that he's lost in his own world, barely listening.

> WILL
> If you keep staring at that it's not going to change, you know?

> MIKE
> Yeah -- I -- I know.

Mike crumples up the letter, then tosses it like a basketball into a nearby garbage bin. It banks off the wall, misses. Will pushes off the bed, grabs it, drops it in for him --

> MIKE (CONT'D)
> Thanks.

Will now crosses to Mike and sits beside him. He waits for his friend -- giving him time. And sure enough, Mike starts to open up...

> MIKE (CONT'D)
> ... Before the cops came -- me and El, we, we got in a bad fight. And we -- we never fight -- I mean we've fought before, you know, but, it was always like, silly fights -- stupid fights -- not like this. This felt like -- an adult fight, like it was about something real. A fight maybe -- you don't come back from.
> (beat)
> And... I -- I should have said something... And I feel like -- if I did -- say it -- she would have wanted me with her -- wherever she is now.

> WILL
> You're going to see her again, Mike. And whatever it is -- *whatever you didn't say* -- you can tell her then.

> MIKE
> ... Yeah.

                    WILL
          And she's going to be okay. She's
          not in Hawkins. That's what we
          should be worried about.

Mike turns to Will.

                    MIKE
          You don't trust Owens?

                    WILL
          I don't know. I mean -- he's been
          good to us, *good to El* -- but he
          wasn't able to protect me, not when
          things got really bad, when I was
          the spy. That was *you guys* who
          saved me.

Mike takes this in, then, realizing --

                    MIKE
          It's going to be up to us again.

                    WILL
          It always is, isn't it?

                    JONATHAN (O.S.)
          Which is why we can't stay here.

Mike and Will look up in surprise to find Jonathan entering.
He shuts the door, kneels down by the boys.

                    JONATHAN (CONT'D)
          Let's assume these "friends of
          Owens" are telling the truth -- we
          can't call Hawkins without alerting
          the military, putting El in danger.
          Fine. Then we'll just have to go to
          them.

                    MIKE
          Go to Hawkins -- ?

                    WILL
          How -- ?

                    JONATHAN
          What are you worried about? Ponch
          and Jon out there? They're half
          asleep right now, watching golf.

                    WILL
          We don't have a car -- or money --

                    JONATHAN
          So we hail ourselves a ride. *A
          cheap one.*

Jonathan tosses them the Surfer Boy Pizza coupon. As Mike and Will look from the coupon to each other, starting to understand, we CUT TO --

INT. BYERS HOUSE - LIVING ROOM - DAY

Our California gang crossing into the living room. The Agents don't even look up from their golf game.

                    WILL
          Excuse me, sir --

                    AGENT HARMON
          What?

                    WILL
          We're hungry.

Off Agent Harmon, finally looking at them, irritated, we PRE-LAP some FAST-PACED "LIVELY ONES" SURFER MUSIC and --

INT. SURFER BOY PIZZA - DAY

The music CRANKS in volume as we move into an ENERGETIC BORDERLINE *EROTIC* MONTAGE OF PIZZA BEING MADE -- dough is tossed -- tomato paste is squirted -- cheese is drizzled -- canned pineapple slices are delicately placed -- the pie is slid into an oven --

WIDEN: We're in a Surfer Boy Pizza kitchen! It's busy as hell in here -- lots of orders for spring break. Half party, half pizza joint.

BRRRRRRRING! A phone blares, adding to the chaos. A hand picks it up off the receiver. It's --

ARGYLE! His eyes are shock-red from weed, of course.

                        ARGYLE
            Surf's up this is Surfer Boy Pizza,
            before ya order, may I strongly
            recommend our Pineapple Pie --
            fruit on pizza is gnarly you say? I
            say -- <u>try before you deny.</u>

INT. BYERS HOUSE - LIVING ROOM - DAY

Off a dumbfounded Harmon, our surfer music CRESCENDOS and we
SMASH TO --

EXT. WHEELER HOUSE - DAY

Quiet outside the Wheeler house. PRE-LAP: SCRIBBLING as --

INT. WHEELER BASEMENT - DAY

Max finishes writing another note. She folds it neatly, slips
it in an envelope, then writes on the front of it: <u>BILLY</u>.

She places the envelope atop a stack of envelopes. *She's been
writing a lot of these.* She now turns to find --

All the boys staring at her from across the room. They
quickly look away --

                        MAX
            I know you guys are staring at me.

They all look up --

                        DUSTIN
            What sorry -- ?

                        LUCAS
            What was that -- you need
            something?

Max just stares at these idiots.

      MAX
   How you think your eyes boring into
   the back of my head is protecting
   me from Vecna, I don't know --

They look away again. Max grabs up the envelopes, walks over to them --

     MAX (CONT'D)
   You can look at me now --

      STEVE
  Yeah --

      DUSTIN
  Right --

                    LUCAS
          Sorry --

                     MAX
          For you -- for you -- *and you.*

She hands each of them an envelope with their name written on it, then passes three additional envelopes to Lucas.

                    MAX (CONT'D)
          Give these to El and Mike and Will.
          If you can ever get ahold of them
          again.

Dustin promptly starts to open his envelope, but --

                    MAX (CONT'D)
          What are you doing??

                    DUSTIN
          Huh -- ??

                    MAX
          Don't open it *now* --

                    DUSTIN
          Oh -- sorry -- *wait* --
               (totally confused)
          What is this?

                    MAX
          It's just... a failsafe... for
          after. If things... don't work out.

Everyone shares looks -- *Jesus that's dark.*

                    LUCAS
          Max, it's gonna w --

                    MAX
               (interrupting)
          No. I don't need you to reassure me
          right now and tell me how it's all
          going to *work out* because people
          have been telling me that my whole
          life and it's almost *never* true. I
          mean -- *of course* this asshole
          curses me. Shoulda seen that one
          coming.

She grabs up the walkie-talkie, spins back to Dustin.

                    MAX (CONT'D)
          -- If we go to East Hawkins, will
          this still reach Pennhurst?

                    DUSTIN
          Of course --

                    STEVE
          Whoa whoa whoa -- what's this about
          East Hawkins?

Off Max, HARD CUT TO --

EXT. WHEELER HOUSE - DAY

Our teens striding out of the basement.

As they head up the hill and toward the driveway, "Dad" Steve pursues, and he's *not happy* --

                    STEVE
          Guys -- seriously -- this isn't a
          joke! I'm not driving you anywhere,
          okay???

                    MAX
              (fast)
          Steve -- if you think I'm going to
          spend what is likely the last day
          of my life in the armpit that is
          Mike Wheeler's basement you're out
          of your mind. So either you take me
          where I need to go -- or you're
          going to have to tie me down which
          is technically *kidnapping of a
          minor* and if live to see another
          day I swear to God I will
          prosecute.

They've now reached Steve's car -- but the doors are locked.

Max fires daggers at Steve.

                    MAX (CONT'D)
          Open the doors.

Steve hesitates.

                    MAX (CONT'D)
          I know a good lawyer.

Steve sighs. *Fuck.* He glares at Dustin.

                    STEVE
          That super walkie of yours *better
          reach Pennhurst*.

He opens the doors. As everyone climbs in, Max suddenly
pauses. She's heard --

THOSE CHIMES. She turns -- looks out toward the power lines.
There's nothing there. *But she knows -- and we know* -- Vecna
is coming. She climbs into the car, slams the door, and --

EXT. PENNHURST ASYLUM - DAY

The Wheeler Wagon speeds under an ominous sign that reads:

PENNHURST MENTAL HOSPITAL. The hospital looms ahead -- it has
massive stone walls and gothic architecture; it looks like it
was ripped out from the pages of a Stephen King book.

EXT. PENNHURST ASYLUM - DAY

Robin and Nancy, now both dressed up in Nancy's conservative,
PREPPY OUTFITS, head toward Pennhurst.

Robin tugs at her tight collar, scratches at her pantyhose,
wildly uncomfortable.

                    ROBIN
          I can't breathe in this thing --
          and I'm itching -- I'm itching all
          over --

                    NANCY
          It's not all about comfort.
          Remember -- we're *academics* --

                    ROBIN
          -- Who are evidently coming
          straight from an Easter brunch --
          also this bra you gave me is like,
          seriously pinching my boobs --

                    NANCY
          Why don't you just -- let me do the
          talking? If that's even possible --

                    ROBIN
          It's not just possible it's
          inevitable, because shortly -- *I'll
          be dead*.

As the girls head up the steps to the entrance...

> DIRECTOR HATCH (PRE-LAP)
> Three point nine GPAs... both of
> you. Impressive.

INT. PENNHURST ASYLUM - DIRECTOR HATCH'S OFFICE - DAY

DIRECTOR HATCH lowers the resumes to reveal our girls sitting across from him. As Robin tugs annoyingly at her collar, Nancy hands him another paper.

> NANCY
> And this is a recommendation from
> Professor Brantley --

> DIRECTOR HATCH
> (interjecting)
> Oh I know Larry. Quite well,
> actually.

The director quickly scans the recommendation --

> DIRECTOR HATCH (CONT'D)
> You know what they say -- those who
> can't do... teach.

He tosses down the recommendation. Robin continues to tug at her collar -- she's being weird. Nancy gives her a look -- *stop it* -- then back to the Director.

> NANCY
> Yes -- that's um... actually why
> we're here. We can only learn so
> much -- in a classroom --

> DIRECTOR HATCH
> And I'm sympathetic to your
> struggle. *Truly*. But there is a
> protocol to visiting a patient like
> Victor. You have to put in a
> request, then you have to undergo a
> screening process at which point
> the board will make a decision.

Robin and Nancy share looks -- this is not going how they hoped. Robin tugs at her collar again. *Jesus, she's a mess.*

> DIRECTOR HATCH (CONT'D)
> I can see you're disappointed. But
> I am more than happy to give you a
> tour of our facility -- perhaps you
> could even speak to some patients
> in our low security wing --

                    NANCY
          Right, we'd -- we'd love that. It's
          just -- our thesis is due next
          month and --

                    DIRECTOR HATCH
          You're out of time. And whose fault
          is that?

                    NANCY
          I -- I know, it's just -- uh...
          yes, our fault, absolutely, and I
          apologize but --

                    ROBIN
          Don't apologize, Ruth. *Screw that.*

Nancy shoots Robin a shocked look. But Robin continues --

                    ROBIN (CONT'D)
          The fact of the matter is we DID
          put in a request months ago and
          were denied and then we reapplied
          and were denied again and coming
          here was our last-ditch effort to
          save our thesis and -- and -- I --
          I can't BREATHE IN THIS THING!

She finally unbuttons the top button, sucks in some air.
Nancy stares at her with wide eyes.

                    NANCY
          Rose -- maybe you should go outside
          and get some air --

                    ROBIN
          Maybe I should, Ruth! Because you
          know what -- I'm starting to think
          this whole thing was a colossal
          mistake -- I'm breaking out in a
          rash -- my boobs hurt --

Nancy shoots daggers -- *WTF* -- Robin is ruining everything!
Yet "Rose" keeps going --

                    ROBIN (CONT'D)
               (fast)
          The truth is, Anthony -- may I call
          you Anthony? -- these aren't
          actually my clothes.
                    (MORE)

                    ROBIN (CONT'D)
          I borrowed them because I wanted
          you to take us seriously because no
          one takes girls like us seriously
          in this field. They _just don't_. We
          don't "look the part" or whatever.
          But let me tell you a story. On the
          night of the twenty-second of May
          nineteen seventy-eight, I was away
          at summer camp, and our counselor
          Drew told me and everyone in Cabin
          C the true story of the "Victor
          Creel Massacre." And Little Petey
          McHew -- you know Petey right
          Ruth?? -- he just started sobbing
          right there on the spot. Like FULL
          ON hyperventilating. And the other
          campers, they couldn't sleep for
          weeks! And I couldn't sleep either
          but not because I was scared --
          because I was obsessed with the
          question: What would drive a human
          to commit such an unimaginable
          act??? Other kids wanted to be
          astronauts and basketball players
          and rock stars -- I _wanted to be_
          you. So forgive me if I'll now try
          anything including wearing this
          ridiculous outfit if it gives me a
          chance to actually speak to the man
          that ignited my passion and learn a
          little bit more about how his
          twisted _but let's be honest here_
          totally fascinating mind works. And
          while I understand we don't have
          official permission -- please don't
          tell me that cry baby Petey McHew
          wouldn't have been granted an
          interview with Victor by now if he
          had asked politely because you and
          I _both know he would have_.
              (_catches_ breath)
          Ten minutes. That's all I ask.

Off Director Hatch, staring, we CUT TO --

INT. PENNHURST - RECEPTION - DAY

WHOOM! The door flies open as the Director leads the girls across reception.

275

>   DIRECTOR HATCH
>   (to secretary)
>   We'll be back in thirty.

A shocked -- but nevertheless *very* impressed -- Nancy gives Robin a *secret underhanded high-five* --

EXT. YURI'S FISH N FLY - ALASKA - DAY

VROOOM! A RENTAL CAR speeds up to a small building, which sits next to a decrepit runway. A rusted sign reads: YURI'S FISH N FLY.

MOMENTS LATER

Murray (carrying the bag of money) and Joyce walk up to the building, but the door is locked. A loud SHRIEKING SOUND drags their eyes toward the runway, where --

A MAN IN A WELDER'S MASK is welding a CARGO PLANE. That is, if you can even call it a plane -- it looks more fit for the junkyard than the skies. This whole situation is *sketchy*.

>   MURRAY
>   If this goes sideways -- I should
>   mention, I'm now a black belt in
>   karate.

Joyce stares. Anything but reassured. And --

INT. YURI'S FISH N FLY - HANGAR - MOMENTS LATER

CLOSE ON: Sparks flying over snow as --

The Welder works on the airplane. Joyce and Murray approach.

>   JOYCE
>   Excuse Me? *EXCUSE ME??*

The Welder finally hears her -- he whips around, hits off his torch, removes his mask. He's a goofy man with big nose, big lips, and a syrup-thick Russian accent. His brow furrows --

>   WELDER
>   Hello -- who are you???
>
>   JOYCE
>   Hi yes, sorry -- to interrupt. We
>   are looking for... Yuri?

The Welder's face darkens.

                    WELDER
          Oh. Why do you need to see Yuri?

                    MURRAY
          Actually -- it's uh --

                    JOYCE
          A private matter. Is Yuri... here?

The Welder removes his helmet completely. Solemn.

                    WELDER
          I am sorry. I do not know how to
          tell you this, but... you are *day
          late.*

Shared looks -- *oh no.* He motions to the plane.

                    WELDER (CONT'D)
          You see damage to this hull? Yuri
          was on sightseeing trip to see
          polar bears -- then bears got into
          plane, pulled him out of cockpit --

                    JOYCE
          Oh God --

                    WELDER
          Killed Yuri. And he loved bears.
          They broke his heart. Or rather --
          punctured it with bear claws.

                    MURRAY
          Oh no -- I'm so sorry --

                    JOYCE
          That -- that's awful --

The Welder suddenly BURSTS OUT LAUGHING. WAHAHAHAHA!

                    WELDER
          Look at your faces -- I got you --
          got you good!!!

Confused looks.

                    WELDER (CONT'D)
          I am Yuri!!! I AM YURI!

More laughter from Yuri. Joyce and Murray try to laugh along.
Yuri holds out his gloved hand. They shake it.

                    YURI
            You must be Joyce -- and --

                    MURRAY
            Murray.

                    YURI
            Murray, Yuri. We RHYME! HA! Come
            come -- I have been expecting you!

Yuri heads toward the office at a brisk pace. Joyce and Murray share looks, then hustle after him and --

INT. YURI'S FISH N FLY - RECEPTION AREA - DAY

WHOOM! Murray drops the bag on a cluttered table, yanks it open it to reveal STACKS OF CASH!

                    MURRAY
            Forty thousand American dollars. *As
            promised.*

Yuri opens the bag. Takes a big whiff.

                    YURI
            Ahhh, I love the smell of cash in
            morning.
                    (laughs, then)
            I hope you do not mind if I count?
            You two seem very nice, very
            trustworthy people but... so did my
            brother -- before he stole my
            wife*!!!*

Another big laugh from Yuri.

                    JOYCE
            Of course -- we understand.

                    MURRAY
            No offense taken.

As Yuri chaotically upends the cash onto his desk -- he notices Joyce clutching her arms, freezing --

                    YURI
            Poor bird, you are freezing.

He motions to a STEAMING COFFEE POT in the corner --

                    YURI (CONT'D)
          Please -- have some coffee -- still
          hot. This could be a while.

                    JOYCE
          Oh, okay -- *thank you.*

As Joyce and Murray happily hurry over for some coffee --

Yuri begins to count.

                    YURI
                 (Russian)
          <And one, and two, and *three,*
          and -- >

EXT. WORKSITE - KAMCHATKA - DAY

WHAM! A spike maul slams into a railroad tie.

WIDEN: We're back with Hopper, who is now working on the
track. As he works, his eyes roam. He sees that the Mean
Guard is distracted, berating another prisoner.

Hopper knows this is his chance -- but he's got to move fast.

He jams the base of his maul handle beneath the railroad
tie, yanks back on it as hard as he can, *straining,* and --

CRACK! The wooden shaft snaps, breaking off from the spike.

The STRONG PRISONER stares at him. Hopper shrugs.

                    HOPPER
          Oops.

A FEW MOMENTS LATER

Hopper walks over to the tool shed --

ACROSS THE WAY,

Dmitri sees him, knows it's happening. A silent prayer as --

BACK BY THE TOOL SHED,

The TOOL SHED GUARD sees Hopper approaching -- holds up his
rifle --

                    TOOL SHED GUARD
          <HEY! Get BACK. *BACK!*>

Hopper freezes, holds up his hands, playing innocent.

He motions to his broken tool --

>   HOPPER
>   <Broke! Broke! Cannot work!>

The Tool Shed Guard lowers his rifle. Sighs.

>   TOOL SHED GUARD
>   <Stay there.>

He stomps back into the tool shed. Hopper looks around, then heads for the shed and --

INT. TOOL SHED - CONTINUOUS

The Tool Shed Guard looks for a replacement tool when --

He hears the crunch of snow behind him. He turns --

Sees Hopper moving toward him -- *fast* --

He starts to raise his rifle but --

Hopper is already swinging his broken spike maul *and* --

WHACK! It SMACKS the Guard hard across the face. The Guard flips, lands hard on the floor, and --

BACK OUTSIDE,

The Mean Guard -- who has finished berating his prisoner -- is now walking back down the line, resuming inspections.

And that's when he notices: Hopper is not by the Strong Prisoner anymore. As he takes this in --

INT. TOOL SHED - DAY

Hopper rips a KEY RING off the guard's belt. *Bingo*. He then drops on the floor, works as fast as he can to remove his leg irons as --

BACK OUTSIDE,

The Mean Guard approaches the Strong Prisoner.

>   MEAN GUARD
>   <Where is the American?!>

The Strong Prisoner shrugs, covering, but then --

The Mean Guard notices the broken tip of the spike mallet -- discarded on the ground. As he lifts it up, his gaze shifts to the tool shed. *Uh oh.*

INT. TOOL SHED - DAY

FWOOM! Hopper pulls off the first leg iron, but struggles with second one -- *the damn thing won't come off --*

                    HOPPER
                    (low)
        Come on come on *come on --*

EXT. TOOL SHED - CONTINUOUS

The Mean Guard approaches the shed, raising that rifle --

ACROSS THE WAY,

Dmitri watches from afar, nervous.

                    DMITRI
                    (low)
        <Watch your back, American...>

INT. TOOL SHED - DAY

Hopper *finally* gets the second leg chain off just as --

CLICK! RACK TO REVEAL: <u>The Mean Guard</u>. Right behind him. His rifle muzzle is aimed right at the back of Hopper's head. *Shit.*

                  MEAN GUARD
        <Where do you think you're going, American?>

Hopper tenses -- then -- in a flash -- he swings the freed chains like a whip at the Mean Guard! The leg iron lashes him across the face, knocking him back. Hopper then leaps to his feet -- *lunges* -- and suddenly --

Hopper and the Mean Guard are fighting for their lives in this small shed, punching and throwing each other against the walls! It's a fairly even back and forth fight, until --

Hopper wraps his chains around the Mean Guard's neck and yanks back as hard as he can -- *strangling the Mean Guard*.

The Mean Guard flails and kicks -- slamming Hopper back against a heavy table and --

BANG! His rifle goes off! Wood SPLINTERS and --

EXT. WORKSITE - DAY

The GUNSHOT RINGS OUT across the worksite. Prisoners and guards alike all whirl toward the commotion, then --

INT. TOOL SHED - DAY

WHUMP! The Mean Guard finally drops to the floor, chains wrapped around his neck, knocked unconscious, but --

Hopper is not out of the woods yet. He can hear SHOUTING GUARDS. *Fuck.*

EXT. WORKSITE - DAY

Guards are now racing for the tool shed.

INT. TOOL SHED - DAY

Hopper's eyes snap around the room. Lock onto -- that HEAVY TABLE. A CRATE OF DYNAMITE. A plan quickly forms as --

EXT. TOOL SHED - DAY

The Guards race up to the tool shed. They go to open the door -- but it won't budge! *The hell?* They slam their shoulders into it, shouting, and --

INT. TOOL SHED - DAY

We cut inside to reveal that Hopper has thrown the heavy table against the door. As the guards struggle against it --

We PAN AWAY from the blockaded door to find Hopper now hauling himself up through a HATCH IN THE CEILING!

EXT. TOOL SHED - DAY

Hopper scrambles onto the snow-blanketed roof. Unnoticed by the guards. That is, *almost* all the guards...

FURTHER DOWN THE TRACKS,

Dmitri watches -- amused and impressed -- as Hopper scurries off the roof, then drops into the soft snow below as --

INT. TOOL SHED - DAY

WHOOM! The Guards at last force their way into the tool shed.

Their eyes move from the two unconscious guards to --

HISSS!! A trail of smoke coming from --

A STICK OF LIT DYNAMITE. Oh *FUCK*.

                    SCARED GUARD
          <RUNN!!!!>

The turn to run, but they're bottlenecked in here and --

EXT. TOOL SHED - DAY

KABOOOOOM! The shed EXPLODES in a FIREBALL OF FLAME AND SMOKE and our guards are HURTLED across the snow -- some *ON FIRE* --

A LITTLE FURTHER AWAY

Hopper doesn't even look back at the mass destruction he's left behind -- he just keeps running until he reaches --

A FLEET OF PARKED SNOWMOBILES.

He mounts one -- jams the stolen keys in -- then --

An EAGLE-EYED GUARD finally spots Hopper --

                    EAGLE-EYED GUARD
          <THERE!! *SNOWMOBILES*!!>

VROOOOOM! Hopper takes off, snow kicking back, as --

Guards open fire. BANG BANG BANG! Hop keeps his body low as bullets whiz around him, pelting snow, *missing*, and --

WHOOM! He explodes into the tree line, VANISHING into the forest. *Escaping*. The prisoners ERUPT IN CHEERS and --

Dmitri watches. A small smile curls on his lips.

                    DMITRI
          A hundred to one... *sonofabitch*.

EXT. WOODS - DAY

A newly FREE Hopper speeds through the forest on his snowmobile. Trees whip past faster and faster *and* --

INT. STEVE'S CAR - DAY

WHOOSH! Trees whip past -- only the trees are now lush and green. We're back in Hawkins.

REVERSE: A CU OF MAX as she looks quietly out the window at the passing landscape.

Lucas sits beside her, clutching the letter she wrote to him.

He clearly wants to say something to Max, but... he doesn't know *what to say*. Or *how to say it*. He looks away.

EXT. MAX'S TRAILER - DAY

Steve's car pulls up to Max's trailer.

INT. STEVE'S CAR - DAY

          STEVE
This better be fast, Mayfield --

          MAX
Twenty seconds.

She exits the car and hurries toward her trailer.

A stressed Steve looks back at Dustin's supercomm.

          STEVE
That things's got batteries in it, right?

          DUSTIN
I'm not answering that.

INT. MAX'S TRAILER - DAY

Max enters her trailer. She opens her backpack and removes the STACK OF LETTERS. She shuffles through them, then places a handful down onto the coffee table, laying them out in a neat row, as to make certain none go unnoticed. We see they are addressed to GRANNY, GRANDPA, DAD, and, lastly, MOM.

Finished, Max starts back for the door when she pauses, eyes narrowing. She has clocked her MOM through the kitchen window. She's outside, hanging some LAUNDRY onto the laundry line. Max is clearly surprised to see her here. She hesitates, takes a breath, then --

EXT. MAX'S TRAILER - LAUNDRY SIDE -- A FEW MOMENTS LATER

THWACK! A clothespin *snaps shut*, pinning a shirt onto the line. We're now with Max's mom as she hangs up the laundry.

                    MAX
-- Mom?

Max's mom looks up to find Max approaching from the back of the house.

                  SUSAN
             (surprised)
Hey sweetie -- I thought you were with your friends today?

                  MAX
I was -- I am --
             (pivoting)
Shouldn't you be at work -- ?

                  SUSAN
Oh -- Mister Bradley let me off early, so -- just catching up on some chores.
             (clocking Max's stress)
I wasn't let go again, sweetie -- *don't worry*.

                  MAX
Oh no -- I know. It's not that. I was -- I was just --
             (not sure if she should be
             honest here)
I put some letters inside. For you -- and Granny and Grandpa. And Dad. If you can -- find him.

Susan takes a step forward, growing concerned --

                  SUSAN
Letters? I, I don't understand --

                  MAX
             (how to explain)
It's just... with everything that's going -- with these murders... It's stupid but I started to think... I don't know -- what if -- what if something happened to me?

Max is trying to fight back an onrush of tears. An increasingly worried Susan takes another step toward Max.

                    SUSAN
          Max -- baby -- <u>nothing</u> is going to
          happen to you --

                    MAX
          I know -- but if -- if it did --
          there are just... so many things I
          want to say, need to say, and...
                (beat, fighting emotion)
          Can you just promise that -- you'll
          give them out -- the letters -- ?

                    SUSAN
          Max -- you're scaring me --

                    MAX
          I'm not trying to scare you --

                    SUSAN
          Is something going on -- ??

                    MAX
          No -- no -- I'm -- I'm sure you're
          right -- I'm sure I'll be fine...
          I'm just being -- silly --

But Max doesn't believe this and she can't hold back the
tears any longer --

                    SUSAN
          Max, *oh, sweetie*!

Max's mom pulls Max into an embrace. As she holds her, gently
stroking the back of her hair --

                    SUSAN (CONT'D)
          Shh, shh... it's going to be okay
          baby -- nothing is going to
          happen, okay, I promise... *nothing
          that you don't deserve...*

Max is startled by this. Then she notices something shocking.
Hanging from the laundry line: A DOZEN VERSIONS OF THE WHITE
TANK TOP THAT BILLY DIED IN. The shirts are soaked with blood
and pierced with ragged holes (from those tentacles). The
wind begins to pick up, blowing the bloody shirts, and the
sky darkens, swallowing us in shadow.

A panicked Max tries to pull away from her mom, but --

Her mother won't let go.

                         MAX
            Mom -- let me go -- mom -- !!

But her mom isn't releasing her. Holding her tight. Worse
still, her mother's left hand is now MUTATED, SLIMY. It's --

VECNA'S HAND. HIS SHARP FINGERNAILS MOVE down the length of
her head, inching their way TOWARD HER EXPOSED NECK --

                      MAX (CONT'D)
            LET GO -- LET GO -- LET GO -- !

A flap of laundry, and like that, her mom is now gone and in
her place -- VECNA. His ROTTEN, BLOODY MOUTH MOVES UP TO
MAX'S EAR. INCHES AWAY. BLACK BILE SPILLS DOWN HIS JAW.

                         VECNA
            You think some letters are going to
            make things right Maxine? You've
            broken everything -- your family --
            your mother -- Billy -- *your life* --

                         MAX
            LET GO -- !!

                         VECNA
            But don't fear -- your time... is
            almost... *at an end* --

His long fingernails begin to DIG INTO HER NECK and --

                         MAX
            NO -- !!

Max finally pries herself free, falling backwards onto the
grass. She looks up in horror, back toward Vecna -- but --

Vecna is gone. And so is her mother. A few (regular) pieces
of laundry sway in a now gentle breeze. A pale-faced Max
scrambles to her feet and hurries away, fleeing --

EXT. MAX'S TRAILER - DAY - MOMENTS LATER

WHOOM! Steve's BMW door flies open as Max leaps into the
car --

                         STEVE
            That wasn't twenty seconds --
                  (noticing tears)
            You alright -- ?

                    MAX
            (catching breath, wiping
              tears)
    I'm fine -- just drive --

                  LUCAS
    Did something happen??

                    MAX
    JUST DRIVE!!

Steve kicks into gear and speeds off.

EXT. PENNHURST ASYLUM - HALLWAY - DAY

MENTAL PATIENTS wandering a lush garden.

Director Hatch escorts Robin and Nancy through these gardens.

>   DIRECTOR HATCH
>   Our gardens -- beautiful, aren't
>   they? We allow them two hours of
>   outside time a day.

Robin eyes the fence -- it isn't very tall.

                    ROBIN
          Can't they -- just escape?

                    DIRECTOR HATCH
          They *could*. But the vast majority
          choose to be here. They *like it
          here.*

He now opens a door and takes them into --

INT. LISTENING ROOM

They now pass A GROUP OF PATIENTS who are listening to a record player -- classical music. Hatch lowers his voice a bit as they move through here, so as to not disturb.

                    DIRECTOR HATCH
          This is one of our more popular
          areas -- the *listening room.* We've
          found that music has a particularly
          calming effect on the broken mind.
          The right song -- particularly one
          which holds personal meaning -- can
          prove a *salient stimulus*. But there
          are some... who are beyond a
          cure...

He now opens a door and takes them into --

A SMALL CORRIDOR - HIGH SECURITY WING - CONTINUOUS

A small, windowless room, with cameras fixed on the ceilings. As a waiting PENNHURST GUARD #1, 40s, begins to unlock a prison door for them, Nancy clears her throat --

                    NANCY
          Doctor Hatch.

Director Hatch turns to them ---

                    NANCY (CONT'D)
          Do you think it might be possible
          for us to speak with Victor...
          alone?

Before a surprised Hatch can respond, Robin blurts out --

                    ROBIN
          We would just *love* the challenge of
          speaking to Victor without the
          safety net of an expert such as
          yourself -- that way we can *really*
          rub it into Professor Bradley's
          face when we get back to campus --

Robin chortles at this, trying to be charming, but --

Something has caught Hatch:

                    DIRECTOR HATCH
          Professor Bradley? I don't believe
          I know a --

                    NANCY
               (jumping in to save)
          Brantley. She meant *Brantley* --

                    ROBIN
                (fast)
            Professor Brantley, yes -- is that
            not what I said? Sorry -- I'm just
            nervous -- excited -- to meet
            Victor. Preferably... *alone?*

Robin forces an awkward smile. The Director stares. Is that a hint of -- *suspicion?* Then -- he matches Robin's smile.

                    DIRECTOR HATCH
            Yes -- why not?? You've caught me
            in a rebellious mood and there's
            something rather urgent I should
            check on anyway.

He looks up at the Guard --

                    DIRECTOR HATCH (CONT'D)
            Keep a close eye on them.

The Guard nods as the Director heads off. Robin shoots Nancy a look -- *sorry!* Then --

INT. HIGH SECURITY WING - CONTINUOUS

Our Guard now leads the girls down the aisle of cells. As they walk, they pass by a ROW OF CREEPY INMATES. One angrily talks to himself while pacing -- one rocks back and forth while clutching his head -- another ogles our girls creepily, licking his lips. Needless to say, it's all rather unpleasant --

                    PENNHURST GUARD #1
            Do not startle him -- do not touch
            him -- do not pass him anything --
            and stay five feet away from the
            bars at all times. Is that clear?

Robin and Nancy nod. Then, at last, they reach --

THE CELL AT THE END OF THE BLOCK.

This is it. The Guard runs his stick across the bars.

                    PENNHURST GUARD #1 (CONT'D)
            Victor, today's your lucky day --
            you got visitors. *Pretty ones.*

REVERSE TO REVEAL: VICTOR CREEL. He's an old man. Not scary at all -- at least not from the back.

He's hunched over a small wooden desk, running a wrinkled hand across an open Bible. He doesn't respond to the Guard. Doesn't even acknowledge him.

                    PENNHURST GUARD #1 (CONT'D)
                (to girls)
            Seems he's in one of his moods
            today. *Have fun...*

And with that, the Pennhurst Guard walks away -- leaving our girls alone with Victor. They share looks -- not quite sure where to even begin here. A tense beat, then --

                    NANCY
            Victor...

No response.

                    NANCY (CONT'D)
            My name is Nancy -- Nancy Wheeler.
            And this -- this is --

                    ROBIN
            Robin Buckley. We have -- some
            questi --

                    VICTOR
                (sharply interrupting)
            I don't talk to reporters. Hatch
            knows that --

                    NANCY
            We're -- not reporters. We're here
            because... we believe your version
            of the story. And because --
                (beat, sincere)
            We need your help.

                    ROBIN
            We think -- whatever killed your
            family -- *is back*.

Now this -- *this* gets Victor's attention. He turns to them.

And now we see that his eyes have been crudely GOUGED OUT WITH SOME JAGGED INSTRUMENT. HORRIBLY SCARRED.

As our shocked girls take this in, HARD CUT TO --

EXT. LENORA ROAD - DAY

VROOOM! Argyle's Surfer Boy Pizzamobile *ROARING* past camera.

INT. PIZZAMOBILE - DAY

Argyle drives slowly, nodding along to a song on the radio, the whole van choked in POT SMOKE. As he drums to the song on the steering wheel, *barely* paying attention to the road --

INT. BYERS HOUSE - WILL'S ROOM - DAY

WHUMP! Clothes drop into a bag. Will is kneeling on the floor, hurriedly packing a bag -- Mike comes up to him, carrying his bag --

>   WILL
> You already packed -- ?

>   MIKE
> Yeah I mean -- I never really...
> unpacked.

Will nods, continues packing.

>   MIKE (CONT'D)
> Thanks, by the way...

>   WILL
> For what -- ?

>   MIKE
> For -- knocking some sense into me.
> I was being -- a total self-pitying
> idiot.

>   WILL
> I didn't say it...

A shared smile between the boys.

> MIKE
> Hey, listen -- about... the past couple of days --

Will looks away, this makes him uncomfortable --

> WILL
> You don't have to say anything. I -- I was a being a jerk to El, I deserved it --

> MIKE
> No. You didn't deserve anything, okay? The truth is... this past year, it's been weird. Dustin and Lucas and Max are great -- but Hawkins -- it just hasn't been the same without you. And I feel like -- I've been so worried about El, that --
> (beat)
> I don't know. I felt like... I almost lost you or something. And... I don't know what's going to happen next. But... I just feel like -- whatever it is -- it'll be easier if we're working together. If we're... friends again. <u>Best friends</u>.

Will finally looks at Mike, emotional --

> WILL
> Yeah?

> MIKE
> Yeah.

This intimate moment is shattered by --

DING DONG! The doorbell rings --

> MIKE (CONT'D)
> That was fast --

> WILL
> Thirty minutes or less --

WHOOM! The door opens and Jonathan hurries in, a backpack slung over his shoulder --

>   JONATHAN
>   You guys ready --?

>   WILL/MIKE
>   Ready --

Jonathan races past them. As he quickly works to unlock and open the window for their escape --

Will clocks his ROLLED UP PAINTING. He jams it into his backpack, zips it up, as --

BACK UPSTAIRS,

The doorbell rings again. DING DONG!

>   AGENT WALLACE
>   Yeah yeah, I'm comin' --

Agent Wallace heads for the door, pulling out his wallet. He swings it open and --

His face drops. It's not Argyle. It's --

ONE OF SULLIVAN'S SOLDIERS.

>   SOLDIER #1
>   Hi there.

He's got a SILENCER. Fuck. Wallace reaches for his gun but --

Too late. BANG! He's shot in the chest. He flies back --

INT. BYERS HOUSE - LIVING ROOM - DAY

Agent Harmon hears it, jolts up from the couch --

BACK IN WILL'S ROOM

Our boys, about to climb out the window, whip around --

>   MIKE
>   The hell was that -- ?

>   JONATHAN
>   *Argyle* --

INT. BYERS HOUSE - STAIRS - MOMENTS LATER

Jonathan races up the steps -- only to crash to a stop as he finds himself in the midst of a GUNFIGHT, as Harmon and the Soldiers begin to exchange fire! SHIT! He U-turns and flees --

INT. BYERS HOUSE - WILL'S ROOM - MOMENTS LATER

-- Back into Will's room, slams the door behind him --

> MIKE
> What's happening -- ??

> JONATHAN
> Soldiers -- in the house --

> MIKE
> What -- ?!

> JONATHAN
> We gotta go -- *we gotta go* --

Jonathan heads back for the window but --

SMASH! The window suddenly explodes, showering glass, scaring the shit out of our teens --

EXT. BYERS HOUSE - OUTSIDE WILL'S ROOM - DAY

A Soldier breaks in, smashing glass with the butt of his rifle --

INT. BYERS HOUSE - WILL'S ROOM - DAY

Jonathan grabs Will --

> JONATHAN
> Follow me -- stay close!!

He leads them --

BACK UP THE STAIRS

Jonathan peers through a railing onto the first floor. The firefight rages on. Glass, pottery, picture frames shatter. *Chaos*. But the Soldiers are focused on Harmon, *distracted* --

> JONATHAN
> This way this way -- !

Jonathan leads the boys into THE FAMILY ROOM, making for the SUNROOM but --

More agents are now entering the sunroom! Including LT. COL. SULLIVAN. FUCK! Our teens scramble away, escaping into --

THE KITCHEN

They duck behind the counters, see --

Harmon, who is exchanging fire with the soldier at the front of the house. Harmon kills him. BAM! As he takes cover behind a dining room partition, reloading, he sees our terrified kids --

>   AGENT HARMON
>   *I START SHOOTING, I WANT YOU TO*
>   *RUN. YOU HEAR ME???*

They nod. Then -- Harmon leaps up and starts to open fire on the sunroom agents. BANG BANG BANG BANG! As glass ERUPTS --

Our kids make a mad dash for the front door. A bullet nails Harmon in the chest but he keeps firing as he runs after them -- and right here, at the PEAK OF CHAOS, we HARD CUT TO --

INT. PIZZAMOBILE - DAY

Argyle. *Stoned* and bobbing his head to music, in great spirits. *When* --

His eyes narrow as he nears the Byers house. A CLUSTER OF BLACK CARS OUTSIDE.

>   ARGYLE
>   Byers -- you have a party and not
>   invite me man?? Not cool NOT cool --

WHAM! A body suddenly slams into the side of his car. Argyle SCREAMS, but it's --

Jonathan!! Pounding on the glass --

>   JONATHAN
>   OPEN UP OPEN THE GODDAMN DOOR!

>   ARGYLE
>   Dude -- the hell -- ??

As a very confused Argyle opens the doors -- the kids and a bleeding Agent Harmon clamber into the back of the truck --

>   ARGYLE (CONT'D)
>   Whoa is that blood man -- ??!

>   JONATHAN
>   DRIVE!!

Argyle now sees a man with a gun approaching --

> ARGYLE
> Oh shit that dude has a gun -- !!

> JONATHAN/WILL/MIKE
> DRIIIVE!!!

Argyle stomps the gas -- the Pizzamobile *SQUEALS OFF*, zigging and zagging down the neighborhood street, crashing through a mailbox, and --

INT. YURI'S FISH N FLY - RECEPTION - DAY

WHAP! Money slaps the table as Yuri finishes counting --

> YURI
> Thirty thousand nine hundred...
> (another hundred)
> And... forty thousand. Wah-lah!

He looks up at Murray and Joyce, sipping their coffees, about to die from boredom. Murray rubs his eyes, trying to focus --

> YURI (CONT'D)
> All there --

> JOYCE
> Now your turn. <u>Go get Hopper</u>.

> YURI
> I will. But first -- I will call
> Enzo. If your friend is dead, I can
> save myself trouble -- *and fuel*.

Joyce stares.

> YURI (CONT'D)
> Kidding! I am sure he is not dead!!
> But still -- I should check, no?

As he heads for his office, whistling --

EXT. KAMCHATKA WOODS - DAY

VROOM! Snowmobiles tear through the forest as RUSSIAN GUARDS search the forest for Hopper -- on vehicle *and* on foot.

EXT. HILL OVERLOOK - NEAR RUSSIAN TOWN - DAY

FWOOM! Snow kicks back at camera as --

Hopper -- alone -- speeds out of the woods on his snowmobile. He slows to a stop. A SMALL TOWN sits in a valley below, not far away. His eyes lock onto a church with a blue steeple. *Bingo*. He hits the gas, zips toward it, and --

EXT. SMALL RUSSIAN TOWN - CHURCH - DAY

Hopper pulls his snowmobile to the hill below the church. Dismounts.

MOMENTS LATER

Hopper climbs up to the church. Scans the ground. Finds the headless statue. Its head rests on the snowy ground nearby. He picks the head up -- finds a RUSTY KEY hiding beneath.

INT. CHURCH - DAY

EEEE. The heavy door to the church opens as --

Hopper enters. The dark and murky space has been converted into a warehouse -- filled with CRATES OF BLACK MARKET GOODS.

MOMENTS LATER

Hopper pries open one of the crates, finds --

LEVI'S JEANS?? *Eh, not very helpful.* He opens another crate. This time, his eyes light up like a kid at Christmas.

IT'S JARS OF PEANUT BUTTER! That's better. *Much better.*

He unscrews the cap, jams his hands into the jar, and BEGINS TO RAVENOUSLY EAT as --

INT. RUSSIAN PRISON - DAY

Dmitri (along with several other guards) frantically works to usher the other prisoners back into their cells, when --

A YOUNG GUARD approaches --

                YOUNG GUARD
    <Antonov, phone for you.>

                DMITRI
    <You realize we just had an
    escape -- ??>

                    YOUNG GUARD
          <They say it is urgent.>

Off Dmitri --

INT. RUSSIAN PRISON - FRONT OFFICE - DAY

Dmitri picks up a phone, answers --

                    DMITRI
          <Hello?>

INT. YURI'S FISH N FLY - OFFICE - DAY - INTERCUT

                    YURI
          <Enzo -- it is Yuri.>

Dmitri is surprised -- and *not* pleased -- to hear from Yuri. He turns so no one can see, drops his voice to an angry whisper --

                    DMITRI
          <Why are you calling here, are you
          mad -- ??!>

                    YURI
          <I know -- I am very sorry. I just
          felt you should know that there has
          been a... <u>slight *change in plans*</u>.>

                    DMITRI
              (suddenly concerned)
          <What -- *what has happened*?>

INT. CHURCH - DAY

Hopper stops mid-peanut butter meal as he sees --

Guards, sweeping past the church windows. *Oh fuck.*

INT. YURI'S FISH N FLY - OFFICE - DAY - INTERCUT

                    YURI
          <I just got off the phone with your
          warden. A very *productive call*. It
          turns out -- escaped prisoners are
          worth quite a bit of money. So Yuri
          thinks -- why not keep the forty
          grand and make <u>*extra money*</u>?>

INT. CHURCH - DAY

Hopper reaches for his rifle as --

WHOOM! Doors are kicked open and guards sweep into the abandoned church from ALL SIDES, surrounding Hopper --

> RUSSIAN GUARD
> <Drop your weapon! DROP IT!!>

A stunned, devastated Hopper drops his rifle --

As the guards move in and take him down --

INT. RUSSIAN PRISON - FRONT OFFICE - DAY

> DMITRI
> <That *wasn't* the deal -- !>

INT. YURI'S FISH N FLY - OFFICE - DAY - INTERCUT

> YURI
> <But it is a better deal for Yuri, yes?? And you know what is worth even more than escaped prisoner? *Corrupt guards*.>

Dmitri looks up through the glass windows of the office -- sees Guards headed this way. *For him.*

> DMITRI
> <What have you done -- ?!>

> YURI
> <And worth *most of all* -- Americans wanted by KGB.>

INT. RECEPTION AREA - DAY

Joyce is refilling her coffee mug when her vision starts to go. She looks down -- sees the coffee is spilling out over the lip of the mug. She looks back at Murray, only to find --

He's slumped in his chair. *Knocked out.* The coffee mug slips out of Joyce's hand and shatters against the floor and --

INT. RUSSIAN PRISON - FRONT OFFICE - DAY

BOOM! Doors kick open and PRISON GUARDS sweep into the main prison office --

Dmitri shouts and tries to run, but they grab him -- SLAM him down onto the table -- the phone clatters away as --

INT. CHURCH - DAY

The Guards slam Hopper down onto a table -- cuff him --

INT. PRISON OFFICE

Dmitri is cuffed too. He shouts as he's dragged away --

INT. YURI'S OFFICE - DAY

Yuri smiles a bit as he listens to the muffled yelling.

>   YURI
>   <Goodbye, Enzo.>

A satisfied Yuri hangs up the phone and --

INT. YURI'S FISH N FLY - RECEPTION AREA - DAY

Yuri strolls back to the reception area, where he finds --

Joyce and Murray. Joyce has now collapsed on the floor.

Yuri kneels down by her. Her eyes are flagging. Still conscious, but only barely.

>   YURI
>   Oh, I'm sorry, poor bird -- did I
>   make your coffee too strong?

He reaches out a hand, gently strokes her hair --

>   YURI (CONT'D)
>   Don't worry -- you will be reunited
>   with your American boyfriend very
>   soon. *Very soon*.

Yuri smiles. As Joyce's vision fades --

INT./EXT. STEVE'S CAR - COUNTRY ROAD - DAY

Steve's BMW speeds down the road.

Steve drives. Everyone silent. Lucas eyes Max -- worried. He can tell something happened to her.

                    MAX
          Turn here --

Everyone shares dark looks as Steve turns the wheel, and we now reveal they're headed into... the <u>HAWKINS CEMETERY</u>.

EXT. HAWKINS CEMETERY - DAY

Steve's car pulls to a stop by a hillside. Max exits, starts to head up a hill, when --

                    LUCAS (O.S.)
          Max --

She turns in surprise to find Lucas walking up to her.

                    MAX
          Lucas -- please just stay in the
          car --

                    LUCAS
               (interjecting)
          I know something happened back
          there -- with your mom.

Max blinks -- he's caught her.

                    LUCAS (CONT'D)
          Was it -- Vecna?

                    MAX
          I -- I told you, *I'm fine*. I mean --
          as fine as someone who's hurtling
          toward a horrific death can be --

A small laugh from Max, trying to play this off -- but Lucas isn't buying it --

                    LUCAS
          Max. You know you can talk to me,
          right -- ?

                    MAX
          Yeah I know that --

                    LUCAS
          Then why are you pushing -- me
          away?

He holds up his letter.

LUCAS (CONT'D)
               I don't need a letter. Or -- want a
               letter. Just -- talk to me. To your
               friends. We're right here.
                    (beat)
               I'm right here.

Max takes this in. For a brief moment we think she might just
open up to him -- even, *that she wants to* -- but then --

                         MAX
               This won't be long. Just -- wait in
               the car.

With that, she heads off, leaving Lucas here, rebuffed,
letter still in hand. We hold on Max -- fighting back emotion
as she winds her way through the graveyard, Lucas growing
smaller and smaller behind her....

                    NANCY (PRE-LAP)
               When he attacks, our friend...
               Described it as... *a trance.*
               Like -- a waking nightmare.
               That's why we think -- *he's coming
               for her next.*

INT. PENNHURST - VICTOR'S CELL - DAY

Victor, now in deep shadow, takes this in. He is listening,
seemingly subdued --

                         NANCY
               Does any of that -- anything we've
               told you -- sound like what
               happened to you and your family?

Still no response from Victor. Nancy and Robin share looks.

                    NANCY (CONT'D)
               Victor -- I know this is hard --

                         VICTOR
                    (snapping, angry)
               You don't KNOW ANYTHING.

His anger is jarring and scary, but Nancy tries to keep her
cool -- speaks calmly, gently...

                         NANCY
               We agree... that's why we're here.
               To learn -- to understand.

> ROBIN
> We just need to know -- how you
> survived that night.

Victor turns toward them.

> VICTOR
> *"Survived"?* Is that what you call
> this? Did I... *"survive"*?

Victor walks close to them now. Moving out of shadow. Creepy.

> VICTOR (CONT'D)
> I am still very much *in Hell*.

As our girls take this in, unnerved, we PRE-LAP FIFTIES MUSIC then CUT TO --

EXT. CREEL HOUSE - DAY (FLASHBACK - 1959)

A shiny 1950s Chevy pulls up a long driveway.

> VICTOR (V.O.)
> I had been back from the war --
> some fourteen years --

The car door opens and out steps YOUNG VICTOR, 40s, his wife, VIRGINIA, 30s, and his two children, HENRY, 12, and ALICE, 11.

> VICTOR (V.O.)
> A great-uncle had died, leaving us
> a small fortune -- enough to buy a
> new home. *A new life.*

The family look toward the CREEL HOUSE. We recognize the house from the Upside Down. Only now -- of course -- it is brand new. What is now scary, was, at this time, beautiful.

> YOUNG VICTOR
> ... What do you think?

Shared, excited looks from the family and --

INT. CREEL HOUSE - DAY (FLASHBACK - 1959)

Everyone heads in, carrying their suitcases, looking around excitedly at this grand, empty house --

The little girl, Alice, races up the stairs to explore --

> VIRGINIA
> Alice, no running -- !!

                         ALICE
                    It's so big!!!

We PUSH IN on Young Victor, who looks on, smiling --

                         VICTOR (V.O.)
                    It was a... magnificent home --

INT. PENNHURST ASYLUM - VICTOR'S CELL - DAY

                         VICTOR
                    Alice said it looked like it was
                    from a fairy tale.

                         NANCY
                    Alice -- she was your daughter?

Victor nods. The talk of her makes him emotional --

                         VICTOR
                    But Henry -- my boy...

INT. CREEL HOUSE - DINING ROOM (FLASHBACK - 1959)

The house is now partially furnished. Henry is drawing in a JOURNAL -- when he looks up.

                         VICTOR (V.O.)
                    He was... a sensitive child. And I
                    could see -- he felt something was
                    wrong.

An overhead light begins to flicker. Spooky.

INT. PENNHURST ASYLUM - VICTOR'S CELL - DAY

                         VICTOR
                    We had one month of peace in that
                    house. And then -- it began.

EXT. PLAYGROUND - DAY (FLASHBACK - 1959)

We PULL BACK from the Creel house to find a PLAYGROUND, which is located directly across the street. Alice climbs up into a RED AND BLUE ROCKET SHIP SLIDE. She readies herself to slide down when -- PLOP -- blood drops onto her arm. She looks up and sees that blood is dripping down from the hole above.

MOMENTS LATER (FLASHBACK - 1959)

A terrified Alice slowly pokes her head through the hole. REVERSE TO REVEAL: A DEAD RABBIT on the upper floor of the rocket. Its insides have been ripped out, its guts unspooled across the cold metal. As Alice's eyes grow wide --

                    VICTOR (V.O.)
          Dead animals -- mutilated, tortured
          -- begin to appear near our home.

MOMENTS LATER (FLASHBACK - 1959)

Alice is suddenly now running across the park, terrified, fleeing back to her house.

                    VICTOR (V.O.)
          Rabbits... squirrels -- chickens...
          even dogs...

EXT. CREEL HOUSE - NIGHT (FLASHBACK - 1959)

Young Victor sits on the back porch with a rifle, watching the yard, keeping vigil --

                    VICTOR (V.O.)
          The police chief blamed the attacks
          on a wild cat. But this was no wild
          cat. This was an evil. An evil
          neither animal nor human.

INT. PENNHURST ASYLUM - VICTOR'S CELL - DAY

                    VICTOR
          This was -- a spawn of Satan. A
          Demon. And it was closer than I
          even realized.

INT. CREEL HOUSE - BATHROOM (FLASHBACK - 1959)

Virginia is drawing a bath. But no water is coming from the faucet. She smacks it. Then her eyes shoot wide as --

A HORDE OF BLACK SPIDERS crawl out of the drain, spilling out into the white tub, more and more and --

INT. PENNHURST ASYLUM - VICTOR'S CELL - DAY

                    VICTOR (V.O.)
          My family began to have encounters,
          conjured by this Demon. Nightmares
          -- _waking, living nightmares_.

MOMENTS LATER (FLASHBACK - 1959)

Young Victor enters the bathroom. But there are no spiders in the tub -- just water -- now overflowing.

VICTOR (V.O.)
This Demon -- it seemed to take
pleasure in tormenting us... even
poor, innocent Alice...

INT. CREEL HOUSE - ALICE'S BEDROOM - NIGHT (FLASHBACK - 1959)

Alice bolts upright, screaming in bed --

Young Victor and Virginia race in, hold her tight, while Henry watches from the doorway...

INT. PENNHURST ASYLUM - VICTOR'S CELL - DAY

VICTOR
It wasn't long before I began to
have... encounters of my own.

INT. CREEL HOUSE - NIGHT (FLASHBACK - 1959)

Young Victor is reading in the living room when he hears the SOUND OF A CRYING BABY. He looks toward the fireplace. In it --

A BURNING CRIB. As his eyes grow wide --

                    VICTOR (V.O.)
      ... I suppose... all evil must have
  a home.

INT. CREEL HOUSE - UPSTAIRS HALLWAY - NIGHT (1959)

Victor is walking to the stairs when he pauses. He looks back. He's noticed that the door at the end of the long hallway is cracked open. Odd...

                    VICTOR (V.O.)
      And though I had not rational
      explanation for it, I could...
      sense this Demon. Always close --

INT. CREEL HOUSE - ATTIC - NIGHT (FLASHBACK - 1959)

Victor climbs the attic steps. Pulls a string, turning on a naked lightbulb that hangs from the ceiling. His heart beats fast as he scrutinizes the darkness... stacks of lonely furniture cast unnerving shadows across the ceilings and walls...

                    VICTOR (V.O.)
      I became convinced it was hiding --
      nesting -- somewhere within the
      shadows of our home.

HIGH ANGLE SHOT OF VICTOR reveals a black widow spider crawling upside down across the rafters --

INT. PENNHURST ASYLUM - VICTOR'S CELL - DAY

                    VICTOR
      It had cursed our town. It had
      cursed our home. It had cursed...
      US.

INT. CREEL HOUSE - DINING ROOM - NIGHT (FLASHBACK - 1959)

The family is now seated around a dining table, when --

THE RADIO KICKS ON, playing Ella Fitzgerald.

Victor crosses to fix it -- when it begins to cycle rapidly through the stations. Then the rest of the house shockingly COMES ALIVE: LIGHTS FLICKER -- THE TV KICKS ON, FLIPPING CHANNELS ON ITS OWN -- EVERYTHING GOING HAYWIRE --

INT. PENNHURST ASYLUM - VICTOR'S CELL - DAY

Victor's voice now begins to shake --

> VICTOR
> It took Virginia first...

INT. CREEL HOUSE - DINING ROOM - NIGHT (FLASHBACK - 1959)

QUICK VIOLENT CUTS through STROBING LIGHTS as Virginia is FLUNG UP INTO THE AIR -- limbs snap -- her eyes SUCK IN -- Alice SCREAMS --

INT. PENNHURST ASYLUM - VICTOR'S CELL - DAY

> VICTOR
> I tried to get the children out --
> to *save them.*

INT. CREEL HOUSE - FOYER - NIGHT (FLASHBACK - 1959)

Young Victor hurries into the foyer with Alice and Henry -- but the front door is locked! He slams his shoulder into it, again and again and --

WHOOM! The door finally bursts open and Young Victor stumbles forward --

INT. OLD WAR-TORN HOUSE - NIGHT (FLASHBACK - 1959)

But he hasn't made it <u>outside</u>. Somehow, impossibly --

He's now <u>inside a small European farmhouse</u>. It's been shelled -- on fire.

>   VICTOR (V.O.)
>   I was -- back to France. Back in --
>   *the war*.

INT. PENNHURST ASYLUM - VICTOR'S CELL - DAY

>   VICTOR
>   It was a... memory. I had...
>   thought German soldiers were
>   inside... I ordered its shelling...

MOMENTS LATER (FLASHBACK - 1959)

A shaken Young Victor walks into a bombed bedroom, only to find a dead family, strewn about the floor. Then he sees --

A crib. On fire. As a horrible scream emanates from within --

>   VICTOR (V.O.)
>   *I was wrong.*

INT. PENNHURST ASYLUM - VICTOR'S CELL - DAY

Victor grows more emotional --

>   VICTOR
>   This... Demon was... *taunting me*. I
>   was sure -- he would now take me --
>   just as he had taken Virginia. But
>   then I heard another voice... a
>   *beautiful* voice. At first, I
>   believed... it *was an angel* --

INT. OLD WAR-TORN HOUSE - NIGHT (FLASHBACK - 1959)

Young Victor turns his head, listening. He can hear a woman singing in the distance.

INT. PENNHURST ASYLUM - VICTOR'S CELL - DAY

>   VICTOR
>   I followed her -- only to find
>   myself in a nightmare... far
>   worse...

INT. CREEL HOUSE - FOYER - NIGHT (FLASHBACK - 1959)

Young Victor suddenly bolts awake -- gasping for air.

He's back in this house, on the floor by the doorway. CUT HIGH AND WIDE TO REVEAL: His children are on the floor at the entryway to the house. Limp. Not moving.

>   VICTOR (V.O.)
>   While I was away -- the Demon took
>   my children --

MOMENTS LATER (FLASHBACK - 1959)

A sobbing Young Victor crawls his way from a dead, eyeless Alice to an unconscious Henry. He lifts Henry's lifeless body into his arms. Henry is bleeding from the eyes and the nose -- but his eyes are still intact. He is still alive.

As Young Victor holds his dying son in his arms, crying --

>   VICTOR (V.O.)
>   Henry slipped into a coma shortly
>   after that. A week later -- he
>   died.

INT. PENNHURST ASYLUM - VICTOR'S CELL - DAY

Victor is shaking now from the memory --

>   VICTOR
>   I-- I tried to join them --

INT. JAIL CELL - NIGHT (FLASHBACK - 1959)

A distraught Young Victor is now in another jail cell. He still has his eyes. He holds a rusty razor blade in his sweaty hand. He slowly brings it toward his left eye...

Just as Victor begins to cut --

INT. PENNHURST - VICTOR'S CELL - DAY

CLOSE ON Victor as he looks back up at the girls with those horrible ragged scars.

>   VICTOR
>   Hatch stopped the bleeding -- he
>   wouldn't... let me join them.

Victor breaks down. He'd be crying -- if he could. Instead, his whole body just shakes.

It's equal parts disturbing and heartbreaking. He begins to
hum to himself as he rocks. Nancy moves closer to the cell,
desperate --

                    NANCY
        This angel -- that you followed
        home -- who was she??

Victor doesn't respond. Just keeps rocking, humming --

                  NANCY (CONT'D)
        Victor? Victor please -- we need
        your help -- _Victor_ --

But Victor is still not responding. He is lost.

                  DIRECTOR HATCH (O.S.)
        Is he everything you hoped he would
        be?

Nancy and Robin whirl to find Director Hatch and two guards
approaching them at a fast clip. Hatch doesn't look pleased.

                  DIRECTOR HATCH (CONT'D)
        I just had a very interesting
        conversation with Professor
        Brantley.
            (beat)
        Perhaps we should discuss in my
        office... <u>while we wait for the
        police</u>.

A smile from Hatch. Off Robin and Nancy, stunned, CUT TO --

EXT. HAWKINS CEMETERY - DAY

It's getting later in the day as --

Max kneels by a GRAVESTONE AT THE TOP OF THE HILL. Our camera
rotates around Max to reveal the name on the headstone:

<u>BILLY HARGROVE</u>.

Max takes a shaky breath here... gathering herself. Then she
removes Billy's letter from the envelope. And <u>_begins to read_</u>:

                  MAX
        Dear Billy.
            (beat)
                (MORE)

                    MAX (CONT'D)
          I don't know if you can even hear
          this. Two years ago, I would've
          said that's ridiculous, *impossible*
          -- but that was before I found out
          about alternate dimensions and
          monsters, so I'm just... going to
          stop assuming I know *anything*.
               (beat)
          So much has happened since you
          left. Your dad -- was a total mess.
          He and my mom started getting into
          fights... *bad fights*. I don't think
          -- he could stand being here
          without you. So he left. And -- he
          didn't leave Mom much. She's taken
          an extra job and we've moved to --
          that *lovely* trailer park off
          Kerley. Any savings we get, Mom
          just blows it at the Hideaway.
          Basically -- ever since you left,
          everything's been... A *total
          disaster*. And the worst part is...
          I can't tell anyone why you're
          gone...
               (beat)
          I can't tell them that you saved
          El's life.
               (beat)
          That you... saved my life.
               (beat)
          I play that moment back -- in my
          head -- all the time. And
          sometimes... I imagine myself
          running to you, pulling you away...
          I imagine -- if I had -- you would
          still be here. And everything would
          be... right again.
               (beat)
          And I imagine we might have
          become... friends. *Good friends*.
          Like a real... brother and sister.
               (beat)
          I -- I know that's silly. You hated
          me -- and I hated you. But I
          thought, maybe, we could try again.

The tears are beginning to fall now --

                    MAX (CONT'D)
          But that's... not what happened. I
          just stood there. Stood... and
          watched. And now...
               (MORE)

                    MAX (CONT'D)
              (beat)
          For a while, I tried to be happy --
          normal -- but I think maybe... a
          part of me died that day too.
              (beat)
          I haven't told... anyone this. I
          just... *can't*. But I had to tell
          you... before it was too late. If
          you can even hear this. I really...
          hope you can.
              (beat)
          I'm sorry. I'm so, so sorry, Billy.
              (beat)
          Love, your shitty little sister --
          Max.

As Max wipes the tears from her eyes and folds up the letter, something strange happens -- the sun drops suddenly, the shadows of the graves moving and shifting as the light goes out of the sky, fog rolls in, and we transition to --

EXT. HAWKINS CEMETERY - MINDSCAPE - NIGHT

In the darkness, a BLURRY FIGURE stirs behind Max.

                    FAMILIAR VOICE (O.S.)
              ...*Max*...

Max turns. Her breath catches. And right here, we HARD CUT TO --

INT./EXT. STEVE'S CAR - HAWKINS CEMETERY - DAY

Steve. It's still day in the real world. Sitting in that car, drumming the steering wheel. He looks at his watch, impatient.

                    STEVE
          Okay it's been long enough --

                    LUCAS
          Give her time --

                    STEVE
          I have -- I'm calling it -- she
          wants to get a lawyer she can --

Steve throws open the door and --

EXT. HAWKINS CEMETERY - LATER - DAY

An anxious Steve hustles up the hill to Max --

                    STEVE
      Max -- time to giddy up, yeah?

She doesn't respond.

                    STEVE (CONT'D)
      Max? *Max?? Max -- come on.*

Steve finally reaches her. He finds her eyes are now half-closed and rapidly fluttering. She's in a trance. *Oh shit* --

He kneels beside her, shakes her --

                    STEVE (CONT'D)
      Max??? MAX???? MAX???

But she's not responding. *VECNA HAS HER.*

EXT. HAWKINS CEMETERY - MINDSCAPE - NIGHT

A stunned, ghost-white Max rises to her feet. Slowly walking toward her from across the dark, fog-choked graveyard:

BILLY. HE'S AS WE LAST SAW HIM, THOSE AWFUL GROTESQUE HOLES PUNCHED IN HIS BODY, WEEPING BLACK BLOOD. YET SOMEHOW, IMPOSSIBLY, *MIRACULOUSLY*, HE IS ALIVE.

Max stares, stunned. His presence is so convincing, so overwhelming, that she can't help but believe that what she's seeing is real. *That she is face to face with the ghost of her brother.* A tear slips down her quivering cheek.

                    BILLY
      I've been waiting to hear those
      words, Max.

Billy reaches her. He smiles softly.

                    BILLY (CONT'D)
      Waiting so very long.

He wipes away a falling tear. Off a shaking Max --

INT./EXT. STEVE'S CAR - HAWKINS CEMETERY - DAY

Lucas and Dustin see now that Steve is trying to wake Max from a distance.

                    LUCAS
          Something's wrong --

They leap out of the car and race up the hill as --

EXT. GRAVEYARD - MINDSCAPE - NIGHT

"Billy" continues to speak to Max.

                    BILLY
          ...But it wasn't the full truth --
          was it, Max?

Max is too shaken to respond.

                    BILLY (CONT'D)
          I think... there is a part of you --
          buried somewhere deep -- that
          wanted me to die that day... That
          was maybe even... relieved...
          happy... that I died?

Max shakes her head. This is her worst nightmare. That can't be true, it *can't be*. Her voice emerges choked, weak --

                    MAX
          No -- no... that -- that's not true
          Billy --

                    BILLY
          That's really why you stood there,
          isn't it? You can admit it now,
          Max, it's okay. No more lies. No
          more hiding.

Max begins to backpedal, shaking her head in denial.

                    MAX
          Billy, no that -- that's just --
          it's not true -- I *swear* --

Billy pursues her. Another step --

                    BILLY
          That's why you feel such guilt --
          why you hide from your friends --

                    MAX
          No -- NO --

                    BILLY
          Why you *hide from the world* --

                    MAX
          No --

                    BILLY
          Why -- late at night... you have
          sometimes wished to follow me --
          follow me into death.

                    MAX
          No *NO* --

More tears fall as those chimes begin to echo out across the
graveyard. DONG. DONG. DONG. Billy's voice begins to deepen --
becoming guttural, *monstrous*.

                    BILLY
          That is why I am here, Max. To end
          your suffering. Once and for all.

DONG! On the fourth and final chime, Max trips over a small
headstone. She falls to the ground with a gasp. Her tear-
stained eyes look back up in horror to find that where Billy
once stood now stands --

VECNA. He towers over her in the darkness.

                    VECNA
          It is time, Max. *Time to join me.*

Max stifles a scream and sprints away as fast as she can,
scrambling past headstones, as --

EXT. HAWKINS CEMETERY - DAY

Back in the real world, Lucas, Steve, and Dustin work
together to wake Max --

                    LUCAS/DUSTIN/STEVE
          MAX! MAX!! MAX! WAKE UP!!!

                    STEVE
          Robin -- Nancy -- call them!! CALL
          THEM!

                    DUSTIN
          Shitshitshit --

Dustin sprints back down the hill --

EXT. HAWKINS CEMETERY - BY STEVE'S CAR - MOMENTS LATER

Dustin grabs his backpack out of the car, removes his
supercomm, yanks up the antenna and --

                    DUSTIN
          Robin, Nancy -- do you copy??? DO
          YOU COPY???? THIS IS A CODE RED!

INT. PENNHURST ASYLUM - LISTENING ROOM - DAY

But of course they <u>don't copy</u>. A furious Director Hatch and guards are now escorting a freaked Nancy and Robin back through the asylum. *They're prisoners.*

Nancy chases behind him -- she's bright red with anger --

                    NANCY
          You're not listening -- <u>our friend
          is in danger</u> --

                    DIRECTOR HATCH
          You *really* expect me to believe
          anything you say at this point -- ?

                    NANCY
            It's _the truth_!

                    DIRECTOR HATCH
            You are free to tell your sob story
            to the police --

As Nancy's frustration grows, our attention turns to Robin. She looks around as they pass back through THE LISTENING ROOM. Patients are listening to a record, heads bobbing slowly, some _humming along_. And suddenly -- _it hits her._

WHOOM! A door flies open and --

EXT. PENNHURST ASYLUM - GARDENS - DAY

The girls are led outside, back through those outdoor gardens.

Robin quickens her pace, grabs Nancy by the arm, whispers --

                    ROBIN
            Victor said the night of the attack
            everything went on in the house,
            right? All the electronics --
                (Nancy nods)
            He made _specific mention of music_ --
            that music was playing --

FLASHBACK TO RECORD PLAYER SPINNING, PLAYING AN OLD-TIMEY TUNE AS THE ATTACK BEGINS.

                    ROBIN (CONT'D)
            And when we asked him about the
            angel -- he started to hum --

FLASHBACK TO VICTOR HUMMING --

                    ROBIN (CONT'D)
            Say "Night-ie night" -- hold me
            tight and tell me you'll miss me --
            While I'm alone and blue as can
            be....

                    NANCY
            Dream a little dream of me.

                    ROBIN
            Ella Fitzgerald --

                    NANCY
            The voice of an angel --

                    ROBIN
            Hatch said music can reach parts of
            the brain words can't -- what if
            music is the key -- a _lifeline_ --

                        NANCY
            A <u>lifeline back to reality</u>.

                        ROBIN
            Worth a shot, right?

Nancy doesn't answer -- doesn't need to. She shifts her gaze
back to the garden. Wide open. She glances back at the
trailing guards real quick, then --

                        NANCY
            I think we can beat them --

                        ROBIN
            What -- ?

                        NANCY
            To the car --

                        ROBIN
            Okay I'm warning you right now I
            have terrible coordination -- like
            it took me six months longer to
            walk than all the other babies --

                        NANCY
            Just -- stay with me --

                        ROBIN
            Oh God -- !

Nancy pulls Robin and suddenly -- THEY'RE RUNNING.

                        PENNHURST GUARDS
            HEY!!

The Guards share looks --

>   DIRECTOR HATCH
>   WHAT ARE YOU STANDING THERE FOR --
>   GET THEM!!!

Our girls sprint across the grass at high speed. Mental patients stare -- shocked --

>   ROBIN
>   Oh my God oh my God -- !!

The Pennhurst guards race after them --

>   NANCY
>   HERE!

Our girls reach the fence. They scramble up and over it as --

EXT. HAWKINS CEMETERY - MINDSCAPE - NIGHT

A panicked Max races through the fog-choked graveyard. She shoots a look over her shoulder, sees nothing through the fog. Has she escaped him? She ducks behind a mausoleum, but has barely caught her breath before --

>   VECNA (O.S.)
>   You cannot hide from me, Maxine...

She looks up, finds he's straight across from her, moving through a sea of fog. Calm. Relentless. Inevitable.

Fuck this. Max turns and begins to run again as --

EXT. PENNHURST ASYLUM - PARKING LOT - DAY

A barefoot Nancy and Robin sprint to their Wheeler Wagon --

>   PENNHURST GUARD #2
>   STOP! STOP!!

The guards have caught up to them --

The girls leap into the Wheeler Wagon, lock the doors --

BAM! The Guards bang on their windows, shouting, and --

INT./EXT. STATION WAGON - DAY

>   ROBIN
>   Go go go GO -- !!!!

Nancy kicks on the ignition, hammers the accelerator, and --

SCREECH! They speed away, <u>leaving the guards in the dust</u>.

>   ROBIN (CONT'D)
>   *Holy shit HOLY SHIT* --

As our girls catch their breath --

>   NANCY
>   You <u>are</u> a weird runner --

>   ROBIN
>   It's like I have to learn again
>   every day --

A small laugh -- the girls feel almost exhilarated from their escape -- *when* --

The supercomm blasts to life, jarring them back to reality --

                    DUSTIN (O.S.)
            This is a code red -- code red!!!
          WE NEED HELP!!! DO YOU COPY???!!!

Oh fuck! A frantic Robin reaches into the backseat, grabs up
the walkie, smashes talk --

                    ROBIN
                (out of breath)
            This -- this is Robin -- we copy!!

EXT. HAWKINS CEMETERY - DAY - INTERCUT

Dustin -- now standing *on top* of Steve's car -- can hardly
believe it's them --

                    DUSTIN
          Holy shit please please *please* tell
          me you have this figured out -- !!

As Robin and Nancy share panicked looks --

EXT. CEMETERY - MINDSACPE - NIGHT

CLOSE ON: *CONVERSES* flying through frame as --

Max sprints across the now *fully dark* cemetery, weaving
through headstones. As she runs, faster, faster, the fog
around her becomes thicker, denser, *enveloping her.* She can
now see only a few feet in front of her. She stops, whirls,
lost, trying to orient herself. She screams through panic,
tears --

                    MAX
            LUCAS??? DUSTIN??? LUCAS???

Nothing. *Wait.* She sees something, just dimly visible in the
fog: a GLOWING RED LIGHT. *Like some sort of beacon.* The hell?
As she moves toward it --

INT./EXT. STEVE'S CAR - HAWKINS CEMETERY - DAY

WHOOM! Dustin upends Max's backpack on the hood of Steve's
car. A bunch of junk spills out, including --

MAX'S WALKMAN and VARIOUS CASSETTE TAPES.

He grabs it all, shoveling them into his arms, then sprints
back up the hill as --

EXT. CEMETERY - MINDSCAPE - NIGHT

Max makes her way toward the light. As she draws closer, the ground beneath her sneakers grows wetter and wetter, as if she is moving through a swamp. Only, this swamp is soaked in --

BLOOD. Her shoes sink down into it. *It's horrible*. But there's nothing to do except keep going. *Keep moving*.

As a terrified Max presses onward, the gravestones become strange rock-like objects, smothered in vines. And then, slowly but surely the fog which envelops her parts way to reveal --

INT. VECNA'S MIND LAIR

A terrible, nightmarish world. This is VECNA'S MIND LAIR.

It is best described as a *HELLISH SWAMP*. There is fog, *lots of fog,* and blood-red water covers the ground as far as the eye can see. Up ahead, not fifty yards away, there is a small island, on which rests the BROKEN PIECES OF AN OLD HOUSE. Large objects FLOAT around and above this house, hovering in the sky. It is haunting... unnerving... *surreal...*

As Max begins to wade through the red water, heading toward this strange house...

EXT. HAWKINS CEMETERY - SUNDOWN

An out-of-breath Dustin races up to Steve and Lucas, who are trying -- *and failing* -- to wake Max, her eyes still fluttering, in that trance. Behind them, the sun has begun to set.

                    DUSTIN
          Guys -- guys -- !!

He races up to Lucas -- passes those cassette tapes --

                    LUCAS
          What is this -- ??

                    DUSTIN
          Her song -- do you know her
          favorite song -- ??

                    LUCAS
          What??? Why???

                    DUSTIN
          Robin said that -- it's too hard to
          explain just WHAT'S HER FAVORITE
          SONG?!

As Lucas frantically digs through the cassette tapes --

INT. VECNA'S MIND LAIR

Max now steps onto the island. She looks around in awe, fear
-- she sees a ruined staircase... the grandfather clock,
drifting through the air... nearby, a broken door with a
stained glass window, also floating.

                    VECNA (O.S.)
          Maxxxxxx... what are you doing in
          here, Max??? Come back to me,
          Max...

CRACK! Something suddenly CRACKS. She looks down and sees she
has stepped onto a HUMAN SKULL. A NASTY SPIDER crawls out of
its twisted jaw. Max backs away in horror and --

WHAM! Slams into something. She whirls, choking back a scream
thinking it's Vecna -- but it's CHRISSY'S EYELESS CORPSE,
which has been strung up on a twisted pillar. Upside Down
vines grow around and *into* her body, taking her over.

As Max backs away -- she sees there are in fact MANY
PILLARS, all displaying Vecna's past victims. We recognize
FRED, but not the others -- their bodies are too rotted to
identify.
                    VECNA (CONT'D)
          How do you like them, Max?

This time -- the voice came from behind her.

She turns. Sees Vecna. Not twenty feet away.

He walks toward her. Methodical.

                    VECNA (CONT'D)
          Would you like -- to join them?

Max turns and starts to run, but she doesn't make it far
before --

THWACK! A vine grabs her leg, sending her splashing face-
first into the gross red water. She tries to scramble up,
but --

THWACK! Another vine snares her right arm. Then another vine snares her left arm. Then --

WHOOM! She's yanked back against a broken wall and --

THWACK! -- a third vine wraps *AROUND HER THROAT*, coiling around it like a boa constrictor, as --

EXT. HAWKINS CEMETERY - SUNDOWN

WHUMP! Lucas opens the Kate Bush *HOUNDS OF LOVE* cassette tape. He slams it into the walkman and --

                        LUCAS
          Go go go -- !

Dustin quickly places the headphones over her ears as --

Lucas smashes [PLAY] and --

INT. VECNA'S MIND LAIR

Max struggles ferociously, trying to tear herself free from these awful vines, but she can't move, can't breathe. She's held in place and forced to watch as --

Vecna approaches, slowly, methodically... *in total control.*

But then, suddenly, she hears her, distant, *but there:*

Kate Bush. "Running Up That Hill." She turns her head as much as she can to the left, toward the source of the music. Then, far away, some of the red fog peels away -- like a storm cloud blown by wind -- to reveal THE GRAVEYARD. Her friends hover around her, in the falling sun, shouting, trying to wake her, but --

                        VECNA
          They can't help you, Max...

Vecna is now upon her. Those awful white eyes bore into her.

                        VECNA (CONT'D)
          There's a reason you hide from
          them. You belong here... *with me* --

                        MAX
               (strained, choked)
          You're not -- really here--

                        VECNA
          But I am -- Max -- I AM.

He hovers his mutated hand over her face, just as he did with Chrissy and Fred. As his eyes roll back into his forehead --

BACK IN THE CEMETERY,

Max begins to lift up into the air, LEVITATING --

The boys back away, startled, eyes wide with horror as --

BACK IN THE MIND LAIR,

Vecna's claws dig deeper into Max's head.

ECU as Max squeezes her eyes tight. She focuses on the music... letting it WASH over her... as the music grows louder and LOUDER, we --

FLASHBACK TO

IMAGES OF FRIENDSHIP FROM THE PAST -- MAX WITH HER FRIENDS -- DANCING WITH LUCAS -- SHOPPING WITH ELEVEN -- SMILING --

BUT BACK IN THE MIND LAIR,

Vecna's fingers begin to curl, a split second from plunging into her forehead when --

                    MAX
      AHHHH!!!!

Max lets out a ferocious scream and rips her right hand from those vines and then--

WHAM! She grabs a tendril on Vecna's neck and pulls with all her strength. THWACK! It snaps in half! Black blood spatters and --

Vecna stumbles back in pain, DROPPING HER. As he releases her, so do the vines and --

Max plummets back down into the blood-red water.

She scrambles back to her feet and begins to run with everything she's got, toward that music, *toward her friends* --

Vecna watches her go. Though he shows little emotion, we sense a hint of surprise -- of <u>anger</u>. But he does not chase her. He does not need to. He simply *curls* his claw and --

Those LARGE OBJECTS begin to FALL FROM THE SKY. They crash into the ground at high speed, narrowly missing Max, shattering into a thousand pieces around her.

Max doesn't slow -- just keeps running -- as Vecna sends more objects crashing down around her. Red water erupts around her like she's in some hellish war zone -- her face spattered with bloodred water now -- but through it all --

She never slows -- just keeps running faster and faster --

Almost to the light -- almost there -- almost --

She lets out a scream and --

BLACK.

Silence. Then --

CEMETERY

WHOOM! Levitating Max suddenly DROPS onto the ground –

She gasps for air, back to reality as --

INT. ATTIC - NIGHT (UPSIDE DOWN)

Vecna's eyes snap open. He's now back in the Upside Down!

The vines detach and he drops to the floor, defeated, as --

EXT. CEMETERY - SUNDOWN

The boys surround Max on the ground, panicked --

>   LUCAS/DUSTIN
>   Max -- MAX???

She's so scared she can hardly breathe. She chokes back tears as a tearful Lucas pulls her into his arms --

>   LUCAS
>   I thought we lost you...

>   MAX
>   I'm still here... *I'm still here...*

Dustin moves in, holding her too --

Steve looks on, fighting tears himself, and we slowly PULL AWAY, until they are all small figures silhouetted in the dying sun.

<u>END EPISODE</u>

EPISODE FIVE

CHAPTER FIVE:
THE NINA PROJECT

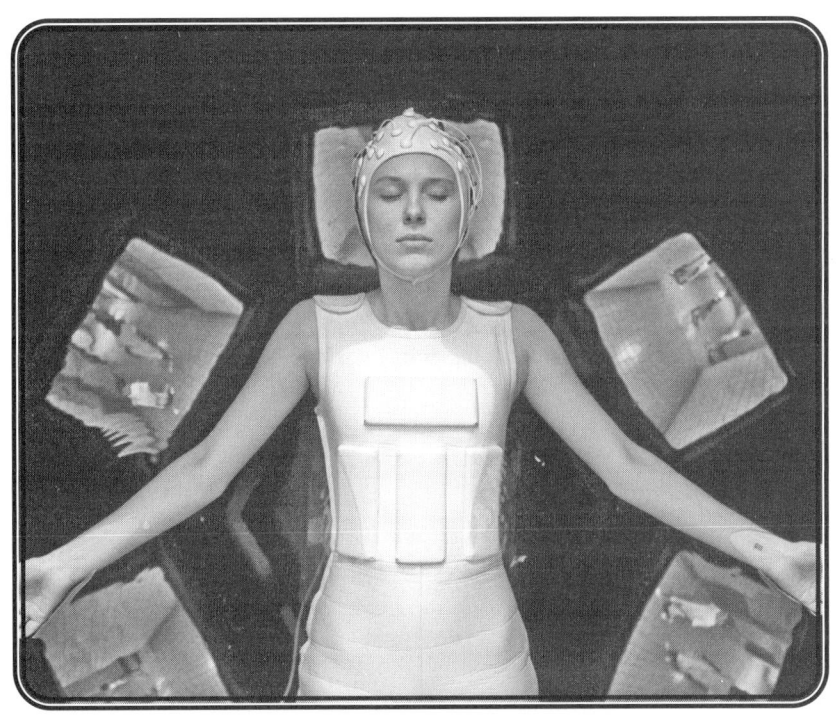

WRITTEN BY **KATE TREFRY**

EXT. LENORA ROAD - NIGHT

We open on a Lenora road. All is quiet. Peaceful. Then --

SCREECH! THE SURFER BOY PIZZAMOBILE swerves into view, tires _squealing_ --

>   ARGYLE (PRE-LAP)
>   Oh my God oh my God OH MY GOD!!!

INT. PIZZAMOBILE - NIGHT

It's pure chaos in the car, surfer music still blasting while ARGYLE drives -- _horribly_. He keeps shooting panicked looks into the back, where --

MIKE, JONATHAN, and WILL are trying to save AGENT HARMON, who is bleeding badly from that gunshot wound to the chest --

They press a stack of SURFER BOY PIZZA NAPKINS against the wound, but blood keeps seeping through the napkins --

>   WILL
>   It's not slowing -- !
>
>   ARGYLE
>   Oh Jesus -- I'm think I'm gonna
>   faint dude -- _I'm gonna faint_ --
>
>   JONATHAN
>   (to Argyle)
>   Just get us to Saint Mary's --
>
>   ARGYLE
>   Dude I don't know if praying is
>   gonna help that dude -- !
>
>   JONATHAN
>   The hospital -- Saint Mary's
>   _hospital_ -- !!
>
>   AGENT HARMON
>   No... _no hospital_ --

All eyes swivel back to Agent Harmon. The color has drained from his face and his voice is choked. He's got very little life left in him, but he is able to get out:

>   AGENT HARMON (CONT'D)
>   You have to -- to _warn Owens_ -- the
>   girl... is in danger --

Mike pales --

> JONATHAN
> How -- how do we find him?

> AGENT HARMON
> (low)
> Nina --

> MIKE
> Nina -- who is Nina??

> AGENT HARMON
> Num... ber...

> JONATHAN
> Number -- we can call her?? This Nina?

Harmon tries to speak -- to get out this last bit of vital information -- but his breathing is now too labored. With a shaky, bloody hand, he removes a BLACK PEN from a pocket.

And suddenly Mike understands --

> MIKE
> He wants to write -- paper -- I need paper -- !!!

Will grabs a nearby magazine (*High Times*, of course) and passes it to Mike, who slides it to Harmon. But it's too late -- Harmon's head is now slumped to his chest. His eyes flutter to a close.

> MIKE (CONT'D)
> Hey, hey -- stay with us -- *stay with us* -- *PLEASE*!

Mike shakes Harmon -- but his body is now totally limp. The pen slips out of his hand and rolls across the truck bed.

Jonathan checks his pulse. Shakes his head. *He's gone.* As our boys take in the gravity of this --

> ARGYLE
> Why it is so quiet back there?! Is he dead -- oh God please tell me that dude isn't dead!!!

Will's face suddenly darkens as he notices --

HEADLIGHTS behind them. And growing. *A tail?*

                    WILL
          We should get off the road --

Jonathan spins to Argyle --

                    JONATHAN
          Argyle -- get us off this road --

                    ARGYLE
          He's dead isn't he?! Oh Jesus man,
          this is bad, this is *REAL BAD* --

                    JONATHAN/MIKE/WILL
          GET OFF THE ROAD -- !!!

Argyle spins the wheel and --

EXT. LENORA ROAD - PIZZAMOBILE - NIGHT

The Pizzamobile swerves off the main road, tires SQUEALING.
As a cloud of dust hits camera, we SMASH TO --

INT. BYERS HOUSE - VARIOUS - NIGHT

A SERIES OF QUICK SHOTS as SOLDIERS sweep through the Byers
house, scouring all the rooms -- opening closets -- flipping
over beds -- shoving aside couches -- just violently tearing
through every inch of the house as they search for Eleven.

INT. ELEVEN'S ROOM - NIGHT

SULLIVAN moves through Eleven's room -- his eyes roam past
Hopper's destroyed cabin to the nearby trashcan. He reaches
in and pulls out a balled-up piece of paper. Unfurls it.

          "Dear Mike. I have gone to become a
          superhero again. From, El."

His face tightens and --

INT. BYERS HOUSE - LIVING ROOM - NIGHT

GLASS CRUNCHES beneath the heel of Sullivan's boot as he
makes his way across the destroyed house and over to --

WALLACE, who is against a wall. His face pale, his breathing
shallow, his shirt soaked in blood. He is alive -- but <u>only
barely</u>.

Sullivan kneels beside him.

                    SULLIVAN
          I know she was just here.
                (beat)
          And if you want to live... you're
          going to tell me where she is.

Off Wallace, trembling, HARD CUT TO --

INT. BLACK SEDAN - DESERT - DAY

A CU OF ELEVEN. Her eyes are shut. *Sleeping.*

Her head jostles, waking her. WIDEN: She is in the back of
the government car. She looks out the window -- she's in a
desert. Nothing around but cacti, sand, low rolling hills.

                    DR. OWENS
          Apologies for the bumpy ride,
          kiddo.

OWENS looks back at her from the passenger seat.

                    DR. OWENS (CONT'D)
          I would've paved a road -- but that
          kinda ruins the whole top secret
          location thing. You get some rest?

                    ELEVEN
          A little.

                    DR. OWENS
          Good. I have a feeling you're going
          to need it.

As Eleven takes this in --

EXT. DESERT ROAD - DAY

VROOM! The sedan roars past camera, driving through an
endless desert, no civilization in sight.

CHYRON: RUTH, NEVADA. 12 HOURS EARLIER.

LATER

The sedan pulls to a stop. The doors open and --

Eleven, Owens, and the DRIVER exit. There is nothing around
save for a SMALL CONCRETE SHED. It is nondescript and
unimpressive, with a metal door and an electronic keypad.

Owens punches a code into the keypad, then --

EEEEE! An electronic lock opens and --

INT. SHED - CONTINUOUS

Owens leads Eleven into the shed. More buttons line the wall. Owens hits one, and a gate shoots down, enclosing them in here, startling El.

> DR. OWENS
> You didn't really think we were working out of a shed, did you?

He punches another button and the room begins to descend. *It's an elevator*. El grabs a railing for support as --

INT. ELEVATOR SHAFT - DAY

The rickety elevator plummets below the earth and...

INT. ELEVATOR - MOMENTS LATER

WHOOM! It rocks to a stop. The doors yawn open and --

INT. SILO LAB - CORRIDOR - DAY

Owens leads El out into a LONG, ROUND, CORRUGATED METAL CORRIDOR. It looks like we're in a spaceship from the 1970s. Grungy, retro, but the scale is nevertheless impressive.

> ELEVEN
> (looking around)
> You... built all this??

> DR. OWENS
> More like... gave it a facelift. You know what an ICBM is?

El shakes her head --

> DR. OWENS (CONT'D)
> Stands for Intercontinental Ballistic Missile --
> (still no help)
> Basically -- a fancy bomb. We used to store them underground in these silos, but we haven't used this one in years. In fact there's no bomb in here at all. It's just a big ol' empty space... So we repurposed it to hold something even more powerful than a missile -- *you*.

A small smile from Owens as they now pass through --

A HIGH-TECH LABORATORY - CONTINUOUS

There are NUMEROUS SCIENTISTS here, working on various machines. Among other things, we see a row of computers, some strange vials containing a MYSTERIOUS DRUG, as well as CAGES FILLED WITH MICE.

The scientists all turn to look at Eleven as she passes.

                    DR. OWENS
          Traci, Dan -- morning.

       SCIENTIST #1   SCIENTIST #2
Morning, Doctor --   Morning --

Their eyes follow Eleven. A few whisper to one another --

                    DR. OWENS
          You'll have to forgive the staring
          -- you're something of a celebrity
          around here.

                    ELEVEN
          I... am?

                    DR. OWENS
            (smiles)
          Absolutely. To them -- you're
          bigger than Madonna.

They now pass by some LIVING QUARTERS.

                    DR. OWENS (CONT'D)
          They've given up their lives, their
          jobs, their families, to come and
          work on this program. All because
          they believe in the cause. Because
          they believe in <u>you</u>.

As El takes this in, not sure how to respond or feel about any of this, Owens leads her through some large doors into --

INT. ANTENNA SILO - DAY

This was once the antenna silo, but is now home to a LARGE BLACK TANK. It looks like some sort of '70s time capsule.

                    DR. OWENS
          We call her Nina.

                    ELEVEN
          What... is it?

                    VOICE (O.S.)
          If we told you, that would ruin the
          surprise, wouldn't it?

Eleven turns toward the voice. Her eyes go wide. Her breath catches. It's...

<u>DR. BRENNER</u>. *PAPA*. HE'S WALKING DOWN SOME METAL STEPS TOWARD HER. HIS FACE IS SCARRED FROM THE DEMOGORGON ATTACK -- BUT HE'S VERY MUCH ALIVE AND WELL.

                    DR. BRENNER
          Hello, Eleven.

Eleven is frozen. She can't speak, can't move.

A look of guilt washes over Owens.

                    DR. OWENS
          I'm sorry, kiddo. If you knew,
          you'd never have come...

Dr. Brenner descends the final step. He is careful, delicate.

                    DR. BRENNER
          I know you are frightened of me.
          Perhaps in our time apart -- you
          have even come to hate me. But I
          have only ever wanted to help you.
          And I think... right now... you
          very much need my help. Your
          gifts... have been stolen from you.
          I believe I know why. And I
          believe... I know how to get them
          back.

He stops. He's now not much more than five feet from El.

                    DR. BRENNER (CONT'D)
          What do you say? Let us work
          together, once again. Papa... and
          daughter.

Dr. Brenner holds out his hand. As Eleven stares at that, her breath quickens and --

WE ARE BOMBARDED WITH IMAGES FROM HER TRAUMATIC PAST WITH BRENNER: SHE IS THROWN INTO THE ISOLATION ROOM -- SCREAMS IN THE TANK -- FINDS THE DEMOGORGON -- THE RIFT OPENS -- AND --

Eleven shakes her head, her fear turning to rage --

                      ELEVEN
          No -- NO -- *NO!*

She breaks into a run, shoving past Brenner, and suddenly --

INT. SILO LAB - MOMENTS LATER

She's racing back down the corridor. But she doesn't make it far before she slams to a stop.

REVERSE TO REVEAL: LAB GUARDS, obstructing her escape.

                LEAD LAB GUARD
         Why don't you go back inside? Play
         nice with the doctor, huh?

Screw it -- she runs, *fast*, trying to blow right past them, but --

WHAM! They catch her in their arms, holding her back. She fights and kicks, ferocious, but without her powers she's no match for these grown men. As they hold her down tight --

SCIENTIST #3, female, approaches. She carries a NEEDLE GUN.

                SCIENTIST #3
         The more you move -- the more this
         will hurt.

Eleven braces herself, biting back a scream, as --

THWACK! The scientist jabs the needle into Eleven's neck and shoots that strange drug into her veins. Her vision begins to go, but in her fading vision, she can just make out...

Dr. Brenner. Approaching. He appears genuinely pained to see her like this.

                DR. BRENNER
         I'm sorry, Eleven. This is not how
         I wanted things to begin.

He reaches out a hand, strokes her hair. Gentle. Loving.

                DR. BRENNER (CONT'D)
         But everything is going to be okay.
         You're home now. *You're home*.

As Eleven's vision goes black, we CRASH TO --

MAIN TITLES

EXT. RUSSIAN PRISON - TORTURE ROOM - NIGHT

Our CAMERA SOARS toward the Kamchatka prison.

INT. RUSSIAN PRISON - TORTURE ROOM - NIGHT

THWACK! A baton smacks HOPPER across the face. He crumples to the cement floor.

WIDEN: PRISON GUARDS are beating HOPPER when --

>   WARDEN MELNIKOV
>   <Enough!>

The guards turn to find WARDEN MELNIKOV approaching, severe --

>   WARDEN MELNIKOV (CONT'D)
>   <He is not yours to kill. *Fools*.>

The guards lower their heads -- apologetic.

The Warden kneels beside Hopper. Their eyes meet.

>   WARDEN MELNIKOV (CONT'D)
>   (broken English)
>   What I tell you, American -- <u>no
>   run</u>. You do not listen. Now... is
>   going to be -- much pain. <u>Much</u>.

Hopper spits blood onto the Warden's shiny black shoe. The Warden barely flinches. He simply wipes the blood away, nods to his guards. They grab Hopper up by the arms and --

INT. RUSSIAN PRISON - CORRIDOR - NIGHT

WHOOSH! Dirty bare feet *scrape* across concrete as the guards drag a weak Hopper down a grimy corridor. They fling open a door as they haul him into a new area we'll call --

THE PIT - CONTINUOUS

It's a very large round room, three stories high. Oddly, there is no roof in this part of the prison, allowing snow to fall from above. Hopper blinks blood out of his eyes, observes his surroundings, sees --

-- FRIGHTENED, HAUNTED PRISONERS looking at him from behind bars on the second floor --

-- A LARGE METAL DOOR.

-- Medieval-style weapons, scattered across the snowy ground -- an AXE, a SWORD, a SPEAR, a MACE.

-- And most of all, BLOOD. LOTS OF BLOOD. Covering the ground, the walls. Whatever this place is... whatever its purpose... *it reeks of death*.

EXT. HOLDING CELL - THE PIT - NIGHT

WHAM! The guards fling Hopper into a large second-story holding cell that contains the other prisoners (six in total, including Hop).

He climbs weakly to his feet. Breathing hard. He then limps to the cell bars, which overlook the pit. As it sinks in that he is once more a prisoner...

>   VOICE (O.S.)
>   It could be worse, American -- at
>   least you have company.

Hopper turns in surprise to find a broken DMITRI stepping out of the shadows of the cell. He is bruised and beaten.

Hopper stares at him, stunned --

>   DMITRI
>   Your eyes don't deceive you --
>   (beat)
>   I am a prisoner now, like you.
>   Yuri, the smuggler... he betrayed
>   me. Betrayed *us*.

A beat as Hopper absorbs this. Then suddenly he SWINGS, and PUNCHES Dmitri, who goes down. The other prisoners launch to their feet, including a gruff prisoner, OLEG, 40s, who seems to be enjoying the entertainment --

>   OLEG
>   <And the moosor's day just gets
>   worse -- *shame*.>

The other prisoners laugh as --

WHAM! Hopper punches Dmitri again, then slams the bleeding Dmitri against a wall -- growls --

>   HOPPER
>   You said we could trust him -- YOU
>   SWORE TO ME -- !!

                    DMITRI
          Because I believed WE COULD!! Do
          you think this is what I planned??
          I have lost everything. EVERYTHING.
          We both knew the risks!!! BOTH OF
          US. We gambled today. And we lost.
          We LOST.

Hopper hesitates, that fist still pulled back --

                    OLEG
          <What are you waiting for,
          American? Do us all the favor --
          finish him.>

And Hopper looks like he might just do as Oleg requests --
might just kill Dmitri here and now. He releases a violent
scream and swings with all his might and --

Punches the wall right by Dmitri's head. Then --

Hopper drops down onto a decrepit bench. Shaken. His knuckles
are now raw, bleeding. Dmitri slumps down weakly against the
wall opposite.

Oleg and the others shake their heads, let down by this
anticlimax, then retreat back into the shadows.

Hopper, head down, is now processing everything, letting that
rage run off him. Then, a dark thought. His trembling eyes
move to Dmitri.

                    HOPPER
               (through heavy breaths)
          ... Joyce? What about Joyce?

Off Dmitri, who clearly has some bad news, HARD CUT TO --

EXT. YURI'S FISH N FLY - MORNING

Snow falling outside Yuri's hanger. The sun is rising. A new
day. PRE-LAP: WHISTLING...

INT. YURI'S FISH N FLY - HANGAR - MORNING

YURI whistles as he works on his plane. He uses a wrench to
screw a part in place. But nothing happens. He frowns, then
kicks the plane hard in its belly, and --

CH-CH-CH-CHOOOOM! The PROPELLER starts to spin. That did it!

A big smile spreads across Yuri's face.

                    YURI
          <There you are, my girl, *there you
          are!*>

INT. YURI'S PLANE - MORNING

A satisfied Yuri hops up into the back of the plane. It's overflowing with CARGO BOXES -- the same kind we saw in the abandoned Kamchatka church. *Smuggled goods*. But this time, Yuri is also bringing along a *different* type of cargo --

JOYCE AND MURRAY. Their hands have been tied to rusted metal seats. *Prisoners*.

                    YURI
          Why the long faces? Are you not
          excited for your journey across the
          iron curtain???

Yuri heads for his cargo boxes, starts opening them, looking for something.

                    JOYCE
          Yuri -- you don't have to do this --

                    YURI
          KGB is expecting you now -- so, I
          think I very much *do* --

                    JOYCE
          I, I have a family -- three kids --
          waiting for me --

                    YURI
          That is touching story, very
          touching --

                    JOYCE
          At least let me call them -- say
          goodbye --

                    YURI
          And *HELLLLLO!*

Yuri yanks a BOTTLE OF CRUNCHY PEANUT BUTTER out of a crate, then spins back to his captives.

                    YURI (CONT'D)
          Did you know peanut butter is
          banned in the Motherland?
                    (starts to unscrew cap)
                    (MORE)

                    YURI (CONT'D)
          I buy for a dollar thirty here --
          sell for *twenty* dollar there.
          Crunchy style sells for *twenty-five*
          -- *everybody* loves crunchy style.

                    MURRAY
          Your mother must be very proud.

Yuri's face turns to anger, sadness.

                    YURI
          My mother is dead.

Murray tenses -- *oops* -- then --

                    YURI (CONT'D)
          Dead TIRED of living like a bum.

Yuri cackles as walks over to them, plops beside them.

                    YURI (CONT'D)
          You see -- Yuri has family too. And
          with money I earn from selling you
          -- I will buy her *new house*. I will
          buy my daughter a pony. I will buy
          my virgin son a large-bosomed
          prostitute. Whatever they desire,
          from now on, they *will have*. And
          yes -- for that -- my mother will
          be very, *very proud*.

With that, Yuri strides away into --

THE COCKPIT - CONTINUOUS

He plops down in the pilot seat, sets down the peanut butter, flips some buttons, and --

EXT. YURI'S FISH N FLY - RUNWAY - MOMENTS LATER

VROOM! The plane speeds down the snowy runway.

INT. YURI'S PLANE - DAY

                    YURI
              (calling back)
          Hold tight, this is not American
          Airlines -- it is going to get bit
          choppy!!!

Joyce and Murray are jostled violently as --

EXT. YURI'S FISH N FLY - RUNWAY - MOMENTS LATER

The plane *achieves takeoff* and suddenly --

EXT. HAWKINS - LOVER'S LAKE - MORNING

We're flying through sky, only now there are lush green trees below us. We're back in Hawkins.

We soar over some trees to find Lover's Lake. A small FISHING BOAT bobs in the water.

ON A DOCK,

We find two FISHERMEN, 50s (both wearing Hawkins Tigers gear, caps, etc.). While one casts out a line, the other squints his eyes, noticing something in the distance.

>   FISHERMAN #1
>   When'd Rick get out of jail -- ?

Fisherman #2 follows his gaze. Across the way, he sees a silhouetted figure moving in the window of Rick's house.

>   FISHERMAN #2
>   Justice system is a *goddamn joke.*

He shakes his head, casts out his line and --

INT. LIPTON HOUSE - KITCHEN - MORNING

We reveal it's not Rick -- it's EDDIE! He's scrounging around the kitchen in search of food. Finds some moldy bread. Some rotten fruit. And... a can of SPAGHETTIOS WITH MEATBALLS.

>   EDDIE
>   ... Guess you'll do...

MOMENTS LATER

FWOOM! The stove kicks on as Eddie heats up the SpaghettiOs in a pot. As it heats, he walks away, making a call on his walkie --

>   EDDIE
>   Hey Dustin -- this is Eddie the
>   Banished, you there?

INT. WHEELER HOUSE - BASEMENT - MORNING

                EDDIE (O.S.)
        (filtered)
  Dusssttin -- you there, man?

We PAN from Dustin's walkie to reveal DUSTIN is fast asleep in Mike's basement. In fact -- the WHOLE GROUP is here, and they're ALL asleep, recovering from their traumatic night.

              EDDIE (O.S.) (CONT'D)
        (filtered)
  Dustin -- earth to Dustin!

Eddie's voice wakes NANCY. She sits up, groggily grabs the walkie --

              NANCY
  Hey, it's Nancy --

INT. LIPTON HOUSE - VARIOUS - INTERCUT

Eddie has now reached the far side of the house; he's looking out a screen door toward Lover's Lake.

              EDDIE
  Wheeler. Hey so -- I'm gonna need
  another food delivery soon -- 'less
  you want me venturing out into the
  world --

              NANCY
  No no -- *don't do that.* Just --
  stay where you are. We'll be there
  as soon as we can --

              EDDIE
  Not to be a pain but there any way
  you can swing me a six-pack? I know
  it seems stupid as shit to be
  drinking right now, but a cold beer
  would actually do a *helluva lot* to
  calm my jangled nerves ya know --

Nancy is now ignoring him -- she's now focused on the couch, which is empty, sheets thrown off --

              NANCY
  Hey -- I'm gonna have to call you
  back --

INT. WHEELER HOUSE - BASEMENT - MOMENTS LATER

She shakes Dustin awake --

                NANCY
        Dustin -- Dustin -- !

He wakes up with a start --

                DUSTIN
        Huh -- what -- ?

                NANCY
        Aren't you on Max watch -- ??

                DUSTIN
        Max watch -- yep, yes, uh huh --

                NANCY
        Okay then where is she -- ?

                DUSTIN
        She's right --
            (he clocks the empty sofa)
        There. A second ago. I swear! I
        just dozed off for --

He checks watch, blinks --

                DUSTIN (CONT'D)
        An hour?

Nancy stares at him in *utter disbelief* and --

INT. WHEELER HOUSE - KITCHEN - DAY

Nancy and Dustin race into the kitchen, where they find --

KAREN merrily cooking pancakes. TED is at the counter, reading the Hawkins Post. A headline reads: "SPRING BREAK KILLER STILL AT LARGE: FRUSTRATION MOUNTS AS NO SUSPECT NAMED."

                KAREN
        Morning, guys -- !
            (noticing concern)
        Everything okay?

Nancy crashes to stop as she reaches the far side of the kitchen -- and breathes a sigh of relief.

                    NANCY
          Yeah... yeah. *Everything's okay.*

REVERSE TO REVEAL: MAX, those Walkman headphones still on,
sitting calmly at the kitchen table alongside HOLLY, who is
playing with a Lite-Brite. <u>Safe</u>.

Karen sidles up to Nancy.

                    KAREN
          ... I think it's so sweet you all
          are sticking together like this --

                    TED
               (behind paper)
          Could try "sticking together" at a
          different house for a change --

Karen shoots Ted a look, then turns to Dustin --

                    KAREN
          You're welcome here *any time* -- you
          know that, right, sweetie -- ?

                    DUSTIN
          Totally. You're like family.
               (re: pancakes)
          May I?

                    TED
          Why not? Just take us for all we're
          worth.

As Dustin starts to heap PANCAKES and BACON onto a plate --

KITCHEN DINING ROOM - MOMENTS LATER

Nancy sits down beside Max. We now see that Max is working on
A SERIES OF DRAWINGS, which are scattered across the kitchen
table -- she's clearly been at this for some time.

She slips off the headphones.

                    MAX
          Hey --

                    NANCY
          Hey... you okay -- ?

                    MAX
          I just... couldn't sleep. People
          kept blasting music in my ears for
          some reason.

A shared smile.

                    MAX (CONT'D)
          But Holly let me borrow some of her
          crayons. We've been having a fun
          morning, right, Holly?

Holly nods as she sticks a light pin into her Lite-Brite.

Nancy's eyes return to Max's work. She's been attempting to
visualize Vecna's disturbing "mindscape." The drawings are
sketchy... but they're nevertheless *unnerving*. Strange shapes
jutting out of red fog, objects floating in the air.

                    NANCY
          Is this -- what you saw last night?

                    MAX
          It's... *supposed* to be. I thought
          it might be easier to draw than
          explain... but -- not so much...

Nancy points to vines stretching across two shapes. Hanging
inside them: *Fred and Chrissy.*

                    NANCY
          Is that...?

Max offers a somber nod.

                    MAX
          It's like they were -- *on display
          or something*. And there was this --
          red fog -- everywhere. It was like
          a dream -- *a nightmare*.

                    HOLLY
          I had a dream where I pooped jelly
          beans --

                    NANCY
              (ignoring this)
          You think Vecna was just trying to
          scare you -- showing you these
          things?

                    MAX
          In Starcourt, with Billy -- yes.
          But when I made it here... I don't
          know. Something was different. He
          seemed -- *surprised almost*. It was
          like, he didn't want me there --

                    DUSTIN (O.S.)
          Maybe you infiltrated his mind --

Dustin now drops by the table with his pancakes, mouth full
as he speaks.

                    DUSTIN (CONT'D)
          I mean -- he invaded *your* mind,
          right? Is it that big of a leap to
          suggest you somehow you wound up in
          his? Like Freddy Krueger's boiler
          room or something ---

                    HOLLY
          Freddy Krueger?

                    DUSTIN
          He's this super burned dude with
          razors for fingers who kills you in
          your dreams --

Holly's eyes go wide.

                    NANCY
          Dustin, *seriously* -- ?

                    DUSTIN
          Sorry. I'm just saying -- what if
          Max stumbled across a back door
          into Vecna's world? Maybe the
          answers we need are right here in
          this...
                    (squints)
          Incredibly vague drawing. Am I
          holding this the right way -- ?

                    MAX
          Yes --

                    DUSTIN
          We *really* need Will --

                    MAX
          Yeah no shit but I tried them again
          this morning, same busy signal --

DUSTIN
So either Joyce starts work earlier
than we thought -- or something
more sinister is going on --

NANCY
What could be "sinister" -- they're
two thousand miles away -- sorry,
can I -- ?

Nancy takes the drawing from Dustin, places it by Max, points
to an object in it --

NANCY (CONT'D)
Is that a window -- ?

MAX
Yeah --

NANCY
Stained glass -- *with roses* -- ?

MAX
Yep.
(to Dustin)
See, I'm not *so* terrible after all.

NANCY
It helps that I've seen it before.

Max and Dustin share surprised looks as --

Nancy grabs a crayon and begins to draw on *top* of Max's
drawing... filling in those strange shapes... adding a door
around the stained glass window... some walls... a roof...
and gradually, the others begin to understand --

MAX
It's... pieces of a house --

NANCY
Not just any house.
(looks up)
<u>Victor Creel's</u>.

Nancy grabs the drawing, hurries off --

DUSTIN
Where are you going -- ??

NANCY
Waking the others.

353

Dustin and Max share looks, then race after her. As they pass the kitchen counter, Dustin sweeps up another strip of bacon.

Ted sighs, snaps his newspaper in irritation, and --

INT. UNKNOWN ROOM - DAY

WHOOM! Eleven shoots awake with a gasp.

She looks around, frightened, her blurry vision gradually coming into focus. She sees white tiled walls... a heavy door... a metal lamp. She's been here before. *She knows this place. We* know this. It's her old room from --

HAWKINS LABS

Eleven looks down to find she's wearing her old hospital gown. She then looks behind her to find a child's drawing, featuring her young self and "Papa," holding hands.

Her breathing quickens. Panicking. *This can't be real...*

She slides off the bed, crosses to that heavy door, and tests the handle. To her surprise -- *it opens*.

INT. HAWKINS LABS - HALLWAY - DAY (MEMORY)

She steps out into a hallway, looks around.

There are cameras mounted on the ceiling, but no people, no guards. She is seemingly all alone in here.

She begins to make her way down the corridor. The audience will recognize this corridor from the season opener. There are rooms on either side, each marked with numbers, in descending order. *010... 09... 08... 07... 06...*

Just as she takes this in, stunned, she hears VOICES.

She rounds a corner and --

INT. HAWKINS LABS - HALLWAY 2 - DAY (MEMORY)

At the far end, there is a door with a familiar RAINBOW painted on it. The voices are coming from behind it.

INT. RAINBOW ROOM - DAY (MEMORY)

Eleven enters the room. REVERSE TO REVEAL --

THE RAINBOW ROOM. The other NUMBERS are here.

There are about fifteen in total. Their ages range from seven to sixteen -- although on average they skew younger. They all wear hospital gowns and their heads are shaved.

They remain laser-focused on various activities -- the youngest Numbers are playing with blocks, puzzles, toys. The older ones (including a boy whom we'll soon come to know as their leader, TWO) are playing chess.

Eleven stares, taking them all in, shocked, when --

>   VOICE (O.S.)
>   Well, well -- look who finally
>   decided to join us.

Eleven turns to find an unfamiliar MALE ORDERLY approaching her. He's young, tall, late 20s, friendly.

>   FRIENDLY ORDERLY
>   Someone's a sleepyhead this
>   morning.

Eleven is so shaken she can barely get the words out.

>   ELEVEN
>   ... Where... am I?

The Orderly smiles a bit at this.

>   FRIENDLY ORDERLY
>   I guess you're still not quite
>   awake, huh?

>   ELEVEN
>   Am I... in Hawkins?

On this question, the Orderly suddenly begins to stutter, shake. The lights flicker, the room warbles, and then --

Everything settles back to normal. Only the Orderly is no longer next to her. He is --

Approaching her again. *It's like we just rewound.*

His movements, his intonations are exactly the same.

>   FRIENDLY ORDERLY
>   Well, well, look who finally
>   decided to join us.

Eleven stares, baffled.

                    FRIENDLY ORDERLY (CONT'D)
               Someone's a sleepyhead this
               morning.

Eleven has heard enough. She stumbles away, scared --

                    FRIENDLY ORDERLY (CONT'D)
               Don't go too far, sleepyhead --
               lessons begin promptly at ten!

Eleven backs up out of the room. In her panic, she knocks over TEN's tower of RED BLOCKS, but she doesn't stop, she just keeps running, blowing past the Numbers and --

INT. HAWKINS LABS - HALLWAY 3 - DAY (MEMORY)

She bursts out into the hallway again, breaks into a sprint.

She looks around as she runs, searching for an escape. She moves down another hallway, and that's when she sees it:

A heavy door. Above it, an EXIT SIGN. *A way out*.

She races for it, throws it open, and --

INT. RAINBOW ROOM - CONTINUOUS (MEMORY)

Eleven crashes to a stop. Her eyes narrow with confusion and horror. REVERSE TO REVEAL:

She's BACK IN THE RAINBOW ROOM. Her eyes dart to Ten's red blocks -- which have been perfectly -- *impossibly* -- stacked back into that tall tower. *As if nothing ever happened*.

The friendly Orderly approaches her *yet again*.

                    FRIENDLY ORDERLY
               Well, well, look who finally
               decided to join us.

She stares at him, dizzy from the déjà vu --

                    FRIENDLY ORDERLY (CONT'D)
               Someone's a sleepyhead this
               morning...

As Eleven begins to realize she's TRAPPED in this moment, her breathing quickens, and we CUT TO --

INT. SILO LAB - OBSERVATION BOOTH - DAY

Her HEAVY BREATHING emanates from a LARGE SPEAKER in an unknown laboratory room. We PULL AWAY from it to find --

SCIENTIST #3 studying a bank of monitors, tracking her vitals.

                    SCIENTIST #3
        Heart rate is now one twenty BPM --

A concerned Owens takes this in, then moves over to a large EEG machine. The needles scratch as paper spits out, tracing unnervingly large arcs. He turns to Brenner --

                    DR. OWENS
        She's rejecting it.

Brenner, for his part, seems unfazed.

                    DR. BRENNER
        Give her time.

                    DR. OWENS
        We shouldn't have just thrown her
        in like this -- she's going to
        drown in there --

                    DR. BRENNER
        No. She's <u>going to swim</u>.

Our camera PANS back to the EEG machine. Those needles sweeping faster and faster and --

EXT. DESERT - CAR GRAVEYARD - DAY

WHAM! A shovel digs into earth. WIDEN OUT --

We're back in the CAR GRAVEYARD from episode #402. Argyle's Pizzamobile is hidden among the dead cars, while a sweating Jonathan, Mike, and Will work to FILL IN A GRAVE. *Oh God --*

They're BURYING AGENT HARMON! It's a grim task.

Argyle paces. Needless to say -- he's *freaking out.*

                    ARGYLE
        This is so messed up, man -- SO
        messed up! Dude's probably got like
        a family and kids and all that
        shit --

Everyone ignores him -- just keeps shoveling.

                  ARGYLE (CONT'D)
I really think we, like, gotta go to the cops. Just lay it all on 'em -- the whole shebang -- everything you told me about this super-powered girlfriend and the bad dudes and the upside dimension planet --

                  MIKE/WILL/JONATHAN
NO --

Argyle storms over to Mike.

                  ARGYLE
But these bad government dudes are after your super girlfriend, right -- *right?* Maybe they can help us find out where she is! 'Cause those dudes are gonna kill her, man -- they're going to kill her then they're gonna kill us -- actually they're gonna kill us first *then* kill her --

                  JONATHAN
Argyle. I think maybe we can figure this out if we... open our minds a bit --

                  ARGYLE
Open our minds -- ?

                  JONATHAN
Purple Palm Tree Delight -- ?

                  ARGYLE
MY MAN! Yes. Yes. It's worn off. Of course!

He heads off to the Pizzamobile to smoke.

                  WILL
          (to Jonathan)
More weed? Is that a good idea?

                  JONATHAN
You have a better way to keep him calm?

Will doesn't. As they continue to shovel, Will looks at Mike. He can see that what Argyle said about El has upset him. *Scared him.* As a worried Will watches Mike shovel --

                  WILL (PRE-LAP)
        You can't let him get to you...

EXT. DESERT - CAR GRAVEYARD - LATER

Mike and Will -- exhausted and sweating heavily post-burial -- are now sitting on the hood of a rusty car, sharing a soda.

Nearby, Jonathan flips through a map, planning a route.

                  WILL
        I mean -- look at him.

A now very stoned Argyle is now folding up a pizza box (???).

                  WILL (CONT'D)
        He's stoned out of his mind -- he
        doesn't know what he's talking
        about --

                  MIKE
        Doesn't mean he's wrong.

Mike looks back at the burial site --

                  MIKE (CONT'D)
        He just had to live one more second
        -- *one more second* -- why didn't he
        just say the number -- ?
            (frustrated)
        Or if I had just -- tried to
        explain myself, El would've taken
        me with her. And then -- then
        everything would be different. I
        just... I didn't know how...

                  WILL
        Sometimes... I think it's just...
        scary to open up like that -- to
        say how we really feel. Especially
        to people you care about the most.
        Because -- what if they don't like
        the truth?

Mike looks at Will, and is about to say something when --

                        ARGYLE (O.S.)
                  HEY ANYONE KNOW THE DEAD DUDE'S
                  NAME???

Everyone spins to Argyle.

                        JONATHAN
                  What? *Why?*

Argyle holds up the pizza box, which we now realize he has
folded into the SHAPE OF A HEADSTONE.

                        ARGYLE
                  I'm making the dude a headstone --

                        JONATHAN
                  You do realize we've spent all
                  morning *hiding* his body, right?

                        ARGYLE
                  Hm. I'll just go with "Unknown Hero
                  Agent Man. Saved Argyle, Jonathan,
                  Will, and Mike from certain death."

Argyle begins to scrawl onto his "headstone," but no ink is
coming out --

                        ARGYLE (CONT'D)
                  Aw *come on man* --

As Mike watches Argyle repeatedly try -- *and fail* -- to write
on the sign, an epiphany forms --

                        MIKE
                     (low)
                  That's his pen --

                        WILL
                  What -- ?

                        MIKE
                  The pen he gave me. *Unknown Hero
                  Agent Man*. Before he died.

Mike spins to Will. Mind racing.

                        MIKE (CONT'D)
                  Why'd he give me a pen that didn't
                  work -- ?

Before Will has a chance to answer, Mike slides off the car hood, newly hopeful. He hurries over to Argyle, then snatches the pen right out of his hand --

                    ARGYLE
          Dude, I'm using that -- !

Mike ignores Argyle and unscrews the cap. It's <u>hollow inside</u>.

Mike flips it around, pops the bottom of it with the palm of his hand, and --

A SCRAP OF PAPER FALLS OUT!

                    ARGYLE (CONT'D)
                (mind blown)
          Something just fell out of that
          pen!

Will and Jonathan, curiosity piqued, cross over as --

Mike grabs up the paper, unfolds it, and...

                    WILL
          -- What is it?

Mike looks back at Will. Stunned.

                    MIKE
          It's the number.
                (looks up)
          <u>We've had it this whole time</u>.

Off the Byers, minds blown, hard cut to --

EXT. RUSSIAN PRISON - THE PIT - DAY

CHOOM! A MEDIEVAL SWORD slots into a WEAPONS LOCKER.

WIDEN: A GUARD is putting the medieval weapons back into place (including a SPEAR and an AWESOME SWORD), while CLEANERS work to wash blood from the walls and floor.

IVAN, 30s, the lead guard, storms up to a cleaner who appears to be taking a break.

                    IVAN
          <Did I tell you it is okay to
          break? Over there -- there is a
          hand -- A HAND. Are we animals?>

The guard slumps off to retrieve the hand. Ivan sighs in irritation, lights a cigarette with a GOLD-PLATED LIGHTER when --

> VOICE
> <Ivan -- Ivan!>

Ivan looks up. It's Dmitri, calling out to him from the cell on the second floor, his hands pressed against the bars.

EXT. THE PIT - SECOND FLOOR - MOMENTS LATER - DAY

Ivan walks up to Dmitri's cell -- irritated.

> IVAN
> <Stop calling my name. You trying to get me in trouble -- ??>

> DMITRI
> <I don't know what they've told you, but it is all lies -- I'm not supposed to be here, it is a mistake!>

> IVAN
> <I'm sorry. I cannot help you.>

He starts to walk away, but --

> DMITRI
> <I can make you *rich*.>

Ivan turns back -- *has Dmitri hooked him?*

> DMITRI (CONT'D)
> <See this American -- he comes from money -- *old money* -->

Dmitri motions to Hopper, who is slumped in a dark corner of the cell --

> DMITRI (CONT'D)
> Tell him, American -- tell him how you will make him rich!

But Hopper doesn't respond -- just looks away.

Ivan shakes his head, walks away.

MOMENTS LATER

Dmitri storms up to Hopper, pissed --

                    DMITRI
          You are *real* help American -- a
          real help -- you know that?

Hopper is unresponsive. Dmitri CLAPS.

                    DMITRI (CONT'D)
          HEY -- you want to die in here??
          YOU want to die?? Is that it??

Hopper finally looks up at Dmitri. He clearly hasn't slept a wink -- dark rings around his eyes. He is lost. Haunted. *Broken.*

                    HOPPER
          I figure that's what we've been
          brought here to do -- *yeah.*

                    DMITRI
          So that is it?? You give up then??

Hopper doesn't answer. Just looks away. Dmitri sits beside him -- tries a new, more hopeful approach--

                    DMITRI (CONT'D)
          What about your woman, huh? She is
          captured, yes -- but *still alive.*
          We can still save her.

Hopper can't help but smile a bit at this.

                    HOPPER
          "Save her"?

                    DMITRI
          That is -- *amusing to you?*

                    HOPPER
          You don't you get it, do you? The
          closer I get to Joyce -- the more
          danger she's in.

                    DMITRI
          You are not thinking straight,
          American --

                    HOPPER
          No. For the first time in my
          life... *I think I am.*

A heavy beat. Hopper looks out toward that falling snow. Then, as he loses himself in a dark memory --

                    HOPPER (CONT'D)
          I used to think... I was cursed.
          Things just -- never seemed to...
          break my way.
                    (beat)
          Two weeks after I turn eighteen, I
          get an induction letter in the
          mail. Uncle Sam wanted me to pack
          my bags for the jungle. Charlie was
          spreading south like a plague, all
          'cause of you commie bastards.
          Anyway -- I was happy enough to go,
          prove to my old man I was worth a
          damn. And I guess I tested well,
          'cause they stuck me in the
          Chemical Corps.
                    (beat)
          Next thing I know, I'm in the bush,
          just a kid you know, eight thousand
          miles from home, and I'm mixing
          fifty-five-gallon drums of Agent
          Orange with these kitchen
          dishwashing gloves, with no masks,
          nothing. We'd hand clean these
          Buffalo turbines after a run and
          we'd be in there just -- inhaling
          the stuff. It wasn't chemical
          warfare -- not really, see -- it
          was just herbicides. To kill plants
          not people. Harmless. That's what
          they told us anyway.
                    (beat, trying to shake it)
          But then we got back to Real
          Life... and... A lot of the guys I
          worked with -- those that made it
          back -- they started trying to have
          families. Just to get back to
          normal, you know? But... things
          went wrong. Kids died in the womb --
          stillborn. Born with crooked
          spines. Popped eyes. The horror --
          it followed us, clung to us. But
          Diane... my wife... she wanted a
          kid -- a family. And... I did too.
          I knew the risks, but I hid them --
          from Diane, my wife. From myself.
                    (beat)
          We had a daughter -- Sara. She was
          born healthy. I thought for once in
          my life -- I got lucky.
                    (beat)
                        (MORE)

                    HOPPER (CONT'D)
          She died. Seven years later. And
          not an easy death. She... suffered.

Hopper chokes up.

                    HOPPER (CONT'D)
          Diane left me. She never blamed me
          -- not with words.
              (beat)
          I hid for a while... in drugs.
          Alcohol.
              (beat)
          But then... people... came into my
          life again. This girl -- El. Then
          Joyce... just happened.
              (beat)
          I thought -- they needed me. I
          convinced myself they needed me.

Hopper is getting angry with himself as he says this --

                    HOPPER (CONT'D)
          But that's not true. That's the
          lie. They didn't need me. I *needed
          them*.

Hopper looks at Dmitri. Heartbroken.

                    HOPPER (CONT'D)
          You were right, last night, what
          you said. I knew the risks,
          breaking out of here. But I hid
          from them -- hid from the truth --
          just like with Sara. The moment I
          sent for Joyce -- the moment I sent
          her that message --
              (beat)
          I sentenced her to death. Just like
          Sara. Everyone I love -- I hurt.
              (beat)
          Do you see now? This whole time --
          I wasn't cursed. <u>I am the curse</u>.

Dmitri takes this in. Shaken. Not sure what to say. How to respond. When --

A MONSTROUS ROAR suddenly echoes out across the Pit.

Dmitri stands, startled. *The hell was that?* He walks over to cell bars as another ROAR echoes out across the Pit. The roars are coming from behind the heavy steel door below.

Dmitri doesn't recognize the roar. But we do.

That's a *FUCKING DEMOGORGON*.

                    DMITRI
              (low)
          I've heard rumors -- of a monster.
          From America...
              (beat)
          I don't know if what you say is
          true, American -- if you are truly
          a cursed man. But you are right
          about one thing...

He turns back to Hopper.

                    DMITRI (CONT'D)
          We are going to die in here.

Off Hopper...

EXT. TRAILER PARK - DAY

A tattered American flag flutters in the breeze. A black sedan weaves through the decrepit trailer park... it is very out-of-place here. It parks alongside Eddie's trailer.

AGENT STINSON steps out, along with two additional men.

They have arrived in Hawkins.

MOMENTS LATER

CLOSE ON: Knuckles RAP on Eddie's trailer. A beat, then --

The door opens, revealing a sleep-deprived WAYNE MUNSON. He tightens a bit as he sees them.

                    WAYNE
          ... Can I help you?

                    AGENT STINSON
          We need to take a look around.

Stinson flashes her BADGE. Off Wayne --

INT. EDDIE'S TRAILER - DAY

BEEP BEEP BEEP. A STRANGE DEVICE beeps, reading EMF and RADIATION LEVELS (it's the same device that Brenner and his men used in season one while searching the Byers' shed).

A nervous Wayne watches as the agents follow the beeping to the center of the trailer. Their gaze shifts to that ceiling where Chrissy died. The rot and mold has now expanded from where we last saw it, the paint now peeling and crumbling.

>WAYNE
>Yeah I think it's some sorta leak.
>Just haven't had time to fix it
>with all that's going on --

The beeping is going nuts now. Agent Stinson turns back to Wayne.

>AGENT STINSON
>Pack your things. We're moving you.

>WAYNE
>Where -- ?

>AGENT STINSON
>Pack your things.

As a shaken Wayne heads off to do just that, Stinson's concerned gaze returns to the ceiling. We SLOWLY PUSH up to that mold and rot. As it begins to spread ever so slightly...

>CHRISSY'S MOM (PRE-LAP)
>... The devil is here... I can...
>feel his presence... growing...
>stronger with each day... and I
>know others feel him too.

INT. HAWKINS CHURCH - DAY

Chrissy's mother, dressed in all black, speaks in a church. Before her -- a CLOSED CASKET COVERED IN FLOWERS and a FRAMED PHOTO OF A SMILING CHRISSY. We're at Chrissy's funeral.

>CHRISSY'S MOM
>But I know Chrissy is in heaven
>now, looking down at us -- and she
>is smiling... happy to see all the
>lives she touched and brightened.

As she speaks, we survey the onlookers. The entire church is filled -- half the town must be here, including, of course, JASON and PATRICK, who sit with their TEAMMATES.

The tension and heartache is palpable.

                    CHRISSY'S MOM (CONT'D)
        But I know she is also frustrated--
        angry -- that the monster that did
        this to her -- is still out there.
        Still... hurting others...

Patrick suddenly looks over, hearing something. A FAMILIAR CHIME. Echoing eerily through the church.

                    CHRISSY'S MOM (CONT'D)
        How does he still live -- while my
        angel is gone? I know God has a
        plan. That there is a -- a reason
        for all this. But I have prayed --
        Lord I have prayed -- and... I just
        do not understand it -- I can see
        no reason.... I see *no reason*...

As the tears begin to fall, she's hustled away, comforted by CHRISSY'S FATHER.

We PUSH IN on Jason, fighting back tears, anger --

                    JASON (PRE-LAP)
        So... I finally got ahold of
        Cappelletti --

INT. CHURCH - BACK ROOM

Nearly the entire basketball team meet in the back of the church together, all still dressed in their Sunday best.

Jason dumps out a backpack. PHOTOS fall out onto the table.

                    JASON
        Photos for the eighty-six yearbook,
        gentlemen.

                    ANDY
        Hot damn...

The boys pass around the photos. They are yearbook pictures of the new Hellfire Club in various poses, including Eddie, Dustin, and Lucas. Andy burns when he sees their "friend" --

ANDY (CONT'D)
Goddamn *traitor* --

JASON
Only one reason he'd lead us to a dead end. The Hellfire Club -- *they're hiding Eddie.*

PATRICK
(hesitant)
... Maybe we should bring all this to the cops --

JASON
The cops who think Chrissy is a drug dealer?? Who are letting this psycho go around killing people?

PATRICK
I'm just saying -- what if this cult is like, doing shit to us -- ?

ANDY
Doing shit?

PATRICK
Like -- they know we're after them. What if they -- cursed us or something -- ?

CHUCKLES from the group --

TEAMMATE
Patrick thinks he's been cursed --

JASON
Hey -- *none of this* is funny. I don't believe in that supernatural crap, but this cult *is* dangerous. We have to be smart about this --

Jason tosses a LIST down --

JASON (CONT'D)
I made a list -- everywhere these freaks've been seen. We divide and conquer, check 'em out one by one, smoke 'em out --

                    FRESHMAN TEAMMATE
                        (looking at list)
                    You should add Reefer Rick's house
                    to this --

Everyone turns to the FRESHMAN TEAMMATE --

                    JASON
                What -- ?

                    FRESHMAN TEAMMATE
                        (a bit nervous now)
                    Reefer Rick? That drug dealer. He
                    supplied Eddie, and my dad, he said
                    he got out of prison early. Timing
                    seemed weird, I don't know, maybe
                    not --

                    JASON
                No. That's good -- good. No stones
                unturned.

As Jason scrawls REEFER RICK onto the list, CUT TO --

EXT. COUNTRY ROAD - DAY

WHOOSH! The Wheeler Wagon speeds down the road --

INT. WHEELER WAGON - DAY

The Hawkins gang is squeezed in here; Nancy drives, Dustin
is on his walkie --

                    DUSTIN
                Hey Eddie the Banished -- you copy?
                Eddie?

INT. BOATHOUSE - DAY - INTERCUT

Eddie -- back in the boathouse -- grabs up the walkie --

                    EDDIE
                Yeah -- I'm here --

                    DUSTIN (ON WALKIE)
                Listen -- we're headed your way --
                but we have a lead on Vecna we need
                to check on first.

                    EDDIE
                You think you can find Vecna, take
                as long as you goddamn need.

EXT. CREEL HOUSE - DAY

SCREECH! The Wheeler Wagon slams to a stop right by camera.

The doors fly open and our Hawkins gang clambers out. They gather together, looking up at something off-screen...

> STEVE
> Yeah okay, that's not creepy at all...

We RISE UP behind the back of our group to reveal... <u>the CREEL HOUSE</u>. The windows are all boarded up, the lawn overgrown, and the paint peels like flaking skin. *A true haunted house.*

EXT. FRONT DOOR - MOMENTS LATER

THWACK! The clawed end of a hammer *tears* out a nail as --

Steve and Nancy work together to remove nails from a plywood sheet which obstructs the front door. As they work --

> STEVE
> I mean -- what exactly are we hoping to find in this shithole?

> NANCY
> We're not sure. We just know this house is important to Vecna...

> STEVE
> Because Max saw it in Vecna's... red soup mind world -- ?

> NANCY
> Basically --

> DUSTIN
> Maybe it holds a clue to where Vecna is -- why he's back -- why he killed the Creels --

> MAX
> <u>Or where he's hiding</u>.

Lucas looks at Max -- suddenly concerned.

                    LUCAS
          We don't think he's in here... do
          we?

                    MAX
          I guess we'll find out.

THWACK! Nancy rips out the final nail and --

WHOOM! She and Steve pull off the plywood, tossing it down the steps behind them, revealing that now very familiar stained glass window behind it. Max takes a beat to catch her breath -- remembering --

Steve tries the door, but --

                    STEVE
          Locked. Should I... knock? See if
          anybody's home?

                    ROBIN (O.S.)
          No need --

They turn to ROBIN.

                    ROBIN (CONT'D)
          I found a key.

She holds up a LARGE ROCK. And --

INT. CREEL HOUSE - A LITTLE LATER

SMASH! Glass SHATTERS as the rock explodes through the window. It skips across a tattered carpet, and then --

MOMENTS LATER

EEEEE... Rusty hinges creak as the door swings open, coughing dust. Our heroes step inside. Due to all those boarded up windows, it's dark in here. *Very dark.*

Lucas tries a light switch, but nothing happens.

                    LUCAS
          Someone forgot to pay their
          electric bill...

One by one everyone hits on flashlights. *Click, click, click.*

                    STEVE
          Where'd everyone get those?

                    DUSTIN
          Do you need to be told everything?
          You're not a child --

Dustin tosses Steve his backpack --

                    DUSTIN (CONT'D)
          Back pocket.

As a grumbling Steve rummages through Dustin's backpack --

The rest of our gang begin to cautiously make their way through the house, sweeping their flashlights around. This house is a time capsule from the 1950s -- nothing much has changed since the Creel flashbacks. It's just... gathered dust and cobwebs.

                    NANCY
          They just *left everything...*

                    ROBIN
          I guess a triple homicide isn't
          great for resale value...

Max suddenly goes very still. And <u>*very pale*</u>.

                    MAX
          Hey guys? You all... *see that,
          right*?

The others step up to Max, following her gaze to --

THE GRANDFATHER CLOCK, STANDING TALL BY A GRAND STAIRCASE.

                    LUCAS/DUSTIN/ROBIN
          Yeah.

                    NANCY
          This is what you saw? In your
          visions?

Max nods. On edge. Robin walks up to the clock, wipes some dust off its face, turns back to the others --

                    ROBIN
          I mean -- it's just, like... a
          clock... a *normal old clock.*

                    STEVE
          Why's this wizard obsessed with
          clocks? Maybe he's like -- also a
          clockmaker -- ?

                        DUSTIN
            I think you just cracked the case,
            Steve --

                        NANCY
            All I know is -- the answers are
            here. *Somewhere*. Stay in groups of
            two. Robin -- upstairs?

Robin nods. *Yep*. As the girls head upstairs --

                        MAX
                      (to Lucas)
            Come on, let's go --

Max grabs Lucas, and they stride off together down the east side of the house, leaving --

<u>Steve with Dustin</u>. Steve sighs.

                        DUSTIN
            Why are you sighing, Steve?

                        STEVE
            I didn't sigh --

                        DUSTIN
            You sighed. That was a <u>*sigh*</u>.

An irritated Dustin heads off in the opposite direction of the house. As Steve chases after him --

We BOOM UP to an overhead light. The filament somehow -- *impossibly* -- begins to glow, HUMMING WITH LIFE.

The humming grows louder and LOUDER, becoming --

EXT. SKY - DAY

WHOOSH! The ROAR of an engine as Yuri's shit plane *PUNCHES* through the sky --

INT. YURI'S PLANE - DAY

Yuri is now snacking on his peanut butter, headphones on, totally oblivious as --

                        MURRAY (O.S.)
            Hey Yuri -- Yuri -- I need to take
            a piss here -- YURI!!

IN THE CARGO AREA,

Murray shouts, his face red from the effort --

> MURRAY
> You want me to just go in my
> pants?? You realize how unsanitary
> that is you SICK SICK BASTARD.

> JOYCE
> Just give it up -- he can't hear
> you -- !

> MURRAY
> I really do have to go, Joyce! This
> isn't some -- ploy to escape!

Joyce's eyes narrow as she watches Yuri lick that that peanut butter off his finger. And suddenly... an idea forms.

> JOYCE
> (low)
> *He can't hear.*

> MURRAY
> What -- ?

> JOYCE
> He *can't hear*.

Joyce's eyes swing to the PEANUT BUTTER CRATE. *Bingo*. She reaches out with her leg, stretching for the crate, those binds tightening painfully against her wrist --

> MURRAY
> Joyce? What are you doing -- Joyce?
> *Joyce??*

WHAP! She kicks the crate. It topples over and SEVERAL JARS OF PEANUT BUTTER ROLL out, GLASS SHATTERING on the floor.

Joyce looks back toward the cockpit -- to Yuri -- but he doesn't turn. He didn't hear that! *So far, so good.*

Although there's a problem: the shattered glass is too far away for her to reach --

> JOYCE
> I'm -- I'm too short. Grab one of
> those shards with your foot, will
> you -- ?

MURRAY
Perhaps we should, you know, talk this through first?

JOYCE
(getting irritated)
What is there to talk through? We cut our bindings, break free --

MURRAY
Yes -- okay -- *then* what?

JOYCE
Then you take Yuri out --

MURRAY
"Take him out -- "?

JOYCE
You said you knew karate -- that you were a black belt --

MURRAY
We're ten thousand feet in the air, Joyce! I take him, who flies this plane??

JOYCE
So don't knock him out -- take his gun, and then we make *him* fly us back home --

MURRAY
"Take his gun," just like that, huh?

JOYCE
Is black *not* the best color -- ??

MURRAY
Yes, yes -- it is, it is the best, it's just --

JOYCE
Just *what* -- ?

MURRAY
I've never fought anyone in a real-world scenario, okay?? I've only sparred with the other students --

                    JOYCE
          How old are these "students" -- ?

                    MURRAY
          They -- range --

                    JOYCE
          How old -- ?

                    MURRAY
          It -- doesn't go younger than
          thirteen --

                    JOYCE
          Thirteen -- ???

                    MURRAY
          But Jeremiah is eighteen. Almost.
          His birthday is next month. And
          Jeremiah is a ferocious fighter.
          Lightning fast. Very skilled.
               (beat)
          I've beaten him -- that one time.
          And certainly Yuri is not strong or
          trained like Jeremiah. So yes --
          yes. You're right. I can defeat
          Yuri. Absolutely. Thank you for
          talking it through. I feel better
          now.

And with that, Murray stretches his foot for that glass.

Off Joyce, staring at Murray, *feeling much worse*, we SMASH TO --

INT. HAWKINS LABS - RAINBOW ROOM - DAY (MEMORY)

WHAM! Bare feet flying across tile as --

A desperate Eleven races through the Nightmare Lab, looking for a way out, like a lab rat in a maze. She finds another door -- *an exit?* -- and throws it open but --

It's the Rainbow Room again. *Shit*. She slams it shut and --

MOMENTS LATER (MEMORY)

Eleven races down the aisle of numbered doors, frantic. She opens the first door -- number two. But once again it leads to the Rainbow Room. *Shit!* She slams it shut and tries --

Room three. Finds the Rainbow Room again. She throws open --

Room four -- room five -- *six* -- *seven* -- *eight* --

But every time she finds the Rainbow Room on the other side.

She slams the final door shut, losing her damn mind in this maze, and --

> VOICE (O.S.)
> Well, well, look who's finally decided to join us --

She whirls. It's that Orderly again. He is approaching exactly as before. *Oh God* --

INT. RAINBOW ROOM (MEMORY)

She's somehow *in* the Rainbow Room again. Like she was teleported there. It's surreal, impossible, MADDENING.

> FRIENDLY ORDERLY
> Someone's a sleepyhead this morning...

FUCK THIS. Eleven storms over toward a security camera, mounted on the ceiling, shouting as she moves --

> ELEVEN
> STOP THIS! LET ME OUT!! LET ME OUT -- !!

Her voice suddenly catches as she steps under the camera. She has noticed something in the rounded lens... something unusual about her reflection. Something about herself... that doesn't look right. Her hair is shaved... she looks *young*.

Eleven turns. Across the room -- a two-way mirror.

She approaches it. Her eyes grow wider with every step.

In the reflection, she is *eight years younger* -- the same age we saw in the opening of the season. Her hair, of course, is shaved.

A stunned Eleven steps right up to the mirror. Now face to face with her past self. She reaches up and touches her cheek. Then her head. Her young reflection matches her movements exactly. It's disorienting, *surreal* --

> DR. BRENNER (V.O.)
> In seventeen eighty-six, Nicolas Dalayrac wrote an opera. Called *Nina*.

She spins. Brenner's voice seems to be coming from nowhere and everywhere, bouncing around the room, echoing eerily.

> ELEVEN
> (low)
> Papa...

She looks around. Searching for him.

But of course, Brenner is not actually here.

INT. OBSERVATION BOOTH - DAY

He is in the control room. He speaks into a microphone.

> DR. BRENNER
> It is about a woman whose lover was killed in a duel. Nina was so traumatized she buried these memories -- it was like... it never happened. She would wait for her lover every day at the train station. For a return that would never be. If only she could know the truth...

INT. HAWKINS LABS - RAINBOW ROOM - DAY (MEMORY) - INTERCUT

Eleven looks around at all those Numbers. It hits her --

> ELEVEN
> This is not... real --

> DR. BRENNER
> No. But it was --

> ELEVEN
> (understanding)
> A... memory.

Brenner smiles.

> DR. BRENNER
> Very good.

> ELEVEN
> H-how -- ?

> DR. BRENNER
> Never mind how.

                    ELEVEN
          I -- I want out -- let me out --

                    DR. BRENNER
          You will need to find your own way
          out. Leave your train station. Stop
          waiting. Focus. Listen. Remember.

                    ELEVEN
          I -- I don't understand --

There is no response from Brenner.

                    ELEVEN (CONT'D)
          I DON'T UNDERSTAND -- !!

But Brenner is now gone.

                    FRIENDLY ORDERLY
          Well, well, look who finally decided
          to join us --

She whips around, finds the Orderly approaching her again.

She has <u>re-looped to the beginning of the memory</u>.

                    FRIENDLY ORDERLY (CONT'D)
          Someone's a sleepyhead this
          morning...

For the first time, Eleven *resists* the impulse to flee. She closes her eyes and focuses like Brenner said, eyelids moving... *remembering*. As she does this, our camera SLOWLY PANS back to the two-way mirror, and we watch --

IN THE MIRROR (MEMORY)

As a YOUNG ELEVEN speaks to the Orderly --

                    YOUNG ELEVEN
          I'm sorry -- am I -- in trouble?

IN THE ROOM (MEMORY)

Eleven opens her eyes. Repeats:

                    ELEVEN
          -- I'm sorry. Am I -- in trouble?

The Orderly smiles.

                    FRIENDLY ORDERLY
          Trouble -- *no no*. Why do you think
          that? You're just missing out on
          all the fun. Training starts any
          minute now.

IN THE MIRROR (MEMORY)

                    YOUNG ELEVEN
          Okay --

Young Eleven looks down anxiously as --

IN THE ROOM (MEMORY)

                    ELEVEN
          Okay --

Present-day Eleven looks down. *She's following the memory.*

                    FRIENDLY ORDERLY
          Hey, there's nothing to be nervous
          about -- you're going to do *great*
          today. I just <u>*know it*</u>.

Eleven looks up at him. Feeling a bit better. When --

The door opens to the Rainbow Room. Eleven turns. It's --

<u>DR. BRENNER</u>. Only he does not have his scar. *This is Dr. Brenner from the past.*

All of the Numbers immediately stop what they're doing and snap to attention, rising to their feet. We do not know yet whether this is out of respect or fear -- or *both*.

                    DR. BRENNER
          Good morning, children.

                    NUMBERS
          Good morning, Papa.

                    DR. BRENNER
          Please. Follow me.

Brenner heads out, and the Numbers follow, filing into a perfect line. Eleven looks around, then, takes a deep breath...

<u>And joins the back of the line.</u>

INT. SILO LAB - OBSERVATION BOOTH - DAY

The EEG needles begin to calm, settling. We PAN from the slowing needles to find Brenner, who is making his way over to an observation window. As he looks out at something we don't yet see, Owens enters the room. He seems a bit pale, on edge.

He sidles up to Brenner, looks out that glass --

>   DR. OWENS
>   ... How is she doing?
>
>   DR. BRENNER
>   Very well. She's swimming now.
>
>   DR. OWENS
>   Good -- because I just got off with
>   Ellen.

Brenner looks at him.

>   DR. OWENS (CONT'D)
>   We don't have much time.

Dr. Brenner quietly absorbs this, nods. He looks back out at the glass.

>   DR. BRENNER
>   Then she will simply have to swim
>   faster.

We PUSH PAST Brenner and for the first time we reveal that they're in an OBSERVATION BOOTH that overlooks the tank in the main lab.

INT. ANTENNA SILO - DAY

An epic overhead shot reveals ELEVEN FLOATING INSIDE THE LARGE BLACK TANK known as NINA. She's wearing a haptic suit (not unlike the one she wore in season one), with electrodes and wires affixed to her scalp. The ceiling of the tank is made up of bulbous television screens -- perhaps a dozen in total -- which play back surveillance tapes from the past.

We PUSH IN on El's closed eyes. They dart under the eyelids. Faster and faster *and* --

EXT. DESERT - LENORA - DAY

The Pizzamobile SLAMS to a stop at a lonely payphone and --

EXT. DESERT - PAYPHONE - DAY

SHOOM! Quarters drop into a payphone's coin slot.

Will feeds Mike the number --

                  WILL
        Two oh two, five six four, nine
        zero eight seven --

Mike quickly punches in the number and --

His brow furrows. It's not ringing -- it's making an ODD FLURRY OF BEEPING SOUNDS.

                JONATHAN
        Is it ringing -- ?

                  MIKE
        No... it's -- making noises --

                  WILL
        Busy -- ?

                  MIKE
        I don't think so. Listen to this --

He passes the phone to Will.

                MIKE (CONT'D)
        What's that remind you of?

It takes Will a second. Then --

                  WILL
        WarGames.

                  MIKE
        Right?

Jonathan grabs the phone now as Argyle, who is eating old pizza atop the hood of his Pizzamobile, calls out:

                ARGYLE
            (mouth full)
        I love that movie. "The only play
        is to move" -- or wait -- the only
        move is to win? Wait -- shit. You
        know this Argyle, come on, dude,
        COME ON --

                    MIKE
          We're not calling a phone --

Jonathan looks up from the phone. Eyes wide.

                    JONATHAN
          We're calling a computer.

Jonathan hangs the phone back up on the receiver and --

MOMENTS LATER

Mike races over to the car and grabs a ROAD MAP out of the glove compartment as he talks --

                    MIKE
          I don't know if Nina is a computer
          like Joshua, or Owens' lab, but
          whatever it is -- Unknown Hero
          Agent Man gave us access to it for
          a reason. If we can get into that
          computer, we can find Owens and
          warn him. *Warn Eleven*. We just need
          a hacker. And the only hacker I
          know --

Mike slams the map down onto the dusty hood of the car--

                    MIKE (CONT'D)
          Lives in Utah.

                    JONATHAN
          Utah -- ?

                    MIKE
          Salt Lake City, to be specific.

It now hits Will like a lightning bolt --

                    WILL
          Oh God --

                    JONATHAN
          Oh God -- why oh God --

                    WILL
          "Turn around... look at what you
          see..."

                        ARGYLE
            NEVERENDING STORY!! That scared the
            shit out of -- the Nothing, man --
            some proper existential shit right
            there --

Jonathan stares at Mike.

                        JONATHAN
            You can't actually be serious.

                        MIKE
            Look -- if we take I-15 north, we
            can be there by morning --

                        JONATHAN
            You're serious.

Mike looks up from the map.

                        MIKE
            I know it sounds insane. But she
            saved the world last year.
                (beat)
            Maybe she can save it again.

And right here, off Jonathan, CUT TO --

INT. BOATHOUSE - DAY

CLANK! A rock skips off the lip of an empty SpaghettiOs soup can.

WIDEN: Eddie is back in the boathouse, attempting (and failing) to toss rocks into the can, when he hears it --

THE SOUND OF TIRES ON GRAVEL. *Shit*. He stands, makes his way to the door, opens it a crack, peers out --

EDDIE POV: It's JASON'S CAR, just now pulling to a stop by the Lipton house.

Eddie's heart leaps in his chest.

                        EDDIE
            ... *Shit* --

EXT. BOATHOUSE - DAY

WHOOM! The doors open and Jason and goons (still dressed in their Sunday best, only now armed with TIRE IRONS AND BATS) are exiting the car.

INT. BOATHOUSE - DAY

Eddie watches as they head toward Reefer Rick's house --

> EDDIE
> (low)
> *Shitshitshitshit...*

EXT. LIPTON HOUSE - DAY

Jason knocks on the door. No answer. Pounds now. Nothing.

He tries the handle. Locked.

INT. BOATHOUSE - MOMENTS LATER

Eddie watches nervously as the jocks now move around the side of the house and --

EXT. HOUSE - MOMENTS LATER

> ANDY
> Hey Jason -- looks like Rick's had company...

Someone has broken into the back door. Shared looks and --

INT. LIPTON HOUSE

The jocks move into the house, weapons up, cautious.

KITCHEN - MOMENTS LATER

As they move into the kitchen, they find the pan, resting on its side in the sink. Jason picks it up -- its base is still slick with SpaghettiO sauce.

> JASON
> It's him. He's here. *I feel it.*

As the jocks begin to fan out through the house --

INT. BOATHOUSE - DAY

A freaked Eddie grabs up his walkie, hits Talk --

                    EDDIE
          Hey -- guys -- Dustin? You there??
          It's Eddie --

INT. CREEL HOUSE - FOYER - DAY

Eddie's muffled voice emanates from Dustin's backpack, which Steve has left by the front door. Goddammit Steve!

                    EDDIE (V.O.)
          I think I might be in real trouble
          here. Hey -- anybody there?
          Wheeler? ANYBODY???

But nobody is around to hear it. They're deep in the house --

INT. CREEL HOUSE - MASTER BATHROOM - DAY

Exploring. WHOOSH! Flashlights sweep across our camera lens as Dustin and Steve investigate the MASTER BATH. Steve seems... lost.

                    STEVE
          Hey, uh, Henderson...

                    DUSTIN
          Yeah --

                    STEVE
          Could you maybe clarify what sorta
          clues we're looking for here?

                    DUSTIN
          "The world is full of obvious
          things which nobody by any chance
          ever observes."

Steve stares, *totally* confused.

                    DUSTIN (CONT'D)
          Sherlock Holmes.

Dustin now heads off, leaving Steve to his own devices.

                    STEVE
          Right -- that's helpful, really
          helpful. *Sherlock Holmes* --

Steve's eyes suddenly narrow -- his flashlight has spotted a loose vent along the tiled floor. Steve kneels down, pries the vent off, and we cut --

INSIDE THE VENT

It's dark in here. *Spooky*. Steve's flashlight pierces the darkness, revealing some MASON JARS that have been stashed away in here, some upright, some on their side. *Strange...*

He reaches in, removes one of the mason jars, and...

IN THE BATHROOM,

Steve shines his light into the glass. There's a rotted branch in there... alongside the mummified corpse of a BLACK WIDOW SPIDER. Steve grimaces. *Ick*. That's when he notices --

ANOTHER BLACK WIDOW spider -- <u>*this one very much alive*</u> -- crawling out of that dark hole. *Shit!* He drops the mason jar and staggers backwards, rising to his feet, only to put his head right through a SPIDERWEB!

                    STEVE
        Aghaghghagh!

Steve frantically brushes the web away as he escapes into --

THE HALLWAY - CONTINUOUS

WHAM! Steve runs SMACK INTO NANCY!! He startles --

                    NANCY
        What's wrong???

                    STEVE
            (embarrassed)
        A spider -- black widow --

He turns around and slams the door --

                  STEVE (CONT'D)
        Just -- don't -- go in there --

In turning around, he's revealed that there is webbing all over the back of his beautiful hair!

                  NANCY
        Hold on, hold on, turn back around,
        don't move --

As Nancy works to pull the webbing away --

> ROBIN
> If a spider's nesting in there you'll never find it until it lays eggs and then a bunch of babies spill out --

> STEVE
> What is wrong with you?? Seriously?

Robin smirks, heads off --

> STEVE (CONT'D)
> She's got problems.

> NANCY
> (smiling)
> Tell me about it.

Steve grimaces as Nancy yanks more webbing from his hair --

> STEVE
> It's cool you two are like -- sorta getting along now. Maybe -- after we find and kill Vecna and you know -- *save the world and stuff* -- we can all go out. I mean, me and Robin and you -- and Jonathan of course -- when he's back. Not that we're dating. Me and Robin I mean -- she told you right? Robin? That we're not --

> NANCY
> Yes. She made it *VERY* clear.

> ROBIN
> (calling from ahead)
> Platonic with a capital P!

> STEVE
> Cool, yeah. Yeah.
> (lowers voice)
> I *would* date her it's just --
> (shut up)
> Friends. Just friends.

> NANCY
> Right.
> (then)
> Okay -- all better!

Steve turns back around to face Nancy. *They're suddenly very close.* Steve's breath catches a little bit --

>   STEVE
>   Great. I guess I'll -- get back to
>   the investigation. "The obvious
>   things are what -- people observe."
>   Or -- "don't observe." Or -- yeah.
>   Sherlock Holmes.

He flashes an awkward smile at Nancy, then hurries off.

Robin crosses back to Nancy.

>   ROBIN
>   I hope you'll eventually share your
>   secret --
>
>   NANCY
>   "Secret" -- ?
>
>   ROBIN
>   To getting everyone to fall in love
>   with you.

And with that, Robin strides off. A bewildered Nancy chases after --

>   NANCY
>   Wait -- what is that supposed mean?
>   Robin?? *Robin?*

As she hurries after Robin, our camera DROPS below the creaking floorboards and into --

INT. CREEL HOUSE - PARLOR - DAY

Where we find Lucas and Max investigating. As Max spotlights an old chess board, suddenly her Walkman tape reaches the end and Kate Bush *stops*. She quickly hits Rewind.

Lucas notices, watches nervously as the tape rewinds --

>   LUCAS
>   Wish we could make that a longer
>   loop --

                    MAX
          Forty-six minutes isn't bad. I
          think there are bigger concerns,
          like -- what if by playing this
          over and over I get sick of it and
          suddenly it's not my favorite song
          anymore -- is it still going to
          work? Or will Kate Bush, like, lose
          her magic power or something?

                    LUCAS
          Kate Bush, _never_.

                    MAX
               (incredulous)
          You're a Kate Bush fan, *really?*

                    LUCAS
          Now I am. A _mega fan_. She saved
          your life.

A smile from Max.

                    LUCAS (CONT'D)
          Besides, we're hot on this creep's
          trail. We're gonna find Vecna and
          kill him before he even thinks of
          messing with you again. Alright?

Max nods -- still scared but feeling a bit reassured.

                    LUCAS (CONT'D)
          In fact...

Lucas crosses to an old piano.

                    LUCAS (CONT'D)
          I bet we hit these suckers in the
          right combo -- it opens a door to
          his secret lair.

Lucas hits a random set of keys, focusing intently, and --

                    LUCAS (CONT'D)
          WAH-LAH!

Nothing happens of course. But it's made Max smile --

                    MAX
          You're such a dork. I thought you
          were, like, one of the cool kids
          now --

                    LUCAS
          You're saying I'm -- not cool?

Max laughs and --

                    LUCAS (CONT'D)
          I've really missed that --

                    MAX
          Missed -- what?

                    LUCAS
          Your laugh.

Max is about to respond, when -- CLICK. The tape stops rewinding. Interrupting the tension.

                    MAX
          All done. Work your magic, Kate.

A soft smile as she hits play on the tape. Kate Bush starts back up. And that's when *it happens* --

BZZZZ! A SOFT ELECTRICAL HUMMING sound fills the room. Lucas and Max turn their heads, their eyes locking on --

A LAMP on the far side of the room. Impossibly, the filament is glowing... pulsing... humming.

                    MAX (CONT'D)
              (low)
          I promise I'm gonna stop asking
          this but -- you're... seeing that
          right?

                    LUCAS
              (low)
          Yeah...

Our kids slowly cross over to the buzzing light. Max reaches out and touches the bulb. And --

It stops glowing. That's weird, but --

                    LUCAS (CONT'D)
          Look --

Max turns, following Lucas's gaze. A light in the connecting hallway is now glowing!

MOMENTS LATER

Max and Lucas step out into the hallway. They watch together as -- one by one -- the lights in the hallway dim then glow.

The electrical current is _traveling down the hallway_.

Lucas and Max share a look, then hurry after the glowing lights, and we CUT TO --

INT. HAWKINS LABS - TRAINING ROOM - DAY (MEMORY)

WHOOM! Lightbulbs glowing with life, one at a time, moving around in a circle, looping around and around. WIDEN:

To our surprise, we're actually _NOT_ in the Creel House. We're back in Hawkins Labs, looking at some sort of strange device known as a LIGHT RING.

The Numbers are lined up, patiently waiting their turn as --

TWO, 16, completes his "session." He is sitting upright in a chair in front of this Light Ring. He wears a white, skintight EEG helmet and his eyes are moving rapidly beneath closed eyelids. _He's clearly making the lights do this._

Brenner observes calmly, with very little expression.

The lights begin to spin faster and faster and --

> DR. BRENNER
> Stop.

Two's eyes snap open. The lights abruptly stop. Going dark.

Two is breathing hard. But he's clearly in control.

> DR. BRENNER (CONT'D)
> Good. _Very good Two._

As Two removes his helmet, Brenner turns back to the others. A small smile curls on his lips.

> DR. BRENNER (CONT'D)
> Now. What brave soul would like to follow that?

No one answers. No one dares.

> DR. BRENNER (CONT'D)
> Eleven.

All eyes swivel to Eleven. A few smirks. She nods, nervous, and --

MOMENTS LATER (MEMORY)

The Orderly affixes the EEG cap to her head (NOTE: we see this same thing happening with YOUNG ELEVEN in a nearby two-way mirror). The Orderly whispers to her -- reassuring.

>   FRIENDLY ORDERLY
>   Remember to stay focused. Find the
>   energy. Feel it.

Eleven takes this in, then closes her eyes -- and begins to focus just like he said. Breathing slow. Constant. Calm.

We PUSH IN on the Light Ring as we wait for something to happen. But... *nothing*.

Some chuckles from the other Numbers. Two looks miffed.

>   TWO
>   (low)
>   Why does he waste so much time with
>   her -- ?
>
>   FRIENDLY ORDERLY
>   Hey -- *quiet* --

Brenner ignores the noise, kneels by Eleven.

>   DR. BRENNER
>   They are laughing at you. They
>   think you are weak. Show them,
>   Eleven. *Show them*.

Her breathing increases and --

BZZZZ! One of the lights begins to glow, humming with life. *Holy shit -- it's working.*

>   DR. BRENNER (CONT'D)
>   Good. Now... *move it*.

We PUSH IN on El, straining with all her might, but --

The light filament once more sputters and fades. *Dead again.*

Eleven opens her eyes. Gasping for breath. Exhausted, unable to do more.

A SCATTERING OF CHUCKLES from the Numbers.

Even Brenner seems disappointed.

Eleven shrinks, embarrassed.

> TWO
> *Waste of time --*

PLOP! A drop of blood falls from Eleven's nose and hits the desk. She reaches up, wipes it away, then --

Her eyes narrow. Somehow -- *impossibly* -- her hand is now SMOTHERED IN BLOOD. Wait -- both hands are. Frightened, she looks to Brenner, only to discover that he has now *vanished*.

She looks behind her -- the other Numbers have vanished too.

She is all ALONE IN HERE. But she hears something: Voices. No -- <u>*SCREAMS*</u>.

INT. HAWKINS LABS - HALLWAY - DAY (MEMORY)

Eleven steps out into the hallway. Her eyes go wide as she finds herself face to face with --

The disaster from the opening of the season. FLICKERING LIGHTS. WRENCHED OPEN DOORS. DEAD SCIENTISTS. BLOOD EVERYWHERE.

AND THOSE SCREAMS. THOSE *AWFUL SCREAMS*.

INT. SILO LAB - OBSERVATION BOOTH - DAY

The EEG reacts violently, the needle making even bigger sweeps than before. FWOOM, FWOOM, FWOOM.

> DR. OWENS
> What's happening -- ?

> DR. BRENNER
> I don't know --

> SCIENTIST #3
> She's going into arrest --

> DR. OWENS
> That's enough -- pull her out --

But Brenner doesn't budge.

> DR. OWENS (CONT'D)
> I SAID PULL HER OUT GODDAMMIT!

INT. ANTENNA SILO - DAY

In the tank, Eleven begins to have a violent paroxysm and her nose and ears spill blood. As blood spills out into the water --

EXT. SKY - DAY

RRRRAOOO! Yuri's plane punches through the sky. As it heads into some dark clouds --

INT. YURI'S PLANE - COCKPIT - DAY

The plane jostles from more turbulence. Yuri flips some buttons to adjust for this, when... he hears a STRANGE NOISE.

He looks down to find it's a loose PEANUT BUTTER JAR rolling into the cockpit. He picks it up, brow furrowing. *That's... odd*. He looks behind him, and his eyes go wide.

Joyce is NOW FREED and working to untie Murray!

Off a shocked Yuri --

IN THE CABIN,

Joyce keeps working to untie Murray's bindings, almost has it, when --

CLICK! THE SOUND OF A COCKED PISTOL.

She turns -- finds Yuri now in the cabin with his pistol aimed right at the side of her head.

> YURI
> *Naughty naughty bird.* Did you fall out of your nest? ON your feet. <u>ON YOUR FEET</u>.

Joyce stands. Begins to slowly backpedal.

                    YURI (CONT'D)
          Where do you think you're going? Be
          a good girl now and get back in
          your chair --

                    JOYCE
          Or *what*? You're going to shoot me?
          The KGB won't like that -- and you
          won't be able to buy your son a --
          a prostitute with big boobs --

Yuri moves toward her.

                    YURI
          You think you are funny. Clever.

Another step.

                    YURI (CONT'D)
          You are right, of course. I cannot
          kill you. But KGB did not *specify
          the condition* you must arrive in.

Joyce is now backed up against the far wall of the plane.

                    YURI (CONT'D)
          You are... *fragile cargo*. You *can*
          still break --

                    MURRAY (O.S.)
          Not if I break you first.

Yuri spins to find a NOW FREED MURRAY IN A KARATE STANCE!!
Before Yuri has a chance to react, Murray CHOPS, sending the
gun flying out of Yuri's hand! It skips between some crates.

Murray gets into position.

                    MURRAY (CONT'D)
          My fingers are like arrows, my arms
          like iron, my feet like spears.
          Resist, and I will end you. But
          turn this plane around -- and I
          will spare you your life.

Yuri stares for a beat. Then -- BURSTS OUT LAUGHING.

Then, very suddenly, he attacks, and before we know it --

MURRAY AND YURI ARE IN A BRUTAL MID-AIR BRAWL!!! As Murray
parries his punches with some impressive karate skills --

Joyce scrambles to the floor, searching for the fallen gun. She finds it, starts to reach for it as --

Murray tries for a kick, but Yuri grabs his leg and --

                    YURI
      AHHHHHHH!

He drives Murray back into --

THE COCKPIT

Murray slams hard into the yoke and --

EXT. SKY - DAY

The plane plummets, *nosing downward* --

INT. YURI'S PLANE - CABIN - DAY

Joyce is thrown, the gun skipping away from her as --

IN THE COCKPIT

WHAM! Yuri grabs Murray's neck, choking him against the window. As Yuri's hands tighten around Murray's throat --

IN THE CABIN

Joyce's hand tightens around the pistol. She finally has it!

She staggers to her feet, aims it at Yuri, but he's too close to Murray. But Murray is dying here and -- *screw it.* She fires! BANG!

IN THE COCKPIT

SMASH! The bullet blows through the windshield. Air begins to suck out of the plane!! As papers in the cockpit fly up and suck back against the window --

Yuri spins around in shock, finds Joyce with that pistol aimed right at his stupid mustache!

                    JOYCE
      TURN THIS PLANE AROUND RIGHT NOW
      OR I'LL KILL YOU WHERE YOU STAND I
      SWEAR TO GOD!!!

Yuri smiles, then he shoves the yoke and --

EXT. SKY - DAY

WHOOM! The plane *SWERVES* and --

INT. YURI'S PLANE - COCKPIT - DAY

Joyce is thrown again, this time into a wall. The gun drops and --

Yuri heads for it. Almost has it when --

WHOOM! A freed Murray kicks him -- hard!! Yuri swings back, but Murray is now driven by a ferocious adrenaline, and he proceeds to PUMMEL Yuri with a ferocity of lightning-quick hits --

> MURRAY
> FINGERS LIKE ARROWS, ARMS LIKE IRON, FEET *LIKE SPEARS* -- !!!

KA-WHAM! A final fearsome kick sends Yuri spiraling to the floor, *OUT COLD*. Murray stands tall -- victorious!!

Joyce staggers to her feet --

> JOYCE
> What did you do???

> MURRAY
> What??? I WON -- !!

> JOYCE
> I said *DON'T* knock him out!!!

Before Murray can respond --

The plane JOSTLES VIOLENTLY. Shared looks -- *oh boy* -- and --

INT. YURI'S PLANE - COCKPIT - MOMENTS LATER

Joyce and Murray drop into the pilot seats. They strap on their seatbelts, then Murray starts to flips some buttons like he's Han Solo or something --

> JOYCE
> I thought you didn't know how to fly -- !

> MURRAY
> I *DON'T* -- !!!

WHOOM! The plane plummets again, Joyce SCREAMS and --

EXT. SKY - DAY

The plane is now soaring dangerously close to the snowy tree line below --

INT. YURI'S PLANE - COCKPIT - DAY

>   JOYCE
>   Pull up -- !!
>
>   MURRAY
>   I *AM* PULLING UP -- !!!

Murray yanks up on the yoke with all his might but it's too late to correct and --

EXT. RUSSIAN TUNDRA - DAY

WHOOM! THE PLANE CRASHES THROUGH SOME TREES --

ITS WINGS *RIP RIGHT OFF ITS BODY -- THEN* --

KACHOOOOOM! THE PLANE CRASHES INTO THE GROUND --

INT. PLANE - DAY

MURRAY AND JOYCE ARE THROWN FORWARD AS --

EXT. TUNDRA

THE PLANE SKIPS VIOLENTLY ACROSS THE WHITE TUNDRA!! A*S A TIDAL WAVE OF SNOW RUSHES OVER CAMERA,* WE HARD CUT TO --

EXT. CREEL HOUSE - NIGHT

BLACK. A few stars punch through the dark. Night has fallen outside the Creel house...

INT. CREEL HOUSE - DINING ROOM - NIGHT

The chandelier glows bright. We TILT DOWN to reveal...

Lucas and Max have gathered the others in the dining room. They all watch the chandelier in awe, their eyes wide.

They keep their voices low, as if to not disturb the "spirit."

>   NANCY
>   It's like the Christmas lights...

                    ROBIN
          The Christmas lights -- ?

                    NANCY
          When Will was in the Upside Down --
          the lights... came to life.

                    LUCAS
          Vecna's here. In this house. Just --
          on the other side.

Before anyone even has much of a chance to absorb this
haunting thought, the chandelier goes dark again.

                    ROBIN
          I think our friend just left the
          room.

                    MAX
          Did he hear us --?

                    STEVE
          Can he -- *see us* -- ?

                    DUSTIN
          Possibly --

Lucas looks at Max --

                    LUCAS
          Headphones --

Max nods, quickly puts on her headphones as --

                    NANCY
              (an idea)
          Everyone turn off your flashlights,
          spread out --

                    STEVE
          How can we see if we turn off
          our -- ?

Too late. Everyone is already following Nancy's direction.
CLICK CLICK CLICK. The room goes dark -- save for Steve's
flashlight. He sighs, reluctantly hits his off, and --

INT. CREEL HOUSE - VARIOUS DOWNSTAIRS ROOMS - MOMENTS LATER

A SERIES OF SHOTS as our teens fan out through the house.

> ROBIN (O.S.)
> I have him -- I HAVE HIM!

Everyone makes their way over to Robin who is in --

THE KITCHEN - CONTINUOUS

Sure enough, her flashlight (now held upright like a candle) is GLOWING. But then -- *choom!* -- it goes dark again.

> ROBIN
> *Had* him.

Steve looks down as his flashlight now glows. It dims again, but Steve tries something different this time -- he takes a step, and his flashlight re-illuminates. *Holy shit.*

As he walks, the flashlight retains its glow.

> STEVE
> ... I think he's *walking* --

> DUSTIN
> *Holy shit* --

> STEVE
> Outta my way, outta my way -- !

Everyone gets out of Steve's way as he "carries" the light out of the kitchen and into --

THE HALLWAY

Our teens now move up the stairs in a clustered group, following Steve, holding onto each other in the dark --

INT. CREEL HOUSE - SECOND FLOOR - CONTINUOUS

They reach the landing. And right here:

The light vanishes.

> STEVE
> I lost him --

> MAX
> No you didn't.

EEEEEE... Max opens a door to reveal a tall, narrow staircase, which leads up into darkness.

A hanging light begins to glow from somewhere above.

                    ROBIN
          The attic... *of course it's the
          attic...*

Steve starts to head up; the others follow as --

                    DUSTIN
          Hold up -- what if he's leading us
          into a trap? Hey, guys -- hey!
               (they're already gone)
          Shitshitshit.

As Dustin scrambles up after them --

INT. BOATHOUSE - NIGHT

CLOSE ON: FRIGHTENED EYES as --

Eddie peers out the boathouse -- watching as the three jocks continue to search and trash Reefer Rick's house --

INT. LIPTON HOUSE

An angry Jason flips over a bed --

                    ANDY
          Dude, seriously, <u>he's not here</u> --

                    JASON
          Shut up and <u>keep looking</u>.

Andy sighs, heads off in frustration. And that's when --

Jason's eyes narrow. *He's seen something.* He walks up to a window. He's spotted... <u>THE BOATHOUSE</u>. Meanwhile...

INT. LIPTON HOUSE - LIVING ROOM - NIGHT

Patrick is searching another room when --

He hears that CHIME again. That *fucking chime*. It's coming from a dark corner of the room. Someone -- *something* -- is standing there. Is that... Vecna??? He kicks on a light and --

It's just a hat rack. *A fucking hat rack* --

WHAM! A hand grabs him from behind. Startling but --

It's Jason -- on edge.

                    JASON
          <u>Come with me</u>.

EXT. LIPTON HOUSE - NIGHT

WIDE SHOT: Moonlight ripples in the inky black water as Jason and Patrick head toward the boathouse, weapons in hand.

INT. BOATHOUSE - NIGHT

WHAM! Jason kicks open the door and --

REVERSE TO REVEAL: The boathouse is empty. *EDDIE IS GONE*.

Jason and Patrick sweep inside. Patrick finds old groceries -- empty beer cans, discarded wrappers --

> PATRICK
> Someone was in here --

Jason's eyes swivel to the dock. The boat isn't there anymore. Tarp tossed aside. The surface is still rippling. *Fuck.*

EXT. BOATHOUSE - NIGHT

Jason races out of the boathouse, scans the lake, and --

HE LOCKS ONTO EDDIE. HE'S ON THE MOTORBOAT IN THE MIDDLE OF THE LAKE, USING THE OAR TO QUIETLY ROW AWAY -- *ESCAPING*. (NOTE: THE WALKIE IS HOOKED TO HIS BELT)

Patrick races up to his side --

> PATRICK
> Holy shit --

> JASON
> HEY FREAK -- WHERE DO YOU THINK YOU'RE GOIN'???!!

ON THE BOAT

Eddie whirls -- sees Jason, panics --

> EDDIE
> Ah shit *shit shit shit* --

Eddie quickly tries to start the motor, yanking the pull string. It sputters but doesn't catch! *Is it out of gas???*

> EDDIE (CONT'D)
> Oh COME ON COME ON -- !!

He tries again -- still nothing --

                    EDDIE (CONT'D)
             COME ON YOU PIECE OF SHIT!!!

As Eddie continues to try to start the motor --

EXT. BACK ON THE SHORE

Jason rips off his tie, frantically starts to strip off his suit. Patrick doesn't move, but --

                    JASON
             You scared of some water??? LET'S
             GO!

Patrick begins to undress too --

EXT. MOTORBOAT

Eddie sees Jason and Patrick, now undressed, heading into the water.

                    EDDIE
             SHITSHITSHIT!!

He gives up with the fucking motor and resumes paddling with his stupid fucking oar, fast as he can as --

EXT. LOVER'S LAKE

Jason and Patrick begin to swim out into the dark lake as --

INT. CREEL HOUSE - ATTIC - NIGHT

Our Hawkins gang ascends into the dark attic.

They gather below the light in the center, which is pulsing.

Their flashlights all begin to glow, brighter, brighter...

                    STEVE
             Okay... what's happening...?

No on answers -- no one knows. Our camera now begins to ROTATE, flipping upside down, and --

FWOOM! The camera MOVES THROUGH the rotted floorboards and suddenly we find ourselves in --

THE UPSIDE DOWN

... Where VECNA is hanging from his terrible web of vines. His eyes are shut tight. *He's casting another spell.*

As his eyes dart back and forth, back --

EXT. LOVER'S LAKE - NIGHT

Eddie frantically continues to paddle away -- but Jason and Patrick are fast swimmers and have nearly reached him.

>   EDDIE
>   Hey stay back -- STAY BACK -- STAY
>   BACK!!!

Eddie pulls his oar back, ready to attack, but --

Patrick abruptly stops swimming. He just doggy paddles in place, looking out at the dark lake, frightened by *something*.

Jason whirls to him, catching his breath --

>   JASON
>   Come on, let's go -- we almost have
>   him! Patrick -- <u>*PATRICK!*</u>

But Patrick isn't listening. His eyes dart around, frantic. *He sees something we don't -- something horrible.*

Eddie watches Patrick with a look of knowing horror. He knows that look -- *he knows that fucking look* --

WHOOM! PATRICK IS SUDDENLY AND BRUTALLY SUCKED BENEATH THE SURFACE OF THE LAKE!

>   JASON (CONT'D)
>   Patrick -- PATRICK????

No response. The surface of the water goes still.

The silence stretches on and on and then....

WHOOM! PATRICK SUDDENLY EXPLODES OUT OF THE WATER AND INTO THE AIR! EDDIE STUMBLES BACK IN HORROR, TOPPLING OVERBOARD INTO THE WATER AS --

<u>PATRICK IS SUSPENDED TEN FEET OVER THE WATER</u> -- IT'S LIKE HE'S BEING HELD UP BY INVISIBLE STRINGS -- WATER STREAMING DOWN HIS BODY.

A TERRIFIED EDDIE AND JASON WATCH FROM THE WATER BELOW AS --

PATRICK SCREAMS IN EXCRUCIATING PAIN THEN --

CRACK! HIS LIMBS SNAP -- HIS EYES SUCK BACK INTO HIS HEAD --
ALL WHILE --

INT. CREEL ATTIC - NIGHT

Our teens' flashlights glow *ever brighter*, the white light overtaking the entire attic, blindingly strong, then --

BOOM! One by one their flashlights SHATTER --

Our teens jump and scream and --

INT. CREEL ATTIC - NIGHT (THE UPSIDE DOWN)

WHOOM! Vecna's eyes snap open -- the vines detach from his body -- as his body drops to the attic floor --

EXT. LOVER'S LAKE - NIGHT

WHOOM! Patrick's broken body drops too, like his strings were just cut. As he breaks the surface of the water --

INT. ANTENNA SILO - LAB - NIGHT

CHOOM! A DEFIBRILLATOR PADDLE sends an electric charge through Eleven's haptic suit and --

WHOOM! SHE JOLTS AWAKE -- GASPING.

WIDEN: She's now outside the tank in her haptic suit, laid out on a small operating table, surrounded by SCIENTISTS and DOCTORS, including Dr. Brenner and a very nervous Owens --

                    DR. OWENS
          Air -- get her some air for
          chrissakes -- !

A scientist straps an oxygen mask over her mouth, begins to
give her air. As Eleven's breathing begins to slow, she looks
to Dr. Brenner. He's a bit blurry, but coming into focus.

                    DR. BRENNER
          It's okay... it's okay. It will
          take time to adjust. But...

He reaches out and takes her hand.

                    DR. BRENNER (CONT'D)
          You're safe now.

Eleven looks at Brenner. She squeezes his hand back. For a
moment, we think she is embracing him. But then we see that
her *other hand* is grabbing the defibrillator and --

WHAM! She swings it with all her might -- slamming Brenner
across the face and before we know it --

Eleven is off the table -- shoving through shocked scientists
-- sprinting away --

As a stunned Brenner shakes off the hit --

Eleven BLOWS through the laboratory doors and --

INT. SILO LAB - CORRIDOR - NIGHT

Eleven is now sprinting down that long, round corridor --
those fluorescent lights whooshing above her. She doesn't
even look back -- she just runs and runs likes she's NEVER
run before until finally she reaches --

THE ELEVATOR

She mashes the call button. But the doors don't open. *Come on
come on* --

The sound of POUNDING FOOTSTEPS causes her to turn --

It's the Lab Guards. They stop, catching their breath.

                    LEAD LAB GUARD (O.S.)
          You're giving us quite the workout
          today. You really want to do this
          again?

Eleven breathes hard, then turns back to the elevator and mashes the button again -- increasingly panicked, but this fucking elevator is taking too long and --

                    LEAD LAB GUARD (CONT'D)
          ... Guess we'll do it the hard way
          then --

The Guards make their move and --

WHAM! They pull Eleven away from the elevator --

She kicks and SCREAMS and throws out her hands and --

WHOOM-SMASH! The GUARDS are suddenly hurtled upward into the ceiling, shattering the overhead lights. Sparks rain down as --

WHUMP! The Guards fall back down and slam to the floor. *Unconscious.*

A stunned Eleven stares at the three bodies which now lie at her feet. *Holy shit. How... did she do that?*

                    DR. BRENNER (O.S.)
          Remarkable.

She looks to find Brenner walking down the long tunnel. He is extra menacing in the now sputtering corridor lights.

Eleven's breathing quickens.

                    ELEVEN
          Stay away -- !

But Brenner keeps coming --

                    ELEVEN (CONT'D)
          I said *STAY AWAY* -- !

She thrusts out a hand, trying to take out Brenner with her powers, but --

Nothing happens. *Not this time.* Brenner is still standing.

                    DR. BRENNER
          You didn't think it would be that
          easy did you?

Eleven catches her breath. Looks at her hands.

                        ELEVEN
                          (low)
                I -- I don't understand.

                        DR. BRENNER
                I do.

He holds out his hand. Then --

CHOOM! A heavy noise echoes out as the elevator at last reaches ground level. The doors grind open.

Eleven looks back at the open elevator, uncertain. She could leave *right now,* and a *big* part of her wants to. The pain Brenner has caused her is... unimaginable. He stole away her childhood. Her *mother*. Her chance for a normal life. And yet...

She needs those answers. *Those powers*. She <u>needs him</u>.

Her face hardens and...

She turns around. Crosses to Brenner. <u>And takes his hand</u>.

As Papa and Daughter walk together down the long corridor, headed back toward the lab -- *toward answers* -- the elevator door shuts, blacking out camera, and we --

<u>END EPISODE</u>

EPISODE SIX

CHAPTER SIX:
THE DIVE

WRITTEN BY **CURTIS GWINN**

EXT. COUNTRY ROAD - NIGHT

WOOPWOOPWOOP! Police sirens blare as TWO COP CARS fly across the road and --

EXT. LIPTON HOUSE - NIGHT

SCREECH! The cars slam to a stop at Reefer Rick's house. CHIEF POWELL and OFFICER CALLAHAN leap out of the lead car where they find --

A panicked ANDY waiting for them --

                    POWELL
    Where is he?

Off Andy --

EXT. LOVER'S LAKE - NIGHT

The cops follow Andy down to the shore of the lake. And that's where they find him --

<u>JASON</u>. He is sitting on the muddy ground. His eyes are stained with tears. He's still shirtless, soaked, body splattered in blood. And most shocking of all --

He's cradling a DEAD PATRICK in his arms. Patrick's eyes are gone. His arms and limbs twisted, broken. *A horrifying sight.*

As Jason looks up at our cops, shaking --

                  POWELL (PRE-LAP)
    ... And where was Eddie when that
    happened?

INT. LIPTON HOUSE - NIGHT

Powell and Callahan question Jason inside Reefer Rick's -- he's dry now, and he's got a blanket over his body. But his eyes are still bloodshot and his voice shakes -- he's still clearly in shock.

> JASON
> W-what?

> POWELL
> Eddie. Where was Eddie when you saw this?

> JASON
> ... In... the boat... like -- like I said.

> CALLAHAN
> Right. Right. But then -- who lifted Patrick up out of the water?

A beat. Jason's shock begins to turn to anger.

> JASON
> You're not listening to me. Why -- why aren't you listening?

> POWELL
> We're listening, Jason --

> JASON
> You're not. You're -- not. Eddie is a... vessel. Just a vessel --

> POWELL
> A vessel?

> JASON
> For Satan. He -- he's made a pact with the devil. Now -- he has his powers.

Powell and Callahan share looks.

A tear slips down Jason's left cheek.

> JASON (CONT'D)
> You don't believe me...

                    POWELL
          We're just -- processing all this,
          that's all, okay?

Jason looks at Powell. He chokes back tears.

                    JASON
          How do you expect to stop the devil
          -- <u>if you don't believe he's real</u>?

As our cops take this in, a light swoops past the window --

EXT. LOVER'S LAKE - NIGHT

A police boat is sweeping the shore with a spotlight, while other cops (some with search dogs) search the area on foot.

As the boat heads off for deeper waters, our CAMERA DROPS DOWN, diving --

BENEATH THE SURFACE OF THE LAKE

The water is turbid -- hard to see much in this underworld. *Wait.* We see...

A FISH. It swims peacefully through the waters, when --

HISSS! A TENTACLE-LIKE VINE shoots out of the murk below and pierces its belly. The fish flails, desperately trying to free itself, but the vine wraps around it like a boa constrictor, then --

WHOOSH! It yanks the fish downward, out of view, into the darkness below, and right here we SMASH TO --

MAIN TITLES

INT. BLACK SITE - HALLWAY - DAY

We are now drifting down a bleak hallway in an abandoned building. Water drips down from the ceiling, and SCREAMS echo from darkness. The screams build, and then we HARD CUT TO --

INT. BLACK SITE - TORTURE ROOM - DAY

ECU ON AGENT WALLACE, as his head slumps to his chest.

WIDEN: He's bleeding badly, weak, miserable, tied to a chair. He's been tortured. There are several men in here, including --

SULLIVAN. He walks forward, kneels before Wallace. Then, gently:

                    SULLIVAN
          I can make this stop. I can make
          the pain end. *Where is the girl?*

                    AGENT WALLACE
               (low, weak)
          I -- told -- you. I -- don't --
          don't know.

Sullivan considers for a moment, then he reaches into a
folder, produces a PHOTOGRAPH.

                    SULLIVAN
          Last night, there was another
          murder.

He holds the photograph up; it features Patrick's mangled,
eyeless body.

                    SULLIVAN (CONT'D)
          Now -- there are two proposed
          explanations for what is happening.
          Explanation one -- an invisible
          boogeyman from another dimension is
          slaughtering these kids.
          Explanation two -- Doctor Brenner's
          special little pet has gone rogue
          again, and he and his lackeys,
          including a fired and disgruntled
          Doctor Owens, are now seeking to
          cover that up. Perhaps in hopes of
          selling their pet to the Soviets.
          The Soviets who -- under Doctor
          Owens' watch -- somehow managed to
          infiltrate our country.
               (beat)
          Now -- which explanation sounds
          more plausible to you?

No answer from Agent Wallace.

                    SULLIVAN (CONT'D)
          You still have a chance to redeem
          yourself, Mister Wallace.
               (beat)
          Where is she?

Agent Wallace stares. For a tense moment we think he will
break -- but then he looks away.

Sullivan breathes deeply. *Okay then*. He stands, nods to his
men.

They grab Wallace and drag him over to a SMALL BLACK
SWEATBOX. As they shove him in and slam the door, we HARD CUT
TO --

INT. SILO LAB - ELEVEN'S ROOM - MORNING

A CU of ELEVEN. She is sitting on a bed in a simple, cramped
bedroom located within the missile silo.

Her eyes shift to the HAPTIC SUIT, hanging on a wall hook.

As we PUSH IN on Eleven, thinking back...

>   DR. BRENNER (PRE-LAP)
>   Do you know what happens when
>   someone has a stroke?

INT. SILO LAB - OFFICE - NIGHT (FLASHBACK)

We have returned to the previous night. BRENNER is talking to
Eleven in his office. Her hair is still damp from her time
inside the tank, but she is back in her civilian clothes.

She scans Brenner's wall, which is plastered with RESEARCH.
Images of stroke victims, brain scans, graphs, charts.

>   DR. BRENNER
>   The blood supply to the brain is
>   cut off. It -- scrambles the
>   brain's signals to the point where
>   the mind can forget how to do
>   things. To speak... to eat... <u>to
>   walk</u>...

INT. SILO LAB - CORRIDOR - MORNING (PRESENT)

CLOSE ON: Bare feet. Walking down the long corridor.

WIDEN: Eleven is now dressed in her haptic suit. She's
flanked by SCIENTISTS and GUARDS. She looks like some kind of
psychic astronaut. As we hold on a CU of Eleven, her
expression some mixture of fear and determination...

>   DR. BRENNER (V.O.)
>   When you were attacked last year, I
>   believe your signals were scrambled
>   in much the same way. But just as
>   the stroke victim can learn to walk
>   again -- I believe you too, can
>   return to your full power.

INT. SILO LAB - OFFICE - NIGHT (FLASHBACK)

Brenner walks up to Eleven. Gently taps her forehead.

                    DR. BRENNER
        Your abilities are still in here.
        You simply need to -- <u>remember</u>.

INT. SILO LAB - OUTSIDE LIBRARY - NIGHT (FLASHBACK)

KA-CHUNK. A key inserts into a lock, opens a door.

INT. SILO LAB - LIBRARY - NIGHT (FLASHBACK)

Brenner now leads Eleven into a dark space. He hits a light switch. Fluorescent lights kick on above us to reveal --

A MASSIVE LIBRARY of VHS tapes -- <u>THOUSANDS OF THEM</u>. Eleven looks around, awed, as Brenner walks her down this impressive corridor of tapes. Each tape is labeled with days and dates.

                    DR. BRENNER
        Everything that took place in my
        lab was captured on videotape.
        Every success. Every failure.

INT. SILO LAB - ANTENNA SILO - MORNING (PRESENT)

Eleven is now seated as scientists affix the EEG cap to her head. It's like a super high-tech swim cap.

                    DR. BRENNER (V.O.)
        It's important for you to not just
        see your past -- but to fully re-
        experience it.

SCIENTIST #1 swabs El's arm with alcohol, while SCIENTIST #2 draws a strange, cloudy medicine into a syringe. As he taps it, clearing an air bubble...

                    DR. BRENNER (V.O.)
        In doing so -- I believe we can
        repair the broken signals. As we
        saw tonight -- that process has
        already begun --

Eleven winces as the substance is injected into her veins.

INT. SILO LAB - OBSERVATION BOOTH - NIGHT (FLASHBACK)

CLOSE ON: A VHS tape slots into a VCR.

WIDEN: We are now in the observation lab above the Nina tank.

Eleven watches through the window as projectors kick on, projecting images of the Numbers performing the light ring test we saw yesterday, now seen from surveillance angles.

As Eleven watches those memories play back --

>   ELEVEN
> If this -- all happened... why
> don't I... remember?

>   DR. BRENNER
> Because you do not want to.

INT. ANTENNA SILO - DAY (PRESENT)

Eleven -- wearing that electrode cap -- now climbs up a spiral staircase as she makes her way to the top of the tank.

>   DR. BRENNER (V.O.)
> Our brain has a defense mechanism
> in place to protect itself from
> painful memories. From trauma. You
> buried these memories, long ago.

INT. SILO LAB - OBSERVATION BOOTH - NIGHT (FLASHBACK)

Eleven looks back at the video. She sees her YOUNG SELF doing the light ring test. As blood drips down her nose --

FLASHCUT TO HER HANDS NOW COVERED IN BLOOD.

>   ELEVEN
> When I was... in there... I saw
> something else.

A VIOLENT FLASHCUT OF THE BLOODY HALLWAY.

>   ELEVEN (CONT'D)
> There was blood -- so much blood.
> Doors. Someone -- had broken all
> the doors. And there were bodies --
> dead bodies.

Brenner darkens. He knows this all too well.

>   DR. BRENNER
> That was... another memory. A more
> powerful one -- invading from your
> subconscious.

This hits Eleven like a sledgehammer.

> DR. BRENNER (CONT'D)
> *There are many demons in your past, Eleven. That is why we must proceed carefully.*

INT. ANTENNA SILO - DAY (PRESENT)

Eleven carefully climbs down into the tank.

> DR. BRENNER (V.O.)
> *One step at a time. One memory at a time. I fear, if we move too fast, you may become... lost in the darkness.*

She pushes out into the dark water.

INT. SILO LAB - OBSERVATION BOOTH - NIGHT (FLASHBACK)

> DR. BRENNER
> *And if you are lost... then <u>so are we all</u>.*

As Eleven takes this in, she looks back toward Nina, and...

INT. ANTENNA SILO - DAY (PRESENT)

We PUSH IN on Eleven, who is now floating inside the tank.

Her bloodshot eyes have begun to flag as that strange drug begins to take hold. Above her, images from the Rainbow Room wash over her, a kaleidoscope of images from her past.

Eleven's eyes close as the sound of her heartbeat <u>*rises*</u> --

Thump thump thump thump, becoming --

EXT. CONSTRUCTION SITE - MORNING

<u>*THUMP*</u>*!* The sound of a hammer striking a nail.

WIDEN: We're at a construction site; WORKERS are building a house. We TRACK WITH A WORKER as he walks past a FOREMAN.

> CONSTRUCTION WORKER
> Erik, I'm taking five --

> FOREMAN
> You just took five --

                    CONSTRUCTION WORKER
          Yeah well tell Milo to take it easy
          on the onions next time --

He slings off his TOOL BELT, tosses it onto a stack of
lumber, and heads into a Porta Potty. We PUSH IN on the tool
belt. A WALKIE is hooked to it. Then suddenly --

WHOOM! A hand reaches from out of frame and grabs the walkie!

It's EDDIE! Clothes dirty. Hair tangled. A mess. He hurries
away, walkie in hand, plunging back into the forest and --

EXT. COUNTRY ROAD - DAY

VROOOM! The Wheeler Wagon speeds down a dark country road.

>   ROBIN (PRE-LAP)
>   Not to be a wimp, but can I maybe
>   stay in the car for today's
>   visit...?

INT./EXT. WHEELER WAGON - DAY

Nancy drives, Robin sits passenger. The rest of our gang is squeezed in the back, with bags of groceries piled atop their laps.

>   ROBIN
>   'Cause this is gonna *totally and
>   royally suck.*
>
>   NANCY
>   It's gonna *be fine* --
>
>   ROBIN
>   I just -- I don't think I can stand
>   watching those doe eyes of Eddie's -
>   - break again. I just -- *can't.*

Steve pulls a SIX-PACK OF BEER out of a grocery bag.

>   STEVE
>   At least he can drink himself into
>   feeling better.
>
>   MAX
>   That's what my mom does.

Dustin holds up some CANDY.

>   DUSTIN
>   Or eat himself into feeling better.
>   That's what -- I do.
>
>   ROBIN
>   Right -- okay -- let's give this a
>   trial run shall we? "Hey Eddie --
>   good news first this time. We got
>   you some Dustin-approved junk food
>   and that six-pack you requested. Oh
>   yeah -- and we found Vecna!
>   (MORE)

                    ROBIN (CONT'D)
          But the bad news -- well -- he's in
          that other scary dimension we told
          you about and the Gate is closed so
          we can't get to him, I mean he's
          completely closed off to us so --
          you're screwed. I mean you were
          already screwed but now you're like
          -- _triply screwed_ -- "

                    LUCAS
          Maybe we -- don't put it like that
          --

                    NANCY
          We're a step closer to finding
          Vecna -- that's what we say --
          that's what's important --

                    STEVE
          See how a positive spin makes all
          the difference Robin?

                    DUSTIN
               (holding up new flashlight)
          Also -- we have way cooler
          flashlights now --

                    LUCAS
          You see they blink if you press the
          button twice?

Lucas makes his flashlight blink --

                    MAX
          Wow. That seems... really useful.

Nancy's eyes suddenly grow wide as she sees something --

                    NANCY
          Shit...

All eyes look out the front window. They've reached the
Lover's Lake crime scene. Police vehicles and NEWS VANS block
the road... it's a total zoo here.

Nancy shifts into park and --

EXT. LIPTON HOUSE - A LITTLE LATER - DAY

WHOOM! Car doors fly open as our panicked teens make their way toward the crime scene; they see crime scene tape, and SEVERAL OFFICERS blocking the way, obstructing onlookers --

              POLICE OFFICER
I want everyone five feet back --
five feet!!

              NANCY
       (to others)
This way -- *come on* --

They make their way away from the officer, duck under some police tape, and take cover behind a ROANE COUNTY NEWS VAN, where they have a good view of --

A NEWS CONFERENCE. Chief Powell (Callahan by his side) is addressing a CROWD OF REPORTERS --

> POWELL
> ... As many of you may know by now -- the Roane County line received a call a little after midnight, reporting a homicide out here on the lake.

Our gang share worried looks. Fearing the worst for Eddie.

> POWELL (CONT'D)
> Officer Callahan here and myself arrived first on the scene. We made our way to the shore of Lover's Lake, about ten yards from that boathouse you see behind me. It was there that we found the victim -- an eighteen-year-old senior from Hawkins High -- *Patrick McKinney*.

A mix of surprise, confusion from our group. But this is a <u>gut punch</u> to Lucas. *Patrick?* Max clocks his reaction, worried --

INT. WHEELER LIVING ROOM - DAY

The press conference plays on the TV in the Wheeler house.

TED and KAREN watch. On edge.

> POWELL (ON TV)
> His limbs -- his body -- it was disfigured in a manner similar to the other victims --

> KAREN
> My God --

> TED
> Where is the FBI? Huh? That's what I want to know -- we got a serial killer on the loose here --

INT. SINCLAIR HOUSE - LIVING ROOM - DAY

The Sinclairs (SUE, CHARLES, ERICA) watch, on edge.

>   POWELL (ON TV)
>   There was an eyewitness, but for
>   his safety we will not be releasing
>   his name at this time. We have also
>   identified a person of interest.

He holds up a PHOTO OF EDDIE MUNSON.

>   POWELL (CONT'D)
>   Eddie Munson, twenty, also a
>   senior at Hawkins High --

>   ERICA
>   *What the fu--*
>   (oops)
>   Dge. *Fudge.*

>   SUE
>   You know him??

Erica shakes her head vigorously.

EXT. LIPTON HOUSE - DAY

Our teens are just as stunned by Eddie's unveiling.

>   STEVE
>   Oh this is not good -- this is
>   *really* not good --

>   POWELL
>   We will provide photos to your
>   stations, and we encourage anyone
>   with information to come forward --

Reporters start to shout questions, but Powell talks over them --

>   POWELL (CONT'D)
>   I understand there are a lot of
>   questions. And I'm going to answer
>   as many as I can -- *two o'clock* at
>   town hall, where anyone from the
>   Hawkins community is welcome. But
>   right now -- I've got some work to
>   do. Appreciate your understanding.

With that, Powell heads off as frantic reporters call after him.

Our gang is in total shock, when --

CHHHH! Dustin's supercomm suddenly blasts to life!

      EDDIE (O.S.)
  Dustin -- you copy -- Wheeler -- ?!

Dustin and the others share looks -- *shit*. They duck back behind the van --

      DUSTIN
  Eddie -- holy shit -- you okay??

EXT. WOODS - SKULL ROCK - INTERCUT

We now reveal Eddie is hiding by a boulder in the woods, talking into the stolen walkie --

      EDDIE
  Nah man. I'm pretty <u>goddamn far
  from okay</u> --

      ROBIN
    (to Dustin)
  Where is he -- ?

      DUSTIN
  Where are you -- ?

      EDDIE
  Skull Rock -- you know it -- ?

      DUSTIN
    (unsure)
  Yeah, uh, near Cornwallis and --

      STEVE
  Garret. <u>I know it</u>.

Steve starts to head off, as do the others.

      DUSTIN
  Just -- hold tight -- okay? We're
  coming -- *we're coming!*

Dustin races after his friends and --

INT./EXT. PIZZAMOBILE - ROAD - MORNING

VROOM! Argyle's Pizzamobile tears down the road, passing a sign that reads --

                    WELCOME TO SALT LAKE CITY!

We crane up to reveal the city and its skyscrapers, nestled
beneath the shadows of those big mountains. Our gang MADE IT!

EXT. SUZIE'S HOUSE - LATER - DAY

The Pizzamobile putters to a stop by a suburban house.

A mailbox reads BINGHAM.

MOMENTS LATER

Doors open and JONATHAN, ARGYLE, MIKE, and WILL stagger out.
They are exhausted from the long drive. Everyone stretches as
they head up the walkway. Argyle massages his butt.

>   ARGYLE
>   I can't feel my butt. Can you guys
>   feel your butts -- ?
>
>   WILL
>   I -- can feel my butt.
>
>   JONATHAN
>   Remember -- everyone needs to be on
>   their best behavior, okay -- ?
>
>   ARGYLE
>   Why'd you look at me when you said
>   that?
>
>   JONATHAN
>   I didn't --
>
>   MIKE
>   They're just -- very religious.
>
>   ARGYLE
>   I'm *super spiritual* dude --
>
>   MIKE
>   Yeah I think they're spiritual --
>   in a *different way*.

They reach the door. Ring the doorbell and --

WHOOM! The door flies open mid-ring to reveal --

A shirtless, barefoot boy, 6. This is CORNELIUS. He's
panting, wearing war paint, and wields a rubber bow and arrow.

He eyes our gang with a feral, ferocious look.

                       MIKE (CONT'D)
        Hi there -- uh -- is Suzie here?

WHACK! Cornelius releases a WAR CRY, then shoots Mike with the arrow, right in the forehead --

                       MIKE (CONT'D)
        -- Ow!

The crazed child now turns and runs away with a scream. Our gang share confused looks, *uhh*, then enter the house --

INT. SUZIE'S HOUSE - VARIOUS - DAY

-- And find themselves in some bizarre combo of *Lord of the Flies* and *Home Alone*! There are children in here -- LOTS OF CHILDREN. And no evidence of adult supervision *whatsoever*.

WHOOSH! Two SWORD-FIGHTING KIDS in Shakespearean garb smack one another with plastic swords --

                       SWORD-FIGHTING KID
        Away, you starvelling, you elf-
        skin, you dried neat's-tongue --!!

                       ARGYLE
        Alright -- this is *my kinda place*!

Off a baffled Mike, we move into a MONTAGE as our gang SEARCHES FOR SUZIE --

INT. SUZIE'S HOUSE - LIVING ROOM - DAY

They enter the living room, where a boy, STERLING, 9, films a girl, TABITHA, 10, with an 8mm camera. She stumbles, a fake wound on her neck.

                       TABITHA
        I've been bitten! HELP!
        Hellllllpppp...

Tabitha drops to the ground, begins to foam at the mouth.

Our kids awkwardly approach Sterling.

                       JONATHAN
        Excuse me -- we're looking for
        Suzie --

                        STERLING
            Can you not see we're filming????
                (beat, back to camera)
            Stay in it, Tabitha!! STAY IN IT!!

Tabitha continues to foam and starts to seize violently and --

INT. SUZIE'S HOUSE - KITCHEN - DAY

They now try the kitchen, where THREE KIDS in chef hats are making a GOURMET MEAL -- chopping onions, breading chicken, grinding pepper.

                        MIKE
            Hi, uh -- we're looking for Suzie --
            ??

                        CHEF KID
            Don't know don't care -- that's too
            much salt, Peter!!!! Father's
            kidneys! Father's KIDNEYS!

WHUMP! The power in the kitchen suddenly goes off. Angry eyes swing over to Cornelius, who is now flipping switches on a CIRCUIT BREAKER like a madman.

                        VOICE
            CORNELIUS!!!

EDEN, 18, storms over and snatches Cornelius by the arm. The clear black sheep of the family, Eden has dyed black hair and wears black clothes and black eyeliner.

                        EDEN
            How many times have I told you --
            that is NOT a toy!

She flips the breaker back on and drags the squirming wild child away. Argyle watches Eden, his eyes wide as saucers. He's in a *love trance*.

                        ARGYLE
            Who is that *goddess*...?

Our kids share baffled looks and --

INT. STUDY - SECOND FLOOR - MINUTES LATER

WHOOM! A scowling Cornelius is slammed down into a chair.

Eden flips a timer to five minutes.

                    EDEN
          You make another escape, I'm
          getting Father!!

As Cornelius hisses, Eden turns to leave the study only to find her path is obstructed by our teens!

                    EDEN (CONT'D)
          Who the *hell* are you?

                    ARGYLE
               (still in love trance)
          Argyle -- and you are -- ?

                    EDEN
               (off guard)
          Eden?

                    ARGYLE
          Like the garden, *nice* --

                    JONATHAN
               (enough of this)
          We're looking for Suzie --

                    WILL
          Do you know where she is?

Eden motions to a door --

                    EDEN
          Third floor, second door on your
          left -- you see her, give that
          selfish little four-eyed shit a
          nice little *shove* for me will ya?

Eden walks away, marching back down the steps. Argyle watches her go.

                    ARGYLE
          Absolutely -- I'll shove her for
          you, Eden. Whatever you desire.

Eden glances back at Argyle (intrigued?) then hurries on her way as --

INT. SUZIE'S HOUSE - THIRD FLOOR - DAY

Our kids scramble up to the third floor, where they find a doorway, half-open. They throw it open the rest of the way --

INT. SUZIE'S ROOM - DAY

>   MIKE
>   Suzie -- ???

His voice catches. <u>The room is empty.</u> *She's not here.*

>   MIKE (CONT'D)
>   The hell??

Argyle opens a closet --

>   ARGYLE
>   She's not in the closet --

>   WILL
>   Why would she be in the closet
>   -- ?

>   ARGYLE
>   (oh!)
>   Under the bed -- !

As Argyle moves to check under the bed, Mike's eyes lock onto the window -- it's wide open, curtains billowing in the wind.

>   MIKE
>   "Give her a shove -- "

Mike and Will share looks, then race over to the window, and --

EXT. SUZIE'S HOUSE - DAY

Thrust their heads out. They look right -- nothing -- then left and --

BINGO! A GIRL (BACK TURNED TO US) IS ON THE ROOF, her waist hooked to a safety cable, wearing a helmet as she fiddles with the CEREBRO ANTENNA.

>   MIKE
>   Suzie???

She turns to them. It's Suzie alright! <u>The one and only</u>!

                        SUZIE
              Yeah? Who _the heck_ are you and what
              are you doing in my room??

                        MIKE
              Yeah -- sorry about that -- it's
              just --

                        WILL
              We're Dustin's friends --

                        MIKE
              And we _really_ need your help.

Off Suzie, stunned, CUT TO --

EXT. RUSSIAN TUNDRA - CRASH SITE - MORNING

A snow-covered tree *BENDING* IN THE WIND. *Back in Russia.*

CLOSE ON: A BOOT stomps through snow as --

MURRAY -- bruised and battered but alive -- hikes his way through snow, scarf around his neck, pushing his way against a HEAVY WIND.

CUT SUPER WIDE TO REVEAL: He is making his way back to the crash site. The plane is half-intact -- buried in snow, metal bent, wings half-ripped off. We see the dim light from a fire, which has been built under one of the broken wings.

EXT. YURI'S PLANE - LATER - DAY

Murray reaches the fire, where he's greeted by --

JOYCE, similarly bruised, keeping warm by the fire --

>   JOYCE
>   You said an hour --

>   MURRAY
>   I underestimated --

>   JOYCE
>   I thought you were dead --

>   MURRAY
>   Might as well be.

Murray drops down on a crate, warms his hands in the fire.

>   MURRAY (CONT'D)
>   We're truly in Hell, if Hell froze
>   over. There's nothing south. But
>   two miles north, I saw some smoke.
>   Could be a town, could be a house --
>   maybe someone there knows where we
>   can find this prison --

>   JOYCE
>   This -- top-secret prison?

Murray sighs.

>   MURRAY
>   Right.

He looks over at YURI -- who is tied to a tree somewhere near the crash site.

>   MURRAY (CONT'D)
>   Any luck with our friend?

>   JOYCE
>   What do you think?

Off Murray, frustration showing --

EXT. YURI'S PLANE - LATER - DAY

Joyce and Murray -- now both carrying BAGS OF SUPPLIES -- stomp their way over to Yuri.

He's... not looking good. He's heavily bruised from the crash, with a big gash on his head, which has been hastily bandaged. He's also, of course, freezing cold out here.

>   MURRAY
>   Hey dipshit --

Murray yanks a gag out of his mouth.

>   MURRAY (CONT'D)
>   We're outta here. Last chance.
>   Where's the prison?

>   YURI
>   I told you. Yuri will help you --
>   for right price.

An annoyed Joyce looks to Murray --

>   JOYCE
>   I told you, we're wasting our
>   time --

>   MURRAY
>   (eyes still on Yuri)
>   Half.

>   JOYCE
>   What -- ??

>   YURI
>   What?

>   MURRAY
>   You heard me you stubborn bastard.
>   Half the reward -- twenty thousand.

                    YURI
          ... Thirty --

                    MURRAY
          Twenty-two --

                    YURI
          Twenty-five --

                    MURRAY
               (satisfied)
          Alright, looks like we've got
          ourselves a --
               (abruptly switching)
          MORON!

Murray suddenly *whaps* Yuri with his glove --

                    MURRAY (CONT'D)
          You thought I was serious??? He
          thought I was serious!
               (leans into Yuri's face
               with a mocking accent)
          "I got you -- I got you GOOD!"

Yuri stares, his face burning from humiliation. He hates the
tables being turned on him like this!

                    MURRAY (CONT'D)
          There is only one thing you get if
          you take this deal -- you <u>get to
          live</u>.

Yuri scoffs.

                    YURI
          You are no killer. If you were I
          would be dead already --

                    JOYCE
          You're right. He's not a killer.
          And I'm just a little bird, right?
          But we don't need to kill you. We
          just need to leave you here.
          There's nothing for miles -- <u>no one
          will find you</u>.

                    MURRAY
          No human, at least.

Murray kneels beside him -- deadly serious now.

                    MURRAY (CONT'D)
               I saw tracks in the woods, Yuri.
               Bears.

Yuri darkens. *Oh no.*

                    MURRAY (CONT'D)
               Remember that story you told us?
               Yuri's heart -- punctured by the
               claws of a bear? Who knew you could
               see your own future?

Yuri tries to mask his fear. But Murray knows he's got him --
got him "good." He turns to Joyce.

                    MURRAY (CONT'D)
               Shall we fly out of here, little
               bird?

She nods. And with that, Murray and Joyce turn heel and walk
away, leaving Yuri behind with this awful thought.

They make it about ten feet when Yuri finally breaks --

                    YURI (O.S.)
               <u>WAIT</u>.

Murray and Joyce spin back --

                    YURI (CONT'D)
               You should head east -- not north.
               My warehouse is there. Supplies.
               Guns. Truck. We will need to reach
               prison by nightfall if you hope to
               save your friend. That is -- if he
               <u>isn't already dead</u>.

Off Murray and Joyce, taking this in, HARD CUT TO --

EXT. DEMOGORGON PIT - HOLDING CELL - DAY

CA-CHUNK! A key turns, opening a lock as --

IVAN opens the holding cell door.

                    IVAN
               <Out -- everyone out!!>

HOPPER and DMITRI share worried looks. This... can't be good.

                    IVAN (CONT'D)
               <LET'S GO!!! MOVE IT!!>

As our prisoners begin to reluctantly rise to their feet --

MOMENTS LATER

Ivan leads Hopper, Dmitri, and the other prisoners down the flight of steps. Armed guards keep watch from the balcony, ready to open fire if any prisoner steps out of line.

THE PIT - CONTINUOUS

Ivan opens a gate below and leads the prisoners out onto the snowy pit, where more guards are stationed. Hopper remains unemotional throughout the walk, but Dmitri and the other prisoners are terrified -- their eyes fixed on that *big metal door...*

                    DMITRI
        This is it American -- I hope you
        are ready.

But then -- something surprising: Ivan *keeps walking*, leading them to a smaller door on the far side of the pit, which he proceeds to unlock. We see only darkness beyond, but we hear music playing within. Is that... <u>Russian Opera</u>?

Our prisoners share confused looks. *The hell?*

Ivan lights up a cigarette with his gold-plated lighter.

                    IVAN
        <What are you all waiting for?
        Move. *Move.*>

Hopper and Dmitri leading the way, they cautiously head past the smoking Ivan, through an open door, and into --

A LARGE ROOM - DAY

We HOLD ON Dmitri as a smile grows across his face --

                    DMITRI
        Am I dreaming, American... or is
        this real??

REVERSE TO REVEAL: A FEAST has been laid out on a long table -- meat, cheese, fruit, potatoes, vodka -- you name it!!! The opera music blasts from the gold horn of an OLD-TIMEY GRAMOPHONE.

Dmitri laughs. Then he and the other prisoners race forward, ecstatic, and our MUSIC RISES and --

MOMENTS LATER

A SERIES OF CLOSE SHOTS as our prisoners devour their meal -- munching grapes -- teeth ripping meat off bones -- ravenous. They are all loving this -- that is, all but Hopper, who is not eating. Rather, he's just downing a bottle of vodka -- which is approximately the size of a glass of Coke. Another empty, already finished bottle sits beside his empty plate.

OLEG eyes him, annoyed.

                    OLEG
              (to Dmitri, mouth full)
      <What is wrong with your American
      friend, moosor?>

                    DMITRI
      <He's not my friend. And he has
      lost his spirit to live.>
              (to Hopper, in English)
      Isn't that right, Cursed One -- you
      have lost to your spirit to live?

                    HOPPER
      Something like that --

Hopper slams down his vodka glass -- he's finished it already. He wipes his mouth, reaches for another -- but he's tipsy and accidentally knocks the glass off the table.

Dmitri watches in disgust as Hopper drops to his knees to retrieve it.

                    DMITRI
      <He is American after all. Big talk
      -- but weak inside.>

                    OLEG
      <Well tell him to eat. Or he
      endangers us all. We have a big
      fight ahead of us.>

                    DMITRI
      <What are you talking about?
      Fight?>

Oleg takes another bite, wipes some grease from his mouth, then --

                    OLEG
          <I have been in this place one
          week. My first night -- I saw --
          six men enter this room. Six, just
          like us. They came out happy and
          fat, faces smothered in grease. But
          when night fell -- they were thrown
          into that pit out there. But not
          alone. You heard those roars, yes?
          That is a monster. Not from this
          world.>

The others share looks, eyes wide as --

WHOOM! A drunk Hopper drops back up into his chair. Only he
doesn't have that vodka -- seemingly couldn't find it? Oh
well. He reaches for another. *What a drunken mess.*

                    OLEG (CONT'D)
          <Thirty seconds it took -- thirty
          seconds -- and all six men were
          dead.>

Scared looks all around but --

                    PRISONER #1
          <You speak no sense. If they plan
          to kill us tonight -- why waste
          this food on us -- ?>

                    OLEG
          <Look around. Everyone in here is
          strong and young, yes? Where are
          the old, the weak, the crippled? I
          believe they have selected us -- to
          train this monster for war. That is
          why they feed us now -- they want
          us strong -- so we can fight it. To
          test its strength. You saw those
          weapons out there, yes?>

The prisoners nod. Hopper just guzzles more vodka. *Jesus.*

                    OLEG (CONT'D)
          <Before they release their monster,
          they give out the key to that
          locker. But -- last week, the men
          got their weapons -- then scattered
          like fools. We stick together,
          perhaps we stand a chance. Perhaps
          -- we live to see another day.>

Nods of agreement and some murmurs of excitement, as hope returns to our prisoners, but --

WHAM! Slams his vodka down. Wipes his mouth.

> HOPPER
> Let me guess. This <beast> -- is around nine feet tall. Thin. White skin. No face. No eyes.

Everyone turns to Hopper, surprised he's speaking.

Dmitri translates for Hopper (and will continue to do so). Oleg stares at Hop, surprised --

> OLEG
> <How do you know this?>

> HOPPER
> Because I've seen one. Fought one. And your theories about it -- they're all wrong. You know why they feed captive predators live prey? Because otherwise the predator gets bored. It needs the thrill of the hunt.
> (beat)
> We're not here to train their monster with swords and axes -- we're here to entertain it.

Hopper picks up a chicken bone.

> HOPPER (CONT'D)
> And the reason for this food? It isn't to make us strong. It's to get us nice and plump so we can provide all the nutrients and protein a growing monster could need.
> (beat)
> So go ahead, boys -- eat up. Enjoy. Because this here --
> (beat)
> This is your last meal.

Hopper tosses the chicken leg back onto the table. As it rattles against a tin plate --

No one else goes to eat. Hop just ruined their appetite. He goes back to drinking as --

The opera song reaches an end. The sound of the needle SCRATCHING across the vinyl becomes --

INT. HAWKINS LABS - RAINBOW ROOM - DAY (MEMORY)

WHOOSH! A RED DISC skipping its way down a wall of pegs --

Eleven is in the Rainbow Room -- *her past*. She's playing PLINKO in the corner. She is alone like usual -- and focusing, trying to mentally direct the disc into a specific slot. She sighs with frustration -- she's clearly failing.

                    VOICE (O.S.)
        What number are you aiming for?

She looks up, sees the FRIENDLY ORDERLY approaching.

                    ELEVEN
    ... Three.

She tries again -- the disc lands in the FIVE slot.

The Orderly kneels beside her.

                    FRIENDLY ORDERLY
    You know... sometimes it's helpful
    to step away for a moment. Let the
    mind clear.

Eleven keeps trying anyway. She gets a six. *Dammit.*

                    FRIENDLY ORDERLY (CONT'D)
    Determined, aren't we?

She tries yet again. As the Orderly watches her --

                    FRIENDLY ORDERLY (CONT'D)
    You know... you remind me of
    someone. Someone I used to know
    really well.

He takes the Plinko coin away from Eleven.

                    FRIENDLY ORDERLY (CONT'D)
    Can you guess who?

Eleven shakes her head. The Friendly Orderly places the Plinko coin in the slot marked ONE. Now this -- *this* gets Eleven's attention.

She looks at him. Eyes wide.

                        ELEVEN
                ... One?

A small nod.

                        ELEVEN (CONT'D)
                Papa said --

                        FRIENDLY ORDERLY
                "He doesn't exist." I know. But...
                can I tell you a secret?

Eleven nods. The Orderly glances at a SECURITY CAMERA --
always watching. Then back to Eleven, his voice a little
lower so no one can hear --

                        FRIENDLY ORDERLY (CONT'D)
                Sometimes... Papa doesn't tell the
                truth.

Eleven stares, stunned. She had never even considered that
possibility.

                        FRIENDLY ORDERLY (CONT'D)
                I spent years with One. Right here
                -- in this very room.

                        ELEVEN
                Where -- is he?

                        FRIENDLY ORDERLY
                Maybe we'll save that story for
                another day. I'm afraid it doesn't
                have a happy ending.

A sad smile, then --

                        FRIENDLY ORDERLY (CONT'D)
                But he was a lot like you. I
                remember... everything was hard for
                him. The other kids, they thought
                he was weak. Slow. So did Papa.
                Then... out of nowhere -- he walked
                in here, and it was like, something
                about him had... *changed*.

Eleven is intrigued now. Really listening.

                        FRIENDLY ORDERLY (CONT'D)
                And I asked him -- what's
                different... and he said --
                        (sad smile as he remembers)
                        (MORE)

                    FRIENDLY ORDERLY (CONT'D)
               He said, he had *figured it out*. He
               wasn't like the others, he said. He
               found his strength in a memory from
               his past -- something that made him
               sad -- but also... *angry*. Do you
               maybe -- have a memory like that?

Eleven shrugs her shoulders. Uncertain.

The Friendly Orderly considers, then --

                    FRIENDLY ORDERLY (CONT'D)
               ... Do you remember that day -- a
               strange woman came to see you? This
               would have been when Eight was
               still here. The woman -- she was
               shouting a name at you -- Jane.

QUICK FLASHCUT OF HER MOTHER PULLED AWAY FROM ELEVEN AND EIGHT -- CALLING OUT JANE --

Eleven gives a small nod.

                    FRIENDLY ORDERLY (CONT'D)
               That was your mother.

Eleven can hardly breathe. That -- *can't be true*.

                    ELEVEN
               My Mama -- died. Making me.

                    FRIENDLY ORDERLY
               And who told you that?

                    ELEVEN
                    (realizing)
               ... Papa. Who -- does not always
               tell the truth.

The Orderly leans in -- his voice a notch lower.

                    FRIENDLY ORDERLY
               This place -- and the people here --
               are *not what you think*.

On this shocking note -- WHOOM! -- the door swings open and Dr. Brenner enters the rainbow room.

                    DR. BRENNER
               Good morning, children.

The children all rise.

                    NUMBERS
            Good morning, Papa.

Eleven can't help but look at "Papa" in a different way now.

Brenner clocks her -- and the Friendly Orderly at her side. He can tell something is going on, but he averts his gaze, burying his concern. *For now, at least.*

                    DR. BRENNER
            I have something very special
            planned for us today. *Follow me.*

Dr. Brenner now leads the Numbers out of the room.

We hold on Eleven, disturbed by all she has learned, and PRE-LAP THE SOUND OF BEEPING AS --

INT. SILO LAB - OBSERVATION BOOTH - DAY

Eleven's heart rate is tracked in the antenna silo.

OWENS is looking out the window at Eleven. *Thinking.*

                    DR. OWENS
            We should have just told her the
            truth...

                    DR. BRENNER
            And risk everything -- no.

Brenner walks over, joins Owens at the window. As he looks out at the tank, some pain, regret in his voice --

                    DR. BRENNER (CONT'D)
            She will find out soon enough.

INT. NINA TANK - DAY

We PUSH back in on Eleven, floating in that black water.

Her eyes dart back and forth. Faster and faster *and* --

EXT. WOODS - BIRD'S EYE - DAY

WHOOSH! We're soaring over the forest. Below us, through an opening in the canopy, we see our Hawkins gang winding their way through the forest, carrying their bags of groceries.

                    STEVE (PRE-LAP)
            Dude, I'm telling you, you're
            taking us the wrong way --

DOWN IN THE FOREST - CLOSER SHOT NOW

We see our gang is walking in pairs, Dustin and Steve leading the way (Dustin has his trusty compass out), then Robin and Nancy, and lastly, Max and Lucas.

>   DUSTIN
>   It's north -- I'm *positive* -- I
>   checked the map.
>
>   STEVE
>   You realize Skull Rock is a super
>   popular make-out spot, right -- ?
>
>   DUSTIN
>   Yeah so -- ?
>
>   STEVE
>   SO it wasn't popular till *I made it
>   popular*. I practically invented it
>   -- and we're heading in the wrong
>   direction.

Steve veers off course, hopping over a fallen tree --

>   DUSTIN
>   Steve -- where are you going?!
>   STEVE!

As Dustin chases after Steve, trying to convince him to turn around --

>   MAX
>   Okay so apparently -- we're going
>   *this way* now. I *swear to God* if
>   they get us lost...

Lucas nods slightly as they follow after the bickering Dustin and Steve. He's tossing a pine cone in his hand, deep in thought. Max, sensing he's hurting in some way, softens --

>   MAX (CONT'D)
>   Hey... are you -- okay?
>
>   LUCAS
>   (nods)
>   Yeah... yeah. Just thinking
>   about... Patrick, you know?
>
>   MAX
>   Yeah.

                    LUCAS
          It's just, like -- why him? Then --
          I remembered, this one day he came
          to practice with a black eye. He
          said he fell, but he was clearly
          lying. It's like -- everyone Vecna
          targets -- has something in their
          life -- something that's --

                    MAX
          Hurting them. *Haunting them.*

Lucas nods. They walk for a beat in silence. Then --

                    LUCAS
          I didn't really know Patrick, so --
          it was easy to just -- look the
          other way, I guess. But I did know
          you, and --
                (turns to Max)
          I'm sorry I wasn't there.

This means a lot to Max, but --

                    MAX
          ... It's not your fault. I
          disappeared.

                    LUCAS
          But you didn't... I just didn't...
          look hard enough. But... I see you
          now. *I see you.*

Max and Lucas share a sweet smile here -- is Lumax blooming again?! We now drop back to --

Nancy and Robin, who are watching them.

                    ROBIN
          God *they're adorable*, I just want
          to squeeze them, you know?
                (Nancy nods, smiles)
          I mean -- if I'm permitted to find
          a silver lining in all this end-of-
          the-world doom and gloom, it's the
          rekindling of some old flames which
          frankly never should have been
          snuffed out --

Nancy shoots her daggers here as Robin realizes she once again put her foot in her mouth --

ROBIN (CONT'D)
That wasn't meant as a -- *a hint* -- or anything --

NANCY
Right.

The girls walk in silence for a beat. Nancy is clearly a bit irritated. And Robin, *well* -- Robin can't help herself --

ROBIN
But if it *was* a hint... would that... be... like, so terrible?? For me to wish happiness for my friends --

NANCY
You think I'm not happy --

ROBIN
Maybe you are. It's just -- in the library, the other day -- when I mentioned Jonathan -- you flinched -- or something. *Winced*.

NANCY
(very defensive)
I didn't *flinch or wince* --

ROBIN
Yeah okay --

NANCY
Me and Jonathan are fine. We're good.

ROBIN
Right. Got it.

A beat. Then Nancy spins to Robin, can't keep it in --

                    NANCY
               (fast)
          It's just -- he was supposed to be
          here for break and then -- he
          pulled out at the last minute for
          some vague, mumbly Jonathan reason
          -- and to be honest I wasn't *that*
          surprised because I've felt him
          pulling away lately and I don't
          know if it's because we're two
          thousand miles away or if he's met
          someone else or *what* -- but I can't
          find out as now he's apparently
          blown up his family's phone or
          something -- so if the mention of
          his name caused some muscle spasm
          in my face -- that's *probably why*.
          Okay?

                    ROBIN
          Yes. A -- uh -- very reasonable
          reason to flinch. Or wince. Wince-
          flinch.

The girls walk another beat. Then, suddenly realizing
something, Nancy turns to Robin --

                    NANCY
          You said happiness for your
          "friends." So -- we're friends now?
          As in, officially?

                    ROBIN
          Yeah -- I mean -- right?

                    NANCY
          Right.

The girls share a soft smile, when --

                    STEVE (O.S.)
          BOOM!!!! BADABADABOOM!!

The girls share looks, then hurry toward the sound. It's --

EXT. SKULL ROCK - CLEARING

Steve -- *celebrating* in a clearing. He's discovered SKULL
ROCK, a large boulder with vague skull-like features. He
dances his way over to Dustin, gets right in his face --

                    STEVE
          There she blows!! SKULL ROCK! IN
          YER FACE, Henderson -- in your
          stupid, cocky little face!!!

Dustin looks back down at his compass, flabbergasted --

                    DUSTIN
          That -- *doesn't make sense* --

                    STEVE
          Even with it staring you right in
          the face, you can't admit it, can
          you?? You can't admit you were
          wrong you butthead -- !

                    EDDIE (O.S.)
          I hate to agree with Harrington but
          I concur --

Eddie suddenly drops out of a tree, startling them --

                    EDDIE (CONT'D)
          You, Dustin Henderson, are a *total
          butthead*.

                    DUSTIN
          Eddie! *Jesus* --

Dustin runs forward and hugs his friend -- but Eddie is too shaken to really hug back.

                    DUSTIN (CONT'D)
          We thought for a second you were a
          goner.

                    EDDIE
          Yeah. Me too, man. Me too.

As the rest of the group moves into the clearing, gathering around Eddie, we SLOWLY PULL AWAY, and --

                    CONCERNED WOMAN (PRE-LAP)
          How long have you known Eddie
          Munson was killing these kids?

INT. TOWN HALL - DAY

A CONCERNED WOMAN stands, mic in hand.

We're in TOWN HALL -- and it's jam-packed with about two hundred townspeople, including Karen, Ted, HOLLY, CLAUDIA, Erica and her parents. Damn -- everyone is here.

The Woman's voice shakes with anger, emotion --

> CONCERNED WOMAN
> It was *his* trailer where Chrissy was killed -- and you expect us to believe that he became a suspect just this morning???

The crowd reacts, clearly angry about this as well.

Chief Powell is on stage behind a podium, flanked by his officers (Callahan, DANIELS), as well as LOCAL GOVERNMENT.

> POWELL
> (ignoring this)
> The truth is we've been following several leads. And yes -- Eddie Munson was one of them -- and we are now doing everything in our power to find him. In the meantime, for your safety, we will be enforcing a strict curfew --

> CONCERNED WOMAN
> That's your solution -- *hide from him* -- ?!

> ANGRY TOWNSPERSON #1
> (shouting)
> We're already doing that -- !

> ANGRY TOWNSPERSON #2
> (shouting)
> It's been days! Days! Why isn't he behind bars *right now* -- !

> POWELL
> I understand you're all upset. But I promise you, we will find him --

> POWERFUL VOICE (O.S.)
> No. YOU WON'T.

Heads swivel to find this powerful voice belongs to --

Jason. He's standing in the back of the room by the entry doors, flanked by Andy and his other teammates.

Powell knows this isn't good. Tries to defuse.

>   POWELL
>   Jason -- son -- how about we talk about this in private -- ?

Jason begins to walk forward. Down the aisle.

>   JASON
>   Why? So you can keep me quiet? So you can keep the truth from coming out?

Some murmurs from the crowd. *Truth?* Jason takes the mic from a MODERATOR, addresses the crowd.

>   JASON (CONT'D)
>   I don't know about the rest of you -- but I can't bear to listen to any more *excuses and lies*.

MURMURS OF APPROVAL --

>   POWELL
>   Son -- that's enough --

>   JASON
>   I agree. I've had "enough". In fact -- I think we've all had ENOUGH.

A RIPPLE OF APPLAUSE now. He's winning over the crowd.

And now -- now Jason starts to get emotional.

>   JASON (CONT'D)
>   Last night -- I saw things... things I -- I can't explain. Things the police don't want to believe. Things... I don't want to believe myself. But I know what I saw. I *know*. And I've come to accept an awful truth -- these murders are *ritualistic sacrifices*.

This sends a shock wave through the crowd -- murmurs, whispers, a few incredulous looks.

Karen exchanges frightened glances with the Sinclairs. Erica looks -- *highly incredulous.*

                    JASON (CONT'D)
          We've all heard about how *satanic
          cults* are spreading through our
          country like some -- some *disease*.
          And Eddie Munson -- he's the leader
          of one of these cults -- a cult
          that operates right here, *in
          Hawkins*. The mall fire -- all those
          unexplained deaths over the years.
          Some people, they say our town is
          cursed -- they just don't know why.
          Now -- now we do. Now we know.

Jason reaches into his letterman jacket, retrieves
something --

                    JASON (CONT'D)
          They call themselves -- Hellfire.

He holds up the most recent YEARBOOK PHOTO OF THE HELLFIRE
CLUB. Karen's heart almost stops. Erica can't believe this --
she leaps out of her seat --

                    ERICA
          That's BULLSHIT! Hellfire's not a
          cult -- it's a CLUB FOR NERDS!

The entire room turns to look at Erica -- including ANGRY
TOWNSPERSON #1. But Erica's mom (Sue) quickly drags Erica
back down into her seat. Jason eyes her, shakes his head --

                    JASON
          A "club." A "harmless club."

Then back to the crowd --

                    JASON (CONT'D)
          That's what they want you think --
          but it's a lie. A lie designed to
          conceal the truth --

Andy and other players now move down the aisle, distributing
photocopies of the Hellfire Club pic to the crowd --

                    JASON (CONT'D)
          And now this cult is protecting its
          leader, Eddie, *hiding him*, allowing
          him to continue his rampage --

Our families (Wheelers, Sinclairs, Henderson) now each get
copies. Karen goes sheet white. *This can't be happening.*

                    JASON (CONT'D)
          Last night -- I became overcome
          with this feeling of...
          hopelessness. But then -- I
          remembered Romans 12:21... *"Do not
          be overcome by evil, but overcome
          evil with good."* And God knows
          there is *good* in this town. <u>So</u> much
          good.
                    (surveys crowd)
          It's in this room -- right here.
          Right now. So I came here today --
          humbly -- to ask for your help. To
          join me in this fight. Let us cast
          out this evil -- and save Hawkins.
          <u>Together</u>.

Jason's "inspiring" speech is met... <u>with silence</u>. We're not
sure if the crowd is with him or not -- but then, ANGRY
TOWNSPERSON #1 shuffles out of his seat and starts to head
for the exit. Then he abruptly stops, turns back to the
crowd --

                    ANGRY TOWNSPERSON #1
          What are you all just standing
          around for? You heard the kid!

He keeps walking, angry, then blows out the exit doors.

MORE TOWNSPEOPLE now begin to follow his lead --

                    POWELL
          Hey -- I want you all to hear me
          loud and clear on this -- anyone
          interfering with this investigation
          will be arrested -- !

A CHORUS OF BOOS directed at Powell fills the room as more
people head for the exits, taking flyers with them. Five
people -- then ten -- then fifteen --

Out of desperation, Callahan races in, grabs the mic --

                    CALLAHAN
          Hey! We *WILL* be enforcing a curfew!
          If you're not in your houses after
          sunset with doors locked, you will
          be written up! It'll go on your
          permanent record -- !

But people keep leaving. Jason locks eyes with Chief Powell. He's won -- and he knows it. He then turns and walks away, joining his new followers out, passing right by --

A shocked Karen. She looks through the line of exiting people to an equally stunned Mrs. Sinclair. As our mothers lock eyes, SMASH TO --

EXT. SUZIE'S HOUSE - DAY

Quiet. We PUSH IN on Suzie's house.

>   SUZIE (PRE-LAP)
>   Okay -- that is A LOT to process.

INT. SUZIE'S HOUSE - SUZIE'S ROOM - DAY

Suzie is sitting on her bed, our Lenora crew across from her. Her eyes wide. She's shaken by what she's heard.

>   SUZIE
>   I mean -- that might be seriously
>   the *craziest* thing I've ever heard.
>
>   MIKE
>   I know it's hard to believe --
>
>   JONATHAN
>   But it's true -- all true.

She holds up the slip of paper with the number.

>   SUZIE
>   I dial into this computer -- and
>   find a location -- and at this
>   location is... the Nina Project?
>
>   WILL
>   Exactly --
>
>   SUZIE
>   And the Nina Project is the
>   code name for...
>   (beat, skeptical)
>   A video game?
>
>   MIKE
>   Console -- a video *game console*.
>
>   WILL
>   It's basically America's answer to
>   Nintendo --

                    ARGYLE
          Americantindo --

Everyone shoots Argyle a look -- *what???*

                    SUZIE
          That's a stupid name --

                    MIKE
          Yeah it's -- *really stupid* -- but
          it's *sixteen bit*, Suzie --

                    SUZIE
          Sixteen bit?! Why have I *never*
          heard of it --

                    MIKE
          Because it's top secret --

                    WILL
          That's why they're doing this --

                    MIKE
          It's part of the promotion -- the
          first person to make it to this
          secret location receives a free --
               (Jesus)
          Americantindo.

                    SUZIE
          So... you drove three thousand
          miles over your spring break so I
          can help you get a new video game
          console no one has ever heard of?

                    MIKE/WILL/JONATHAN
          ... Yes.

Suzie stares at them skeptically.

                    WILL
          But it's not for us -- it's for --
          for Dustin --

                    MIKE
               (picking up)
          Yeah -- for his birthday, which is
          --

                    SUZIE
          In two months three days and five
          hours.

WHOOM! The door flies open and Eden bursts into the room --

>   EDEN
> Suzie, I don't know WHAT you're
> doing, but I'm not spending my
> entire day BABYSITTING! PULL YOUR
> DAMN WEIGHT!!!

>   SUZIE
> *Language* -- !

>   EDEN
> Oh no, am I gonna burn in Hell now?

>   ARGYLE
> You tell her, Eden.

>   SUZIE
> OUT OF MY ROOM!

Suzie pushes off the bed, slams the door on Eden, and spins the lock.

>   WILL
> So, can you... help?

Suzie catches her breath, then turns back to the others, who are looking at her like lost puppy dogs, but --

>   SUZIE
> I would do *anything for Dustybun*...
> but... I'm afraid there's been...
>   (how to put this?)
> An... unfortunate development.

INT. SUZIE'S BEDROOM - FLASHBACK - NIGHT

It's night now. We swing from the cross over Suzie's bed to find Suzie, who is tossing and turning in bed, her pale skin covered in sweat.

>   SUZIE (V.O.)
> After changing Dusty's grade, I was
> wracked with the most awful guilt.

INT. SUZIE'S BEDROOM - FLASHBACK - DAY

Father talks to Suzie, pacing in front of her as she sits at her desk. She looks like a prisoner of war.

                    SUZIE (V.O.)
          Father could see my soul was
          tortured and he wrenched a
          confession out of me. Not only was
          I breaking the law -- I was dating
          an agnostic! AN AGNOSTIC! I've
          never seen father so angry.

LATER

Suzie's very angry Father carries her computer out of the room. As we push in on a tearful, guilty Suzie --

                    SUZIE (V.O.)
          Naturally, after learning the
          terrible truth, he confiscated my
          computer --

BACK TO SCENE

                    SUZIE
          I'm as likely to see it again as I
          am my poor Dustybun --

                    JONATHAN
          Where is it -- ?

                    SUZIE
          His study -- he uses it for work
          now -- and Father is always working
          -- and his door is, like,
          permanently locked. I'm *really
          sorry*. Truly. But it looks like you
          came all the way here <u>for nothing</u>.

As everyone shares defeated looks --

WHUMP! The power goes out in the room, followed promptly by--

                    EDEN (O.S.)
          CORNELIUUUUUUS!!!!

CH-WHUMP! The power sputters back on. Suzie's mind races -- this gave her an idea. She walks away from the boys, a plan forming...

                    SUZIE
          Unless...

Our boys lean forward.

                    MIKE
          Unless...?

                        SUZIE
              There might be a way.

She turns back to look at them.

                        SUZIE (CONT'D)
              But we're gonna need help. *A lot of*
              help.

Off our teens, newly hopeful, CUT TO --

EXT. WHEELER HOUSE - DAY

SSSCCEEEE!!! A CARAVAN OF FAMILY CARS screeches to a stop outside the Wheeler house.

The doors fly open as our various parents (plus Holly and Erica) race out and into the house --

>   KAREN (PRE-LAP)
>   Guys hello, hello??

INT. WHEELER HOUSE - BASEMENT - DAY

Our anxious parents race down into the basement, Karen in the lead --

>   KAREN
>   GUYS -- ARE YOU DOWN HERE?? GUYS?

As she reaches the landing, we WIDEN TO REVEAL:

It's EMPTY. *Shit.*

>KAREN (CONT'D)
>(freaked)
>They should be back by now -- they should be back --

>SUE
>What time was the movie -- ?

>KAREN
>Four hours ago --

>ERICA
>Hate to break it you Missus Wheeler -- but they lied to you --

>HOLLY
>LIAR LIARS PANTS ON FIRES!!

>CLAUDIA
>We don't think they're actually involved with this Eddie guy, do we?

>TED
>At this point anything is possible.

>KAREN
>Our children are not murderers, Ted!

>TED
>Don't put words in my mouth.
>(to Charles)
>She does that. Twists my words.

Karen dials a number on the basement phone.

>ERICA
>You calling the theater -- ?

>KAREN
>The police --

As the phone begins to RING --

EXT. WOODS - SKULL ROCK - DAY

Our camera pushes through the dense forest, finds --

A shaken Eddie leaning against the boulder, smoking a camel while he talks to our gang. That is, all but Dustin, who paces nearby, still obsessing with his compass.

> EDDIE
> ... When I got to shore, I tried calling you guys, but my walkie was drenched, busted. So I just -- did what I guess I do now. *I ran.*

A beat as our group takes everything in. Then...

> NANCY
> Do you know what time this was -- the attack...?

> EDDIE
> Yeah. As it so happens -- I know *exactly.*

Eddie starts to unhook his watch from his wrist.

> EDDIE (CONT'D)
> My walkie wasn't the only thing that got soaked.

He tosses the watch to Nancy. She flips it over. It's digital, and it's stuck at --

> NANCY
> Nine twenty-seven.

> ROBIN
> Same time our flashlights went kabloowie --

> STEVE
> Right -- so that means... what exactly?

> NANCY
> That surge of energy was Vecna *attacking* Patrick -- casting his spell.

> ROBIN
> What do yah know -- Nance is right. We *are* a step closer -- we now understand how Vecna attacks --

> LUCAS
> And *where* he attacks from --

                    MAX
So now we just need to sneak into
his secret lair in the Upside Down
and drive a stake through his
heart --

                    ROBIN
If he even *has* a heart --

                    STEVE
Why a stake? He's not a vampire --

                    MAX
It was a *metaphor* --

                    EDDIE
Bullets should work on him right?

                    LUCAS
I say we chop off his head --

                    NANCY
I say all of the above. But we
can't do *any of it* until we find a
way into the Upside Down --

                    MAX
We need El to get her powers back --

                    STEVE
               (to Eddie)
Everything was, like, way easier
when we had this girl with --

                    EDDIE
Superpowers. You've mentioned her.

Eddie's eyes now swivel to Dustin, still pacing around like a
madman.

                    EDDIE (CONT'D)
Henderson's... not cursed, is he?

                    STEVE
Cursed, no. Mental. *Absolutely*.

Dustin whirls back to the group --

                    DUSTIN
BOOM! BADABADA BOOM!

He stomps over to Steve.

DUSTIN (CONT'D)
I was right -- Skull Rock WAS north!!!

STEVE
Seriously -- you're serious???
This IS Skull Rock, dude -- you were absolutely a hundred-percent totally WRONG --

DUSTIN
Yes -- and NO.
(holds up compass)
This compass was working correctly when we left the Wheelers -- it was correct when we got in the car on Kerley. But it started to slip the further east we got -- and now it's, like, *way off*. So when I was leading us here -- I wasn't wrong -- the compass was.

STEVE
Okay -- so you were using faulty equipment, you were *still wrong* --

DUSTIN
Except it's *not* faulty. Lucas -- you remember what can affect a compass, right -- ?

LUCAS
An electromagnetic field --

DUSTIN
Yep --

ROBIN
Sorry, I must've I skipped that class --

DUSTIN
If there's a presence of a more powerful magnetic field, the needle deflects to that power. So either there's a super strong magnet near here, or --

LUCAS
There's a Gate.

Chills go through the group. But --

                        NANCY
            We're *nowhere* near the lab --

                        DUSTIN
            But what if -- somehow -- there's
            another gate -- a gate we don't
            know about. It'd have to be
            smaller, less powerful --

                        ROBIN
            A snack-sized gate -- ?

                        STEVE
            Where -- how -- why -- ?

                        DUSTIN
            No idea. All I know is *something* is
            causing this disturbance, and last
            time we saw something like this, it
            was a Gate. And I hope it is --
            because then we'd have a way to
            Vecna.

On that note, Dustin sweeps up his backpack and starts to
head off, following his compass --

                        STEVE
            Dude, Eddie's still a wanted man --
            we can't just be hiking around --

Dustin turns back, hold up the compass.

                        DUSTIN
            This little steel capsule here --
            might just be the key to saving
            Eddie.
                    (he looks to Eddie)
            What say you, Eddie the Banished?

Eddie takes a hard drag of his cigarette.

                        EDDIE
            I say you're asking me to follow you
            into Mordor. Which... if I'm bein'
            totally straight -- sounds like a
            real bad idea.
                    (beat)
            But the Shire --

He stands, tosses his cigarette. Stomps it out --

                    EDDIE (CONT'D)
              The Shire is burning.

Eddie grabs his stuff.

                    EDDIE (CONT'D)
              So Mordor it is.

He starts to head off with Dustin. The others share looks, then push to their feet and hustle after them and --

INT. HAWKINS LABS - TRAINING ROOM - DAY (MEMORY)

ECU: WHITE CHALK scrapes across a linoleum floor as--

Brenner draws a circle on one side of the training room as the Numbers -- all standing in a row -- look on.

                    DR. BRENNER (V.O.)
              We are going to play a game today.
              The rules of this game are simple.

We INTERCUT this with --

A LITTLE EARLIER (MEMORY)

As Brenner addresses the Numbers.

                    DR. BRENNER
              Stay in your circle. You leave your
              circle -- you lose.

LATER (MEMORY)

He draws another chalk circle on the other side of the room.

EARLIER (MEMORY)

                    DR. BRENNER
              The last one standing in a circle
              gets to spend an extra hour of free
              time in the Rainbow Room.

Numbers share looks, excited by this small reward, and --

LATER (MEMORY)

TWO steps into one circle, while SIX steps into the other. As the Friendly Orderly and ANOTHER ORDERLY work to blindfold the Numbers --

> DR. BRENNER (V.O.)
> Even though you are now competing with one another, I want you to approach this no differently than our tests.

EARLIER (MEMORY)

> DR. BRENNER
> If you allow emotion or anger to invade your thoughts, I promise -- you will fail. Do you understand?

> NUMBERS
> Yes, Papa.

Brenner nods. *Good.*

LATER (MEMORY)

The Orderlies finish blindfolding the Numbers, then step away, and --

> DR. BRENNER
> Begin.

Nothing seems to happen. Our Numbers are just standing there. But then, suddenly --

Six's feet begin to slide back a bit across the floor as if he is being pushed by an invisible person, and --

FWOOM! His body suddenly does a full spin and he falls, crashing hard to the ground -- and out of the circle.

He pulls off his blindfold, breathing hard. He looks to Two, who hasn't moved at all in his circle. His breathing calm.

> DR. BRENNER (CONT'D)
> (to Six)
> Take a seat. By the wall.

As Six goes to take a seat, Brenner turns to the other waiting Numbers. Looks them over. And --

> DR. BRENNER (CONT'D)
> Ten.

WE NOW MOVE INTO A MONTAGE (MEMORY)

As the Numbers take their turns against Two, attempting to knock him out of the circle. But one by one, they *fail* --

TEN is *THROWN* -- FIVE *STUMBLES* -- THREE *TOPPLES* -- SEVEN *SLIDES* -- each of them banished to the wall -- our cutting gets faster and faster as we show close, graphic shots of limbs hitting the concrete -- bodies blasting through frame -- one after the next -- until eventually --

<u>All the Numbers</u> are sitting against the wall.

That is, all *except* for --

                DR. BRENNER
  <u>Eleven</u>.

Eleven steps into her circle. Visibly nervous. As the Friendly Orderly blindfolds her, he whispers into her ear.

              FRIENDLY ORDERLY
  ... *Good luck.*

Brenner clocks this exchange. A flash of suspicion, concern.

The Friendly Orderly pulls her blindfold tight, then steps away.

CUT WIDE to reveal Eleven and Two standing inside opposite circles.

              DR. BRENNER
  <u>Begin</u>.

WHOOSH! Right away, Eleven's feet begin to slide across the floor. She is being pushed out of the circle by Two, same as the others. But just as her feet near the chalk line --

Her feet halt, *locking*. Brenner is surprised. The other Numbers are too. *They can't believe what they're seeing.*

CLOSE ON ELEVEN, breathing calmly, intently focused as she remembers back to what the Friendly Orderly told her --

            FRIENDLY ORDERLY (V.O.)
    (heavy reverb)
  ... *This place -- and the people here -- are not what you think...*

QUICK FLASHCUTS OF ELEVEN'S MOTHER BEING VIOLENTLY REMOVED FROM THE LAB, then --

            FRIENDLY ORDERLY (V.O.)
  Papa -- doesn't tell the truth...

Two's feet suddenly begin to slide backwards.

                    FRIENDLY ORDERLY (V.O.)
               Remember... that was your mother...

One inch... Two inches... *Three* --

                    FRIENDLY ORDERLY (V.O.)
               Your mother --

And -- WHOOM! Two is suddenly HURLED violently backwards -- his feet lifting off the ground -- and -- !

BAM! The back of his head SLAMS into the observation window, hard. He CRUMPLES weakly to the ground.

The Numbers are all clearly stunned.

As a confused Two staggers to his feet, yanking off his blindfold, breathing hard, we PUSH PAST him and into --

THE OBSERVATION WINDOW - CONTINUOUS

Where we find a YOUNG ELEVEN, removing her blindfold, clearly stunned herself. As blood trickles down her nose --

Our CAMERA PANS and finds Brenner. He glances at the Friendly Orderly, suspicious, then turns back to Eleven.

                    DR. BRENNER
               It looks like... we have ourselves
               a winner.

Off Young Eleven, breathing hard, HARD CUT TO --

EXT. RUSSIAN TUNDRA - DAY

WHOOSH! We're soaring over a white tundra. Far below us, we see three figures marching across the snow.

CLOSER NOW

It's Joyce, Murray, and Yuri -- his hands are still bound, but the gag is now loose around his neck. He is leading the way. They are all exhausted from the journey.

MOMENTS LATER

They stop as they crest a hill. Yuri breaks into a smile.

                    YURI
               And I present you -- Kyrzran.

As Joyce and Murray walk up beside him, REVERSE TO REVEAL:

Our familiar KAMCHATKA TOWN! A blue steeple peaks up above the rest of the houses --

> YURI (CONT'D)
> See that blue steeple there? That is Yuri's warehouse --

> MURRAY
> That looks like a church.

> YURI
> Can it not be both? Let us see what miracles it holds -- yes??

With that, Yuri heads toward the town. Joyce and Murray share looks, then scurry after him, and --

INT. KAMCHATKA CHURCH - LATER

EEEE! The heavy wooden door groans open as our ragtag group enters the dusty, abandoned church. They head into --

THE SANCTUARY.

They see all the boxes -- including the peanut butter Hopper took out --

> YURI
> Tsk tsk -- someone has been in my peanut butter. Very popular, as I say.

> MURRAY
> Weapons -- where are the weapons?

MOMENTS LATER

WHOOM! A crate is wrenched open, revealing --

A MASSIVE STOCKPILE OF WEAPONS.

> MURRAY
> Oh Jesus --

> YURI
> Not in church!

As Murray searches through the weapons, Yuri sidles up to him, pleased.

                    YURI (CONT'D)
          You like all this, wait until you
          see my flamethrower --

                    JOYCE
          We don't have time for a show-and-
          tell. We need to get going.

                    YURI
               (to Murray)
          She always this bossy?

Murray pulls out a pistol.

                    MURRAY
               (unamused)
          You heard her. Keys. Map. *Let's go*.

He slams a mag into the pistol and --

INT. CHURCH - SANCTUARY - A LITTLE LATER

WHAM! A WELL-WORN MAP hits the top of a crate. As they gather around, Yuri taps an empty area with his bound, dirty hands.

                    YURI
          So -- prison is here, hidden
          between these mountains -- perhaps
          a two-hour drive --

                    MURRAY
          I don't see anything --

                    YURI
          Because it is not on the map. But
          it is there.

                    JOYCE
          And how do we know you're not just
          leading us into a trap -- ?

                    YURI
          A "trap"??? Why -- because I do not
          need to. After all -- what sort of
          trap could I set more treacherous
          than this?? You want to break into
          the deadliest prison in all the
          Motherland -- it is *suicide*.

                    MURRAY
          Who said anything about breaking
          in?

                    YURI
          Oh. You expect to just knock --
          "hello, let me in please!"

Yuri laughs --

                    JOYCE
          Something like that, actually,
          yeah.

                    MURRAY
          You were planning to turn us over
          to the warden. Today, if I'm not
          mistaken.

Yuri starts to pick up on the plan now.

                    YURI
          AHH -- I see now! I bring you in as
          prisoners, then set you free *inside
          walls*. It is risky. Crazy. You will
          probably still die. Yet -- I like
          it!!! But for this to work --

He flashes his bound hands --

                    YURI (CONT'D)
          Yuri cannot be tied. Hard to turn
          over prisoners when I am prisoner
          myself!!! I think the warden might
          find that suspicious, no -- ??

                    MURRAY
          He certainly would. He'll also be
          suspicious of your injuries.

                    JOYCE
          Which is why from here on out --
          you're going to play Murray.

                    MURRAY
          And I'm going to play Yuri.

Yuri's eyes swivel between them --

                    YURI
          I -- do not follow --

                    MURRAY
          Don't worry.

He grabs the bandana around Yuri's neck --

                    MURRAY (CONT'D)
          It's a *silent role*.

Murray shoves the bandana back into Yuri's mouth.

Yuri SCREAMS beneath the gag and --

INT. RUSSIAN PRISON - LARGE ROOM - DAY

CHOOM! A flame leaps out of Ivan's gold-plated lighter as he lights his cigarette again.

As Ivan smokes, he eyes the gloomy prisoners who are now (rather unenthusiastically) finishing their "feast." Drunk Hopper glances at him, then looks away. As we hold on Hopper...

                    DMITRI (PRE-LAP)
          You want to make a fool of yourself
          -- go ahead.

EXT. THE PIT - LATER

Ivan now leads our newly "fattened" prisoners back across the pit. Their frightened eyes go to that metal gate now... now knowing the horrible truth that lies within.

Dmitri and Hopper speak as they walk --

                    DMITRI
          But to bring down these men --
          leaving them with no hope? What is
          the purpose of that?

                    HOPPER
          I give them -- the *truth*. You --
          you feed their delusions.

                    DMITRI
          Not delusions -- *hope*. I believe we
          can fight. I believe we can win. I
          must. I have a son. Mikhail. I
          cannot leave this world with him
          believing his father is a traitor.
          I need to get back to him. And -- I
          will -- I *will* get back to him.

A beat as Hopper absorbs this new info. But he's not... exactly moved by Dmitri's story.

                    HOPPER
          Is he slow?

                    DMITRI
          What -- ?

The prisoners all come to a stop as Ivan works to unlock the
gate by the stairs, searching for the key --

                    HOPPER
          Mikhail -- your son. Is he slow?
          Stupid? Like you?

Dmitri smirks. *He must be joking.*

                    DMITRI
          As a matter fact, he is very smart.
          Top of his class.

                    HOPPER
          So then you are not his father?

Dmitri's smile fades.

                    DMITRI
          You are drunk, American. I would
          stop speaking unless you wish to
          die sooner.

                    HOPPER
          I can. Doesn't matter. One way or
          another -- I'm dying today. And I
          know who I am and what I've done.
          But you -- you're just like these
          men -- you can't face the truth.
          That you're the reason we're in
          here. That you're going to die
          tonight. That your son is not
          really yours. And that your wife --
          your wife is a whore.

A beat. Then --

                    DMITRI
          ... *Sooner it is.*

WHAM! Dmitri SOCKS Hopper in the face, and before we know it
our two men are *VICIOUSLY FIGHTING* in the pit --

                    GUARD #1
          <STOP -- STOP!!!>

But they do not stop, both men in a blind rage. Oleg and the others watch, clearly amused, as Dmitri gets the upper hand, pins Hopper to the ground, and begins to punch him repeatedly when --

WHOOM! A GUARD grabs Dmitri and YANKS him off Hopper. But then Hopper, still enraged, lunges for Dmitri but --

Ivan grabs him, pulls him back. Hopper struggles with Ivan now, wrestling him to the ground and --

WHACK! GUARD #2 cracks Hopper across the ribs with a baton. Hopper drops hard, gasping for air, weakened --

WHACK! The Guard then hits Hopper with the baton again, this time knocking him to the ground.

Ivan turns to the other prisoners -- furious --

                    IVAN
        <WHAT ARE YOU ALL STARING AT! GET
        IN YOUR CELLS -- IN YOUR CELLS!>

They start to head up as a guard grabs Hopper's limp body and --

EXT. PIT - HOLDING CELL - LATER

WHAM! A bloodied Dmitri and Hopper are tossed into the cell.

                    IVAN
        <You do that again we will shoot
        you dead on the spot!!! Fools!>

The cell door slams shut -- locking them back in here with the other prisoners.

Dmitri is breathing hard, nose spilling blood. He glares at Hopper, shouts --

                    DMITRI
        You happy now American?! Was that
        worth it?? Huh???? Was that worth
        it??

Hopper looks up, wipes some blood from his mouth. Then, through heavy breaths --

                    HOPPER
        We call it... a Demogorgon.

Dmitri blinks, surprised. Oleg and the other prisoners move toward him, listening curiously as he continues --

                    HOPPER (CONT'D)
    I don't know how they got it here --
    or what the hell they're doing with
    it... But everything I said about
    it was true. Except -- it does have
    a weakness. *Fire*. It... *hates fire.*
    So -- we actually want a shot at
    killing this thing -- I figured
    we'd need some fuel --

Hopper reaches into his jacket and removes --

A "COKE" BOTTLE OF VODKA. He tosses it to a stunned Dmitri.

                    HOPPER (CONT'D)
    And... something to light it...

He then reaches into his pocket and pulls out Ivan's gold-plated lighter. He strikes it -- making *a small flame*.

                    HOPPER (CONT'D)
    So to answer your question -- yeah
    -- yeah... <u>I think it was worth it</u>.

He snaps the lighter closed. Slips it back in his pocket.

Dmitri can't help but smile --

                    DMITRI
    You sonofabitch -- you <u>*sonofabitch*</u>.

Dmitri begins to laugh. Hopper laughs too. But it *hurts.*

                    HOPPER
    My ribs -- I -- I think they're
    broken --

This makes Dmitri laugh louder. Off the sound of our men, bleeding and laughing in their cell, we HARD CUT TO --

EXT. SUZIE'S HOUSE - DAY

Suzie's house, where --

INT. SUZIE'S HOUSE - STUDY - DAY

Fingers tap away on a computer. TILT UP to find...

SUZIE'S FATHER, late 40s, diligently working away when --
CHOOM! The power in his study suddenly goes off.

INT. SUZIE'S HOUSE - HALLWAY - DAY

Suzie's Father exits the study, calling for --

> SUZIE'S FATHER
> Cornelius!! Cornelius!!

As he vanishes down the hall, we find Suzie, Mike, Will, and Jonathan peeking out from behind a door. Suzie motions to them -- *now* -- and they sneak out and head into the now vacant --

STUDY - CONTINUOUS

They shut the door, lock it. Made it. Then it hits Will --

> WILL
> Where's Argyle -- ?

> JONATHAN
> (oh shit)
> I -- don't know --

Suzie drops down by the computer. It still doesn't have power, but Suzie checks her watch --

> SUZIE
> And... *three, two* --

INT. DINING ROOM - DAY

WHOOM! Cornelius flips the circuit breaker back on and --

INT. STUDY - CONTINUOUS

FWOOM! The study lights and computer power kick back on.

> MIKE
> Way to go Cornelius!

Suzie dials the Nina "number" on a rotary phone as --

INT. SUZIE'S HOUSE - STAIRS - DAY

Suzie's Father heads downstairs, only to find his path obstructed by the sword fighters, now dueling on the stairs.

> SUZIE'S FATHER
> Tanner, Tatum -- out of the way!!!

                    SWORD-FIGHTING KID
               Away, you moldy rogue, away!!!

Plastic swords continuing to clash as --

INT. STUDY - DAY

WHAP! The receiver drops onto an ACOUSTIC COUPLER and --

BEEP! A screen labeled NINA pops up.

                    SUZIE
               And -- *we're in* --

                    MIKE
               Holy shi -- heck. Holy heck!

                    SUZIE
               Hold your applause. I don't see an
               address --

She's right -- below NINA, a bunch of options: FILES, COMMUNICATION, OFFICE, as well as more obscure SCIENTIFIC categories. But nothing that indicates an address.

                    JONATHAN
               Office -- *try office* --

Suzie does. Hundreds of lines of green code fill the screen.

                    SUZIE
               What... *is all this* -- ?

Worried looks all around as --

INT. SUZIE'S HOUSE - STAIRS - DAY

An annoyed Father finally squeezes past the two sword-fighters and --

INT. SUZIE'S HOUSE - HALLWAY - MOMENTS LATER

He makes his way to the circuit breaker. The switch to the STUDY is flipped "on." <u>Huh</u>? WHAP! A rubber arrow suddenly whaps him across the brow. He whirls to find --

Cornelius, bow in hand. Cornelius HISSES, then races away -- successfully drawing Father's attention to --

THE KITCHEN,

Where THE PAN OF CHICKEN IS ON FIRE!! Off Suzie's horrified Father --

INT. STUDY - DAY

Suzie continues to scroll, but -- *no address.*

> JONATHAN
> Maybe it's hidden in the code somehow?

> MIKE
> What you just said makes no sense --

> SUZIE
> Hold your butts. I'll just trace the IP --

> WILL
> The what -- ?

> SUZIE
> The Internet Protocol Address.
> (typing as she talks)
> It's a unique numerical label given to all information technology connected to the internet --

> JONATHAN
> What's the internet -- ?

> SUZIE
> Don't worry about it. It's just going to *change the world.*

As Suzie's fingers fly across keyboards --

INT. SUZIE'S HOUSE - KITCHEN - DAY

WHOOSH! Suzie's Father frantically puts out the fire with a fire extinguisher. He sighs, relieved, only to panic *again* as he sees --

Tabitha, seizing and foaming at the mouth!!!

> SUZIE'S FATHER
> TABITHA -- ???

As he sprints forward to rescue his "dying" daughter --

STUDY

Suzie continues to code.

>   MIKE
>   What's going on now -- ?
>
>   SUZIE
>   I'm running the IP through a
>   geolocation software, basically a
>   form of data mining --

As Suzie continues to type, green code filling the screen --

INT. LIVING ROOM - DAY

Suzie's Father shakes Tabitha --

>   SUZIE'S FATHER
>   Tabitha -- *Tabitha???*
>
>   STERLING (O.S.)
>   And... *CUT!*

Suzie's dad whirls to find Sterling filming the whole thing on his 8mm camera!

>   STERLING (CONT'D)
>   Incredible. Just incredible,
>   Father! Your terror looked *genuine!*

Suzie's Father stares, unamused as --

INT. SUZIE'S HOUSE - STUDY - DAY

Suzie hits enter and --

>   SUZIE
>   BINGO!

A list of coordinates pops up!!! Region, longitude, latitude.

>   JONATHAN/WILL
>   Nevada -- ??
>
>   MIKE
>   Can you print that -- ?
>
>   SUZIE
>   No, my skills end at IP geolocation.

She rolls her eyes, smashes [PRINT] and --

EEEEEE. Paper begins to spit out of a bulky printer and --

INT. SUZIE'S HOUSE - STAIRS - DAY

Our *enormously stressed* Father now marches back toward the steps when --

WHOOM! Suzie and our boys suddenly explode down the steps past him --

>   SUZIE
>   Hi, Father! You look like you need a
>   nap --

>   FATHER
>   SLOW DOWN!

He sighs, then continues on his way, totally oblivious to the great heist that just took place and --

MOMENTS LATER

WHOOM! Our heroes burst outside and slam the door -- safe! Suzie smiles, exhilarated, as she hands Mike the printout, hot off the presses! Mike can hardly believe it --

                              MIKE
                    Dustin's right -- you're a
                    certified genius.

Suzie beams, practically glowing, when -- her smile fades.

                              SUZIE
                    I think we just spooked a skunk!

Our boys turn toward the Pizzamobile and --

MOMENTS LATER

WHOOM! They fling open the back of the truck to reveal --

Argyle and Eden inside -- half undressed beneath a HAZE OF POT SMOKE! Argyle turns to them, high as a fucking kite.

                              ARGYLE
                    YO! My dudes!!! Any luck??

As Suzie's jaw literally *drops*, WE SMASH TO --

EXT. KERLEY ROAD - NIGHT

VROOM!!!!! A LARGE TRUCK speeds down a country road. Its flatbed is packed with men, all armed with rifles. VIGILANTES. Several of them throw waves and a mocking salute as they pass by --

A COP CAR, driving on the opposite side of the road.

INT. COP CAR - NIGHT

Callahan watches them pass over his shoulder --

                              CALLAHAN
                    They're mocking us now -- you see
                    that Chief? *Openly mocking us* --

                              POWELL
                    Stay calm.

                              CALLAHAN
                    A bunch of angry, armed
                    vigilantes are out hunting kids,
                    openly defyin' us -- and you want
                    me to stay calm -- ??

Before Powell can fire back, the radio crackles --

                              OFFICER DANIELS (OVER RADIO)
                    Hey, Chief -- you copy?

Powell rips the radio up into his hand --

                    POWELL
          Yeah I copy --

EXT. WOODS - SIDE OF ROAD - NIGHT

Officer Daniels is standing by the side of the road. His flashlight is aimed at the Wheeler family STATION WAGON, which is half-hidden beneath some brush.

>   OFFICER DANIELS
>   I found their station wagon, hidden
>   out by Skull Rock --

INT. COP CAR - NIGHT

Callahan and Powell share looks.

>   CALLAHAN
>   Skull Rock -- isn't that a make-out
>   spot --
>
>   POWELL
>   Yeah. And it's also a stone's throw
>   from Lover's Lake --
>
>   CALLAHAN
>   The hell would they go back there
>   for -- ?
>
>   POWELL
>   One way to find out --
>   (into radio)
>   Hold tight, on our way --

Powell hits the siren, then spins the wheel hard and --

EXT. COUNTRY ROAD - NIGHT

The cop car makes a U-turn, sirens flashing, and --

EXT. WOODS - NIGHT

WHOOSH! Our kids now shove through foliage of their own. Flashlights out, beams cutting through the dark night.

But Dustin isn't even looking where he's going -- his eyes are glued to the compass, following it north, when --

The needle begins to quiver. *Uh oh.*

>   DUSTIN
>   Something's happening --

Dustin quickens his pace --

                    EDDIE
          Hey, Dustin, slow down -- *Dustin* --

                    DUSTIN
          I think we're close -- !

Dustin bursts out of the tree line and --

EXT. LOVER'S LAKE - SHORELINE - NIGHT

WHOOM! Eddie suddenly *GRABS* the back of his shirt, halting him in his tracks.

                    EDDIE
          Watch your step, Henderson.

Dustin's eyes shoot wide. WE NOW REVERSE TO REVEAL:

They've reached the SHORE OF LOVER'S LAKE, opposite Reefer Rick's house. The lake is mist-covered, beautiful but spooky.

The others join up with Dustin and Eddie.

> STEVE
> You *gotta be shitting me* --

> EDDIE
> I thought these woods were...
> *familiar.*

> DUSTIN
> This is... confounding.

> MAX
> So there's a gate -- in Lover's Lake?

> LUCAS
> Almost rhymes --

> MAX
> Except it doesn't --

Nancy looks out at the misty water. Mind racing.

> NANCY
> When the Demogorgon attacked... he always left an opening. Maybe it's the same with Vecna --

> STEVE
> ... One way to find out.

EXT. WOODS - NIGHT

WHOOM! The group flings foliage off something, revealing --

REEFER RICK'S (BROKEN) MOTORBOAT.

A LITTLE LATER

WHOOSH! Water kicks back as they push the boat into the water.

Nancy, Robin, Eddie, and Steve climb in first. The kids start to follow but --

                    EDDIE
          Whoa whoa -- you wanna sink us???
          This sucker holds three people tops
          -- we're already pushing it --

                    NANCY
          That's better anyway --
               (to kids)
          Stay back with Max, keep an eye out
          for trouble --

                    DUSTIN
          You keep an eye out. This was *my*
          goddamn theory -- !

Dustin tries to get on the boat, but Robin blocks him.

                    ROBIN
          You heard Nance --

                    DUSTIN
          Seriously?? Who put her in charge?

                    ROBIN
          Me.

Nancy holds out a hand.

                    NANCY
          Compass.

Dustin sighs, tosses her the compass.

Steve and Eddie then push with their oars, shoving the boat out into the water.

                    ROBIN
          And remember, kiddies -- in bed
          before nine.

Dustin flips her off as --

The boat rows out into the darkness. As mist envelops the boat, PRE-LAP the sound of clacking plastic --

INT. HAWKINS LABS - RAINBOW ROOM - NIGHT (MEMORY)

CLOSE ON: A familiar RED DISC skips down pegs.

WIDEN: Eleven is playing Plinko again in the Rainbow Room. She is all by herself in here, "enjoying" her reward. But she still can't get that damn disc to fall in the THREE SLOT.

She focuses. Trying to use her memory as before when --

THE SOUND OF SHOUTING interrupts. Off Eleven...

INT. HAWKINS LABS - HALLWAY - NIGHT (MEMORY)

EEEEEE. The Rainbow Room door creaks open as Eleven creeps out into the hallway. It's dark out here. Spooky.

MORE SHOUTING. A SCREAM. Louder this time. *Nearby*.

Eleven tracks the sound down --

A DARK CORRIDOR (MEMORY)

Through a square window at the end of the hall, she sees Brenner and SEVERAL GUARDS.

She ducks back into hiding, then peers out around the corner, watching. *What are they doing??*

ELEVEN POV: The Guards have SHOCK STICKS. At Brenner's direction, they are repeatedly electrocuting an off-screen man. He screams in pain. Then -- abruptly -- he goes silent.

After a beat, the door opens and they drag a limp body out.

IT'S THE FRIENDLY ORDERLY. *Holy shit.* He's bleeding badly from the nose and ears.

Brenner, somehow sensing something, looks up and locks eyes with Eleven. His eyes are cold. <u>He looks like the devil.</u>

Eleven's heart almost stops. She races away and --

MOMENTS LATER (MEMORY)

We track a terrified Eleven as she races back down the hallway. She shoots a look behind her to see if Brenner or the guards are pursuing -- doesn't see anything.

INT. HAWKINS LABS - RAINBOW ROOM - NIGHT (MEMORY)

WHOOM! She bursts back into the Rainbow Room and slams the door behind her. Catches her breath. Made it. *Then --*

>   TWO (O.S.)
>   You shouldn't be wandering the
>   halls.

She whirls, startled, finds she's no longer alone in here --

Four, Two, Three, and Five are all here. They step away from the walls, surrounding her on all sides.

> FOUR
> It's against the rules.

> TWO
> And not safe.

Two walks closer to her, intimidating.

> TWO (CONT'D)
> You shamed me today.

> ELEVEN
> I -- I am sorry --

> TWO
> I did not want to hurt you -- you are weak and pathetic. I was holding back. And then you do that? Before everyone -- *before Papa?*

Eleven doesn't respond -- too scared. Then suddenly --

WHOOM! Two throws out an arm and shoves Eleven across the room. She stumbles backwards and falls through the tower of red blocks, crashing hard to the floor. Hard.

> TWO (CONT'D)
> How did that feel? Did you like that?

Eleven staggers to her feet, her frightened eyes dart to a camera but --

> TWO (CONT'D)
> See a light? I don't.

> THREE
> Strange. Something must have happened to the power.

WHAM! Five then uses his powers to push her again. She is about to fall when --

Three pushes her the opposite direction with his powers. Then Four pushes her. Before we know it all the Numbers are pushing her back and forth between them like psionic hot potato. It's whiplash-inducing and dizzying and it gets faster and more violent until finally Two throws his hand out and --

WHOOM! Eleven goes flying through the air and SLAMS hard into the rainbow wall, her head cracking against those bright colors. She crumples to the ground. Weak, bloodied, dazed.

Two walks over and kneels beside her. Wipes blood from his nose.

> TWO
> You tell Papa we did this -- <u>we will kill you</u>.

And with that, Two and the other Numbers leave.

Dazed and gasping for air, crying from pain, Eleven grabs a chair, hauls herself back to her feet. Then suddenly -- her eyes go wide and her breath catches as <u>she sees something</u>.

She walks across the room -- toward the TWO-SIDED MIRROR.

IN THE REFLECTION: We see her younger self. Only something is different: Her face and body are now DRENCHED IN BLOOD.

The lights begin to flicker. Eleven whirls, startled. In the flickering light she now sees --

DEAD BODIES ALL AROUND HER. CLOSE SHOTS reveal the bodies of Four, Two, Three, and Five -- her tormentors. But there are also higher Numbers dead here. The *children*. *It's a massacre.*

> DR. BRENNER (O.S.)
> What have you done?

Eleven turns to find a shaken, injured Brenner in the doorway. <u>We've looped back to the climax of this season's opener</u>.

Brenner looks right at Eleven. Those eyes boring into her.

> DR. BRENNER (CONT'D)
> What have you done?

The lights begin to flicker more and more and --

INT. ANTENNA SILO - NIGHT

Eleven's eyes shoot open! She jolts up --

She's out of the tank -- back on the <u>operation table</u> in the lab, gasping for air, fighting tears, drenched. Brenner and Owens hover over her, as well as the other scientists.

As Eleven fights to catch her breath --

                    DR. OWENS
          Easy. Deep breaths. Deep breaths.

As Eleven's breathing begins to slow, Brenner takes her hand.

                    DR. BRENNER
          You did well, Eleven. You did very
          well.

But Eleven doesn't feel relieved. Or proud. She just feels... *scared*. Her eyes shake. Her voice trembles.

                    ELEVEN
          I -- I -- know what happened now.
               (catches breath)
          I killed them -- didn't I?
               (beat)
          <u>I killed them all</u>.

Off Brenner, his face darkening, we SMASH TO --

EXT. LOVER'S LAKE - NIGHT

An overhead shot of Rick's boat gliding through dark water.

ON THE BOAT,

Steve rows, while Nancy keeps an eye on the compass. The compass needle goes haywire -- spinning around and around.

                    NANCY
          Whoa, slow down -- slow down.

Steve and Eddie stop oaring. The boat eases to a stop.

BACK AT SHORE,

Lucas keeps an eye on them with his trusty binoculars.

                    LUCAS
          They're stopping.

Dustin brings up his walkie --

                    DUSTIN
          Talk to us -- what's going on?

BACK ON THE BOAT,

Robin brings up her walkie, answers.

                    ROBIN
              (into walkie)
          Compass just went, uh, from wonky
          to Wonky with a capital W.

Steve and the others peer over the lip of the boat and into
the water -- but they see only a black void.

Steve starts taking off his shoes and socks --

                    NANCY
          What are you doing?

                    STEVE
          Someone needs to go down and check.
          And unless someone else here can
          top being a Hawkins High Swim co-
          captain and certified lifeguard,
          then, uh, no complaints, alright?

                    EDDIE
          Shit I'm not complaining. I don't
          want to go down there. Knock
          yourself out man.

Steve pulls his shirt off. Nancy can't help but look. That's
kinda... *hot*. Robin clocks this. *Interesting*. But --

ON SHORE,

Lucas, watching Steve through the binoculars, grimaces.

                    LUCAS
          When'd Steve get so hairy?

                    DUSTIN
          Right? I told him he should tame
          that jungle. But he claims the
          ladies dig it.

                    MAX
          Let me see --

Max snatches the scopes -- looks out at Steve.

                    LUCAS
          You like that he's all hairy like
          that?

She doesn't answer --

                    LUCAS (CONT'D)
              Max -- earth to Max? *Max?*

ON THE BOAT,

Eddie double wraps a flashlight in one of the grocery bags, hands it to Steve.

                    EDDIE
              Good luck.

Steve nods, crosses to edge of boat, and --

                    NANCY
              Steve?

He turns to Nancy --

                    NANCY (CONT'D)
              Be careful.

A nod. A connection even? Then -- in a flash -- Steve turns and dives into the water. He vanishes --

BELOW THE SURFACE OF THE LAKE,

We stay with Steve as he swims down into the lake, sweeping his arms, pushing his body down through those murky waters, that bagged flashlight guiding his way.

BACK ON SHORE,

Our "children" watch, on edge, Max still with the binoculars.

                    DUSTIN
              You realize, if I'm right about
              this and there's a Gate down there,
              then technically -- it's a water
              gate.

Lucas looks at him --

                    DUSTIN (CONT'D)
              Get it -- Watergate?

Lucas just... stares. And --

BACK UNDERWATER,

Steve swims further down, his hair flowing beautifully in this underwater world. He finally reaches the lake floor.

It's littered with a GRAVEYARD OF DEAD, ROTTED FISH. And -- about twenty yards away --

A RED SHAFT OF LIGHT, pushing up through the turbid green water. Holy shit. He kicks his legs, swimming toward it, and --

ON THE BOAT - NIGHT

Silence. Nancy, Robin, and Eddie nervously watch the water.

> ROBIN
> Where are we at Wheeler?

> NANCY
> (checks watch)
> Closing in on a minute.

BACK ON THE SHORE,

Max and the others watch, waiting for him --

> DUSTIN
> Come on, Steve... *come on*...

Suddenly -- they hear something. VOICES, FOOTSTEPS. They turn -- see flashlights moving through the woods behind.

> LUCAS
> Down -- down -- !!

They duck, taking cover behind a tree as--

BACK UNDER THE WATER,

Steve continues to swim until he reaches --

A TEN-FOOT WIDE THROBBING MEMBRANE. A RIFT. This is, uh... "WATERGATE." The whole thing is creepy but almost... beautiful.

Steve reaches out, lays a hand down on the surface of the membrane. It groans, throbs. *Whoa.*

But Steve's seen enough. He releases the membrane, then kicks back toward the surface. As Steve swims away from camera, a TENTACLE slithers up from below camera and slowly begins to "swim" its way up toward Steve like some sort of disgustingly long underwater snake as --

BACK ON THE BOAT,

Our anxious teens wait, and wait. The surface is quiet. Still. And --

WHOOM! Steve suddenly explodes up onto the surface, about fifteen feet away, startling them.

> EDDIE
> (relieved)
> *Jesus Christ --*

He gasps for air, but he's okay! He flashes a thumbs up --

> NANCY
> You found it???

> STEVE
> (catching breath)
> FOUND IT -- !

An excited Robin makes a call on the walkie --

> ROBIN
> Dustin, you're a goddamn Einstein --

BACK ON SHORE,

> ROBIN (OVER WALKIE)
> Steve found it -- he found the Gate --

Dustin quickly hits off the walkie, silencing Robin. As much as he'd like to join in the celebration -- <u>he can't</u>. Max peers out from behind their cover, sees the approaching people are <u>Powell, Callahan and Daniels</u>. *Shit!*

She drops back into hiding.

> MAX
> *Cops --*

> DUSTIN
> (low)
> Shitshitshitshit...

> LUCAS
> (low)
> We can't let them find Eddie.

Shared looks. Suddenly Max has an idea --

                    MAX
          Stay with me --

                    LUCAS
          Wait -- Max --

Too late. She's already on her feet, leaping out from behind her cover, waving her hands like crazy.

                    MAX
          HEY OFFICERS!! OFFICERS!

The cops spin to Max, spotting her with their flashlights --

                    MAX (CONT'D)
          I FOUND THE KILLER! HE'S THIS WAY!!

Max suddenly breaks into a sprint. Our boys share looks, WTF, then race after her. As our baffled cops give chase --

BACK ON THE LAKE,

Steve swims back over to the boat, grabs the side. Nancy holds out a hand to help him up. Steve takes it, still catching his breath --

                    STEVE
          It's pretty wild -- it might be
          snack-sized compared to mama Gate
          but it's still pretty damn bi--

WHOOM! Steve is suddenly and violently yanked backwards out of a shocked Nancy's hand and dragged back --

UNDER THE WATER,

That SNAKE-LIKE VINE is coiled around his leg -- yanking him down. Steve desperately tries to kick free -- but the thing has a firm grip and keeps pulling him down --

BACK ON THE SURFACE,

Our teens look in horror at the rippling surface --

                    EDDIE
          THE HELL WAS THAT -- ???

                    ROBIN
          WHAT HAPPENED -- WHAT JUST
          HAPPENED??!

UNDERWATER

The vine continues dragging Steve back through the water and toward Watergate!!! He lets out an underwater scream as he's dragged through the membrane and --

WHAM! He grabs hold of the slimy lip of the membrane at the last second -- desperately trying not to be pulled all the way through. As Steve struggles, our camera begins to ROTATE, turning all the way upside down just as his grip slips and --

THE UPSIDE DOWN - CONTINUOUS

WHOOM! Steve is yanked up through the Rift and into the Upside Down. There is no water on this side -- just dry, craggy land. We HOLD TIGHT on a terrified Steve as he is dragged across this rough land, fighting for a handhold, not finding one, as --

INT. REEFER RICK'S BOAT - NIGHT

Nancy starts to KICK off her shoes, pulls off her overshirt.

                    EDDIE
          You're not going in there are you??

                    NANCY
          Just, *wait here* --

                    ROBIN
          Nancy -- !!!

Too late. She dives in -- SPLASH!

UNDERWATER

As Nancy begins to swim, kicking, moving fast --

INT. WOODS - SHORELINE - NIGHT

WHOOSH! Dustin, Lucas, and Max sprint through the woods -- leaping over roots, shoving through foliage --

The cops give chase --

                    CALLAHAN
          Hey -- get back here! HEY!

WHAM! Dustin suddenly trips over a ROOT, goes tumbling.

                         MAX
          DUSTIN -- !!

Max and Lucas double back, but they're too late and --

WHOOM! Dustin is suddenly yanked away into the arms of --

                         POWELL
                    Hey there.

Callahan and Daniels come up in the rear. Callahan is wheezing.

                         CALLAHAN
                    Okay -- what was the point of
                    that??

Off our kids, caught, HARD CUT TO --

INT. REEFER RICK'S BOAT - NIGHT

Robin kicks off her shoes, yanks off her jacket --

                         EDDIE
                    What are you doing -- she said
                    wait!

                         ROBIN
                    Yeah I heard her --

                         EDDIE
                    She's in charge --

                         ROBIN
                    Are you kidding me? I made that
                    shit up.

Robin leaps off the boat, diving in. Leaving <u>Eddie all alone</u>.

                         EDDIE
                    Oh, *for chrissakes* --

Eddie begins to yank off his shoes and --

EXT. LAKEBED - NIGHT (UPSIDE DOWN)

WHOOM! Steve is violently dragged across land, screaming, faster and faster until suddenly --

The vine releases him. He skids to a stop, gasping for air. The vine slithers away. The hell?

Steve slowly pushes to his feet. Takes in his surroundings. He's in LOVER'S LAKE -- but in the Upside Down.

Meaning -- it's an enormous dry lakebed, the ground cracked like dry skin, surrounded on all sides by a skeletal forest. A few old boats and their oars line the bed and spores choke the air but -- most unsettling of all -- there are BONES all around him. *Lots* of bones. Fish bones, along with the skeletal remains of creatures we don't recognize from the Upside Down. This is... a GRAVEYARD. Then --

A SHRIEK. Steve whirls, sees --

THREE DEMOBATS. HURTLING THROUGH THE SKY. FLYING RIGHT FOR HIM. A flash of lightning, and for the first time, we get a good look at these ugly fuckers. They have no eyes. Long, sea creature tails. Huge, leathery bat-like wings. Fish-like mouths with rings of razor-sharp teeth.

Steve runs across the dry bed -- trying to escape -- but these creatures are fast and --

WHAM! They dive-bomb Steve -- slamming into him -- knocking him flat onto the lake bed!

Steve tries to fight back, but they quickly overwhelm them. As one of the Demobats wraps its long tentacle-like tail around Steve's throat, silencing his screams --

The others open their mouths --

And begin to feed.

END EPISODE

EPISODE SEVEN

CHAPTER SEVEN:
THE MASSACRE AT HAWKINS LAB

WRITTEN BY **THE DUFFER BROTHERS**

EXT. LAKEBED - NIGHT (UPSIDE DOWN)

We pick up right where we left off -- WITH THE DEMOBATS FEEDING ON STEVE!

CLOSE ON: Their nasty little razor-sharp mouths rip skin from his bare body like supernatural vultures. It's awful --

Steve screams, trying to fight them off, but every time he pushes one away, it snaps right back. To make matters worse, a bat's squid-like tail remains still wrapped around his throat and he is rapidly running out of air. He can't breathe -- he can't breathe -- he can't b --

FWOOM!!! A fast-moving object suddenly comes out of nowhere and SMACKS Demobat #1, swatting it off Steve!!

The bat shrieks in pain as it tumbles across the dry lakebed. The remaining Demobats spin with a SHRIEK to find --

NANCY AND ROBIN AND EDDIE! They're barefoot and drenched and spattered in membrane mucus. But they're alive and they're in the Upside Down and better yet --

Eddie and Nancy have those OARS from the boat!

                NANCY
    HEY THERE!

She swings her oar and -- WHAM! -- she swats Demobat #2 off Steve! But before they can knock Bat #3 off Steve --

A pissed Demobat #1 flies back toward them! It attacks Eddie! Eddie swings his oar, slamming it with all his might! WHAM! As Eddie and Bat #1 fight --

Nancy and Robin try to free Steve from Bat #3 -- Nancy jabs her oar at it, while Robin tugs at that tentacle, but the Demobat is holding holds on tight and --

EEEEEE! Bat #2 now attacks, burying its claws into Nancy's back. She cries out in pain --

                ROBIN
    NANCY -- !

Robin grabs the screeching Demobat and yanks it off Nancy. As it flaps around Robin's arms like a crazed chicken --

Steve -- out of desperation -- *bites* down on Demobat #3's squid-like tail. Black blood sprays and the monster shrieks in pain, then it releases its grip on Steve's throat.

Steve, finally free, grabs the bat by its slimy tail -- rips it off of him -- then begins to repeatedly swing it into the ground as --

-- Nancy pins Bat #2 down with her oar -- then stomps on her oar. THWACK-SPLAT! The Demobat's body SEVERS IN HALF!! As --

-- Eddie hammers Bat #1 so hard his oar breaks. Eddie now thrusts the broken tip of the oar through the bat's mouth, shish-kabobing the fucker as --

-- Steve continues to swing Demobat #3 into the ground -- over and over, turning its body to mush, until finally

ALL THREE BATS ARE DEAD. And at last, we have *silence*.

      EDDIE
  Jesus Christ -- *JESUS H. CHRIST.*

As an exhausted and wide-eyed Eddie drops his skewered bat and looks around, taking in his spore-choked post-apocalyptic surroundings --

Nancy hurries to Steve's side, examining his wounds. He spits black bat blood from his mouth -- *gross* --

      NANCY
  You okay -- ???

      STEVE
   (catching breath)
  I think I lost about a pound of
  flesh but other than that -- yeah --
  never better.

A freaked Robin studies one of the mashed up bats --

      ROBIN
  You think they carry rabies -- ?

      STEVE
  What -- ?

      ROBIN
  It's just rabies is my number one
  fear because by the time symptoms
  set in you can't do anything you're
  already dead.

Steve just stares at her --

                    ROBIN (CONT'D)
          I just think we should get checked
          out by a doctor sooner rather than
          later is all I'm saying --

                    STEVE
          Oh really 'cause I was thinking we
          should stick around here a little
          longer, see the sights --

                    EDDIE
          Yeah well -- we may not have a
          choice in that matter. They seem to
          be, uh, blocking the door.

The others now step up to Eddie, following his gaze to
Watergate, where they find SIX MORE DEMOBATS, all perched by
Watergate. In the red glow of the membrane, they look like
little demons. They glare at our teens, SHRIEK ANGRILY.

                    STEVE
          Alright -- uh -- we can take them,
          it's not that many --

An EAR-PIERCING shriek echoes out, as if in response to
Steve. All eyes move up, then widen, as they clock the source
-- a MASSIVE SWARM OF DEMOBATS, headed their way across the
scorched sky. Must be at least a hundred of the fuckers.

                    ROBIN
               (to Steve)
          ... You were saying?

Nancy's eyes swivel to the woods --

                    NANCY
          We can take cover in the woods --
          come on -- !

Nancy tosses her oar and starts to break. The others follow --

                    ROBIN
          More running -- _awesome_ --

As our teens scramble up a slope and into the dense dark
woods, our CAMERA CRANES UP AND UP AND UP, revealing --

OUR MOST EPIC SHOT OF THE UPSIDE DOWN YET. WE SEE <u>ALL OF
HAWKINS</u> -- ROTTING AND CHOKED IN SPORES AND VINES. AS THUNDER
BOOMS AND RED LIGHTNING SLASHES THE SKY, HARD CUT TO --

MAIN TITLES

INT. BLACK SITE - TORTURE ROOM - NIGHT

CLOSE ON: An INDUSTRIAL HEAT LAMP. BUZZING LOUDLY.

WIDEN TO REVEAL a bevy of heat lamps are aimed at the SWEATBOX, which towers in the middle of this room like some vampire coffin.

SULLIVAN and his men enter the room. As his men move about the room, switching off those heat lamps, Sullivan strides up to the sweatbox. He calmly unlocks it with a key and --

WHOOM! AGENT WALLACE'S body drops out of the box and crashes to the floor, limp as a rag doll. He is still conscious -- but only barely. He's gasping for air, his whole body heaving, dripping sweat. Sullivan kneels beside him, studies him with uncaring eyes.

> SULLIVAN
> How was your sleep, Mister Wallace?

Wallace continues to suck in that oxygen.

> SULLIVAN (CONT'D)
> Lots of time to think, I would imagine. Have you... reconsidered your position?

Wallace still doesn't answer. Just trying to breathe.

> SULLIVAN (CONT'D)
> Where is the girl?

Still no answer. Sullivan sighs.

> SULLIVAN (CONT'D)
> Perhaps you need more time.

Sullivan stands and nods to his men, who lift Wallace up by the arms and drag him back over to the sweatbox. They almost have him inside when a panicked Wallace releases a choked --

> AGENT WALLACE
> *Wait.*

Sullivan turns back to Wallace.

> AGENT WALLACE (CONT'D)
> *Wait...*

Sullivan slowly walks up to Wallace. Face to face.

Wallace fights back tears. Then, through heavy breaths:

> AGENT WALLACE (CONT'D)
> Just... don't... kill her. Promise
> -- you won't -- kill her.

Off Sullivan, *victorious*, we CUT TO --

INT. SILO LAB - TEST ROOM - NIGHT

ELEVEN. A pair of electrodes affixed to her temple.

She's sitting at a desk, focusing on a COKE CAN, trying to crush it. *The classic test.* But as she focuses, she's hit with *subliminal flashes of* ALL THE MURDERED NUMBERS and --

She loses focus. The Coke can remains undamaged.

IN A NEARBY OBSERVATION ROOM,

OWENS and BRENNER watch her through a glass window. Owens is clearly frustrated.

> DR. OWENS
> We're running out of time here,
> Martin. Hawkins is running out of
> time.

> DR. BRENNER
> I understand the stakes quite well.

Owens turns to him.

> DR. OWENS
> You know -- sometimes I wonder if
> you do -- or if you're just doing
> all this just because you missed
> father-daughter time.

Brenner tightens. *This* really pisses him off. But he keeps his emotions bottled. Owens, however, does not; he takes a step closer to Brenner.

> DR. OWENS (CONT'D)
> I've given you all the resources
> you've asked for, I've given you
> your people, I've compromised my
> principles, I've risked my life, my
> family's life, all because you
> assured me *this would work*.
> (MORE)

                    DR. OWENS (CONT'D)
               That this was the only way.
                    (motions to glass)
               But I don't see progress out there.
               You know what I see, Martin?
                    (beat)
               I see a scared, *traumatized little
               girl.*

On that note, Owens heads out, Brenner just... keeps his gaze trained on Eleven. And Owens is not wrong... she looks distant. *Lost. Scared.*

                    DR. BRENNER (PRE-LAP)
               The truth is, Eleven... you are
               regressing. *Going backwards.*

INT. ELEVEN'S ROOM - NIGHT

Brenner is now seated beside Eleven in her room. Eleven looks away, ashamed.

                    DR. BRENNER
               Eleven. Look at me.

She looks at him. We now see she's fighting tears. It pains Brenner to see her like this...

                    DR. BRENNER (CONT'D)
               ... I know you are frightened --
               terribly frightened by what you
               have seen. But it is this very fear
               that is now holding you back. If
               you wish for Nina to succeed, you
               can't hide from the truth. No
               matter *how scary* it may seem.

Eleven looks away again and we get --

A FEW SHOCKING, FAST SHOTS OF BLOODY HALLWAYS, DEAD BODIES --

                    ELEVEN
               I saw what -- I did.

MORE NIGHTMARISH FLASHES JOLT US.

                    ELEVEN (CONT'D)
               I am -- a <u>monster</u>.

Brenner takes this in. When he speaks again, we get the impression that he is not just speaking for Eleven -- but <u>also for himself</u>.

                    DR. BRENNER
               You speak of monsters... of
               superheroes. Those are the stuff of
               myth and fairy tales, Eleven.
               Reality -- truth -- is rarely so
               simple. People are not so easily
               defined. Only by facing all of
               ourselves -- *the good and the bad* --
               can we become whole.

Eleven considers this. Then, looks back at Papa --

                    ELEVEN
               What if -- I don't want to
               become... whole?

                    DR. BRENNER
               Then that is a choice. *Your choice.*
               The door is always open, Eleven.
               This place -- is not a prison.

He taps her head.

                    DR. BRENNER (CONT'D)
               This is.

A beat as Eleven absorbs this.

                    DR. BRENNER (CONT'D)
               You chose to trust me once. And now
               I am asking you trust me again.
               Journey with me into the past. One
               last time.
                    (beat)
               No more hiding, Eleven.

Eleven takes this in, then her gaze shifts to the haptic suit hanging on the wall, lit by a single lamp. As her face gradually shifts from uncertainty to determination, we PRE-LAP THE SOUND OF BEEPING MACHINERY AND MOVING GEARS AS --

INT. ANTENNA SILO - NIGHT

EEEE! Chains and gears turn as the roof to the Nina tank is slowly opened. Then --

INT. ANTENNA SILO - NIGHT

HISS! Strange liquid filling a syringe as --

Eleven, once more dressed in her haptic suit, is prepared for re-entry. A scientist jabs the needle into her arm.

She doesn't even flinch. <u>She seems ready</u>. Owens is here, looking somewhat *less ready*, but Brenner is elsewhere...

INT. SILO LAB - LIBRARY - NIGHT

... Making his way down that long corridor of VHS tapes. He walks to the far end of the room. Kneels down by the last tape on the bottom shelf. A date reads: September 8 -- 1979.

As his hand grazes the sleeve of the VHS tape --

QUICK FLASHCUTS FROM THE OPENING OF OUR SEASON -- BRENNER DRESSING FOR THE DAY -- WORKING WITH TEN -- SMILING -- THEN ALARMS -- THE DOOR TO THE LAB EXPLODES INWARD -- AND --

Brenner hesitates, his hand still on that VHS sleeve. Now that he is here, a part of him is afraid to continue. But then he gathers his composure, takes the tape, and --

INT. SILO LAB - OBSERVATION BOOTH - NIGHT

Brenner slots the tape into the VCR. His finger hits play -- the tape reels spin and --

INT. ANTENNA SILO - NIGHT

Video begins to play in the bulbous televisions mounted inside the Nina tank. We TILT DOWN from this wall of TVs to find --

Eleven wearing her EEG cap, floating in that the darkness.

INT. SILO LAB - OBSERVATION BOOTH - NIGHT

Brenner and Owens watch from the observation window.

                    DR. OWENS
          How many months did you skip?

                    DR. BRENNER
          You wanted progress. I'm giving it
          to you.

Off Owens, his anxiety building...

INT. ANTENNA LAB - NINA TANK - NIGHT

We PUSH toward Eleven's eyes as they to flutter to a close. As her heartbeat quickens, images of that violent day flash past us -- faster and faster and FASTER and --

EXT. WHEELER HOUSE - NIGHT

Quiet. TWO COP CARS are now parked outside the Wheeler house.

As our camera slowly pushes toward the house...

> POWELL (PRE-LAP)
> And what exactly were you all doing at the lake -- ?

INT. WHEELER HOUSE - LIVING ROOM - NIGHT

DUSTIN, MAX, and LUCAS are sandwiched on the living room couch, while POWELL, CALLAHAN, OFFICER DANIELS, as well as the WHEELERS, the SINCLAIRS, CLAUDIA, and ERICA hover nearby.

The cops are pissed; the parents, anxious; Erica, *suspicious*.

> MAX
> We were just... going for a walk --

> CALLAHAN
> A "walk"? *At nine pm* --

> DUSTIN
> (jumping in)
> To the lake. We wanted to take a swim -- a night swim --

> CLAUDIA
> Dusty someone was just murdered there -- !

> DUSTIN
> Yeah we realized that like, right when we got there --

> LUCAS
> Which is why we didn't swim --

> KAREN
> And Nancy, was she with you on this "night swim" -- ?

DUSTIN		MAX
Yes --		No --

> LUCAS
> We're not sure.

DUSTIN
She was, then she -- left. At some
point. It was very confusing --

LUCAS
And then you guys came and --

MAX
They dared me to say that -- about
the killer --

TED
You're lucky you weren't shot --

POWELL
Have you had any contact with
Eddie -- ?

DUSTIN
That psycho freak killer??? Oh God
no no no -- *absolutely not* --

MAX
We haven't heard from him in --
ages --

LUCAS
Barely know him --

ERICA
Oh <u>BULLSHIT</u> --

SUE	CHARLES
Erica -- !	Erica -- !

ERICA
Right -- get mad at me! I mean --
you all realize they're lying
right??? The whole couch is on fire
-- like just call the *goddamn fire
department* already --

SUE	CHARLES
ERICA -- !	ERICA -- !

ERICA
Just the facts -- !!

CLAUDIA
Are you lying to these policemen,
Dusty -- ??

                    DUSTIN
          No -- I -- I would never lie to an
          authority figure -- !!

                    CHARLES
          Lying to a cop is a crime, son --

                    LUCAS
          We're not lying -- !

                    ERICA
          The fire is consuming us now --
          it's _consuming us_ --

                    TED
          Threaten them with a little jail
          time, see if that loosens their
          lips --

Everyone now starts talking over one another, the cacophony building and building until finally --

                    POWELL
          Hey -- everyone shut up -- SHUT
          UP!!!

Everyone finally quiets. Powell takes a beat to compose himself, then --

                    POWELL (CONT'D)
          We're gonna try a more _civilized_
          approach. _One at a time_.

He eyes the kids, then locks on to Max.

                    POWELL (CONT'D)
          You first. Follow me.

                    MAX
          What -- why me??? I'm not even in
          Hellfire --

                    CALLAHAN
          I need to cuff you?

As Max reluctantly stands, following the cops, HARD CUT TO --

EXT. WOODS - NIGHT (UPSIDE DOWN)

EEEE! The cloud of screeching Demobats soar over the woods.

EXT. SKULL ROCK - NIGHT (UPSIDE DOWN)

We TILT DOWN from the sky as the swarm of Demobats pass overhead to reveal --

Our teens, HIDDEN BENEATH VARIOUS SKULL ROCK OUTCROPPINGS. They listen in fear as the swarm passes overhead. As the SCREECHING fades, our terrified teens slowly peek out from hiding, watching as the swarm continues to recede.

And, at long last, they can finally breathe --

              ROBIN
   ... Okay that was close --

              EDDIE
   Yeah *too close* --

WHOOM! Steve suddenly slumps back down against a rock, woozy.

              NANCY
   Steve? Jesus --

              STEVE
   I -- I'm fine --

              NANCY
   No, you're not fine -- you're
   losing blood. Sit down -- SIT.

As Steve sits, leaning his back against a rock, Nancy kneels down beside him, tears a strip of cloth from her shirt. We now get our first real good look at Steve's wounds. They're not large -- but they're quite nasty, blood just running freely down his bare chest.

              ROBIN
   So the good news here is I'm pretty
   sure wooziness is not like a common
   rabies symptom but if you start to
   have muscle spasms or like
   hallucinations or if you suddenly
   feel super aggressive like you want
   to punch me or something then
   totally let us know --

              STEVE
   I... kinda want to punch you --

              ROBIN
   Okay, so you still have your sense
   of humor, that's a good sign --

Nancy wraps the torn cloth around Steve's bare, wounded chest. They're... *very* close right now. Inches away. Steve tenses a bit from the contact --

                    STEVE
Thanks.

                    NANCY
Yeah.

They lock eyes for a moment. Tension is high --

                    NANCY (CONT'D)
Can you, uh -- turn around -- ?

Steve turns around. As Nancy goes to tie the bandage off in the back, Eddie scales a rock for a better look --

                    EDDIE
So this place -- it's just like Hawkins, except -- with monsters and nasty shit?

                    NANCY
Pretty much --
    (watching Eddie)
Hey watch out for those vines -- it's all a hive mind.

                    EDDIE
What?

                    STEVE
All the creepy crawlies here are like -- one, or something. Step on a vine -- you're stepping on a bat -- you're stepping on Vecna.

                    EDDIE
Oh shit --

                    ROBIN
But everything in our world -- is still here, right? Except people obviously?

                    NANCY
As far as I understand, yes --

                    ROBIN
          So then theoretically we could,
          like -- just go to the police
          station or whatever -- grab guns
          and grenades or whatever we need,
          and blow up those bat things that
          are guarding the Gate --

                    STEVE
          I kinda doubt the Hawkins police
          have grenades -- but guns, sure --

                    NANCY
          Yeah well -- we don't need to go
          all the way downtown for guns --

Nancy yanks the bandage tight -- finished. She stands.

                    NANCY (CONT'D)
          I have guns... in my bedroom --

Eddie hops off the rock, dropping right by Nancy.

                    EDDIE
          You, Nancy Wheeler -- have guns,
          plural -- in your bedroom -- ?

                    ROBIN
          Full of surprises isn't she -- ?

                    NANCY
          A Russian Makarov -- and Lonnie
          Byers' revolver --

Steve pushes to his feet.

                    STEVE
          You almost shot me with that one --

                    NANCY
          And you almost deserved it.

A smile between them. Then -- interrupting the moment --
Eddie tosses Steve his cut-off denim vest here --

                    EDDIE
          For your modesty, dude.

Before Steve has a chance to respond --

BOOOOOMM!!! THE ENTIRE GROUND SUDDENLY SHAKES AS IF FROM AN
EARTHQUAKE.

Everybody grabs onto the rock and one another for support -- including, of course, Steve and Nancy, who cling to one another. *Uh oh.* But there are bigger problems than sexual tension -- as soon as the earthquake ends, a CHORUS OF MONSTROUS ROARS fills the air, as if calling in response, like animals in the jungle. They are SEEMINGLY EVERYWHERE.

A MOMENT OF SILENCE before anyone dares speak, then...

>   EDDIE (CONT'D)
>   Hey yeah so guns seem like a pretty
>   good idea to me.
>
>   ROBIN
>   Me too.
>
>   STEVE
>   So what are we waiting for?

Steve lets go of Nancy, pulls on his new denim vest --

Robin gawks at his new look. Her mouth begins to open --

>   STEVE (CONT'D)
>   Whatever you're about to say --
>   *don't*.

With that, Steve heads off. The others share looks, then quickly follow, heading deeper into the Upside Down woods. As thunder BOOMS, CUT TO --

EXT. DEMO PIT - KAMCHATKA - NIGHT

Quiet. Blood splatters the walls of the Pit. Snow falls gently across lens. We're back in Russia.

EXT. THE PIT - SECOND FLOOR - HOLDING CELL - NIGHT

HOPPER is busily ripping the lining out of his jacket, while DMITRI is by the cell bars, looking out at the Pit, toward that falling snow, thinking of the task that lies ahead...

>   DMITRI
>   You know -- what we are to attempt
>   is quite mad -- even by your
>   standards, American.
>
>   HOPPER
>   Yeah. You got odds for us this
>   time?

                    DMITRI
          I think -- *a thousand to one*. Even
          if we somehow kill this beast -- we
          still must escape. We fail there, I
          don't think they will be so kind as
          to throw us back in a cell -- they
          will shoot us on sight --

                    HOPPER
          But then we die as monster slayers.
          You'll be a legend.

                    DMITRI
          But still a "traitor," you forgot
          "traitor."

                    HOPPER
          Eh, come on -- monster slayer
          trumps traitor. I bet Mikhail will
          be impressed with his pops at
          least.

Dmitri just shakes his head, smiling softly.

                    DMITRI
          Mikhail, *no.* I can do nothing right
          with him anymore it seems. He will
          say -- "Papa, I bet that bald
          American did most of the monster
          slaying!"

                    HOPPER
          He's that age huh?

                    DMITRI
          He's that age.

Dmitri now crosses over, sits on a bench near Hopper.

                    DMITRI (CONT'D)
          It is same for you, American? With
          your new daughter?

Hopper nods. Then, remembering back --

                    HOPPER
          Last time I was with El -- she
          wanted just about nothing to do
          with me. I was just -- in her way,
          really. But I think back and...
                    (small smile)
          I was the same way with my father.
                    (MORE)

                    HOPPER (CONT'D)
          Same exact way. I think... it must
          be hardwired into us -- to reject
          our fathers, you know? So that we
          can grow, move on -- become
          something of our own. Hopefully --
          that's what she's doing now. Coming
          into her own. But still --

                    DMITRI
          You worry.

Hopper doesn't answer, doesn't have to. We can tell from his
face that *shit yeah* he's worried.

                    DMITRI (CONT'D)
          To worry for our sons and daughters
          -- that is natural, isn't it?

                    HOPPER
          Yeah -- except nothing about what
          El's had to deal with is natural.

Hopper pushes to his feet, slipping his now lining-free coat
on as he makes his way to the bars of the cell. He looks out
at that large door from where those Demogorgon roars came.

                    HOPPER (CONT'D)
          That beast in there, that
          monster... it's a part of... of
          something -- something that wants
          to hurt El. Kill her.

Dmitri, of course, is confused by this --

                    DMITRI
          But -- she is not here.

                    HOPPER
          No --

                    DMITRI
          I -- do not understand --

                    HOPPER
          Yeah well, truth is -- I don't
          either. Not really. All I know is --
          this monster -- it shouldn't be
          here. It shouldn't be alive. And if
          it is -- that means it's still not
          over.
               (beat)
          I was convinced this place was...
                    (MORE)

                    HOPPER (CONT'D)
          My purgatory. But now -- now I'm
          thinking -- maybe there was another
          reason I was put here. Maybe I can
          still help El. Even if it's the
          last damn thing I do.

                    DMITRI
          You almost sound religious,
          American --

                    HOPPER
          Religious --
               (small scoff)
          I don't know about that. But I
          guess I might as well give that
          prayer thing a try.

He turns back to Dmitri.

                    HOPPER (CONT'D)
          Because if we're gonna get out of
          here... if we're gonna get back to
          El and Mikhail... you and me?
               (beat)
          We're gonna need a miracle.

EXT. RUSSIAN PRISON - NIGHT

VROOM! An OFF-ROAD VAN kicks up snow as it pulls up to a guard booth.

A PRISON GUARD exits the booth, approaches.

                    PRISON GUARD
          <Can I help you, comrade?>

We reverse to reveal: MURRAY BEHIND THE WHEEL!! Only it's not the Murray we know -- he has SHAVED HIS BEARD, leaving only a big bushy mustache!!!! He *really* looks like Yuri now!!!

Is this... Hopper's miracle???

                    MURRAY
          <Yes -- my name is Yuri Ismaylov.>

Murray passes him IDENTIFICATION. As the Prison Guard inspects it, checking that picture of Yuri...

                    MURRAY (CONT'D)
          <The Warden is expecting me. I have
          a very special delivery for him --
          a *rare import* from America.>

Murray chuckles as the Guard glances into the back of the van, where he clocks JOYCE and YURI, bound and gagged.

The Guard hesitates, then hands back the ID, and --

MOMENTS LATER

EEEE! Gears turn as the gate swings open! Murray hits the gas. As the van putters forward, coughing black smoke from a shuddering exhaust pipe, we CRANE UP TO REVEAL --

The looming prison, not two hundred yards away! And right here, with our two stories *primed to collide*, we CUT TO --

INT. ANTENNA SILO - NIGHT

A SLOW PUSH-IN on the Nina tank.

INT. TANK - NIGHT

Eleven floats in the darkness. As her eyes begin to close, drifting off...

>   DR. BRENNER (V.O.)
>   (heavy reverb)
>   *Keep your eyes open, okay?*

INT. HAWKINS LABS - INFIRMARY - DAY (MEMORY)

WHOOSH! A small penlight flares lens, pointed right at us. It sweeps back and forth, then we WIDEN TO REVEAL --

Dr. Brenner examining Eleven, checking her dilation. We have once more *traveled back in time*, and now we're in some kind of unassuming INFIRMARY ROOM. Eleven is noticeably bruised from the bullies' attack.

>   DR. BRENNER
>   ... Any more headaches, nausea this
>   morning?

Eleven shakes her head. "No."

>   DR. BRENNER (CONT'D)
>   How about your memory? Can you
>   remember what happened now?

Eleven shakes her head, quickly looks away.

Brenner considers, then --

                    DR. BRENNER (CONT'D)
          Perhaps someone else -- can fill in
          those gaps for us, yes?

Off Eleven, tensing at the thought of this...

INT. HAWKINS LABS - HALLWAY - DAY (MEMORY)

Dr. Brenner leads Eleven down the hallway. Hands clasped.

We focus on Eleven. With each step, she grows more nervous.

                    DR. BRENNER (PRE-LAP)
          Today -- our lesson is going to be
          about <u>rules</u>.

INT. TRAINING ROOM - DAY (MEMORY)

Dr. Brenner is now speaking in front of the Numbers, who are lined up per usual, including Eleven.

As Brenner speaks, El clocks the FRIENDLY ORDERLY, standing nearby. Something seems... *off* about him. He averts his gaze from her, as Brenner continues to address his "children" --

                    DR. BRENNER
          For many of you, this lesson will
          seem redundant. For others -- it
          seems a refresher is required.

He looks at Eleven.

                    DR. BRENNER (CONT'D)
          Eleven. Please step forward.

She nervously steps forward. *Uh oh.*

                    DR. BRENNER (CONT'D)
          Last night, your sister Eleven
          suffered a concussion during her
          alone time in the Rainbow Room.

TWO and the OTHER BULLIES shoot El looks -- threatening. Eleven quickly averts her gaze -- *this isn't good* --

                    DR. BRENNER (CONT'D)
          She claims to have no memory of the
          event. But injuries of this nature
          do not simply occur on their own.
          Someone did this. Someone in this
          room.

He looks over the group. Eyes piercing.

                    DR. BRENNER (CONT'D)
    Who would like to tell me what
    happened?

The Numbers all remain silent. More eyes go to the floor. The tension is palpable. Then --

                    TWO
    ... She must have fallen.

Dr. Brenner looks at Two.

                    DR. BRENNER
    "Fallen"?

                    TWO
    Yes. You have seen her Papa -- she
    is clumsy. Stupid.

Some giggles from FOUR and THREE. But Brenner is not amused.

                    DR. BRENNER
    Eleven, you may step back.
        (she does)
    Two, step forward please.

Two's smile fades. He shares a glance with his friends, then steps forward. Brenner looks to a STERN ORDERLY, who approaches Two with a METAL COLLAR.

Two's face drops. *Oh fuck, oh no.* In fact -- the whole room reacts. Whatever this is -- it isn't good.

                    DR. BRENNER (CONT'D)
    You believe that -- because you
    demonstrate talent -- you are
    somehow... immune? Is that it?

                    TWO
    No, Papa --

CHOOM. The Stern Orderly snaps the collar around Two's neck.

                    DR. BRENNER
    That the rules do not apply to you
    in the same way that they apply to
    your brothers and sisters --

                    TWO
    No, Papa --

Brenner now removes a STRANGE ELECTRONIC REMOTE from his pocket. Though quite compact, the device has a small antenna, a frequency dial, and a trigger.

>   DR. BRENNER
> Then why did you attack Eleven?

>   TWO
> Did she tell you that?

>   DR. BRENNER
> Are you asking questions or am I?
> Did you attack Eleven?

>   TWO
> If she told you that she's lying.

Brenner begins to rotate a dial on the remote with his thumb, clicking it forward. *Tick, tick, tick.*

>   TWO (CONT'D)
> Papa, you have to believe me --

Tick, tick --

>   TWO (CONT'D)
> She's LYI --

Brenner squeezes a trigger on that creepy remote and --

We hear a HIGH-FREQUENCY HUM and Two *SCREAMS*, grasping at his collar. As he drops to his knees from extreme pain --

Brenner releases the remote's trigger.

>   DR. BRENNER
> Now -- shall we try again? What
> happened?

Two looks up at Brenner. Breathing hard. Then, through tearful eyes --

>   TWO
> It -- it was an accident --

Wrong answer. Brenner pulls the trigger again.

WHUMP! Two's body folds to the floor and shudders, his jaw locking, seizing. It's awful, and Brenner is not releasing that trigger. As Two begins to SCREAM --

Our CAMERA PANS from a disturbed Friendly Orderly to --

Eleven. She *can't bear to watch*. As she looks away, horrified, Two's screams grow LOUDER and LOUDER and --

EXT. WOODS - NIGHT (UPSIDE DOWN)

BOOOOM! A FORK OF RED LIGHTNING scars the sky. We're back in the Upside Down, where --

Our teens are walking through the Upside Down forest. They look around as they walk, nervous, keeping an eye out for monsters and Demobats. As they walk, Steve sidles up to Eddie, and -- in a very awkward "guy" way --

> STEVE
> Hey -- Eddie -- uh... just wanted to say -- thanks -- you know, for saving my ass like that --

> EDDIE
> Shit. You saved your own ass, man. I mean, that was a real Ozzy move you pulled back there --

> STEVE
> Ozzy -- ?

> EDDIE
> When you took a bite outta that bat.

Steve stares, totally lost --

> EDDIE (CONT'D)
> Ozzy Osbourne. Black Sabbath? Bit a bat's head off on stage? Doesn't matter. It was very metal, what you did, all I'm saying. Henderson told me you were a badass -- insisted on it matter of fact -- I just didn't believe him --

> STEVE
> (incredulous)
> Dustin -- said I was "badass"?

> EDDIE
> Oh yeah. Shit. Kid WORSHIPS you, man. Like, you got no idea. It's rather annoying to be honest.

We can tell this means a lot to Steve --

                    EDDIE (CONT'D)
          I don't know why I even care what
          that little shrimp thinks, but, uh
          -- I actually got like, a little
          jealous about it. I just couldn't
          accept that Steve Harrington was
          actually a good dude. Rich parents,
          popular, girls love 'em, not a
          douche? No way man, NO WAY, that
          like, flies right in the face of
          the laws of the universe and my own
          personal Munson Doctrine. I'm still
          super jealous as hell by the way
          which is why I'd NEVER have jumped
          in that lake to save your ass, not
          under normal circumstances. Outside
          of D&D, I'm no hero. I see danger
          -- I turn heel and run, least
          that's what I discovered about
          myself this week. Truth is, I came
          in here 'cause --
              (points to Nancy and Robin)
          Those ladies jumped in after you --
          and I was too damn ashamed to be
          the one who stayed behind. Wheeler
          there -- she didn't waste a second.
          I mean *not a split second*. She just
          -- dove right in.

Steve tries to hide the fact that this means a lot to him.

                    EDDIE (CONT'D)
          I don't know what happened between
          you two but... I'd get her back,
          man. Whatever it takes. 'Cause that
          -- that was as unambiguous a sign
          of true love as these cynical eyes
          have ever seen.

Before a flustered Steve has a chance to respond --

BOOOM! The ground begins to shakes beneath their feet. The
boys grab nearby trees to steady themselves as --

                    STEVE
          Jesus --

                    EDDIE
          Here we go again --

Robin nearly topples, but catches a tree at the last second.

                    ROBIN
              (to Nancy)
          Second on my list of least favorite
          things -- earthquakes. Like
          seriously I'm unsteady enough as it
          is --

Nancy is about to respond when her eyes narrow: She's clocked
something. She hurries forward, ignoring the fact that the
ground is still trembling a bit beneath a bit her feet --

                    ROBIN (CONT'D)
          Nancy -- where are you going?
          Nancy??

Nancy doesn't answer, she just keeps moving until she bursts
out of the tree line and into --

A FAMILIAR OVERGROWN FIELD - CONTINUOUS (UPSIDE DOWN)

Nancy stops, looks ahead. REVERSE TO REVEAL:

A FIELD OF TOPPLED POWER LINES, overgrown with vines. Beyond
it: The Wheeler House. Choked in spores. Shared looks and --

                    NANCY
          Come on -- !

As they head forward -- making for the Wheeler house, we fly
past them, swooping over the power line, toward the house --

                    DUSTIN (PRE-LAP)
          Steve, do you copy? Nancy? Robin?

INT. WHEELER HOUSE - DOWNSTAIRS BATHROOM - NIGHT

Dustin is in the bathroom, sitting on the closed lid of the
toilet, calling on the walkie, his voice low but urgent --

                    DUSTIN
          It's Dustin! Where are you?! We've
          been collared by the law. I repeat,
          we've been COLLARED by the law --
          do you copy?!

Nothing. Shit. He sighs, flushes the toilet, FLOOSH, and --

INT. WHEELER HOUSE - NIGHT

A frustrated Dustin exits the bathroom and crosses to the TV
room.

He passes by HOLLY, who is playing with a LITE-BRITE, past anxious parents talking to Officer Daniels, and rejoins Lucas in --

THE KITCHEN - CONTINUOUS

      LUCAS
  Anything?

      DUSTIN
 Nothing.

      LUCAS
 You don't think they... went
 through, do you?

      DUSTIN
 Through *Watergate?* Without us?
 Without a plan? *Without weapons?*
 They wouldn't be that stupid.
   (Lucas nods, of course not)
 They must just be staying low
 because they know the law got us --

      ERICA (O.S.)
 "The law"??? What is this --
 Gunsmoke? The Stupid and the Ugly?

Our boys look up to see Erica making a beeline for them, sucking on a grape juice box.

      ERICA (CONT'D)
 Should I round up the posse? Saddle
 the horses --

      LUCAS
 Erica -- *please* just -- go away --

      ERICA
 I'd rather not.

She leans against the counter, looks right at Lucas.

      ERICA (CONT'D)
 Here's the deal -- either you tell
 me what's really going on, or --
   (to Lucas)
 I'll tell Dustin what I found under
 your bed.

                    LUCAS
                (horrified)
    _NO_ --

                    ERICA
    Then spill yer guts, cowpuncher --

                    DUSTIN
    What'd she find under your bed???

                    LUCAS
    Nothing --

                    DUSTIN
                (to Erica)
    Is it gross, how gross would you
    say, scale of one to ten --

                    ERICA
    A hundred --

                    LUCAS
    The serial killer's a dark wizard
    from the Upside Down and we've been
    looking for him but he's in the
    Upside Down which we can't reach at
    least we thought we couldn't until
    we found a Gate at Lover's Lake
    which is why we were there but then
    we got grabbed by these stupid cops
    and if you say anything about this
    to ANYONE and that includes Mom and
    Dad and Tina -- especially TINA --
    I will smother you in your sleep *do
    you copy?!*

Erica stares. Processing. Lucas leans in, right in his
sister's face.

                    LUCAS (CONT'D)
    Do. You. Copy??

                    ERICA
    The smothering in the sleep part
    yeah, but -- not much else. Why
    would they open a Gate in Lover's
    Lake?

                    LUCAS
    What -- ?

ERICA
The commies --

LUCAS
The commies didn't do this --

ERICA
Then *who* did it -- ??

LUCAS
Nobody --

ERICA
It just opened up -- for fun???

LUCAS
Erica you have NO idea what you're talking about --

DUSTIN
No she doesn't YET she brings up an *essential question*. How did Watergate open? Two Gates have opened so far as we know -- one by El, one by the commies -- and we know it's not the commies or El this time so --
(lightbulb!)
Holy shit, *wait* wait *wait* --

LUCAS
Wait *what* -- ?

Dustin starts pacing around, his mind racing.

DUSTIN
There's one thing we've never understood -- which is why is Vecna killing people? What's his motive? Killing teens? It's always seemed too random, too prosaic. On top of that -- how does the Mind Flayer figure into all this? Maybe this is it, *THIS* is the answer --

LUCAS
What is the answer -- ?

Before Dustin can respond, Karen enters with Officer Daniels.

                    KAREN
          You sure you just want water?
               (opens fridge)
          We've got Coke, Sprite, Dr.
          Pepper...

As Karen opens the fridge, Dustin drags Lucas down --

THE HALLWAY - CONTINUOUS

Away from earshot of the adults. Erica tags along, of course.

Dustin is excited, almost manic here --

                    DUSTIN
          Okay, so just -- *hear me out*. How
          did El open the Mother Gate -- ??

                    LUCAS
          She -- made... contact with the
          Demogorgon --

                    DUSTIN
          Psychic contact -- just like --

                    LUCAS
               (realizing)
          Vecna, when he casts his spells --

                    DUSTIN
          Exactly. So what if -- with every
          kill -- he's not simply killing --
          he's making a powerful psychic
          connection with his victims -- a
          connection *so powerful* it's tearing
          a hole in the fabric in time and
          space --

                    LUCAS
               (shocked)
          -- He's opening gates.

                    DUSTIN
          Bingo. And why?

                    LUCAS
          To take over the world.

                    DUSTIN
          And who do we know who wants to
          take over the world -- ?

                    LUCAS
          The Mind Flayer.

                    DUSTIN
          If the Demogorgon is a foot soldier
          -- Vecna is his five-star general.
          A five-star general with the power
          to open Gates.

                    LUCAS
          Holy shit.

                    DUSTIN
          Holy shit.

                    ERICA
          Holy shit that was
          incomprehensible. You lost me at
          Mother Gate. Please be kind,
          rewind.

As our frustrated boys turn to Erica and begin to "rewind,"
WE PUSH PAST THEM TOWARD THE FRONT DOOR --

The voices of our kids slowly fade as we become aware that
the front porch light is blinking, stuttering, and then --

INT. WHEELER HOUSE - FOYER (THE UPSIDE DOWN)

WHOOM! Sound SUCKS OUT and the door handle turns and --

WIDEN: Our teens open the door, stepping into the same area
as Dustin, Lucas, and Erica. Only they're in the Upside Down
version of our house.

Nancy looks around, takes it in. This is... *weird*.

                    ROBIN
          When's the last time you got a
          maid, Wheeler.

                    NANCY
               (ignoring this)
          Come on, I don't wanna stay in here
          any longer than we have to --

Nancy leads our teens up the decrepit stairs, but --

Steve pauses on the second step. He's heard something. A
voice. Ghostly. *Familiar...*

INT. NANCY'S ROOM (UPSIDE DOWN)

WHOOM! Nancy throws open her closet and --

She pulls a SHOEBOX off the upper shelf -- drops it onto her bed -- rips off the top -- and -- her face *drops*. Inside --

A PAIR OF PINK DRESS SHOES.

                EDDIE
     Those... don't look like guns --

Robin grabs one of the shoes from Nancy.

                ROBIN
     I mean yeah, Nance these heels are
     a bit pointy -- but I was hoping
     for something along the lines of...
     could fire deadly projectiles --

                NANCY
     I don't understand --

                EDDIE
     Maybe you hid them somewhere else
     -- ?

                NANCY
     We have a six-year-old in the
     house, I know where I keep my guns.
     Also, I threw these out years ago.

Nancy's eyes narrow. She's spotted something peeking out from under the shoebox. She pushes the shoebox aside to reveal a CHEMISTRY TEXTBOOK and a stack of FLASHCARDS. She grabs up the cards and flips through them, her confusion building --

QUICK FLASHCUT TO NANCY AND STEVE STUDYING ON THE BED FROM SEASON ONE -- READING THE *SAME FLASHCARDS* --

                ROBIN
     I know grades are important to you
     but perhaps studying can wait until
     we're outta here -- ?

                NANCY
        (ignoring this)
     These are from sophomore chemistry
     --

Nancy looks around.

                    NANCY (CONT'D)
          And this wallpaper -- this is my
          old wallpaper.

Nancy crosses to her dresser mirror --

                    NANCY (CONT'D)
          This mirror went to the yard sale --

She grabs a stuffed animal off of the bed.

                    NANCY (CONT'D)
          And you -- I gave you to cousin
          Joanna -- *two years ago.*

She crosses to the other side of the room and grabs up a
DIARY which sits on the nightstand beside her bed. She flips
through it, faster, faster, panic rising, until she arrives
at the last entry. A bolded date reads: NOVEMBER 6, 1986.

Her breath catches in her throat.

                    ROBIN
          What is it?

Nancy doesn't respond right away, just stands there, reading
that date over and over, as if it might just change. *It can't
be right...* Robin takes a step closer, really worried now --

                    ROBIN (CONT'D)
          Nancy -- you're freaking me out --

Finally Nancy speaks. She's not sure how to put this...

                    NANCY
          I think... my guns aren't here...
          because... they don't *exist* here
          yet.

Robin and Eddie share confused looks.

                    EDDIE
          Don't... *exist?*

Nancy turns back to them. Holds up the diary.

                    NANCY
          This diary... it should be filled.
          But it's not. The last entry is
          November sixth, nineteen eighty-
          three. That's the day Will went
          missing. The day the Gate opened.
                    (MORE)

                    NANCY (CONT'D)
                (beat)
          We're in the past.

Just as Robin and Eddie take in this mind-blowing
revelation --

                    STEVE (O.S.)
          DUSTIN??!?! CAN YOU HEAR ME??!
          DUSTIN!!!

They share looks, now realizing Steve isn't with them, and --

INT. WHEELER HOUSE - STAIRCASE (UPSIDE DOWN)

They race back downstairs to find Steve still in the foyer.
He's shouting at... *nothing*. He looks like an angry old man
yelling at the sky or something --

                    STEVE
          DUSTIN!?!??!?!? DUSTIN?!
          HELLOOOO?!?!

                    NANCY
          Steve what are you doing -- ???!!

                    ROBIN
          Maybe he really does have rabies --

                    STEVE
          The little shit's here -- he's like
          -- in the walls! Listen, listen!

They do. And sure enough, they hear Dustin:

                    DUSTIN (V.O.)
                (filtered, heavy reverb)
            *And this finally brings us to the
            question you first raised.*

INT. WHEELER HOUSE - FOYER - NIGHT

Dustin is now catching up Erica, totally oblivious to the
teens' peril in the Upside Down --

                    DUSTIN
            How and why is there a new Gate in
            Lover's Lake?? Now, let's analyze --
            what do Vecna and Eleven have in
            common -- ?

THE UPSIDE DOWN

                    NANCY/ROBIN/EDDIE
            DUSTIN???! DUSTIN! HELLOO??!
            HELLOO! DUSTIN!???!

They wait for a response. But Dustin just keeps yapping away
to Erica.

                    STEVE
            Okay so either he's being a real
            douchebag or he can't hear us --

                    NANCY
            Will found a way.

                    STEVE
            What -- ?

                    NANCY
            Will. He found a way. To talk to
            Joyce.

Nancy makes her move into --

THE LIVING ROOM (UPSIDE DOWN)

She hits a light switch -- nothing happens. Eddie tries
another, Robin another, but --

                    ROBIN
            Everything's dead --

                    STEVE
            Hold up -- back up, *back up* --

Steve shines his flashlight at the lamp near Robin --

>   STEVE (CONT'D)
>   You guys see that??

Robin narrows her eyes. Sure enough, she sees a weird "SHIMMER," distorting the air around the light bulb. It's hard to discern, only *just* visible in the beam of Steve's light.

Nancy reaches out, runs her hand through the shimmer, and --

Strange particulates begin to dance around her fingers.

>   EDDIE
>   Whoa....

As the particulates light up --

INT. WHEELER HOUSE - NIGHT

The lamp in the real world glows in response, then dims again as --

INT. WHEELER HOUSE - NIGHT (UPSIDE DOWN)

Nancy removes her hand from the shimmer.

Steve now tries it, moving his hand through the "shimmer."

>   STEVE
>   It *tickles* --

As the others take turns --

>   ROBIN
>   Kinda... *feels good* --

>   NANCY
>   Anyone know morse code?

>   ROBIN/STEVE
>   No --

>   EDDIE
>   Does S.O.S. count?

Shared looks and --

INT. WHEELER HOUSE - NIGHT

As Dustin continues explaining to Erica, Erica suddenly notices the blinking light in the living room.

> DUSTIN
> Hey -- are you even listening to me?

> ERICA
> Yeah I'm listening. It's just... you said you followed Vecna through lights, right?

> DUSTIN
> Yeah, why -- ?

> ERICA
> Because I think he's here.

Dustin and Lucas now turn, following Erica's worried gaze to the blinking lamp. Lucas's face drops. Scared now. But Dustin isn't scared -- he's *curious*. He crosses into THE LIVING ROOM, moving toward that blinking light, eyes narrowing as --

INT. WHEELER HOUSE (UPSIDE DOWN)

Eddie moves his hand in and out of the light in rhythm --

> ROBIN
> It's working --

He's making --

WHEELER HOUSE

> DUSTIN
> S.... O.... S....
> (realizing, stunned)
> Hey so -- you remember when I said they wouldn't be stupid enough to go through Watergate?

> LUCAS
> Yeah --

Dustin turns back to Lucas --

> DUSTIN
> I overestimated them.

EXT. RUSSIAN PRISON - NIGHT

WHOOSH! We're suddenly soaring over a snow-swept landscape, back toward the Russian prison where --

INT. PRISON - ABANDONED ROOM - NIGHT

Murray (disguised as Yuri), Joyce and Yuri (disguised as prisoners), wait in an abandoned section of the prison.

Murray is practicing removing his gun from his jacket. He drops it. *Shit!* As he fumbles for it, Joyce tries to say something to him, but can't beneath her gag --

>   JOYCE
> UMMMMGMGM -- MGMMGG --

Murray crosses over to Joyce, yanks out her gag --

>   MURRAY
> WHAT -- ??

>   JOYCE
> Would you please STOP playing with
> that??

>   MURRAY
> I am not playing I am practicing
> and will you please STOP trying to
> talk to me and stay in character!
> Remember -- you're frightened,
> scared, confused --

>   JOYCE
> I am frightened and scared and
> conffff-fff!

Murray has shoved the gag back in, silencing her just as --

WHOOM! A door opens up -- Murray spins, startled. He frantically stuffs the pistol back into his pants as --

WARDEN MELNIKOV enters. He's joined by a SCARY GUARD. He locks eyes with Murray as he approaches.

Murray tries to stay calm -- and stay *in character.*

>   WARDEN MELNIKOV
> <Yuri Ismaylov. At last, we meet.>

>   MURRAY
> <Comrade Major.>

As the two men shake hands, the Warden clocks the bound and gagged Yuri. He approaches him. He seems... a little thrown.

                    WARDEN MELNIKOV
          <This is the Bauman spy? He
          looks... different.>

                    MURRAY
          <Uglier in person I know.>

Yuri begins to make noises beneath this gag --

                    MURRAY (CONT'D)
          <He also shaved his beard to
          disguise himself. *Tricky bastard.*>

Yuri continues to shout through his gag, trying to warn the warden, but -- WHAP! Murray SLAPS him across his cheek!

                    MURRAY (CONT'D)
                 (accented English)
          Silence American scum!! Enough from
          you! ENOUGH!

Yuri burns under the gag, but the Warden is already bored with him and has moved on to Joyce.

                    WARDEN MELNIKOV
          <Now this one... this one I would
          recognize a continent away. She was
          more beautiful in our uniform, but
          still... quite striking, isn't
          she?>

                    MURRAY
          <Yes -- very pleasing to the eyes,
          comrade. But not so pleasing to the
          ears I am afraid.>

Murray removes her gag. Joyce immediately starts to "act" in character --

                    JOYCE
          Where is he?! What did you do to
          Hopper! You -- STUPID -- UGLY --
          COMMIE PIG!!

                    MURRAY
          <As I said -- unpleasant.>

Murray quickly gags her again --

                    MURRAY (CONT'D)
          <But... I must say -- I too am
          curious. The other American. What
          did you do to him? Lobotomy? Pluck
          out his tongue? I do not know why,
          but I imagine him on a rack, in the
          cold, stretched thin, birds pecking
          his eyeballs. Am I -- close?>

Needless to say, this catches the Warden's attention.

                    WARDEN MELNIKOV
          <I have heard stories of Yuri
          Ismaylov -- the *Peanut Butter
          Smuggler*. And you -- you are not
          the Yuri I have heard of.>

Murray swallows. *Uh oh.*

                    MURRAY
          <I am -- not?>

                    WARDEN MELNIKOV
          <No. No. The Yuri I was told of --
          had a screw loose. And you -->
                    (beat)
          <Have many screws loose!!>

The Warden starts laughing. Murray laughs too.

                    WARDEN MELNIKOV (CONT'D)
          <But do not worry -- we have
          something special planned for the
          American.>

The Warden checks his watch, grins --

                    WARDEN MELNIKOV (CONT'D)
          <And -- as it happens -- you are
          just in time to see for yourself.>
                    (turns to Joyce)
          And to see what fate awaits you,
          princess -- if you do not watch
          that *tongue*.

Off Joyce, now terrified, we CUT TO --

INT. PRISON CORRIDOR / CONTROL ROOM - NIGHT

A metal door swings open as the Warden now leads Murray and his "prisoners" through an EERIE PRISON LABORATORY. Joyce and Murray inspect their surroundings; there are many SCIENTISTS here, all staring at them... a LARGE METAL DOOR... and a CONTROL PANEL, with lights and switches, manned by a TECH.

                WARDEN MELNIKOV
                  (to Tech)
      <I hope we have not missed the
      show.>

                TECHNICIAN
      <On the contrary -- just in time.>

The Tech hits a button and a BUZZER goes off as a door on the far side of the lab unlocks. The Warden leads his prisoners through this door and up a FLIGHT OF STAIRS and --

EXT. THE PIT - NIGHT

Out into the third-floor balcony above the Pit! They're immediately met by blustery, cold wind, and falling snow.

The Warden leads them to a balcony railing. Murray and Joyce's eyes go wide as they take in the scene below --

<u>Hopper and the other prisoners</u> are out of their cells now and <u>IN THE PIT</u>, kneeling in the snow! *Oh no.* They're too late!! IVAN paces back and forth in front of them, speaking.

Joyce's eyes well with emotion as she sees Hopper -- he is a shell of the man she remembers. Murray, meanwhile, chokes back his own emotions, struggling to stay "in character."

                MURRAY
                  (to Warden)
      <What -- what is happening?>

                WARDEN MELNIKOV
      <They are being told the rules.>

                MURRAY
      <Rules for what?>

                WARDEN MELNIKOV
      <I could tell you -- but that would
      spoil the fun, now, wouldn't it?>

DOWN IN THE PIT,

Ivan finishes addressing the prisoners --

                    IVAN
          <You wait for the buzzer. You WAIT.
          You move before the buzzer -- you
          will be shot. Is that understood??>

The Prisoners all nod. Mutter "<yes>."

                    IVAN (CONT'D)
          <I'd wish you luck -- but it won't
          help you.>

On that note, Ivan drops a KEY into the snow and then heads
off with the other guards, leaving the prisoners behind.

                    DMITRI
          Let us hope your prayers have been
          heard, American.

Before Hop can respond, an EARTH SHATTERING ROAR ECHOES
ACROSS THE PIT. Our prisoners turn toward the big door. They
are scared, but they have heard this roar before, whereas...

UP ON THE BALCONY

Joyce *hasn't*. As her whole body tenses upon hearing the sound
of a monster she had thought was long dead, we HARD CUT TO --

INT. RAINBOW ROOM (MEMORY)

PLUNK! A Plinko tile dropping down a series of pegs. Quiet.

WIDEN: Eleven is back in the Rainbow Room. And though she is
going about her daily routine, we can tell that she is
nervous, on edge. She looks around. Two is not here, but the
other bullies keep looking her way. Clearly furious. El
suddenly drops a Plinko. She goes to pick it up but --

Another hand scoops it up for her. It's the Friendly Orderly.
As he passes it back to her --

                    FRIENDLY ORDERLY
          You open for something -- a little
          more challenging?

Off Eleven --

INT. RAINBOW ROOM - MOMENTS LATER (MEMORY)

A CHESS BOARD is now set up. Eleven and the Friendly Orderly
sitting across from one another. As they begin to play --

                    FRIENDLY ORDERLY
               Try not to show any emotion as I
               speak, okay?

Eleven tenses a bit.

                    FRIENDLY ORDERLY (CONT'D)
               Just... keep playing the game if
               you understand.

El does as he says -- keeps playing. She can't help but be a
bit nervous.

                    FRIENDLY ORDERLY (CONT'D)
               Two is still recovering in the
               infirmary -- he's being watched
               now, but once he is released, he
               and the others are going to attempt
               to kill you. Right here, in this
               room.

Eleven's heart skips -- *oh God.*

                    FRIENDLY ORDERLY (CONT'D)
               And Papa will allow it to happen.
               In fact, he wants it to happen.
               He's been planning it for some time
               now.

This hits Eleven like a gut punch -- she can't not look at
the Orderly here --

                    FRIENDLY ORDERLY (CONT'D)
               Stay calm. Focus on the game.

Eleven returns to the game. Slides a piece forward.

                    FRIENDLY ORDERLY (CONT'D)
               There's a reason Two and the others
               were able to escape their room last
               night. Why the security cameras
               were turned off. Why Papa punished
               Two today. They don't even realize
               it, but Papa is moving them -- like
               the pieces on this board here --
               driving them to do exactly what he
               wants. Which is...

He jumps one of her pawns with his knight, then knocks it off
the board.

                    ELEVEN
        W-why?

                    FRIENDLY ORDERLY
        You frighten him. He knows you're
        more powerful than the others.
        And he also knows he can't control
        you. That's all he wants. *Control*.
        I saw all this happening... That's
        why I wanted to help you, but -- I
        only made things worse...

Eleven is beginning to understand --

                    ELEVEN
        Helping me -- is why... Papa hurt
        you?

QUICK FLASHBACK TO THE ORDERLY GETTING SHOCKED LAST NIGHT --

The Friendly Orderly gives a small nod.

                    FRIENDLY ORDERLY
        And it is why you must escape --
        today. But they are watching us
        closely. If you wish to make it out
        of here alive -- you will need to
        do exactly as I say, do you
        understand?

Eleven nods, but then, she looks back at him one last time.

                    ELEVEN
        Why... do you -- still help me?

                    FRIENDLY ORDERLY
        Because I believe in you. And it's
        time you are free from this Hell.

Slyly, he slips an ELECTRONIC KEYCARD to El under the table. As her hand curls around the KEYCARD, we CUT TO --

INT. WHEELER HOUSE - TV ROOM - NIGHT

A peg GLOWS as Holly places it in the Lite-Brite. She's almost finished with a cute BUNNY RABBIT DESIGN, when --

ZOOP! The Lite-Brite suddenly ZAPS out. Holly looks up in shock to find Lucas holding the power cord --

                    HOLLY
        Hey -- !

                    DUSTIN
          Sorry, emergency, we need to borrow
          this --

Dustin yanks the Lite-Brite away from Holly, Lucas grabs the
Lite-Brite box, filled with loose pegs, while Erica tosses
Holly a BAG OF SKITTLES --

                    ERICA
          For your understanding.

As a slack-jawed Holly stares at the Skittles --

INT. WHEELER HOUSE - NANCY'S ROOM - NIGHT

WHOOM! Dustin drops the Lite-Brite onto Nancy's bed and we
move into a QUICK MONTAGE as our kids work to plug ALL OF
THE PEGS into the holes, covering the entire panel.

The second they finish, Dustin plugs the Lite-Brite into the
wall. As the panel lights up, projecting a rainbow of colored
light back at our kids, Dustin projects his voice --

                    DUSTIN
          OKAY -- ARE YOU GUYS SEEING THIS???

INT. NANCY'S ROOM (UPSIDE DOWN)

Nancy, Robin, Steve, and Eddie -- who we find also gathered
in Nancy's room -- can, in fact, see a "shimmer" above exactly
where Dustin placed the Lite-Brite.

Nancy reaches out, touches the shimmer with her hand, and --

INT. NANCY'S ROOM - NIGHT

The Lite-Brite glows brighter, casting a more powerful
rainbow of colors over our awed kids' faces.

                    ERICA
          Holy shit --

                    DUSTIN
          Okay, okay -- I'm not moving it,
          but we're going to unplug it,
          okay?? Stand by!

Lucas drops down by the outlet and unplugs the Lite-Brite.

INT. NANCY'S ROOM (UPSIDE DOWN)

The shimmer dissipates on the bed, though a few particles still linger, almost like a burn-in on a TV or something.

REAL WORLD - INTERCUT

>   DUSTIN
> Okay, try it now --

UPSIDE DOWN - INTERCUT

Nancy reaches out with her finger and traces the air where the Lite-Brite was and --

REAL WORLD

The Lite-Brite pegs glow in such a way that spells: H.I.

>   DUSTIN/LUCAS/ERICA
> *Hi.*

The kids share stunned looks --

>   DUSTIN
> Okay okay -- um -- that worked!!!

UPSIDE DOWN

>   EDDIE
> *Hot damn --*

Nancy is already tracing more letters, writing --

REAL WORLD

>   LUCAS/DUSTIN/ERICA
> S.T.U.C.K.

>   LUCAS
> "Stuck" -- okay *they're stuck in the Upside Down* --

>   DUSTIN
> You can't you get back through Watergate -- ?

UPSIDE DOWN

>   STEVE
> Watergate -- ?

                    ROBIN
          Oh because -- the Gate's -- in
          water.

                    STEVE
          Jesus --

                    EDDIE
          Cute.

Nancy starts writing back and

REAL WORLD

More letters appear:

                    LUCAS/DUSTIN/ERICA
          G -- U -- A -- R -- D -- E -- D.

                    DUSTIN
          "Guarded." Watergate is -- *guarded*.
          Okay, okay -- um -- well --
                  (projecting voice)
          We have a theory that maybe could
          help with that. We think Watergate
          isn't the only Gate -- that there's
          a Gate at *every* murder site --

UPSIDE DOWN

Teens share totally confused looks --

                    NANCY
          Does anyone understand what he's
          talking about -- ?

                    STEVE/ROBIN/EDDIE
          No --

Nancy draws a question mark --

NANCY'S ROOM

A "?" glows on the Lite-Brite, much to Dustin's frustration.

                    DUSTIN
          Okay. Seriously -- how many times
          do I have to be right on the money
          before you JUST TRUST ME --

UPSIDE DOWN

> STEVE
> Okay his ego is, like, way out of control at this point --

> NANCY
> (to Eddie)
> How far to your trailer?

> EDDIE
> I don't know -- seven miles, give or take --

> ROBIN
> Nancy -- I get your house in here is like, weirdly, creepily frozen in time and shit, but -- you've always had bikes right?

Off Nancy, HARD CUT TO --

INT. WHEELER HOUSE - TV ROOM - NIGHT

WHOOM! The basement door opens, and Powell and Callahan lead Max back upstairs. As she puts her headphones back on, she notices Dustin, urgently waving at her from the stairs. *Come on!* As she sneaks off, weirded out --

Worried parents (accompanied by Daniels) approach Powell for an update.

> KAREN
> Anything?

> POWELL
> No --

> CALLAHAN
> Honestly -- shouldn't have gone with her first. She's like -- *kinda mean*.

> POWELL
> (ignoring him)
> We'll find your daughter, Missus Wheeler. Don't worry --

> CALLAHAN
> One of those little brats is gonna squeal, I can just feel it. Where are they?

> OFFICER DANIELS
> Upstairs. Moping.

INT. WHEELER HOUSE - UPSTAIRS LANDING - NIGHT

Callahan stomps upstairs to Nancy's room.

> CALLAHAN
> Little pigs, little pigs -- let Officer Callahan in.

INT. WHEELER HOUSE - NANCY'S ROOM - NIGHT

Callahan enters the room, and freezes. The Lite-Brite is on the bed, filled with pegs. But there are no kids, and --

The window is WIDE OPEN. Callahan's face falls. He races over to the window, sees --

OUT THE WINDOW - CALLAHAN POV:

The kids pushing bikes up the driveway -- escaping!!

> CALLAHAN
> HEY!! HEY!!!

EXT. WHEELER HOUSE - NIGHT

The kids stop by the cop car.

> DUSTIN
> Do it -- !

Erica removes a SWISS ARMY knife. Flips out the blade.

> ERICA
> I guess it's just a minor misdemeanor.

She stabs it into the cop car tire like a fucking ninja!! As the blade plunges through rubber, air HISSING --

> CALLAHAN
> HEYYYYYYYY!!!

EXT. WHEELER HOUSE - NIGHT

WHOOM! The front door to the house blows open as --

A mess of cops and parents tumble out of the house and race across the lawn, after our kids -- but they are too late.

SHOOOOM! Our kids are far away now, escaping "the law" on their bikes. As they pedal, triumphant, their hair whipping in the wind, we can't help but notice that their bike lights are pulsing, _flickering_. Wait a minute...

OUR CAMERA NOW BEGINS TO ROTATE, FLIPPING <u>UNDER THE ROAD</u> AND THEN RE-EMERGING IN --

THE UPSIDE DOWN - NIGHT

Where we find our teens biking too -- that's right, they're biking in the Upside Down, right along with our kids!!!!

As they pedal down the post-apocalyptic street, spores whipping and swirling around them, we CRANE UP to find --

<u>A DEMOBAT</u>, landing on a crooked electrical wire. _Watching them, breathing._ It releases a sharp SHRIEK and --

INT. CREEL HOUSE - FIRST FLOOR (UPSIDE DOWN)

<u>VECNA suddenly turns toward camera</u>. <u>Alerted by his spy</u>.

And right here, MAKE A HARD CUT TO --

INT. RAINBOW ROOM - DAY (MEMORY)

Quiet. _Unnerving quiet._ Looking at that painted rainbow.

We PULL AWAY to find a nervous Eleven. As she fidgets with a chess piece -- _the queen_ -- she looks up at the clock. The clock nears 3 pm when --

WHOOM! The door opens. She whirls, on edge, to find --

<u>Dr. Brenner</u>. _Oh God._ She turns away, trying to stay calm as he heads in her direction. But he stops short of reaching her, and instead kneels by --

TEN, who is playing with a Magic 8 Ball. And now we realize... we've LOOPED BACK TO THE BEGINNING OF OUR SEASON. _The day of the massacre._ Only now we're experiencing it from Eleven's POV. She watches out of the corner of her eye as Brenner and Ten speak --

> DR. BRENNER
> That's your favorite, isn't it?

Ten nods shyly.

                    DR. BRENNER (CONT'D)
               How are we feeling today?

                         TEN
               Okay.

                    DR. BRENNER
               Up for some more lessons?

Ten shakes the 8 Ball again. Holds it up for Brenner. It
reads: "Decidedly so."

Dr. Brenner takes Ten's hand and they exit the room. As soon
as the door shuts behind them, Eleven's eyes dart back to the
clock. The minute hand moves to three now.

She takes a deep breath, then pushes off her seat and --

MOMENTS LATER

Eleven walks up to the Stern Orderly --

                         ELEVEN
                    (clearly rehearsed)
               I -- feel dizzy.

                    STERN ORDERLY
               Dizzy?

                         ELEVEN
               Yes. And the light -- the light is
               hurting my head.

Off the Orderly, clearly concerned --

INT. HAWKINS LABS - HALLWAY - MOMENTS LATER (MEMORY)

The Stern Orderly takes Eleven down a hallway and into --

INT. HAWKINS LABS - INFIRMARY - CONTINUOUS (MEMORY)

There is a ROW OF BEDS here, but only one is occupied by...

<u>Two</u>. Still recovering from this morning. The NURSE -- who is
caring for him -- looks up as the Stern Orderly approaches --

                         NURSE
               Hey -- everything alright -- ?

                    STERN ORDERLY
               Not sure. She says she's still
               dizzy -- lights are hurting her --

                    NURSE
         ... Who is?

He turns, sees that Eleven is no longer with him.

Off the Orderly's *stunned face*, CUT TO --

INT. HAWKINS LABS - HALLWAY - DAY (MEMORY)

Eleven hurrying away down a hallway, her hand clutching tight to that keycard. She reaches a door at the end of the hallway, swipes the keycard across an ELECTRONIC KEYPAD.

BEEP! A red light turns green. She shoves through the door, and --

INT. HAWKINS LABS - STAIRWELL - DAY (MEMORY)

Eleven hurries down a dark staircase, bare feet taking two steps at a time and --

INT. HAWKINS LABS - BOILER ROOM - DAY (MEMORY)

-- She enters the BOILER ROOM. We recognize this from Bob's heroic journey in season 2. It's scary down here, and without a flashlight, it's very difficult to see. She hears a gurgling noise, turns, and --

HISSS! Steam blasts out at her from some jagged pipe, shrieking like a monster. She startles back and --

WHAM!! Slams into someone. She starts to scream but it's just the Friendly Orderly. He holds a finger to his lips.

                    FRIENDLY ORDERLY
          Quiet. Follow me.

MOMENTS LATER

The Friendly Orderly leads her to a SMALL PIPE in the wall.

He grabs a grate, pulls it off.

                    FRIENDLY ORDERLY
          It's going to be a bit scary in
          here -- but this will take you
          beyond the lab fence, to the woods.

She looks at him, confused --

                    ELEVEN
          You -- are too big --

The Friendly Orderly hesitates. He has to break it to her --

> FRIENDLY ORDERLY
> I am not going with you, Eleven.

This is a gut punch -- her eyes fill with tears, fear --

> FRIENDLY ORDERLY (CONT'D)
> I meant what I said when I called this lab a prison. And everyone here... is a prisoner. Not just you. Not just your brothers and sisters. The guards too. The Nurses. *Me.*

He removes his hand from hers and pulls back his hair, revealing --

A SMALL SCAR BEHIND HIS EAR. He then pushes down on the skin around this scar, revealing the outline of a small object. It's shaped almost like a pill capsule. Very odd but... it seems like this capsule has been... *sewn into his neck.*

> FRIENDLY ORDERLY (CONT'D)
> Your "Papa" -- he calls it "an Inhibitor." It weakens me -- tracks me. Even if there were another way out -- he *will* find me. And if he finds me -- he will find you.

Eleven takes this in. Mind racing. Then, a thought --

> ELEVEN
> What if I make it -- go away?

The Friendly Orderly looks at Eleven, surprised.

> ELEVEN (CONT'D)
> You -- help me. I -- *help you.*

Off the Friendly Orderly, moved by this, more steam BLASTS from the pipe, and we SMASH TO --

EXT. RUSSIAN PRISON - NIGHT

An aerial shot soars toward the "Pit." Beneath HOWLING WIND, we can hear a GUTTURAL ROAR. It's echoing out from --

EXT. THE PIT - NIGHT

That large, bloody door. Our prisoners listen to the roars, tense, scared.

                    DMITRI
               (to prisoners)
          <Stay calm. Stay close. Stick to
          the plan.>

EEEEEE! A HORRIBLE BUZZER suddenly blasts from a loudspeaker
Game on. Dmitri grabs up the key as our prisoners sprint
across the Pit for the WEAPONS LOCKER.

Dmitri thrusts the key into the locker's keyhole, throws it
open. As the prisoners grab weapons --

UP ON THE THIRD-FLOOR BALCONY,

A pleased Warden sidles up to Murray.

                    WARDEN MELNIKOV
          <I enjoy this part... when they
          believe there is still hope.>

Joyce shoots Murray a desperate look as --

IN THE PIT BELOW,

Dmitri grabs a SPEAR from the locker. He crosses to Hopper,
who wastes no time, frantically wrapping that lining around
the sharp tip of the spear, making what appears to be a
MAKESHIFT TORCH, when --

AN EAR-PIERCING METALLIC SOUND echoes across the Pit.

The prisoners, now all holding weapons, whirl to find that
the large door is now grinding open. Inside this yawning
door, they see nothing, just blackness, but they hear that
awful, familiar sound of the Demogorgon's CLICKING.

                    DMITRI
          <Whatever comes out of there --
          hold your ground. HOLD YOUR
          GROUND!>

But the men seem TERRIFIED. Hopper pulls out the stolen vodka
and begins to douse that now cloth-covered end of the spear.

UP ON THE BALCONY,

The Warden sees Hopper doing this, turns to the TALL GUARD.

                    WARDEN MELNIKOV
          <What is that -- what is the
          American doing?>

                    TALL GUARD
          <I don't know -- >

                    WARDEN MELNIKOV
          <*Find out*.>

The Tall Guard nods and hurries away, moving down some steps to the second floor balcony, as --

Joyce shoots a look at Murray -- now is their chance. As a nervous Murray wraps his hand around the gun...

BACK IN THE PIT,

CLOSE ON: Hands wrapping tight around weapons as our prisoners brace for battle. Something stirs in the darkness of the now wide open door. *Oh Jesus, it's coming.*

Hopper tosses the empty Vodka bottle into the snow, pulls out the lighter, flicks it, but --

It doesn't catch.

                    HOPPER
          Oh come on come on --

                    DMITRI
          Tell me that's not out of fluid --

As Hopper continues to flick the lighter, the other prisoners react... anxiety *ratcheting*... this is NOT good.

BACK ON THE BALCONY,

Murray removes his pistol as practiced, thrusts it into the Warden's back.

                    MURRAY
          <You move so much as an inch, I'll
          kill you.>

The Warden is -- naturally -- blindsided by this. He starts to turn, but Murray cocks the pistol --

                    MURRAY (CONT'D)
          <I said you move you die,
          understand??>

                    WARDEN MELNIKOV
          <What is this? Some kind of sick
          joke -- ?>

                    MURRAY
          <It's no joke. As I said --> the
          Americans are *very tricky*.

Joyce now steps up to him, slipping out of her "bindings."

                    JOYCE
          You want to live -- whatever this
          game is -- you're going to stop it.
          And you're going to free our
          friend.

                    WARDEN MELNIKOV
          If that is the case... then I'm
          afraid you're going to have to kill
          me.

He looks back toward the Pit.

                    WARDEN MELNIKOV (CONT'D)
          Because your friend... is already
          dead.

IN THE PIT,

We see some stirring in that darkness. Then, very suddenly --

THE DEMOGORGON FLIES OUT OF THE PIT AT AN EXTREME HIGH SPEED, MOVING ON ALL FOURS, LIKE A COUGAR. WE'VE NEVER SEEN IT MOVE LIKE THIS AND WE'VE BARELY PROCESSED IT BEFORE --

WHAM! It leaps onto a terrified prisoner, slamming him to the ground. Its claws PLUNGE through the prisoner's chest, killing him instantly. Blood splatters across snow as --

ON THE THIRD-FLOOR BALCONY,

Murray and Joyce watch in horror. *Holy shit.* The Warden can't help but smile a touch as --

IN THE PIT,

The Demogorgon rises from its first kill, standing now. Its pale body now spattered in blood. It looks almost regal in that falling snow. It surveys the terrified prisoners, who surround him with their now rather pitiful looking weapons --

                    DMITRI
          <NOW!!!>

Our prisoners attack, swinging their weapons, but the Demogorgon easily evades.

It SLASHES a prisoner in the arm, then slashes a second prisoner across the neck, killing him instantly. It's a brutal and fast and insane display of power and suddenly our remaining prisoners -- even OLEG -- are fleeing in terror --

> DMITRI (CONT'D)
> <WHAT ARE YOU DOING?? STAY TOGETHER, YOU FOOLS!!>

ON THE BALCONY,

Murray's eyes snap from the battle to the lower balcony, where he sees the Tall Guard arguing with Ivan. He snaps back to the Warden --

> MURRAY
> <Order your men to shoot -- to kill it!!!>

> WARDEN MELNIKOV
> <If I give that order, I will be shot tomorrow, and I will die a traitor. You want to kill me -- <u>do it</u>.>

Murray is at a dead end with this guy. *Fuck it* --

He grabs the Warden, dragging him back across the balcony, toward the exit. Yuri yelps under his gag, then hurries after them as --

IN THE PIT,

Dmitri charges the Demo and swings his axe, but the Demo slashes, splintering his axe. Fuck! The Demo roars and lunges for Dmitri, but right before it gets him --

FWOOM!!! Hopper's lighter catches and the torch lights and --

WHOOM! HE THRUSTS HIS FLAMING TORCH INTO THE DEMO'S HEAVING BACK. AS SPARKS FLY, THE DEMO SHRIEKS, WHIRLING TO HOPPER --

> HOPPER
> (to Demo)
> BACK!! GET THE HELL BACK!!!

As Dmitri scrambles away, Hopper continues to thrust the torch at the shrieking monster --

The Demo HISSES -- then starts to *BACK AWAY*. It's WORKING! The monster's attention now swivels, moving from Hopper and Dmitri to easier prey -- the fleeing prisoners. It charges after them, LEAPS onto Oleg. As Oleg lets out a SCREAM --

INT. CONTROL ROOM - NIGHT

WHOOM! Murray bursts down the steps and back into the control room -- his gun now shoved up to the Warden's temple.

The posted GUARD reaches for his gun but --

> MURRAY
> <I'll kill him -- I'll KILL HIM!>

The Guard moves his hand away from his gun --

> MURRAY (CONT'D)
> <TOSS YOUR GUN! OVER TO ME -- OVER TO ME!>

The Guard places his gun on the ground and kicks it to Murray. As Joyce scoops it up, Murray drags his hostage over to the Tech --

> MURRAY (CONT'D)
> <You -- open all the doors below -- you understand???! OPEN THE DOORS!!>

The Tech's eyes go to the Warden, who remains defiant --

> WARDEN MELNIKOV
> <You open all the doors, that monster will get loose in this prison -- and we are all dead -->

> MURRAY
> <I will pull this trigger! OPEN. THE. DOORS!>

Off the Technician, trapped between a rock and a hard place--

BACK IN THE PIT

Feet fly as Hopper and Dmitri scramble across the Pit. Dmitri sweeps a pickaxe off the ground from a dead prisoner as they approach --

THE CLOSED DEMO DOOR. Hopper jams the butt of his torch into a grate, leaving it there for now, as --

                    DMITRI
          HERE -- !!

Dmitri tosses Hop his axe. Our men now go about executing what is clearly a well-thought-out plan: Dmitri positions the pickaxe into the crevice between the closed double doors, then Hopper follows it up with a powerful hit from the butt of the axe. They're HAMMERING the pickaxe into the door --

ON THE SECOND-FLOOR BALCONY,

The guards watch. The Tall Guard is clearly concerned --

                    TALL GUARD
          <You're just going to stand there
          and watch??>>

                    IVAN
          <What else would we do? Why are you
          so concerned, huh? They would need
          a battering ram to open that door.>

BACK BELOW

The pickaxe is now hammered into the door. Dmitri and Hopper pull back on it with all their might -- but the door doesn't budge. *Seems Ivan may be right.* As they continue to strain --

CONTROL ROOM

CLICK! Murray cocks his gun, growing desperate --

                    MURRAY
          <You think I'm playing?? You think
          I won't do it?? OPEN THE DOOR!>

The Technician fights back panic -- and *finds courage*:

                    TECHNICIAN
          <If I open those doors, I condemn
          not just myself, but all of my
          comrades to death. In good
          conscience I cannot. *I will not.*>

The Warden is clearly pleased. Murray -- not so much.

                    MURRAY
          I gotta give it to you commies...
          you're *committed* --

WHAM! Murray slams the Warden in the head with the butt of his gun -- knocking him down and out.

The Tech then charges to attack but -- WHAM! -- Murray slams the Tech once, twice, then KICKS him, sending him spinning to the floor as --

BACK IN THE PIT,

The Demogorgon finishes devouring another prisoner. Its flesh petals now DRIPPING WITH FRESH BLOOD. Now only two victims remain: Hop and Dmitri. It charges them, going for the kill, but Hopper grabs the torch up out of the grate and --

>   HOPPER
>   BACK BACK!!!

He jabs that flame at the monster. The tactic works again -- but not as well. The torch's flame is sputtering, dying, that jacket lining burning away, and with less heat, the Demo is able to get closer to Hopper -- it SLASHES HIM IN THE ARM!

Hopper recoils in pain, jabs it back with the torch.

>   HOPPER (CONT'D)
>   (to Dmitri)
>   RUNNING OUTTA TIME HERE!!!

>   DMITRI
>   ALMOST -- HAVE IT -- !

Dmitri throws all his weight behind the pickaxe and -- THWACK! The pickaxe handle SNAPS IN HALF. Shit! As a baffled Dmitri stares at the now broken handle in his hand --

CONTROL ROOM

Murray drops down into the chair, frantically scans the various buttons. It looks... *complicated.*

>   JOYCE
>   What are you doing -- ???

>   MURRAY
>   I have NO IDEA!! There are a -- a
>   lot of buttons here -- gimme a
>   second --

>   JOYCE
>   We don't have a second -- !!

Joyce begins to flip switches and hit buttons AT RANDOM as --

EXT. THE PIT - SECOND-FLOOR BALCONY - NIGHT

ZZZZAP! The electrified barbed-wire fence around the Pit *LOSES POWER*. Ivan clocks it, startled by this as --

IN THE PIT,

The Demogorgon continues to get closer to Hop -- *almost on him now* -- its mouth opens, baring its bloody teeth as --

INT. CONTROL ROOM - NIGHT

WHUMP! Joyce flips another switch and --

BACK IN THE PIT,

EEEE! THE DOOR BEGINS TO OPEN --

Hopper and Dmitri share looks. They can hardly believe it.

INT. CONTROL ROOM - NIGHT

And neither can Murray!

>MURRAY
>That did it -- THAT DID IT!!!!

EXT. THE PIT - NIGHT

Hopper and Dmitri backpedal through the opening door.

>DMITRI
>*And we have your miracle.*

But their relief is *short-lived* as they find themselves in --

THE DEMOGORGON PEN,

A containment cell for the Demogorgon. Solid metal on all sides.

>DMITRI
>*Out of one prison into another...*

Making matters worse, Hopper's torch SPUTTERS OUT. *Oh no.*

BACK OUTSIDE

The Demogorgon -- sensing opportunity -- lowers itself onto all fours, then, with a TERRIFYING ROAR, pounces toward our men at high speed --

CONTROL ROOM

>   MURRAY
>   CLOSE IT!! CLOSE IT!!!

Joyce mashes the button and --

BACK OUTSIDE

The door starts to close, almost shut when --

INT. DEMOGORGON PEN - NIGHT

WHAM! The Demogorgon CATCHES the door with its claws, then begins to pry it open in an amazing display of strength --

Hopper lowers his spear and charges the beast --

>   HOPPER
>   AHHHHHHH!!!!!

HE DRIVES THAT SPEAR STRAIGHT INTO THE DEMOGORGON'S GAPING MOUTH!!! *THWAACK*! THE DEMOGORGON SHRIEKS IN PAIN AND --

UP ON THE BALCONY

The wounded Demo stumbles backwards into the Pit, black blood spewing all over the ground from its wounded mouth, and --

THE DEMOGORGON PEN

CHOOOOOM! The DOOR FINALLY SNAPS SHUT. And --

BZZZZ! A LOUD BUZZER sounds, startling our two men. They whirl to find that the heavy metal door behind them is *rising*. They raise their weapons, bracing for another battle, but then...

Hopper's weapon lowers, his breath catches. He can hardly believe what he is seeing. It's --

JOYCE. TIME SEEMS TO SLOW as they meet eyes for the first time since that fateful day last summer. As music and emotions rise, tears filling those eyes, we HARD CUT TO --

EXT. TRAILER PARK - NIGHT (UPSIDE DOWN)

Tires RIPPING past the camera as our teens continue their epic bike trip through the Upside Down. As they bike, they slow a bit as they clock something ominous in the distance:

THE CREEL HOUSE, perched atop its hill, overlooking the playground. That now familiar army of Bats circles overhead, guarding it. It's unnerving -- sends a chill down their spines. They pedal faster, heading away from it, and --

EXT. TRAILER PARK - NIGHT (UPSIDE DOWN)

Our teens now bike their way through the empty, vine-covered, post-apocalyptic trailer park, biking more slowly now. Everything is eerily quiet here. *Too quiet.*

EXT. TRAILER PARK - EDDIE'S TRAILER - NIGHT (UPSIDE DOWN)

They pull to a stop as they near Eddie's trailer. As they dismount, catch their breaths --

>   ROBIN
> Okay, so I feel like -- that's
> gotta be, like some Guinness
> record: most miles traveled --
> interdimensionally --

>   STEVE
>   (hacking)
> Shit -- I got that stuff all in my
> throat -- I think some of it's
> stuck --

They make for Eddie's trailer and --

INT. EDDIE'S TRAILER (UPSIDE DOWN)

EEEEEE... the door to Eddie's trailer creeps open as --

Our teens head in. They are met almost immediately by a red glow, emanating from above them. As their eyes lift --

                    STEVE
        Goddamn...

WE PUSH PAST THEM TO REVEAL A SMALL RIFT ON THE CEILING. IT PULSES... *ALIVE*...

                    EDDIE
        That's where Chrissy died -- *right*
        where she died...

                    ROBIN
        Something's in there...

Sure enough, a SHADOW is moving beneath the membrane. No wait -- *multiple shadows. Monsters?*

WHOOOM! Something SUDDENLY *EXPLODES* out of the Rift, lunging right at them, scaring the shit out of everyone, but --

It's just a BROOM HANDLE! It sweeps around, scraping away the mucus to create a SMALL HOLE in the ceiling, revealing --

<u>Dustin</u>! He's standing in the real world trailer; Lucas and Erica gathered around him.

To clarify -- both groups are standing on the same floor, in the same trailer, *ONLY IN OPPOSITE DIMENSIONS.*

> ROBIN (CONT'D)
> *Holy shit this is trippy.*

Off our two groups, staring at one another, CUT TO --

INT. HAWKINS LABS - BOILER ROOM - DAY (MEMORY)

CLOSE ON: Teeth bite down on leather as --

The Friendly Orderly places his belt between his teeth. He is now sitting down, his back against one of the machines.

Eleven stands across from him. And she looks nervous.

> FRIENDLY ORDERLY
> Remember -- you can't hurt me more than they already have.

Eleven nods. Then she closes her eyes... holds out a hand... and focuses. She's using her powers. *But why?* Then we see --

The skin around the Friendly Orderly's scar begins to throb... *move*. And we realize: El is pulling on his Inhibitor -- attempting to remove it! This is a crude, early version of psychic surgery, and it's painful -- terribly painful.

CLOSE ON: THE ORDERLY'S TEETH CLAMPING DOWN ON THE BELT -- his eyes squeezing shut -- his fists clenching -- and --

SHOOOM! A SMALL METAL DEVICE SUDDENLY rips out of the Friendly Orderly's neck, scattering across the floor. As Eleven falls against a machine, totally drained --

The Friendly Orderly -- now holding his bleeding neck -- staggers to his knees, walks over, and picks up --

THE INHIBITOR. It's a strange, small metallic device -- so small that he can hold it between his thumb and forefinger.

> FRIENDLY ORDERLY (CONT'D)
> (almost to himself)
> Who knew something so small...
> *could cause so much trouble...*

He turns back to El. Grateful.

> FRIENDLY ORDERLY (CONT'D)
> Thank you.

She gently wipes the blood from her nose, then, suddenly, we hear a door -- voices -- footsteps -- flashlights -- GUARDS.

The Friendly Orderly spins back to El --

                 FRIENDLY ORDERLY (CONT'D)
    We have to go. *Now*.

He grabs El's hand and --

INT. STAIRCASE - DAY (MEMORY)

They race through the boiler room, weaving through the maze of machines, then scramble up some stairs, but --

The GUARDS have spotted them --

                 GUARD #1
    HEY STOP!! STOP!!

They don't look back. Just keep running. They burst through a door and into --

INT. HAWKINS LABS - HALLWAY - DAY (MEMORY)

They don't make it far before they crash to a halt. There are other Guards in front of them, blocking their path, including someone we will call LEAD GUARD.

                 LEAD GUARD
    Where do you think you're going?

WHOOM! The basement door flies open behind them as --

The three guards now catch up to them. They are now surrounded. The guards remove shock sticks, hit them on. Electricity CRACKLES.

                 LEAD GUARD (CONT'D)
    Against the wall. Both of you. NOW.

A frightened Eleven starts to obey their orders but --

                 FRIENDLY ORDERLY
    No. You don't have to be afraid of
    them, Eleven. Not anymore.

The Guards share looks then --

                 LEAD GUARD
    Take them.

The Guards move in to take him out. Then, it happens --

WHOOM! Our Friendly Orderly THROWS OUT HIS LEFT HAND and --

WHAM! TWO GUARDS ARE POUNDED WITH A PSIONIC FORCE WHICH SENDS THEM HURTLING ACROSS THE HALLWAY AT HIGH SPEED, FLIPPING THROUGH THE AIR, THEN BAM! THEY SLAM THE FAR WALL SO HARD TILE SHATTERS, THEN, IN A FLASH --

THE FRIENDLY ORDERLY SWINGS AROUND, THROWS OUT HIS HAND AGAIN, AND -- FWOOM! -- HE TAKES OUT THE TWO GUARDS BEHIND THEM -- FLINGING THEM INTO THE CEILING -- SHATTERING THE OVERHEAD LIGHTS -- AND SUDDENLY --

Only the Lead Guard remains. And he is *terrified*.

                    LEAD GUARD (CONT'D)
          Don't --

Too late. The Orderly cocks his neck and -- and THWACK! -- the Guard's neck snaps. He folds to the floor like a rag doll.

Eleven stares at the dead bodies around them. Stunned.

The Orderly turns to her. He's barely broken a sweat.

                    FRIENDLY ORDERLY
          Come.

He grabs a *shocked Eleven's* hand and --

INT. LAB ROOM - NIGHT - MOMENTS LATER (MEMORY)

-- Ushers her into a dark, empty room.

                    FRIENDLY ORDERLY
          Wait here -- don't move -- I'll
          find us a way out.

He is about to leave but can't help but notice the way Eleven is staring at him. A small smile.

                    FRIENDLY ORDERLY (CONT'D)
          Like I said... we're alike, you and
          I.

He rolls up his sleeve, revealing a tattoo: <u>001</u>.

And with that, One exits. As the door closes on a stunned Eleven, CRASH TO --

INT. EDDIE'S TRAILER - NIGHT

SHOOM! Two different colored bedsheets are tied together.

WIDEN: Dustin and Erica are working to build a makeshift rope with old sheets while --

Max and Lucas carrying a stained (and now sheetless) mattress across the trailer.

INT. EDDIE'S TRAILER (THE UPSIDE DOWN)

Our teens watch this from what is an overhead view as our kids drop the mattress into place below the Gate. We're starting to understand -- they're creating a <u>landing pad</u>.

> EDDIE
> Those stains are -- I don't know what those stains are.

Our teens stare at Eddie and --

IN THE TRAILER,

Dustin and Erica yank a knot tight, completing their "bedsheet" rope.

> DUSTIN
> Okay... not quite sure how these physics are gonna work but, uh -- here goes nothing.

Dustin swings the "rope" like a lasso and tosses it upward. WHOOSH! The rope soars through the ceiling Gate and into --

THE UPSIDE DOWN

Gravity *SHIFTS* as the rope passes through the hole -- dragging the rope downward and --

PLOP! It lands on the floor below.

IN THE RIGHT-SIDE UP

Dustin is still holding the other end.

> DUSTIN
> But if my theory is correct...

He releases the rope, steps back, and... the sheet stays in place. The gravity is holding it in place.

                    DUSTIN (CONT'D)
          Abracadabra.

                    MAX
          Holy shit.

                    DUSTIN
               (calling through the hole)
          Pull on it -- see if it holds!

UPSIDE DOWN

Robin pulls on the sheet. Sure enough, it holds firm while --

RIGHT-SIDE UP

The other end keeps just... floating in mid-air.

                    ERICA
          Okay this is the craziest shit I've
          ever seen in my life and I've seen
          some *crazy shit.*

UPSIDE DOWN - MOMENTS LATER

CLOSE ON: Hands grab the bedsheet as --

Robin starts to climb, pulling herself up and up and up. The second her body is through the Gate, gravity *shifts* and --

RIGHT-SIDE UP

WHOOM! Robin flips backwards and tumbles down and --

WHOMP! She lands on the grimy mattress.

                    ROBIN
          That was... fun!!!

She pops back onto her feet!

UPSIDE DOWN

Eddie goes now, climbing up those sheets, and --

RIGHT-SIDE UP

WHUMP! He falls onto the mattress. Pops back up --

                    EDDIE
          That *was* fun -- *shit* --

As Robin and the kids help Eddie to his feet --

UPSIDE DOWN

Steve motions to the sheet --

                   STEVE
         See you on the other side --

                   NANCY
        On the other side --

Nancy grabs onto the sheet and climbs up, pulling herself through the trailer Gate, and --

EXT. UNKNOWN - NIGHT (MINDSCAPE)

Nancy's body flips just like the others and she falls and --

She keeps falling -- *too far* -- further than the others and --

WHAM! She lands not on Eddie's mattress but on a HARD CONCRETE SURFACE. She screams in pain. *That fucking hurt.* As she staggers weakly to her feet, holding her arm, her eyes go wide as she finds she's not in the trailer at all. She's in --

AN EMPTY SWIMMING POOL (MINDSCAPE)

A *very* familiar one. Spores float in the air --

INT. EDDIE'S TRAILER (UPSIDE DOWN)

Back in Eddie's trailer we find that Nancy is <u>not climbing</u> -- she's <u>standing in place by the rope</u>. Her eyes are half-closed, fluttering. *She's in a trance.*

                   STEVE
         Nancy -- Nancy?!

INT. EDDIE'S TRAILER (RIGHT-SIDE UP)

The others begin to realize something is wrong --

We PUSH IN on Max, terrified --

                   MAX
     <u>*Vecna*</u>.

INT. CREEL HOUSE - ATTIC (UPSIDE DOWN)

BOOM! Thunder crashes, revealing Vecna hanging from the attic ceiling like a spider. His eyes dart back and forth.

EXT. POOL - UPSIDE DOWN (MINDSCAPE)

A terrified Nancy looks around the pool, scanning for an escape --

A FLASH OF RED LIGHTNING reveals something lying on the bottom of the pool. Nancy moves toward it, heart-in-chest, tears in her eyes. It's...

BARB'S DEAD BODY. IT LOOKS JUST LIKE WHAT ELEVEN SAW IN SEASON ONE. A SLUG CRAWLS OUT OF HER OPEN, ROTTED MOUTH.

> VECNA (O.S.)
> (heavy reverb)
> Do you remember what you did, Nancy? Or have you -- already -- forgotten?

Nancy whirls around, fighting back those tears. That *AWFUL GUTTURAL VOICE* is coming from all around her.

> VECNA (O.S.) (CONT'D)
> When I kill someone -- I NEVER FORGET...

Suddenly BLOOD begins to pump out of the pool drain then --

SHHHH! BLOOD GUSHES OUT of the pool skimmers along the wall -- filling this pool with blood.

Nancy GASPS IN HORROR and scrambles away, clambering up the slimy rungs of this ladder, escaping as --

INT. HAWKINS LABS - LAB ROOM - DAY (MEMORY)

Eleven continues to wait for One, when --

WAAAH! WAAAH! SIRENS suddenly begin to blare. She hears panicked voices, shouting. *What is going on?*

INT. HAWKINS LABS - HALLWAY - DAY (MEMORY)

She steps back out into the hallway. The voices are coming from one of the dead guard's walkies. She picks it up, turns up the volume. She hears more panicked shouting -- then SCREAMS.

Eleven can't just stand here and wait. *She has to help.*

She drops the walkie, presses forward...

INT. HAWKINS LABS - HALLWAY - DAY (MEMORY)

She heads down an empty hallway. Lights are sputtering. She sees a dead guard -- slumped on the ground -- head twisted around. She continues past him, turns a corner and --

INT. HAWKINS LABS - HALLWAY - NUMBERED ROOMS - DAY (MEMORY)

She freezes, her breath catching.

She has reached the hallway of numbered rooms. The dead bodies of orderlies and guards line the floor, BLOOD EVERYWHERE. But more disturbingly, doors have been violently wrenched open, some completely blown off their hinges.

As Eleven walks slowly forward, she looks into the various rooms and, to her horror, she finds --

DEAD NUMBERS, murdered in their own beds. As she continues down the corridor, horror growing with every step, she reaches --

A FAMILIAR TEST ROOM - ELEVEN POV (MEMORY)

Inside, she sees Brenner, unconscious; Ten's mangled dead body lies near him. We've nearly come full circle. And that's when she hears it: SCREAMS. THE SCREAMS OF CHILDREN.

She turns. They are coming from...

THE RAINBOW ROOM. *Oh no...*

INT. HAWKINS LABS - HALLWAY - MOMENTS LATER (MEMORY)

CLOSE ON: Eleven's bare feet race through blood as --

She makes her way to the Rainbow Room. She shoves open the door and --

INT. RAINBOW ROOM - DAY (MEMORY)

Eleven's heart all but stops. Before her --

THE REST OF THE NUMBERS. ALREADY DEAD. THOSE COLORFUL WALLS PAINTED IN BLOOD.

Wait... someone is still alive. <u>Two</u>. He is pinned to the wall, screaming in pain, his veins visible, and his eyes... his <u>eyes are bleeding</u>. As he continues to thrash helplessly against the wall, we PAN away from him to find...

<u>One</u>. His white uniform is now painted in blood... his hand is outstretched toward Two... and his eyes are closed. And it now hits Eleven like a sledgehammer:

<u>ONE IS DOING THIS. ONE DID... ALL OF THIS.</u>

We hear the SOUND OF SNAPPING BONES, then a QUICK SHOT of Two's body hitting the floor.

One slowly opens his eyes. He seems invigorated by his kill. But then, sensing something, he turns calmly to --

<u>Eleven</u>. She is still standing on the opposite side of the room. Too scared to breathe. Too scared to move.

                    ONE
      ... I asked you to wait.

Eleven spins around, making for the door, but --

WHOOM!! One slams the door with his powers, bolts the lock.

Eleven is now trapped in here. She turns back around as --

One now begins to walk toward her. Slow, methodical. Something about his gait is now... *eerily familiar*. As he nears Eleven, our CAMERA PUSHES PAST One and moves --

INTO THE MIRROR - CONTINUOUS (MEMORY)

Where Eleven once again looks seven years old. One steps up to Young Eleven, towering over her. But he doesn't seem angry -- if anything, he seems confused -- perhaps *disappointed*.

                    ONE
      Why do you cry for them, Eleven?
      After *all* they did to you?

He reaches out a hand and gently wipes a tear from her cheek, we move out of the mirror, matching the movement with <u>present-day Eleven</u>. She looks shocked, trapped, helpless...

                  ONE (CONT'D)
      You think you need them... but you
      don't. You don't. But I know you're
      just scared. I was once scared too.
         (beat)
      I know what it is like, Eleven. To
      be different. To be... alone in
      this world.

As he runs a hand across Eleven's face, sweeping away another falling tear --

EXT. STEVE'S POOL - UPSIDE DOWN (MINDSCAPE)

WHAM! A hand slams down onto a bloody surface as a terrified Nancy climbs out of the nightmare pool. As she rises to her feet, she finds herself in --

VECNA'S MIND LAIR

The same nightmarish world that Max explored. A stained glass door floats past her. Nancy watches in awe and fear as it drifts away from her, spinning in space...

>   VECNA (O.S.)
>   I see you've been looking for me,
>   Nancy. You were so close -- *so
>   close* to the truth.

We now PULL OUT to reveal Nancy is in fact standing on the top landing of the Creel staircase...

>   VECNA (O.S.) (CONT'D)
>   How was old, blind, dumb Victor?
>   Did he miss me? I've been meaning
>   to check back in...

As a frightened Nancy begins to cautiously make her way down the rotting staircase, she sees the dead bodies Max saw, wrapped in vines, displayed like medieval trophies.

>   VECNA (CONT'D)
>   But I've been busy... so *very*
>   busy...

We see close-up shots of dead FRED -- CHRISSY -- PATRICK.

As Nancy reaches the bottom of the steps, she sees the front door to the Creel house, wide open. Through it -- a rectangle of BRIGHT SUNLIGHT. We hear voices -- *happy voices*.

>   VIRGINIA (O.S.)
>   And you are certain this is the
>   right house???
>
>   YOUNG VICTOR (O.S.)
>   (laughing)
>   I am certain, darling --

As Nancy walks up to the door, WALLS BEGIN TO FORM around the
door and the red fog dissipates as we are transported into --

INT. CREEL HOUSE - FOYER - DAY - (MINDSCAPE)

WHOOM! The front door swings open and THE CREEL FAMILY
ENTERS, carrying their luggage. We've been here before; we're
in the flashback.

>   ALICE
>   It looks like a fairy tale -- a
>   dream!!!

As an excited Young Alice races for the stairs, our camera
swings around to find Nancy -- she is now IN the flashback.
The Creels, however, do not notice her; she is just an
observer, a ghost.

>   VIRGINIA CREEL
>   No running Alice!!
>
>   ALICE
>   It's so big!!

Our camera now leaves Nancy and PANS BACK to the family. We
PUSH in on a miserable Young Henry, hovering by the door with
his luggage, looking as if this is the last place on earth he
wants to be.

>   ONE (V.O.)
>   Like you, I didn't fit in with the
>   other children. Something was wrong
>   with me, all the teachers and
>   doctors said.

INT. RAINBOW ROOM - DAY (MEMORY)

One continues to talk to Eleven.

>   ONE
>   I was _broken_, they said. My parents
>   hoped a change of scenery -- a
>   fresh start in Hawkins -- might
>   cure me. It was absurd -- as if the
>   world would be any different here.

INT. CREEL HOUSE - UPSTAIRS - NIGHT (MINDSCAPE)

Nancy follows the Creel family as they fan out upstairs with their luggage, retreating into their respective bedrooms.

>   ONE (V.O.)
>   But then -- to my surprise -- our
>   new home led to a discovery... and
>   a new... _sense of purpose_.

Nancy abruptly stops. Through a cracked bathroom door, she spies Young Henry, kneeling on the tiled floor, prying open a vent -- the same vent that Steve found.

Inside this vent: a NEST OF BLACK WIDOW SPIDERS.

>   ONE (V.O.)
>   I found a nest of black widows,
>   living inside a vent...

Young Henry reaches out a hand and a large black widow crawls up onto his palm, then up his arm. As an unsettled Nancy observes --

>   ONE (V.O.)
>   Most people fear spiders. They --
>   detest them even. And yet -- I
>   found them endlessly fascinating.
>   More than that -- I found great
>   comfort in them. A _kinship_.

WHOOM! A SUDDEN MOVEMENT BEHIND HER. Nancy, whirls, started. It's just Young Henry, hurrying behind her, cradling a MASON JAR. _She's now in a new memory._ She watches as he heads upstairs and into the darkness of the attic --

INT. CREEL HOUSE - ATTIC (MINDSCAPE)

Nancy enters the attic to find Young Henry has the black widow spiders lined up in mason jars on the floor, lit by candles. He lies beside them, studying them with great curiosity...

>   ONE (V.O.)
>   Like me, they are solitary
>   creatures. And deeply
>   misunderstood. They are *gods of our
>   world*, the most important of all
>   predators.

Young Henry pulls out a notebook, begins to sketch his new "friends"...

>   ONE (V.O.)
>   They immobilize and feed on the
>   weak, bringing balance and order to
>   an unstable ecosystem.

INT. RAINBOW ROOM - DAY (MEMORY)

>   ONE
>   But the human world... was
>   disrupting this harmony. Humans are
>   a unique type of pest, multiplying
>   and poisoning our world, all while
>   enforcing a structure of their own
>   -- a deeply *unnatural structure*.
>   All unchecked, all *unchallenged*.

INT. CREEL HOUSE - DAY (MINDSCAPE)

Nancy now watches as Young Victor walks over to the Grandfather clock. Studying it. Seemingly... *angered by it.*

>   ONE (V.O.)
>   Where others saw order, I saw a
>   straightjacket -- an oppressive,
>   cruel world dictated by made-up
>   rules. Minutes, days, months,
>   years, decades, every life a faded,
>   lesser copy of the one before. Wake
>   up -- work -- eat -- sleep --
>   reproduce -- die --

INT. RAINBOW ROOM (MEMORY)

>   ONE
> Everyone is just waiting -- waiting
> for it to all be over, distracting
> themselves while performing in a
> silly, terrible play, day after
> day. And I could not do that. I
> couldn't close off my mind and join
> the madness. I couldn't... pretend.
> And I realized -- I didn't have to.

INT. CREEL HOUSE - DAY (MINDSCAPE)

Young Henry focuses on the clock, his eyes closed, and, suddenly, the clock <u>stops ticking</u>. Then, the clock begins to wind backwards, those second and minute hands reversing, faster, *faster* --

>   ONE (V.O.)
> I could... make my own rules --

As the clock begins to CHIME --

INT. RAINBOW ROOM - DAY (MEMORY)

>   ONE
> I could restore balance to a broken
> world. A predator -- *<u>but for good</u>*.

INT. CREEL HOUSE - DAY (MINDSCAPE)

Nancy hears a PAINED SHRIEKING, coming from behind her. She whirls, and suddenly --

EXT. CREEL HOUSE (MINDSCAPE)

Nancy has been transported <u>outside</u>, to the backyard of the Creel house. The shrieking comes from a RABBIT, caught in a snare trap. As it desperately tries to free itself --

YOUNG HENRY steps out from a hiding spot. He watches, totally emotionless, as the rabbit struggles. He kneels by the rabbit and holds out his hand. We get a QUICK FLASH of the Rabbit's BONES SNAPPING. Then OFF-SCREEN, we continue to hear the awful sound of BONES SNAPPING. *He's torturing it.*

The rabbit's screams are awful and relentless, but --

Henry keeps going, seemingly fascinated by its suffering.

                    ONE (V.O.)
          As I practiced, I found I could do
          more than I possibly imagined. I
          could *reach into others*. Into their
          minds. *Their memories.*

INT. RAINBOW ROOM - DAY (MEMORY)

                    ONE
          I became... an explorer. I saw my
          parents as they truly were. To the
          world, they presented themselves as
          normal people, *good* people. But
          like everything else in this world,
          it was all a lie -- a terrible lie.
          They had done things -- such *awful*
          things --

INT. CREEL HOUSE - DAY (MINDSCAPE)

Nancy escapes back in the house and slams the door, shutting out the screams of that dying rabbit, only to hear MORE SCREAMS. This time -- the SCREAMS OF AN INFANT.

THE LIVING ROOM - CREEL HOUSE - MOMENTS LATER (MINDSCAPE)

Nancy steps into the living room, where she finds Young Victor by the fireplace, frozen in horror as he looks at that BURNING CRIB. As a tear slips down his cheek --

Our CAMERA CRANES UP, rising through floors, up and up until at last we reach --

THE ATTIC (MINDSCAPE)

Where we find Young Henry, sitting cross-legged, his eyes shut tight. He is surrounded by his jars of spiders, candles.

As we PUSH IN on him...

                    ONE (V.O.)
          The more I practiced, the stronger
          I became. And, in time, I was ready
          to take the next step.

INT. CREEL HOUSE - LIVING ROOM - NIGHT (MINDSCAPE)

Nancy now hears music -- Ella Fitzgerald, "Dream a Little Dream of Me." She trails it into...

THE DINING ROOM - CONTINUOUS (MINDSCAPE)

Where the Creel family is now seated for dinner. The lights flicker, the RADIO GOES HAYWIRE. As Victor heads to fix the radio, we PUSH IN on Young Henry. Shutting his eyes. Focusing. And --

WHOOM! Virginia is suddenly flung into the ceiling. Her limbs snap, her eyes suck out, and then her LIMP BODY *CRASHES* back into the dining table. Henry opens his eyes, observing his dead mother with cold fascination --

> ONE (V.O.)
> With each life I took, I grew stronger, more powerful. They were becoming *a part of me.*
> (beat)
> But I was still a child... I did not yet know my limits. And it almost killed me.

INT. CREEL HOUSE - FOYER - NIGHT (MINDSCAPE)

Young Henry, the color drained from his face -- collapses on the ground alongside his dead sister.

MOMENTS LATER (MINDSCAPE)

As Young Victor takes him into his arms, holding him, sobbing, our camera PULLS AWAY --

> ONE (V.O.)
> If my weak father suspected me, he did not show it. He simply lied to himself. As he always did...

EXT. CREEL HOUSE - NIGHT (MINDSCAPE)

Police escort a shocked Victor toward waiting police cars.

> ONE (V.O.)
> I had finally escaped my family -- but I was far from free.

INT. LAB ROOM (MINDSCAPE)

Young Henry blinks awake --

ONE (V.O.)
               I woke up to find myself in the
               care of a different kind of doctor
               -- a doctor not interested in
               fixing -- but _studying_.

A Young Dr. Brenner steps out of the shadows.

RAINBOW ROOM (MEMORY)

                    ONE
               But -- the truth is -- he did not
               just want to study me... he wanted
               more. He wanted -- to _control_.

INT. UNKNOWN ROOM - DAY (MINDSCAPE)

Nancy now watches as DR. BRENNER, now wearing a surgical
mask, uses a crude tattoo device to ink a tattoo into Young
Henry's wrist.

                    ONE (V.O.)
               When Papa couldn't control me -- he
               tried to recreate me instead. He
               began a program.

We now see the tattoo reads 001.

                    ONE
               Soon, others were born.

INT. RAINBOW ROOM - DAY (MEMORY)

                    ONE
               You were born.
                    (beat)
               And I'm so glad you were, Eleven.
               So very glad.

Eleven fights tears as One's story reaches an end. Her eyes
move past One to all those dead Numbers. For the first time,
we really see their bodies -- and what One has done to them.
Their eyes are gone... their limbs have been snapped... just
like the Creel family.

                    ONE (CONT'D)
               They're not gone, Eleven. They're
               still with me.
                    (motions to temple)
               In here.

                    ELEVEN
          You -- tricked me --

                    ONE
          Saved you. You are a prisoner here,
          Eleven, just like me. To your
          "Papa," you are nothing but a lab
          rat, <u>a monster to be tamed</u>.

A beat as Eleven absorbs this -- there is <u>truth here</u>. One
sees that he has sunk his hooks into her, softens:

                    ONE (CONT'D)
          But the truth... the truth is *just
          the opposite*. You are better than
          they are. Superior. That is why you
          frighten him. If you come with me --
          for the first time in your life --
          you will be free. *Truly free.*
               (beat)
          Imagine what we could do together.
          We could reshape the world --
          remake it -- however we see fit.

Eleven takes this in. Tears in her eyes. For a moment, we
think she is persuaded. She looks down... then back up at
One. And...

                    ELEVEN
          ... No.

Eleven throws out a hand. WHOOM! ONE IS HURLED ACROSS THE
ROOM. He hits the observation window, then crashes to the
floor. He's visibly shaken, surprised by her power. As he
rises to his feet, we CUT TO --

A WIDE SHOT: One and Eleven facing one another on opposite
sides of the room. Visually, this "face-off" is just like the
circle test -- only now the stakes are far more real.

                    ONE
          I thought you were different.

He throws out a hand but so does Eleven. And suddenly --
we're in a POWER FIGHT!

Electricity starts to go nuts as Eleven starts to slide
backwards across the floor -- One is easily winning. But
then, Eleven's feet stop sliding, locking into place, just
like when she faced off with Two and --

WE PUSH IN on Eleven, as MEMORIES BEGIN TO FLASH before her:

TWO LAUGHING AT HER -- THE BULLIES BEATING HER -- HER MOTHER TAKEN AWAY, CALLING HER NAME -- THE DEAD NUMBERS -- ALL THESE PAINFUL MEMORIES RACE PAST HER, FASTER AND FASTER -- AND --

WHOOM! She is suddenly overpowered. Her back slams into the wall, head clapping against the wall, then she drops hard to the ground. Almost as soon as she lands --

WHOOM! An invisible force begins to drag her across the blood-stained floor. She grasps at fallen tables, trying to stop herself -- but the force of the pull is too strong and --

Her now blood-spattered body is LIFTED UP INTO the air -- floating now in the middle of the room, unable to move as --

One calmly steps up to her.

      ONE (CONT'D)
  It wasn't supposed to end like
  this.

He holds out a hand to finish Eleven off. She gasps in horrible pain as her limbs begin to contort and her eyes begin to bleed and then abruptly we CUT TO --

BLACK

We hear a HEARTBEAT. A VOICE echoes through the darkness. Calling to us...

      TERRY IVES (V.O.)
 Jane...

INT. HOSPITAL ROOM (FLASHBACK)

A baby emerges into the world, lifted into the arms of a nurse. Doctors (including Dr. Brenner) watch. We recognize this from season 2 -- it's Eleven's birth. We're now in baby Eleven's POV as --

TERRY IVES looks at her daughter -- at us. Her eyes are filled with tears. And a deep, powerful, transcendent love.

      TERRY IVES
 Jane...

She reaches for Eleven, for us, and --

BLACK AGAIN

A HEARTBEAT THUMPS FASTER AND FASTER AS A KALEIDOSCOPE OF COLORS AND SHAPES MOVE PAST US, AND --

INT. RAINBOW ROOM - DAY (MEMORY)

Eleven -- still bleeding out from her eyes -- throws out her hands and lets out an EAR-PIERCING SCREAM and --

One is suddenly lifted off his feet and thrown violently back into the two-way mirror! So hard the MIRROR CRACKS!

Eleven is released from his grip, dropping to her hands and knees and --

INT. NINA TANK - NIGHT

Back in the tank, Eleven's eyes dart back and forth and --

INT. SILO LAB - OBSERVATION BOOTH - NIGHT

The EEG machine goes wild and lights flicker.

We PUSH PAST Owens, into a CU of Dr. Brenner.

> DR. BRENNER
> *It's happening.*

INT. RAINBOW ROOM (MEMORY)

As One struggles, now <u>pinned</u> to the mirror, we PUSH PAST him, back --

INTO THE MIRROR (MEMORY)

So that we once again see Eleven as her YOUNG SELF. She lifts her head as she rises to her feet. She no longer looks timid, or scared, or small. She looks <u>powerful</u>. Her skin is ghostly pale, and dark veins flare across her forehead. It's exactly how she looked when she killed the Demogorgon. This is Eleven in her most heightened state. *A phoenix rising.*

One looks at her, helpless, as she walks up to him. As soon as she is face to face with this evil, she calmly holds out a hand, palm up, and --

One screams in pain as a powerful light begins to emanate from his chest -- spreading outward across his body -- up his chest -- overtaking him -- brighter and brighter -- he screams then -- WHOOSH! His body ERUPTS INTO BLACK ASH.

The lights stop flickering. Everything calms.

WIDEN: Eleven is alone now. Breathing hard. The ash dissipates to reveal that One is gone.

A glowing Rift scars the mirror -- where One was just pinned -- *just like when El killed the Demogorgon.* As this Rift slowly -- ever so slowly -- begins to close, our camera pushes toward the throbbing Rift, then dives *INTO* it, and suddenly --

EXT. HELLSCAPE (FLASHBACK)

WHOOM! We are hurtling backwards through a bizarre, inter-dimensional HELLSCAPE. And tumbling through this space --

One. Red lightning crashes all around him, striking his body, burning him, ripping off his clothes, searing his flesh, his hair. Vines begin to crawl up his scorched body and --

Second by second, shot by shot, he transforms into something that is no longer human. Into a monster. Into --

INT. CREEL HOUSE - ATTIC (UPSIDE DOWN)

VECNA. We've now come full circle. We're back in the attic, where Vecna continues to hang from his web, digging and worming his way into Nancy's mind with his ranged attack.

Our camera slowly drops below his wrist. Vines slither, briefly parting to reveal the bare, rotted skin, beneath. Then -- in a bright flash of RED LIGHTNING -- we finally see it:

THE TATTOO. 001.

Henry is Vecna.

Vecna is One.

And right here, with a final BOOM OF THUNDER, we --

END EPISODE

EPISODE EIGHT

CHAPTER EIGHT:
PAPA

WRITTEN BY **THE DUFFER BROTHERS**

We hold on BLACK for a few uncomfortable beats. Then --

INT. HAWKINS LABS - RAINBOW ROOM (MEMORY)

WHAM! We slam into a CU OF YOUNG ELEVEN. She's right where we left her. Face pale. Breathing hard. Spattered in blood.

Her bloodshot eyes are fixed on the Rift. There is no sign of One. He is lost somewhere in there. *Banished to Hell*. As Eleven's breathing begins to slow --

The Rift closes. Its edges shrinking. *Healing, scabbing*. And as suddenly as this nightmare began, it's over. *It's all over*. Then -- footsteps. Eleven turns, finds --

DR. BRENNER. He is just now entering the Rainbow Room. He, too, is bloodied and dazed from One's attack.

He pales as he takes in the scene before him. All of his "children"... *dead*. It's almost too much to bear. As the only "child" standing is Eleven -- spattered in blood -- it seems clear to him in this moment that *she* is the culprit.

As he looks at her with disbelief, anger, he now utters those lines which began our season:

>   DR. BRENNER
>   What have you done?
>   (beat)
>   *What have you done?*

Before Young Eleven can answer, the life seems to drain out and she folds to the floor. As she lies there on the floor, her eyes fluttering to a close, we slowly PUSH IN. As we draw ever closer to her, a strange mechanical sound begins to overtake the soundscape. CH-CH-CH-CH! Louder and louder and --

INT. HAWKINS LABS - ROOM - DAY (MINDSCAPE)

CHHHHH! EXTREME CLOSE ON: A TATTOO GUN. Its cluster of tiny needles are repeatedly *STABBING* into flesh, filling it with ink. CH-CH-CH-CH!

WIDEN OUT: YOUNG HENRY is strapped to a chair somewhere in Hawkins Labs, receiving his tattoo from a MASKED BRENNER. Henry is -- quite literally -- becoming One.

NANCY is still watching from the corner, still in this nightmarish trip down memory lane. Her eyes are glassy with tears, overwhelmed by all she has seen.

> DR. BRENNER
> And... *all done.*

Brenner begins to clean the tattoo, washing that blood away.

> DR. BRENNER (CONT'D)
> Not so bad now, was it?

Young Henry shakes his head. *Not so bad.*

> DR. BRENNER (CONT'D)
> See -- there's nothing to be afraid of, Nancy.

Nancy's heart jumps -- *did he just say her name??* And then, suddenly, Brenner turns to face Nancy. His eyes are solid white and his voice emerges from his throat as deep, guttural -- half Brenner, half Vecna.

> BRENNER/VECNA
> Why don't you... *take a seat?*

Fuck this. Nancy turns, throws open the door and escapes --

INT. HAWKINS LABS - HALLWAY - DAY (MINDSCAPE)

But she has simply escaped into another memory. *A worse one.* She's now in --

The aftermath of One's massacre. Blood all over the walls. Doors wrenched off.

Nancy turns and runs and, sprinting away down the dark, bloodied hallways. We now CUT from a running Nancy to --

INT. EDDIE'S TRAILER (UPSIDE DOWN)

A <u>very still</u> Nancy in the trailer. Still locked in that trance. Blood drips out of her nose. A hand wipes it away --

WIDEN TO REVEAL: The hand belongs to STEVE -- who is still down here with her, trying his best not to panic.

                        STEVE
            Nance -- just stay with me okay --
            stay with me, okay??

He shoots a panicked look up through the Trailer Gate. The
other teens are gone, but ERICA is still there, keeping
watch --

                        STEVE (CONT'D)
            Whatever the hell they're doing
            tell them to *hurry up* -- !!!

INT. EDDIE'S TRAILER - NIGHT (REAL WORLD)

Erica now hurries away, weaving her way to the back of the trailer and into --

INT. EDDIE'S ROOM - CONTINUOUS

Where we find the OTHERS frantically searching for music, more or less ransacking the room --

> ERICA
> Steve says you need to hurry -- !

> DUSTIN
> Yeah no shit -- !!

ROBIN is sifting through tapes -- Anthrax, Iron Maiden, Slayer, Metallica, Megadeth --

> ROBIN
> What is all this shit -- seriously????

> EDDIE
> What are we even looking for -- ??

> ROBIN
> I don't know like Madonna -- Blondie -- Bowie -- Beatles -- the BEATLES -- MUSIC -- WE NEED MUSIC -- !!

> EDDIE
> This IS music -- !!

As tossed tapes clatter across the floor, CUT TO --

INT. HAWKINS LABS - DAY (MINDSCAPE)

Feet flying as Nancy sprints for her life, desperately searching for a way out of this nightmare lab.

She reaches a door, *an exit*, but it's boarded up with ROTTING WOOD PLANKS -- the same planks that barred the door of the Creel house. She frantically pries off one of the planks --

> VECNA
> Nancy... what are you doing...?

She shoots a look back, sees VECNA (in his full Vecna state) walking toward her. He moves with that now familiar methodical gait.

                    VECNA (CONT'D)
          It's not time for you to leave.
          Now that you have seen where I've
          been... I'd like very much to show
          you where I am going...

She tears off the last board, pushes through the door, and --

INT. HAWKINS LABS - LAB ROOM - DAY (MINDSCAPE)

-- Crashes to a halt. She's back in the room she started in.

Young Henry is now gone from the chair. But our MASKED BRENNER is still here, standing next to that chair. Only now his eyes are scarred -- missing.

                    DR. BRENNER
          Take a seat, Nancy.

The lights suddenly CUT OUT and all goes --

BLACK

For a beat, we can only hear Nancy's PANICKED BREATHING, then the lights sputter back on to reveal --

INT. HAWKINS LABS - ROOM - DAY (MINDSCAPE)

Nancy is now *in* the chair, held in place not by leather straps but by SLITHERING VINES.

Vecna emerges from the shadows. Nancy desperately tries to free herself, but the vines tighten their grip, *HISSING*.

                    VECNA
          I want you to... tell Eleven. I
          want you to tell her... everything
          you see.

He hovers his mutated, clawed left hand over Nancy's head and his white eyes roll back into his head like some feeding shark and --

WHOOM! NANCY'S EYES SHOOT WIDE WITH HORROR and her JAW DROPS as she enters a STATE OF SHOCK. We get QUICK FLASHCUTS of FOUR RIFTS CLEAVING THEIR WAY ACROSS HAWKINS -- OF THE GRANDFATHER CLOCK PENDULUM SWINGING -- A CHIME RINGS OUT --

Her breathing gets faster and faster -- A SECOND CHIME RINGS OUT --

Vecna leans right up to her ear -- A THIRD CHIME RINGS OUT --

                    VECNA (O.S.) (CONT'D)
          <u>Tell her...</u> *what you see.*

A FOURTH CHIME --

Nancy SCREAMS as tears slip down her face --

                    NANCY
          NOOOOO -- !!!

WHOOM! Vecna's sharp nails yank out of Nancy's head and --

INT. EDDIE'S TRAILER (UPSIDE DOWN)

Nancy's eyes SNAP OPEN and she is RELEASED. Her body falls but --

WHOOM! Steve catches her just before she hits the floor --

                    STEVE
          Nancy -- NANCY??

As Steve cradles her in his arms and lap, she looks at him, shaken, her eyes wet with tears, her face white as a ghost.

                    STEVE (CONT'D)
          Are you okay??? Are you okay???

Off a stunned, shell-shocked Nancy, clearly a LONG WAY from okay, we HARD CUT TO --

MAIN TITLES

EXT. RUSSIAN PRISON - NIGHT

We drift toward the prison, pushing through falling snow.

It's quiet. Almost... peaceful. But then --

EXT. DEMO PIT - NIGHT

RAAAR! The DEMOGORGON lets out a VICIOUS ROAR as its body SUDDENLY *FLAILS* across screen --

It's still bleeding from where Hopper stabbed it and it's clearly pissed about it. It thrashes about the pit, taking its anger out on anything and everything, ripping open a cell door, flinging it --

UP ON THE BALCONY ABOVE,

Terrified guards helplessly watch as it throws its tantrum. Their guns are raised, ready.

We find IVAN pacing, shouting into a walkie, desperate --

>   IVAN
> <What is going on down there?!!!
> GET THE POWER BACK ON!!!>

INT. RUSSIAN PRISON - CONTROL ROOM - NIGHT

Ivan's voice blasts out of a Guard's walkie, but the GUARD can't answer because --

He's cuffed to a table. MURRAY rips the Guard's walkie out, holds it up to him --

>   MURRAY
> <Tell him that the prisoners are
> contained and you're working on the
> power.>

The Guard glares. Murray aims his gun at him.

>   MURRAY (CONT'D)
> <TELL HIM.>

As the Guard reluctantly passes on Murray's message, our CAMERA PULLS BACK to find a gagged YURI, trying to yelp through his gag, but no one's listening. We keep pulling back past Yuri to find --

DMITRI, who has a SCIENTIST against the wall. He's got his axe blade to the Scientist's neck, interrogating him --

>   DMITRI
> <... And that door there -- where
> does it lead -- ?>

>   SCIENTIST
> <To -- to cell block two -->

>   DMITRI
> <No -- NO cell blocks. I need a
> safe way out of here -->

As Dmitri continues to interrogate the Scientist, our CAMERA continues to PULL BACK until at last we find --

HOPPER and JOYCE. Joyce is quickly working to stanch Hopper's slashed arm with MEDICAL TAPE.

> HOPPER
> I guess... you got my message?

Joyce looks up at him. A slight smile.

> JOYCE
> No, I've just -- always wanted to visit Kamchatka. With Murray.

Hopper glances at Murray --

> HOPPER
> You two getting along?

> JOYCE
> Peas in a pod.

Another smile, then the tone turns serious...

> HOPPER
> I thought you were dead. I -- I... thought I had lost you --

> JOYCE
> I did lose you. For eight months.

A beat as Hopper takes in the weight of this.

> JOYCE (CONT'D)
> Even had your funeral.

> HOPPER
> ... Anyone show?

> JOYCE
> A few. You're a hero. Back in Hawkins.

We can tell this surprises Hop a bit --

> HOPPER
> I always figured I'd be easier to like when I'm dead.
> (beat)
> And -- El?

> JOYCE
> She's good. She's good. But... she misses her dad.
> (MORE)

                    JOYCE (CONT'D)
              (beat)
          We all do.

Before a moved Hopper has a chance to respond --

                    MURRAY (O.S.)
          Okay -- uh -- that's not good.

Their eyes now swivel to Murray. He's looking at the BANK OF SECURITY MONITORS.

Hopper, Joyce, and Dmitri cross to his side.

                    MURRAY (CONT'D)
          Apparently they can *climb* too...

ON THE BANK OF MONITORS

Sure enough, the Demogorgon is now CLIMBING its way out of the pit, scaling that (de-electrified) wire!!!

EXT. THE PIT - NIGHT

The Demogorgon drops onto the balcony, landing on all fours. It then rises to its feet, towering over --

Our terrified guards. Fingers tremble on triggers.

                    IVAN
          <Lower your weapons -- LOWER YOUR
          WEAPONS -- DO NOT SHOOT -- THAT'S
          AN ORD -- !!>

A scared Guard opens fire anyway. BANGBANGBANG!!! And then the rest of the Guards follow suit. As bullets pummel the Demogorgon, it recoils, SHRIEKING IN PAIN --

INT. CONTROL ROOM - NIGHT

The SHRIEK is so loud that everyone can hear it in the control room. But then, strangely, there is another SHRIEK -- almost like an echo. Only *not quite*. This shriek is different. Higher in pitch. Louder, clearer... *CLOSER*. It's coming from --

A CLOSED DOOR on the far side of the room. *Uh oh.*

As a concerned Hop grabs up his spear --

EXT. THE PIT - NIGHT

CLIUCK! The gunfire ends. The Guards are out of ammo. Only --

The Demo is still alive. And now EVEN MORE PISSED. Our guards frantically try to reload but it's too late -- IT CHARGES AND ATTACKS them with a FEROCIOUS ROAR --

Our camera (DEMO POV) rushes in on a horrified Ivan --

BLOOD *splats* the wall -- and --

INT. CONTROL ROOM - NIGHT

Quiet as ... Hopper slowly makes his way toward the ominous door, hands clutching tight to that spear. The SHRIEKING persists, louder with every step. The Scientist watches Hopper, frightened --

                    SCIENTIST
      <You can't go in there -- it's not
      safe -- it's not safe!!>

Hopper ignores him, nudges the door open with his spear, and enters...

A MYSTERIOUS LABORATORY - NIGHT

His eyes go wide, his breath catches.

REVERSE TO REVEAL: A DEMODOG is strapped to a steel operating table. Its chest is cut open, its ribs exposed, seemingly abandoned mid-operation. Yet somehow the creature is still alive, shrieking in pain.

Around it, a NUMBER OF TANKS, all containing creatures from the Upside Down. More DEMODOGS... DEMOSLUGS... DEMOBATS... all suspended in an odd clear liquid, floating unconscious. And in the back, perhaps worst of all: a tank filled with MIND FLAYER PARTICLES. The particles swirl, alive, whipping around inside that glass like an imprisoned tornado.

The others now step up behind our disturbed Hop, taking in this nightmare room...

                    JOYCE
      My God...

                    MURRAY
      ... The hell are they doing?

Hopper finally can't take it anymore -- he strips Murray's gun from him, strides into the room, and -- BANG! -- shoots the writhing creature in the head, putting it out of its misery. And -- at last -- the wailing stops.

Hop -- breathing hard -- now notices something beneath the operating table. He shoves the table aside, revealing --

A BLOOD-SPATTERED GRATE ON THE FLOOR.

Hopper looks back at Dmitri --

                      HOPPER
        You think this'll take us out?

Dmitri strides over, studies the grate for a beat.

                      DMITRI
        I give it -- a hundred to one odds.

A small, knowing smile between the men, then --

WHAM! Dmitri jams his axe into the blood grate, pries it open. Our camera dives into the blood grate and the screen goes --

BLACK - UNKNOWN

                      DISTANT VOICE (V.O.)
        And one -- two -- three -- and -- again -- one -- two --

INT. ANTENNA SILO - LAB - NIGHT

CHOOM! A DEFIBRILLATOR PADDLE sends an electric charge through Eleven's haptic suit and --

WHOOM! SHE JOLTS AWAKE -- GASPING.

WIDEN: She's in her haptic suit, laid out on that operating table. She looks around. Her vision is blurry, but she can see that she is surrounded by SCIENTISTS and DOCTORS, including Brenner and OWENS -- just like in episode five.

One DOCTOR straps an oxygen mask over her face, as another checks her vitals --

                    SCIENTIST #3
          Pulse is dropping, one fifty
          now, BP's one sixty palp --

                    DR. BRENNER
                    (distant)
          ... How do you feel, Eleven?

                    DR. OWENS
                    (distant)
          Eleven, can you hear us? Eleven?

Eleven doesn't answer anyone. Instead, she just removes her
oxygen mask. Scientist #3 tries to put it back on but Eleven
pushes it away -- doesn't want it.

                    DR. BRENNER
          Leave her -- leave her.

As Scientist #3 backs off, Eleven slides her legs off the
operating table. Her bare feet hit the floor. And then she --

Stands. She's steadier than we expect. She seems different
somehow. Stronger. More confident. *Driven by something.*

Brenner, Owens, and the others watch as she walks away from
them, about ten feet or so, and then she turns to face --

THE NINA TANK. Taking it in. Then...

She HOLDS OUT A HAND. Narrows those eyes. Nothing happens at
first. But as El concentrates, we hear a LOW RUMBLING and...

The lights in the lab begin to flicker and --

The bolts at the base of the tank begin to shudder... then
the body of the tank itself begins to quake... then...

CHOOM! The bolts RIP RIGHT OUT OF THE CONCRETE and...

THE ENORMOUS TANK BEGINS TO LIFT UP OFF THE GROUND.

ELEVEN LIFTS THE TANK TEN FEET IN THE AIR. THEN SHE JUST...
HOLDS IT THERE. AS IT HOVERS IN THAT FLICKERING LIGHT, IT
LOOKS LIKE A UFO OR SOMETHING. THEN, EVER SO GENTLY, ELEVEN
LOWERS IT BACK TO THE FLOOR, PUTTING IT RIGHT BACK IN ITS
PLACE, THOSE BOLTS SLOTTING INTO THE GROUND. A PERFECT
LANDING. AS HER HAND LOWERS, RELEASING IT...

The lights stop flickering. The water inside the tank
settles. And...

Eleven -- a thin trail of blood now spilling from her nose -- finally turns to face Brenner and Owens.

Needless to say, the men are stunned. It's clear -- the Nina Project has been a success. And Eleven...

<u>Eleven is reborn.</u>

Off Eleven, calmly wiping away that blood, we CUT TO --

EXT. DESERT - VARIOUS - SUNRISE

The sun rises over the desert as --

The Pizzamobile speeds down a near-empty freeway.

INT. PIZZAMOBILE - SUNRISE

JONATHAN is driving, rubbing his eyes, trying to stay awake. ARGYLE sits in the passenger seat --

                    ARYGLE
        Holy shit dude. *Check it out!*

He points. Jonathan follows his gaze to find a SURFER BOY PIZZA BILLBOARD. It features our now familiar surfer boy riding his giant wave of cheese. Beneath, bold letters read: LAST PIZZA BEFORE VEGAS!!

                    ARGYLE
        I didn't know they expanded into
        Nevada -- watch out Domino's, your
        dominos gonna *faaall!*

As Jonathan sighs to himself, we move --

INTO THE BACK OF THE VAN,

Where we find MIKE and WILL. The mood is a bit more somber back here.

                    WILL
        How far is Nina from Vegas?

Mike consults a ROAD ATLAS, where they've marked a spot on the map using latitude and longitude --

                    MIKE
        As long as Suzie's coordinates are
        right -- about another... ninety
        miles.

                    WILL
          Once we save her -- El -- we should
          stop on the way back. At Vegas. El
          could make us, like, super rich and
          we'd never have to work, right? We
          could just -- retire and play D&D
          and Nintendo for the rest of our
          lives.

                    MIKE
          Yeah. Totally.

Will smiles, but Mike doesn't offer much of a smile back.
He's worried. Will tries to offer reassurance here --

                    WILL
          We're gonna make it, Mike. She's
          going to be okay.

                    MIKE
          Yeah... I know. I know she is.

Mike looks out the window for a beat. Just watching the
passing desert...

                    MIKE (CONT'D)
          But... what if... after all this...
          she doesn't need me anymore.

                    WILL
          Of course she'll still need you,
          Mike. She'll *always need you.*

                    MIKE
          Yeah that's what I keep telling
          myself, but the truth is -- I don't
          believe it. Not really.

He looks to Will.

                    MIKE (CONT'D)
          She's... special. She was *born
          special*. Maybe I was one of the
          first to realize that -- but the
          truth is I just stumbled on her in
          the woods when she needed someone --
          it's not fate, it's not destiny, it
          was *simple dumb luck* -- and one day
          she's going to realize that, she's
          going to realize that deep down I'm
          -- I'm just some random nerd who
          got lucky that Superman landed on
          his doorstep.
                    (MORE)

                    MIKE (CONT'D)
          She's already beginning to
          understand she doesn't need me. I
          saw it -- I saw it in her eyes,
          that last time we talked. I mean --
          at least Lois Lane was like -- an
          ace reporter for the *Daily Planet* --
               (shaking it off)
          Sorry -- I know this sounds stupid
          given everything right now, it's
          just, I don't know --

                    WILL
          You're scared of losing her.

Mike nods. *Yeah.* Will just nailed it. Will hesitates, then --
screw it --

                    WILL (CONT'D)
          Can I... show you something?

Mike nods. Will unzips his backpack and hands him his (now
slightly crumpled) ROLLED-UP PAINTING. Mike removes the twine
that clasps it, then unfurls it. His breath catches. IT'S AN
INCREDIBLY DETAILED, STYLIZED IMAGE OF MIKE, WILL, AND THE
OTHERS -- DRESSED AS THEIR D&D CHARACTERS -- FIGHTING OFF A
THREE-HEADED DRAGON. MIKE IS LEADING THE CHARGE, THRUSTING
HIS SWORD BRAVELY AT THE DRAGON.

                    MIKE
          This is -- *amazing*. You *painted
          this?*

                    WILL
               (a little flustered)
          Yeah -- I mean -- El asked me to.
          Commissioned it basically. She told
          me what to -- draw.

Jonathan in the front seat clocks this lie. He now begins to
observe his brother in the rearview...

                    WILL (CONT'D)
          The point is -- see how you're
          leading here? You're guiding the
          party. *Inspiring us.* That's --
          that's what you do. And your coat
          of arms here -- it's a heart. I
          know it's sort of on the nose but --
          that's what holds the whole party
          together. *Heart.* Because see,
          without heart, we'd all fall apart.
          Even El. *Especially El.*
               (beat)
                    (MORE)

                            602

                    WILL (CONT'D)
          These past months, she's been...
          lost without you. She's so
          different from other people and...
          it's really scary to be different.
               (beat)
          When you're different...
          sometimes... you feel like... a
          mistake.

Jonathan now begins to sense that Will is not just talking
about El -- but also himself.

                    WILL (CONT'D)
          But... you make her feel like...
          she's not a mistake at all -- like
          she's *better* for being different.
          And that gives her the courage to
          fight on. And if she was mean to
          you or -- or she seemed like she
          was pushing you away -- it's
          probably just because she was
          scared of losing you, just as
          you're scared of losing her. And...
          if she was going to lose you, I
          think... she'd rather just... get
          it over with quick... like ripping
          off a Band-Aid... Because losing
          you -- it just hurts -- it hurts
          too much.
               (beat, emotional)
          So yeah -- El needs you Mike. And
          she always will.

Mike takes this all in. Emotional now too.

                    MIKE
          ... You really think so?

                    WILL
          I know so.

Mike smiles a bit, looking back at that drawing, feeling
better now. Will gives a small smile back -- but then he
turns and looks out the window and that smile fades -- giving
way to melancholy.

Jonathan clocks this in the rearview. It pains him that he
can't comfort his brother here. His eyes turn back to the
road, to that endless freeway stretching before them, and --

EXT. FREEWAY - SUNRISE

As the Pizzamobile speeds off down the freeway, a large rainbow slowly overlays itself across the highway. For a moment it looks real. But then the rest of the landscape DISSOLVES and we realize we are in fact back in --

INT. RAINBOW ROOM - DAY (FLASHBACK)

WE PAN FROM THE BLOOD-SPATTERED RAINBOW... past the carnage of the massacre... and up to the now scarred two-way mirror where the Rift once was. A hand reaches out, touches it.

It's Young Brenner. He turns, looks back down at --

Young Eleven. On the floor. Blood spattered. Unconscious.

>   DR. BRENNER (V.O.)
>   After the attack, you fell into a
>   coma...

INT. SILO LAB - BRENNER'S OFFICE - DAY

We find present-day Eleven still in her haptic suit, a towel wrapped around her shoulders. She is sitting across from Brenner and Owens, who are filling her in on the rest of the story.

>   DR. BRENNER
>   Like One, you had pushed yourself
>   beyond your limit -- and it very
>   nearly destroyed you. But that is
>   where your similarities ended.

INT. HAWKINS LABS - CONTROL ROOM (FLASHBACK)

A horrified Young Brenner is now watching a tape of ONE killing Two. Learning the terrible truth for himself. Then horror turns to wonder as he sees Young Eleven defeat One -- propelling him out of this world. The light from her powers is so bright that the television screen goes SOLID WHITE. As that white light projects back onto an awed Brenner, dancing across his eyes...

>   DR. BRENNER (V.O.)
>   What you displayed that day was
>   beyond anything I had ever seen. A
>   potential I had only dreamed of...

INT. HAWKINS LABS - INFIRMARY - DAY (FLASHBACK)

Young Eleven blinks awake from her coma to find Young Brenner at her bedside. She blinks, confused, disoriented. As he begins to comfort her...

>			DR. BRENNER (V.O.)
>		But when you awoke... something had
>		been lost. Your memories -- but
>		also -- whatever you had found
>		within yourself that day.

INT. SILO LAB - BRENNER'S OFFICE - DAY

>			DR. BRENNER
>		But I knew then -- just as I knew
>		today -- that your powers had not
>		left you. They just... needed a
>		*spark.*

WE NOW CUT TO FLASHBACKS OF ELEVEN'S VARIOUS SEASON ONE TRAINING MOMENTS: ELEVEN CRUSHES THE COKE CAN... THROWS A GUARD... LISTENS TO THE RUSSIAN IN THE VOID... BRENNER PICKS HER UP AND CARRIES HER DOWN THE HAWKINS LABS HALLWAY --

>			DR. BRENNER (CONT'D)
>		But that day... you had awakened
>		something else -- a doorway to
>		another world --

FLASHBACK TO THE RIFT RIPPING OPEN IN THE LAB WALL -- SCIENTISTS RUNNING AWAY IN FEAR --

>			DR. BRENNER (CONT'D)
>		I always thought... Henry was out
>		there... hiding in that darkness...

FLASHBACK TO BRENNER SENDING MEN INTO THE UPSIDE DOWN --

>			DR. BRENNER (CONT'D)
>		But I didn't know. Not beyond a
>		feeling. Until now.

This is Owens' cue -- he opens a folder and then begins to lay out PHOTOGRAPHS OF CHRISSY, FRED, PATRICK... LIMBS TWISTED, EYES GONE. THE MARK OF VECNA. THE MARK OF *ONE*...

Eleven can hardly breathe as she takes it all in.

>			DR. OWENS
>		He's claimed three victims so far.
>		As soon as I saw their eyes -- I
>		knew. I knew it was him.
>			(MORE)

                    DR. OWENS (CONT'D)
               He was sending us a message,
               letting us know he's back. That's
               when I came to you in Lenora.

Eleven looks up from the photos, eyes wide --

                    ELEVEN
               My friends --

                    DR. OWENS
               We haven't risked contact -- but as
               far as we know -- they're safe.

                    DR. BRENNER
               But I won't lie to you, Eleven --
               they are in terrible danger. With
               each victim he takes, One is
               chiseling away at the barrier which
               exists between our two worlds.

                    ELEVEN
               "Chiseling"?

                    DR. BRENNER
               Puncturing. *Weakening.*

Brenner moves toward her, removing a PENCIL from his desk. He
grips the pencil between two hands, and holds it out toward
Eleven, horizontally.

                    DR. BRENNER (CONT'D)
               Imagine -- if you will -- that the
               barrier between our worlds is a
               concrete dam. One is putting cracks
               in this dam. Cracks in dams allow
               pressure to build.

Brenner begins to bend the pencil, applying pressure.

                    DR. BRENNER (CONT'D)
               Left unchecked, this pressure will
               build and build, and eventually it
               will reach a breaking point and --

CRACK! The pencil snaps.

                    DR. BRENNER (CONT'D)
               The dam will burst. And when that
               happens, <u>Hawkins will fall</u>.

Eleven has heard enough. She tosses the photos and hurries
out of the office. Owens watches her go, then --

                    DR. OWENS
          Well... I think that went nicely,
          doc. You eased her into it, real
          gentle, just like we talked
          about. Not ominous at all.

Off an unamused Brenner, we CUT TO --

INT. ANTENNA SILO - DAY

A scared Eleven, quickly weaving her way through the lab, racing by the tank, passing scientists and guards, and --

INT. ELEVEN'S ROOM - DAY

WHOOM! Eleven bursts into her room. She shuts the door and locks it with a flick of the wrist, then --

She hits on her sink -- sits on her bed -- shuts her eyes --

And FOCUSES. She's *traveling*. We cut CLOSE to her eyes, darting beneath those eyelids -- then we TILT to her mouth as she works to slow her breathing. A DEEP EXHALE becomes --

EXT. TRAILER PARK - DAY

Crime scene tape fluttering in the wind.

WIDEN: We're outside Eddie's trailer. We SLOW PAN AWAY from the trailer, then begin to DOLLY toward Max's trailer as...

                    NANCY (PRE-LAP)
          He showed me... things that haven't
          happened yet... *the most awful
          things*...

INT. MAX'S TRAILER - MAIN ROOM - DAY

Nancy is on the couch, her worried friends all close by. She looks like a corpse, face pale, voice low, shaky, choking back tears.

                    NANCY
          I saw a dark cloud, spreading over
          Hawkins... downtown on fire... dead
          soldiers... a giant creature...
          with this... *gaping mouth*.

Disturbed looks here.

                    NANCY (CONT'D)
          And this... creature wasn't alone.
          There were so many monsters...
                    (MORE)

                    NANCY (CONT'D)
          an *army*. And they were coming into
          Hawkins... into our neighborhood...
          our *homes*. And then... he showed me
          my mom... Holly... Mike. And they
          were... they were all...

She can't finish her sentence here; it's too upsetting to
say. But we know what she was about to say. They were all
<u>dead</u>. More terrified looks are exchanged, as no one is sure
what to say. Steve finally breaks the silence --

                    STEVE
          Okay, but... he's just trying to
          scare you, right? I mean -- that's
          not real.

Nancy locks eyes with Steve.

                    NANCY
          Not yet. But... there was something
          else. He showed me Gates... <u>four
          Gates</u> -- spreading across Hawkins.
          These Gates, they looked like what
          we saw outside Eddie's trailer, but
          -- they didn't stop growing. And it
          wasn't Upside Down Hawkins. It was
          -- our Hawkins. *Our home* --

                    MAX
          ... Four chimes.

Everyone turns to Max, surprised.

                    MAX (CONT'D)
          Vecna's clock. It -- it always
          chimes four times. *Four exactly.*

                    NANCY
          I heard it too.

                    MAX
          He's been telling us his plan this
          whole time.

                    LUCAS
          Four kills. Four Gates. End of the
          world.

                    DUSTIN
          If that's true -- he's just one
          kill away.

                              EDDIE
                Jesus Christ -- *JESUS CHRIST*.

                              STEVE
                         (to Max)
                    Try them again.

A panicked Max heads to a phone, grabs the receiver, starts to dial a number. As Max dials, we PUSH PAST her, toward the wall of the trailer, which DISSOLVES, giving way to --

INT. THE VOID

Where we find Eleven walking through the WATERY DARKNESS. As she walks toward us, we hear the voices of her friends, echoing around her, distorted but coming into focus...

                              DUSTIN (O.S.)
                    Anything?

                              MAX (O.S.)
                    No, nothing, still a busy signal --

                              LUCAS (O.S.)
                    How's that possible -- ?

Our camera now ROTATES AROUND El, revealing her friends, who are NOW IN THIS VOID WITH HER. She's found them.

                              DUSTIN
                    Joyce has a new telemarketer job,
                    she's on the phone all the time,
                    Mike won't stop whining about it --

                              MAX
                    Yeah okay but that phone's been out
                    busy for, what, three days straight
                    now? That's not Joyce. No way.
                    Something is wrong.

Eleven desperately wants to speak here, to reassure her friends that she's okay, but she can only watch as --

INT. MAX'S TRAILER - DAY - INTERCUT

Nancy, freaked, stands up and walks over to the trailer window. She peers through the dirty blinds, toward Eddie's trailer, toward that Gate...

                    NANCY
          Whatever's happening in Lenora...
          it's connected to all this, I'm
          sure of it. But Vecna can't hurt
          them -- not if he's dead.

She turns back to the others.

                    NANCY (CONT'D)
          We're going to have to go back in
          there... back to the Upside Down.

Steve pushes to his feet -- freaked.

                    STEVE
          Whoa whoa -- let's think this
          through --

                    NANCY
          What is there to think though -- ??

                    STEVE
          We barely made it outta there in
          one piece --

                    NANCY
          Because we *weren't prepared*. This
          time we will be. We'll get weapons,
          protection. Then we go through that
          Gate, get to his lair -- and *kill
          him*.

                    STEVE
          Or -- he'll kill *us*. The only
          reason you survived is because he
          wanted you to. He's not scared of
          us --

                    ROBIN
          And for good reason. We were wrong
          about Vecna -- Henry -- One -- wait
          sorry what are we calling him now?

DUSTIN		ERICA
One.	Vecna.	
NANCY		**LUCAS**
Henry.	One.	

ROBIN
Right. My point is -- now we know something new about Vecna-slash-Henry-slash-One -- he's a Number, like Eleven -- only, like, an evil, sick, male, child-murdering version of her with... really bad skin. My point is -- he's super powerful and could probably turn us inside out with a *snap of his fingers*. It's not a fair fight --

DUSTIN
So then we don't fight fair.

Everyone now turns to Dustin.

DUSTIN (CONT'D)
You're right -- he's like Eleven. But that gives us an upper hand -- we know Eleven's strengths -- and *weaknesses*.

ERICA
"Weaknesses" -- ?

DUSTIN
(nods)
When El remote travels... she goes into a trance-like state. I bet the same is true of Vecna --

LUCAS
That would explain what he was doing in that attic --

DUSTIN
Exactly. When he attacks his next victim, I'll bet you he's back in that attic -- and his physical body will be defenseless, *vulnerable*.

STEVE
Defenseless? You forgetting about that *army of bats* --

DUSTIN
Right true we'll have to find a way past them, distract them somehow --

EDDIE
And how we gonna do that -- ?

                    DUSTIN
          No idea. But once they're gone, he
          won't stand a chance. It'll be like
          slaying sleeping Dracula in his
          coffin.

                    ROBIN
          Yeah I think this is all -- good *in
          theory* -- but there's no real
          pattern to his killings, at least
          not one that I can decipher -- we
          don't know when he's going to
          attack again or even *who* he's gonna
          attack --

                    MAX
          Yes we do.

All eyes swivel back to Max. What??

                    MAX (CONT'D)
          I can still feel him...
               (motions to head)
          In here. I'm still... marked.
          Cursed. I ditch Kate Bush -- I can
          draw his focus back to me.

INT. THE VOID

We return to Eleven. Her heart jumps - *oh no* -- Max...

BACK IN THE TRAILER

                    LUCAS
          Max, you *can't* -- he'll *kill you* --

                    MAX
          I survived before. I can survive
          again. I just need to keep him busy
          long enough for you guys to get
          into that attic and chop off his
          head or stab him in the heart or
          blow him up with some homemade
          explosive that Dustin cooks up -- I
          honestly really don't care how you
          put this asshole in his grave --
          just... whatever it is... whatever
          you do...
               (beat)
          Try not to miss.

As everyone takes this in --

INT. THE VOID

We PUSH IN on Eleven. *Terrified for her friends but helpless to stop them.* Off her frightened look, we CUT TO --

EXT. RUSSIAN PRISON - ESTABLISHING - MORNING

WHOOM! A sewer grate suddenly pops up and out then --

WHAM! A grimy hand hits cement as --

Hopper pulls himself up out of the darkness below! He staggers to his feet and looks around, blinking in the rising sun. WIDEN TO REVEAL: HE'S MADE IT OUTSIDE THE PRISON.

Holy shit!!! He drops back down by the grate, where --

Joyce and the others are waiting anxious below --

     DMITRI
 And...?

     HOPPER
 We made it --

He smiles a bit, holds out a hand. Joyce takes it. As their <u>hands CLASP</u>, CUT TO --

INT. RUSSIAN PRISON - GUARD BOOTH - MORNING

WHUMP! A PLAYING CARD hits a fold-out table.

WIDEN: TWO PRISON GUARDS are holed up in the guard booth, playing a popular Russian card game, Durak, while listening to terrible Soviet pop music on a radio.

Prison Guard #1 sheds his last card. Announces victory --

     PRISON GUARD #1
 <u>*Durak*</u>!

He flashes a dirty-toothed smile, but then --

His smile fades. He's <u>*seen something*</u> out the window.

EXT. RUSSIAN PRISON - GUARD BOOTH - DAY

The guard exits the booth, eyes wide. GUARD POV: Yuri's van is zooming their way at HIGH SPEED -- what the hell??? And the van is not slowing down -- in fact, it's ACCELERATING. *Shit!* The guard races back into the booth as --

BOOM-SMASH! THE VAN BLOWS THROUGH THE GATE, SPLINTERING THAT WOOD INTO A THOUSAND PIECES --

INT. YURI'S VAN - OUTSIDE PRISON - DAY

          MURRAY
  SAYONARA!!!!

EXT. GUARD BOOTH - DAY

Our guards grab their rifles, scramble back out of their booth, and open fire on the van --

INT. YURI'S VAN - OUTSIDE PRISON - DAY

BANGBANGABANG!! Gunfire rips through the back of the van.

Hopper pulls a screaming Joyce down, protecting her as the back windshield shatters, glass raining down. BANGBANGBANG! Bullets continues to punch holes in the van until finally --

GUARD BOOTH

CLICK! The guards run out of ammo.

          PRISON GUARD #1
    <SHIT!!!>

INT. YURI'S VAN - DAY

The van flies down the road, swiss-cheesed but still driving! As Hopper and Joyce untangle from one another, sitting back up --

          HOPPER
  You okay -- you okay??

She nods as --

          MURRAY
  WHOOOO! Nothing like a little
  prison escape to get your day
  started am I right or am I right??

          DMITRI
  We are not out of the woods yet. My
  people do not take kindly to
  escapes. They will be hunting us --

          HOPPER
  Yeah well we weren't exactly
  planning on sticking around.
  Where's the plane you came in on?

                    JOYCE
          Oh the plane. Yeah. That -- um --

Joyce makes a downward motion with her hand --

                    JOYCE (CONT'D)
          Crashed.

                    HOPPER
          Crashed?

                    MURRAY
          With *us* in it.

                    JOYCE
          His fault --

Joyce motions to Yuri. Hopper scowls. *That* <u>motherfucker</u>. Hopper slides over to him, then reaches to take out his gag, but --

                    MURRAY
          Word of warning, Jim -- that man is
          more slippery than an eel dipped in
          baby oil. I wouldn't trust *a word*
          out of his mouth --

                    HOPPER
          Yeah -- I know what his word means.

Hopper now removes Yuri's gag. Yuri immediately starts gagging, smacking his mouth, trying to feel his tongue -- it's all very dramatic and VERY Yuri.

                    YURI
          My tongue -- I can't feel my
          tongue, GAAHHHH!

                    HOPPER
          We need a way out of here, back to
          the States. Can you get us to
          another plane?

                    YURI
          Ah -- now -- NOW -- you ask for
          Yuri's help?? After dragging him
          though miles of *shit* tunnel -- I
          could have told you we were going
          wrong way *hours ago* you -- *you*
          Neanderthal --

                    HOPPER
          You don't watch your mouth --
               (holds up rag)
          I'm gonna wipe this off on my shoe
          and jam it back down your throat --

                    YURI
          Go ahead -- but then you will never
          make it out of my country alive ---

                    JOYCE
          So you can get us out -- ?

                    YURI
          ... For a glass of water, a
          steaming hot bath -- and a five-
          inch stack of American dollars --
          Yuri will <u>fly you to moon</u> --

CLICK! A startled Yuri whips around to find --

Dmitri. He's leaning over from the front seat -- and he's got
the <u>barrel of his gun aimed right at Yuri's nose</u>.

                    DMITRI
          You make another demand, you double-
          crossing *mudak*, I will decorate the
          roof of this van with your brains --

                    YURI
          Dmitri, tsk, tsk -- why so angry,
          comrade? Rough couple of days for
          you, I am sure. But now -- you are
          free. Everything works out, happy
          ending for everybody, no?

Yuri flashes a big smile. Dmitri doesn't return one.

                    DMITRI
          For you -- that will very much
          depend on how you answer. *Comrade.*

Dmitri's finger tightens around the trigger.

                    DMITRI (CONT'D)
          Will you take us to America? Yes.
          <u>Or no</u>.

Off Yuri, that grin of his slowly fading, we SMASH TO --

EXT. TRAILER PARK - DAY

An American flag waves in the growing wind. We're back in America -- specifically, the trailer park.

INT. MAX'S TRAILER - DAY

WHOOM! Eddie slams down a PHONE BOOK, open to an ad for THE WAR ZONE: ARMY/NAVY SURPLUS. It features a cheap RAMBO LOOK-ALIKE, posing in front of an American flag. Naturally, he's armed to the teeth.

                    EDDIE
Okay so check this out -- the War Zone. I've been there once -- it's huge, and they've got everything you'd need for -- well -- killing basically --

                    ROBIN
Think fake Rambo there has enough guns there --? Is that a grenade?? I mean how is any of this legal -- ?

                    EDDIE
Well good for us it is. I figure this place, it's just far enough outside of Hawkins -- long as we steer clear of the main roads, we oughta be able to avoid cops or angry hicks --

                    ERICA
We're trying to steer clear of angry hicks, maybe we shouldn't go to some store called "the War Zone" --

                    NANCY
Normally I'd agree -- but we need weapons -- I say it's worth the risk --

                    LUCAS
Me too --

                    DUSTIN
But is it worth the time? It'll take all day to bike there and back --

                    EDDIE
          Who said anything about bikes?

                    STEVE
          You have a car here we don't know
          about?

                    EDDIE
          Ehhh... it's not exactly a car. And
          it's not mine. But -- uh -- it
          might just have to do.
               (then, to Max)
          Red -- you got a bandana or ski
          mask or something?

Off Max, we CUT TO --

EXT. TRAILER PARK - A LITTLE LATER

WHOOM! Eddie -- now wearing Max's MICHAEL MYERS MASK from Halloween! -- suddenly pops out from behind a trailer. *The hell?* He turns back and motions to the rest of our Hawkins gang! They follow his lead as he presses forward, staying low, trying to stay hidden.

OUTSIDE A NEARBY WINNEBAGO,

We find a LOWER-CLASS MAN and WIFE (ANNOYED NEIGHBOR from episode two) camped outside. They drink beers and clean guns as they listen to a local talk show on a beat-up radio...

We DOLLY AROUND to find our gang sneaking up to the back of the Winnebago. Eddie pries open a window, crawls inside, and --

INT. WINNEBAGO - DAY

WHUMP! He lands inside! He tears off the mask --

                    EDDIE
          Jesus that thing is suffocating...

He tosses the mask aside. As the others begin to climb in behind him, Eddie quietly locks the Winnebago door, then --

MOMENTS LATER

WHOOM! Eddie drops down behind the enormous wheel. He uses a screwdriver to pop off the steering column, then rips out a BUNDLE OF WIRES. He's hot-wiring this sucker!!!

As he works, Steve walks up, leaning over, impressed.

                    STEVE
          Where'd you learn how to do this?

                    EDDIE
          When the other dads were teaching
          their kid how to fish or play ball
          -- my old man was teaching me how
          to hot-wire. I swore to myself I'd
          never wind up like him. Now I'm
          wanted for murder and soon *grand
          theft auto*, so, uh -- really living
          up to that Munson name. In fact, I
          think I might just have my old man
          beat --

                    ROBIN
          Hey Eddie -- you know, I'm not
          really sure I love the idea of you
          driving --

                    EDDIE
          Oh I'm just starting this sucker --
          Harrington's got her, donchya
          Harrington?

Before Steve has a chance to respond, Eddie twists two wires together and --

VROOM! The Winnebago's engine SUDDENLY ROARS TO LIFE!!! CREEDENCE CLEARWATER begins to BLAST from the radio --

EXT. TRAILER PARK - WINNEBAGO - DAY

The neighbors whirl, leaping off their fold-out chairs --

                    ANNOYED NEIGHBOR #2
          The hell -- ?!

INT. WINNEBAGO - DAY

Eddie leaps out of the way, letting Steve slide down behind the big wheel --

                    STEVE
          Okay shit -- shit shit -- just a
          car -- just a car --

He shifts into drive --

                    STEVE (CONT'D)
          EVERYONE GRAB ONTO SOMETHING --

He PUNCHES THE GAS and --

EXT. TRAILER PARK - WINNEBAGO - DAY

VROOM! The Winnebago suddenly tears away. The WHOLE HOUSE IS MOVING, with that awning still jutting out!!

>   ANNOYED NEIGHBOR #2
>   HEYYYY!!! HEYYY!!!

The shocked owners race after their home --

INT. WINNEBAGO - DAY

Everyone holds on for dear life in the back. Dustin watches the couple chasing after them out the back window.

>   DUSTIN
>   Oh shit they look *pissed*!!
>
>   ROBIN
>   Not every day you lose your house
>   and car in one fell swoop!!
>
>   STEVE
>   HOLD ON!!!

Steve pumps the brakes and spins the wheel, hand over hand, making a hard right, and the Winnebago squeals out of the trailer park and onto the road, leaving --

EXT. TRAILER PARK - WINNEBAGO - DAY

Our angry couple in the dust!!!

EXT. COUNTRY ROAD - DAY

The Winnebago fishtails a bit, then straightens out as it rockets away from the trailer park. The awning finally folds in. As the ROCK MUSIC fades into the distance...

>   ELEVEN (PRE-LAP)
>   You told me -- they were safe...

INT. ANTENNA SILO - DAY

Eleven is now back in the office with Brenner and Owens -- and she's *pissed*.

>   ELEVEN
>   They are -- <u>not safe</u>.

Brenner and Owens are listening. They're clearly worried.
They also know they have to tread carefully here.

>   DR. OWENS
>   First things first, we won't let
>   anything happen to your friends,
>   okay, kiddo? I'll make sure of it
>   personally. You see where they
>   were?

>   ELEVEN
>   They were... at Max's house --

>   DR. OWENS
>   This Max have a last name?

>   ELEVEN
>   May--field --

>   DR. OWENS
>   Okay so -- here's what's gonna
>   happen...

Owens moves closer to Eleven, reassuring.

>   DR. OWENS (CONT'D)
>   I have people in Hawkins -- I'll
>   send some them to, uh, Max
>   Mayfield's, and they will stop her
>   and the rest of them -- from
>   whatever foolish but well-
>   intentioned mission they're
>   attempting here, alright?

Owens smiles softly, but Eleven is not on the same page.

>   ELEVEN
>   No. Do not send "your men." Send
>   me.

Before Owens has a chance to respond, a voice interrupts:

>   DR. BRENNER (O.S.)
>   Your friends are not prepared for
>   this fight, Eleven. But neither are
>   you.

Eleven turns to Brenner. This hits her hard.

Brenner now makes his way over to her.

                    DR. BRENNER (CONT'D)
          You must understand. When One
          kills... he does not simply kill.
          He _consumes_. He takes everything
          from his victims -- everything they
          are and everything they ever will
          be. Their memories... their
          abilities. And we do not know where
          he has been these lost years -- but
          if he has survived this long, we
          can only assume he has grown in
          strength. To underestimate him --
          to act rashly in this moment --
          would be very dangerous.

Dr. Brenner is right by Eleven now.

                    DR. BRENNER (CONT'D)
          I am not trying to upset you,
          Eleven. What you've achieved here
          is nothing short of a miracle. You
          came to us broken -- and you have
          learned to _walk again_. But if you
          want to stop One, you will need to
          do more than walk. You will need to
          do more than run. You will need to
          fly.
                    (beat)
          You are not ready.

Eleven takes this in, stunned to hear this. A part of her wonders if Papa is right. She looks away. But then --

She looks back at Brenner. Determined.

                    ELEVEN
          My friends -- need me.
                    (beat)
          I stopped him -- before. I will
          again.

Brenner takes this in. Obviously frustrated.

                    DR. BRENNER
          I'm sorry. But you can't. It's
          impossible --

                    DR. OWENS (O.S.)
          Nothing's impossible.

Brenner turns to Owens, surprised. He expected resistance from Eleven -- _but not this_.

                    DR. OWENS (CONT'D)
          I can call Stinson -- she's got
          connections at Nellis, that's two
          hours away -- we hustle, I bet we
          can get to Hawkins by --
              (looks at watch)
          Nightfall I bet.

                    DR. BRENNER
          That would be a grave mistake --

                    DR. OWENS
          Waiting might be an ever graver
          one. What if One makes his move and
          we haven't even had a chance to
          throw a punch -- then what's the
          point of all this -- ?

                    DR. BRENNER
          That's a risk we're going to have
          to take --

Owens moves closer to Brenner, it's getting a bit heated.

                    DR. OWENS
          We pushed her before, and look what
          happened? She lifted a ten thousand
          pound tank into the goddamn air --

                    DR. BRENNER
          You don't understand what's he's
          capable of --

                    DR. OWENS
          Yeah, maybe I don't. Or maybe
          you're overestimating him. Either
          way, doesn't matter, because this
          isn't our choice. We agreed this
          wasn't going to be a prison. We
          show her what this is, what we can
          offer, then it's _her choice_ whether
          or not to stay or go, right, doc?
          Well -- you may not agree with it,
          but here she is, standing right
          before us -- _making a choice_.

Owens doesn't wait for Brenner to respond. He just turns back
to Eleven, softer now...

                    DR. OWENS (CONT'D)
          You _sure_ about this, kiddo?

She nods. *Abso-fucking-lutely.*

                    DR. OWENS (CONT'D)
            Then get your things -- say your
            goodbyes. *I'll hail us a ride.*

As Owens heads off, Eleven turns back to Brenner. A final, tense look between then. It's a strange feeling, going so directly against him. He instilled in her an obedience to him that is difficult to shake. But her love for her friends overrides it. She tears her gaze from him and walks away.

Off Brenner, his face *darkening*, CUT TO --

EXT. COUNTRY ROAD - LATER

WHOOSH! Our Winnebago speeds down a country road. Bob Dylan (or something similar but cheaper!) is now on the radio...

INT. WINNEBAGO

Nancy glances at Steve. Slightly amused. It looks like he's driving a *bus*.

                    NANCY
            ... How's it handle?

                    STEVE
            Actually... *not that bad.* I mean --
            considering this is a... *house.*
                    (small smile)
            You know, it's silly, but... I
            always had this dream that I'd
            have, like, this really big family.
            I'm talking -- like a full brood of
            Harringtons, six little nuggets --

                    NANCY
            Six -- ???

                    STEVE
            Three boys, three girls. And every
            summer, I figured all us
            Harringtons, we'd just -- take off
            in one of these things and just...
            see the country. Rockies, Grand
            Canyon, Yellowstone -- and then
            we'd end up at some California
            beach, spend a few weeks parked in
            the sand, learn how to surf or
            something.

Nancy lets this wash over her. Right now, given the dire situation, she has to admit...

                    NANCY
          That sounds... *nice*.

                    STEVE
          Yeah?

                    NANCY
          Well -- not the six kids part.
          That's a total nightmare.

                    STEVE
          Yeah, well -- if only I had some
          practice...

He glances back in the rearview, at his brood of "children."

                    NANCY
          Alright -- fair. *That's fair.*

She smiles. Steve smiles back. And...

BACK OF THE WINNEBAGO,

We now survey his "brood of children." Land on Max. She seems lost in her own head, her own dark thoughts, when --

Lucas makes his way over to her, sits beside her...

                    LUCAS
          Hey. So -- I've been thinking...
          two of the three of Vecna's victims
          were seeing Miss Kelley, right?

                    MAX
          Yeah --

                    LUCAS
          So I figure there's a good chance
          Vecna cursed another one of her
          students. We go back into her
          office, read all the files, look
          for mentions of headaches or
          nosebleeds or nightmares. We
          identify his most likely next
          victim, stake out their house and --

                    MAX
          Lucas -- Lucas --

                    LUCAS
          When Vecna strikes, we send a
          signal to the group in the Upside
          Down and --

                    MAX
          LUCAS. *Stop*. We don't have time for
          ANY of that. Okay? And even if we
          did -- *even* if your plan worked --
          we'd be putting a total stranger at
          risk. A stranger who would have *no
          idea* what they're up against. I *do*.

Deep down, Lucas knows that she's right -- but he's still
terrified. Max, sensing this, softens her tone --

                    MAX (CONT'D)
          ... I think there's a way -- a way
          I can hide from him. Last time...
          when I was in the mall -- running
          from him, I went into those service
          corridors -- that go behind the
          stores you know?

FLASHBACK TO MAX RUNNING INTO THE SERVICE CORRIDOR -- THEY
SPLIT OFF IN TWO DIRECTIONS.

                    MAX (CONT'D)
          Only, I was panicked and -- I took
          a wrong turn.

MAX REACHES A DEAD END AT THE END OF THE LONG CORRIDOR.

                    MAX (CONT'D)
          I hit a dead end. I was trapped.

MAX TRIES TO OPEN NEARBY SHOP DOORS -- ALL LOCKED. AND VECNA
IS COMING.

                    MAX (CONT'D)
          But then -- suddenly -- the
          elevator -- it was just... there.

THE CARGO ELEVATOR APPEARS IN THE FLUTTERING LIGHT.

                    LUCAS
          I don't understand --

                    MAX
          Yeah I don't either -- not exactly.
          I just know I was -- thinking about
          it and -- and it's like, it just
          manifested. I think... maybe just
          as Vecna can control things in
          there -- maybe I can too. It's my
          mind after all. *Not his*.

Lucas is feeling a bit better here, but --

                    LUCAS
            The second you start to lift -- I'm
            calling in Kate Bush.

Max considers. Holds out her hand.

                    MAX
            ... *Deal.*

Lucas takes her hand, shakes it. They share a small smile,
then Max turns her gaze out the window... and that small
smile gradually erodes. There is an unmistakable undercurrent
of uncertainty in her eyes. *Fear.* As ominous music builds, we
CUT TO --

EXT./INT. YURI'S VAN - KAMCHATKA CHURCH - DAY

Yuri's shot-up van putters through town, that tailpipe
coughing black smoke. We PAN to reveal that it's headed
toward Yuri's church hideout.

EXT. KAMCHATKA CHURCH - DAY

The van parks behind the church. The doors slide open and --

Hopper, Joyce, Murray, Yuri, and Dmitri hop out.

                    YURI
            This way -- come on --

Yuri leads them away from the church, toward a large SNOW-
COVERED SHED around back. Everyone's a bit on edge; Dmitri
walks close to Yuri, his gun still out --

                    DMITRI
            <I get a whiff of any funny
            business, smuggler, I will not
            hesitate to kill you. In fact -- I
            am just looking for a reason. Do
            you understand?>

                    YURI
            <Are you parrot, *ment*? You have two
            things you can say -- just repeat?>

Yuri snorts, then approaches the shed. As he thrusts a key
into a padlock, he shoots a glance at Hopper --

                    YURI (CONT'D)
            You were trapped in a cell with
            this dull man and did not take the
            opportunity to smother him?

Yuri *tsks tsks* as he dramatically rolls open the metal door.

INT. SHED - DAY

Yuri lights up. Delighted.

>   YURI
>   AHHHH! Beautiful yes?

He excitedly strides forward into the hangar. But the others do not share his enthusiasm -- in fact, quite the opposite.

They look *horrified*.

>   MURRAY
>   Please tell me this is another poor
>   joke...

WE NOW REVERSE TO REVEAL: THE SHITTIEST HELICOPTER you've ever seen. It is very small, very orange, and very round -- *bubble shaped in fact* -- with three, *max four* seats in there. To top it off, several parts of the chopper appear to be missing and a latch on the side is flung open, mid-repair.

A pissed Joyce storms up to Yuri --

>   JOYCE
>   You told us you had a plane --
>
>   YURI
>   No no no -- I told you I could fly
>   you home. And Katinka can fly you
>   home, little bird. She is named
>   Katinka after my first lover.

He strokes her bulbous metallic body as he remembers --

>   YURI (CONT'D)
>   Katinka had very beautiful, very
>   round buttocks, much like this --
>
>   DMITRI
>   This cannot fly us to America--
>
>   YURI
>   Why not, you miserable pouty boring
>   unimaginative man? As long as winds
>   are not too strong and your
>   military friends do not shoot us
>   out of sky, we can make it to the
>   coast.
>   (MORE)

                    YURI (CONT'D)
          There, while we refuel, we skinny
          dip in icy cold water and wash off
          this *muck* -- then fly her rest of
          way. Happy ending!

                    JOYCE
          How far have you flown -- Katinka
          before?

                    YURI
          Ah well... she is still a virgin.
          Not real Katinka -- hahahaha
          nononono goodness not THAT Katinka
          -- but yes, this Katinka is very
          much unspoiled! But I have no doubt
          she will soar when given the
          chance. She just needs a little
          tune-up --

As Yuri heads to grab some TOOLS, the others share horrified
looks.

                    MURRAY
          I did warn you, Jim...

                    DMITRI
          Should I shoot him now -- or later?

Joyce turns to Hopper --

                    JOYCE
          What about Owens? The military must
          have contacts here -- spies --
          someone who could help us.

Hopper turns to Dmitri --

                    HOPPER
          Can we do that -- make a call to
          the States?

Off Dmitri, hesitating --

INT. KAMCHATKA CHURCH - DAY

WHOOM! A BULKY PHONE RECEIVER is pulled off its cradle.

WIDEN: A tense Dmitri, Hopper and Joyce are now huddled
around a small desk at the back of the church. Dmitri dials
07. A few rings, then a MUFFLED OPERATOR answers --

> DMITRI
> <Good afternoon, Comrade. I'd --
> I'd like to place a call to the
> United States. A very sick
> relative.>
> (beat)
> <Correct. Yes -- the number is...>

Dmitri cups the phone, motions urgently to Joyce --

> JOYCE
> Six one eight, six two five,
> eight three two six --

> DMITRI (CONT'D)
> (repeating)
> <Six one eight, six two five,
> eight three two six -- >

> DMITRI (CONT'D)
> <Thank you.>

Dmitri hangs up the phone receiver.

> JOYCE
> What are you doing??

> DMITRI
> How exactly do you think this
> works? They will make the call for
> us and then call us back.

> HOPPER
> And how long will that take?

> DMITRI
> Five minutes. Five hours. Five
> days. Who knows. And when we do get
> a return call -- assume the KGB
> will be on the other line,
> listening to everything you say. So
> I suggest talking in code. Say the
> wrong thing, they will be on us
> like flies on shit.
> (beat)
> <u>Welcome to the Soviet Union</u>.

And with that, Dmitri heads off, leaving a frustrated Joyce and Hopper behind. As they settle in and begin their *wait*, we CUT TO --

EXT. THE WAR ZONE ARMY/NAVY SURPLUS - DAY

We PUSH IN on the War Zone. The parking lot is jam packed.

INT. THE WAR ZONE ARMY/NAVY SURPLUS - DAY

DING! A bell chimes as Steve, Robin, Erica, Max, and Nancy enter the War Zone. Their faces fall. It feels like the entire town is here. Even worse -- Jason's WANTED POSTERS are plastered all over the walls. *Oh boy.*

                  ROBIN
        So much for avoiding angry hicks.

                  NANCY
        Let's... be fast.

            ROBIN   ERICA
                        Definitely --

Yep --

They fan out and --

MOMENTS LATER

Max examines a DISPLAY OF HUNTING KNIVES. We DOLLY PAST HER, moving into --

ANOTHER AISLE

Where we find Erica grabbing BUG LIGHTS. As she plops them into a cart, our CAMERA CONTINUES TO DOLLY, sweeping into --

ANOTHER AISLE,

Where we find Robin and Steve placing GASOLINE and KEROSENE into a grocery cart, when suddenly --

Robin freezes, her heart leaping in her chest. We think it must be something bad, but then we REVERSE TO REVEAL it's --

VICKIE!!! Her crush. She's about thirty feet away, checking out some MACE. Steve notices too.

                    STEVE
          You just gonna stand there and gawk
          or -- ?

                    ROBIN
          Shut up --

Robin takes a breath and starts to move toward Vickie, almost there, when --

WHOOM! A COLLEGE BRO WEARING A PURDUE T-SHIRT suddenly swoops in and wraps his hand around Vickie's waist. Vickie smiles, pushes him back, joking. Then -- THEY KISS.

Robin can hardly breathe. Crushed. Her eyes well with tears. And now, at just the worst moment --

Vickie looks up and sees Robin. *Fuck*. Robin turns and walks away, brushing past Steve --

                    STEVE
          Robin -- *Robin* --

As a concerned Steve chases after her --

WITH VICKIE NOW,

Vickie watches her go. She looks... concerned.

                    COLLEGE BRO
          Who is that -- ?

                    VICKIE
          Oh -- uh -- just someone from band.

Vickie smiles, playing it off, and --

THE GUN COUNTER,

Nancy examines a DOUBLE-BARREL SHOTGUN. She looks up at the CLERK --

                    NANCY
          How much is this -- ?

                    CLERK
          One-twenty, ninety-nine -- but I'll
          throw in twenty rounds of buckshot
          for ya --

As Nancy considers, SOMEONE settles beside her, just out of focus --

                  VOICE (O.S.)
          Could I see that real pretty three
          fifty-seven?

Nancy *knows* that voice. She turns to find --

JASON. He looks like a mess since we last saw him at the town hall -- he hasn't changed his outfit, and also clearly hasn't slept, dark rings around his eyes. The clerk passes him a .357 MAGNUM REVOLVER. As Jason rolls it around in his hand, he looks over Nancy, who is doing her best to pretend she doesn't see him.

                  JASON
          ... Nancy Wheeler.

Fuck.

                  JASON (CONT'D)
          Wouldn't have expected to find you
          here.

She turns to him, tries to play it cool.

                  NANCY
          Oh yeah -- well -- it's just --
          scary times.

AN AISLE OPPOSITE,

Erica spots Jason talking to Nancy from her aisle. She goes stone still, heart-in-throat.

BACK WITH NANCY,

> NANCY
> ... I'm so -- sorry about -- Chrissy.

Jason takes this in, then a small nod, then --

> JASON
> You want my advice -- shotguns are not good for much of anything past killing small birds. They got power, sure, but not much range, and that's gonna force you into close-range combat, and then someone can just grab that barrel like this --
> (he suddenly grabs her barrel, forcefully)
> And redirect it.

BACK WITH ERICA,

Erica's eyes swivel from Jason and Nancy as she spots Andy, milling about the store. Then another jock. *Another*. This place is swarming with <u>the enemy.</u>

BACK WITH NANCY,

As Jason remains close to Nancy, not letting go of that shotgun barrel, that tension steadily rising...

> JASON
> You look nervous --

> NANCY
> I told you -- *scary times* --

> JASON
> Your brother -- he here with you by chance?

> NANCY
> Mike -- no --

> JASON
> I ask because -- he's in Hellfire, isn't he?

> NANCY
> I don't know what you're talking about.

                    JASON
          What about his friends? They here
          with you?

                    NANCY
          Would you let go.

Jason doesn't.

                    NANCY (CONT'D)
          Let. Go.

Off Jason, suspicion rising, *not letting go*, HARD CUT TO --

INT./EXT. WINNEBAGO - ALLEY BEHIND WAR ZONE - DAY

The Winnebago idling behind the store.

Dustin, Lucas, and Eddie wait anxiously inside. Dustin, paces, checks his watch.

                    DUSTIN
          The hell is taking them so long?

No one answers. No one knows. When --

WHOOM! The door to the Winnebago suddenly explodes open. Everyone startles but it's just --

Nancy and the others. They all leap in, clutching their bags of goods --

                    LUCAS
          What happened -- ?

                    STEVE
          We gotta go --

                    ERICA
          Your old friends are here --

                    LUCAS
          Shit --

Steve leaps back behind the wheel and --

EXT. WAR ZONE - FRONT OF STORE - MOMENTS LATER - DAY

SCREEECH! The Winnebago squeals away as we PAN to find --

Jason in CLOSE UP. Watching them go. Suspicious. Our music *rises* and --

EXT. NEVADA ROAD - DAY

VROOM! The Pizzamobile speeding down an empty Nevada road. They're now off the freeway and in the middle of the desert.

                MIKE (PRE-LAP)
        Okay -- it should be coming up on
        the left --

INT. PIZZAMOBILE - DAY

Jonathan looks around, sees nothing but vast desert --

                JONATHAN
        There's *nothing* out here...

Argyle, woken by the chatter, rubs his bloodshot eyes --

                ARGYLE
        Whoa -- we there already?

                WILL
        Already? It's been *nine hours*.

                MIKE
        It has to be here -- *somewhere* --

                ARGYLE
        What exactly are we looking for, my
        dudes -- ?

                WILL
        Some sort of facility --

                MIKE
        A building -- fencing --

JONATHAN
Any signs of life, really --

ARGYLE
When did we decide Nina is like a physical building and not a woman? It sounds like a woman --

MIKE
It's *not* a woman --

ARGYLE
A woman would be hard to see out in this desert. Especially if she's a small woman.

WILL
How is he still high?

JONATHAN
(ignoring this)
Are you sure your measurements were right -- ?

MIKE
Yes, they're right --

JONATHAN
You're a <u>hundred percent</u> sure -- ?

MIKE
YES --

JONATHAN
Maybe the latitude and longitude are wrong --

MIKE
You're questioning Suzie now -- ?

WILL
She's a *genius*, Jonathan --

JONATHAN
Even geniuses makes mistakes --

MIKE
She <u>*didn't*</u> --

ARGYLE
If this woman is small enough she could be hiding in that brush right there --

SCREECH! Jonathan -- who has finally had enough -- slams on the brakes.

>   MIKE
>   What are you doing??

>   JONATHAN
>   Stopping us before we get more
>   lost.

He shifts into park and --

EXT. PIZZAMOBILE - DESERT - DAY

WHAM! The road map hits the now dusty hood of the car. Jonathan places a ruler on the map, readies a pen --

>   JONATHAN
>   Alright, give me the coordinates --

As Will reads the coordinates from Suzie --

We turn our focus to Argyle, who is stomping off into the desert, making his way over to that brush! He checks behind it, hopeful, but he doesn't find a small woman. DAMMIT! But then his eyes narrow as he spots *something else* --

>   ARYGLE
>   *Holy macaroni...*

BY THE PIZZAMOBILE,

Jonathan now runs his finger down from the longitude mark --

>   JONATHAN
>   Okay now straight across, *straight
>   straight straight* --

Will and Jonathan run their fingers from the latitude mark, until their fingers meet, pinpointing a location that is --

<u>Already</u> marked with an X.

>   MIKE
>   Right on the money, *as I said* --

Before Jonathan can respond --

>   ARGYLE
>   Yo dudes! MY DUUUDES!!!

They turn to find Argyle excitedly waving to them.

                    ARGYLE (CONT'D)
          Come check this shit out!!!

                    MIKE
          What is it -- ?

                    ARGYLE
          YOU GOTTA SEE IT TO BELIEVE IT, MY
          DUDES!!

Our group sighs and --

MOMENTS LATER

They stomp unenthusiastically over to Argyle.

                    ARGYLE
          So okay, no small woman named Nina
          -- but you said *any signs of life*,
          am I right dudes? Well...

Argyle excitedly gestures to the ground where we find --

TIRE TRACKS. LOTS OF THEM. THEY LEAD OFF THE MAIN ROAD AND CUT ACROSS THE OPEN DESERT. Argyle kneels down, running his fingers across them like he's some sort of master tracker.

                    ARGYLE (CONT'D)
          And these are no regular tire
          tracks, mi amigos -- they're
          fatties.

                    MIKE
          Military --

                    JONATHAN
          Come on -- !

As they race back to the van, our camera RACKS BACK to those tire tracks and we PRE-LAP the SOUND OF ROARING ENGINES -- an ominous sound which builds until suddenly we HARD CUT TO --

EXT. NEVADA DESERT - DAY

CLOSE ON: "FATTY" TIRES cutting through desert as --

A CONVOY OF BLACK MILITARY HUMVEES MAKE THEIR WAY ACROSS THE OPEN DESERT. A CHOPPER SOARS ABOVE.

INT./EXT. HUMVEES - DESERT - DAY

We survey various soldiers. All armed to the teeth. Sitting passenger in the lead Humvee: LT. COLONEL SULLIVAN. He looks very much in his element here. *Ready to finish this.*

As the chopper soars past camera, we SMASH TO --

INT. ANTENNA SILO - VARIOUS - DAY

Quiet. Establishing shots at Nina Lab. Scientists calmly move down corridors. Unaware of the impending danger.

>   DR. OWENS (PRE-LAP)
>   I wouldn't be doing this if I
>   didn't think she was ready --

INT. SILO LAB - MAIN LAB - DAY

>   DR. OWENS
>   But either way -- I don't see we
>   have much of a choice here, do you?

We now CUT TO --

EXT. PHONE BOOTH - HAWKINS - DAY

AGENT STINSON, who is in a phone booth in the middle of nowhere, Hawkins.

>   AGENT STINSON
>   No. I don't.
>   (beat)
>   It might take me some time though --

INT. SILO LAB - MAIN LAB - DAY

>   DR. OWENS
>   Just as fast as you can, it's gonna
>   take us two hours to get to Nellis
>   as it is. Also -- I need another
>   favor -- can you send someone to a
>   Max Mayfield's house, there are
>   some kids there that need checking
>   on. Mayfield spelled like -- well,
>   like it sounds.

Owens waits for a response --

>   DR. OWENS (CONT'D)
>   Ellen, you there? Ellen? *Ellen?*

EXT. PHONE BOOTH - HAWKINS - DAY

Stinson speaks into the dead phone --

>   AGENT STINSON
>   Sam? *Hello* -- *??*

INT. SILO LAB - MAIN LAB - DAY (FMR. PT. OF SC. 86)

Owens hears APPROACHING FOOTSTEPS. Looks up, sees --

TWO GUARDS walking toward him. *Fuck.* Sensing that something is wrong, Owens quickly moves in the other direction only to find --

THE LEAD LAB GUARD blocking his path.

>   LEAD LAB GUARD
>   Why the long face doc? We just
>   wanna talk...

Off Owens, face darkening, HARD CUT TO --

INT. SILO LAB - ELEVEN'S ROOM - DAY

CHOOM! A wire hanger drops onto a hook.

WIDEN: Eleven has hung up her haptic suit. She has dressed back into her civilian clothes. She takes one last look at the haptic suit, then exits her room. We PUSH toward the suit, hanging there like a discarded superhero cape, as...

INT. SILO LAB - OUTER RING - ANTENNA SILO - DAY

Eleven heads down the stairs into the hallway which encircles the Nina lab. She pushes on a door to exit -- but it doesn't open. Confused, she pushes it again, but -- no go.

>   DR. BRENNER (O.S.)
>   You can't leave, Eleven.

Eleven turns, finds --

Brenner, standing behind her, all alone in the antenna silo. Eleven's heart skips --

>   ELEVEN
>   ... Where is Doctor -- Owens?

>   DR. BRENNER
>   Doctor Owens... had a change of
>   heart.

INT. SILO LAB - MAIN LAB - DAY

WHAM! Owens is suddenly slammed down into the desk by the Lead Guard. He shouts in anger as they handcuff him and --

INT. SILO LAB - ANTENNA SILO - DAY

Eleven tenses, weighing her options --

> DR. BRENNER
> I know you wish to go to him. And I can't stop you from forcing open that door. But if my men hear you coming, they <u>will</u> kill him. And alone, you will never make it out of this desert to your friends.

As Eleven takes this in, *now trapped* --

Brenner begins to walk toward her. He has <u>regained control</u>.

> DR. BRENNER (CONT'D)
> This is what is going to happen. We are going to finish our work together. When I decide you are ready, we will leave for Hawkins. Together. Papa and daughter.

Eleven fights tears, rage -- betrayed.

> ELEVEN
> Why -- are you doing this?

> DR. BRENNER
> Because there is no other choice.

Eleven shakes her head. *No.*

> ELEVEN
> There is -- there is a choice.

> DR. BRENNER
> Only one that is right.

> ELEVEN
> And you -- make the -- right choices?

A beat -- this catches Brenner off-guard.

> DR. BRENNER
> I try.

Eleven steps toward him -- as all of those bottled-up emotions inside her finally begin to spill out --

              ELEVEN
       Did you make the right choice --
       with Mama?

FLASHCUT TO "MAMA" GETTING ELECTROSHOCKED --

              DR. BRENNER
       Your mother was sick, Eleven. She
       was a danger, to herself and
       others. She brought a gun into a
       hospital, killed a man --

              ELEVEN
       A hospital? No -- *a prison* --

              DR. BRENNER
       Everything I have done was for your
       own good -- your own protection --

              ELEVEN
       And Henry... you -- you kept Henry
       in the lab. With the children. Was
       that for our *good*? You knew -- *you*
       knew what he was. Was that -- a
       <u>*right choice*</u>?

              DR. BRENNER
       I had no idea what he would do,
       Eleven. I cared for you -- I loved
       you -- <u>all of you</u> --

              ELEVEN
       ... Even Henry?

Brenner tightens. This question makes him uncomfortable.

              DR. BRENNER
       I was trying to help Henry, Eleven
       -- to understand him.
           (then, the truth)
       Yes... I cared for him.

              ELEVEN
       Even after -- what he did?

              DR. BRENNER
       Yes. Because I knew I had failed
       him.

                    ELEVEN
          This morning -- you said you always
          believed... He was still alive --
          in the darkness... Is that why -- I
          was searching -- the darkness?

FLASHCUT TO YOUNG ELEVEN WALKING THE VOID--

                    ELEVEN (CONT'D)
          Was... I looking -- for him -- for
          Henry?

                    DR. BRENNER
               (firm)
          No. *No*. We were focused on the
          Soviets, Eleven, you know that --

                    ELEVEN
          "Papa does not tell the truth."
          Henry said that.

                    DR. BRENNER
          And you trust Henry now? Henry who
          manipulated you like some puppet.
          YOU are the one who released him
          from his prison, Eleven. And now
          you are angry at yourself, and you
          are taking that anger out on me --
          and you are risking *everything* --

                    ELEVEN
          NO -- you, YOU risked *everything*.
          YOU have lied. YOU made me look for
          him --

FLASHCUT TO YOUNG BRENNER SLIDING A PHOTO OF HENRY TO YOUNG
ELEVEN -- ELEVEN GOING IN THE ORIGINAL ISOLATION TANK --
ELEVEN WALKING UP TO THE DEMOGORGON --

The puzzle pieces are beginning to click --

                    ELEVEN (CONT'D)
          The Gate --

FLASHCUT TO THE GATE OPENING --

                    ELEVEN (CONT'D)
          The Mind Flayer --

FLASHCUT TO THE MIND FLAYER GOING INSIDE WILL --

                    ELEVEN (CONT'D)
          So many -- dead --

FLASHCUT TO BOB -- BARB -- BILLY -- ALL OF OUR DEAD --

> ELEVEN (CONT'D)
> All -- because of you. Because you -- you could not stop. You could not -- let him go.

Brenner is shaken here -- she's nailing him --

> ELEVEN (CONT'D)
> I came here -- because I wanted... to understand... who I was. To see if I -- if I was the monster.

FLASHCUTS AGAIN TO MAMA -- DEAD NUMBERS -- BRENNER SHOCKING HENRY -- ELEVEN DRAGGED DOWN THE HALLWAY --

Eleven is tearing up now --

> ELEVEN (CONT'D)
> And now -- now I know the truth. It is not me. It is *you*.

A tear slips down her cheek.

> ELEVEN (CONT'D)
> You -- you are the monster.

It rips Brenner apart to hear her say this. She's thrust a dagger into his heart. And for once -- *for once* -- Brenner has nothing to say. He seems -- defeated.

> ELEVEN (CONT'D)
> I am going to open that door. And then -- I am going to leave. *With Owens*. If you try to stop us -- I will kill you and your men.

And with that, Eleven walks away from Brenner, turning to the door, and holds out her hand. The door starts to wrench open, lights flickering from her power usage, and --

CHOOM! It rips off its hinges. Badass. But right then -- in the flashing lights -- we suddenly see that Brenner is now directly behind Eleven and --

THWACK! HE SWINGS A NEEDLE INTO HER NECK --

Eleven whirls -- fast -- throws out her hand, and --

WHOOM! A PSIONIC BLAST HITS BRENNER HARD, KNOCKING HIM OFF HIS FEET AND SENDING HIM FLYING BACK INTO THE HARD METAL OF THE NINA TANK. HE CRASHES TO GROUND BUT IT'S TOO LATE --

The needle is stuck in Eleven's neck. She yanks it out. Half the liquid is out of vial -- and *in her bloodstream.*

She tosses the needle, then staggers, dazed now, her vision beginning to blur and stutter as --

Dr. Brenner pushes weakly to his feet --

> DR. BRENNER
> You will soon see the truth,
> Eleven. This was the only way --

WHAM! She SCREAMS and throws out a hand again and slams Brenner back up against the tank. *Hard.* She keeps him pinned there as she walks toward him, her eyes filled with rage. He gasps for air as his neck muscles tighten. She's *choking him... killing him.* But the vision waivers as the drug takes hold and her hand falls and her knees buckle, and --

WHUMP! She folds to the floor.

Brenner drops at the same time as he is released from her physic grip. As he gasps, grasping at his bruised throat --

EXT. FIELD - HAWKINS - DAY

BAM! A NAIL punches through the trash can lid. Another. BAM!

WIDEN TO REVEAL: Eddie and Dustin making a "spike" shield!

WIDEN FURTHER: The Winnebago is parked in an empty field. Our gang is spread out, working in pairs to assemble weapons as they prepare for the upcoming battle. We survey each group...

Nancy saws the barrel of her shotgun with a hacksaw, while Max holds it in place --

> MAX
> Is this -- legal...?

> NANCY
> Actually -- I think it's a felony.

> MAX
> Right.

> NANCY
> But -- it guarantees one thing.
> (beat)
> *I won't miss.*

> DUSTIN (PRE-LAP)
> How's she feel?

NEARBY,

Eddie has now finished a spike shield, swings it around --

                    EDDIE
          Light, but durable, deadly, but
          reliable. I'll tell ya one thing --
          there'll be <u>no more retreating</u> for
          Eddie the Banished.

                    DUSTIN
          You're ready for Bat-tle. Get it?
          Bat-- tle? B. A. T. -- battle?

Eddie stares at Dustin --

                    DUSTIN (CONT'D)
          ... No?

Eddie breaks into a big smile. He grabs Dustin, pulls him into a hug, then looks him firm in the eyes --

                    EDDIE
          Don't you ever change Henderson --
          <u>*never*</u>, you got me?

                    DUSTIN
          Wasn't... planning on it.

                    EDDIE
          Good -- *good*.

Eddie then looks over, calls across the field --

                    EDDIE (CONT'D)
          HEY SINCLAIRS! How are those spears
          coming??

Erica and Lucas look up from their work -- sure enough, they're crafting MAKESHIFT SPEARS, tying HUNTING KNIVES to the tip of wooden branches. Lucas gives a thumbs up, but --

                    ERICA
          Flip that damn thumb around --

                    LUCAS
          What -- ?

                    ERICA
          It's *too loose, Lucas!* This isn't a
          basketball game where they blow the
          whistle when your shoes fall off --

She crawls over to Lucas, starts to untie his rope and show him how it's done --

                    LUCAS
          Okay -- for the record -- my shoes
          never fell off --

                    ERICA
          Okay -- "for the record" -- it's
          hard for your shoes to fall off
          when you're *riding the bench* --

                    LUCAS
          Yet -- for some reason... you still
          came to every game.

                    ERICA
          Except the one that mattered. Plus
          Mom and Dad forced me.

                    LUCAS
          Bull. Mom and Dad can't force you
          to do shit.

Erica can't deny this. He's got her here.

                    ERICA
          Well... even when you're a bench-
          riding loser... you're still my
          brother. Just the facts.

That's as much of a compliment as Erica will give, but Lucas will take it! As Erica begins to tie that knife, wrapping that rope *nice and TIGHT* --

NEARBY,

Gasoline splashes over the rim of a bottle as Steve and Robin make MOLOTOV COCKTAILS. As they work --

                    STEVE
          It just... it doesn't make sense.

                    ROBIN
          What doesn't make sense?

                    STEVE
          That was *Danny Simmons* -- he
          graduated *two years ago*.

                    ROBIN
          So --

                    STEVE
          So he's in college -- meaning he's
          visiting here over spring break.
          Fast Times was returned <u>LAST WEEK</u> --

                    ROBIN
          Steve --

                    STEVE
          I mean -- who was getting off on
          Phoebe Cates if not Vickie? Unless
          she's got some horndog little
          brother we don't know about or
          she's like -- super into *Judge
          Reinhold??*

                    ROBIN
          STEVE --

                    STEVE
          What --?

                    ROBIN
          <u>I</u>. <u>DON'T</u>. <u>CARE</u>. And I don't see why
          you do either with everything
          that's going on. Actually, if you
          think about it -- this was the
          <u>*perfect*</u> time for that little pull
          of the rug because in the face of
          the world ending the stakes of my
          love life seem <u>SPECTACULARLY LOW</u>.

                    STEVE
          Yeah, okay, fair enough. But...

Steve stuffs a kerosene-soaked rag into a bottle.

                    STEVE (CONT'D)
          <u>I still think there's hope</u>.

Robin sighs.

                    ROBIN
          Not everything has a happy ending
          you know?

Steve glances at Nancy.

                    STEVE
          Yeah. Believe me -- *I know*.

                    ROBIN
          I'm not talking about failed
          romance here, Steve.

A dark cloud seems to pass over Robin here. She seems *scared*.

                    ROBIN (CONT'D)
          I just... I don't know... I have
          this... terrible... awful...
          gnawing feeling that... things
          might... not work out for us this
          time.

Steve takes in the weight of what she said.

                    STEVE
          You think... we shouldn't be doing
          this?

Robin hesitates. She looks around at the others, all still working on their various weapons. All still so... hopeful.

                    ROBIN
          I think we're mad fools. The lot of
          us. But then I think -- if we
          don't stop him -- *who will?*

She turns back to Steve. Determined now.

                    ROBIN (CONT'D)
          We have to try.

Steve holds up his now finished Molotov cocktail --

                    STEVE
          To killing Vecna.

                    ROBIN
          Slash Henry --

                    STEVE
          Slash One.

A small smile. They clink their Molotov cocktails together. But as they go back to work, we push back in on Steve -- what Robin said left a mark on him, and he feels a little uneasy about it all now. As OMINOUS MUSIC begins we CUT TO --

INT. SILO LAB - ELEVEN'S ROOM - DAY

A PAIR OF EYES fluttering open.

It's Eleven. She's back in the bedroom. She's groggy from the drugs, her vision still blurry. But she can *feel* something around her neck. She reaches up, touches it. It's METAL --

<u>A SHOCK COLLAR</u>. The same device Brenner used on Two. As the horror of this new development settles in --

                    VOICE (O.S)
          It is only a precaution.

Eleven looks toward the voice, her blurry vision coming into focus just long enough to make out Brenner, standing in the doorway to her room. His neck is bruised from her attack, but he now is calm.

                    DR. BRENNER
          I never expect to use it. I very
          much hope our fighting is at an
          end.

He walks over and sits down beside Eleven. Eleven wants to leave so badly, to flee this man, but the drugs weigh her down, trapping her here...

                    DR. BRENNER (CONT'D)
          I know you are angry at me. But
          this is the best way. The only way.

He gently strokes her hair, "comforting" her, when --

WAH! WAH! WAH! AN ALARM BEGINS TO BLARE.

Brenner looks back toward the door, startled.

INT. SILO LAB - OUTER RING - DAY

Brenner heads out of Eleven's room into the outer ring. He sees his scientists fleeing down the hallway. *The hell?*

The Lead Guard pushes his way through the crowd, makes his way over to Brenner --

                    DR. BRENNER
          What is this??

                    LEAD LAB GUARD
          <u>They've found us</u>.

Off Brenner, face darkening, we CUT TO --

EXT. SILO LAB - ENTRANCE - DAY

CLOSE ON: Military boots stomping through dirt.

WIDEN TO REVEAL: SULLIVAN and his soldiers are racing toward Nina Lab, their guns raised and ready, their Humvees parked behind them, that chopper circling above.

INT./EXT. HELICOPTER - DAY

A SNIPER is positioned by the open door, his rifle resting in some prefabricated straps. He watches through his scope as --

INT. SILO LAB - SUPPLY ROOM - DAY

The Lead Guard and his men grab ASSAULT RIFLES from a weapons locker, arming up as

EXT. SILO LAB - ENTRANCE - DAY

An EXPLOSIVES SPECIALIST now plants an EXPLOSIVE CHARGE on the door. He unspools a wire, backing away from the door.

SPECIALIST
Five, four, three, two, one --

He pulls a TRIGGER and BOOM! The door EXPLODES!!

SULLIVAN
MOVE MOVE MOVE --

Our Soldiers swarm into the silo as --

INT. SILO LAB - MAIN LAB - DAY

The Lead Guard and his men now take positions in the central lab, aiming their guns down the tunnel, toward the elevator door. And then they wait. Fingers on triggers.

We hear the sound of feet on metal. Then silence. Then --

BOOM! The stairwell door suddenly explodes, blown right of its hinges, coughing smoke, and --

The Soldiers storm into the corridor!

The guards open fire on them -- BANGBANGBANGBANG!!! -- but the soldiers have BALLISTIC SHIELDS to protect them. Bullets ricochet off the metal as the soldiers fire back on the guards -- and begin to slowly ADVANCE down the corridor.

INT. SILO LAB - ELEVEN'S ROOM - DAY

Brenner races back into Eleven's room. She has now pushed herself up in the bed, but her vision is still blurry, her body weak. She can hear the din of GUNFIRE --

                    ELEVEN
        What... what is -- happening?

                    DR. BRENNER
        They have come to kill you. We have
        to go. Hold on, Eleven -- *hold on* --

He lifts Eleven up into his arms, carrying her --

INT. SILO LAB - OUTER RING - DAY

-- through that outer ring of the Nina Lab. He reaches a heavy closed door, punches a code into a keypad, pushes it open --

INT. SILO LAB - ESCAPE STAIRWELL - DAY

-- And carries Eleven into an ESCAPE STAIRWELL. The stairs are spiral, very narrow and very steep, but they'll have to do. As he begins to carry Eleven up --

INT. SILO LAB - MAIN LAB - DAY

The soldiers fight their way into the central lab and --

BANGBANG! They finish off the Lead Guard and his remaining men. Sullivan sweeps in, motions to his men --

                    SULLIVAN
        Quarter and search by twos --
        Hicks, take the upper level --

As our teams break now off into pairs, we move into a FAST MONTAGE as Sullivan and his Soldiers search the lab --

-- They fly down CORRIDORS -- burst into THE NINA LAB -- search BRENNER'S OFFICE -- THE LIBRARY -- and --

INT. SILO LAB - ELEVEN'S ROOM - DAY

Sullivan scours Eleven's bedroom with some men -- clearly miffed. *Where is she??* A soldier races in --

>   SOLDIER
>   Sir -- we found something you're
>   gonna wanna see.

INT. SILO LAB - BARE ROOM - DAY

The Soldier leads Sullivan into a bare room.

Sullivan freezes. He can barely believe his eyes. REVERSE TO REVEAL: Owens, bruised and battered, handcuffed to a pipe!

>   SULLIVAN
>   Well well... what happened here?
>   Are mommy and daddy fighting?

Sullivan walks over, kneels down by Owens. Menacing.

>   SULLIVAN (CONT'D)
>   Let's try this again.
>   (beat)
>   Where is the girl??

Off Owens, hardening, we CUT TO --

EXT. DESERT - DAY

Silence. We're out in the empty desert. Then suddenly --

WHOOM! Dirt scatters as a SMALL HATCH DOOR on the ground flies open. It's like a bomb shelter door, hidden a hundred yards from the silo entrance. Rising up out of it...

Brenner, with Eleven still cradled in his arms. He's exhausted from the long climb, but he's relieved to have escaped. But the relief quickly leaves him as he sees --

THE OTHER SCIENTISTS. THEIR BODIES LITTER THE DESERT. ALL DEAD. JUST BEYOND THEM, THE GOVERNMENT SEDANS -- ALL ON FIRE.

BANG! A bullet suddenly RIPS through Brenner's shoulder. His body jerks and he stumbles, nearly dropping Eleven --

He looks up, sees the helicopter, hovering ominously above him. We see a GLINT OF LIGHT in the open window, then --

BANG! Another gunshot. It misses him, punching dirt. Fuck.

Brenner turns, and starts to make his way across the desert as fast as he can -- but he is slowed by the weight of Eleven and the gunshot wound.

INT./EXT. HELICOPTER - DAY

The Sniper calmly tracks the fleeing Brenner.

>   SNIPER
>   Where you think you're goin', doc?

The crosshairs vibrate from the shake of the helicopter, making it hard to keep the running Brenner centered and --

EXT. DESERT - DAY

BAM-THUNK! The bullet *whizzes* past Brenner, punches the ground near him.

INT./EXT. HELICOPTER - DAY

>   PILOT
>   Give him some lead --
>
>   SNIPER
>   I got it --

The Sniper adjusts, gives more lead, fires again, and --

EXT. DESERT - DAY

BANG! This time the bullet SLAMS Brenner right in the back. BAM! Another hit in the back. BAM! Another and --

Brenner CRASHES TO THE GROUND, dropping Eleven as he falls.

As Eleven's limp body tumbles across the dirt --

INT./EXT. HELICOPTER - DAY

>   SNIPER
>   And *down he goes*.

Our sniper ejects his mag, works to load ANOTHER as --

EXT. DESERT - DAY

The weakened Eleven coughs dirt, gasping for air. In her BLURRED VISION, she can make out --

Brenner lying next to her, bleeding out. *Dying*. Her glassy, bloodshot eyes move from Brenner to the sky, where she sees that evil chopper, hovering overhead in the dying afternoon sun. Its rotor blades stutter in her drugged vision.

INT./EXT. HELICOPTER - DAY

The sniper finishes reloading, then looks back into his scope. He shifts the crosshairs from Brenner to --

Eleven.

> PILOT
> (into headset)
> Victor-Two-Sierra, this is Charlie-Lima-Golf. Do you copy, over?

INT. SILO LAB - OWENS' OFFICE - DAY

Sullivan, still with Owens, grabs his walkie --

> SULLIVAN
> Victor-Two-Sierra I copy, over --

INT./EXT. HELICOPTER - DAY

> PILOT
> We have the target in sights. Requesting permission to take the shot, over.

INT. SILO LAB - OWENS' OFFICE - DAY

Owens looks at Sullivan, desperate --

> DR. OWENS
> *Jack. You don't have to do this* --

> SULLIVAN
> It's over, Sam.

Sullivan stands, starts to answer on the walkie but --

> DR. OWENS
> I can put her in a -- a coma -- a medically induced coma --

Sullivan turns back to Owens -- taken aback. Owens doesn't give him a chance to respond, just keeps talking, fast --

> DR. OWENS (CONT'D)
> We've got the drugs right here to do it.
> (MORE)

                    DR. OWENS (CONT'D)
            We see if these murders keep
            happening. If you're right, the
            killing ends, and you pull the plug
            on her. In fact, I'll *pull it
            myself*. But if you're wrong about
            this... we are going to need her.
            God are we going to need her.
                    (beat, emotional)
            Don't do this, Jack. I am begging
            you.

Sullivan considers. For a moment we think he's been
convinced, but then he raises the walkie back to his mouth,
and --

                    SULLIVAN
            Take it.

                    DR. OWENS
            YOU SONOFABITCH!!! YOU
            SONOFABITCH!!! HEY!!! HEY!!!

Owens yanks violently against his cuffs and --

INT./EXT. HELICOPTER - DAY

                    PILOT
            Greenlight.

The sniper wraps his finger around that trigger, struggling
against the movement of the chopper to get that crosshair
positioned over Eleven. Just as he's ready --

HONNNK!!! A HORN interrupts, distracting him. HOOONK!

                    SNIPER
            The hell is that -- ?

                    PILOT
            Civie -- two o'clock -- !!!

Our sniper swings the crosshairs up and right to find a van
speeding toward them through the desert. On the side of it, a
surfer boy rides a wave of cheese. Holy lord, it's --

THE PIZZAMOBILE!!!

                    SNIPER
            What the fu -- ??

INT./EXT. PIZZAMOBILE - DESERT - DAY

VROOOOM! We're now in the Pizzamobile with our Lenora gang coming to the rescue! Needless to say, they're panicked --

>   MIKE
> I see her -- I SEE HER -- !
>
>   JONATHAN
> What -- where -- ??
>
>   MIKE
> There, *there* -- on the ground -- !
>
>   ARGYLE
> Why are all those dudes on the
> ground -- is that blood, man, is
> that blood -- ???!!
>
>   MIKE
> Faster -- *drive faster* -- !!!

Jonathan punches the gas, the speedometer shuddering as it inches its way toward 75 mph. But they're still far away -- they're not going to get to Eleven in time...

>   PILOT (V.O.)
> Victor-Two-Sierra. We've now got a
> civie heading our way --

INT. SILO LAB - DAY - INTERCUT

Sullivan is now striding back through the lab with his men --

>   SULLIVAN
> What??? We're in the middle of <u>the
> goddamn desert</u> --
>
>   PILOT
> I don't know, sir. It looks like
> some kind of... *pizza delivery
> truck.*

Sullivan's face hardens as he realizes who it is --

>   SULLIVAN
> I'll handle it. Just <u>take out the
> girl</u>.

INT. HELICOPTER - DAY

                     PILOT
              (to sniper)
    Ignore the civie. Take the shot.

The sniper swings his rifle away from the pizza truck, moving those crosshairs back over to Eleven, only --

<u>She's not there anymore</u>. *The hell?* He moves the sights around and --

<u>Locates her</u>. Only -- she's NOW STANDING. She is still clearly drugged, woozy, breathing hard, her body hunched a bit as she struggles to stand -- but she's powered by rage. And --

<u>SHE'S GOT A HAND OUT</u>. *Uh oh.*

WHOOM! The chopper rocks slightly, causing the crosshairs to JERK and -- BANG! The Sniper fires and *misses*, dirt puffing behind Eleven.

                    SNIPER
    The hell are you doing, hold her
    steady -- !

                    PILOT
    Something's wrong -- !!!

Sure enough his instruments are going haywire because --

EXT. DESERT - DAY

Eleven has a GRIP ON THIS FUCKING THING.

BANG! BANG! BANG! More sniper shots fire around Eleven -- narrowly missing -- puffing dirt -- but her focus never breaks. Her eyes narrow, blood slips down from her nose, and --

INT./EXT. HELICOPTER - DAY

Instrument alarms BLARE as the pilot struggles to regain control of the chopper --

                    PILOT
  SHIT!!

The crosshairs jerk and the sniper is thrown as --

THE CHOPPER BEGINS TO ROTATE VIOLENTLY, spinning like a top in the desert sky, faster and faster, spiraling down, down, down toward the parked military Humvees below --

EXT. DESERT - DAY

WIDE SLOW MOTION shot from behind Eleven as that helicopter continues to spiral down and down and then --

INT./EXT. HELICOPTER - DAY

The pilot SCREAMS and --

EXT. SILO LAB - ENTRANCE - DESERT - DAY

KABOOOOOOOM! THE CHOPPER SLAMS INTO THE HUMVEES AND EVERYTHING EXPLODES IN A MASSIVE FIREBALL!!! SHATTERED ROTORS AND METAL SHRAPNEL FLY AND DARK SMOKE PLUMES INTO THE AIR.

Eleven remains standing, breathing heavily, not moving --

IN THE PIZZAMOBILE

The kids watch from the front windshield -- eyes wide --

> ARYGLE
> DUDDDDEEE!

EXT. SILO LAB - ENTRANCE - DESERT - DAY

Eleven -- drained -- drops to her knees as the chopper burns in front of her. The Pizzamobile speeds up behind her, slams to a stop, coughing up dirt --

MOMENTS LATER

WHOOM! The door flies open and Mike and the others leap out. They race across the desert to Eleven's side --

> MIKE
> Eleven! ELEVEN!!!

Mike pulls her into an embrace. She can hardly believe he's here. In the daze of the drugs, he seems like... *a mirage.*

> ELEVEN
> ... *Mike...??*

> MIKE
> Yeah -- it's me. It's me. *I'm here...* we're <u>all here</u>.

El's eyes move to Will and Jonathan. Will goes up to her now, hugs her tight, while Argyle puts his hands on his head, taking in all the carnage --

                    ARGYLE
          Oh man -- oh man -- oh man!

As Will and Eleven pull out of the embrace, Will notices the
shock collar --

                    WILL
          Are -- are you okay?

Eleven manages a small nod --

                    JONATHAN
          Guys, we need to get out of here --
          we need to go, okay??

El nods, but then her eyes and mood shift as she sees --

Brenner. *Papa.* Still alive. But only *just*. Mike and others
now see him too. *Fuck...* Eleven leaves them, staggers over to
Brenner. As she kneels down beside him, we move into --

CLOSE-UPS. All sounds drop away except for their voices. For
a moment, it seems like time has been suspended, like it's
just the two of them out here in the desert, a blood-red sun
setting between them...

                    ELEVEN
          Papa...

Brenner reaches out and takes her hand. A shaky inhale as he
works up the strength to speak...

                    DR. BRENNER
          I need... you to know... I am... so
          proud of you... so proud...
              (beat)
          You are... my family... *my child...*

Eleven chokes back her tears, heartbroken...

                    DR. BRENNER (CONT'D)
          I have only ever... wanted to help
          you... to protect you... everything
          I did... I did *for you...*

His hand tightens around hers.

                    DR. BRENNER (CONT'D)
          Please tell me... you understand...
          I... I need to know... you
          understand...

We think for a moment Eleven is going to give him this. But then, she gathers her remaining strength, hardens, and...

Pulls her hand away from his.

> ELEVEN
> Goodbye, Papa.

She pushes to her feet, wipes away her tears, turns, and...

<u>WALKS AWAY. LEAVING HIM.</u>

Off Brenner, emotionally shattered, gasping for breath...

INT. PIZZAMOBILE - DAY

Mike helps Eleven into the back of the Pizzamobile, Will shuts the door behind them, Jonathan hits the gas, and --

EXT. DESERT - DAY

The Pizzamobile drives off toward the setting sun.

Brenner now finds himself all alone, that massive fire raging behind him. His breathing slows. Then his eyes close. Then...

He is gone. EMOTIONAL MUSIC SWELLS AS --

EXT. SILO LAB - A LITTLE LATER

WHOOM! Sullivan and his soldiers race back outside.

Sullivan's eyes go wide as he finds his convoy in flames. His eyes move from this destruction to the Pizzamobile -- now just a distant blot. *Escaping*...

Off a stunned, *defeated Sullivan* --

INT. PIZZAMOBILE - DESERT - DAY

Jonathan's hands clutch tight on the steering wheel as he pushes this sucker as fast as it will go, while --

Mike consoles Eleven. But there's no time to mourn --

> ELEVEN
> Hawkins -- we need to -- <u>to get to Hawkins</u>.

                    MIKE
          I know -- and *we will* -- but right
          now we need to get you somewhere
          safe, okay? They're going to be
          right behind us --

                    ELEVEN
          No. We need to get to Hawkins.
          Tonight.

                    JONATHAN
          We can't make it there tonight --
          it's two thousand miles away --

                    ELEVEN
          We have to find -- a way.
               (beat)
          If we don't -- they are... going to
          die.

                    MIKE
          Who is going to die?

El hesitates.

                    MIKE (CONT'D)
          El -- *who is going to die?*

Off Eleven, scared to say, we CUT TO --

EXT. COUNTRY ROAD - SUNSET

The Winnebago speeding down a road at sunset.

INT. WINNEBAGO - SUNSET

Our Hawkins group sits inside. They're all geared up now, wearing a hodgepodge of "armor" -- flak jackets, military boots, some helmets, some bandanas, some arm and knee pads. As for weapons, Dustin and Eddie have their spike shields and spears... Nancy's got her sawed off shotgun... Steve's got an axe strapped to his back... and Robin cradles a A MILITARY RUCKSACK in her lap, its cargo pockets jammed with SIX MOLOTOV COCKTAILS, just waiting to be lit...

It's a real *Red Dawn/Lost Boys* vibe. *Our teens are going to war*. But the mood is by no means triumphant -- it is somber, tense. A few looks between them that say everything. They all know that this is it... that their fate -- and the fate of Hawkins -- depends on each and every one of them.

Steve pumps the brakes as he pulls to a stop. Everyone in the back rocks a bit as the Winnebago settles, and then --

EXT. WINNEBAGO - DAY

EEEE. The Winnebago door opens and Erica, Lucas, and Max silently climb out. The doors shut behind them, then --

The Winnebago drives away, leaving them here.

The three kids now look out and up toward...

THE CREEL HOUSE. It towers over them. Ominous. That bloodred sun is setting behind it. A deep breath. Then... *screw it.*

Max walks toward the house.

Erica and Lucas share looks, then follow. They head up the steps and enter the house. Lucas shuts the door.

And right here, as that red sun begins to dip below the horizon, we --

END EPISODE

EPISODE NINE

CHAPTER NINE:
THE PIGGYBACK

WRITTEN BY **THE DUFFER BROTHERS**

EXT. KAMCHATKA CHURCH - SHED - NIGHT

Snow falls across the night sky. We follow it down to find --

Yuri's shitty, bulbous chopper, which has now been wheeled outside of the shed. A greasy YURI is working on the open engine. As he does, he glances over at --

DMITRI and MURRAY, leaning against the shed, talking. *Not looking his way*. He removes a PART from the engine, <u>slips it into his pocket</u>, and shuts the hatch. WHAM!

          YURI
Good news, my friends -- Katinka is feeling better!! Shall we give her another try??

Yuri hops up into the cockpit. As Dmitri and Murray walk over, skeptical but hopeful, Yuri turns on the engine and pushes the throttle. EEEEE! The chopper makes a horrible shrieking sound. But Yuri doesn't stop, just keeps pushing that throttle. The sound gets worse and worse --

          MURRAY
That's enough -- *that's enough*. HEY!

WHAM! Murray grabs him, yanking his hand off the throttle --

          MURRAY (CONT'D)
The hell you think you're doing???

          YURI
Get your hands off me, potato head!

          MURRAY
You're trying to break her, aren't you? Get us captured again so you can get your reward, that it -- ?

          YURI
You have big stupid imagination --

          DMITRI
He's lying. He's up to something.

          MURRAY
Yeah no shit --

          YURI
What do you two lizard brains know? You are engineers now?

                    DMITRI
          I know that sound is not good --

                    YURI
          On contrary, snoozy man. Those
          noises you hear -- that *eeeeee* --
          is *very* good sign.

                    MURRAY
               (scoffs)
          Good sign -- ??

                    YURI
          Yes -- my women make noise when I
          please them. You would not know
          what that is like, I understand --
          but for those like me who know what
          and where to touch -- MUCH NOISE!!!

On that note, Yuri rips his arm away from Murray, and resumes cranking the engine. As Katinka continues to SHRIEK with "pleasure," we CUT TO --

INT. KAMCHATKA CHURCH - NIGHT

CLOSE ON: The phone in the church. Still not ringing.

We PULL AWAY from the phone to find JOYCE pacing, impatiently waiting, dragging hard on a cigarette. We PULL BACK further to find HOPPER rummaging through crates, searching through those Levi jeans, checking sizes. He finds a PAIR --

                    HOPPER
          These are the smallest I can find--

Hopper tosses Joyce the jeans, then a T-shirt --

                    HOPPER (CONT'D)
          And this was it for shirts.

It's a bright red T-shirt with a picture of Hulk Hogan! It reads I AM A REAL AMERICAN.

                    JOYCE
               Cute.

                    HOPPER
          Yuri's got good taste. What can I
          say?

Hopper walks past Joyce, carrying his own change of clothes (same shirt, same jeans). He moves behind a shelf to change.

We now INTERCUT between Joyce and Hopper as they undress. Though they can't see each other, they are less than ten feet away from one another; the sexual tension is *thick*.

As Joyce pulls on her Hulk Hogan shirt, she clocks a dirty mirror, resting against a wall. In the reflection, she can see Hopper, just visible through some gaps in the shelf. He is now shirtless and working to re-dress his bandaged arm. But it's not just his arm that's wounded; his rail-thin body is covered in scars and bruises.

BEHIND THE SHELF - MOMENTS LATER

Hopper finishes redressing his wound, when --

>   JOYCE (O.S.)
>   ... What did they do to you?

A still-shirtless Hopper turns to find Joyce moving toward him. She now sees that more scars cover his chest and body.

>   JOYCE (CONT'D)
>   ... My God...

>   HOPPER
>   It's not all bad. I've been meaning
>   to lose weight. The Gulag Diet
>   wasn't my top choice -- it's got
>   some nasty side effects -- but,
>   hey, can't deny the results, right?

Hopper smiles. Joyce smiles too, but she's still clearly worried for him. Hopper takes a step toward her, as the mood turns serious.

>   HOPPER (CONT'D)
>   It's also... given me time. Time to
>   think... About the way I've been...
>   about... the things I've done...
>   (beat, then, locking eyes)
>   I never should've sent you that
>   message.

>   JOYCE
>   ... Why not? I've always wanted to
>   get kidnapped -- crash a plane --
>   stage a prison break.

She smiles. But Hopper won't let her play this off. He takes a step closer to her, looks her deep in the eyes, then --

>   HOPPER
>   I'm sorry.

A beat. This means a lot to Joyce, but --

                    JOYCE
          You didn't know what would happen --

                    HOPPER
          I knew it was dangerous --

                    JOYCE
          So did I. I chose to do this. And
          if I had to make the choice again,
          knowing what I know now -- I'd do
          it again. After all -- we still
          have a date to get to, remember?

                    HOPPER
                (a smile)
          Remember? Shit. I've been dreaming
          about it.

                    JOYCE
          Yeah?

                    HOPPER
          Oh yeah. So -- I've got it all
          planned out. I'm getting two orders
          of breadsticks -- those things will
          knock your socks off. Enzo, he's
          got this spice on them, I don't
          know what it is, but it's good, you
          dip it in olive oil, just *forget
          it*. And then -- for the main course
          -- I'm wavering between the veal
          and the lasagna, but I think I have
          to go with the lasagna.

Joyce just... stares.

                    JOYCE
          That's what you've been dreaming
          about? Breadsticks... and lasagna?

                    HOPPER
          I've been on a diet of watery soup,
          moldy bread, and maggots. So, yeah.
          I've been dreaming about
          breadsticks and lasagna -- sue me.
                (beat, then)
          Should I have been dreaming about
          something else?

                    JOYCE
          You tell me.

HOPPER
Well. There's... the wine --

JOYCE
Yeah -- wine is good.

HOPPER
I was thinking Cheeanti --

JOYCE
Chianti --

HOPPER
Chianti. Yeah. Then maybe... an after-dinner cocktail? What do they call that one again -- ?

JOYCE
Amaretto.

HOPPER
Amaretto. Yeah. *And dessert* --

JOYCE
Can't forget dessert --

HOPPER
Can't forget that. I hear their tiramisu is pretty great --

JOYCE
And after dessert?

HOPPER
I pay the bill --

JOYCE
We split it --

HOPPER
We argue about that --

JOYCE
I win. And then -- ?

HOPPER
And then -- then... I don't know --

JOYCE
... Use your imagination.

Hopper looks at her. He can barely breathe. Neither can she. He reaches out, pushes a stray hair away from her face.

                    HOPPER
              (low)
          Who needs imagination.

Hopper leans forward. And, at last, THEY KISS. Holy shit! FINALLY. They fall back against a shelf. Hands exploring bodies... lips pressed tight... but just as things start to get REALLY HOT --

RIIIIINNNGG! THE PHONE BLARES, SHATTERING THE MOMENT. OH -- you have _got_ to be fucking kidding!!

MOMENTS LATER

A flustered, bare-chested Hopper races to the phone. He pauses as he reaches the receiver, catching his breath, and --

                    JOYCE
          Whatever you say -- they're
          listening.

Hopper nods. _Got it._ He takes a deep breath, grabs up the phone, and --

EXT. SIDE OF ROAD - NIGHT

We dolly toward the Winnebago, which is now parked in the woods near the trailer park.

                    NANCY (PRE-LAP)
          Okay -- I want to go through it one
          more time.

INT. WINNEBAGO - NIGHT

Our weaponed-up, armored TEENS talk in the Winnebago.

                    NANCY
          Phase one?

                    ROBIN
          We meet Erica at the playground.

                    NANCY
          Phase two?

                    STEVE
          Max baits Vecna.

                    NANCY
          Phase three?

                    DUSTIN
          Me and Eddie draw the bats away.

                    NANCY
          Four?

Robin holds up the backpack full of Molotovs.

                    ROBIN
          Flambé.

                    NANCY
          No one moves into a new phase until
          we've all copied. And no one
          deviates from the plan. No matter
          what. Got it?

                    EDDIE/DUSTIN/ROBIN
          Got it.

Nancy nods. Good. She flings open the door and --

EXT. TRAILER PARK - NIGHT

Our teens head out of the woods and into the trailer park.

EXT. EDDIE'S TRAILER - NIGHT

They scurry into Eddie's trailer.

INT. EDDIE'S TRAILER - NIGHT

Steve climbs the bedsheet, scaling his way into --

INT. EDDIE'S TRAILER (UPSIDE DOWN)

As he falls, he flips his body like he's somersaulting off a diving board. He lands on two feet! *Perfect landing.*

INT. EDDIE'S TRAILER - NIGHT

Nancy can't help but react. That was... *kinda hot*. Robin, meanwhile, rolls her eyes -- *showoff*.

INT. EDDIE'S TRAILER (UPSIDE DOWN)

Steve drags a tattered mattress below the Rift, and --

MOMENTS LATER

WHUMP! Nancy drops onto the mattress. Steve helps her to her feet then we go to CLOSE UP SHOTS as the rest of our teens join them: Dustin drops into frame -- followed by his spear -- followed by Eddie -- then a battle shield -- then Robin -- then a backpack stuffed with Molotov cocktails -- then --

EXT. EDDIE'S TRAILER (UPSIDE DOWN)

BOOM! Thunder booms and red lightning scars the sky as --

Our now weaponed-up group steps out into the spore-choked trailer park. Steve looks back at Dustin and Eddie, who are hanging back in the trailer. He's concerned; like he doesn't want to leave them. He steps toward them --

> STEVE
> Hey -- if things here go south here
> -- I mean *at all* -- you *abort*. Even
> if we haven't walkied.
> (points at Dustin)
> I'm talking mostly to you, short
> stack. Don't be cute and try and be
> a hero or something. You're just --

> DUSTIN
> *Decoys*. Don't worry -- you can be
> the hero, Steve.

> EDDIE
> Absolutely. Agreed. I mean -- look
> at us. We are... *not heroes*.

Steve nods. Feeling better now. And with that, Steve turns back and joins Robin and Nancy. A shared look, and then they set off on their journey. But about ten feet out --

> EDDIE (CONT'D)
> Hey.

The teens turn back to Eddie.

> EDDIE (CONT'D)
> Make him pay.

Understanding nods from our trio and then they turn back and resume their march across this post-apocalyptic landscape.

EXT. CREEL HOUSE (UPSIDE DOWN)

BOOM! Thunder crashes outside the Creel House. That swarm of bats circles overhead. *Guarding Vecna's lair.*

INT. CREEL HOUSE (UPSIDE DOWN)

We snake through the house, making our way over vines as we move into a CLOSE UP of the Grandfather Clock. Beneath the ticking of the second hand, we hear groaning floorboards... a raspy breathing... then, in the reflection of the clock face, he appears:

VECNA. He patiently watches the time tick away.

Tick. Tock. Tick. Tock. Tick tock.

MAIN TITLES

EXT. NEVADA ROAD - NIGHT

Stars blanket the night sky. Below us, a GAS STATION sits like some sort of neon-soaked oasis in the middle of the black desert. We CRANE DOWN toward --

ARGYLE, who whistles as he fills up the Pizzamobile's tank.

> JONATHAN (O.S.)
> Okay and -- uh -- what about a smaller airline?

We swing past Argyle to find JONATHAN on a payphone. An anxious MIKE and WILL and ELEVEN hover behind him, listening.

> JONATHAN (CONT'D)
> It doesn't have to be one-way --
> I'll take *one seat* if you have it --

As Jonathan continues to plead on the phone, we zero in on Eleven, who has clocked something off-screen. She walks away from the others and looks up at...

A SUN-FADED BILLBOARD. It reads: SCENIC ROUTE AHEAD - NEXT RIGHT and features a family gathered at a canyon overlook. A Young Girl rides piggyback atop her big sister's shoulders.

As Eleven studies the photo, her mind races, and we flashback to several significant moments from her life: *EL TAKES MAMA'S HAND -- ENTERS HER MIND -- BILLY GRABS HER IN THE VOID -- SHE ENTERS HIS MIND -- THROWS BILLY ACROSS THE CABIN -- AND --*

BACK AT PAYPHONE

WHOOOM! Jonathan hangs up the phone, frustrated.

> WILL
> What'd they say?

                    JONATHAN
               Earliest is tomorrow.

               MIKE   WILL
Tomorrow --- ??   Seriously -- ?

                    MIKE (CONT'D)
               That's *too late* --

                    JONATHAN
               I *know* --

Argyle saunters over --

                    ARGYLE
               You ask if we can go in the baggage
               compartment --

                    JONATHAN
               The baggage compartment -- ?

                    MIKE
               We'd *suffocate* --

                    ARGYLE
               Dogs ride in there all the time --
               they don't suffocate.

Before anyone can respond to this inanity --

                    ELEVEN (O.S.)
               There is another way.

The others turn to find Eleven walking back toward them.

                    ELEVEN (CONT'D)
               A way to protect Max... from here.

Off the others --

MOMENTS LATER

WHAM! THE BACK OF THE MAP slams down onto the Pizzamobile
hood. Eleven messily draws out a plan using a colored pen.

                    ELEVEN
               This -- is Max.

She draws a CRUDE STICK FIGURE. *Max.*

                    ELEVEN (CONT'D)
               When One attacks -- he will be...
               in her mind.

She draws a thought bubble over Max's head, then draws a stick figure of One inside the bubble. *Sharing the mindspace.*

>   ELEVEN (CONT'D)
>   But I can do that too... I went
>   into Mama's mind. Into *Billy's*. I
>   can go into Max's. Into -- her
>   mind. Max can carry me to Vecna. I
>   can -- *piggyback*.

She now draws a stick figure of herself in the thought bubble. Right next to One.

>   ELEVEN (CONT'D)
>   I can... protect her from One.
>   Fight him. *From here.*

>   ARGYLE
>   Mind fight -- *righteous* --

>   MIKE
>   That'll actually work?

>   ELEVEN
>   I... think so. A bathtub would --
>   help --

>   ARGYLE
>   Yeah you gotta be clean to enter
>   the mind --

>   MIKE
>   No no -- it's a sensory deprivation
>   tank -- it relaxes the mind, so El
>   can focus her powers --

>   WILL
>   Didn't we just pass a motel?
>   They'll have a tub --

>   MIKE
>   Yeah, but not salt --

>   ARGYLE
>   How much salt we talking about here,
>   my dudes -- ?

>   JONATHAN
>   Depends on how large the tub is.
>   But -- *a lot* --

>   ARGYLE
>   Six hundred pounds suffice?

Everyone stares at Argyle.

> MIKE
> *You* know where to get *six hundred pounds of salt??*

Argyle doesn't answer; he just walks over to El and starts to measure her in relation to himself.

> ARGYLE
> Mmm hmmm, yep -- yep. It'll work --

> ELEVEN
> What... will work?

> ARGYLE
> I know of a magical place that has all you need, my brave little superpowered friend! Mind fight is on. VAMANOS!

On that note, Argyle heads back to the van. The others share baffled looks, then hurry after him. As the van door slams shut --

EXT. CREEL HOUSE - NIGHT

Quiet outside the Creel house.

INT. CREEL HOUSE - ATTIC - NIGHT

CLOSE ON: Socked feet making their way across the attic.

WIDEN: MAX is carrying a bug light through the dark attic. Waiting for it to light up. *Searching for Vecna.* As she searches, our CAMERA DROPS DOWN THROUGH THE FLOORBOARDS TO --

THE SECOND-FLOOR STUDY - CONTINUOUS

LUCAS crosses into frame, carrying another bug light, also in socks, searching the bathroom. Our camera doesn't stop, but rather continues its downward journey, dropping down into --

THE FIRST-FLOOR PARLOR - CONTINUOUS

Where we land on ERICA, searching with her own bug light. She heads toward the dining room when her bug light comes to life. As the ultraviolet light blooms, illuminating her awed face --

INT. CREEL HOUSE - SECOND-FLOOR STUDY - NIGHT

Erica quickly but quietly makes her way over to Lucas. She holds up a small notepad, on which she's scratched out a note with red marker. It reads: <u>FOUND VECNA</u>. Off Lucas, his breath catching, CUT TO --

INT. CREEL HOUSE - PARLOR - NIGHT

Max, Lucas, and Erica now step together into the ultraviolet room, their eyes on that glowing bug light, which Erica has placed atop the piano. Lucas and Max share looks -- *that's him alright*.

Lucas takes the notepad from Erica, scribbles another note. Holds it up. This one reads:

<u>PHASE ONE</u>

Erica nods, *copy that*, then --

EXT. CREEL HOUSE - NIGHT

Erica exits the Creel house and hurries across the street, making her way toward her new destination: <u>THE PLAYGROUND</u>.

THE PLAYGROUND - MOMENTS LATER

We DOLLY with Erica as she hustles across the playground, abandoned and spooky at this time of night. As she climbs up a metal ladder and into the caged belly of the RED ROCKET SLIDE, a BLURRY FIGURE appears in our foreground.

It's ANGRY TOWNSPERSON #1 from town hall, walking his dog -- and eyeing Erica. His gaze shifts from Erica to the Creel House. He sees that strange blue light emanating from the window. It's... <u>undeniably odd</u>.

He tosses his cigarette, yanks his dog --

                    ANGRY TOWNSPERSON #1
        Come on -- *come on* --

As the dragged dog YELPS, HARD CUT TO --

EXT. BENNY'S BURGERS - NIGHT

BANG! A powerful bullet slams into the foam head of a FOOTBALL TACKLE DUMMY.

WIDEN: A SLED OF DUMMIES has been placed along the edge of the woods behind Benny's Burgers. As bullets and stuffing continue to fly, REVERSE TO REVEAL:

JASON, firing his newly purchased .357. He is laser-focused, intense, *scary*. BANG! He fires a final shot. This bullet hammers the final dummy in the neck, and its head nearly comes clean off. As Jason begins to calmly reload --

ANDY bursts out of the back screen door behind him --

                    ANDY
        Hey -- I think we got something.

Jason doesn't even look back at Andy, just keeps reloading --

                    JASON
        Send Ryan -- I don't want to waste
        more time on bullshit leads --

                    ANDY
        Yeah I don't know if we want to
        send Ryan out on this one.

Jason turns to Andy. He's got his attention.

                    ANDY (CONT'D)
        You know the old murder house on
        Morehead?

                    JASON
        Yeah -- what about it?

Off Andy, about to tell all, we CUT TO --

EXT. KAMCHATKA CHURCH - NIGHT

Snow falling outside the dreary Russian church.

                    MURRAY (PRE-LAP)
        Okay, and uh -- *who* exactly was
        this woman?

INT. KAMCHATKA CHURCH - NIGHT

Inside, we find a shaken Hopper downloading Murray and Dmitri in the church, phone now back on the cradle.

Joyce stands in the back, looking lost in the shadows.

                    HOPPER
        I'm not sure -- she wasn't exactly
        miss talkative. Took me five
        minutes just to convince her I was
        real. I'm supposed to be dead,
        remember?
                    (MORE)

                        HOPPER (CONT'D)
            Anyway, I finally get her halfway
            convinced, to open up a bit, and
            she tells me she's --

EXT. HAWKINS - PHONE BOOTH - NIGHT (FLASHBACK)

STINSON is in the phone booth on the side of the road.

                        STINSON
            ... A friend of the doc's --

INT. KAMCHATKA CHURCH - NIGHT (FLASHBACK)

                        HOPPER
            Great. So am I. Now put me on the
            phone with him --

EXT. HAWKINS - PHONE BOOTH - NIGHT (FLASHBACK)

                        STINSON
            I'm afraid the doc is...
            indisposed at the moment --

INT. KAMCHATKA CHURCH - NIGHT (PRESENT)

                        MURRAY
            "Indisposed" -- ?

                        HOPPER
            It gets worse. She says the doc was
            with "the girl" -- that she was
            going off to fight some -- evil in
            Hawkins. And then they all just
            went off grid. The doc, the girl --
            everyone.

                        MURRAY
            The girl, meaning El -- ?

                        HOPPER
            Has to be.

                        DMITRI
            This is your daughter, American?

                        HOPPER
                 (nods)
            And she's not alone. She's with
            Joyce's kids.

All eyes move to Joyce. She's still in the back, looking spooked.

                    MURRAY
          Okay, I see that the mood here is
          bleak. And understandably so. But I
          think we need to consider the very
          real possibility that this mystery
          woman is in fact KGB --

                    JOYCE
          No. She's _telling the truth_. In
          that lab, those particles we saw
          were alive.

FLASHCUT TO PARTICLES SWIRLING IN THE LAB.

                    JOYCE (CONT'D)
          And if they're alive, it means a
          Gate has opened in Hawkins.

Murray swallows. That is indeed, not _good_.

                    DMITRI
          Gate -- what does this mean -- ?

                    HOPPER
          It means we have to get home. _Right
          now_.

Hopper crosses over to a church window. He looks out, sees
Yuri still working away on Katinka. Murray joins him --

                    HOPPER (CONT'D)
          What is taking so long -- I thought
          he was close --

                    MURRAY
          Close to _sabotaging_ us you mean --

                    DMITRI
          We think he's playing us again --

                    HOPPER
          So then put a gun to his _goddamn_
          head --

                    DMITRI
          And then what? He just spits out
          more lies. We kill him, we never
          escape here.

                    MURRAY
          It's moot anyway -- if your kids
          are truly in some kind of imminent
          danger -- even if we were to leave
          this very moment, we wouldn't make
          it in time. The earliest we'd get
          there is late tomorrow.

Hopper darkens. He knows that Murray is right. Everyone's at
a loss, when --

                    JOYCE (O.S.)
          Maybe we don't have to make it
          back. *Not tonight.*

All eyes return to Joyce. She steps forward, moving out of
those shadows, a confidence now replacing her panic --

                    JOYCE (CONT'D)
          Whatever this... evil is -- chances
          are it's connected to the hive
          mind. And now we know a part of
          that hive mind is here -- *in
          Russia*. We don't have to be in
          Hawkins to fight it.

                    HOPPER
               (picking up)
          We just need to destroy those
          particles.

                    JOYCE
          If we're lucky, it'll hurt it
          enough to give El and the kids the
          upper hand --

                    MURRAY
          Wait wait -- *time out* -- we're
          talking about the particles *in the
          prison*? The prison we just narrowly
          escaped from -- ??

                    HOPPER
          We broke out. We can break back in.

On that note, Hopper moves across the church. A flabbergasted
Murray pursues --

                    MURRAY
          Jim, Jim -- the entire Soviet army
          is looking for us -- !

                    HOPPER
          Sure -- and we'll be going where
          they will <u>least expect us</u> --

Hopper grabs up a crowbar, yanks open a crate, begins to grab
weapons --

                    MURRAY
          There is a fine line between
          courage and stupidity -- and this
          falls *very far* on the side of
          stupid! This is *Dirty Dozen* stuff
          except there are   uh -- four of
          us --

                    HOPPER
          Three. I figure getting back in
          will be easier than getting back
          out -- we're gonna need an
          airlift --

Hopper turns to Dmitri --

                    HOPPER (CONT'D)
          That's where you come in. I don't
          care *what it takes*. Get Yuri in
          line and get that bird in the air.

Dmitri nods, then heads out to handle Yuri. As Hopper loads a
mag into an AK, Joyce turns to Murray --

                    JOYCE
          Yuri, he mentioned a flamethrower,
          right?

INT. KAMCHATKA CHURCH - NIGHT

WHOOM! A crowbar pries the lid off a crate, revealing --

YURI'S FLAMETHROWER. IT'S GOT A PROTON-BLASTER-LIKE FIRING
MECHANISM, WHICH IS HOOKED TO A LARGE METAL FUEL TANK. It's
bulky and retro -- and yes, very, very fucking cool.

                    HOPPER
          Yeah. This'll do. *This'll do just
          fine.*

As Hop hoists the flamethrower out of the crate, CRASH TO --

INT./EXT. PIZZAMOBILE - NIGHT

SCREECH! The Pizzamobile squeals to a stop in an unknown
parking lot. The van doors slide open and --

Our Lenora gang step out. They take in the sight before them.

>   MIKE
>   You have gotta be kidding me...

REVERSE TO REVEAL: A SURFER BOY PIZZA JOINT!

>   ARGYLE
>   Trust me on this one, my dudes.

Argyle strides confidently toward his "home." The others share incredulous looks, then follow, but Jonathan has a thought. He doubles back, grabs Argyle's BACKPACK out of the van, and --

INT. SURFER BOY PIZZA - NEVADA - NIGHT

DING! A door chime rings as they head inside. Argyle saunters up to the counter, where an EMPLOYEE is cleaning up, his back toward us --

>   ARGYLE
>   Surf's up, my dude!

The worker turns to face us. His eyes are bloodshot, his hair hangs down to his waist, and he wears a colorful hat. Holy hell, he could be Argyle's long lost twin! Let's call him --

>   ARGYLE 2.0
>   Nice shirt my dude -- !

>   ARGYLE
>   Thanks my dude --   !

>   ARGYLE 2.0
>   Listen I'd love to feed a fellow
>   Surfer Boy, but I got some gnarly
>   news -- kitchen closed five minutes
>   ago. No more pies tonight --

>   ARGYLE
>   That's alright my dude, we're not
>   here for your tasty pies -- but we
>   do come to you in a time of great
>   danger -- and _great need_.

Argyle 2.0 stares -- *huh?* Argyle motions to Eleven, who stands awkwardly behind him.

                    ARGYLE (CONT'D)
          See this weird girl behind me? She
          needs a tub with a buncha salt so
          we can enhance her psychic powers
          so she can save the world from this
          super bad dude. And to make this
          salty tub, we require your kitchen.

ARGYLE 2.0 stares. *WTF?* He's about to speak up, when --

                    ARGYLE (CONT'D)
          Before you say something you might
          regret, my dude, I ask that you
          recall *what makes a Surfer Boy a
          Surfer Boy*. Is it our tasty pies?
          No. Is it our righteous vans? No.
          It is our SURFER BOY SPIRIT. No
          matter how gnarly the waves are on
          a given day, we find balance, we
          conquer that wave, and we surf that
          tasty pie to shore in *thirty
          minutes or less*. Now -- I want you
          to imagine that today's pie is not
          a pie -- it is our beautiful
          planet. And the wave -- the wave is
          a tsunami the scale of which you
          have never seen. It will drown all
          you know and love. But with your
          help, I believe we can conquer this
          wave -- and together we can surf
          our planet to the sandy shore.

Argyle 2.0 hesitates. Checks his watch.

                    ARGYLE 2.0.
          Uh -- it's just -- I'm supposed to
          meet Chaz at Taco Bell in ten.

Before a flabbergasted Argyle can respond --

                    JONATHAN (O.S.)
               (jumping in)
          We're not asking you to help for
          free, *my dude*.

Jonathan tosses Argyle's backpack down onto the counter.

                    JONATHAN (CONT'D)
          You ever partake in the Purple Palm
          Tree Delight?

He reaches in, pulls out Argyle's BAG OF WEED. Waves it.

                    JONATHAN (CONT'D)
                It'll make your troubles float
                away... *like the seed pods of a
                dandelion in the wind.*

Off Argyle 2.0, his eyes growing saucer-wide as he takes in
all those beautiful (*off-screen*!) buds, FAST-PACED MUSIC
BEGINS AS WE CUT TO --

INT./EXT. SURFER BOY PIZZA - NIGHT

DING! Argyle 2.0 strides out of the store, pleased as punch,
that bag of weed in hand. Jonathan swings the sign to CLOSED
and --

INT. SURFER BOY PIZZA - NIGHT

Argyle leads the gang through the kitchen and over to --

A LARGE PIZZA DOUGH FREEZER. He flings it open. *Ta-da!*

                    ARGYLE
                The first ever Mind Fight held in a
                pizza dough freezer. Rad, right?

Shared looks. And now DRIVING SYNTH MUSIC begins as we
crosscut TWO PREPARATION MONTAGES. In one, our Surfer Boy
group readies their MAKESHIFT "ISOLATION TANK." In the other,
Dustin and Eddie ready their trailer for battle.

INT. SURFER BOY / EDDIE'S TRAILER (UPSIDE DOWN)

-- Jonathan and Argyle work to empty out the freezer, tossing
bags of frozen dough across the tiled floor.

-- Eddie and Dustin use a hammer to rip the panels of metal
skirting off the base of his trailer --

-- Will hooks up a WATER HOSE to a faucet -- begins to fill
up the freezer --

-- Dustin holds the metal skirting over the trailer window,
Eddie drills the panel into place --

-- Argyle tosses pizza dough -- Mike steals his sunglasses --

-- Eddie drills skirting over a second window --

-- Argyle tosses pineapple onto a pizza --

-- Another window is fortified -- *another* --

-- Jonathan slices open a bag of salt --

-- Argyle tosses his pizza into the oven -- spins a dial -- as flames rise --

EXT. TRAILER PARK - NIGHT (UPSIDE DOWN)

Dustin and Eddie step back and take in their work, wiping sweat from their brows. REVERSE TO REVEAL: Eddie's trailer now looks like a <u>killer Mad Max-style fortress</u>.

>   EDDIE
>   Not bad.
>
>   DUSTIN
>   ... Not bad at all.
>
>   EDDIE
>   Now for the fun part.

Eddie strides back into the trailer and --

INT. EDDIE'S TRAILER - EDDIE'S ROOM - NIGHT (UPSIDE DOWN)

-- Throws open the door to his room. Dustin sidles up beside him, following Eddie's gaze to something across the room.

>   EDDIE
>   ... Jesus. It's like she was
>   destined for an alternate
>   dimension.

REVERSE TO REVEAL: EDDIE'S B.C. RICH WARLOCK ELECTRIC GUITAR!! It's mounted on the wall like a piece of art. And goddamn if Eddie isn't right. The guitar's flame paint job and stark design makes it look like it just... *belongs here*.

>   EDDIE (CONT'D)
>   Whaddaya say, Henderson? You ready
>   for the most metal concert in the
>   history of the world?
>
>   DUSTIN
>   That a rhetorical question?

Eddie walks forward, grabs the guitar off its mount, and right here, as THUNDER BOOMS, we CUT TO --

EXT. WOODS - NIGHT (UPSIDE DOWN)

The thunder reverberates through the forest, where --

The weaponed-up Nancy, Steve, and Robin march through the Upside Down.

They keep an eye out for Demobats and other monsters while stepping over vines, careful not to alert the hive mind.

> ROBIN
> Okay, I don't want to freak anyone out, but I swear we've already seen that tree --

> NANCY
> That's impossible --

> ROBIN
> That would be just perfect right? This asshole destroys the world because we *get lost in the woods* --

> NANCY
> We're *not* lost, Robin --

Robin picks up her pace, anxious, plowing ahead --

> NANCY (CONT'D)
> Watch out for vines -- hive mind, remember?

Robin keeps charging ahead. Nancy sighs, frustrated.

> STEVE
> She's just stressed. Scared.

> NANCY
> Yeah, I know. I know. It's just --

> STEVE
> She's a super klutz?

> NANCY
> (smiles, nods)
> She told me she took longer than other babies to walk.

A small laugh but --

> STEVE
> I really -- shouldn't laugh. So -- this is super embarrassing alright, and if you tell Robin I'll kill you -- but when I was a baby... I crawled backwards.

> NANCY
> *Crawled backwards?*

                    STEVE
          Yeah. I -- uh -- I pushed with my
          hands, like this --
               (Steve demonstrates)
          Beep beep. Always in reverse. I
          mean, it kinda makes sense, right?
          You push to move --

                    NANCY
               (laughs)
          No it doesn't make sense --

                    STEVE
          Well, it did to my tiny Harrington
          brain. But then one day I reversed
          my baby butt down a flight of
          stairs and I thumped my head real
          good. And aren't baby brains like
          super squishy or something? Anyway,
          my mom thought I was a total goner --

                    NANCY
          Wow. That... explains -- SO much--

A soft smile from Steve.

                    STEVE
          I think it actually... kinda does.
          I think, like, right out of the
          gate, I'm super confident -- but
          I'm also an idiot, right? Which is
          a brutal combination. But the good
          news is -- I get a big enough thump
          on the head -- I can change. I can
          learn. I can *crawl forward*.

Nancy begins to realize -- he's talking about them now.

                    STEVE (CONT'D)
          So -- I think -- what I'm trying to
          say in a really stupid, roundabout
          way is -- <u>thank you</u>.

                    NANCY
          Thank me -- for -- ?

                    STEVE
          -- Giving my squishy head the
          biggest thump of its life two years
          ago. I needed it. It changed my
          life. And... I'm -- <u>crawling
          forward now</u>.

Nancy looks away. Not sure what to say to this.

                    STEVE (CONT'D)
          I just wonder sometimes -- if some
          other girl had given me a proper
          thump before we met -- would things
          have turned out different? Like --
          if we were meeting for the first
          time right now... a part of me... I
          don't know... *thinks we would've
          made it.*

Nancy pauses, turns to Steve --

                    NANCY
          Steve --

                    STEVE
          You remember that dream I told you
          -- about the Winnebago. About
          seeing the country with my six
          little nuggets?

Nancy nods.

                    STEVE (CONT'D)
          That's all true. Every last word.
          But... I left one part out. The
          most important part.
               (beat)
          You're there, Nance.
               (beat)
          You've always been there.

Nancy's heart skips. She is about to respond when --

                    ROBIN
          Hey guys! YOU GUYS!

They look up to find Robin racing back toward them. She
wobbles a bit as she crashes to a stop, catches her breath.

                    ROBIN (CONT'D)
          Awesome news! We weren't going the
          wrong way after all!

Our teens share looks, then --

EXT. FOREST CLEARING - MOMENTS LATER - NIGHT (UPSIDE DOWN)

They push out of the forest clearing to find --

A street up ahead. And maybe half a mile away, they see the Creel House. Those bats circling overhead. Across the street from this house, the park. An orange glow emanates from the metal rib of the rocket ship.

                  STEVE/NANCY
    Erica --

They press forward, moving fast, and --

EXT. RUSSIAN ROAD - NIGHT

VROOM! Yuri's van speeds down the icy road.

INT. YURI'S VAN - NIGHT

Hop is in the driver's seat, Joyce passenger, Murray in back. As the van makes a turn, the guard booth comes into view.

                  JOYCE
    Slow down...

Hopper pumps the brakes, Murray tightens his grip on his AK-47, bracing for violence, Joyce tenses. But as they draw closer to the booth, they see that the guards are gone, their playing cards abandoned, blowing in the wind, the radio emitting static. And so they pass, completely unhindered.

                  MURRAY
    That was -- easy.

                  HOPPER
    Yeah. *Too easy.*

Hopper's eyes go to the prison. Unnervingly quiet. And --

EXT. RUSSIAN PRISON - BACK - NIGHT

WHAM! Murray wrenches off the sewer grate using a crowbar.

WIDEN TO REVEAL: The van is now parked along the back of the prison. Hopper, the flamethrower now strapped to his back, climbs down into the sewer. Murray follows, then Joyce.

Two rungs down, Joyce pauses. Listening. In the distance, beneath a gust of wind, she hears a FAINT ROAR, coming from deep within the prison. She tenses. Takes a breath. Then --

Descends. As her body vanishes into the darkness --

EXT. KAMCHATKA CHURCH - SHED - NIGHT

A cigarette stub burns, illuminating the night. WIDEN: We're back with Dmitri. He is standing outside the shed, smoking, watching calmly as Yuri fumbles around with the engine. He seems to be doing a lot while also *doing very little*.

Dmitri tosses his cigarette, stomps it out.

               DMITRI
     <I have a question.>

               YURI
     <And I am sure I do not want to
     hear it.>

               DMITRI
     <Have you always been a coward?>

Yuri spins to Dmitri. Seething. He stomps over to him.

               YURI
     <Yuri Ismaylov is many things,
     traitor -- but he is no coward.>

               DMITRI
     <If that is so -- why do you
     continue to stall?>

               YURI
     <And what if I am stalling? *Huh?* I
     owe nothing to the Americans --
     NOTHING -- and they are on a
     suicide mission. You know this -->

               DMITRI
     <I've underestimated the American
     before -- I won't again. He says he
     can do it. *He can.*>

               YURI
     <Listen to yourself -- you are
     Ronald Reagan now -- ???>

Yuri spits a big gob of saliva onto the ground, disgusted --

               DMITRI
     <This isn't just about *America*,
     smuggler. They have told us a story
     -- a story of *great evil*. An evil
     that does not rest, that does not
     respect borders.
               (MORE)

>   After it has consumed their home,
>   it will come for us, for our
>   families -- for our *Motherland*. You
>   saw it with your own eyes -- you
>   know it to be true. And yet you
>   continue to *play tricks*.>

We can tell that Dmitri is getting to Yuri. *Is there a heart in there, buried somewhere deep?*

>   DMITRI (CONT'D)
>   <I was told the Peanut Butter
>   Smuggler, before he lost his ways
>   to drink and cards, was once a
>   *great man*. That he led his men to
>   victory over the Chinese in
>   Damansky. That he was awarded the
>   Order of the Red Banner. Is it
>   true?>
>
>   YURI
>   <... It is true.>
>
>   DMITRI
>   <That hero -- where is he now?
>   Because I do not see him.>

And with that, Dmitri walks away. Yuri watches him go, then turns back to Katinka. He slips the helicopter part out of his pocket, rolls it in his hand, uncertain as...

INT. CREEL HOUSE - PARLOR - NIGHT

BZZZZ! The bug light is still glowing in the Creel house. Humming. *Vecna*. We DRIFT AWAY from it and move into --

THE STUDY - CONTINUOUS

Max and Lucas sit silently, nervous -- *waiting*.

Max scribbles something on her notepad. Holds it up:

>   Hi.

Lucas grins, surprised. He writes a response on his own notepad, holds it up.

>   Hi :)

Max scribbles another note:

>   I'm glad you're here

Lucas:

                Me too.

Lucas considers, scratches another note:

                Movie Friday?

Max's breath catches. A beat as she considers, then she looks down and scribbles something new on her notepad. She's taking a long time on this note, looking very serious and very focused as she does so. Lucas deflates; this can't be good.

At last Max finishes. She holds up the notepad. To Lucas's surprise, she hasn't *written* anything. Instead, she's *drawn* something:

TWO STICK FIGURES AT A MOVIE THEATER, SEATED SIDE BY SIDE, A BAG OF POPCORN WEDGED BETWEEN THEM. THEY ARE <u>HOLDING HANDS</u>.

Lucas beams. And so does Max. They are as happy as they have been in a long, long time, and for a moment, they forget about the impending battle. But the moment is fleeting: Lucas's smile fades as he notices a light out of the corner of his eye. He stands up and crosses to the window.

LUCAS POV: A small light, emanating from the park grounds, blinks on, off, on, off. *A signal*. It's --

EXT. PLAYGROUND - ROCKET SHIP - NIGHT

<u>Erica</u>. She's in the playground rocket ship, blinking her flashlight in a steady rhythm. *On, off, on, off.*

                ERICA
        Come on, come on --

INT. CREEL HOUSE - STUDY - NIGHT

Max steps up to Lucas. They share a look. Then Lucas holds up his flashlight and sends a return signal. *On, off, on, off.*

EXT. PLAYGROUND - ROCKET SHIP - NIGHT

Erica observes the blinking light, then speaks --

                ERICA
        Alright, the lovebirds copied. Max
        is moving into Phase Two --

EXT. PLAYGROUND - NIGHT - INTERCUT (UPSIDE DOWN)

Erica's voice carries into the Upside Down, where we find --

Steve, Robin, and Nancy huddled near the rocket ship. They made it! Erica is not visible, but the ethereal shimmer from her flashlight warms the belly of the rocket ship.

> ROBIN
> Okay... so far so smooth --

> STEVE
> Yeah, we're not to the hard part yet.

Nancy's eyes look toward the Creel house.

> NANCY
> Take the bait you sonofabitch...
> *take the bait...*

INT. CREEL HOUSE - FOYER - NIGHT

Shoelaces tighten as Max ties her sneakers back on.

INT. CREEL HOUSE - PARLOR - NIGHT

The hardwood floor GROANS NOISILY beneath the weight of Max's sneakers as she makes her way to the glowing bug light. She now carries her own bug light. Lucas, still in his socks, steps up beside her. They share a knowing look. *This is it.*

Max reaches down to her Walkman. Her finger hovers over the STOP button, hesitating. A deep breath, and then, *screw it* --

CLICK. She hits it off. ECU on cassette tape stopping and --

TOTAL SILENCE. We play no music here, very little sound. We just sit in the suffocating silence. Max now hands the Walkman off to Lucas. As his hands clasp tightly around it...

Max turns to the bug light... gathers her courage... and...

> MAX
> HEY. ASSHOLE.

Her voice echoes throughout the house.

> MAX (CONT'D)
> I'm here. No more music. No more games.

The bug light doesn't change... doesn't react.

> MAX (CONT'D)
> Hey! Do you hear me?? What are you waiting for? You want me or not?!!

For a moment, it seems like it's not going to work, but then --

The bug light fades in response. A beat, then Max's bug light glows. It's Vecna -- *he's on the move.* Max begins to walk, "carrying" the light, just as Steve did before.

INT. CREEL HOUSE - FOYER - NIGHT

As a tense Max "carries" the light up the stairs, Lucas close behind, the silence all but unbearable, we CUT TO --

INT. SURFER BOY PIZZA - KITCHEN - NIGHT

WHOOSH! A KNIFE slicing through a BAG OF SALT --

WIDEN: Jonathan empties salt into the freezer, which is now filled with water. Will stirs the salt with a large spoon.

Our CAMERA PANS from the brothers to find Argyle pulling a pineapple pizza out of the oven. He eyes that melted cheese and toasted pineapple with a look of deep satisfaction.

                    ARGYLE
     ... Sei bello! *SEI BELLO!*

As he begins to slice up the pizza, we CUT TO --

INT. SURFER BOY PIZZA - DINING AREA - NIGHT

Mike and Eleven, seated together at one of the dining tables. Mike has cut up a cardboard pizza box and is now taping it to the side of the Argyle's sunglasses.

                    MIKE
     Okay, so -- hopefully this blocks
     out any peripheral light.

Finished, he tries on the cardboard sunglasses. It is as silly looking as you expect.

                  MIKE (CONT'D)
     So -- it's super dark in here.
     Which is good. But the more
     important question --
          (cocks his head at El)
     How do 1 look? Because I feel like
     I look *pretty cool*.

Eleven giggles.

                    MIKE (CONT'D)
          You're giggling because I'm so cool
          right?

He slips off the glasses. El takes his hand.

                    ELEVEN
          Mike...

                    MIKE
          Yeah?

                    ELEVEN
          I... missed you.

                    MIKE
          ... I missed you too.
               (beat, then serious)
          And I've had some time these past
          days... to think... you know about
          -- about the last talk we had?
          Before the cops came and, like, the
          whole world went to shit. And... I
          just... I wanted to say --

                    ARGYLE
          SURF'S UP, Romeo!

They spin to find Argyle approaching with the pizza.

                    ARGYLE (CONT'D)
          Too much flavor awesomeness can't
          overpower your battery can it???

He tosses El a slice of pizza. Mike grimaces.

                    MIKE
          Pineapple -- ?

                    ARGYLE
          Try before you deny --

Eleven, curious, takes a hesitant bite. Her eyes light up a bit as she chews. Surprised.

                    ELEVEN
          Good. *Really good.*

                    MIKE
          Oh *come on* --

As El tries to persuade Mike to taste it, CUT TO --

INT. SURFER BOY PIZZA - KITCHEN - NIGHT

Will, who is watching Mike and El flirt through the porthole-style window of the pizza kitchen. Unable to watch them anymore, he returns his eyes to the dissolving salt.

Jonathan eyes Will. He knows his brother too well. *Knows he's hurting.*

>JONATHAN
>... Remember that time you told me that you had a Lego stuck up your nose?

Will looks up, surprised. That came out of nowhere --

>WILL
>*What -- ?*

>JONATHAN
>I think it was like -- one of those construction guys or something --

>WILL
>Yeah -- vaguely --

>JONATHAN
>Well I remember it like it was yesterday. I mean, I was freaked -- 'cause this guy, this construction worker, he was way, *way* up there -- I don't even know how you got him so far in -- I had to use tweezers to dig him out --

>WILL
>*Bull --*

>JONATHAN
>Swear on my life.

The boys chuckle. Then, Jonathan turns more serious --

>JONATHAN (CONT'D)
>I just... I don't know... I feel like... you used to come to me more for help. Or just to -- talk, you know? But it feels like... you don't do that much anymore. Not like before.

Will doesn't respond. He isn't sure how to feel about this --

                    JONATHAN (CONT'D)
          And a lot of that's... probably my
          fault. This year... I know I've
          been kinda... distant.

                    WILL
          Or stoned.

                    JONATHAN
               (small smile)
          Or stoned. Yeah. But that has
          nothing to do with you, okay?
          That's just me dealing with my own
          shit, hiding from my own problems.
          And the truth is -- I miss talking
          to you. *I really miss it*. And I
          think we need to talk more than
          ever because things are just
          getting... complicated. Like -- way
          more complicated than Legos up the
          nose, you know? And, I just... I
          don't want you to forget that I'm
          here. And I'll always be here. <u>No
          matter what</u>.

The brothers' eyes meet.

                    JONATHAN (CONT'D)
          Because you're my brother... and I
          love you... and there's nothing in
          this world -- *absolutely nothing* --
          that can <u>ever change that</u>. *You got
          that?*

We can tell this means the world to Will. He nods. Then, pushing back tears, he asks --

                    WILL
          I'm here -- for you too.

                    JONATHAN
          Yeah. I know you are. *I know you
          are.*

A teary smile between brothers, then Jonathan looks down at the water, then back to his brother.

                    JONATHAN (CONT'D)
          I think it's ready.

INT. SURFER BOY PIZZA - DINING AREA - MOMENTS LATER

WHOOM! Kitchen doors swing open as the Byers boys step back out into the dining area.

                    JONATHAN

    <u>It's time</u>.

Off El, pineapple drooping from her mouth, music rises and

INT. SURFER BOY PIZZA - KITCHEN - NIGHT

-- Eleven removes her tennis shoes.

-- Straps on her one-of-a-kind pizza-box blackout goggles.

-- Jonathan kicks on a radio, spins a dial, pumps static.

-- Mike and Will take Eleven's hand and help her into the water-filled pizza dough freezer. It's tight and looks a bit like a coffin, but Argyle wasn't wrong -- <u>she fits</u>.

Our gang gathers around the floating Eleven. As she focuses, the overhead lights flicker. Argyle looks around in awe --

                    ARGYLE
    ... *Wild*...

We PUSH IN on Eleven. We hear the sound of her heartbeat: *Thump -- thump -- thump.* And very suddenly the world goes --

BLACK.

We hold for a beat in the darkness. Then --

INT. BLACK VOID

A beautiful blue light emerges out of the blackness. In the glow of this blue light, we can make out the faces of:

Max and Lucas. They are far away, walking through this big black void. Max carries that UV bug light as if it were a lantern. A blurred body steps into the foreground of our shot. The CAMERA SWINGS AROUND to reveal it is Eleven.

                  ELEVEN
    ... I found them. They are --

INT. SURFER BOY PIZZA - KITCHEN - NIGHT

                    ELEVEN (CONT'D)
        (low)
  -- Carrying a light. A... blue
  light.

The others share looks, not sure what this means.

INT. CREEL HOUSE - ATTIC - NIGHT

Max follows Vecna to the center of the attic, then stops. Her bug light begins to pulse, glowing brighter. Max and Lucas share knowing looks, bracing for Vecna's attack.

INT. BLACK VOID

Eleven walks over to Lucas and Max. As she nears them, the pulsing blue light washes over her too, but then --

INT. CREEL HOUSE - ATTIC - NIGHT

The bug light stops pulsing and its glow returns to normal. And... Max is still not in a trance. That's... *odd*.

                    MAX
  What are you waiting for?! I'm
  right here you asshole! I'm RIGHT
  HERE!

INT. VOID

Eleven looks on, worried, as Max's voice echoes around her.

                    MIKE (O.S.)
        (heavy reverb)
  What's happening?

                    ELEVEN
  It's not working.

INT. SURFER BOY PIZZA - KITCHEN - NIGHT

                    WILL
  What's not working?

                    ELEVEN
  Max's plan.

INT. CREEL HOUSE - ATTIC - NIGHT

                    MAX
I don't know what you're waiting for -- but *I know* you're there. I know you can hear me. And I know... you can read my thoughts.
        (beat)
Even the worst ones. Maybe -- *mostly the worst ones...*

She sets the lantern down, then sits down beside it. She looks at that glowing light. A long beat, then --

                MAX (CONT'D)
I've... thought... about what you said. That -- I *wanted* my brother to die. I thought you were just trying to upset me... to anger me, but... you weren't, were you?
        (beat)
You were just telling the truth.

Lucas looks at Max, surprised by this revelation. But Max doesn't look at him, she can't. Instead, she keeps her eyes focused on that blue light, on Vecna.

                MAX (CONT'D)
I was happy. In California. So happy. Then... it was like, I blinked and -- everything I loved was gone. My dad was gone. My home was gone. My friends were gone. And... I was mad -- I was *so mad* --
        (beat)
I didn't blame it on Billy. But Billy -- he blamed it on me. He made my life... *living Hell*. Every chance he got.
        (beat)
And sometimes, when I would lie in bed at night, I would pray -- I would pray for something to happen to him. Something... *awful*.
        (beat)
I knew he drove too fast, so -- I would imagine him crashing. Dying in that *stupid car*. I just -- I wanted him out of my life -- forever. I wanted him... *to disappear*.

INT. BLACK VOID

Eleven listens to Max's confession. She so badly wants to reach out and comfort her friend, but she can only listen.

> MAX
> The day he died -- I think -- that's why I just -- stood there and watched.

INT. CREEL HOUSE - ATTIC

> MAX
> Not because I was scared. Not because I was weak. But because I didn't know if he *deserved* to be saved. Maybe... all my prayers... were finally answered.
> (beat)
> And... I -- I can't forgive myself. I've tried, and... I can't. *I can't.* Now... when I lie in bed at night -- I pray, I pray that something terrible will happen <u>to me</u>.

She looks back up at that glowing blue light. Her eyes are wet with tears.

> MAX (CONT'D)
> So that's why I'm here. Because... I want you to... take me away. I want you --
> (beat)
> <u>To make me disappear.</u>

A tear slips down her cheek. But, still, the light does not react.

> LUCAS (O.S.)
> ... Is that -- all true?

Max looks back at Lucas, surprised.

> LUCAS (CONT'D)
> You wanted Billy to die?

> MAX
> ... *Why are you talking* -- ?

> LUCAS
> Do you ever have thoughts like that about me -- ?

Max pushes to her feet --

                    MAX
        No... Lucas -- *never* --

                    LUCAS
        Normal people don't fantasize about
        killing people, Max. You realize
        that right?

                    MAX
        Lucas, please --

                    LUCAS
        I thought you were getting
        better... but you're not -- are
        you? You're sick --

Lucas moves toward her. More tears fall now -- this is her worst nightmare; she's exposed the deepest, darkest part of herself, and Lucas is judging her for it.

                    MAX
        Lucas, *you don't mean that* --

                    LUCAS
        Maybe it's good he takes you. Maybe
        it's for the best.

Lucas's voice is now a bit deeper. Something is wrong...

                    LUCAS (CONT'D)
        In fact -- I'm glad it's going to
        be you. I'm glad it's going to be
        you who breaks the world.

And it begins to dawn on Max -- *this isn't Lucas...*

INT. CREEL HOUSE - ATTIC - NIGHT

The real Lucas is crouched beside Max, terrified. He shakes her --

                    LUCAS
        Max, can you hear me -- MAX???

No response. Her eyelids flutter, and her eyes are rolled back. *She's in a trance.*

INT. BLACK VOID

Eleven's breath catches --

                    ELEVEN
          He has her.

INT. SURFER BOY PIZZA - KITCHEN - NIGHT

Our boys share frightened looks as --

INT. CREEL HOUSE - ATTIC - NIGHT (MINDSCAPE)

Max, now realizing this too, backpedals away from "Lucas."

                    LUCAS
          Where are you going? Don't be
          scared --

                    MAX
          Stay away from me --

                    LUCAS
          I thought you said you were ready?
          Ready to disappear...

                    MAX
          I SAID STAY AWAY -- !!!

Max grabs an old lamp, swings it, and -- SMASH! -- crashes it across Lucas's head, knocking him away. As Max scrambles away, fleeing back down the attic steps, our camera swings around and pushes in on Lucas. Only... it's not Lucas anymore. <u>It's Vecna</u>. There is a gleam in his eye.

He enjoys this part -- *the thrill of the hunt*.

As he slowly rises back to his feet...

INT. BLACK VOID

A scared Eleven kneels beside the tranced Max.

                    ELEVEN
          I'm coming, Max. I'm *coming*. Just--
          hold on. *Hold on a little longer.*

She takes Max's hand, then closes her eyes and focuses her powers. As our camera (remaining in close-up) begins to WRAP AROUND Eleven, Max's memories begin to flash past us --

We see Max crying at Billy's grave -- passing the letter to her mom -- singing "NeverEnding Story" with Lucas -- crying over Billy's grave -- playing Dig Dug -- trick or treating with the boys --

INT. SURFER BOY PIZZA - KITCHEN - NIGHT

The lights in the kitchen flicker like crazy and --

INT. VOID / UNKNOWN

We complete our rotation, landing back on El's face, and here the memories stop and El's eyes snap open. A harsh sun shines on her face. As she squints, adjusting to the new light --

INT. SURFER BOY PIZZA

Mike leans over the tub, on edge, gently probes.

                    MIKE
          El -- *what's happening?*

                    ELEVEN
          I think I am in... a memory. *A Max
          memory...*

EXT. GRUNGY PARKING LOT - CALIFORNIA - DAY (MINDSCAPE)

WE NOW REVERSE TO REVEAL HER ENVIRONMENT: a grungy California parking lot, which is overrun with longhaired SKATERS and PUNKS. Some just observe from behind fences and graffitied concrete barriers, while others skate around, zooming up a makeshift wooden ramp, performing impressive tricks, which are met with cheers and whistles from the observing crowd.

                    WILL
          Do you see her? Do you see Max?

                    ELEVEN
          No. But she's here -- she *has to be
          here*.

As Eleven begins to wade into the memory, searching for her friend, our CAMERA TILTS UP to the blinding sun. The glare of the sun becomes --

INT. CREEL HOUSE - ATTIC - NIGHT

A FLASHLIGHT, blinking into the lens, o*n, off, on, off.*

WIDEN OUT: Lucas is now once again signaling to --

EXT. PLAYGROUND - ROCKET SHIP - NIGHT

Erica, who remains nestled in her rocket ship. She signals back to Lucas, then speaks to her "invisible" friends --

>   ERICA
> Okay, she's in. Initiate Phase
> Three.

EXT. PLAYGROUND - NIGHT (UPSIDE DOWN)

Robin raises up her walkie, hits talk --

>   ROBIN
> She's in. Move into Phase Three --

EXT. EDDIE'S TRAILER - NIGHT (UPSIDE DOWN)

Dustin answers on his walkie.

>   DUSTIN
> Copy that. Initiating Phase Three.

Our CAMERA WIDENS OUT TO REVEAL that Dustin and Eddie have positioned themselves <u>on the roof of the trailer</u>. Eddie has his Warlock guitar strapped on and they have set up SPEAKERS and an AMPLIFIER. Dustin kneels down and grabs an extension cord which has been fed through a drilled hole in the trailer roof. He plugs it into the amp and cranks a dial and --

EEEEE!!! FEEDBACK SHRIEKS. Dustin nods to Eddie. *Greenlight*.

Eddie kisses his guitar pick for good luck. Then...

>   EDDIE
> This is for you, Chrissy.

WAHHHH! Eddie strums his lucky guitar pick across the Warlock's strings. The FIRST POWER CORDS of Metallica's "Master of Puppets" reverberate across the trailer park. Holy shit, it's <u>A HEAVY METAL METALLICA CONCERT IN THE UPSIDE DOWN</u>!! At first Eddie plays a bit timid, but he soon grows more confident, losing himself in the music, head thrashing, long hair whipping, red lightning flashing in the sky! It's EPIC AF and even Dustin can't help but bob his head.

EXT. CREEL HOUSE - NIGHT (UPSIDE DOWN)

The MASSIVE SOUND carries all the way to the Creel house. A bat -- hearing this noise -- shrieks and takes off in the direction of the sound. And it is not alone: more and more bats follow its lead, shrieking too, heading for the "concert."

EXT. PLAYGROUND - NIGHT (UPSIDE DOWN)

Our teens, who have taken cover behind the rocket ship, watch in awe as the swarm of bats fly over them. There are so many of them it's like a dark cloud passing overhead. Holy shit -- *it's working*. As soon as the bats are safely out of sight --

>   NANCY
>   *Let's go* --

They move out, heading for the Creel House, all while --

EXT. EDDIE'S TRAILER - NIGHT (UPSIDE DOWN)

Eddie continues to rock on. As he plays, we lay in crashing drums and James Hetfield's vocals, bringing the song to full life. THE SONG NOW CARRIES US THROUGH AN EPIC SEQUENCE AS --

INT. CREEL HOUSE - NIGHT (MINDSCAPE)

Max scrambles down the winding staircase to the front door.

She throws it open only to find a wall of ROTTEN BOARDS. It's just like what happened to Chrissy. She pounds on the boards to no avail -- *she's trapped in here. In Vecna's mind...*

>   VECNA (O.S.)
>   Where do you think you're going,
>   Maxine?

Max spins, looking up at the top of the stairs, where --

A familiar silhouette looms. *Vecna*.

Max scrambles away in horror and we SMASH TO --

EXT. PLAYGROUND - NIGHT

Erica hears the SHRIEK OF TIRES. She looks up, sees a pair of HEADLIGHTS. Coming her way. Fast. It's --

EXT. ROAD - NEAR PLAYGROUND - NIGHT

A FAMILIAR BLACK JEEP, tearing down the road.

INT. JASON'S JEEP - NIGHT

Jason is behind the wheel, his hands gripping tight to the wheel, his eyes wide, *scary*. A tense Andy sits passenger.

> JASON
> You see her -- ?

> ANDY
> Yeah I see her.

Jason accelerates, shifting into a higher gear, and --

EXT. PLAYGROUND - NIGHT

WHOOM! The Jeep *jumps* the curb and speeds across the playground, driving straight toward the rocket ship!

Erica's jaw goes slack -- FUCK. She slides out of the rocket, scrambles to her feet, and BEGINS TO RUN! As she sprints for the woods, the Jeep blows through a sandbox and skids to a stop. Andy leaps out and chases Erica --

EXT. WOODS - NIGHT

Erica sprints through the woods, shoving through brush, as --

INT. CREEL HOUSE - VARIOUS - NIGHT (MINDSCAPE)

Max *sprints* through the Creel house, moving room to room, searching for escape. She flings open a door only to find more rotted boards. *Shit.*

She tries a second door. More boards.

INT. CREEL HOUSE - MUSIC ROOM - NIGHT (MINDSCAPE)

She tries a third door. And --

Freezes. This door isn't boarded. Instead, it has revealed... another door. An eerily *familiar* one.

THE SAUNA DOOR. Before she can even process this --

WHOOM! BILLY SUDDENLY LEAPS UP AND SLAMS HIS HAND INTO THE GLASS AND SCREAMS --

                    BILLY
        MAX!! LET ME OUTTA HERE!! LET ME
        OUT!!

(NOTE: THIS IS REUSING FOOTAGE FROM SEASON 3.)

Max startles back -- terrified, and also fighting a new rush of tears as she is confronted by yet another painful memory.

                  BILLY (CONT'D)
        OPEN THE DOOR! OPEN THE GODDAMN
        DOOR!!

As her brother continues to beg for his life, Max turns to flee, only to find the exit to this room now obstructed by a SOLID BRICK WALL. Off Max, horrified --

EXT. EDDIE'S TRAILER - NIGHT (UPSIDE DOWN)

Eddie continues to rock out on top of the trailer! As he plays, Dustin scans the skies with his binoculars --

BINOCULAR POV: SWIVEL ACROSS THE SKY, THEN, WE SEE THEM -- DEMOBATS, LIT UP BY LIGHTNING. HUNDREDS. HEADED THEIR WAY.

Dustin drops the scopes, shouts over the music --

                    DUSTIN
      EDDIE THEY'RE COMING! WE GOTTA LOCK
      DOWN IN T-MINUS THIRTY SECONDS!

Eddie gives a small nod, acknowledging, but he keeps his focus on playing for now as --

EXT. PLAYGROUND - NIGHT

Erica continues to run through the woods, but Andy is bigger and faster and he's hot on her heels and --

WHAM! He tackles her to the ground. She tumbles, eats dirt.

                    ERICA
      GET OFF -- GET OFF!!!

Erica, shoves and kicks, scrappy as always, but Andy easily overpowers her, pinning her shoulders to the dirt as --

EXT. SKY - NIGHT (UPSIDE DOWN)

We SWOOP *through* the scorched sky, flying *with* the Demobats. We can see Dustin and Eddie far below us, standing on the roof of that trailer. *They're almost on them.*

EXT. EDDIE'S TRAILER - NIGHT (UPSIDE DOWN)

                    DUSTIN
      T-MINUS TWENTY SECONDS!!!

Eddie reaches the climax of the song, his fingers flying across those guitar strings at breathtaking speed, as --

INT. CREEL HOUSE - MUSIC ROOM - NIGHT (MINDSCAPE)

WHAM! An infected Billy begins to drive his shoulder into the sauna door. The door jerks against the chain lock. We know he's going to break out because we've been here before.

But Max doesn't move. *Doesn't panic*. Instead, she simply closes her eyes. *And focuses*. Remembering back to a happier time. *The SNOW BALL DANCE*. IMAGES FROM THAT MEMORY FLASH through her mind: *DANCING WITH LUCAS* --

EXT. EDDIE'S TRAILER - NIGHT (UPSIDE DOWN)

      DUSTIN
  T-MINUS TEN -- !!!

INT. SNOW BALL DANCE - NIGHT (FLASHBACK)

SHARING A SMILE --

EXT. EDDIE'S TRAILER - NIGHT (UPSIDE DOWN)

      DUSTIN
  FIVE -- !!!

INT. SNOW BALL DANCE - NIGHT (FLASHBACK)

HER FIRST KISS --

EXT. EDDIE'S TRAILER - NIGHT (UPSIDE DOWN)

      DUSTIN
  ONE -- !!

INT. CREEL HOUSE - MUSIC ROOM - NIGHT (MINDSCAPE)

BOOOM! Infected Billy smashes through the sauna door. The heavy metal frame of the door flies right at Max as --

EXT. EDDIE'S TRAILER - NIGHT (UPSIDE DOWN)

EEEEE! Eddie brings "Master of Puppets" to a dramatic close with an EPIC POWER CHORD and --

INT. HAWKINS MIDDLE GYM - SNOW BALL - NIGHT (MINDSCAPE)

WHOOM! Max opens her eyes. As that last chord echoes out, our CAMERA PULLS OUT TO REVEAL Max has transported herself out of the weight room and into the Snow Ball!!! And she is all alone here. No Billy. No Vecna. Safe. *For now*. As --

EXT./INT. EDDIE'S TRAILER - NIGHT (UPSIDE DOWN)

WHAM! Dustin and Eddie leap off the roof and scramble into the trailer. WHAM! They slam the door behind them just as the SWARM OF BATS fly into the fortified walls of the trailer, shrieking and gnawing but unable to get in!!!

INT. EDDIE'S TRAILER - NIGHT (UPSIDE DOWN)

Dustin and Eddie drop against the door, exhausted, catching their breath. Like Max, they, too, are safe. *For now.*

DUSTIN
Dude...

Eddie, breathing hard, sweating, looks to Dustin.

DUSTIN (CONT'D)
Most. Metal. *Ever*.

As Eddie grins, exhausted but *exhilarated*, we CUT TO --

INT. RUSSIAN PRISON - MYSTERIOUS LABORATORY - NIGHT

WHOOM! The blood grate slides open, scattering across tiles. A grimy hand slaps onto tile, then another as --

Hopper hauls himself up into the lab. His face pales as he takes in the scene before him. *Oh dear God.* Straight ahead --

The tank with the Mind Flayer particles has been shattered. The particles are GONE. As Murray and Joyce climb into the lab, equally shocked, Hopper turns around to take in the rest of the lab. OUR CAMERA PULLS BACK AWAY FROM HIM TO REVEAL --

ALL OF THE TANKS HAVE BEEN SHATTERED. THE CREATURES, LIKE THE PARTICLES, HAVE ESCAPED.

MURRAY
Oh dear God...

Their plan, like this laboratory, lies in ruin. Then --

A METALLIC CLATTERING. Somewhere close by. *Shit.*

Everyone spins. Hopper primes his flamethrower, Murray his AK, and --

INT. RUSSIAN PRISON - CONTROL ROOM - NIGHT

Our heroes creep out into the control room. It's a MASSACRE in here. Scientists and guards have been killed, bodies slashed, *eaten*. But they see no sign of life; no monsters.

Wait. They hear RASPY BREATHING. With Hop in the lead, they track the sound, edging around the control monitor, but --

It's just WARDEN MELNIKOV. He is on the floor, his back resting against the desk, his face pasty and clammy -- *he is dying*. Hopper kicks off his flamethrower, preserving that gas, as --

Murray kneels down beside him.

>   MURRAY
>   <What happened here?>

The Warden can barely speak, because his throat is so choked with blood. But he manages to eke out some words. As he speaks, Murray translates for Hopper and Joyce:

>   MURRAY (CONT'D)
>   ... The monster got in --
>   (listens, then)
>   The guards, they tried to stop
>   it...
>   (listens, then)
>   Their gunfire -- shattered the
>   tanks. The others... came alive...

Hopper tenses.

>   JOYCE
>   The particles. Ask him about *the
>   particles*.

Murray nods, turns back to the Warden.

>   MURRAY
>   <What happened to the particles?
>   The black particles, in the far
>   tank, looks like dust?>

He listens a beat, then back to Hopper and Joyce --

>   MURRAY (CONT'D)
>   He says -- they call it "the
>   Shadow." "The Shadow"... went into
>   them.
>
>   HOPPER
>   Into who?
>
>   MURRAY
>   (back to the Warden)
>   <Into -- who? Into who??>

But the Warden cannot respond. He has passed. But we get an answer of another kind: a CACOPHONOUS ROAR. Off our trio, a chill running down their spines --

MOMENTS LATER

Joyce, Hopper, and Murray walk up to the control monitor.

The monitors feed us LIVE FOOTAGE from rooms across the prison. The quality is black and white and quite degraded, but we can see the monsters plain enough: There are SIX DEMODOGS, along with THE DEMOGORGON, who is still very much alive. They are scattered throughout the prison, feasting on the remains of guards and prisoners.

>   MURRAY
>   I think that answers your question.
>   (beat)
>   The Shadow is in *them*.

EXT. CREEL HOUSE - NIGHT (UPSIDE DOWN)

BOOOM! Red electricity crackles over the now bat-free Creel House. Our CAMERA DROPS to find --

Steve, Nancy, and Robin heading into the house.

INT. CREEL HOUSE - NIGHT (UPSIDE DOWN)

EEEEEE... Steve gently opens the door to the house. And...

>   STEVE
>   (low)
>   ... *That's not good.*

REVERSE: There are FLESHY VINES everywhere -- on the walls, the banister, the furniture, and worst of all, the rotting floor, slithering like snakes. A *supernatural booby trap.*

Steve takes a deep breath, then -- *screw it* -- he enters the house, cautiously stepping over a nasty vine, then another. His agility is astounding. Robin watches, intimidated.

Nancy clocks her anxiety, takes her hand.

>   NANCY
>   (low)
>   *Don't worry -- I got you.*

Robin nods gratefully, and the friends begin to follow Steve's lead. As they delicately step over a *hissing* vine --

EXT. GRUNGY PARKING LOT - CALIFORNIA - DAY (MINDSCAPE)

WHAM! A SKATER eats it, tumbling across concrete.

Eleven walks through the parking lot as skaters zip around her. Her eyes roam, still searching for Max. Finally, she spots a YOUNG REDHEAD, 8 years old, smothering a scraped, bleeding knee with Band-Aids. As an OLDER SKATER rolls past, he taunts --

>   OLDER SKATER
>   Shouldn't you be playing with dolls
>   or somethin'?
>
>   YOUNG MAX
>   Shouldn't you bag your face??

She flips him off. Yep, it's YOUNG MAX alright!!

>   ELEVEN
>   ... Max?

But Young Max just hops on her skateboard.

>   ELEVEN (CONT'D)
>   Max --

But Young Max doesn't respond; she just skates forward, passing Eleven. Eleven whips around, watching as Max skates away from her, fearlessly joining those older boy skaters.

>   ELEVEN (CONT'D)
>   I found her, but -- *she's young.*

INT. SURFER BOY PIZZA - INTERCUT

>   ELEVEN
>   And she can't -- hear me. Can't see
>   me.

Shared looks. *That's not good*. Will's mind races --

>   WILL
>   Do you see anything -- weird in
>   this memory? Any sign of Vecna --
>   or the Mind Flayer?

EXT. GRUNGY PARKING LOT - CALIFORNIA - DAY (MINDSCAPE) - INTERCUT

>   ELEVEN
>   No -- no -- everything is...

Her voice catches as she notices something...

                    ELEVEN (CONT'D)
               (low)
          Normal...

On the far side of the skate park, a DJ STAND decorated with silver streamers. "Every Breath You Take" plays from some speakers. It's not the weirdest thing in the world, but something about it definitely seems out-of-place.

                    ELEVEN (CONT'D)
          There is... something -- that
          doesn't fit. I think... it is
          another memory.

INT. SURFER BOY PIZZA - INTERCUT

                    ARGYLE
               (whoaaaa)
          A memory within a memory...

EXT. GRUNGY PARKING LOT - CALIFORNIA - DAY (MINDSCAPE) - INTERCUT

As El begins to walk toward the music, that music growing in volume, we RETURN TO --

INT. HAWKINS MIDDLE GYM - SNOWBALL - NIGHT (MINDSCAPE)

The empty Snowball, where THE SAME SONG is playing.

We find Max, nervous, sitting on the bleachers in her Snowball hideout. Her sneakers nervously tap the gym floor. She looks down at her watch to check on the time and --

Her eyes narrow. The face of her watch is now THE CREEL GRANDFATHER CLOCK. The second hand ticks loudly. *Tick tock tick tock.* A nightmare. She rips off the watch and tosses it to the ground and stomps on it when --

EEEE! THE SOUND OF SHRIEKING FEEDBACK draws her eyes to the DJ stand. "Every Breath You Take" begins to distort and --

EXT. GRUNGY PARKING LOT - CALIFORNIA - DAY (MINDSCAPE)

The music distorts at the parking lot too, the lyrics and instrumentation morphing and twisting into a very different song; an eerily familiar one. It's --

INT. HAWKINS MIDDLE GYM - SNOWBALL - NIGHT (MINDSCAPE)

... "Dream a Little Dream of Me." The song that Henry played as he murdered his family. Just as Max takes this in, the gym walls around her begin to deteriorate, peel, rot.

<u>Vecna is coming.</u>

BOOM! THUNDER rattles the gymnasium, startling Max. She looks up at the windows, sees red lightning flashing outside, crackling, and --

EXT. GRUNGY PARKING LOT - CALIFORNIA (MINDSCAPE)

BOOM! Eleven hears the crashing thunder too, only it's not nearly as close for her. She looks up; off in the distance, maybe two miles away, she sees a massive dark storm cloud, alive with red electricity, very much out-of-place in the bright blue California sky.

                    ELEVEN
          ... Max

She begins to hurry across the parking lot, weaving through skaters, making for the storm, but she's got a long way to go. She quickens her pace as thunder booms again and --

INT. CREEL HOUSE - ATTIC - NIGHT

Tranced Max is now breathing faster. *Scared*.

Lucas sees this. *Shit*. He crosses to the window and blinks his flashlight, signaling to Erica, but --

EXT. WOODS OUTSIDE PLAYGROUND - NIGHT

Erica is not there to answer -- she is in the woods, held by Andy. He's got her arms twisted behind her back.

                    ERICA
          Let me go YOU MEATHEAD!!!

Andy pulls her arms tighter --

                    ANDY
          You don't shut your mouth I'll
          break your arms! You hear me, you
          little shit??!

INT. CREEL HOUSE - ATTIC - NIGHT

Lucas hears CREAKING FLOORBOARDS. He turns to find --

<u>Jason</u>, stepping up into the attic. *Oh no*. His eyes go wide as he takes in the scene before him: the glowing blue bug lamp... Max, frozen in place, her eyelids fluttering, her eyes rolled back... it looks like an honest-to-God *satanic ritual*.

His horrified eyes finally land on Lucas --

>   JASON
> The hell have you done?

>   LUCAS
> Jason, you need to leave --

Jason moves up to Max --

>   JASON
> Is *this* what you did to Chrissy?

He kneels beside her, studying those eyes in fear --

>   JASON (CONT'D)
> Hey -- can you hear me?! HEY!

He waves his hands in front of Max. Shakes her. Gets nothing in response. Lucas starts to stride toward Jason --

>   LUCAS
> Jason, I'm not messing around --
> it's not safe, you need to lea --

Lucas's voice catches and his body goes very still.

REVERSE: Jason's revolver is now out and trained at Lucas. He rises to his feet, slow, so the gun's aim never leaves Lucas.

>   JASON
> Not another step.

>   LUCAS
> You don't have to do this --

>   JASON
> I hope you're right. Is there anyone else in the house?
>   (Lucas shakes his head)
> Turn around. *Turn around* --
>   (Lucas turns around)
> Now empty your pockets -- *your pockets* --
>   (Lucas empties his pockets)
> Okay. This is what's going to happen. I am going to back away, just to the top of the stairs there. Then I will watch as you wake her up from whatever the *hell* this is.

Lucas swallows. *How to put this...?*

LUCAS
... I, I can't. If I wake her too
soon, *we all die* --

JASON
No. You don't wake her up, *right
now*, you die, Sinclair.
         (beat)
Just. YOU.

CLICK. Jason COCKS his gun. Off Lucas, trapped, we CUT TO --

INT. RUSSIAN PRISON - CONTROL ROOM - NIGHT

Boots crunch snow as Hopper strides into the Demo pit, which
is still littered with the bloody bodies of dead prisoners.

He stops in the middle of the arena and looks around. His
eyes move from one of the lower-level prison cells to the
electrified fencing above.

HOPPER
That fence -- you switched it off,
right?

JOYCE
Yeah --

HOPPER
Good. So you can get it back on.

MURRAY
Jim -- you want to clue us in on
what you're thinking here or we
supposed to read your mind --

HOPPER
This pit was designed to trap
monsters. We get them in here, lock
them in, then --
    (motioning to balcony)
-- we reign fire from above. And we
hope like hell that gives El and
the kids an upper hand.

MURRAY
I'm with you except for the, uh --
getting them all in here part.

HOPPER
This is a hive mind. We draw one, we
draw them all.

Hopper removes his flamethrower and passes it to Murray. It's so heavy he almost drops it --

>HOPPER (CONT'D)
>You're grillmaster--
>>(to Joyce)
>And you're jailer -- get the fence on. Then, soon as they're all in, you lock that door behind them.

>JOYCE
>And what about you?

>HOPPER
>I'm the bait.

As this terrifying notion hits Joyce, CUT TO --

INT. CONTROL ROOM - MINUTES LATER

Hopper leads Joyce back up to the monitors.

>HOPPER
>That one there, you see him? In the cafeteria --

He motions to the feed of a lone Demodog in the cafeteria.

>HOPPER (CONT'D)
>That's not far from here. And he's all alone. He's our target.

But Joyce is barely listening. Her eyes are fixed on that Demodog, feeding on a prisoner. *FLASHCUT TO DOGS KILLING BOB -- JOYCE SCREAMING -- HOPPER HOLDS HER BACK -- AND --*

>HOPPER (CONT'D)
>Hey.

She snaps out of her dark reverie.

>HOPPER (CONT'D)
>I'm gonna die someday -- but not today. I still got a date to make.

>JOYCE
>You had a date to make last time.

>HOPPER
>And I'm still here, aren't I?

A beat. A deep look into his eyes and --

                          JOYCE
                I'm not having a second funeral.

Hopper nods. He squeezes her hand, then heads for the door.
Off Joyce, watching Hopper go, scared as hell, and --

INT. EDDIE'S TRAILER - NIGHT (UPSIDE DOWN)

Eddie and Dustin hold tight to their spears and shields,
rotating around, their eyes fixated on those shuddering
barricades. We can't see the bats but we can *hear them* --
SHRIEKING in anger, SCRABBLING at the metal with their
talons. There must be *hundreds* of them out there. And
they're PISSED. The cacophony grows louder and louder until
abruptly --

Silence.

                          EDDIE
                            (low)
                ...The hell...?

                          DUSTIN
                Hey DIPSHITS -- you give up that
                easy??? HUH?

                          EDDIE
                Hey, perhaps let's not -- aggravate
                them more than necessary?

Suddenly -- a SCRABBLING SOUND. Coming from above.

                          EDDIE/DUSTIN
                Roof --

Their eyes swivel up, scanning the ceiling. Dustin's eyes
land on a small round vent above the kitchen.

                          DUSTIN
                They can't get in there can th -- ?

BAM-SMASH! The vent grate suddenly EXPLODES open and an ugly
bat head bursts in. It shrieks as it flashes sharp fangs!
Dustin charges and thrusts his spear into the mouth of the
bat, driving it back! Eddie joins him and they both jam their
spears into the vent --

                          DUSTIN (CONT'D)
                GET BACK YOU BASTAAAAARD!!!

As black blood rains down out of the vent, we SMASH TO --

INT. CREEL HOUSE - STAIRS - LANDING - NIGHT (UPSIDE DOWN)

The Teens, who are taking longer than expected to reach Vecna thanks to those damn vines. In stark juxtaposition to Eddie's trailer, it's very quiet here, unnervingly so, as our teens very carefully work their way up the booby-trapped stairs.

But by taking it slowly, at last they all reach --

THE SECOND-FLOOR LANDING - CONTINUOUS

Their eyes turn to the attic door at the end of the hall. This is it. They made it. Shared looks. A deep breath. Then --

They start to head for it, but not one step in and --

BOOOOM! AN EARTHQUAKE HITS, SHAKING THE ENTIRE HOUSE! OUR TEENS GRAB ONTO ONE ANOTHER FOR BALANCE, NEARLY FALLING. But they barely manage to catch and steady themselves. *Holy shit that was too close!* A shared smile of disbelief! But then --

Robin's smile fades as she feels something. She looks down. The edge of her foot has landed on a vine. It slithers and hisses and wraps itself around her ankle. *Oh God* --

She pries her foot loose and staggers away but in doing so she loses her balance and stumbles back into a wall where --

THWACK! Another vine snares her arm! Then another snares her other arm! Then her foot! She shrieks, panicking, as --

                NANCY
        Hold still -- !!

WHAM! Nancy mashes one of the vines with the butt of her shotgun as --

THWACK! Steve chops at the base of the vine with his axe, but as he raises the axe to swing a second time, a vine snares his lower arm, yanking it back. The axe scatters out of his hand at the same time as --

HISSS! Vines grab at Nancy. More vines come for Steve. Before we know it, the entire hallway has come to slithering, horrifying life, vines snaring limbs, and soon --

ALL OF OUR TEENS ARE PINNED TO THE WALL. *They're trapped.*

Robin's eyes goes wide as a vine slithers over her neck. As she lets out a choked scream, SMASH TO --

INT. RUSSIAN PRISON - HALLWAY - NIGHT

A DEAD GUARD. A boot steps over the body as --

Hopper makes his way through a prison corridor. The floor is littered with bodies; the walls are spattered with blood.

INT. RUSSIAN PRISON - CONTROL ROOM - NIGHT

An anxious Joyce watches him on a security monitor...

INT. RUSSIAN PRISON - HALLWAY - NIGHT

Hop uses the barrel of his AK to ease open the door to --

INT. RUSSIAN PRISON - CAFETERIA - NIGHT

In the stuttering light, he can make out the lone Demodog, which is still feeding on that dead guard.

A deep breath. *Now or never.*

      HOPPER
  Hey -- <u>DIPSHIT</u>.

The Demodog snaps to Hop. Its ugly face peels open. Snarling. Then, in a flash, it pounces, charging for Hop --

But Hopper is ready. He races out of the cafeteria and --

INT. RUSSIAN PRISON - HALLWAY - NIGHT

WHAM! Throws the door shut behind him. He continues to race down the hall, as fast as he can, BAM! THE DEMO BREAKS through the door behind him with a FEROCIOUS ROAR and --

INT. EDDIE'S TRAILER - NIGHT (UPSIDE DOWN)

WHACK! Dustin and Eddie continue to stab their spears into the vent, fending off more SHRIEKING off-screen bats.

      EDDIE
  Shield -- GIMME YOUR SHIELD -- !!

As Eddie continues to stab, Dustin passes him his nail-studded shield. Eddie promptly flings it up and over the vent with all his strength, driving those nails both into the head of the bat and into the ceiling. In one swoop, he's killed a bat -- and covered the hole!

      DUSTIN
  Nice --

                        EDDIE
            Thanks --

                        DUSTIN
                  (wait)
            Are there other vents -- ??

Eddie doesn't answer, but a look of dread flashes across his
face. *Fuck.* He sprints down the hallway and bursts into --

INT. EDDIE'S BEDROOM - TRAILER - NIGHT

Too late. A floor vent EXPLODES OPEN and a VORTEX OF BATS
explode up into the bedroom with a horrible SHRIEK --

                        EDDIE
            SHIT -- !!!

Eddie scrambles back out of the room, slams the door, and --

INT. EDDIE'S TRAILER - NIGHT (UPSIDE DOWN)

BAM! Off-screen bats slam into the door. The thin wood
splinters.

Eddie backs up toward Dustin. They watch in horror as the
wood withers away further. BAM!

                        DUSTIN
            That's not gonna hold -- !!

                        EDDIE
            Let's go -- let's go -- !

They scramble back toward the rift. Dustin grabs onto the
bedsheet, climbs through the rift and --

INT. EDDIE'S TRAILER - NIGHT (RIGHT SIDE UP)

WHOOSH! Tumbles safely down onto the mattress. He scrambles to his feet --

                    DUSTIN
          EDDIE, COME ON!! COME ON!!!

INT. EDDIE'S TRAILER - NIGHT (UPSIDE DOWN) - INTERCUT

Eddie leaps onto the mattress. He is about to climb when --

He pauses. He looks back at that shuddering door. His face hardens. *A decision is made.*

                    DUSTIN
          EDDIE -- what are you doing?? Come
          on!! EDDIE!!

But Eddie doesn't. Instead he swings his spear and -- CHOP! -- SLICES THE BEDSHEET IN HALF!!!

A shocked Dustin watches the rope fall onto the mattress.

                    DUSTIN (CONT'D)
          WHAT ARE YOU DOING?!!

                    EDDIE
          BUYING THEM SOME MORE TIME! STAY
          WHERE YOU ARE!!

Eddie kicks the mattress away from the hole, robbing Dustin of his means of return.

                    DUSTIN
          EDDIE!!! NO!! *EDDIE!!!*

Eddie sprints away and --

EXT. TRAILER - CONTINUOUS (UPSIDE DOWN)

WHOOM! He bursts out of the trailer. There are bats all around him, nasty heads peeling off the trailer to look at him, shrieking. But he doesn't stop to fight -- he grabs up a bike, begins to push it while running, then leaps on, his feet searching, finding the pedals, and before we know it --

HE'S BIKING THROUGH THE TRAILER PARK AT TOP SPEED!

The bats lift off the walls and roof of the trailer and SWOOP AFTER him with a GUTTURAL SHRIEK and --

INT. HAWKINS MIDDLE GYM - NIGHT (MINDSCAPE)

The gymnasium continues to rot, spores now falling from the ceiling, "Dream a Little Dream" still creepily playing as --

Max, breathing hard, slings a chair over her shoulder and carries it across the length of the gymnasium. She throws it at the front door, where it joins a mess of other chairs and tables. She's BARRICADED the front door! Max storms back across the gym, grabs another chair, turns back, and --

The barricade is gone. In its place, the Creel House Door.

>   VECNA (O.S.)
>   You can't hide from me, Max.

His voice reverberates through the gym. Then...

EEEE! Hinges squeak as the door begins to inch open.

Max closes her eyes, blocking it out, instead trying to locate another memory. Memories flash by until she lands on --

HER SLEEPOVER WITH EL AT HOP'S CABIN. *THE GIRLS DANCE TO MADONNA. READ TEEN MAGAZINES. PLAY SPIN THE BOTTLE.*

>   VECNA (O.S.) (CONT'D)
>   You think I can't see what you're
>   doing, Max? You think... I don't
>   see everything?

Max struggles to shut him out, to stay inside that memory. But the memories are stuttering now. *Her focus is slipping.*

>   VECNA (O.S.) (CONT'D)
>   You thought you could trick me. You
>   thought... your friends could stop
>   me. But I see them Max, I see your
>   friends -- as clear as I see you...
>   I can... feel them.
>   (beat)
>   I feel them... dying.

Max's happy memories are overtaken by present-day images of --

INT. CREEL HOUSE (UPSIDE DOWN)

STEVE, NANCY, AND ROBIN, AS THEY ARE CHOKED BY VINES. THEY GASP, GAG, EYES FLAGGING, DYING, AND --

INT. GYM - SNOWBALL - NIGHT (MINDSCAPE)

Max can't take it anymore. Her eyes snap open to find --

The Creel door is now wide open. But no sign of Vecna.

>   VECNA (O.S.)
>   It's time, Max.

That came from behind her. She whirls. The decayed snowball streamers are undulating. *Is he hiding there?* She stares, frightened, slowly backing away, when...

A DARK SHAPE APPEARS BEHIND HER. *VECNA.*

>   VECNA (CONT'D)
>   It's time.

Max spins back around just as he hits her with a powerful psychic blast. She flies backwards, punching through the streamers. Her back slams into a wall. But instead of falling, she stays pinned. As she struggles --

Vecna begins his methodical march toward her, those spores drifting around him, red lightning flashing, thunder booming.

>   LUCAS (PRE-LAP)
>   We call him... Vecna... He's a dark
>   wizard -- a monster... he has
>   powers -- *terrible powers.*

INT. CREEL HOUSE - ATTIC - NIGHT

A frantic, desperate Lucas is explaining all to Jason. We cannot tell exactly how Jason is processing this information; we only know that his revolver remains trained on Lucas.

>   LUCAS
>   He lives in another dimension,
>   that's why you can't see them --
>
>   JASON
>   And Eddie Munson and his Hellfire
>   acolytes... you all summoned this --
>   Vecna -- ?

LUCAS
No, NO, you're not listening to me -- *there's no cult,* there *never* was --

JASON
You expect me to *believe that* --

LUCAS
It's the truth --

JASON
Then why was Chrissy at Eddie's trailer -- ??

LUCAS
... She was buying drugs --

JASON
LIAR!

Jason steps toward Lucas, furious. But Lucas holds firm.

LUCAS
Chrissy was seeing things, *terrible things*, things Vecna forced her to see. She was cursed, she was scared -- she *needed help* --

JASON
See -- that's how I know you're lying. If Chrissy wanted help, if she was scared, she would've come to me -- not Eddie. *Not that freak.* NEVER.

LUCAS
You're wrong about Eddie --

JASON
No. But I *was* wrong about you.
    (beat)
I never should have let you in the door --

LUCAS
And I never should have knocked.

Lucas steps forward. *Unafraid.*

LUCAS (CONT'D)
I thought I wanted to be like you. Popular. *Normal*. But, turns out --
    (MORE)

                    LUCAS (CONT'D)
              (beat)
          Normal is a raging psychopath.

Jason glares. Then he hits off the safety. CLICK.

                         JASON
              You have five seconds to wake her.

His finger touches the trigger.

                         JASON (CONT'D)
              Four --

Lucas stares. Not moving --

                         JASON (CONT'D)
              Three --

WHAM! Lucas springs forward. He swats Jason's arm and --

BLAM! The revolver goes off. The bullet punches a hole in the ceiling and the gun scatters to the floor and --

EXT. WOODS OUTSIDE PLAYGROUND - NIGHT

Andy and Erica hear the gunshot. *Oh God.* Andy is now distracted and --

Erica tears free from his grip.

                         ANDY
              HEY -- !!

She spins and kicks him right in the ballsack, as promised!!! Andy doubles over in pain. Erica now races over and scoops his flashlight up off the dirt and --

                         ERICA
              CRIT HIT!!!!

WHACK! She clocks him with the flashlight, sending him reeling into a tree. His head CLANKS a branch, then he drops, out cold. Erica turns and starts to sprint through the woods, back to the Creel house, flashlight jerking up and down as --

INT. CREEL HOUSE - ATTIC - NIGHT

Lucas and Jason continue to fight, fists flying. They crash into junk. The impact sends the Walkman scattering away. Our camera moves past it and up to the tranced-out Max, her breath racing as --

INT. HAWKINS MIDDLE GYM - SNOWBALL - NIGHT (MINDSCAPE)

Vecna walks right up to her. Only a few feet away now. She squirms, desperate but unable to escape his psychic grip.

                    VECNA
          You are brave, Maxine. Much braver
          than your brother. But, in the
          end...

He runs a long fingernail along her face, drawing blood.

                    VECNA (CONT'D)
          ... You are weak and fragile, like
          him. Like all the rest of them. And
          you will break.

He then starts to dig his nail into her forehead when --

WHOOM! Vecna is suddenly and violently ripped backwards by some psionic force, away from Max, pulled into the middle of the gym. Max is released and crumples to the ground while --

Vecna hovers in mid-air, struggling, unable to move. *He's* now the one pinned by an invisible force. *The hell is going on?*

SLOW MOTION: Max looks up from the floor, her eyes going wide. Through a drifting curtain of spores she sees --

Eleven. Walking across the gym. Her hand is held out, angled slightly up. *She is holding Vecna*. With a subtle twist of the wrist, she rotates him around so that he is looking at her.

We now register an emotion from him that we have not before:

Surprise.

                    ELEVEN
          Hi.

Eleven throws her hand. WHOOM! Vecna is flung sideways. He slams into the nearby bleachers with so much force that he blows through the wood, and right here, we HARD CUT TO --

EXT. OUTSIDE TRAILER PARK - NIGHT (UPSIDE DOWN)

WHOOSH! Bike wheels tearing across dirt as --

Eddie bikes as fast as he can through the trailer park. He's flying, his long hair flowing in the wind, but as we WIDEN OUT we see that cloud of bats is right on his tail.

> EDDIE
> Come and get me you sonsabitches!!!

He takes a sharp left, turning out of the trailer park and onto the road. As bike tires SQUEAL --

INT. EDDIE'S TRAILER - NIGHT (RIGHT SIDE UP)

A panicked Dustin drags a chair under the Gate. He clambers on top then looks through the hole. There is no soft mattress waiting to catch him this time. *Screw it.* He grabs the slimed lip of Gate, then pulls himself up and through and --

INT. EDDIE'S TRAILER - NIGHT (UPSIDE DOWN)

He tumbles into the Upside Down and WHOOMP-CRACK! He lands on the floor at an awkward angle and his leg twists beneath his body. Dustin lets out a PAINED SCREAM as --

EXT. OUTSIDE TRAILER PARK - NIGHT (UPSIDE DOWN)

EEEE! The lead Demobat dive-bombs Eddie. It slams him and --

WHOOM! Eddie tumbles off the bike, rolling across pavement. Shit! He grabs the Demobat, rips it off him, and stabs it with his spear. But then, in a flash, the other bats are on him, enveloping him like some dark, leathery cloud. As he fights them off with his spear and shield, we CUT TO --

INT. RUSSIAN PRISON - HALLWAY - NIGHT

Hopper, who is sprinting down a maze of prison corridors, that Demodog hot on his tail! *It's gaining ground* --

INT. RUSSIAN PRISON - CONTROL ROOM - NIGHT

Joyce clocks all this from the monitors. *Oh God.*

Her gaze shifts to those SHOCK STICKS on the far wall, *and* --

EXT. PLAYGROUND - ROCKET SHIP - NIGHT

Erica races across the playground, making for the Creel house, *for her brother*, as --

INT. CREEL HOUSE - ATTIC - NIGHT

Jason and Lucas continue to fight. It's a fairly even fight as both boys land solid hits, but then Jason grabs a vase from atop a cluttered mound of furniture and swings it and --

WHAM! Shatters it across Lucas's head. Lucas staggers back, dazed, bleeding from the head. As Jason lands another powerful punch, Lucas goes crashing to the floor and --

INT. HAWKINS MIDDLE GYM - SNOWBALL - NIGHT (MINDSCAPE)

CLOSE ON: A PAIR OF HANDS CLASP together as --

Eleven helps a dazed Max to her feet.

>   ELEVEN
>   Are you -- okay?

Max just stares at El. Dumbfounded.

>   ELEVEN (CONT'D)
>   Max?
>
>   MAX
>   Huh?
>
>   ELEVEN
>   *Are you okay?*
>
>   MAX
>   Yeah.
>   (still confused)
>   Are you -- real? Or did I... *make
>   you?*
>
>   ELEVEN
>   I'm real.

Max reaches out, touches Eleven's face, just to make sure.

>   MAX
>   How...?
>
>   ELEVEN
>   I -- piggybacked from a pizza dough
>   freezer.
>
>   MAX
>   *What?*

Before El can respond, they hear MOVEMENT. Eleven turns around to find Vecna slowly rising up from the wreckage of the bleachers. His body heaves. He looks very, very angry.

>   ELEVEN
>   (to Max)
>   Stay back.

Eleven steps away from Max and moves toward Vecna.

We move into an EPIC WIDE SHOT as hero and villain walk toward one another from across opposite sides of the spore-choked gym. They stop about ten feet away from one another.

Eleven stays strong, determined, her eyes fierce.

>   ELEVEN (CONT'D)
>   Touch her again... I'll kill you
>   again.

Vecna studies her with very little emotion.

>   VECNA
>   Is that -- what you did? Did you --
>   kill me?

A thick vine snarls its way up the back of his neck.

>   VECNA (CONT'D)
>   I am very glad you're here.
>   (beat)
>   It will be beautiful, Eleven. So...
>   very beautiful. And it's all --
>   thanks to you.

Wood shards from the shattered bleachers suddenly rise up behind him. They angle at Eleven like projectiles, then --

WHOOSH! The dagger-like wood shards fly at Eleven. She easily swats them away with her powers but she's distracted and --

Vecna moves his hand and Eleven is hurtled backwards across the gym. Her body crashes through a table, upending a punch bowl. A dazed Eleven has barely recovered before --

Vecna lifts her back up into the air and flings her again, this time using a full hand motion. Her body flips 180 degrees as she hurtles like a rocket across the length of the gym. As her back slams hard into a cement wall --

INT. SURFER BOY PIZZA - KITCHEN - NIGHT

Eleven twitches in the freezer. Her breathing quickens. Blood streams from her nose. Mike and the others look on, worried.

                    MIKE
        She's fighting him.

EXT. TRAILER PARK - NIGHT (UPSIDE DOWN)

WHOOM! The door to Eddie's trailer bursts open as Dustin races out. He's now limping from his fall. In the distance, he can see that swarm of Demobats attacking Eddie.

                    DUSTIN
    EDDIE!!!

Dustin limps toward his friend and --

EXT. OUTSIDE TRAILER PARK - NIGHT (UPSIDE DOWN)

We're now *inside* the cloud of bats as Eddie battles on.

                    EDDIE
      COME ON!!!

He drops his shield and resorts to spear only, slashing and killing with both ends. It is a heroic effort, but there are so many, *too many*, and they overwhelm him. As lamprey-like mouths attach to his body, Eddie screams and --

INT. HAWKINS MIDDLE GYM - SNOWBALL - NIGHT (MINDSCAPE)

WHOOM! Eleven lets out a cry as her body crashes through another table. As she struggles to lift herself up off the ground, bloodied and weak, Vecna calmly walks over to her. He's toying with her now, a cat with a mouse. He is almost upon her when he hears POUNDING FEET. He turns to find --

Max charging, a jagged wood bleacher shard held like a dagger. She screams and swings it at him, but Vecna calmly moves his hand and sends Max flipping sideways through the air. Her head slams a wall and she drops. *Unconscious*. But Max's heroics have bought Eleven precious time and --

She's on her feet now and throws out her hand fast, but Vecna is *faster*. Without even looking back at her, he moves his hand and -- WHOOOM -- her wrist twists around. Bones SNAP.

Eleven SCREAMS and --

INT. SURFER BOY PIZZA - KITCHEN - NIGHT

Her scream translates into a muffled cry in the real world. Blood streams now from her second nostril. *This isn't looking good*. Mike takes her hand, squeezes it --

                    MIKE
          El, can you hear me?! EL!!!! You
          need to get out of there -- EL -- !

INT. HAWKINS MIDDLE GYM - SNOWBALL - NIGHT (MINDSCAPE)

Vecna uses his powers to lift and reel Eleven toward him. They are now face to face. Her feet dangle three feet off the ground. She is dazed, limp as a rag doll.

                    VECNA
          Before I kill you -- I want you *to
          watch*.

He throws her. She flies across the gym again but as she moves through the air a thick red fog envelops her body and--

INT. VECNA'S MIND LAIR

Eleven lands on a foggy, bloody ground. As she rolls to a stop, we WIDEN TO REVEAL that she is no longer in the Snowball. She is in VECNA'S MIND LAIR. We CUT TO --

AN EPIC OVERHEAD SHOT as vines slither toward her through the red water like sea snakes. They snare her legs, her arms, her neck, then hoist her limp body up onto a broken wall. Her eyes flag. Her consciousness now hangs by a thread.

ELEVEN POV: In her dazed vision, she takes in her nightmarish surroundings. Those broken elements from the Creel house... the strange rock formations, floating in the sky... Vecna's victims, hanging on pillars... and lastly...

Vecna, who is now dragging an unconscious Max through his lair with his oversized mutant hand. He drops her alongside a wall. As vines take her, lifting her, pinning her to the wall, Eleven at last finds the strength to call out:

                    ELEVEN
          Papa is dead.

Vecna turns to El. For the second time tonight, she has surprised him. Eleven keeps her eyes fixed on him.

                    ELEVEN (CONT'D)
          I know... I know what he did to
          you.
                         (MORE)

                    ELEVEN (CONT'D)
          (beat)
     You were different, just like me.
     And he -- hurt you. He *made you --
     into this*.
          (beat)
     He is the monster, Henry. Not you.
     Not... you.

Vecna slowly walks over to Eleven. His emotions are
difficult, if not impossible, to read.

                    VECNA
     You are right. You and I -- we *are*
     different. And Papa hurt me. But he
     was no monster. He was just a man.
     An ordinary, *mediocre man*. That is
     why he sought greatness in others.
     In you -- and me.

Vecna reaches Eleven.

                    VECNA (CONT'D)
     But, in the end, he could not
     control us. He could not change us.
     He could not shape us.
          (beat)
     Do you not see, Eleven? He did not
     make me into this.
          (beat)
     You did.

As Eleven takes this in, her breath catching, we're suddenly
thrust BACKWARDS IN TIME as --

INT. RAINBOW ROOM - DAY (FLASHBACK)

Eleven uses her power to push One out of our dimension --

EXT. HELLSCAPE (FLASHBACK)

*Henry/One flies backwards through space and time. Lightning
crashes all around him, searing his flesh, transforming him --*

                    VECNA (V.O.)
     At first, I believed you had sent
     me to my death... to *purgatory*...
     But I was wrong. I was somewhere...
     new.

EXT. DIMENSION X (FLASHBACK)

Rocky red objects, like the ones from Vecna's mind lair, float like nightmare islands in a scorched sky. CRANE DOWN TO FIND Henry, wandering a desolate landscape. His clothes have been torn from his body and his skin is scorched, bloodied. He is half-monster, half-human, not yet Vecna, but well on his way to becoming him. Through the fog, he spots a Demogorgon, wandering the land like some bear in the wilderness...

                  VECNA (V.O.)
      I became an explorer... an explorer
      of a realm unspoiled by mankind.

INT. VECNA'S MIND LAIR

                  VECNA
      I saw so many things, Eleven -- so
      many extraordinary things. And then
      -- one day -- I found the most
      extraordinary thing of all...

EXT. DIMENSION X - HILL (FLASHBACK)

Henry stumbles up a fleshy hill. Lightning flashes, illuminating a very familiar cloud of particles. It undulates, moving against the wind, amorphous. <u>Alive</u>.

Off Henry, his eyes wide...

                  VECNA (O.S.)
      Something that would change...
      <u>everything</u>...

INT. CREEL HOUSE - ATTIC - NIGHT (FLASHBACK)

Young Henry sits in the attic, lit by candlelight. The Mason jars are laid out before him, his idolized spiders resting inside. He scribbles in his notepad with a charcoal pencil, focused, drawing them --

EXT. DIMENSION X (FLASHBACK)

Henry now holds out his hand and the particles begin to move. He's using his psionic powers to mold the particle cloud into a shape... a very _familiar shape_...

INT. CREEL HOUSE - ATTIC - NIGHT (FLASHBACK)

Young Henry finishes his drawing. As he brushes away excess charcoal we reveal the drawing: It is a giant spider, with grotesquely long limbs. An early, crude version of somehing we have to come to know quite well...

EXT. DIMENSION X (FLASHBACK)

The particles finish forming. They now resemble the drawing Henry made as a child. We know it as... _the Mind Flayer_.

INT. VECNA'S MIND LAIR

Eleven can barely breathe as the truth hits her.

                    ELEVEN
        It was... you... always... you...

Vecna somehow answers "yes" without words.

                    VECNA
        All I needed was someone to open
        the door. You did that for me --
        without even realizing it, didn't
        you?

FLASHBACK TO Eleven touching the Demogorgon in season one. The Gate tears open --

                    VECNA (CONT'D)
        When you did realize -- you chose
        to resist.

FLASHBACK TO Eleven killing the Demogorgon, forcing the door closed in season two --

                    VECNA (CONT'D)
        So I sought out a means to open my
        own doors. I sought -- _your power_.

FLASHBACK TO Billy telling Eleven how they built the flesh monster just for her -- we see the people melting -- the monster grabbing Eleven with the tentacle -- her powers vanishing --

A tear slips down Eleven's cheek. Everything is now coming together -- the last puzzle pieces snapping in place.

> VECNA (CONT'D)
> So don't you see? Once again --
> (beat)
> *You have freed me*.

Eleven shakes her head, fighting tears --

> ELEVEN
> You don't have to do this -- *you can -- still stop this.*

> VECNA
> It is over, Eleven.

As a suite of DARK MUSIC swells --

EXT. OUTSIDE TRAILER PARK - CONTINUOUS (UPSIDE DOWN)

The Demobats overwhelm Eddie, taking him to the ground. His spear scatters, out of his reach, as that swarm of Demobats latch onto his body and begin to FEED. As Eddie screams --

EXT. TRAILER PARK - NIGHT (UPSIDE DOWN)

Dustin limps across the trailer park, as fast as he can, but he's not halfway to Eddie. *He'll never make it in time.* He calls out to Eddie, though we can't hear him: The soundscape is now muted, driven by that dark music, and Vecna's voice --

> VECNA (V.O.)
> Your friends... have lost --

INT. RUSSIAN PRISON - NIGHT

The Demodog leaps through the air and slams Hopper, tackling him to the ground. Hopper uses his arms to fend it off. Its jaws bury into his skin. As Hop cries out in pain --

> VECNA (V.O.)
> There is nothing -- nothing you can do to stop it now.

INT. CREEL HOUSE - NIGHT (UPSIDE DOWN)

Those vines continue to choke our helpless teens --

> VECNA (V.O.)
> Hawkins will fall...

INT. CREEL HOUSE - ATTIC - NIGHT

Jason now has Lucas against a wall. He is pummeling him with his fists, over and over, splitting Lucas's nose as --

> VECNA (V.O.)
> Then the rest of this senseless, broken world...

INT. CREEL HOUSE - SECOND-FLOOR HALLWAY - NIGHT

Erica sprints up the stairs to the attic door, but it has been locked with a chain. She bangs on it, desperate --

> VECNA (V.O.)
> And I will be there, waiting -- to pick up the pieces --

INT. VECNA'S MIND LAIR

> VECNA
> And I will *remake this world*... into something... *beautiful*.

He reaches out and touches Eleven, who is now crying.

> VECNA (CONT'D)
> Once, I had hoped to have you at my side. But now...
> (beat)
> Now... I only wish for you to *watch*.

With that, Vecna turns away and walks back to Max.

Eleven, panicked, focuses on her vine restraints. They loosen, but then tighten. She's drained, helpless as --

Vecna steps up to Max. Her eyes flutter. She's awake, just barely, but she is too weak to fight.

> VECNA (CONT'D)
> Don't be afraid. Try and stay very still. *It will be over soon.*

Vecna places his mutated hand over her forehead and...

INT. CREEL HOUSE - ATTIC - NIGHT

Max lifts up off the attic floor, levitating. The bug light strobes wildly in response, drawing the attention of --

Lucas, bruised and bloodied, still getting beaten by Jason --

INT. VECNA'S MIND LAIR

Vecna's claws dig deeper into Max's skull. Eleven screams, struggling with all her might to free herself, but a thick vine tightens around her neck, choking her, and --

INT. CREEL HOUSE - ATTIC - NIGHT

Lucas watches as Max continues to lift. He has to do something -- and *fast*. Fueled by an explosion of adrenaline, he ducks a punch, then swings and clocks Jason across the jaw. Jason stumbles, stunned, and Lucas doesn't let up. He swings again, again, in a display of strength we didn't know he had, and --

BAM! A final, powerful punch from Lucas sends Jason crashing to the floor, out cold.

Lucas doesn't waste a beat. He races across the attic and grabs up the fallen Walkman and --

His face falls. The plastic casing was shattered in the fight, and a ribbon of tape dangles out of a splintered cassette tape. *Oh no...* His panicked eyes return to Max, who continues to lift higher, out of his reach now, as --

INT. VECNA'S MIND LAIR

Vecna's eyes begins to roll in to the back of his head. We've seen this look before. *He's going for the kill*. El continues to watch in horror, but she still cannot move, cannot breathe --

INT. SURFER BOY PIZZA - KITCHEN - NIGHT

Eleven gasps for air from within the freezer. She is very pale; the blood from her nose has begun to turn the water red.

                    MIKE
       El, can you hear me? El??

Mike rips off her blackout goggles. Her eyes beneath her eyelids dart faster than we've ever seen them before.

                    MIKE (CONT'D)
      El wake up! Please. El! *EL!!! EL!!*

No response. *She is trapped in there.* Mike plunges his hands into the water and works to lift her up out of the tank --

                    MIKE (CONT'D)
               Help me -- help me!!

Jonathan, Argyle, Will help him raise her out of the tub.
They set El down on the tile floor. OVERHEAD SHOT as our
panicked gang circles her. Her eyes continue to move rapidly.

Mike leans in close, takes her hand --

                    MIKE (CONT'D)
               El, can you hear me? El?? El??

INT. VECNA'S MIND LAIR

El hears Mike's voice, echoing faintly through the mindscape.
Her eyes flutter as she fights to hold onto consciousness.

INT. SURFER BOY PIZZA - KITCHEN - NIGHT

Mike tears up as El seems not to hear him. But --

                    WILL
               Don't stop.

Mike looks up at Will.

                    WILL (CONT'D)
               You're the heart. *You're the heart.*

Mike looks back down at Eleven. His determination builds. He
squeezes her hand.

                    MIKE
               El... I don't know if you can hear
               this... but if you can... I just..
               I want you to know... That I'm
               here... I'm right here... and...
                    (beat)
               I love you.

INT. VECNA'S MIND LAIR

El's eyes blink again as Mike's words give her strength.

INT. SURFER BOY PIZZA - KITCHEN - NIGHT - INTERCUT

                    MIKE
               I'm sorry I haven't said it more.
               It's not because I'm scared of you.
               I've never felt that way about you.
               Never. But I am scared...that one
               day, you'll realize -- you don't
               really need me.
                    (MORE)

> MIKE (CONT'D)
> And I thought that if I said how I felt -- it would make that day somehow hurt *more*. Because the truth is -- I don't know how to be without you, El.

INT. VECNA'S MIND LAIR

Eleven is tearing up now as his words begin to draw her back toward consciousness. It's as though she were drowning, and Mike's voice is a hand, pulling her back toward the surface.

> MIKE
> I feel like -- my life started that day we found you in the woods. It was pouring rain, you remember? And you -- you were wearing that yellow Benny's Burgers shirt -- it was so big it almost swallowed you whole. And I knew somehow then -- in that moment -- that I loved you. And I've loved you *every day since.* I love you on your good days and your bad days. I love you with your power... and without. I love you for *exactly who you are.*

Eleven's hands tighten around his. She's listening.

> MIKE (CONT'D)
> And I'm not ready to lose you -- you hear me?? You can do anything -- you can fly, you can move mountains. I *believe* that. I really do. You -- you just have to keep fighting.

El's tears slow and color begins to return to her face. She looks over at Max, dying at the hands of Vecna.

> MIKE (CONT'D)
> So you -- you need to fight, El. Do you hear me?? *FIGHT.*

El closes her eyes. Focusing her strength. And it happens: The vines holding her begin to loosen, *uncoiling.* Lights strobe in the pizza kitchen. As the others look up in awe, Mike keeps focused on El, more determined, *it's working* --

> MIKE (CONT'D)
> That's it, EL! FIGHT!! FIGHT!! FIGHT!!!

Vines continue to unravel as Eleven begins to free herself. But is it too late?? As DRAMATIC MUSIC builds, Vecna's fingers plunge into Max's skull...

INT. CREEL HOUSE - ATTIC - NIGHT

MAX'S LIMBS BEGIN TO SNAP ONE BY ONE... LUCAS SCREAMS...

INT. RUSSIAN PRISON - HALLWAY - NIGHT

THE DEMODOG STRETCHES FOR HOP'S NECK, ABOUT TO GET HIM...

EXT. CREEL HOUSE (UPSIDE DOWN)

THE VINES CONTINUE TO CHOKE THE TEENS -- THEY SHARE FINAL DESPERATE LOOKS...

EXT. TRAILER PARK - NIGHT (UPSIDE DOWN)

BATS ASSAIL EDDIE. DUSTIN LIMPS TOWARD HIM, SHOUTING FOR HIS FRIEND...

INT. CREEL HOUSE - ATTIC - NIGHT

MAX'S LIMBS CONTINUE TO SNAP. HER EYES BEGIN TO POUR BLOOD AND...

INT. SURFER BOY PIZZA - NIGHT

                     MIKE
        FIIIIIIIIIGHT!

INT. VECNA'S MIND LAIR

EL UNLEASHES A POWERFUL SCREAM AND -- WHOOSH! -- THE VINES RIP FREE AND SHE DROPS TO THE BLOOD-SOAKED GROUND AND --

BLACK

WE HOLD FOR A LONG, SILENT BEAT. THEN --

INT. VECNA'S MIND LAIR

We're suddenly watching in SLOW MOTION as --

VECNA'S BODY HURTLES BACKWARDS ACROSS THE FOGGY MINDSCAPE.

WIDEN TO REVEAL: Eleven, now back on her feet, hand outstretched, using her powers to throw him as --

INT. RUSSIAN PRISON - HALLWAY - NIGHT

ZZZZT!!! The Demodog lurches away from Hopper, shrieking as a powerful electrical current surges through its body.

WIDEN TO REVEAL: Joyce, standing tall, thrusting a SHOCK STICK into its ribcage. As its body folds to the floor --

INT. VECNA'S MIND LAIR

Vecna's body slams against a rotted wall, so hard the wall *dents*. With Vecna knocked back, the vines at last release Max's broken body and she drops into the red swamp below --

INT. CREEL ATTIC - NIGHT

Max's broken body drops in the real world. Lucas catches her in his arms as --

INT. RUSSIAN PRISON - NIGHT

Joyce helps a dazed Hopper back onto his feet. Before Hop can offer a thanks, a CHORUS OF ROARS erupts behind them. They spin, eyes wide, to find THE REST OF THE MONSTERS stampeding down the long prison corridor, headed right for them. Leading the pack: THE DEMOGORGON, *the alpha*, flying on all fours.

Hopper and Joyce take hands and <u>run for their lives</u>.

INT. RUSSIAN PRISON - CONTROL ROOM - NIGHT

They sprint through the control room --

EXT. THE PIT - NIGHT

-- And race out into the snow-swept pit. Murray spots them from the balcony. *This is it.* As he readies the flamethrower, kicking on the gas --

The Demogorgon explodes into the pit, the Demodogs right behind him, almost on Hopper and Joyce. They race into an open prison cell and slam it shut. The bolt locks just a half-second before the Demogorgon reaches them. Its open maw collides with the bars of the cell, and right here --

Murray pulls the flamethrower's trigger and --

FWOOM!! SOUND RETURNS AS THE FLAMETHROWER ROARS TO LIFE, UNLEASHING A TIDAL WAVE OF FIRE UPON THE MONSTERS BELOW.

INSIDE THE CELL,

Hopper and Joyce duck into the corner of the cell, turn their backs to the pit, and cling to one another as the hot flames fill the arena, enveloping the Demogorgon and the Demodogs. The monsters SHRIEK in terrible pain, a pain that ripples out, affecting all monsters in the HIVE MIND, including --

INT. VECNA'S MIND LAIR

Vecna, who SCREAMS, still pinned against that wall as --

EXT. TRAILER PARK - NIGHT (UPSIDE DOWN)

The Demobats SHRIEK, falling off Eddie and out of the sky.

Dustin watches in awe as the sky rains bats.

INT. CREEL HOUSE - ATTIC - NIGHT (UPSIDE DOWN)

Vines SHRIEK and throb, loosening their vice-like grips on Steve, Nancy, and Robin, slithering away like skittish snakes and --

WHOMP! Our teens all suddenly plummet to the ground. As hands and knees collide with floor --

EXT. THE PIT - NIGHT

Murray continues to flame-throw the trapped monsters, sweeping that massive funnel of flames back and forth across the pit.

Inside the cell, Hopper and Joyce continue to hold on to one another, hands clasped tight, dripping sweat, until eventually the flamethrower sputters and dies out. Out *of gas*. And it is here, at last, that Murray's <u>reign of fire ends</u>.

Hopper and Joyce peel away from one another and look out across the pit, which is now choked in a dense cloud of black smoke. The smoke slowly dissipates, revealing a GRAVEYARD OF MONSTERS. Their bodies are withered. Smoking. <u>DEAD</u>.

INT. CREEL HOUSE - ATTIC - NIGHT (UPSIDE DOWN)

Steve, Nancy, and Robin catch their breath and stagger weakly to their feet. They look behind them, watching as the vines slither back down those steps.

>   ROBIN
>   Okay, I don't really believe in, like,
>   a higher power or divine intervention or
>   anything like that --
>   (beat)
>   But that -- that was a miracle.

Nancy turns back toward the attic door. Wide open.

>   NANCY
>   Then let's not let it go to waste.

>   STEVE
>   Phase four.

>   ROBIN
>   Flambé.

With that our teens begin to march toward the attic, *ready to end this once and for all*, as --

EXT. THE PIT - NIGHT

Hopper nudges the hot prison cell door open with his rifle. Joyce watches, on edge, as he cautiously enters the smoke-filled pit. He sees those Demodogs, dark smoke curling from their bodies. But he is not looking for Demodogs.

A GUTTURAL CLICKING nearby. He turns. Across the smoky pit, he finally sees it: The Demogorgon. It is downed, weak, burnt, but somehow, impossibly, still alive. Slowly but surely it begins to rise back to its feet.

Hopper's eyes lock onto a MEDIEVAL SWORD, still on the ground from the previous day's gladiatorial battle. He tosses his AK and takes the sword instead. We TRACK BEHIND HOPPER as he marches across the pit toward the rising Demogorgon as --

INT. VECNA'S MIND LAIR

Eleven marches toward Vecna, hand outstretched, keeping him pinned to that wall. It's a mirror image of their climactic confrontation in the Rainbow Room, only this time --

Vecna does not appear scared. Nor does he struggle. Instead, he seems almost *amused,* wearing the faintest of smiles.

                    VECNA
          You and your friends... believe you
          have won -- don't you??

INT. CREEL HOUSE - ATTIC (UPSIDE DOWN)

Steve, Nancy, and Robin step into the attic. Their eyes move up. Vecna is hanging from that disgusting fleshy spiderweb. Holy shit. *This is it...*

As they remove Molotovs from Robin's backpack --

INT. VECNA'S MIND LAIR

                    VECNA
          But this... is only the beginning,
          Eleven. The beginning... *of the
          end*.

INT. CREEL HOUSE - ATTIC (UPSIDE DOWN)

The teens light them. Gas-soaked cloth catches fire.

INT. VECNA'S MIND LAIR

                    VECNA
          You have already lost.

Eleven steps right up to him. Then --

                    ELEVEN
          No. *You have*.

INT. CREEL HOUSE - ATTIC (UPSIDE DOWN)

WHOOM! Our teens toss their Molotovs. The flaming bottles soar through the air in SLOW MOTION as --

EXT. THE PIT - NIGHT

Hopper and the Demo charge one another in SLOW MOTION. The Demo ROARS, swings a claw, going for Hop's throat. Hop ducks, evading, then swings his sword. Metal meets flesh and --

CHOOM! The DEMO howls as its right arm is severed from its body. As black blood sprays out across the white snow --

INT. CREEL HOUSE - ATTIC (UPSIDE DOWN)

SMASH! Glass bottles shatter against Vecna's body. As fuel and flame meet, Vecna's physical body goes UP IN FLAMES --

INT. VECNA'S MIND LAIR

In the mindscape, Vecna's face twists in agony and he lets out an awful, earth-shattering scream, and then he and Max and his ENTIRE MIND LAIR are WIPED AWAY leaving only darkness behind as they are thrust back to --

INT. CREEL HOUSE - ATTIC (UPSIDE DOWN)

-- The physical world. Vecna's eyes snap open and those awful tentacles slurp back into those creases in his back and his flaming body plummets to the floor.

INT. CREEL HOUSE - ATTIC - NIGHT

Max's eyes snap open as she, too, now returns to the physical world. Lucas, cradling her in his arms, gasps with relief --

>   LUCAS
>   Max??? MAX!!!

INT. CREEL HOUSE - ATTIC (UPSIDE DOWN)

Vecna, still on fire, rises to his feet, his eyes narrowed in anger as he locks onto the teens, who stand opposite him. But they're not intimidated. Nancy's got her shotgun ready and --

BLAM!! She unloads the sawed-off into his flaming torso. BLAM! The force of the blast drives him backwards as --

EXT. THE PIT - NIGHT

The Demo reels backwards in extreme pain, dark blood spewing from the bloody appendage that was once its arm. But Hopper is not done. He pulls the sword back for one final swing as--

INT. CREEL HOUSE - ATTIC (UPSIDE DOWN)

BLAM!! Nancy continues to unload on Vecna. BLAM! BLAM! The powerful blasts drive the burning Vecna back and back as --

EXT. THE PIT - NIGHT

WHOOM! Hopper screams, swings that sword with all his might, and -- SHOOOM! -- SEVERS THE DEMO'S HEAD FROM ITS BODY AS --

INT. CREEL HOUSE - ATTIC (UPSIDE DOWN)

BOOOM! A final shotgun blast sends Vecna exploding out of the attic window!

EXT. CREEL HOUSE - NIGHT

A flaming Vecna plummets down, down, down the length of the Creel house. As his body meets the brick walkway below --

EXT. THE PIT - NIGHT

The headless Demogorgon crashes into the snow-covered ground.

Hopper, heaving from the effort, now becomes aware of another sound, a SHUFFLING. He turns. It is Joyce, moving toward him. He drops his bloodied sword, moves toward her, and --

They embrace. As they hold tight to one another, the smoke begins to dance around them, and their clothes billow, as a ROAR overtakes them. Only it is not a monster. It is distinctly *mechanical* in nature. They look up to find...

A FAMILIAR HELICOPTER, swooping into view above them. KATINKA!!! Holy shit -- she's flying!! Inside --

INT. KATINKA - NIGHT

Yuri and Dmitri! Dmitri waves. Yuri throws a salute.

EXT. THE PIT - NIGHT

Murray shakes his head in disbelief.

> MURRAY
> *Sonofabitch*...

Joyce and Hopper continue to hold on to one another as the chopper begins its descent, coming to their rescue as...

EXT. OUTSIDE TRAILER PARK - NIGHT (UPSIDE DOWN)

Dustin limps over to Eddie, *coming to his rescue*.

Eddie's limp body is encircled by flapping, wounded Demobats, but Dustin doesn't even seem aware of the creatures. He is not worried for himself, only his friend.

He drops down beside Eddie. He sees that his white Hellfire shirt is soaked through with blood; on the visible skin, we glimpse a number of deep bite marks.

                    DUSTIN
          Oh God -- *Eddie* --

                    EDDIE
          ... That... bad, huh...?

                    DUSTIN
          No no... we just, we need to get
          you some help -- get you to a
          hospital. You're *going to be fine* --
          okay??

We get the strong feeling that Dustin is trying to convince
himself here just as much as he's trying to convince Eddie.

                    EDDIE
          Okay...

                    DUSTIN
          You think -- you can move? If I
          help?

                    EDDIE
          Yeah... yeah... I think so... I
          just, I... I need a... a second...

Another gasping breath. Then, a surprising smile as Eddie
realizes something --

                    EDDIE (CONT'D)
          Hey... I didn't... run this time...
          did I?

A soft, sad smile from Dustin.

                    DUSTIN
          No... you didn't run...

                    EDDIE
          Make sure you keep... saving
          those... those lost sheep for me...
          yeah?

Dustin shakes his head. Refusing to accept this.

                    DUSTIN
          No. *No.* You can save them yourself.
          You can save them yourself.

                    EDDIE
          ... Nah. I think... I think I'm
          actually gonna graduate... I
          think...
                    (MORE)

                    EDDIE (CONT'D)
          it's finally my year, Henderson. I
          think... it's... *finally my year...*

Eddie smiles one final time. Then the light leaves his eyes
and his body goes very very still. Eddie Munson has left us.
As Dustin begins to cry, emotional MUSIC SWELLS as --

INT. CREEL HOUSE - SECOND-FLOOR HALLWAY - NIGHT

A chain lock breaks as Erica at last shoves her way through
the attic door. She hurries up the stairs.

INT. CREEL HOUSE - ATTIC - CONTINUOUS

She pulls to a stop as she takes in the shocking scene before
her: Jason, flat on the ground, knocked unconscious. Nearby,
a distraught Lucas cradles a limp, broken Max in his arms.

He looks up at his sister, then, through choked sobs --

                    LUCAS
          We need a doctor -- call an
          ambulance -- an AMBULANCE. HURRY!!!

A shocked Erica nods, then hurries back down the steps. We
don't follow her, but rather stay behind with Lucas and Max.

Max's voice quivers. She's scared --

                    MAX
          Lucas...

He squeezes her hand.

                    LUCAS
          Yeah, I'm here -- *I'm here* --

But Max can't seem to locate him. Her eyes seem unnaturally
cloudy. They search, frantic.

                    MAX
          I -- I can't see -- or -- or feel
          anything...

Lucas tries to fight off the panic he feels when he hears
this. He needs to stay strong for her.

                    LUCAS
          I know -- it's okay. We're going to
          get you help. Just hold on okay. I
          just need you to -- *to hold on.*
          Okay??

                    MAX
          I'm -- scared Lucas -- I'm... so
          scared --

                    LUCAS
          I know, I know --

                    MAX
          I -- I don't want to die... I don't
          want to die -- I'm not ready --

                    LUCAS
          You're not going to die -- just
          hang on -- *hang on* --

As Max struggles to breathe, to hang on --

INT. VOID

Eleven cradles the broken Max in her arms in the black void, crying here too as Lucas's voice echoes around her --

                    LUCAS (V.O.)
          Just hang on... *hang on* --

EXT. CREEL HOUSE - (UPSIDE DOWN)

The front door to the Creel house opens up and --

Our teens step out, Nancy leading the way with her shotgun. They pull to a stop on the porch. Their faces fall.

There are glass shards and blood all over the brick walkway. This is where Vecna fell -- but Vecna is nowhere in sight. Gone. As our teens take this in, scanning the darkness for him, but not finding him...

INT. CREEL HOUSE - ATTIC - NIGHT

Max's eyes begin to flag. She is slipping away.

                    LUCAS
          Max -- you have to -- stay with me
          -- STAY WITH ME --

Max's face goes very still. Her hand goes limp.

She is gone.

Lucas shakes her.

                    LUCAS (CONT'D)
          MAX??? MAX???? MAX!!!!

INT. VOID

Eleven watches as Max passes away in the void too. Lucas's desperate calls reverberate all around her. As a shocked Eleven breaks down --

INT./EXT. CREEL HOUSE - NIGHT (UPSIDE DOWN)

AN OMINOUS CHIME REVERBERATES ACROSS THE NIGHT. Our teens turn toward the sound, looking back into the house, back at --

THE GRANDFATHER CLOCK. Its heavy gold pendulum swings as it chimes once more. And then it chimes again. And then one final time.

Four chimes.

>   ROBIN
> That's four --
>
>   NANCY
> ... Max --

BOOM! A MASSIVE EARTHQUAKE SUDDENLY ASSAULTS THE UPSIDE DOWN, FAR MORE VIOLENT THAN ANY OF THE EARTHQUAKES THAT CAME BEFORE. THE TEENS HOLD ONTO ONE ANOTHER.

INT. CREEL HOUSE - ATTIC (UPSIDE DOWN)

We move into the attic, where we see a RIFT opening up across the floor. The fourth Gate. As floorboards split apart --

INT. CREEL HOUSE - ATTIC - NIGHT

The massive earthquake carries into the real world.

A grieving Lucas, still cradling Max, watches in shock as the rift begins to form across the floor, in the same place as in the Upside Down. A powerful red glow shines from within.

The commotion wakes Jason. His eyes blink open just in time to see the Rift racing right for him. He tries to scramble away, but it's too late --

WHOOM! The Rift passes over his chest, searing his body. He SCREAMS IN AGONY. As a bright red glow erupts from his body, Lucas averts his gaze and --

EXT. CREEL HOUSE - NIGHT

The Rift continues to expand, cleaving its way down the face of the Creel house.

It is a surreal sight, as if the house itself is being carved in half by some massive, invisible knife. When the Rift reaches the ground, it begins to expand across the yard, resuming its horizontal growth --

INT. EDDIE'S TRAILER - NIGHT

The Rift in Eddie's trailer begins to grow and spread too --

EXT. TRAILER PARK - NIGHT

Trailers shake like crazy as the Rift travels out of the Munson trailer and across the trailer park --

EXT. LOVER'S LAKE - NIGHT

The Lover's Lake Rift grows too... we can see the glow traveling under the water, almost beautiful.

EXT. COUNTRY ROAD - NIGHT

The Rift expands from the site of Fred's murder... traveling across the road and into the woods...

EXT. HAWKINS - NIGHT

We now cut to an EPIC BIRD'S-EYE SHOT, where we see ALL FOUR RIFTS carving their way across the town of Hawkins, demolishing anything and everything in their path. We see now that they are now racing toward one another, *on a collision course*, and --

INT. WHEELER HOUSE - LIVING ROOM - NIGHT

The Wheeler house shakes. HOLLY screams as framed pictures fall from the mantel and walls. KAREN runs in, pulling her daughter into her protective arms as --

INT. CREEL HOUSE - LIVING ROOM - NIGHT (UPSIDE DOWN)

The teens continue to hold tight to one another, bracing themselves, and --

EXT. DOWNTOWN HAWKINS - NIGHT

KAAAAABOOM! The four Rifts crash together as they meet in a single point on deserted Main Street. The asphalt rises, then falls, as a MASSIVE sinkhole plunges through the street. And then, at long last --

The earthquake ends, *settling*.

INT. CREEL HOUSE - ATTIC - NIGHT

Lucas looks up as the last dust falls around him.

INT. SURFER BOY PIZZA - KITCHEN - NIGHT

Mike continues to hold El's hand. She's still unconscious, but her eyes continue to dart rapidly back and forth beneath her eyelids. *She isn't back yet.* She's still in --

INT. THE VOID

-- Where she is holding Max in her arms. But as she looks down at her lifeless friend, she hears Mike's voice again:

>   MIKE (V.O. FLASHBACK)
>   Fight, El... you can do anything...
>   you can fly... you can move
>   mountains... I believe that...

El's eyes narrow with determination.

>   ELEVEN
>   No -- no -- you're not going.
>   (beat, firm)
>   No.

She places a hand on Max's chest. *On her heart.* She focuses her breathing. Shuts her eyes. And --

QUICK FLASHBACKS of Eleven with Max, *dancing, laughing, playing*, then a BRILLIANT KALEIDOSCOPE OF COLORS fly at camera. *Just like when Eleven sent One into another dimension.* The colors rush past us faster and faster and --

BLACK

Total silence.

A TITLE CARD slowly fades onto screen:

>   TWO DAYS LATER.

EXT. HAWKINS ROAD - DAY

We FADE UP on the LEAVING HAWKINS sign.

WHOOSH! A sedan suddenly blows past camera, heading out of town. A stack of suitcases have been strapped to its roof. Then, after a beat, another car passes camera, also packed with luggage. Then another car passes. Then *another*. As cars continue to pass, a *mass exodus*, we notice an aberration:

A LONE VAN, driving in the opposite direction, heading *into* Hawkins. We would recognize this van anywhere. It's --

The Pizzamobile.

INT./EXT. PIZZAMOBILE - COUNTRY ROAD - HAWKINS - DAY

Jonathan drives, Argyle sits passenger. A solemn Mike, Will, Eleven, sit in the back, watching out the windows as cars continue to pass them, fleeing their town.

We CRANE UP behind the Pizzamobile to reveal a devastated Hawkins. We see the Rift cutting across forest and buildings; we see scattered plumes of smoke; we see military choppers buzzing in the sky; we see chaos.

>   TV REPORTER (V.O.)
>   ... It's been less than forty-eight
>   hours since a seven-point-four
>   magnitude earthquake rocked the
>   quaint town of Hawkins, eighty
>   miles outside of Indianapolis, in
>   an event seismologists are calling
>   a natural disaster of near
>   unprecedented scale.

INT./EXT. PIZZAMOBILE - HAWKINS - VARIOUS - DAY

Our kids look out the car windows as they drive through a devastated post-Rupture Hawkins. Directly ahead, a SOLDIER guards a military blockade, obstructing people from entering downtown Hawkins. The Soldier hand signals aggressively.

>   TV REPORTER (V.O.)
>   As of last night, the president has
>   declared the site a federal
>   disaster. Military, FEMA, and the
>   National Guard are now working
>   together in a courageous effort to
>   rescue this small community.

-- Eleven looks past the military barricade, glimpsing the destruction that lies beyond; we see collapsed buildings, fallen power lines, toppled street lights, and the burnt lip of the massive rift. Excavators lift slabs of broken concrete as hard-hatted workers climb rubble, searching for survivors.

-- Jonathan watches paramedics carry a bloody white body away on a stretcher.

> TV REPORTER (V.O.)
> The death toll now stands at twenty-two, but with hundreds more filling Roane County hospitals, and many more still missing, officials expect those numbers to rise.

-- Mike looks out the window as they drive past Hawkins High. Families stream out of a school bus, joining a growing line of people waiting outside the gym...

> TV REPORTER (V.O.)
> Thousands of residents have been forced to evacuate homes and businesses; local schools and warehouses have been outfitted to provide temporary shelter.

-- Will looks out the window to his left, sees some residents packing cars outside the driveways of their houses, preparing to flee.

> TV REPORTER (V.O.)
> Some have chosen to leave, with many telling us they plan to never return, as this is only the latest tragedy to befall their once safe town...

-- They now pass by a church, where a throng of frightened citizens flock inside. The sign outside the church reads: "Do not be overcome with evil, but overcome evil with good."

> TV REPORTER (V.O.)
> Most recently, a string of high school students were killed in a series of ritualistic murders, which have been linked to a local satanic cult known as Hellfire.

INT. WHEELER HOUSE - TV ROOM - DAY

We are now watching the REPORTER on a small TV set. She is positioned by a military barricade, and she is not alone. Scattered around her, a caravan of news vans and reporters here from all across the country; helicopters buzz overhead.

> TV REPORTER (ON TV)
> Eddie Munson -- the leader of this cult, and prime suspect in the murders -- has been missing since the earthquake and is presumed dead.
> (MORE)

                    TV REPORTER (ON TV) (CONT'D)
               But this offers little comfort to
               the people of Hawkins, who are
               scared, angry -- and searching for
               answers.

We PULL BACK from the TV, panning past Holly, who is lying on
the carpet, playing contentedly with her Lite-Brite...

                    TV REPORTER (ON TV) (CONT'D)
               Why their town? What have they done
               to deserve so much suffering? A
               growing chorus believes the two
               recent tragedies are linked,
               claiming the Munson Murders opened
               a doorway between worlds -- a
               doorway, they say, into Hell
               itself.

Our camera at last lands on TED, who is watching the TV from
his La-Z-Boy with a look of obvious irritation. He calls out
to Karen, who is just now walking behind him, cradling a BOX
filled with stuffed animals, dolls, and clothing.

                    TED
               You hear that Karen? They're now
               calling it "a doorway into Hell."

                    KAREN
               Great, more hysteria, just what we
               need.

                    TED
               The news is now indistinguishable
               from the tabloids, I tell you --
               indistinguishable.

Karen nods as she carries the box out the door and --

EXT. WHEELER HOUSE - GARAGE - DRIVEWAY - DAY

-- Onto the driveway, where we find Nancy, Dustin, Steve, and
Robin loading DONATION boxes into the trunk of Steve's BMW.
The trunk is so crammed the boxes won't all fit, leading to
some bickering.

                    KAREN
               Nance -- found some more of your
               old stuff in the attic --
                    (seeing the disaster)
               You should really just take my
               car --

                    STEVE
          No no -- we'll find room, Missus
          Wheeler, don't you worry --

As Nancy looks through the box, she's flooded with memories.

                    NANCY
          Mister Rabbit...

                    KAREN
          It's okay if you want to save him,
          you know?

                    NANCY
          No, no. He'll be more loved in a
          new home.

Nancy smiles softly, takes the box when --

                    KAREN
          Someone order pizza?

                    DUSTIN
          Pizza??

All eyes turn to the top of the driveway, where --

The Pizzamobile is now pulling to a creaking stop.

CLOSE ON: The van door opening. Then CLOSE ON dusty sneakers stepping out onto concrete as --

MIKE, ELEVEN, WILL, AND JONATHAN EXIT THE VAN. Time seems to slow as our two groups of friends lock eyes, seeing one another for the first time in what feels like a *lifetime*.

EXT. WHEELER HOUSE - DRIVEWAY - MOMENTS LATER

WIDE SHOT as our characters hurry toward one another from opposite sides of the driveway. They meet halfway, crashing together, falling into embraces. We survey various reunions:

Karen squeezes Mike, not letting him go. As she at last breaks away from her son, her relief turns to frustration.

                    KAREN
          Where have you been??

                    MIKE
          We went on a kind of a... spur-of-
          the-moment... road trip.

                    KAREN
          What? Where is Joyce -- ??

                    MIKE
          She's -- at some encyclopedia
          conference -- in Alaska --

                    KAREN
          And you don't think to call?? You
          realize how scared we've been??

                    MIKE
          I'm sorry --

                    KAREN
          Not good enough, mister -- not even
          close -- you're never going on
          vacation again, you hear me?? In
          fact -- you can just FORGET
          college. You're staying right here.
          Right here.

As Karen pulls Mike into another fierce hug, we DOLLY over to
Jonathan and Nancy, who are pulling out of their own embrace.

                    JONATHAN
          Are you -- okay?

                    NANCY
          Yeah -- I, I'm okay. But Jonathan --

                    JONATHAN
          This isn't an earthquake, I know...
          I know a lot more than you think.

Nancy is stunned by this --

                    NANCY
          How? You've been -- MIA all week --

                    JONATHAN
          Yeah -- *not exactly*. We just -- we
          couldn't risk contact.

                    NANCY
          Couldn't "risk contact" -- ?

                    JONATHAN
          I'll tell you everything soon, I
          promise, okay? But right now -- I'm
          just -- *I'm glad you're safe.*

Jonathan kisses her sweetly on the forehead. Steve, standing nearby, averts his gaze and walks away, passing by Robin, who clocks all; she knows her friend's pain all too well. The retreating Steve finally carries our camera over to...

Dustin and Eleven, who are hugging. As they pull away --

                        ELEVEN
          Where is... Lucas?

                        DUSTIN
          He's... still at the hospital.

Eleven blinks, worried.

                        ELEVEN
          He is... hurt?

                        DUSTIN
          No, no, he's...

Dustin pauses as he realizes --

                        DUSTIN (CONT'D)
          Oh. God. You don't know...

Off Eleven, confused, we CUT TO --

INT. HAWKINS HOSPITAL ROOM - DAY

A familiar drawing hangs from the wall, featuring two stick figures watching a movie together. *It's Max's drawing...*

                        LUCAS (O.S.)
          "I've got some innocent bystanders
          to save," she thinks. "Wonder Woman
          now throws out her lasso -- and
          grabs hold of the Atom Galaxy!"

We PULL AWAY from the drawing to find Lucas, seated in a hospital chair. MAX'S MOM is in the back, listening on as Lucas reads from *The Legend of Wonder Woman* comic.

                        LUCAS (CONT'D)
          Wonder Woman calls out, unafraid --
          "All right, Atomia, if I remember
          right, only magnetic force can
          imprison your pocket galaxy... but
          that's *just what I've got*,
          augmented by the power of my magic
          lasso..."

We CONTINUE TO PULL BACK, at last revealing his audience:

Max. She's lying on a hospital bed. Her skin is ashen... her eyes covered by bandages... her frail limbs are encased in casts... tubes feed fluid into her veins... and a hulking ventilator breathes for her. She is not awake, but Lucas reads as though she were, giving it his dramatic all:

> LUCAS (CONT'D)
> "So set those people you kidnapped free -- or I'll stick you in a lead box and use you for a footwarmer!"
> (chuckles a bit)
> I gotta use that sometimes. "Stick you in a lead box..."

Lucas smiles, instinctively looking to Max for a reaction... but, of course, there is none. As his smile fades a bit, he hears the CREAK of a door opening. He looks up to find --

Mike, Will, and Jonathan. Lucas can't believe his eyes.

> LUCAS (CONT'D)
> Oh my God --

He drops the comic, races forward. He hugs Will, then Mike --

> LUCAS (CONT'D)
> We've been calling you guys like crazy --

> MIKE
> I know. I'm sorry. We just got in -- we came as soon as we heard.

Lucas is about to respond when he sees Eleven. She is standing a few feet behind Will and Mike, wearing a dark hoodie. She takes a breath and then walks forward, stepping into the hospital room. Her breath catches as she takes in Max for the first time. It is painful and terrifying to see her friend like this, but there is relief too. She is alive.

> ELEVEN
> Do they know -- when she will wake?

Lucas steps up beside Eleven. Shakes his head.

> LUCAS
> No... they say -- she might not. Her heart stopped for over a minute. She died. I mean -- clinically. But then... she came back. The doctors, they don't know how. They say -- it's a *miracle*.

Mike and Will share looks. They know the truth here -- that this was no miracle. At least, not an unexplained one.

Eleven did this... <u>she brought Max back to life</u>.

Eleven steps up to the hospital bed. Then she reaches out, takes Max's hand, and closes her eyes. We PUSH IN on Eleven, and the sounds of the hospital fade into the background, giving way to the gentle thump of El's heartbeat. *Thump... Thump... Thump...*

EXT. HAWKINS HIGH - GYM - DAY

VROOM! Steve's BMW drives past camera, headed toward the school gym. It pulls to a stop by the curb. Then --

MOMENTS LATER

The trunk pops open. WIDEN: Robin, Dustin, and Steve grab their DONATION boxes and --

INT. HAWKINS HIGH - GYM - DAY

Our teens carry the boxes through the crowded gym, which we now see has been converted into a disaster relief center for displaced families. Row upon row of makeshift cots are lined up across the gym, and every single one is occupied; it's so packed that sleeping bags have been wedged between cots.

Some families seem content enough -- talking, reading. Others are distraught; we see a mother consoling her daughter, a baby crying in the arms of his mother. Dustin looks over and sees that one of the gymnasium walls has been wallpapered with MISSING PEOPLE posters. *So many still lost...*

Our gang reaches a table at the far end, marked "Donations." They drop their boxes in front of a FRIENDLY VOLUNTEER --

      ROBIN
  Blankets and sheets here -- toys in
  there -- clothes there.

     FRIENDLY VOLUNTEER
  Wow -- already so organized, we
  appreciate that! Do you want a tax
  receipt form?

      ROBIN
  Nah. That's okay. But, uh...

Robin glances back at the chaos behind her, then --

                    ROBIN (CONT'D)
          Is there anything else we could do
          to -- help?

Off the Volunteer's "are you *kidding*" look, we CUT TO --

INT. HAWKINS HIGH - CAFETERIA - DAY

Steve in the cafeteria, standing before a mountain of donated clothes. ANOTHER VOLUNTEER explains the process to him --

                    VOLUNTEER #2
          Okay so first we need to make sure
          everything's folded. Then we're
          sorting by age -- baby clothes go
          here -- ages three to five here,
          six to eight over there...

As an overwhelmed Steve attempts to keep track of everything, our CAMERA PULLS BACK over a counter into --

THE KITCHEN - CONTINUOUS

Where we find Robin slapping together peanut butter and jelly sandwiches alongside volunteers. As she slips a finished sandwich into a bag, a familiar voice pipes up behind her:

                    VOICE (O.S.)
          I found another jar of peanut
          butter! Crunchy style!

Robin looks up to find... VICKIE! *Holy shit.* Vickie crashes to a stop, clearly surprised to see Robin here --

                    VICKE
          Robin -- ?

                    ROBIN
          Hey --

                    VICKIE
          What are -- you doing here?

                    ROBIN
          Oh just -- uh --
              (holds up baggie)
          Making some PB and Js --

                    VICKIE
          Right -- yeah. Duh. Of course.
              (holds up peanut butter)
              (MORE)

                    VICKIE (CONT'D)
          I'm also making PB and Js, as it
          so happens!

Robin smiles as Vickie settles into position beside her. The
girls now begin to work side by side, making those PB and Js.
Robin is acutely aware of Vickie's proximity. She's *nervous
as hell*. She is about to finally say something when --

                    VICKIE (CONT'D)
          Hey -- uh -- sorry if that came out
          weird -- "What are you doing
          here???" It wasn't, meant
          like, "What are YOU doing here?" I
          meant it like "What are you doing
          here?" Like -- *wow* -- nice
          surprise, awesome to see you --

                    ROBIN
          Oh yeah, I didn't take it as
          anything -- negative --

                    VICKIE
          Okay, good, it's just -- I don't
          know -- my brain, it's a little
          frazzled lately because well --

                    ROBIN
          Everything.

                    VICKIE
          Yeah. And also -- Dan. He's my
          boyfriend. *Was* -- my boyfriend. He
          was visiting and he took one look
          at all this and let's just say it
          was not what he envisioned for his
          spring break, so he was like -- I'm
          outta here. Back to Purdue. Good
          luck, Vick! Which ultimately, you
          know, is fine, bordering on good
          because he was really grating on
          me. I mean, he chews really loudly,
          like right over my shoulder, and he
          just has all around bad taste --
          he's the kinda person who trashes
          Fast Times because it doesn't have
          a "plot," I mean as soon as he said
          that I should have just ended it
          right then and there and --
               (catching herself)
          Oh God -- sorry. I'm totally
          rambling about my dumb boyfriend as
          people are out there suffering and
          -- need food.
                    (MORE)

                    VICKIE (CONT'D)
          AND I just made a peanut butter on
          peanut butter monstrosity. *Awesome.*

Vickie starts to scrape away the excess peanut butter from
the sandwich. Smiles a bit to herself.

                    VICKIE (CONT'D)
          I don't know what's wrong with me --
          sometimes -- I don't know -- it's
          like my mouth is moving faster than
          my brain, like this runaway train,
          and I can't seem to stop it no
          matter how hard I try -- you know
          what I mean?

Robin just looks at her, and smiles.

                    ROBIN
          Yeah... I think I know what you
          mean.

Vickie smiles back, then our girls return to making their
sandwiches.

IN THE CAFETERIA

Steve, folding clothes, watches from afar. He grins softly to
himself, then returns to folding clothes as we CUT TO --

INT. HAWKINS HIGH - GYM - CONTINUOUS

Dustin. He is making his way down a row of cots, carrying a
tray of water cups.

                    DUSTIN
          Water anyone? H2O? Vital for all
          forms of life.

A few people take the cups, thanking him, when Dustin
abruptly stops. He's clocked --

Eddie's UNCLE WAYNE. He is standing in front of the missing
poster wall, pulling down a missing person poster of Eddie
that has been vandalized; Eddie's been given devil horns.

Dustin slowly approaches, watching as Wayne crumples up the
poster, then works to replace it with a new, clean poster.

                    DUSTIN (CONT'D)
          ... Mister Munson?

Wayne mumbles a response, continues stapling, not even
looking back.

DUSTIN (CONT'D)
I -- I'm Dustin Henderson -- can
we... talk?

Wayne finishes stapling the poster, turns around.

WAYNE
Can't imagine we got anything to
talk about. My nephew is innocent,
and he's still missing. And I'll
put up as many posters as I need
til he's found. Good day to ya.

And with that, Wayne strides past Dustin, but --

DUSTIN
I was with him.

This stops Wayne cold in his tracks. He turns back to Dustin.

DUSTIN (CONT'D)
I was with Eddie. When the
earthquake hit.

Wayne swallows. Still stoic, but we can see his whole body is tense.

WAYNE
And... where's Eddie now?

Dustin can't get the words out. He fishes Eddie's guitar pick necklace out of his pocket and hands it over to Wayne. As Wayne rolls it in his hand, he sees it is stained with blood. He looks back up at Dustin, who finally finds words:

DUSTIN
I'm sorry. I'm *so... sorry*.

The life seems to drain from Wayne's body. He sinks down onto a cot. That guitar pick still gripped tightly in his hand.

Dustin sits beside him. His eyes move to the photograph of Eddie that Wayne just tacked up on the wall. Eddie is smiling big in the photo, all goofy and fun -- *just a kid*.

DUSTIN (CONT'D)
I wish everyone had gotten to know
him... I mean -- *really know him*.
Because they would've loved him,
Mister Munson. *They would've loved
him*. Even in the end -- he... he
never stopped being Eddie.
(MORE)

                    DUSTIN (CONT'D)
          Despite everything -- I never even
          saw him get mad.

Wayne manages a faint nod.

                    DUSTIN (CONT'D)
          He could've run... he could've
          saved himself. But... he fought...
          he fought and died to protect this
          town -- this town *that hated him.*

Dustin looks back from the photo to Wayne.

                    DUSTIN (CONT'D)
          He's not just innocent, Mister
          Munson.
                    (beat)
          He's a hero.

Wayne takes this in, those tears falling now despite his best
effort. We now begin to PULL AWAY from Wayne and Dustin,
drifting backwards through the crowd, music swelling, and --

EXT. WOODS - DAY

Spring leaves flutter in the wind. We CRANE DOWN to find the
Pizzamobile pulling to a stop in an opening in the woods.

MOMENTS LATER

The door slides open and our group (Argyle, Nancy, Jonathan,
Will, and Mike) step out. As others move forward, Eleven
hangs back, emotional as she takes in their destination:

HOPPER'S CABIN. A deep breath, then El presses forward and --

INT. HOPPER'S CABIN - DAY

Our group enters the cabin. Their faces drop.

                    JONATHAN
          Oh *Jesus...*

REVERSE TO REVEAL the wreckage still stands from the Fourth
of July attack: There is a massive hole punched in the roof,
two gaping holes in the walls, windows are shattered,
furniture lies in splinters, and it's been battered by three
seasons worth of rain and snow.

                    ARGYLE
          Yeah I mean... I get we gotta hide
          Supergirl and stuff, but this isn't
          exactly a Fortress of Solitude.
                    (MORE)

                    ARGYLE (CONT'D)
          More like a Fortress of --
          Grodiness.

                    NANCY
          Come on, guys, seriously? I've seen
          Mike's room look worse.

                    ARGYLE
                (to Mike)
          Brutal, dude.

Nancy moves into the kitchen, hits on the faucet.

                    NANCY
          Water still works --

She opens a cabinet. It's still got stuff in here. She takes out some vinegar, baking soda, and baking powder.

                    NANCY (CONT'D)
          And -- wa-lah -- cleaning supplies.

She slams the supplies down onto the counter and turns back to the group, who are still just... standing there. Staring.

                    NANCY (CONT'D)
          It's not going to fix itself up.
          Come on -- Let's go.

She grabs a broom, tosses it to Mike. As he catches it --

LATER

WHOOSH! The broom sweeps across the floor, gathering glass.

WIDEN: Mike sweeps, while Will scrubs the walls, Eleven, meanwhile, gathers up trash, placing it all in a trash bag. As they work, we TILT UP to that massive hole in the ceiling just as a LARGE PIECE OF PLYWOOD drops on top of it.

ON THE CABIN ROOF,

Jonathan and Nancy are on the roof, repairing that hole.

                    JONATHAN
          Alright, that's good, hold it right
          there --

As Jonathan begins to hammer the plywood in, Nancy looks up, noticing something: Argyle is wandering the woods. He kneels down, plucks a mushroom off the ground. He seems excited by his discovery. *Righteous.*

                    NANCY
          ... What's ... he doing?

Jonathan follows her gaze to Argyle. Smiles a bit.

                    JONATHAN
          Looks like... gathering mushrooms?
          Either that or he's searching for a
          very small person --

                    NANCY
          What -- ?

                    JONATHAN
          Nothing. He kinda just... does his
          own thing. He's a little on the
          eccentric side --

                    NANCY
          I guess welcome to the club, right?

                    JONATHAN
          Yeah. *Welcome to the club.*

They share a smile. Jonathan grabs for a nail, but before he hammers it in, he looks back up at Nancy. Turning serious.

                    JONATHAN (CONT'D)
          Hey. Nance --

                    NANCY
          Yeah -- ?

                    JONATHAN
          I'm... sorry... I wasn't here --

                    NANCY
          To be honest -- I'm glad you
          weren't.
               (catching herself, wincing)
          I just mean -- I'm glad you were
          with Mike, and Will. They don't
          think they need a babysitter -- but
          they do.

                    JONATHAN
          Yeah well -- I guess it's good you
          were here too. Otherwise, who'd've
          been in charge? Steve?

Jonathan smiles. But Nancy is surprisingly defensive --

                         NANCY
               He's grown up a lot, you know --

                         JONATHAN
               Yeah. I -- I'm sure.

Okay... this is getting awkward. Jonathan returns to
hammering, but his mind is now swimming with thoughts. He
finishes driving in the nail, then looks back up at Nancy --

                         JONATHAN (CONT'D)
               Hey...

Their eyes meet again.

                         JONATHAN (CONT'D)
               Are we... okay?

                         NANCY
               Yeah -- totally. Right? It's just --
               it's hard -- life just seems to
               keep getting in the way of our big
               plans doesn't it -- ?

                         JONATHAN
               Yeah -- sure seems that way --

                         NANCY
               Is it too late to add "saving the
               world" to your college resume, you
               think?
                    (small smile, then)
               Your acceptance letter -- not that
               it even really matters anymore, but
               -- did it ever come?

Jonathan hesitates. Moment of truth here. But --

                         JONATHAN
               No -- not yet.

Jonathan quickly looks away, resumes hammering, and --

INT. CABIN - DAY

WHOOM! An old board game is dropped into a trash bag.

We're with Eleven now, who is collecting trash around the
house, lost in a dark reverie. She passes by our boys, who
are still cleaning. They watch as she disappears into her
room, with nary a glance their way. She's clearly not doing
well. As she shuts the door with her powers (leaving it open
just a crack), a concerned Will turns to Mike.

WILL
... Did she... talk to you at all?

MIKE
Not much. A little. She said Brenner -- he told her she wasn't ready. Now she thinks -- he was right.

WILL
That's *crap*. If it wasn't for her, if she hadn't left the lab, Max wouldn't be alive right now --

MIKE
I know -- it's just... she's never... lost before. Not -- like this.

WILL
She'll have another chance.

MIKE
Let's hope not -- let's hope he's dead and rotting --

WILL
He's not.

The certainty in Will's voice spooks Mike.

WILL (CONT'D)
Now that I'm here -- in Hawkins -- I can... feel him. <u>One</u>. He's hurt. *Hurting*... but -- he's still alive.

Will moves, sits down on a dusty bed. Mike joins him.

WILL (CONT'D)
It's strange, knowing now... who it was this whole time.
    (beat)
I can still remember... what he thinks... how he thinks -- and --

Will looks Mike dead in the eyes. Frightened.

WILL (CONT'D)
He's not going to stop, Mike. Ever. Not until he's taken everything. *Everyone*.
    (beat)
<u>We have to kill him.</u>

                    MIKE
          I know. And we will. _We will_.

Will nods. But he seems less confident than Mike somehow. Then Will's face suddenly darkens. He stands and moves over to a window, looks out. There is --

A BLACK SEDAN, weaving its way down the road, headed for the cabin. As a nervous Mike joins Will's side --

EXT. HOPPER'S CABIN - ROOF - DAY

Nancy and Jonathan stand up on the roof -- they've clocked the sedan now too. Shared looks and --

                    JONATHAN
          Government.

INT. HOPPER'S CABIN - ELEVEN'S ROOM - DAY

WHOOM! Eleven, tossing some junk into a bag, oblivious to the coming danger. As she cleans, she notices a glass Coke bottle. As she picks it up, she remembers back, and we hear distant sounds of her and Max giggling together last summer:

Eleven places the bottle down, then spins it. As the bottle rotates, its glass belly drumming gently against the wood, we hear her heartbeat again... thump... thump --

INT. HOSPITAL ROOM - DAY (FLASHBACK)

Thump. _We're now back in time, back in the hospital_. Eleven, holding Max's hands, has her eyes closed, focusing. As our camera PUSHES IN on her, the lighting shifts, darkening.

THE BLACK VOID - CONTINUOUS (FLASHBACK)

When Eleven opens her eyes, she is no longer in the hospital. She is in _the Black Void_. Her eyes roam the darkness --

                    ELEVEN
          ... Max?

Her voice echoes out. Unanswered.

                    ELEVEN (CONT'D)
          Max?? MAX???

As Eleven continues to call out for her friend, the CAMERA PULLS AWAY from her, further and further, revealing _she is all alone in here, no sign of Max_. As our camera continues to pull back, Eleven smaller and smaller, an airy sound begins to dominate the soundscape. Whoo-whooo-whoo --

INT. HOPPER'S CABIN - ELEVEN'S ROOM - DAY

Whoomp. The spinning Coke bottle slows to a stop.

A tear slips down Eleven's cheek. She begins to cry, all alone in here. Then she hears it: SLAMMING CAR DOORS. *VOICES.* THEN THE CABIN DOOR OPENS AND HEAVY FOOTSTEPS APPROACH.

Someone is coming. Her chest tightens as a shadow fills the gap below her cracked bedroom door.

KNOCK. KNOCK. KNOCK. Knuckles pound against the bedroom door. Then the door opens. And Eleven all but faints. It's --

HOPPER. STANDING TALL IN THE DOORWAY.

                        HOPPER
        Hey, kiddo.

It takes Eleven a moment to process that he's here; that he's *real*. Then, in a flash, she runs and leaps into his arms. Hopper hugs her tight.

                        ELEVEN
        I -- I kept it open. Three inches.
        I never -- never stopped...
        believing --

Hop's got tears in his eyes now too.

                        HOPPER
        I know, kid. *I know.*

As they break their embrace, Hop reaches out, wipes a tear from her cheek.

                        HOPPER (CONT'D)
        I'm here now. And I'm not going
        anywhere, ever again, okay? <u>I'm
        here</u>.

Eleven gives a shaky nod, trying to push back those tears. A heavy weight seems to lift; she feels so much less alone now. Then, looking him over, for the first time she really notices his change in appearance --

                        ELEVEN
        You are --

                        HOPPER
        Not fat? I know.

                    ELEVEN
          And -- your -- hair --

                    HOPPER
          Oh yeah... that too --

Hopper runs a hand back over his scalp.

                    HOPPER (CONT'D)
          I guess... I kinda stole your look,
          huh?

El smiles, nods. *He totally did.*

                    HOPPER (CONT'D)
          What do you think?

                    ELEVEN
          ... *Bitchin'.*

Hopper laughs. Eleven smiles. Then, as Hop's laughter quiets, she hears more VOICES. *HAPPY VOICES.*

EXT. HOPPER'S CABIN - DAY

Eleven and Hopper step onto the porch to find that Hopper did not arrive alone -- Joyce is here too! She is embracing Will and Jonathan, her face stained with tears.

                    HOPPER
          You weren't the only one who didn't
          stop believing...

The puzzle pieces begin to click for El. Joyce now looks up and sees her. *Oh my God --*

                    JOYCE
          El --

El and Joyce now move toward one another and fall into an embrace. As Joyce holds her tight, stroking her hair --

                    ELEVEN
          I am happy -- you went to your
          conference --

Joyce smiles through her tears.

                    JOYCE
          Oh -- right. *My conference.*
              (a quick look to Hopper)
          Yeah -- it was -- *more exciting
          than I expected.*

Hopper, smiling, now looks past them to Agent Stinson, who is standing by the black sedan. A knowing nod between them, then Stinson climbs into her sedan and drives off, leaving our family to their happy reunion.

                    MIKE
          Hey --

Hopper turns to find Mike approaching him. Man and boy eye one another.

                    HOPPER
          You've grown.

                    MIKE
          You've shrunk.

They both break into smiles, then hug. As our reunion continues, our CAMERA DOLLIES over to Will, whose smile fades as he senses something. He reaches up and touches the nape of his neck. THOSE GOOSEBUMPS ARE FLARING.

A dark shadow now envelops our characters. Will and the others look up to find a DARK SMOG rapidly expanding across the blue spring sky. BOOM! DISTANT THUNDER CLAPS.

Eleven walks up to the Pizzamobile. Something has landed on the car hood. She reaches out, touches it. A small white particle is now stuck to the tip of her finger. It is...

SPORES. As the others begin to notice spores too, falling around them...

INT. WHEELER HOUSE - DAY

An excited Holly watches falling spores from the window...

                    HOLLY
          Mom -- it's snowing!!! MOM!!

Karen walks up, watching, a look of concern on her face...

EXT. HAWKINS HIGH - GYM - DAY

Dustin, Wayne, and a crowd of others exit from the gym to watch the falling spores. As Dustin's face darkens...

INT. HAWKINS HIGH - CAFETERIA - DAY

Steve watches the falling spores through the cafeteria window. Robin and Vickie cross to his side...

INT. HOSPITAL ROOM - DAY

Lucas and Erica watch from out the hospital window...

EXT. HOPPER'S CABIN - DAY

We now return to the cabin, as Hopper steps out onto the dirt road. In the distance, perhaps a mile away, he sees a plume of darkness, rising into the sky. As Mike, Will, Jonathan, and Nancy gather around Hop, seeing it now too, we CUT TO --

EXT. WOODS - MOMENTS LATER

Our group walking together through the woods. The spores are falling heavier now, clinging to their hair and clothes.

MOMENTS LATER

They step out of the woods and into --

A FIELD OF FLOWERS - CONTINUOUS

In the valley below, we get a wide view of the town.

At the center of the four Rifts, where the Rift is widest, a dark mushroom cloud billows upward, like smoke rising from a volcano, spewing darkness and spores across the sky. Military choppers circle the dark cloud, showing us the sheer, massive scale of this thing.

As a tense Hopper and Joyce take hands...

Eleven walks deeper into the field. Here, flowers and grass are rotting. *The evil is spreading across both ground and sky.*

Eleven kneels down and plucks up a dead flower. Her hand curls around its stem. She looks up again, and we see her face is now a mask of anger and determination. As she rises back to her feet, CUT TO --

An epic shot of Eleven, Hopper, Joyce, Mike, Will, Nancy, and Jonathan, standing together -- *united* -- in this half-dead field of flowers, bracing themselves for *one last fight*.

And right here, as our music crescendos, we --

<u>END SEASON</u>